Juvenile Delinquency

The Core

SECOND EDITION

LARRY J. SIEGEL
University of Massachusetts–Lowell

BRANDON C. WELSH
University of Massachusetts–Lowell

THOMSON

WADSWORTH

Australia · Canada · Mexico · Singapore · Spain · United Kingdom · United States

THOMSON
WADSWORTH

Senior Executive Editor, Criminal Justice: Sabra Horne
Development Editor: Shelley Murphy
Assistant Editor: Jana Davis
Editorial Assistant: Elise Smith
Technology Project Manager: Susan DeVanna
Marketing Manager: Terra Schultz
Marketing Assistant: Annabelle Yang
Advertising Project Manager: Stacey Purviance
Project Manager, Editorial Production: Jennie Redwitz
Art Director: Vernon Boes/Carolyn Deacy
Print/Media Buyer: Karen Hunt
Permissions Editor: Sarah Harkrader

Production Service: Linda Jupiter
Text Designer: Liz Harasymczuk
Photo Researcher: Linda L Rill
Copy Editor: Sandra Beriss
Illustrator: John and Judy Waller, Scientific Illustrators
Proofreader: M. Kate St. Clair
Indexer: Medea Minnich
Cover Designer: Yvo
Cover Image: © Polyakov/SIS
Compositor: Thompson Type
Text and Cover Printer: Quebecor World/Dubuque

For more information about our products, contact us at:
Thomson Learning Academic Resource Center
1-800-423-0563

For permission to use material from this text or product, submit a request online at **http://www.thomsonrights.com.**

Any additional questions about permissions can be submitted by email to **thomsonrights@thomson.com.**

Library of Congress Control Number: 2003116393

Student Edition: ISBN 0-534-62982-2

Instructor's Edition: ISBN 0-534-62983-0

Thomson Wadsworth
10 Davis Drive
Belmont, CA 94002-3098
USA

Asia
Thomson Learning
5 Shenton Way #01-01
UIC Building
Singapore 068808

Australia/New Zealand
Thomson Learning
102 Dodds Street
Southbank, Victoria 3006
Australia

Canada
Nelson
1120 Birchmount Road
Toronto, Ontario M1K 5G4
Canada

Europe/Middle East/Africa
Thomson Learning
High Holborn House
50/51 Bedford Row
London WC1R 4LR
United Kingdom

Latin America
Thomson Learning
Seneca, 53
Colonia Polanco
11560 Mexico D.F.
Mexico

Spain/Portugal
Paraninfo
Calle Magallanes, 25
28015 Madrid, Spain

To my wife, best friend, and confidante, Therese J. Libby,

my children, Eric, Andrew, Julie, and Rachel,

my grandson Jack, my son-in-law Jason, and

our newest family member, Watson the Wonder Dog.

—LJS

To my wife, Jennifer, and our son, Ryan.

—BCW

About the Authors

Larry J. Siegel

Larry Siegel was born in The Bronx, New York. He attended the City College of New York, where he took the criminology and deviance courses taught by Charles Winick, an experience that convinced him to pursue an academic career. After graduating with a degree in sociology and social welfare, he became a member of the first-ever criminal justice class at the State University at Albany; he received his Ph.D. in 1975. Since then he has taught in criminal justice programs at Northeastern University, University of Nebraska–Omaha, St. Anselm College, and currently the University of Massachusetts–Lowell. During his career, Siegel has written more than a dozen books on topics related to crime and justice, including criminology, criminal procedure, and juvenile law. He is a court-certified expert on police behavior and has testified in numerous cases. He currently lives with his wife, Terry, in Bedford, New Hampshire.

Brandon C. Welsh

Brandon C. Welsh was born in Canada. He received his undergraduate and M.A. degrees at the University of Ottawa and his Ph.D. from Cambridge University in England. He is currently an assistant professor at the University of Massachusetts–Lowell. He teaches graduate and undergraduate courses on crime prevention, juvenile delinquency, policing, and international criminology. His research interests focus on the prevention of crime and delinquency and the economic analysis of crime prevention programs. Welsh has published extensively in these areas and is the author or editor of five books. He lives in Brookline, New Hampshire, with his wife and son.

Brief Contents

Contents

Chapter Nine

Schools and Delinquency 209

Chapter Ten

Drug Use and Delinquency 231

Chapter Fourteen

Juvenile Corrections: Probation, Community Treatment, and Institutionalization 337

Preface

Northern New Hampshire is known for its beautiful scenery and laid-back lifestyle, not for violent crime. So when Dartmouth College professors Half Zantop, sixty-two, an economic geologist, and his wife Susanne, fifty-five, who chaired the German Studies department, were found dead in their home on January 27, 2001, the killings shocked the state. The murders had been carried out in a particularly grisly fashion; the couple had been stabbed repeatedly in the neck, chest, and head with a military-style knife. Police quickly traced the weapons used in the killings to Robert Tulloch, seventeen, and James Parker, sixteen, who lived in Chelsea, Vermont, a town of about twelve hundred people located twenty miles northwest of the Zantops' home.

The murders seemed to make no sense to the people who knew the boys. Chelsea is a peaceful village. Robert Tulloch was a student council president, champion debater, and good student who did well in tough courses such as precalculus and physics. James Parker played on the high school basketball team and was known as a fun-loving jokester. Both Parker and Tulloch came from families who were well respected in the community.

The Zantop murders raise many issues concerning youth crime and juvenile delinquency. What could possibly motivate two young people with no history of violent crimes to commit such ghastly acts? These boys were not inner-city youth growing up in poverty and despair. Those familiar with the case were baffled by their outburst of violence. And considering their youth and immaturity, what would be a fitting punishment for their act? Life in an adult prison? The death penalty? The boys pleaded guilty and received a very long prison sentence.

Cases such as this have sparked interest in the study of juvenile delinquency. Considering the national concern with the problems of youth, it is not surprising that courses on juvenile delinquency have become popular offerings on college campuses across the country. We have written *Juvenile Delinquency: The Core* to help students understand the nature of juvenile delinquency and its causes and correlates, as well as the current strategies being used to prevent or control its occurrence. This brief version of our more comprehensive text, *Juvenile Delinquency: Theory, Practice, and Law,* also reviews the legal rules that have been set down either to protect innocent minors or to control adolescent misconduct: Can children be required to submit to drug testing in school? Can teachers search suspicious students or use corporal punishment as a method of discipline? Should children be allowed to testify on closed-circuit TV in child abuse cases? Should a minor be given a death penalty sentence?

Because the study of juvenile delinquency is a dynamic field of scientific inquiry, and because the theories, concepts, and processes of this area of study are constantly evolving, we have updated *Juvenile Delinquency: The Core* to reflect the changes that have taken place in the study of delinquent behavior during the past few years.

Like its predecessor, the second edition includes a review of recent legal cases, research studies, and policy initiatives. It aims at providing the groundwork for the study of juvenile delinquency by analyzing and describing the nature and extent of delinquency, the suspected causes of delinquent behavior, and how a child's relationships with key social institutions such as the family, school, and peer group influence youthful misbehavior. Though it is concise and to the point, it covers what most experts believe are the critical issues in juvenile delinquency and analyzes the critical policy issues as well, including the use of pretrial detention, waiver to adult court, and restorative justice programs.

GOALS AND OBJECTIVES

Our primary goals in writing this edition remain the same as in the previous edition:

1. To be as objective as possible, presenting the many diverse views and perspectives that characterize the study of juvenile delinquency and reflect its interdisciplinary nature.

2. To maintain a balance of theory, law, policy, and practice. It is essential that a text on delinquency not solely present theory while neglecting to cover the juvenile justice system, or provide sections on current policies without examining legal issues and cases.

3. To be as thorough and up to date as possible. We have attempted to include the most current data and information available.

4. To make the study of delinquency interesting as well as informative. We want readers to become interested in the study of delinquency so that they will pursue it further on an undergraduate or graduate level.

We have tried, in a brief format, to provide a text that is both scholarly and informative, comprehensive yet interesting, well organized and objective, yet provocative and thought provoking.

ORGANIZATION OF THE TEXT

The second edition of *Juvenile Delinquency: The Core* has fourteen chapters:

- **Chapter 1** contains extensive material on the history of childhood and the legal concepts of delinquency and status offending. This material enables the reader to understand how the concept of adolescence evolved over time and how that evolution influenced the development of the juvenile court and the special status of delinquency.

- **Chapter 2** covers the measurement of delinquent behavior, examines trends and patterns in teen crime, and discusses the correlates of delinquency, including race, gender, class, age, and chronic offending.

- **Chapter 3** covers recent individual-level views of delinquency that focus on choice, biological, and psychological theories.

- **Chapter 4** looks at theories that hold that economic, cultural, and environmental influences control delinquent behavior.

- **Chapter 5** covers the newly emerging developmental theories of delinquency, including such issues as the onset, continuity, paths to, and termination of a delinquent career.

- **Chapter 6** explores the sex-based differences thought to account for the gender patterns in the delinquency rate.

- **Chapter 7** reviews the family's influence on delinquency and pays special attention to child abuse and its control.

- **Chapter 8** reviews the effect peers have on delinquency and covers the topic of teen gangs.

- **Chapter 9** looks at the influence of schools and the education process, as well as delinquency in the school setting.

- **Chapter 10** reviews the influence drugs and substance abuse have on delinquent behavior and what is being done to reduce teenage drug use.

- **Chapter 11** examines the emergence of state control over children in need and the development of the juvenile justice system. It also covers the contemporary juvenile justice system, including major stages in the justice process, the role of the federal government in the system, and the differences between the adult and juvenile justice systems.

- **Chapter 12** reviews the history of juvenile policing, covers legal issues such as the *Miranda* rights of juveniles, examines race and gender effects on police discretion, and discusses the major policing strategies to prevent delinquency.

- **Chapter 13,** which covers the juvenile court process, contains information on plea bargaining in juvenile court, the use of detention, and transfer to the adult system. It also examines the juvenile trial, sentencing, and the critical factors that influence the transfer decision.

- **Chapter 14,** which covers juvenile corrections, discusses probation and other community dispositions, including restorative justice programs and secure juvenile corrections. It also reviews legal issues such as the right to treatment.

WHAT'S NEW IN THIS EDITION

A number of important features have been added to this edition and we have focused on three key areas: improving the balance of depth and breadth of coverage and organization, increasing accessibility and providing more applications of key concepts, and increasing the integration of technology in the text and supplements.

Learning Tools

The following features were designed to help students learn and comprehend the material:

- Each chapter now begins with a **Chapter Outline** and a new list of **Chapter Objectives** for students to follow.

- New **Chapter Opening Vignettes** are based on a CNN news item. Students can view the CNN story by accessing the video clip on the enclosed **Student CD-ROM,** which is also new to this edition.

- We have added new **Internet activities** to each chapter.

- We have put a greater focus on the juvenile justice strategy of today, provided more information on the differences between the juvenile and adult justice systems, and included more discussion of the future of juvenile justice. We have also placed more emphasis on delinquency prevention and increased the coverage of juvenile justice policies and programs through examples in two new features called **Focus on Delinquency** and **Preventing and Treating Delinquency.** For example, in chapter 3 a Focus on Delinquency box entitled "Are You What You Eat?" discusses whether nutrition can affect children's behavior.

- **What Does This Mean to Me?** is a new feature designed to help students understand risk factors contributing to delinquency and to provide them with even more applied and personalized learning opportunities.

- More visual aids, including new **Concept Summary** tables to help students review the material in an organized fashion, have been added throughout the text to make it even more visually appealing and student-friendly.

- **Checkpoints** are placed at strategic points throughout each chapter to help students retain key concepts.

- **Web Links** in the margins of every chapter provide links to Web sites that students can use to enrich their understanding of important issues and concepts discussed in the text.

- Each chapter ends with a **Chapter Summary** to reinforce key concepts. These summaries are presented in a new format for this edition so they are more closely tied to the chapter objectives. Thought-provoking **Questions for Discussion** are provided after each summary. New **Applying What You Have Learned** sections appear next, presenting hypothetical cases for students to analyze. These are followed by new **Doing Research on the Web** sections that contain information on relevant Web sites and articles available online.

- **Key Terms** are defined in a **Running Glossary** throughout the text at their first appearance and are listed at the end of each chapter.

- Three new **New Directions in Preventing Delinquency** essays, which describe the three levels of efforts being made to prevent delinquency, bookend the text into three main sections. The first essay, on primary prevention, explains how programs are designed to help kids avoid delinquent behaviors before they actually get involved; the second, on secondary prevention, reviews programs aimed at kids at risk for delinquency because of personal or social problems; and the third, on tertiary prevention, discusses those programs attempting to help kids who have committed delinquent acts and are involved with the juvenile justice system.

- The **Glossary** sets out and defines the key terms used in the text.

Chapter-by-Chapter Additions

- In **chapter 1** we present recent data from the Centers for Disease Control and Prevention (CDC) showing that teens in the United States are risk takers. There is new information on the problems of youth, including health care, poverty, and education.

- **Chapter 2** contains new (2003) data showing that at-risk teens who live in stable families are much less likely to engage in violent behaviors than those lacking family support. Evidence is also presented that shows that racial differences in the delinquency rate would evaporate if minorities had the same lifestyle currently enjoyed by Whites. Data are presented from a 2003 study that addresses the critical issue of the number of adolescents who experience extreme physical and sexual violence and the effects these experiences have on their lives.

- **Chapter 3** now looks at a provocative issue: Does delinquency pay? Is it possible that the delinquent lifestyle can be profitable? There is also recent research (2003) on ADHD and delinquent activity. Updated findings are presented from the Minnesota Study of Twins Reared Apart, and findings are discussed from a recent (2003) long-term study of the association between children's exposure to TV violence and their involvement with violent behavior as adults. There is also important new research on the effect of adolescent work experiences and delinquency that shows that kids who get jobs may actually be more likely to violate the law than those who shun after-school and weekend employment.

- In **chapter 4,** recent data on the effects of collective efficacy (communities that use mutual trust, a willingness to intervene in the supervision of children, and maintenance of public order) are presented. There is a Preventing and Treating Delinquency box on SafeFutures, a program that uses community resources to prevent and control youth crime and victimization. There is also a review of recent research that shows that the loss of a girlfriend or boyfriend can produce strain.

- **Chapter 5** presents new research on the effects of problem behavior syndrome, including new data (2003) indicating that traumatized youths have high rates of suicidal thoughts and attempts. There is also new research showing that delinquents may travel more than a single road in their delinquent career. There is a new Preventing and Treating Delinquency feature on the Across Ages program, a community-based drug prevention effort.

- **Chapter 6** presents a new Preventing and Treating Delinquency box on preventing teen pregnancy. New (2003) data show that girls who are more physically developed than their male peers are more likely to socialize at an early age and get involved in deviant behaviors, especially "party deviance" such as drinking, smoking, and substance abuse.

- **Chapter 7** discusses the relationship between parental deviance and children's antisocial behaviors. Recent data (2003) showing that deviant behavior is intergenerational and that the children of deviant parents produce delinquent children themselves are discussed. A Preventing and Treating Delinquency box looks at the relationship between substance abuse and child maltreatment.

- In **chapter 8** we cover the concept of controversial status youth—aggressive kids who are either highly liked or intensely disliked by their peers and are the ones most likely to become engaged in antisocial behavior. The chapter contains recent (2004) data showing that deviant peers amplify the likelihood of a troubled teen getting further involved in antisocial behaviors. The chapter has the most recent data on gang migration, numbers, and activities. It also contains data and findings from Terence Thornberry and colleagues' new (2003) book, *Gangs and Delinquency in Developmental Perspective*.

- **Chapter 9** presents the latest data available on school crime, which shows that students ages twelve through eighteen are the victims of about 2 million school-based crimes each year, including more than 125,000 serious violent crimes such as rape, sexual assault, robbery, and aggravated assault. There are sections covering the nature and extent of school shootings, including research now being conducted to determine trends and patterns among school shooters. A Preventing and Treating Delinquency box focuses on Keeping Truants in School; another feature discusses Bullying in School.

- **Chapter 10** presents the latest findings on teen substance abuse reported by national surveys along with the latest findings from the National Institute of Justice's ADAM program for drug use among juvenile arrestees. The most recent evaluation findings of the effects of D.A.R.E. on teen substance abuse and delinquency are reviewed. There is an expanded and up-to-date discussion of drug control strategies.

- In **chapter 11** we present state comparisons of key juvenile justice legal issues. The latest findings on court processing of juvenile offenders are included, and new evaluations of the effects of teen courts on subsequent involvement in delinquency are reviewed. There is an expanded and up-to-date discussion of the future of juvenile justice.

- **Chapter 12** brings together the latest findings on what works when it comes to police efforts to prevent juvenile crime. There is expanded coverage of police innovations, including police in schools, community-based policing, and problem-oriented policing. The chapter also provides a number of new profiles of successful policing practices to prevent juvenile crime.

- **Chapter 13** discusses findings from a recent (2003) American Bar Association study on problems facing public defender services for indigent juveniles. The latest findings on delinquency cases waived to juvenile court are presented. There is an expanded discussion of the death penalty for juveniles, with the latest national statistics on juveniles on death row.

- In **chapter 14** we present the latest findings on juvenile probation and correctional population trends. New evaluation findings of probation innovations and correctional treatment for juveniles, including wilderness programs and boot camps, are reviewed. There are new state comparisons of juvenile offenders and minority representation in custody and an expanded discussion of barriers facing juvenile female inmates.

ANCILLARIES

A number of supplements are provided by Thomson Wadsworth to help instructors use *Juvenile Delinquency: The Core* in their courses and to help students prepare for exams. Available to qualified adopters. Please consult your local sales representative for details.

For the Instructor

Instructor's Manual The manual includes lecture outlines, learning objectives, discussion topics, key terms, student activities, relevant Web sites, media resources, and a test bank that will not only help time-pressed teachers communicate more effectively with their students but also strengthen the coverage of course material. Each chapter has multiple choice, true-false, and fill-in-the-blank test items, as well as sample essay questions.

WebTutor™ ToolBox Preloaded with content and available free via pin code when packaged with this text, WebTutor ToolBox for WebCT pairs the content of this text's rich book companion Web site with all the sophisticated course management functionality of a WebCT product. Instructors may assign materials (including online quizzes) and have the results flow automatically to their gradebook. ToolBox is ready to use at log-on, or the preloaded content can be customized by uploading images and other resources, adding Web links, or creating unique practice materials. Students only have access to student resources on the Web site. Instructors enter a pin code for access to password-protected instructor resources. Contact your Thomson Wadsworth representative for information on packaging the WebTutor ToolBox with this text.

ExamView® This computerized testing software helps instructors create and customize exams in minutes. Instructors can easily edit and import their own questions and graphics, change test layouts, and reorganize questions. This software also offers the ability to test and grade online. It is available for both Windows and Macintosh.

CNN® Today Videos Exclusively from Thomson Wadsworth, the CNN Today video series offers compelling videos that feature current news footage from the Cable News Network's comprehensive archives. Juvenile Delinquency Volumes I through IV each provide a collection of two- to eight-minute clips on hot topics in juvenile delinquency. Available to qualified adopters, these videotapes are great lecture launchers as well as classroom discussion pieces.

Wadsworth Criminal Justice Video Library The Wadsworth Criminal Justice Video Library offers an exciting collection of videos to enrich lectures. Qualified adopters may select from a wide variety of professionally prepared videos covering various aspects of policing, corrections, and other areas of the criminal justice system. The selections include videos from *Films for the Humanities & Sciences, Court TV* videos that feature provocative one-hour court cases to illustrate seminal high-profile cases in depth, *A&E American Justice Series* videos, *National Institute of Justice: Crime File* videos, *ABC News* videos, and *MPI Home Videos*.

Opposing Viewpoints Resource Center (OVRC) This online center allows instructors to expose their students to all sides of today's most compelling issues, including gun control, media violence, genetic engineering, environmental policy, prejudice, abortion, health care reform, and dozens more. The OVRC draws on Greenhaven Press's acclaimed social issues series, as well as core reference content from other Gale and Macmillan Reference USA sources. The result is a dynamic online library of current event topics. Special sections focus on critical thinking (and walk students through how to critically evaluate point-counterpoint arguments) and researching and writing papers. To take a quick tour of the OVRC, visit www.gale.com/OpposingViewpoints/index.htm.

For the Student

Student CD-ROM (packaged free with text)—NEW to this edition Included on the CD are the CNN video clips linked to the Chapter Opening Vignettes with critical thinking questions relating to key points from the text. Student responses can be saved and e-mailed to instructors.

Student Study Guide An extensive study guide has been developed for this edition. Because students learn in different ways, a variety of pedagogical aids are included. The guide outlines each chapter, includes key terms, and provides learning objectives and practice tests.

Companion Web Site This Web site provides chapter outlines and summaries, tutorial quizzing, a final exam, textbook glossary, flashcards, crossword puzzle, concentration game, InfoTrac College Edition exercises, Web links, a link to the OVRC, and the multistep **Concept Builder,** which includes review, application, and exercise questions on chapter-based key concepts.

InfoTrac® College Edition Students receive four months of real-time access to InfoTrac College Edition's online database of continuously updated, full-length articles from hundreds of journals and periodicals. By doing a simple key word search, they can quickly generate a list of related articles, then select relevant articles to explore and print out for reference or further study.

Crime Scenes: An Interactive Criminal Justice CD-ROM This highly interactive program casts students as the decision makers in various roles as they explore all aspects of the criminal justice system. Exciting videos and supporting documents put them in the midst of a juvenile murder trial, a prostitution case that turns into manslaughter, and several other scenarios. This product received the gold medal in higher education and the silver medal for video interface from *NewMedia Magazine's Invision Awards.*

Mind of a Killer CD-ROM Based on Eric Hickey's book *Serial Murderers and Their Victims,* this award-winning CD-ROM offers viewers a look at the psyches of the world's most notorious killers. Students can view confessions of and interviews with serial killers, and examine famous cases through original video documentaries and news footage. Included are 3-D profiling simulations, which are extensive mapping systems that seek to find out what motivates these killers.

Careers in Criminal Justice Interactive CD-ROM Version 3.0 This engaging self-exploration CD-ROM provides an interactive discovery of the wide range of careers in criminal justice. The self-assessment helps steer students to suitable careers based on their personal profile. Students can gather information on various careers from the job descriptions, salaries, employment requirements, sample tests, and video profiles of criminal justice professionals presented on this valuable tool.

Seeking Employment in Criminal Justice and Related Fields, Fourth Edition by J. Scott Harr and Kären Hess. This practical book helps students develop a search strategy to find employment in criminal justice and related fields. Each chapter includes "insiders' views," written by individuals in the field and addressing promotions and career planning.

Guide to Careers in Criminal Justice   This concise sixty-page booklet provides a brief introduction to the exciting and diverse field of criminal justice. Students can learn about opportunities in law enforcement, courts, and corrections and how they can go about getting these jobs.

Criminal Justice Internet Investigator III   This handy brochure lists the most useful criminal justice links on the Web. It includes the popular criminal justice and criminology sites featuring online newsletters, grants and funding information, statistics, and more.

Internet Guide for Criminal Justice   Developed by Daniel Kurland and Christina Polsenberg, this easy reference text helps newcomers as well as experienced Web surfers use the Internet for criminal justice research.

Internet Activities for Criminal Justice   This sixty-page booklet shows how to best employ the Internet to do research via searches and activities.

ACKNOWLEDGMENTS

It would not have been possible to prepare this text without the aid of our colleagues, who helped by reviewing the manuscript and making important suggestions for improvement. These colleagues include, for this edition:

Patricia Grant, Virginia Commonwealth University
Julia Glover Hall, Drexel University
Eric L. Jensen, University of Idaho
Brian A. Perusek, Lakeland Community College
Shela Vanness, University of Tennessee at Chattanooga
Charles M. Vivona, SUNY College at Old Westbury
Lisa Hutchinson Wallace, University of Alaska Fairbanks

We also gratefully acknowledge reviewers who helped us on the first edition: Bruce Berg, California State University Long Beach; Sue Bourke, University of Cincinnati; Jerald C. Burns, Alabama State University; Ann Butzin, Owens State Community College; John R. Cross, Oklahoma State University; Brendan Maguire, Western Illinois University; Jane Kravitz Munley, Luzern County Community College; Rebecca D. Peterson, University of Texas San Antonio; and Cheryl Tieman, Radford University.

Our colleagues at Wadsworth did their usual outstanding job of aiding in the preparation of the text. Sabra Horne, our wonderful editor, is always there for us when we need her. Shelley Murphy, our great developmental editor, kept us on track throughout the writing and editing stages. Jennie "From the Block" Redwitz, project manager, somehow manages to pull everything together. Linda Rill did her usual thorough, professional job in photo research and is an honorary Siegel family member. Linda Jupiter, who managed the book's production, has been great to work with. Sandra Beris was a fantastic copyeditor, M. Kate St.Clair was a terrific proofreader, and Medea Minnich did an outstanding job indexing. And Susan DeVanna, technology project manager, worked tirelessly on the development of the new CD-ROM and the text Web site. We are also grateful to Terra Schultz, a tireless worker on the marketing front who has and will continue to make a huge difference, and to Joy Westberg.

Larry J. Siegel
Bedford, NH

Brandon C. Welsh
Brookline, NH

Childhood and Delinquency

CHAPTER OUTLINE

CHAPTER OBJECTIVES

**After reading this chapter
you should:**

1. Be familiar with the problems of youth in American culture.
2. Be able to discuss the concept of adolescence and risk taking.
3. Develop an understanding of the history of childhood.
4. Be familiar with the concept of *parens patriae.*
5. Be able to discuss development of a special status of minor offenders.
6. Know what is meant by the terms *juvenile delinquent* and *status offender.*
7. Be able to describe the differences between delinquency and status offending.
8. Be able to discuss what is meant by parental responsibility laws.
9. Be familiar with juvenile curfew laws.
10. Identify the efforts being made to reform status offense laws.

1

In 1999 the nation was shocked when a twelve-year-old boy, Lionel Tate, was arrested for beating to death a six-year-old girl, Tiffany Eunick, a family friend. Lionel's attorneys argued that the incident was an accident, and that the boy was merely imitating wrestling moves he had seen on television.

Tiffany's autopsy revealed that she had suffered a crushed skull, broken ribs, and more than thirty internal bruises. Her liver had been shredded and pushed through her rib cage. She must have screamed in agony before her death, but her cries were unheeded. The thought that Lionel was merely "playing" seemed ludicrous considering the damage done.

Before his trial in adult court, Lionel's mother and defense attorney turned down a plea bargain offer for a three-year sentence followed by counseling and treatment. At trial, the boy was sentenced to life in prison with no chance of parole. Many were surprised that such a young child could be given a lifetime prison sentence. Three years later the conviction was overturned on appeal, and a new trial ordered on the grounds that Lionel had not been given a competency evaluation before his trial. Because Tiffany's family was favorable to clemency, the prosecutor offered Lionel the option of pleading guilty to second-degree murder with a sentence of the three years he had already served, another year of house arrest, and ten years probation. He also must receive counseling, perform a thousand hours of community service, and wear a monitoring device. Lionel walked out of prison on January 26, 2004.

CNN. VIEW THE CNN VIDEO CLIP OF THIS STORY AND ANSWER RELATED CRITICAL THINKING QUESTIONS ON YOUR JUVENILE DELINQUENCY: THE CORE 2E CD.

There are about seventy-three million children under age eighteen in the United States, making up 25 percent of the population, down from a peak of 36 percent at the end of the baby boom, in 1964.[1] Children are projected to remain a substantial percentage of the total population, expected to reach eighty million or about 24 percent of the population in 2020.[2] The present generation of adolescents has been described as cynical, preoccupied with material acquisitions, and uninterested in creative expression.[3] By age eighteen they have spent more time in front of a TV set than in the classroom; each year they may see up to one thousand rapes, murders, and assaults on TV.

In the 1950s teenagers were reading comic books, but today teens are listening to rap CDs such as Fifty Cent's "In Da Club," whose lyrics routinely describe substance abuse and promiscuity. They watch TV shows and movies that rely on graphic scenes of violence as their main theme, and cyberspace has exposed them to images that their parents could not imagine. How will this exposure affect them? Should we be concerned? Can the media be blamed for Lionel Tate's violent act?

THE ADOLESCENT DILEMMA

The problems of American society have had a significant effect on our nation's youth. Adolescence is a time of trial and uncertainty, a time when youths experience anxiety, humiliation, and mood swings. During this period, the personality is still developing and is vulnerable to a host of external factors. Adolescents also undergo a period of rapid biological development. During just a few years' time, their height,

Older But Wiser

"When I was a boy of fourteen, my father was so ignorant I could hardly stand to have the old man around. But when I got to be twenty-one, I was astonished at how much he had learned in seven years" (Mark Twain, "Old Times on the Mississippi," *Atlantic Monthly*, 1874).

Do you agree with Mark Twain? When you look back at your adolescence are you surprised at how much you thought you knew then and how little you know now? Did you do anything that you now consider silly and immature? Of course, as they say, "Hindsight is always 20/20." Maybe there is a benefit to teenage rebellion. For example, would it make you a better parent knowing firsthand about all the trouble your kids get into and why they do?

weight, and sexual characteristics change dramatically. A hundred and fifty years ago girls matured sexually at age 16, but today they do so at 12.5 years of age. Although they may be capable of having children as early as 14, many youngsters remain emotionally immature long after reaching biological maturity. At age 15 a significant number of teenagers are unable to meet the responsibilities of the workplace, the family, and the neighborhood. Many suffer from health problems, are underachievers in school, and are skeptical about their ability to enter the workforce and become productive members of society.

In later adolescence (ages sixteen to eighteen), youths may experience a crisis that psychologist Erik Erikson described as a struggle between ego identity and role diffusion. **Ego identity** is formed when youths develop a firm sense of who they are and what they stand for; **role diffusion** occurs when youths experience uncertainty and place themselves at the mercy of leaders who promise to give them a sense of identity they cannot mold for themselves.[4] Psychologists also find that late adolescence is dominated by a yearning for independence from parental control.[5] Given this mixture of biological change and desire for autonomy, it isn't surprising that the teenage years are a time of conflict with authority at home, at school, and in the community.

Youth in Crisis

Problems in the home, the school, and the neighborhood have placed a significant portion of American youths at risk. Youths considered at risk are those who engage in dangerous conduct such as drug abuse, alcohol use, and precocious sexuality. Although it is impossible to determine precisely the number of **at-risk youths** in the United States, one estimate is that 25 percent of the population under age seventeen, or about seventeen million youths, are in this category. Of these, seven million are extremely vulnerable to delinquency and gang activity.[6] An additional seven million adolescents can be classified as at moderate risk.[7] The most pressing problems facing American youth revolve around five issues.[8]

Poverty As Figure 1.1 shows, children have a higher poverty rate than any other age group.

And though the poverty rate has declined in recent years, the number of African-American children living in extreme poverty is at its highest level in twenty-three years; nearly one million African-American children in 2001 lived in a family with an annual income of less than half the federal poverty level (disposable income below $7,064 for a family of three).[9]

Hundreds of studies have documented the association between family poverty and children's health, achievement, and behavior impairments.[10] Children who grow up in low-income homes are less likely to achieve in school and less likely to complete their schooling than children with more affluent parents.

Health Problems Many children are now suffering from chronic health problems and receive inadequate health care. Poverty influences health. Children living below the poverty line are less likely than children in higher-income families to be in very good or excellent health: 71 percent of poor children are considered in good or excellent health versus 86 percent of more-affluent children who enjoy good health.[11]

The number of U.S. children covered by health insurance is declining and will continue to do so for the foreseeable future. A recent (2003) national survey found that

ego identity
According to Erik Erikson, ego identity is formed when persons develop a firm sense of who they are and what they stand for.

role diffusion
According to Erik Erikson, role diffusion occurs when youths spread themselves too thin, experience personal uncertainty, and place themselves at the mercy of leaders who promise to give them a sense of identity they cannot develop for themselves.

at-risk youths
Young people who are extremely vulnerable to the negative consequences of school failure, substance abuse, and early sexuality.

in more than half the states, at least 10 percent of children have no health insurance. The percentage of children without health coverage ranged from more than 20 percent in Texas to 5 percent in Vermont, Rhode Island, and Wisconsin.[12] Without health benefits or the means to afford medical care, these children are likely to have health problems that impede their long-term development.

Family Problems   Divorce strikes about half of all new marriages, and many families sacrifice time with each other to afford more affluent lifestyles. In 2002, 69 percent of children under age eighteen lived with two married parents, down from 77 percent in 1980. However, the percentage has remained stable since 1995, ending a decades-long downward trend. In 2003, about one-fifth of children lived with only their mothers, 5 percent lived with only their fathers, and 4 percent lived with neither of their parents.[13] Children are being polarized into two distinct economic groups: those in affluent, two-earner, married-couple households and those in poor, single-parent households.[14] Kids whose parents divorce may increase their involvement in delinquency, especially if they have a close bond with the parent who is forced to leave.[15]

Substandard Living Conditions   Many children live in substandard housing—such as high-rise, multiple-family dwellings—which can have a negative influence on their long-term psychological health.[16] Adolescents living in deteriorated urban areas are prevented from having productive and happy lives. Many die from random bullets and drive-by shootings. Some adolescents are homeless and living on the street, where they are at risk of drug addiction and sexually transmitted diseases (STDs), including AIDS. Today about one third of U.S. households with children had one or more of the following three housing problems: physically inadequate housing, crowded housing, or housing that cost more than 30 percent of the household income.[17]

| Figure 1.1 | Poverty Rates by Age, 1959–2002 |

Note: The data points represent the midpoints of the respective years.
Data for people ages 18 to 64 and 65 and older are not available from 1960 to 1965.

Source: *Current Population Survey, 1960–2003, Annual Social and Economic Supplements* (Washington, DC: U.S. Census Bureau, 2003).

Inadequate Education   The U.S. educational system seems to be failing many young people. We are lagging behind other developed nations in critical areas such as science and mathematics. The rate of *retention* (being forced to repeat a grade) is far higher than it should be. Retention rates are associated with another major problem: dropping out. It is estimated that about 14 percent of all eligible youths do not finish high school.[18] In addition, poor and minority-group children attend the most underfunded schools, receive inadequate educational opportunities, and have the fewest opportunities to achieve conventional success.

Considering that youth are at risk during the most tumultuous time of their lives, it comes as no surprise that, as the Focus on Delinquency box entitled "Teen Risk Taking" suggests, they are willing to engage in risky, destructive behavior.

Is There Reason for Hope?

Despite the many hazards faced by teens, there are some bright spots on the horizon. Teenage birthrates nationwide have declined substantially during the past decade, with the sharpest declines among African-American girls. Over the past decade, the birthrate dropped 19 percent while the abortion rate was down 39 percent in this age group. More recent data indicate the teen birthrate has continued to drop through 2002—down 28 percent during the past decade.[19] These data indicate that more young girls are using birth control and practicing safe sex. Fewer children with health risks are being born today than in 1990. This probably means that fewer women are drinking or smoking during pregnancy and that fewer are receiving late or no prenatal care. In addition, since 1990 the number of children immunized against disease has increased. The infant mortality rate for the United States is seven deaths per one thousand live births; infant mortality has dropped for all racial and ethnic groups since 1983.[20]

Education is still a problem area, but more parents are reading to their children, and math achievement is rising in grades four through twelve. More students are receiving degrees in math and science than were doing so in the 1970s and 1980s.[21] There are also indications that youngsters may be rejecting hard drugs. Teen smoking and drinking rates remain high, but fewer kids are using heroin and crack cocaine and the numbers of teens who report cigarette use has been in decline since the

Maria Sanchez, shown here with her family, lives in Starr County, Texas, one of the poorest communities in the United States. Do you think there is a relationship between delinquency and growing up in an area with high levels of substandard housing and high rates of poverty?

© Lara Jo Regan/Getty Images

Teen Risk Taking

The Centers for Disease Control and Prevention (CDC) reports that, in the United States, 70 percent of all deaths among youth and young adults from ten to twenty-four years of age result from only four causes: motor vehicle crashes, unintentional injuries, homicide, and suicide. The reason may be that many high school students engage in risky behaviors that increase their likelihood of death from violence, accident, or self-destruction. The CDC found that high school students engaged in the following risky behaviors described in Table A.

Why do youths take such chances? Criminologist Nanette Davis suggests there is a potential for risky behavior among youth in all facets of American life. *Risky* describes behavior that is emotionally edgy, dangerous, exciting, hazardous, challenging, volatile, and potentially emotionally, socially, and financially costly—even life-threatening. Youths commonly become involved in risky behavior as they negotiate the hurdles of adolescent life, learning to drive, date, drink, work, relate, and live. Davis finds that social developments in the United States have increased the risks of growing up for all children. The social, economic, and political circumstances that increase adolescent risk taking include these:

1. *The uncertainty of contemporary social life.* Planning a future is problematic in a society where job elimination and corporate downsizing are accepted business practices, and divorce and family restructuring are epidemic.
2. *Politicians who opt for short-term solutions while ignoring long-term consequences.* For example, politicians may find that fighting minimum wage increases pleases their constituents. Yet a low minimum wage reinforces the belief that economic advancement cannot be achieved through conventional means; the politicians' actions

may undermine the working poor's belief in the American Dream of economic opportunity. Lack of legitimate opportunity may lead to delinquent alternatives such as drug dealing or theft.

3. *Emphasis on consumerism.* In high schools, peer respect is bought through the accumulation of material goods. Underprivileged youth are driven to illegal behavior in an effort to engage in conspicuous consumption. Drug deals and theft may be a shortcut to getting coveted name-brand clothes and athletic shoes.
4. *Racial, class, age, and ethnicity inequalities.* These discourage kids from believing in a better future. Children are raised to be skeptical that they can receive social benefits from any institution beyond themselves or their immediate family.
5. *Lack of adequate child care.* This has become a national emergency. Lower-class women cannot afford adequate child care. New welfare laws that require single mothers to work put millions of kids in high-risk situations. Children in low-quality care can have delayed cognition and language development. They behave more aggressively toward others and react poorly to stress.
6. *Access to dominant social institutions and persons in authority.* For some, this access is barred. The inability to have access—most often a function of social class and occupation—decreases the ability to manage risk.
7. *The "cult of individualism."* This makes people self-centered and hurts collective and group identities. Children are taught to put their own interests above those of others.

As children mature into adults, the uncertainty of modern society may prolong their risk-taking behavior. Jobs have become unpredictable, and many undereducated and undertrained youths find themselves competing for the same low-

mid-1990s.[22] Although these are encouraging signs, many problem areas remain, and the improvement of adolescent life continues to be a national goal.

THE STUDY OF JUVENILE DELINQUENCY

The problems of youth in modern society are an important subject for academic study. This text focuses on one area of particular concern: **juvenile delinquency,** or criminal behavior engaged in by minors. The study of juvenile delinquency is important both because of the damage suffered by its victims and the problems faced by its perpetrators.

Almost 1.6 million youths under age eighteen were arrested in 2002 for crimes ranging from loitering to murder.[23] Though most juvenile law violations are minor, some young offenders are extremely dangerous and violent. More than eight hundred thousand youths belong to street gangs. Youths involved in multiple serious criminal acts, referred to as *repeat,* or **chronic juvenile offenders,** are considered a

juvenile delinquency
Participation in illegal behavior by a minor who falls under a statutory age limit.

64%	Ever smoked cigarettes		24%	Used marijuana during the past month
28%	Smoked cigarettes during the past month		9%	Ever used cocaine
14%	Rarely or never used safety belts		15%	Ever sniffed or inhaled intoxicating substances
31%	Rode with a drinking driver during the past month		46%	Ever had sexual intercourse
			14%	Had had four or more sex partners
17%	Carried a weapon during the past month		33%	Had sexual intercourse during the past three months
33%	Were in a physical fight during the past year		42%	Did not use a condom during last sexual intercourse
9%	Attempted suicide during the past year		82%	Did not use birth control pills during last sexual intercourse
47%	Drank alcohol during the past month			
30%	Reported episodic heavy drinking during the past month			

paying job as hundreds of other applicants; they are a "surplus product." They may find their only alternative for survival is to return to their childhood bedroom and live off their parents. Under these circumstances, risk taking may be a plausible alternative for fitting in in our consumer-oriented society.

CRITICAL THINKING

1. Davis calls for a major national effort to restore these troubled youths using a holistic, nonpunitive approach that recognizes the special needs of children. How would you convince kids to stop taking risks?
2. Do you agree that elements of contemporary society cause kids to take risks, or do you think that teens are natural risk takers who are actually rebelling against a society that discourages their behavior?

INFOTRAC COLLEGE EDITION RESEARCH

Why do kids take risks? Could it be that they believe their parents will never find out? To read more, go to N. R. Saltmarsh, "Adolescent Risk Taking Tied to Perceived Parental Monitoring," *B & Outbreaks Week*, June 26, 2001, p.NA. To find out more, use "teenage risk taking" as a key term in InfoTrac College Edition.

Sources: Jo Anne Grunbaum et al., *Youth Risk Behavior Surveillance: United States, 2001* (Atlanta, GA: Centers for Disease Control, *Morbidity and Mortality Weekly Report*, June 28, 2002); Nanette Davis, *Youth Crisis: Growing Up in the High-Risk Society* (New York: Praeger/Greenwood, 1998).

chronic juvenile offenders (also known as chronic delinquent offenders, chronic delinquents, or chronic recidivists)
Youths who have been arrested four or more times during their minority and perpetuate a striking majority of serious criminal acts; this small group, known as the "chronic 6 percent," is believed to engage in a significant portion of all delinquent behavior; these youths do not age out of crime but continue their criminal behavior into adulthood.

juvenile justice system
The segment of the justice system including law enforcement officers, the courts, and correctional agencies that is designed to treat youthful offenders.

serious social problem. State juvenile authorities must deal with these offenders while responding to a range of other social problems, including child abuse and neglect, school crime and vandalism, family crises, and drug abuse.

Clearly, there is an urgent need for strategies to combat juvenile delinquency. But formulating effective strategies demands a solid understanding of the causes of delinquency. Is it a function of psychological abnormality? A reaction against destructive social conditions? The product of a disturbed home life? Does serious delinquent behavior occur only in urban areas among lower-class youths? Or is it spread throughout the social structure? What are the effects of family life, substance abuse, school experiences, and peer relations?

The study of delinquency also involves the analysis of the **juvenile justice system**—the law enforcement, court, and correctional agencies designed to treat youthful offenders. How should police deal with minors who violate the law? What are the legal rights of children? What kinds of correctional programs are most effective with delinquent youths? How useful are educational, community, counseling, and vocational development programs? Is it true, as some critics claim, that most

The study of juvenile delinquency is important both because of the damage suffered by its victims and the problems faced by its perpetrators. Here young girls in California place roses on the coffin of a friend killed in a drive-by shooting. Hundreds of teens are killed each year in gang-related crimes.

© A. Ramey/PhotoEdit

efforts to rehabilitate young offenders are doomed to failure?[24] The reaction to juvenile delinquency frequently divides the public. People want to insulate young people from a life of crime and drug abuse. Research suggests that a majority still favor policies mandating rehabilitation of offenders.[25] Evidence also exists that many at-risk youths can be helped successfully with the proper treatment.[26] However, many Americans are wary of teenage hoodlums and gangs. How can we control their behavior? Should we embrace a "get tough" policy in which violent teens are locked up? Or should we continue to treat delinquents as troubled teens who need a helping hand? Many juvenile court judges today base their sentencing decisions on the need to punish offenders and are more concerned about protecting the rights of victims of crime than rehabilitating juveniles.[27] Similarly, the Supreme Court has legalized the death penalty for children once they reach age sixteen.[28] Should the juvenile justice system be more concerned about the long-term effects of punishment? Can even the most violent teenager one day be rehabilitated?

In summary, the scientific study of delinquency requires understanding the nature, extent, and cause of youthful law violations and the methods devised for their control. We also need to study environmental and social issues, including substance abuse, child abuse and neglect, education, and peer relations. All of these aspects of juvenile delinquency will be discussed in this text. We begin, however, with a look back to the development of the concept of childhood and how children were first identified as a unique group with their own special needs and behaviors.

THE DEVELOPMENT OF CHILDHOOD

paternalistic family
A family style wherein the father is the final authority on all family matters and exercises complete control over his wife and children.

Treating children as a distinct social group with special needs and behavior is a relatively new concept. Only for the past 350 years has any formal mechanism existed to care for even the neediest children. In Europe during the Middle Ages (A.D. 700–1500), the concept of childhood as we know it today did not exist. In the **paternalistic family** of the time, the father exercised complete control over his wife and children.[29] Children who did not obey were subject to severe physical punishment, even death.

Should we embrace a get-tough policy in which violent teens are locked up? Or should we continue to treat delinquents as troubled teens who need a helping hand? Can we combine both approaches? Chandra Soh, pictured here, has used her contacts with the community of Khmer Buddhist Monks in North Chelmsford, Massachusetts, to help coordinate a youth violence prevention program for Southeast Asian runaways with the Lowell Police Department.

Custom and Practice in the Middle Ages

During the Middle Ages, as soon as they were physically capable, children of all classes were expected to take on adult roles. Boys learned farming or a skilled trade such as masonry or metalworking; girls aided in food preparation or household maintenance.[30] Some peasant youths went into domestic or agricultural service on the estates of powerful landowners or became apprenticed in trades or crafts.[31] Children of the landholding classes also assumed adult roles at an early age. At age seven or eight, boys born to landholding families were either sent to a monastery or cathedral school or were sent to serve as squires, or assistants, to experienced knights. At age twenty-one, young men of the knightly classes received their own knighthood and returned home to live with their parents. Girls were educated at home and married in their early teens. A few were taught to read, write, and do sufficient mathematics to handle household accounts in addition to typical female duties such as supervising servants.

Some experts, most notably Philippe Aries, have described the medieval child as a "miniature adult" who began to work and accept adult roles at an early age and were treated with great cruelty.[32] In a new work, *Medieval Children* (2003), historian Nicholas Orme disagrees with this standard vision. Orme finds that the medieval mother began to care for her children even before their delivery. Royal ladies borrowed relics of the Virgin Mary from the Church to protect their unborn children, while poorer women used jasper stones or drawings of the cross, which were placed across their stomachs to ensure a healthy and uneventful birth. Parents associated their children's birthdays with a saint's feast day. As they do today, children devised songs, rhymes, and games. Some used cherry pits and hazelnuts in their games. They had toys, including dolls, and even mechanical toys made for royalty.[33]

Child Rearing and Discipline   In many families, especially the highborn, newborns were handed over to *wet nurses* who fed and cared for them during the first two years of life; parents had little contact with their children. Discipline was severe. Young children of all classes were subjected to stringent rules and regulations. Children were beaten severely for any sign of disobedience or ill temper, and many would be considered abused by today's standards. Children were expected to undertake responsibilities early in their lives, sharing in the work of siblings and parents. Those thought to be suffering from disease or retardation were often abandoned to churches, orphanages, or foundling homes.[34]

The impersonal relationship between parent and child can be traced to the high mortality rates of the day. Parents were reluctant to invest emotional effort in relationships that could so easily end because of violence, accident, or disease. Many believed that children must be toughened to ensure their survival, and close family relationships were viewed as detrimental to this process. Also, since the oldest male child was the essential player in a family's well-being, younger male and female siblings were considered liabilities.

The Development of Concern for Children

Throughout the seventeenth and eighteenth centuries, a number of developments in England heralded the march toward the recognition of children's rights. Among them were changes in family style and child care, the English Poor Laws, the apprenticeship movement, and the role of the chancery court.[35]

Changes in Family Structure

Family structure began to change after the Middle Ages. Extended families, which were created over centuries, gave way to the nuclear family structure with which we are familiar today. It became more common for marriage to be based on love rather than parental consent and paternal dominance. This changing concept of marriage from an economic arrangement to an emotional commitment also began to influence the way children were treated. Although parents still rigidly disciplined their children, they formed closer ties and had greater concern for the well-being of their offspring.

Grammar and boarding schools were established in many large cities during this time.[36] Children studied grammar, Latin, law, and logic. Teachers often ruled by fear. Students were beaten for academic mistakes as well as for moral lapses. Such brutal treatment fell on both the rich and the poor throughout all levels of educational life, including boarding schools and universities. This treatment abated in Europe during the Enlightenment, but it remained in full force in Great Britain until late in the nineteenth century.

Toward the close of the eighteenth century, the work of such philosophers as Voltaire, Rousseau, and Locke launched a new age for childhood and the family.[37] Their vision produced a period known as the Enlightenment, which stressed a humanistic view of life, freedom, family, reason, and law. These new beliefs influenced the family. The father's authority was tempered, discipline became more relaxed, and the expression of affection became more commonplace. Upper- and middle-class families began to devote attention to child rearing, and the status of children was advanced.

As a result of these changes, children began to emerge as a distinct group with independent needs and interests. Serious questions arose over the treatment of children in school. Restrictions were placed on the use of the whip, and in some schools academic assignments or the loss of privileges replaced corporal punishment. Despite such reforms, punishment was still primarily physical, and schools continued to mistreat children.

Poor Laws

As early as 1535, the English passed statutes known as **Poor Laws.**[38] These laws allowed for the appointment of overseers to place destitute or neglected children as servants in the homes of the affluent, where they were trained in agricultural, trade, or domestic services. The Elizabethan Poor Laws of 1601 created a system of church wardens and overseers who, with the consent of justices of the peace, identified vagrant, delinquent, and neglected children and put them to work. Often this meant placing them in poorhouses or workhouses or apprenticing them to masters.

The Apprenticeship Movement

Apprenticeship existed throughout almost the entire history of Great Britain.[39] Under this practice, children were placed in the care of adults who trained them in specific skills, such as being a blacksmith or a farrier (a shoer of horses). *Voluntary apprentices* were bound out by parents or guardians in exchange for a fee. Legal authority over the child was then transferred to the apprentice's master. The system helped parents avoid the costs and responsibilities of child rearing. *Involuntary apprentices* were compelled by the legal authorities to serve a master until they were twenty-one or older. The master-apprentice relationship was similar to the parent-child relationship in that the master had complete authority over the apprentice and could have agreements enforced by local magistrates.

Poor Laws

English statutes that allowed the courts to appoint overseers for destitute and neglected children, allowing placement of these children as servants in the homes of the affluent.

As soon as they were physically capable, children of the Middle Ages were expected to engage in adult roles. Among the working classes, males engaged in peasant farming or learned a skilled trade, such as masonry or metalworking; females aided in food preparation or household maintenance. Some peasant youth went into domestic or agricultural service on the estate of a powerful land-owner or into trades or crafts, such as blacksmith or farrier (horseshoer).

chancery courts
Court proceedings created in fifteenth-century England to oversee the lives of highborn minors who were orphaned or otherwise could not care for themselves.

parens patriae
The power of the state to act on behalf of the child and provide care and protection equivalent to that of a parent.

Chancery Court   Throughout Great Britain in the Middle Ages, **chancery courts** were established to protect property rights and seek equitable solutions to disputes and conflicts. Eventually, its authority was extended to the welfare of children in cases involving the guardianship of orphans. This included safeguarding their property and inheritance rights and appointing a guardian to protect them until they reached the age of majority.

The courts operated on the proposition that children were under the protective control of the king; thus, the Latin phrase **parens patriae** was used, which refers to the role of the king as the father of his country. The concept was first used by English kings to establish their right to intervene in the lives of the children of their vassals.[40] In the famous 1827 case *Wellesley v. Wellesley*, a duke's children were taken away from him in the name and interest of *parens patriae* because of his scandalous behavior.[41] Thus, the concept of *parens patriae* became the theoretical basis for the protective jurisdiction of the chancery courts acting as part of the Crown's power. As time passed, the monarchy used *parens patriae* more and more to justify its intervention in the lives of families and children.[42]

The chancery courts did not have jurisdiction over children charged with criminal conduct. Juveniles who violated the law were handled through the regular criminal court system. Nonetheless, the concept of *parens patriae* grew to refer primarily to the responsibility of the courts and the state to act in the best interests of the child.

For more information on the early history of childhood and the development of education, go to "Factors Influencing the Development of the Idea of Childhood in Europe and America," by Jim Vandergriff. Find this Web site by clicking on Web Links under the Chapter Resources at http://cj.wadsworth.com/siegel_jdcore2e.

Checkpoints

✔ *The problems of American youth have become a national concern and an important subject of academic study.*

✔ *There are more than seventy million youths in the United States, and the number is expected to rise.*

✔ *American youth are under a great deal of stress. They face poverty, family problems, urban decay, inadequate education, teen pregnancy, and social conflict.*

✔ *The concept of a separate status of childhood has developed slowly over the centuries.*

✔ *Early family life was controlled by parents. Punishment was severe and children were expected to take on adult roles early in their lives.*

Childhood in America

While England was using its chancery courts and Poor Laws to care for children in need, the American colonies were developing similar concepts. The colonies were a haven for people looking for opportunities denied them in England and Europe. Along with the adult early settlers, many children came not as citizens but as indentured servants, apprentices, or agricultural workers. They were recruited from workhouses, orphanages, prisons, and asylums that housed vagrant and delinquent youths.[43]

At the same time, the colonists themselves produced illegitimate, neglected, and delinquent children. The initial response to caring for such children was to adopt court and Poor Law systems similar to those in England. Poor Law legislation requiring poor and dependent children to serve apprenticeships was passed in Virginia in 1646 and in Massachusetts and Connecticut in 1673.[44]

It was also possible, as in England, for parents to voluntarily apprentice their children to a master for care and training. The master in colonial America acted as a surrogate parent, and in certain instances apprentices would actually become part of the family. If they disobeyed their masters, they were punished by local tribunals. If masters abused apprentices, courts would make them pay damages, return the children to the parents, or find new guardians for them. Maryland and Virginia developed an orphans' court that supervised the treatment of youths placed with guardians. These courts did not supervise children living with their natural parents, leaving intact parents' rights to care for their children.[45]

By the beginning of the nineteenth century, the apprenticeship system gave way to the factory system, and the problems of how to deal with dependent youths increased. Early settlers believed hard work, strict discipline, and education were the only reliable methods for salvation. A child's life was marked by work alongside parents, some schooling, prayer, more work, and further study. Work in the factories, however, often placed demands on child laborers that they were too young to endure. To alleviate this problem, the *Factory Act* of the early nineteenth century limited the hours children were permitted to work and the age at which they could begin to work. It also prescribed a minimum amount of schooling to be provided by factory owners.[46] This and related statutes were often violated, and conditions of work and school remained troublesome issues well into the twentieth century. Nevertheless, the statutes were a step in the direction of reform.

A century ago, work in the factories often placed demands on child laborers that many were too young to endure. Here children work in a North Carolina cotton mill in 1908.

© Corbis

Controlling Children

In the United States, as in England, moral discipline was rigidly enforced. Stubborn child laws were passed that required children to obey their parents.[47] It was not uncommon for children to be whipped if they were disobedient or disrespectful to their families. Children were often required to attend public whippings and executions because these events were thought to be important forms of moral instruction. Parents referred their children to published writings on behavior and expected them to follow their precepts carefully. The early colonists, however, viewed family violence as a sin, and child protection laws were passed as early as 1639 (in New Haven, Connecticut). These laws expressed the community's commitment to God to oppose sin, but offenders usually received lenient sentences.[48]

Although most colonies adopted a protectionist stance, few cases of child abuse were actually brought before the courts. This neglect may reflect the nature of life in extremely religious households. Children were productive laborers and respected by their parents. In addition, large families provided many siblings and kinfolk who could care for children and relieve the burden on parents.[49] Another view is that although many children were harshly punished, in early America the acceptable limits of discipline were so high that few parents were charged with assault. Any punishment that fell short of maiming or permanently harming a child was considered within the sphere of parental rights.[50] ✔ Checkpoints

THE CONCEPT OF DELINQUENCY

Until the twentieth century, little distinction was made between adult and juvenile offenders. Although judges considered the age of an offender when deciding on punishment, both adults and children were eligible for prison, corporal punishment, and even the death penalty. In fact, children were treated with extreme cruelty at home, at school, and by the law.[51]

Over the years this treatment changed as society became sensitive to the special needs of children. Beginning in the mid-nineteenth century, there was official recognition that children formed a separate group with their own special needs. In New York, Boston, and Chicago, groups known as **child savers** were formed to assist children. They created community programs to service needy children and lobbied for a separate legal status for children, which ultimately led to development of a formal juvenile justice system. The child-saving movement will be discussed more fully in chapter 11.

child savers
Nineteenth-century reformers who developed programs for troubled youth and influenced legislation creating the juvenile justice system; today some critics view them as being more concerned with control of the poor than with their welfare.

delinquent
Juvenile who has been adjudicated by a judicial officer of a juvenile court as having committed a delinquent act.

best interests of the child
A philosophical viewpoint that encourages the state to take control of wayward children and provide care, custody, and treatment to remedy delinquent behavior.

Delinquency and *Parens Patriae*

The current treatment of juvenile delinquents is a by-product of this developing national consciousness of children's needs. The designation *delinquent* became popular at the onset of the twentieth century when the first separate juvenile courts were instituted. The child savers believed that treating minors and adults equally violated the humanitarian ideals of American society. Consequently, the emerging juvenile justice system operated under the *parens patriae* philosophy. Minors who engaged in illegal behavior were viewed as victims of improper care at home. Illegal behavior was a sign that the state should step in and take control of the youths before they committed more serious crimes. The state should act in the **best interests of the child.** Children should not be punished for their misdeeds but instead should be given the care necessary to control wayward behavior. It makes no sense to find children guilty of specific crimes, such as burglary or petty larceny, because that stigmatizes them as thieves or burglars. Instead, the catchall term *juvenile delinquency* should be used because it indicates that the child needs the care and custody of the state.

The Legal Status of Delinquency

The child savers fought hard for a legal status of juvenile delinquent, but the concept that children could be treated differently before the law can actually be traced to the British legal tradition. Early British jurisprudence held that children under the age of seven were legally incapable of committing crimes. Children between the ages of seven and fourteen were responsible for their actions, but their age might be used to excuse or lighten their punishment. Our legal system still recognizes that many young people are incapable of making mature judgments and that responsibility for their acts should be limited. Children can intentionally steal cars and know that the act is illegal, but they may be incapable of fully understanding the consequences of their behavior. Therefore, the law does not punish a youth as it would an adult, and it sees youthful misconduct as evidence of impaired judgment.

Today, the legal status of *juvenile delinquent* refers to a minor child who has been found to have violated the penal code. Most states define *minor child* as an individual who falls under a statutory age limit, most commonly seventeen or eighteen years of age. Juveniles are usually kept separate from adults and receive different treatment under the law. Most large police departments employ officers whose sole responsibility is delinquency. Every state has some form of juvenile court with its own judges, probation department, and other facilities. Terminology is also different. Adults are *tried* in court; children are *adjudicated*. Adults can be *punished;* children are *treated*. If treatment is mandated, children can be sent to secure detention facilities, but they cannot normally be committed to adult prisons.

Children also have a unique legal status. A minor apprehended for a criminal act is usually charged with being a juvenile delinquent regardless of the offense. These charges are confidential, and trial records are kept secret. The purpose of these safeguards is to shield children from the stigma of a criminal conviction and to prevent youthful misdeeds from becoming a lifelong burden.

Legal Responsibility of Youths

In our society the actions of adults are controlled by two types of law: criminal law and civil law. Criminal laws prohibit activities that are injurious to the well-being of society, such as drug use, theft, and rape; criminal legal actions are brought by state authorities against private citizens. In contrast, civil laws control interpersonal or private activities, and legal actions are usually initiated by individual citizens. Contractual relationships and personal conflicts (torts) are subjects of civil law. Also covered under civil law are provisions for the care of people who cannot care for themselves—for example, the mentally ill, the incompetent, and the infirm.

Today juvenile delinquency falls somewhere between criminal and civil law. Under *parens patriae,* delinquent acts are not considered criminal violations. The legal action against them is similar (though not identical) to a civil action that, in an ideal situation, is based on their **need for treatment.** This legal theory recognizes that children who violate the law are in need of the same treatment as are law-abiding citizens who cannot care for themselves.

Delinquent behavior is treated more leniently than adult misbehavior because the law considers juveniles to be less responsible for their behavior than adults. Compared with adults, adolescents are believed to (1) have a stronger preference for risk and novelty; (2) be less accurate in assessing the potential consequences of risky conduct; (3) be more impulsive and more concerned with short-term consequences; (4) have a different appreciation of time and self-control; and (5) be more susceptible to peer pressure.[52]

Even though youths have a lesser degree of legal responsibility, like adults they are subject to arrest, trial, and incarceration. Their legal predicament has prompted the courts to grant children many of the same legal protections conferred on adults accused of criminal offenses. These include the right to consult an attorney, to be free from self-incrimination, and to be protected from illegal searches and seizures.

need for treatment
The criteria on which juvenile sentencing is based. Ideally, juveniles are treated according to their need for treatment and not for the seriousness of the delinquent act they committed.

© Sherman Zent/Palm Beach Post

Although most children who break the law are considered salvageable and worthy of community treatment efforts, there are also violent juvenile offenders whose behavior requires a firmer response. Some state authorities have declared that these hard-core offenders cannot be treated as children and must be given more secure treatment that is beyond the resources of the juvenile justice system. This recognition has prompted the policy of **waiver**—also known as **bindover** or **removal**—that is, transferring legal jurisdiction over the most serious juvenile offenders to the adult court for criminal prosecution. To the chagrin of reformers, waived youth may find themselves serving time in adult prisons.[53] So although the *parens patriae* concept is still applied to children whose law violations are considered not to be serious, the more serious juvenile offenders can be treated in a manner similar to adults.

STATUS OFFENDERS

A child can become subject to state authority for committing actions that would not be considered illegal if committed by an adult. Conduct that is illegal only because the child is under age is known as a **status offense.** Exhibit 1.1, showing the status offense law of Maryland, describes typical status offenses. Eleven states classify these youths using the term *child in need of supervision,* whereas the remainder use terms such as *unruly child, incorrigible child,* or *minor in need of supervision.*[54] The court can also exercise control over dependent children who are not being properly cared for by their parents or guardians.[55]

State control over a child's noncriminal behavior supports the *parens patriae* philosophy because it is assumed to be in the best interests of the child. Usually, a status offender is directed to the juvenile court when it is determined that his parents are unable or unwilling to care for or control him and that the adolescent's behavior is self-destructive or harmful to society.

A historical basis exists for status offense statutes. It was common practice early in the nation's history to place disobedient or runaway youths in orphan asylums, residential homes, or houses of refuge.[56] When the first juvenile courts were established in Illinois, the Chicago Bar Association described part of their purpose as follows:

> The whole trend and spirit of the [1889 Juvenile Court Act] is that the State, acting through the Juvenile Court, exercises that tender solicitude and care over its neglected, dependent wards that a wise and loving parent would exercise with reference to his own children under similar circumstances.[57]

waiver (also known as bindover or removal)
Transferring legal jurisdiction over the most serious and experienced juvenile offenders to the adult court for criminal prosecution.

status offense
Conduct that is illegal only because the child is under age.

Until relatively recently, however, almost every state treated status offenders and juvenile delinquents alike, referring to them either as **wayward minors** or delinquent children. A trend begun in the 1960s has resulted in the creation of separate status offense categories that vary from state to state: children, minors, persons, youths, or juveniles in need of supervision (CHINS, MINS, PINS, YINS, or JINS). The purpose is to shield noncriminal youths from the stigma attached to the juvenile delinquent label and to signify that they have special needs and problems. (See Concept Summary 1.1.) But even where there are separate legal categories for delinquents and status offenders, the distinction between them has become blurred. Some noncriminal conduct may be included in the definition of delinquency, and some less serious criminal offenses occasionally may be labeled as status offenses.[58] In some states the juvenile court judge may substitute a status offense for a delinquency charge.[59] This possibility can be used to encourage youths to admit to the charges against them in return for less punitive treatment.

The Status Offender in the Juvenile Justice System

Separate status offense categories may avoid some of the stigma associated with the delinquency label, but they have little effect on treatment. Youths in either category can be picked up by the police and brought to a police station. They can be petitioned to the same juvenile court, where they have a hearing before the same judge and come under the supervision of the probation department, the court clinic, and the treatment staff. At a hearing, status offenders may see little difference between the treatment they receive and the treatment of the delinquent offenders sitting across the room. Although status offenders are usually not detained or incarcerated with delinquents, they can be transferred to secure facilities if they are considered uncontrollable.

Aiding the Status Offender

To learn more about the efforts to remove status offenders from secure lockups, go to Gwen A. Holden and Robert A. Kapler, "Deinstitutionalizing Status Offenders: A Record of Progress." Find this Web site by clicking on Web Links under the Chapter Resources at http://cj.wadsworth.com/siegel_jdcore2e.

Efforts have been ongoing to reduce the penalties and stigma borne by status offenders. In 1974, the U.S. Congress passed the Juvenile Justice and Delinquency Prevention Act (JJDPA) that provides the major source of federal funding to improve states' juvenile justice systems. Under the JJDPA and its subsequent reauthorizations, in order to receive federal funds, states were and are required to remove status offenders from secure detention and lockups in order to insulate them from more serious delinquent offenders. The act created the **Office of Juvenile Justice and Delinquency Prevention (OJJDP),** which was authorized to distribute grants and provide support to those states that developed alternate procedural methods.[60] Title III of the JJDPA, referred to as the Runaway and Homeless Youth Act (RHYA) of 1974, provides funds for nonsecure facilities where status offenders who need protection can receive safe shelter, counseling, and education until an effective family reunion can be realized.[61]

wayward minors
Early legal designation of youths who violate the law because of their minority status; now referred to as status offenders.

Office of Juvenile Justice and Delinquency Prevention (OJJDP)
Branch of the U.S. Justice Department charged with shaping national juvenile justice policy through disbursement of federal aid and research funds.

Exhibit 1.1	Status Offense Law: Maryland

(d) Child. "Child" means an individual under the age of 18 years.

(e) Child in need of supervision. "Child in need of supervision" is a child who requires guidance, treatment, or rehabilitation and:

(1) Is required by law to attend school and is habitually truant;

(2) Is habitually disobedient, ungovernable, and beyond the control of the person having custody of him;

(3) Deports himself so as to injure or endanger himself or others; or

(4) Has committed an offense applicable only to children.

Source: Maryland Courts and Judicial Proceedings Code Ann. § 3-8A-01 (2002).

	Juvenile Delinquents	*Status Offenders*
Act	Burglary, shoplifting, robbery	Truancy, running away, disobedient
Injured party	Crime victim	Themselves, their family
Philosophy	*Parens patriae*	Best interests of the child
Legal status	Can be detained in secure confinement	Must be kept in nonsecure shelter
Is there resulting stigma?	Yes	Yes

 Do curfew laws work in reducing the rate of youth crime? To find out, visit the Web site of the Justice Policy Institute. Find this Web site by clicking on Web Links under the Chapter Resources at http://cj.wadsworth.com/siegel_jdcore2e.

This has been a highly successful policy, and the number of status offenders kept in secure pretrial detention has dropped significantly during the past three decades. Nevertheless, juvenile court judges in many states can still detain status offenders in secure lockups if the youths are found in contempt of court. The act that created the OJJDP was amended in 1987 to allow status offenders to be detained for violations of valid court orders.[62] At last count, about forty-four states were in compliance with the OJJDP mandate and were eligible for receiving federal funds.[63]

Changes in the treatment of status offenders reflect the current attitude toward children who violate the law. On the one hand, there appears to be a movement to severely sanction youths who commit serious offenses and transfer them to the adult court. On the other hand, a great effort has been made to remove nonserious cases from the official agencies of justice and place these youths in community-based treatment programs.

Reforming Status Offense Laws

For more than twenty years national crime commissions have called for limiting control over status offenders.[64] In 1976 the National Advisory Commission on Criminal Justice Standards and Goals, created by the federal government to study the crime problem, opted for the non-judicial treatment of status offenders by arguing that the only conduct that should warrant family court intervention is conduct that is clearly self-destructive or otherwise harmful to the child. The commission suggested that juvenile courts confine themselves to controlling five status offenses: habitual truancy, repeated disregard for parental authority, repeated running away, repeated use of intoxicating beverages, and delinquent acts by youths under the age of ten.[65]

These calls for reform prompted a number of changes. Kentucky, for example, has amended its status offense law in order to eliminate vague terms and language. For example, instead of labeling a child who is "beyond control of school" as a status offender, the state is now required to show that the student has repeatedly violated "lawful regulations for the government of the school," with the petition describing the behaviors "and all intervention strategies attempted by the school."[66] A few

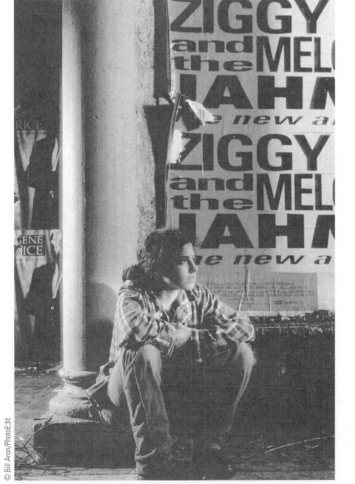

© Bill Aron/PhotoEdit

Delinquency experts who favor removing status offenders from juvenile court authority charge that their experience with the legal system further stigmatizes these already-troubled youths. Would a young runaway, such as the one shown here, be better served by the justice system or a social service agency?

Increasing Social Control over Juveniles and Their Parents

Those in favor of retaining the status offense category point to society's responsibility to care for troubled youths. Others maintain that the status offense should remain a legal category so that juvenile courts can force a youth to receive treatment. Although it is recognized that a court appearance can produce stigma, the taint may be less important than the need for treatment. Many state jurisdictions, prompted by concern over serious delinquency, have enacted laws that actually expand social control over juveniles.

Curfew Laws

Since 1990 there has been an explosion in the passage of curfew laws aimed at restricting the opportunity kids have for getting in trouble. A survey of seventy-seven large U.S. cities found that fifty-nine of them have such laws. Each year about sixty-thousand youths are arrested for curfew violations. As of yet, there is little conclusive evidence that curfews have a significant impact on youth crime rates. Evaluations of the benefits of curfews yield mixed results. Andra Bannister and her associates surveyed more than four hundred police agencies and found that most had curfew ordinances in effect for several years. In the vast majority of cases, police felt that curfew was an effective tool to control vandalism, graffiti, nighttime burglary, and auto theft. Those jurisdictions that did not have curfew laws reported that their absence was a result of political objections rather than perceived ineffectiveness. However, although this research is supportive of curfews, other efforts have found that juvenile arrests and juvenile crime do not seem to decrease significantly during curfew hours. Some research efforts have even found that, after curfews were implemented, victimizations increased significantly during noncurfew hours. This indicates that, rather than suppressing delinquency, curfews merely shift the time of occurrence of the offenses. Some studies have found that strict enforcement of curfew laws actually increases juvenile crime rates. The failure of curfews to control crime coupled with their infringement on civil rights prompted the American Civil Liberties Union to condemn the practice and say in part:

> *Curfews are just the latest in a long line of misguided anticrime strategies that divert public attention from the real root causes of crime. The fact is that such laws are empty political gestures: they will do nothing to make our streets safer. It is absurd to think that any teenager who is selling drugs or carrying a gun—crimes that could lead to years in prison—would rush home at 11:00 to avoid violating curfew, or that this same teenager won't have a false ID. And certainly any crime that would be committed after midnight can just as easily be committed earlier. In fact, most juvenile crimes are committed right after school, between 3:00 and 6:00 P.M.*

Disciplining Parents

Since the early twentieth century, there have been laws aimed at disciplining parents for *contributing to the delinquency of a minor*. The first of these was enacted in Colorado in 1903, and today all states have some form of statute requiring parents to take some responsibility for their children's misbehavior. All states, for example, make it either mandatory or discretionary for the juvenile court to require a parent or guardian to pay at least part of the support costs for a child who is adjudicated delinquent and placed out of the home. Even when the payment is required, however, payment is based on the parent's financial ability to make such payments. During the past decade, approximately one-half of the states enacted or strengthened existing parental liability statutes that make parents criminally liable for the actions of their delinquent children. Such laws allow parents to be sanctioned in juvenile courts for behaviors associated with

Checkpoints

✔ *The concept of delinquency was developed in the early twentieth century. Before that, criminal youths and adults were treated in almost the same fashion.*

✔ *A group of reformers, referred to as* child savers, *helped create a separate delinquency category to insulate juvenile offenders from the influence of adult criminals.*

✔ *The separate status of juvenile delinquency is based on the* parens patriae *philosophy, which holds that children have the right to care and custody and that, if parents are not*

states, including Maine, Delaware, and Idaho, have attempted to eliminate status offense laws and treat these youths as neglected or dependent children, giving child protective services the primary responsibility for their care.

There is serious debate over the liberalization of status offense laws. Some juvenile court judges believe that reducing judicial authority over children will limit juvenile court jurisdiction to hard-core offenders and constrain its ability to help youths before they commit serious antisocial acts.[67] Their concerns are fueled by research that shows that many status offenders, especially those who are runaways living on the streets, often have serious emotional problems and engage in self-destructive behaviors ranging from substance abuse to self-mutilation.[68]

Some states have resisted weakening status offense laws and gone in the opposite direction by mandating that habitual truants and runaways be placed in secure detention facilities, and if found to be in need of supervision, placed in secure treatment facilities. There has been a call for greater rather than less control over way-

their child's misbehavior. Some states (Florida, Idaho, Virginia) require parents to reimburse the government for the costs of detention or care of their children. Others (Maryland, Missouri, Oklahoma) demand that parents make restitution payments—for example, paying for damage caused by their children who vandalized a school. All states except New Hampshire have incorporated parental liability laws in their statutes, though most recent legislation places limits on recovery at somewhere between $250 (Vermont) and $15,000 (Texas); the average is $2,500. Other states (Colorado, Texas, Louisiana) require parents as well as children to participate in counseling and community service activities.

Parents may also be held civilly liable, under the concept of *vicarious liability*, for the damages caused by their child. In some states, parents are responsible for up to $300,000 damages; in others the liability cap is $3,500 (sometimes homeowner's insurance covers at least some of liability). Parents can also be charged with civil negligence if they should have known of the damage a child was about to inflict but did nothing to stop them—for example, when they give a weapon to an emotionally unstable youth. Juries have levied awards of up to $500,000 in such cases. Since 1990 there have been more than eighteen cases in which parents have been ordered to serve time in jail because their children have been truant from school.

Some critics charge that these laws contravene the right to due process because they are unfairly used only against lower-class and minority parents. As legal scholar Elena Laskin points out, imposing penalties on these parents may actually be detrimental. Fining a delinquent's mother removes money from someone who is already among society's poorest people. If a single mother is sent to jail, it leaves her children, including those who are not delinquent, with no parent to raise them; the kids may become depressed, lose concentration and sleep. Even if punishment encourages the parent to take action, it may be too late because by the time a parent is charged with violating the statute, the child has already committed a crime, indicating that any damaging socialization by the parent has already occurred.

CRITICAL THINKING

1. Does punishing parents for the behavior of their children violate their rights to be free from vague and undefined punishments? Should children be punished for the behavior of their parents? (They were in the Middle Ages.) Should a husband be held responsible for the actions of his wife or a wife for her husband?
2. At what age should a child be subject to a curfew law? Should the cutoff be sixteen, seventeen, or eighteen?

INFOTRAC COLLEGE EDITION RESEARCH

To learn more about these issues, use "curfew laws" in a key word search on InfoTrac College Edition. Also read Elena Laskin, "How Parental Liability Statutes Criminalize and Stigmatize Minority Mothers," *American Criminal Law Review* 37:1195–1217 (2000).

Sources: Linda Szymanski, "Parental Support Obligation of Institutionalized Delinquents," *NCJJ Snapshot* 6.6 (Pittsburgh, PA: National Center for Juvenile Justice, 2001); Andra Bannister, David Carter, and Joseph Schafer, "A National Police Survey on the Use of Juvenile Curfews," *Journal of Criminal Justice* 29:233–240 (2001); Jerry Tyler and Thomas Segady, "Parental Liability Laws: Rationale, Theory, and Effectiveness," *Social Science Journal* 37:79–98 (2000); Elena Laskin, "How Parental Liability Statutes Criminalize and Stigmatize Minority Mothers," *American Criminal Law Review* 37:1195–1217 (2000); American Civil Liberties Union, *Curfews: A National Debate*, www.aclu-or.org/national/curfew1.html (2003); Mike Reynolds, Ruth Seydlitz, and Pamela Jenkins, "Do Juvenile Curfew Laws Work? A Time-Series Analysis of the New Orleans Law," *Justice Quarterly* (2000); William Ruefle and Kenneth Mike Reynolds, "Curfews and Delinquency in Major American Cities," *Crime and Delinquency* 41:347–363 (1995); Gilbert Geis and Arnold Binder, "Sins of Their Children: Parental Responsibility for Juvenile Delinquency," *Notre Dame Journal of Law, Ethics, and Public Policy* 5:303–322 (1991).

capable of providing that care, the state must step in to take control.

✔ Delinquents are given greater legal protection than adult criminals and are shielded from stigma and labels.

✔ More serious juvenile cases may be waived to the adult court.

✔ Juvenile courts also have jurisdiction over noncriminal status offenders. Status offenses are illegal only because of the minority status of the offender.

To quiz yourself on this material, go to questions 1.8–1.20 on the Juvenile Delinquency: The Core 2e Web site.

ward youth, a policy that has spawned both curfew laws and parental responsibility laws, discussed in the Preventing and Treating Delinquency feature above.

Though this debate will not end soon, we cannot lose sight of the fact that a majority of youths engage in some status offenses.[69] Illegal acts such as teen sex and substance abuse have become commonplace. Does it make sense, then, to have the juvenile court intervene in cases when no criminal act occurred? The predominant view today is that many status offenders and delinquents share similar problems, and that both categories should fall under the jurisdiction of the juvenile court.

✔ Checkpoints

SUMMARY

- The study of delinquency is concerned with the nature and extent of the criminal behavior of youths, the causes of youthful law violations, the legal rights of juveniles, and prevention and treatment.
- The problems of American youths have become an important subject of academic study. Many children live in poverty, have inadequate health care, and suffer family problems.
- Adolescence is a time of taking risks, which can get kids into trouble.
- Our modern conception of a separate status for children is quite different than in the past. In earlier times relationships between children and parents were remote. Punishment was severe, and children were expected to take on adult roles early in their lives.
- With the start of the seventeenth century came greater recognition of the needs of children. In Great Britain, the chancery court movement, Poor Laws, and apprenticeship programs helped reinforce the idea of children as a distinct social group. In colonial America, many of the characteristics of English family living were adopted.
- In the nineteenth century, delinquent and runaway children were treated no differently than criminal defendants.
- During this time, however, increased support for the *parens patriae* concept resulted in steps to reduce the responsibility of children under the criminal law.
- The concept of delinquency was developed in the early twentieth century. Before that time, criminal youths and adults were treated in almost the same fashion. A group of reformers, referred to as *child savers,* helped create a separate delinquency category to insulate juvenile offenders from the influence of adult criminals.
- The status of juvenile delinquency is still based on the *parens patriae* philosophy, which holds that children have the right to care and custody and that if parents are not capable of providing that care, the state must step in to take control.
- Juvenile courts also have jurisdiction over noncriminal status offenders, whose offenses (truancy, running away, sexual misconduct) are illegal only because of their minority status.
- Some experts have called for an end to juvenile court control over status offenders, charging that it further stigmatizes already troubled youths. Some research indicates that status offenders are harmed by juvenile court processing. Other research indicates that status offenders and delinquents are quite similar.
- There has been a successful effort to separate status offenders from delinquents and to maintain separate facilities for those who need to be placed in a shelter care program.
- The treatment of juveniles is an ongoing dilemma. Still uncertain is whether young law violators respond better to harsh punishments or to benevolent treatment.

KEY TERMS

ego identity, p. 3
role diffusion, p. 3
at-risk youths, p. 3
juvenile delinquency, p. 6
chronic juvenile offenders, p. 7
juvenile justice system, p. 7
paternalistic family, p. 8

Poor Laws, p. 10
chancery courts, p. 11
parens patriae, p. 11
child savers, p. 13
delinquent, p. 13
best interests of the child, p. 13
need for treatment, p. 14

waiver, bindover, removal, p. 15
status offense, p. 15
wayward minors, p. 16
Office of Juvenile Justice and Delinquency Prevention (OJJDP), p. 16

QUESTIONS FOR DISCUSSION

1. Is it fair to have a separate legal category for youths? Considering how dangerous young people can be, does it make more sense to group offenders on the basis of what they have done rather than on their age?

2. At what age are juveniles truly capable of understanding the seriousness of their actions?

3. Is it fair to institutionalize a minor simply for being truant or running away from home? Should the jurisdiction of status offenders be removed from juvenile court and placed with the state's department of social services or some other welfare organization?

4. Should delinquency proceedings be secretive? Does the public have a right to know who juvenile criminals are?

5. Can a "get tough" policy help control juvenile misbehavior, or should *parens patriae* remain the standard?

6. Should juveniles who commit felonies such as rape or robbery be treated as adults?

You have just been appointed by the governor as chairperson of a newly formed group charged with overhauling the state's juvenile justice system. One primary concern is the treatment of status offenders—kids who have been picked up and charged with being runaways, sexually active, truant from school, or unmanageable at home. Under existing status offense statutes, these youth can be sent to juvenile court and stand trial for their misbehaviors. If the allegations against them are proven valid, they may be removed from the home and placed in foster care or even in a state or private custodial institution.

Recently, a great deal of media attention has been given to the plight of runaway children who live on the streets, take drugs, and engage in prostitution. At an open hearing, advocates of the current system argue that many families cannot provide the care and control needed to keep kids out of trouble and that the state must maintain control of at-risk youth. They contend that many status offenders have histories of drug and delinquency problems and are little different from kids arrested on criminal charges; control by the juvenile court is necessary if the youths are ever to get needed treatment.

Another vocal group argues that it is a mistake for a system that deals with criminal youth also to handle troubled adolescents, whose problems usually are the result of child abuse and neglect. They believe that the current statute should be amended to give the state's department of social welfare (DSW) jurisdiction over all noncriminal youths who are in need of assistance. These opponents of the current law point out that, even though status offenders and delinquents are held in separate facilities, those who run away or are unmanageable can be transferred to more secure correctional facilities that house criminal youths. Furthermore, the current court-based process, where troubled youths are involved with lawyers, trials, and court proceedings, helps convince them that they are "bad kids" and social outcasts.

- Should status offenders be treated differently than juvenile delinquents?
- Should distinctions be made between different types of status offenders? That is, are runaways different from truants?
- Are these behavioral problems better handled by a social service or mental health agency than a juvenile court?
- What recommendations would you make to the governor?

For reports on deinstitutionalization and respite care for status offenders, and to read about the problems of high-risk kids, click on Web Links under the Chapter Resources at http://cj.wadsworth.com/siegel_jdcore2e.

Pro/Con discussions and Viewpoint Essays on some of the topics in this chapter may be found at the Opposing Viewpoints Resource Center: www.gale.com/OpposingViewpoints.

The Nature and Extent of Delinquency

Courtesy of CNN

CHAPTER OBJECTIVES

After reading this chapter you should:

1. Know what is meant by the term *official delinquency.*
2. Understand how the FBI's Uniform Crime Report (UCR) is compiled.
3. Be familiar with recent trends in juvenile delinquency.
4. Understand how self-report data are collected and what they say about juvenile crime.
5. Recognize the factors that affect the juvenile crime rate.
6. Be aware of gender patterns in delinquency.
7. Appreciate the factors that cause racial differences in delinquency.
8. Be able to debate the issue of class position and delinquency.
9. Be aware of the debate over the role age plays in delinquency.
10. Understand the concept of the chronic persistent offender.
11. Be familiar with the relationship between childhood and victimization.

In late August 2003, players from the varsity and junior varsity football teams of Mepham High School in Bellmore, Long Island, New York, went to a four-day training camp in Pennsylvania. While there, three varsity players, ages sixteen and seventeen, began hazing several junior varsity players, ages thirteen and fourteen. The hazing soon began to resemble a bizarre sexual ritual. The young boys were sodomized with a broomstick, pinecones, and golf balls.

After the trip, when one of the boys told his parents what had happened, his mother complained to school authorities but was told it was her responsibility to call the police. It was not, she found out, school policy to notify authorities about incidents that happened off campus. The press soon got hold of the story, and it made headlines around the nation.

The Bellmore-Merrick school board decided to cancel all of the Mepham team's football games. Later, the district charged the senior boys with offenses including involuntary deviate sexual intercourse, kidnapping, aggravated assault, unlawful restraint, and false imprisonment. On November 13, 2003, a Pennsylvania juvenile court judge decided to refuse the prosecution's attempts to try the case in adult court and ordered the boys be tried in juvenile court, where they could receive appropriate treatment. One of the teens was ordered to spend time in a detention center, another sent to a military-style boot camp, and the third received probation. All three were barred from returning to school once their sentence was completed; they were to be home-schooled for the remainder of their high school career.

 VIEW THE CNN VIDEO CLIP OF THIS STORY AND ANSWER RELATED CRITICAL THINKING QUESTIONS ON YOUR JUVENILE DELINQUENCY: THE CORE 2E CD.

Federal Bureau of Investigation (FBI)
Arm of the U.S. Department of Justice that investigates violations of federal law, gathers crime statistics, runs a comprehensive crime laboratory, and helps train local law enforcement officers.

Uniform Crime Report (UCR)
Compiled by the FBI, the UCR is the most widely used source of national crime and delinquency statistics.

Part I offenses (also known as index crimes)
Offenses including homicide and nonnegligent manslaughter, forcible rape, robbery, aggravated assault, burglary, larceny, arson, and motor vehicle theft; recorded by local law enforcement officers, these crimes are tallied quarterly and sent to the FBI for inclusion in the UCR.

The Mepham hazing incident is but one of millions of serious illegal acts committed by young people each year. Who commits delinquent acts, and where are they most likely to occur? Is the juvenile crime rate increasing or decreasing? Are juveniles more likely than adults to become the victims of crime?[1] To understand the causes of delinquent behavior and to devise effective means to reduce its occurrence, we must seek answers to these questions.

Delinquency experts have devised a variety of methods to measure the nature and extent of delinquency. We begin with a description of the most widely used sources of data on crime and delinquency. We also examine the information these resources furnish on juvenile crime rates and trends. These data sources will then be used to provide information on the characteristics of adolescent law violators.

OFFICIAL STATISTICS

Each year the U.S. Justice Department's **Federal Bureau of Investigation (FBI)** compiles information gathered by police departments on the number of criminal acts reported by citizens and the number of persons arrested. This information is published in the annual **Uniform Crime Report (UCR),** which is the most widely used source of national crime and delinquency statistics.

The UCR is compiled from statistics sent to the FBI from more than seventeen thousand police departments. It groups offenses into two categories. **Part I offenses,** also known as **index crimes,** include homicide and non-negligent manslaughter,

forcible rape, robbery, aggravated assault, burglary, larceny, arson, and motor vehicle theft. Police record every reported incident of these offenses and report them on a quarterly basis to the FBI. Data are broken down by city, county, metropolitan area, and geographical divisions. In addition, the UCR provides information on individuals who have been arrested for these and all other criminal offenses, including vandalism, liquor law violations, and drug trafficking. These are known as **Part II offenses.** The arrest data are presented by age, sex, and race.

The UCR uses three methods to express crime data. First, the number of crimes reported to the police and arrests made are expressed as raw figures (for example, 16,204 murders occurred in 2002). Second, crime rates per 100,000 people are computed. That is, when the UCR indicates that the murder rate was 5.6 in 2002, it means that about 6 people in every 100,000 were murdered between January 1 and December 31, 2002. Third, the FBI computes changes in the number and rate of crime over time. For example, murder rates declined 4.5 percent between 1998 and 2002.

Crime Trends in the United States

The U.S. index crime rate skyrocketed between 1960 (3.3 million index crimes reported to police agencies) and 1981 (13.4 million index crimes recorded). By 1991 the FBI was recording more than 14 million crimes annually. Both the number and rate of crimes have been declining ever since. In 2002 about 11.8 million crimes were reported to the police, a number almost identical to that of the year before. Despite this recent stabilization, the number of reported crimes has declined by about 3 million from the 1991 peak, and as Figure 2.1 shows, the crime rate has also declined.[2] But despite this dramatic decline, millions of serious criminal incidents still occur each year.

Measuring Official Delinquency

Because the UCR arrest statistics are **disaggregated** (broken down) by suspect's age, they can be used to estimate adolescent crime. Juvenile arrest data must be interpreted with caution, however. First, the number of teenagers arrested does not represent the actual number of youths who have committed delinquent acts. Some offenders are

Part II offenses
All crimes other than Part I offenses; recorded by local law enforcement officers, arrests for these crimes are tallied quarterly and sent to the FBI for inclusion in the UCR.

disaggregated
Analyzing the relationship between two or more independent variables (such as murder convictions and death sentence) while controlling for the influence of a dependent variable (such as race).

| Figure 2.1 | Crime Rate Trends, 1960–2002 |

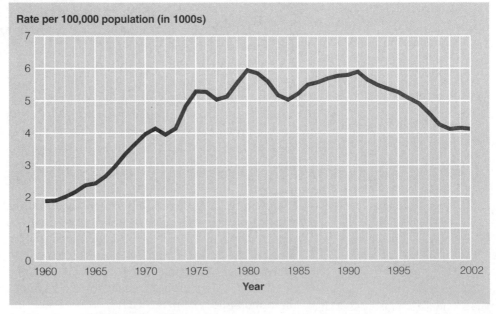

Source: FBI, *Crime in the United States, 2002*, pp. 9–12.

More than 350,000 youth are arrested each year for serious crimes, including rape, murder, and robbery. Here, David P. Socha, 17, (center) of Paxton, Massachusetts, covers his head while being escorted past his family, after Socha's arraignment on a charge of making a false bomb threat while boarding a flight with his family at Logan International Airport. Socha was released on his own recognizance.

© 2003 AP/Wide World Photos

never counted because they are never caught. Others are counted more than once because multiple arrests of the same individual for different crimes are counted separately in the UCR. Consequently, the total number of arrests does not equal the number of people who have been arrested. Put another way, if two million arrests of youths under eighteen years of age were made in a given year, we could not be sure if two million individuals had been arrested once or if five hundred thousand chronic offenders had been arrested four times each. In addition, when an arrested offender commits multiple crimes, only the most serious one is recorded. Therefore, if two million juveniles are arrested, the number of crimes committed is at least two million but it may be much higher.

Despite these limitations, the nature of arrest data remains constant over time. Consequently, arrest data can provide some indication of the nature and trends in juvenile crime. What does the UCR tell us about delinquency?

Official Delinquency   In 2002 (the latest data available), about 13.7 million arrests were made, or about 5,000 per 100,000 population. Of these, about 2.2 million were for serious Part I crimes and 11.5 million for less serious Part II crimes. Juveniles under eighteen who make up about 26 percent of the population were responsible for about 26 percent of all arrests for index crimes, including 16 percent of the violent crime arrests and about 31 percent of the property crime arrests (see Table 2.1).

Table 2.1	Arrests by Age of Offender		
	Under 15	**Under 18**	**Over 18**
Part I or Index violent crime	5%	15%	85%
Part I or Index property crime	11%	30%	70%
Part I or Index total	9%	26%	74%
Total all crimes	5%	16%	85%

Because of rounding, percentages may not add to 100.
"Under 18" includes "Under 15."
Source: FBI, *Crime in the United States, 2002*, p. 222.

About 1.2 million juvenile arrests were made in 2002 for Part II offenses. Included in this total were 90,000 arrests for running away from home, 139,000 for disorderly conduct, 133,000 for drug-abuse violations, and 103,000 for curfew violations.

Juvenile Crime Trends   Juvenile crime continues to have a significant influence on the nation's overall crime statistics. As Figure 2.2 shows, the juvenile arrest rate began to climb in the 1980s, peaked during the mid-1990s, and then began to fall; it has since been in decline. Even the teen murder rate, which had remained stubbornly high, has undergone a decline during the past few years.[3] For example, 1,700 youths were arrested for murder in 1997, a number that by 2002 had declined by almost half (to 973). Similarly, 3,800 juveniles were arrested for rape in 1997, and 3,300 in 2002. This decline in juvenile violence is especially welcome considering that its rate was approaching epidemic proportions.

Though juvenile crime rates have been in decline for the past decade, they tend to ebb and flow over long periods of time. What factors account for change in the crime and delinquency rate? This is the topic of the Focus on Delinquency box entitled "The Rise and Fall of Juvenile Crime Rates."

What the Future Holds   Some experts, such as criminologist James A. Fox, predict a significant increase in teen violence if current population trends persist. The nation's teenage population will increase by 15 percent, or more than nine million, between now and 2010; the number in the high-risk ages of fifteen to seventeen will increase by more than three million, or 31 percent. There are approximately fifty million school-age children in the United States, many younger than ten—more than we have had for decades. Although many come from stable homes, others lack stable families and adequate supervision; these are some of the children who will soon enter their prime crime years. As a result, Fox predicts a wave of youth violence even greater than that of the past ten years.[4]

In contrast, economist Steven Levitt believes that even though teen crime rates may eventually rise, their influence on the nation's total crime rate may be offset by the growing number of crime-free senior citizens.[5] Levitt also believes that punitive policies such as putting more kids behind bars and adding police may help control delinquency. One problem on the horizon remains the maturation of "crack babies," who spent their early childhood years in families and neighborhoods ravaged by crack cocaine. Coupled with a difficult home environment, these children may turn out to be extremely prone to delinquency activity, producing the increase in the delinquency predicted by James A. Fox.[6]

Figure 2.2   **Juvenile Arrest Rates for All Crimes, 1980–2002**

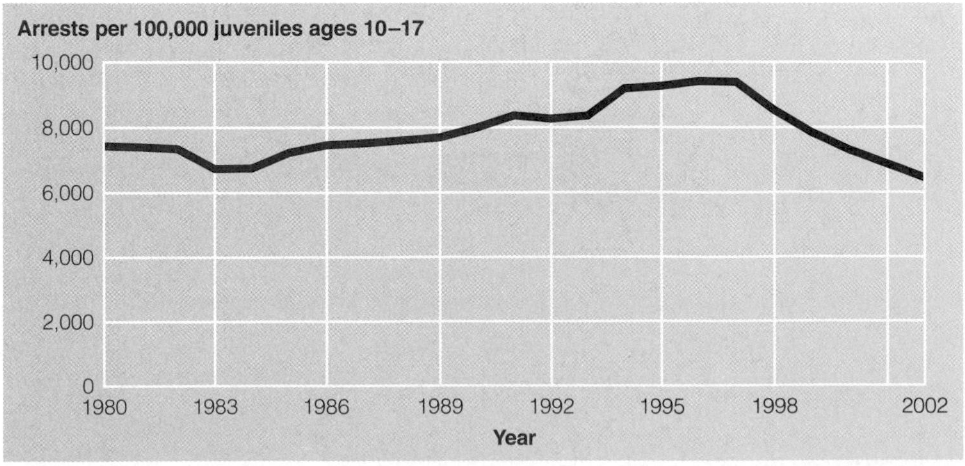

Source: Adapted from Howard Snyder, *Juvenile Arrests 2001* (Washington, DC: Office of Juvenile Justice and Delinquency Prevention, 2003, updated).

ARE THE UCR DATA VALID?

Questions have been raised about the validity and accuracy of UCR's "official" crime data. Victim surveys show that less than half of all victims report the crime to police. Because official data are derived entirely from police records, we can assume that a significant number of crimes are not accounted for in the UCR. There are also concerns that police departments make systematic errors in recording crime data or manipulate the data in order to give the public the impression that they are highly effective crime fighters.[7]

Using official arrest data to measure delinquency rates is particularly problematic. Arrest records count only adolescents who have been *caught,* and these youths may be different from those who evade capture. Victimless crimes such as drug and alcohol use are significantly undercounted using this measure. Another problem is that arrest decision criteria vary among police agencies. Some police agencies practice full enforcement, arresting all teens who violate the law, whereas others follow a policy of discretion that encourages unofficial handling of juvenile matters through social service agencies.

Although these questions are troubling, the problems associated with collecting and verifying the official UCR data are consistent and stable over time. This means that, although the absolute accuracy of the data can be questioned, the trends and patterns they show are probably reliable. In other words, we cannot be absolutely sure about the actual number of adolescents who commit crimes, but it is likely that the teen crime rate has been in a significant decline.

Victim surveys show that less than half of all victims report the crime to police. Because official data are derived entirely from police records, we can assume that a significant number of crimes are not accounted for in the UCR. What is the likelihood that the vandalism being committed by these juveniles will be reported to the police?

The National Incident-Based Reporting System (NIBRS)

The FBI is currently instituting a new program that collects data on each reported crime incident. Instead of submitting statements of the kinds of crime that individual citizens reported to the police and summary statements of resulting arrests, the new program will require local police agencies to provide at least a brief account of each incident and arrest, including the incident, victim, and offender information. Under NIBRS, law enforcement authorities will provide information to the FBI on each criminal incident involving forty-six specific offenses, including the eight Part I crimes, that occur in their jurisdiction; arrest information on the forty-six offenses plus eleven lesser offenses is also provided in NIBRS. These expanded crime categories would include numerous additional crimes, such as blackmail, embezzlement, drug offenses, and bribery; this would allow a national database on the nature of crime, victims, and criminals to be developed. So far, twenty-two states have implemented their NIBRS program and twelve others are in the process of finalizing their data collections. When this new UCR program is fully implemented and adopted across the nation, it should provide significantly better data on juvenile crime than exists today.

The Rise and Fall of Juvenile Crime Rates

Crime rates climb and fall, reflecting a variety of social and economic conditions. Although there is still disagreement over what causes crime rate fluctuations, the following factors are considered to play a major role in determining patterns and trends.

Age

Change in the age distribution of the population deeply influences crime and delinquency rates. Because juvenile males commit more crime than any other population segment, as a general rule the crime rate follows the proportion of young males in the population. The postwar baby-boom generation reached their teenage years in the 1960s, just as the crime rate began a sharp increase. With the "graying" of society and a decline in the birthrate, it is not surprising that the overall crime rate began to decline in the mid-1990s. Some criminologists fear crime rates will begin to climb when (and if) the number of juveniles in the population begins to increase.

Economy

In the short term, a poor economy may actually help lower crime rates. Unemployed parents are at home to supervise children and guard their homes. Because there is less to spend, a poor economy means that there are actually fewer valuables worth stealing. Recent research (2002) on the relationship between unemployment and crime conducted by Gary Kleck and Ted Chiricos discovered that there was no relationship between unemployment rates and the rate of most crimes desperate kids might commit, including robbery, shoplifting, residential burglary, theft of motor vehicle parts, and automobile theft.

Despite the weak association, it is possible that long-term periods of economic weakness and unemployment eventually lift crime rates. Chronic teenage unemployment rates may produce a perception of hopelessness that leads to crime and delinquency. Violence may be a function of urban problems and the economic deterioration in the nation's inner cities. Our nation's economy is now fueled by the service and technology industries. Youths who at one time might have obtained low-skill jobs in factories and shops find that these legitimate economic opportunities no longer exist. Low-skill manufacturing jobs have been dispersed to overseas plants; most new jobs that don't require specialized skills are in the low-paying service area. Lack of real economic opportunity may encourage drug dealing, theft, and

violence. Experts fear that a long-term economic downturn coupled with a relatively large number of teens in the population will produce the high delinquency rates of the late eighties and early nineties.

Drugs

Drug use has been linked to fluctuations in the crime and delinquency rate. Abusers are particularly crime-prone, so as drug use levels increase, so too do crime rates. When teen violence skyrocketed in the 1980s, it was no coincidence that this period also witnessed increases in drug trafficking and arrests for drug crimes. Teenage substance abusers commit a significant portion of all serious crimes and inner-city drug-abuse problems may account in part for the persistently high violent-crime rate. Groups and gangs that are involved in the urban drug trade recruit juveniles because they work cheaply, are immune from heavy criminal penalties, and are daring and willing to take risks. Arming themselves for protection, these youthful dealers pose a threat to neighborhood adolescents, who in turn arm themselves for self-protection. The result is an "arms race" that produces an increasing spiral of violence.

Drug abuse may also have a more direct influence on teen crime patterns—as when alcohol-abusing kids engage in acts of senseless violence. Users may turn to theft and violence for money to purchase drugs and support drug habits. Increases in teenage drug use may be a precursor to higher violence rates in the future.

Media

Some experts argue that violent media can influence youth crime. As the availability of media with a violent theme skyrocketed with the introduction of home video players, DVDs, cable TV, computer and video games, and so on, so too did teen violence rates. According to a recent analysis of all available scientific data conducted by Brad Bushman and Craig Anderson, watching violence on TV is correlated to aggressive behavior, especially among kids with a preexisting tendency toward crime and violence.

Ongoing Social Problems

As the level of social problems increase—divorce, school dropout, teen pregnancy, and racial conflict—so do crime and delinquency rates. For example, cross-national research indicates that child homicide rates are greatest in those nations, including the United States, that have the highest rates of children born out of wedlock and with teenage mothers. Children living in single-parent homes are twice as likely to

SELF-REPORTED DELINQUENCY

Official statistics are useful for examining general trends, but they cannot tell us how many youth commit crime but are never arrested. Nor do they reveal much about the personality, attitudes, and behavior of individual delinquents. To get information

be impoverished than those in two-parent homes, and are consequently at greater risk for juvenile delinquency. The number of teen pregnancies is on the decline and so too are teen crime rates.

Abortion

In a controversial work, John J. Donohue III and Steven D. Levitt found empirical evidence that the recent drop in the crime rate can be attributed to the availability of legalized abortion. In 1973, *Roe v. Wade* legalized abortion nationwide. Within a few years of the *Roe v. Wade* decision, more than one million abortions were being performed annually, or roughly one abortion for every three live births. Donohue and Levitt suggest that the decrease in the crime rate that began approximately eighteen years later, in 1991, can be related to the fact that the first group of potential offenders affected by the abortion decision began reaching the peak age of criminal activity. It is possible that the link between crime rates and abortion is the result of two mechanisms: (1) selective abortion on the part of women most at risk to have children who would engage in delinquent activity, and (2) improved child-rearing or environmental circumstances caused by better maternal, familial, or fetal circumstances because women are having fewer children. If abortion were illegal, they find, crime rates might be 10 to 20 percent higher than they currently are with legal abortion.

Guns

Another important influence on violence rates is the number of weapons in the hands of teens. In 2002, twenty-five thousand kids were arrested on weapons-related charges. More than 60 percent of the homicides committed by juveniles involve firearms. Guns can turn a schoolyard fight into a homicide. Their presence creates a climate in which kids who would otherwise shun firearms begin to carry them to "protect" themselves. As the number of guns in the hands of children increases, so do juvenile violence rates.

Gangs

The explosive growth in teenage gangs has also contributed to teen violence rates. Surveys indicate that there are more than 750,000 gang members in the United States. There is evidence that a significant portion of murders in some cities, such as Chicago and Los Angeles, are gang-related. A large and growing number of juveniles who kill do so in groups of two or more; multiple-offender killings have doubled since the mid-1980s. Gang-related violence is frequently compounded by the use of firearms. Research indicates that in major cities about one-third of kids who are gang members carry a gun all or most of the time.

Juvenile Justice Policy

Some law-enforcement experts have suggested that a reduction in crime rates may be attributed to a recent get tough attitude toward delinquency and drug abuse. Police have become more aggressive. New laws call for mandatory incarceration for juvenile offenders. Juveniles may even be eligible for the death penalty. Putting potentially high-rate offenders behind bars may help stabilize crime rates.

CRITICAL THINKING

1. Are there any other factors, in addition to those mentioned here, that influence juvenile crime rates? For example, do you believe that pop culture icons who seem to embrace drugs, sex, and rebellion influence adolescent behavior?
2. How has the post-9/11 world, with its emphasis on security and patriotism, influenced teens? Does a national calamity such as the 9/11 attacks encourage or discourage youthful misbehavior?

INFOTRAC COLLEGE EDITION RESEARCH

To find out more about the factors that influence *juvenile arrest rates,* use the term as a key word search on InfoTrac College Edition.

Sources: William Wells and Julie Horney, "Weapon Effects and Individual Intent to Do Harm: Influences on the Escalation of Violence," *Criminology* 40:265–296 (2002); Jeffrey Johnson, Patricia Cohen, Elizabeth Smailes, Stephanie Kasen, and Judith Brook, "Television Viewing and Aggressive Behavior During Adolescence and Adulthood," *Science* 295:2468–2471 (2002); Brad Bushman and Craig Anderson, "Media Violence and the American Public," *American Psychologist* 56:477–489 (2001); Gary Kleck and Ted Chiricos, "Unemployment and Property Crime: A Target-Specific Assessment of Opportunity and Motivation as Mediating Factors," *Criminology* 40:649–680 (2002); John J. Donohue III and Steven D. Levitt, "Legalized Abortion and Crime" (June 24, 1999, unpublished paper, University of Chicago); Donald Green, Dara Strolovitch, and Janelle Wong, "Defended Neighborhoods, Integration, and Racially Motivated Crime," *American Journal of Sociology* 104:372–403 (1998); Robert O'Brien, Jean Stockard, and Lynne Isaacson, "The Enduring Effects of Cohort Characteristics on Age-Specific Homicide Rates, 1960–1995," *American Journal of Sociology* 104:1061–1095 (1999); Scott Decker and Susan Pennell, *Arrestees and Guns: Monitoring the Illegal Firearms Market* (Washington, DC: National Institute of Justice, 1995); G. David Curry, Richard Ball, and Scott Decker, "Estimating the National Scope of Gang Crime from Law Enforcement Data," in C. Ronald Huff, ed., *Gangs in America,* 2nd ed. (Newbury Park, CA: Sage, 1996).

self-reports
Questionnaire or survey technique that asks subjects to reveal their own participation in delinquent or criminal acts.

at this level, criminologists have developed alternative sources of delinquency statistics, with the most commonly used source being **self-reports** of delinquent behavior.

Self-report studies are designed to obtain information from youthful subjects about their violations of the law. Youths arrested by police may be interviewed at the station house; an anonymous survey can be distributed to every student in a high school; boys in a detention center may be asked to respond to a survey; or youths randomly selected from the population of teenagers can be questioned in their homes. Self-report information can be collected in one-to-one interviews or through a self-administered questionnaire, but more commonly this information is gathered through a mass distribution of anonymous questionnaires.

Self-report surveys can include all segments of the population. They provide information on offenders who have never been arrested and are therefore not part of the official data. They also measure behavior that is rarely detected by police, such as drug abuse, because their anonymity allows youths freely to describe their illegal activities. Surveys can also include items measuring personality characteristics, behavior, and attitudes.

Table 2.2 shows one format for self-report questions. Youths are asked to indicate how many times they have participated in illegal or deviant behavior. Other formats allow subjects to record the precise number of times they engaged in each delinquent activity. Note that the reporting period is limited to the previous twelve months here, but some surveys question lifetime activity.

Questions not directly related to delinquent activity are often included in self-report surveys. Information may be collected on self-image; intelligence; personality; attitudes toward family, friends, and school; leisure activities; and school activities. Self-report surveys also gather information on family background, social status, race, and sex. Reports of delinquent acts can be correlated with this information to create a much more complete picture of delinquent offenders than official statistics can provide.

Criminologists have used self-report studies of delinquency for more than forty years.[8] They are a valuable source of information on the activities of youths who have had contact with the juvenile justice system as well as on the **dark figures of crime**—that is, those who have escaped official notice.

What Self-Report Data Show

Most self-report studies indicate that the number of children who break the law is far greater than official statistics would lead us to believe.[9] In fact, when truancy, alcohol consumption, petty theft, and recreational drug use are included in self-report scales, delinquency appears to be almost universal. The most common offenses are truancy, drinking alcohol, using a false ID, shoplifting or larceny under five dollars, fighting, using marijuana, and damaging the property of others. In chapter 10, self-report data will be used to gauge trends in adolescent drug abuse.

dark figures of crime
Incidents of crime and delinquency that go undetected by police.

Table 2.2   **Self-Report Survey Sample**

Please indicate how often in the past twelve months you did each act. (Check the best answer.)

	Never Did Act	One Time	2–5 Times	6–9 Times	10+ Times
Stole something worth less than $50	___	___	___	___	___
Stole something worth more than $50	___	___	___	___	___
Used cocaine	___	___	___	___	___
Was in a fistfight	___	___	___	___	___
Carried a weapon such as a gun or a knife	___	___	___	___	___
Fought someone using a weapon	___	___	___	___	___

To find out more about the Institute for Social Research, click on Web Links under the Chapter Resources at http://cj.wadsworth.com/siegel_jdcore2e.

Researchers at the University of Michigan's Institute for Social Research (ISR)[10] conduct an annual national self-report survey, called Monitoring the Future (MTF), that involves a sample of about three thousand youths. Table 2.3 contains some of the data from the 2002 MTF survey.

A surprising number of these *typical* teenagers reported involvement in serious criminal behavior: about 12 percent reported hurting someone badly enough that the victim needed medical care (6 percent said they did it more than once); about 29 percent reported stealing something worth less than $50, and another 10 percent stole something worth more than $50; 28 percent reported shoplifting; 11 percent had damaged school property.

If the MTF data are accurate, the juvenile crime problem is much greater than official statistics would lead us to believe. There are approximately forty million youths between the ages of ten and eighteen. Extrapolating from the MTF findings, this group accounts for more than 100 percent of all the theft offenses reported in the UCR. Some 3 percent of the students said they had used force to steal (which is the legal definition of a robbery). At this rate, high school students commit 1.2 million robberies per year. In comparison, the UCR tallies about 240,000 robberies for all age groups in 2002. Over the past decade, the MTF surveys indicate that with a few exceptions, self-reported teenage participation in theft, violence, and damage-related crimes seems to be more stable than the trends reported in the UCR arrest data.

There is also some question about the accuracy of self-report data. For example, there is evidence that reporting accuracy differs between racial, ethnic, and gender groups. One recent study found that although girls are generally more willing than boys to disclose drug use, Hispanic girls are significantly more likely than Hispanic boys to *underreport* their use of cocaine. Such gender-cultural differences might provide a skewed and inaccurate portrait of criminal and or delinquent activity. In this case, self-report data might delude delinquency experts into believing that there is not much risk that Hispanic females will become substance abusers, but in reality their abuse rates are inaccurate because they are reluctant to admit their drug usage.[11]

✔ Checkpoints

Checkpoints

✔ The FBI's Uniform Crime Report is an annual tally of crime reported to local police departments; it is the nation's official crime data.

✔ Crime rates peaked in the early 1990s and have been in decline ever since.

✔ The murder rate has undergone a particularly steep decline.

✔ A number of factors influence crime rate trends, including the economy, drug use, availability of guns, and crime control policies.

✔ The number of youths arrested for delinquent behavior has also declined, including a significant decrease in those arrested for violent offenses.

✔ Self-report surveys ask respondents about their criminal activity. They are useful in measuring crimes such as drug usage that are rarely reported to police.

✔ Self-reports show us that a significant number of kids engage in criminal acts, far more than is measured by the arrest data.

✔ It is difficult to gauge future trends. Some experts forecast an increase in juvenile crime, while others foresee a long-term decline in the crime rate.

To quiz yourself on this material, go to questions 2.1–2.7 on the Juvenile Delinquency: The Core 2e Web site.

Table 2.3 Self-Reported Delinquent Activity of High School Seniors, 2002

Type of Crime	Total (%)	Committed Only Once (%)	Committed More Than Once (%)
Set fire on purpose	3	1	2
Damaged school property	11	5	6
Damaged work property	7	3	4
Auto theft	5	2	3
Auto part theft	5	2	3
Breaking and entering	23	10	13
Theft (under $50)	29	12	17
Theft (over $50)	10	5	5
Shoplifting	28	11	17
Was involved in gang fight	17	9	8
Hurt someone badly enough that they needed medical care	12	6	6
Used force to steal	3	1	2
Hit teacher or supervisor	3	1	2
Got into a serious fight	12	6	6

Source: *Monitoring the Future, 2002* (Ann Arbor, MI: Institute for Social Research, 2003).

CORRELATES OF DELINQUENCY

An important aspect of delinquency research is measurement of the personal traits and social characteristics associated with adolescent misbehavior. If, for example, a strong association exists between delinquent behavior and family income, then poverty and economic deprivation must be considered in any explanation of the onset of adolescent criminality. If the delinquency-income association is not present, then other forces may be responsible for producing antisocial behavior. It would be fruitless to concentrate delinquency control efforts in areas such as job creation and vocational training if social status were found to be unrelated to delinquent behavior. Similarly, if only a handful of delinquents are responsible for most serious crimes, then crime control policies might be made more effective by identifying and treating these offenders. The next sections discuss the relationship between delinquency and the characteristics of gender, race, social class, and age.

Gender and Delinquency

Males are significantly more delinquent than females. The teenage gender ratio for serious violent crime is approximately four to one, and for property crime approximately two to one, male to female.

One relationship reverses this general pattern: girls are more likely than boys to be arrested as runaways. There are two possible explanations for this. Girls could be more likely than boys to run away from home, or police may view the female runaway as the more serious problem and therefore more likely to process girls through official justice channels. This may reflect paternalistic attitudes toward girls, who are viewed as likely to "get in trouble" if they are on the street.

Between 1993 and 2002, the number of arrests of male delinquents decreased about 16 percent, whereas the number of female delinquents arrested actually increased about 6 percent. The change in serious violent crime arrests was even more striking: that for males decreased by 33 percent, while females' violent crime arrests remained relatively stable during this period of declining juvenile crime, decreasing only 2 percent. However, as Figure 2.3 shows, both the male and female juvenile arrest *rates* are down from their peak. Though the number of crimes committed

Girls from the 18th Street Gang in Los Angeles mug for the camera. Female delinquency has risen during the past decade while at the same time the male rate has declined substantially.

© A. Ramey/PhotoEdit

Figure 2.3 | Juvenile Arrest Rates for All Crimes, by Gender, 1980–2002

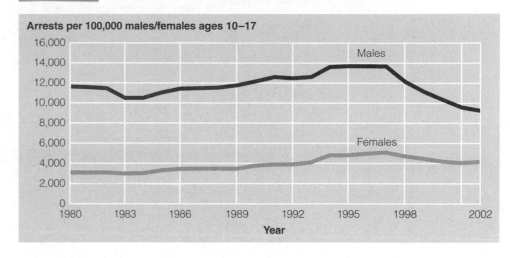

Arrests per 100,000 males/females ages 10–17

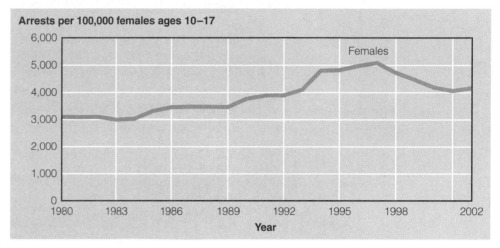

Arrests per 100,000 females ages 10–17

Source: Howard Snyder, *Juvenile Arrests 2001* (Washington, DC: Office of Juvenile Justice and Delinquency Prevention, 2003, updated); FBI, *Crime in the United States, 2002,* p. 239.

by young girls is higher now than a decade ago (because the number of girls in the population has increased) the average girl is actually "less delinquent" than her older sisters.

Self-report data also seem to show that the incidence of female delinquency is much higher than believed earlier, and that the most common crimes committed by males are also the ones most female offenders commit.[12] Table 2.4 shows the percentages of males and females who admitted engaging in delinquent acts during the past twelve months in the latest MTF survey. As the table indicates, about 33 percent of boys and 26 percent of girls admit to shoplifting, 14 percent of boys and 5 percent of girls said they stole something worth more than $50, and 18 percent of boys and 5 percent of girls said they hurt someone badly enough that they required medical care. Although self-report studies indicate that the content of girls' delinquency is similar to boys', the few adolescents who reported engaging frequently in serious violent crime are still predominantly male.[13] However, as the official arrest data show, over the past decade girls have increased their self-reported delinquency whereas boys report somewhat less involvement. Because the relationship between gender and delinquency rate is so important, this topic will be discussed further in chapter 6.

Table 2.4 Self-Reported Delinquent Activity of High School Seniors, by Gender, 2002

Type of Crime	Males (%)	Females (%)
Serious fight	17	10
Gang fight	19	14
Hurt someone badly	18	5
Used a weapon to steal	5	1
Stole (under $50)	33	25
Stole (over $50)	14	5
Shoplifted	30	26
Breaking and entering	26	19
Committed arson	4	1
Damaged school property	20	6

Source: *Monitoring the Future, 2002* (Ann Arbor, MI: Institute for Social Research, 2003).

Figure 2.4 Juvenile Arrest Rates for All Crimes, by Race, 1980–2002

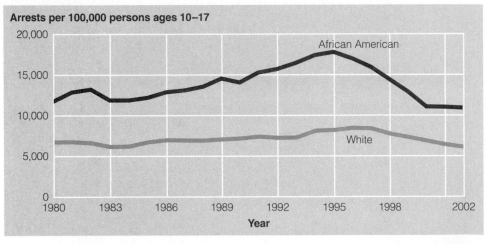

Source: Howard Snyder, *Juvenile Arrests 2001* (Washington, DC: Office of Juvenile Justice and Delinquency Prevention, 2003, updated).

Race and Delinquency

There are approximately 41 million White and 8.5 million African-American youths ages five to seventeen, a ratio of about five to one. Yet racial minorities are disproportionately represented in the arrest statistics (see Figure 2.4). African-American youths are arrested for a disproportionate number of murders, rapes, robberies, and assaults, while White youths are arrested for a disproportionate share of arsons. Among Part II crimes, White youths are disproportionately arrested for alcohol-related violations.

Self-Report Differences   Official statistics show that minority youths are much more likely than Whites to be arrested for serious criminal behavior. To many delinquency experts, this pattern reflects discrimination in the juvenile justice system. In other words, African-American youths are more likely to be formally arrested by the police, who, in contrast, will treat White youths informally. One way to examine this issue is to compare the racial differences in self-reported data with those found in the official delinquency records. Given the disproportionate numbers of African

Americans arrested, charges of racial discrimination would be supported if we found little difference between the number of self-reported minority and White crimes.

Early researchers found that the relationship between race and self-reported delinquency was virtually nonexistent.[14] This suggests that racial differences in the official crime data may reflect the fact that African-American youths have a much greater chance of being arrested and officially processed.[15] Self-report studies also suggest that the delinquent behavior rates of African-American and White teenagers are generally similar and that differences in arrest statistics may indicate discrimination by police.[16] The MTF survey, for example, generally shows that offending differences between African-American and White youths are marginal.[17] However, some experts warn that African-American youths may underreport more serious crimes, limiting the ability of self-reports to be a valid indicator of racial differences in the crime rate.[18]

Bias Effects?   How can the disproportionate number of African-American youngsters arrested for serious crimes be explained? One view is that it is a result of bias by the police and courts. According to this view, ethnic minority group members are more likely to be formally arrested than Whites.[19] Police routinely search, question, and detain all African-American males in an area if a violent criminal has been described as "looking or sounding Black"; this is called *racial profiling*. African-American youth who develop a police record are more likely to be severely punished if they are picked up again and sent back to juvenile court.[20] Consequently, the racial discrimination that is present at the early stages of the justice system ensures that minorities receive greater punishments at its conclusion.

Juvenile court judges may see the offenses committed by African-American youths as more serious than those committed by White offenders. They seem more willing to give White defendants lenient sentences or dismiss their cases.[21] As a result, African-American youths are more likely to get an official record.

According to this view then, the disproportionate number of minority youth who are arrested is less a function of their involvement in serious crime and more the result of the race-based decision making that is found in the juvenile justice system.[22] Institutional racism by police and the courts is still an element of daily life in the African-American community, a factor that undermines faith in social and political institutions and weakens confidence in the justice system.[23]

Race Matters   The other point of view holds that although evidence of racial bias does exist in the justice system, there is enough correspondence between official and self-report data to conclude that racial differences in the crime rate are real.[24] If African-American youths are arrested at a disproportionately high rate for crimes such as robbery and assault, it is a result of offending rates rather than bias on the part of the criminal justice system.[25]

Some experts believe that racial differences in the juvenile arrest rate are a function of police officer bias. While African-American and White juveniles commit crimes at the same rate, the former are much more likely to get arrested and maintain an official record. Here, Lonnell McGhee of Oakland, California, listens to speakers at a rally against racial profiling at the state capitol in Sacramento, California. Hundreds of others were there to show support for SB1389, the so-called "DWB Bill," or "Driving While Black/Brown Bill."

According to this view of race and delinquency, racial differentials in the crime rate are tied to the social and economic disparity suffered by African-American youths. Too many are forced to live in the nation's poorest areas that suffer high crime rates.[26] The burden of social and economic marginalization has weakened the African-American family structure. When families are weakened or disrupted, their ability to act as social control agents is compromised.[27]

Even during times of economic growth, lower-class African Americans are left out of the economic mainstream, causing a growing sense of frustration and failure.[28] As a result of being shut out of educational and economic opportunities enjoyed by the rest of society, this population may be prone, some believe, to the lure of illegitimate gain and criminality. However, even among at-risk African-American kids growing up in communities characterized by poverty, high unemployment levels, and single-parent households, those who do live in stable families with reasonable incomes and educational achievement are much less likely to engage in violent behaviors than those lacking family support.[29] Consequently, racial differences in the delinquency rate would evaporate if the social and economic characteristics of racial minorities were improved to levels currently enjoyed by Whites, and African-American kids could enjoy the same social, economic, and educational privileges.[30]

In summary, official data indicate that African-American youths are arrested for more serious crimes than Whites. But self-report studies show that the differences in the rates of delinquency between the races is insignificant. Therefore, some experts believe that official differences in the delinquency rate are an artifact of bias in the justice system: police are more likely to arrest and courts are more likely to convict young African Americans.[31] To those who believe that the official data have validity, the participation of African-American youths in serious criminal behavior is generally viewed as a function of their socioeconomic position and the racism they face.

Social Class and Delinquency

Defining the relationship between economic status and delinquent behavior is a key element in the study of delinquency. If youth crime is purely a lower-class phenomenon, its cause must be rooted in the social forces that are found solely in lower-class areas: poverty, unemployment, social disorganization, culture conflict, and alienation. However, if delinquent behavior is spread throughout the social structure, its cause must be related to some non-economic factor: intelligence, personality, socialization, family dysfunction, educational failure, or peer influence. According to this line of reasoning, providing jobs or economic incentives would have little effect on the crime rate.

At first glance, the relationship between class and crime seems clear. Youths who lack wealth or social standing are the most likely to use criminal means to achieve their goals. Communities that lack economic and social opportunities produce high levels of frustration. Kids who live in these areas believe that they can never compete socially or economically with adolescents being raised in more affluent areas. They may turn to criminal behavior for monetary gain and psychological satisfaction.[32] Family life is disrupted in these low-income areas, and law-violating youth groups thrive in a climate that undermines and neutralizes adult supervision.[33]

Research on Social Class and Delinquency
The social class–delinquency relationship was challenged by pioneering self-report studies, specifically those that revealed no direct relationship between social class and the commission of delinquent acts.[34] Instead, socioeconomic class was related to the manner of official processing by police, court, and correctional agencies.[35] In other words, although both poor and affluent kids get into fights, shoplift, and take drugs, only the indigent are likely to be arrested and sent to juvenile court.[36] This finding casts doubt on the assumption that poverty and lower-class position is a significant cause of delinquent behavior.

To get information on the economic status of America's children, go to the federal government's Web site by clicking on Web Links under the Chapter Resources at http://cj.wadsworth.com/siegel_jdcore2e.

Those who fault self-report studies point to the inclusion of trivial offenses—for example, using a false ID—in most self-report instruments. Although middle- and upper-class youths may appear to be as delinquent as those in the lower class, it is because they engage in significant amounts of such status offenses. Lower-class youths are more likely to engage in serious delinquent acts.[37]

In sum, there are those experts who believe that antisocial behavior occurs at all levels of the social strata. Other experts argue that, while some middle- and upper-class youths engage in some forms of minor illegal activity and theft offenses, it is members of the underclass who are responsible for the majority of serious delinquent acts.[38] The prevailing wisdom is that kids who engage in the most serious forms of delinquency (for example, gang violence) are more likely to be members of the lower class.

Age and Delinquency

It is generally believed that age is inversely related to criminality: as people age, the likelihood that they will commit crime declines.[39] Official statistics tell us that young people are arrested at a disproportionate rate to their numbers in the population, and this finding is supported by victim surveys. Youths ages fifteen to nineteen make up about 7 percent of the total U.S. population, but they account for 27 percent of the index crime arrests and 21 percent of the arrests for all crimes. In contrast, adults age fifty and older, who make up slightly less than a third of the population, account for only about 6 percent of arrests. Figure 2.5 shows that even though the number of arrests have been in decline, the peak age for arrest remains the teen years.

Why Age Matters   Why do people commit less crime as they age? One view is that the relationship is constant: regardless of race, sex, social class, intelligence, or any other social variable, people commit less crime as they age.[40] This is referred to as the ***aging-out process,*** sometimes called ***desistance from crime*** or ***spontaneous remission.*** According to some experts, even the most chronic juvenile offenders will commit less crime as they age.[41]

There are also experts who disagree with the concept of spontaneous remission. They suggest that age is one important determinant of crime but that other factors

aging-out process (also known as desistance from crime or spontaneous remission) The tendency for youths to reduce the frequency of their offending behavior as they age; aging out is thought to occur among all groups of offenders.

Figure 2.5   **The Relationship Between Age and Serious Crime Arrests**

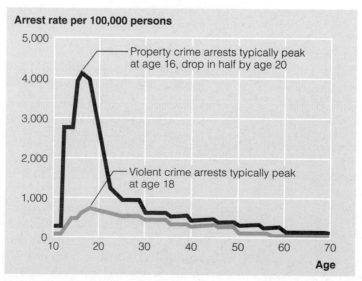

Source: FBI, *Crime in the United States, 2002.*

Delinquency rates tend to go down as people mature. Increasing levels of responsibility result in lower levels of criminality. Young people who marry, enlist in the armed services, or enroll in vocational training courses are less likely to pursue criminal activities. Although having a baby will place great stress upon them, this teen couple will simply have less time to get in trouble than before their child was born.

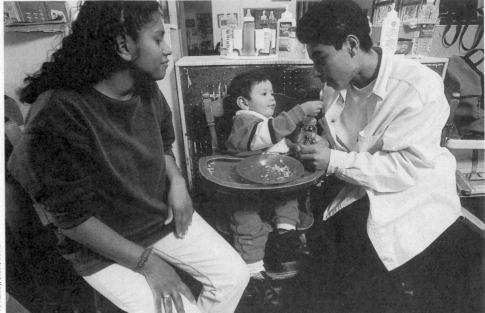

© A. Ramey/Stock, Boston

directly associated with a person's lifestyle, such as peer relations, also affect offending rates.[42] The probability that a person will become a persistent career criminal is influenced by a number of personal and environmental factors.[43] Evidence exists, for example, that the **age of onset** of a delinquent career has an important effect on its length: those who demonstrate antisocial tendencies at a very early age are more likely to commit more crimes for a longer period of time. This is referred to as the *developmental view of delinquency.*

In summary, some criminologists believe youths who get involved with delinquency at a very early age are most likely to become career criminals. These researchers believe age is a key determinant of delinquency.[44] Those opposed to this view find that all people commit less crime as they age and that because the relationship between age and crime is constant, it is irrelevant to the study of delinquency.[45]

Why Does Crime Decline with Age?

Although there is certainly disagreement about the nature of the aging-out process, there is no question that people commit less crime as they grow older. Delinquency experts have developed a number of reasons for the aging-out process:

- *Growing older means having to face the future.* Young people, especially the indigent and antisocial, tend to "discount the future."[46] Why should they delay gratification when faced with an uncertain future?

- *With maturity comes the ability to resist the "quick fix" to their problems.*[47] Research shows that some kids may turn to crime as a way to solve the problems of adolescence, loneliness, frustration, and fear of peer rejection. As they mature, conventional means of problem solving become available. Life experience helps former delinquents seek out nondestructive solutions to their personal problems.[48]

- *Maturation coincides with increased levels of responsibility.* Petty crimes are risky and exciting social activities that provide adventure in an otherwise boring world. As youths grow older, they take on new responsibilities that are inconsistent with criminality.[49] For example, young people who marry, enlist in the armed services, or enroll in vocational training courses are less likely to pursue criminal activities.[50]

age of onset
Age at which youths begin their delinquent careers; early onset is believed to be linked with chronic offending patterns.

chronic juvenile offenders (also known as chronic delinquent offenders, chronic delinquents, or chronic recidivists)
Youths who have been arrested four or more times during their minority and perpetuate a striking majority of serious criminal acts; this small group, known as the "chronic 6 percent," is believed to engage in a significant portion of all delinquent behavior; these youths do not age out of crime but continue their criminal behavior into adulthood.

- *Personalities can change with age.* As youths mature, rebellious youngsters may develop increased self-control and be able to resist antisocial behavior.[51]

- *Young adults become more aware of the risks that accompany crime.* As adults, they are no longer protected by the relatively kindly arms of the juvenile justice system.[52]

Of course, not all juvenile criminals desist as they age; some go on to become chronic adult offenders. Yet even they slow down as they age. Crime is too dangerous, physically taxing, and unrewarding, and punishments too harsh and long-lasting, to become a way of life for most people.[53]

CHRONIC OFFENDING: CAREERS IN DELINQUENCY

Although most adolescents age out of crime, a relatively small number of youths begin to violate the law early in their lives (early onset) and continue at a high rate well into adulthood (persistence).[54] The association between early onset and high-rate persistent offending has been demonstrated in samples drawn from a variety of cultures, time periods, and offender types.[55] These offenders are resistant to change and seem immune to the effects of punishment. Arrest, prosecution, and conviction do little to slow down their offending careers. These *chronic offenders* are responsible for a significant amount of all delinquent and criminal activity.

Current interest in the delinquent life cycle was prompted in part by the "discovery" in the 1970s of the **chronic juvenile** (or delinquent) **offender.** According to this view, a relatively small number of youthful offenders commit a significant percentage of all serious crimes, and many of these same offenders grow up to become chronic adult criminals.

Chronic offenders can be distinguished from other delinquent youths. Many youthful law violators are apprehended for a single instance of criminal behavior, such as shoplifting or joyriding. Chronic offenders begin their delinquent careers at a young age (under ten years, referred to as early onset), have serious and persistent brushes with the law, and may be excessively violent and destructive. They do not age out of crime but continue their law-violating behavior into adulthood.[56] Most research shows that early, repeated delinquent activity is the best predictor of future adult criminality.

A number of research efforts have set out to chronicle the careers of serious delinquent offenders. The next sections describe these initiatives.

Chronic offenders do not age out of crime but continue their law-violating behavior into adulthood. James Justin Sledge, a man once tied to the 1997 Pearl High School shootings, is escorted from the federal courthouse in Jackson, Mississippi, in 2003, after pleading guilty to possessing an unregistered machine gun ordered over the Internet. Sledge was sentenced to four months in federal prison, four months of house arrest, three years probation, and a $100 fine.

Delinquency in a Birth Cohort

The concept of the chronic career offender is most closely associated with the research efforts of Marvin Wolfgang.[57] In 1972, Wolfgang, Robert Figlio, and Thorsten Sellin published a landmark study, *Delinquency in a Birth Cohort.* They followed the delinquent careers of a cohort of 9,945 boys born in Philadelphia from birth until they reached age eighteen. Data were obtained from police files and school records. Socioeconomic status was determined by locating the residence of each member of the cohort and assigning him the median family income for that area.

About one-third of the boys (3,475) had some police contact. The remaining two-thirds (6,470) had none. Those boys who had at least one contact with the police committed a total of 10,214 offenses.

The most significant discovery of Wolfgang and his associates was that of the so-called chronic offender. The data indicated that 54 percent (1,862) of the sample's delinquent youths were repeat offenders. The repeaters could be further categorized as nonchronic recidivists and chronic recidivists. *Nonchronic recidivists* had been arrested more than once but fewer than five times. In contrast, the 627 boys labeled *chronic recidivists* had been arrested five times or more. Although these offenders accounted for only 18 percent of the delinquent population (6 percent of the total sample), they were responsible for 52 percent of all offenses. Known today as the "chronic 6 percent," this group perpetrated 71 percent of the homicides, 82 percent of the robberies, and 64 percent of the aggravated assaults.

Arrest and juvenile court experience did little to deter chronic offenders. In fact, the greater the punishment, the more likely they were to engage in repeat delinquent behavior. Strict punishment also increased the probability that further court action would be taken. Two factors stood out as encouraging recidivism: the seriousness of the original offense and the severity of the punishment. The researchers concluded that efforts of the juvenile justice system to eliminate delinquent behavior may be futile.

Wolfgang and his colleagues conducted a second cohort study with children born in 1958 and substantiated the finding that a relatively few chronic offenders are responsible for a significant portion of all delinquent acts.[58] Wolfgang's results have been duplicated in a number of research studies conducted in locales across the United States and also in Great Britain.[59] Some have used the records of court-processed youths and others have employed self-report data.

Stability in Crime: From Delinquent to Criminal

Do chronic juvenile offenders grow up to become chronic adult criminals? One study that followed a 10 percent sample of the original Pennsylvania cohort (974 subjects) to age thirty found that 70 percent of the "persistent" adult offenders had also been chronic juvenile offenders. Chronic juvenile offenders had an 80 percent chance of becoming adult offenders and a 50 percent chance of being arrested four or more times as adults.[60] Paul Tracy and Kimberly Kempf-Leonard conducted a follow-up study of all the subjects in the second 1958 cohort. By age twenty-six, Cohort II subjects were displaying the same behavior patterns as their older peers. Kids who started their delinquent careers early, committed a violent crime, and continued offending throughout adolescence were most likely to persist in criminal behavior as adults. Delinquents who began their offending careers with serious offenses or who quickly increased the severity of their offending early in life were most likely to persist in their criminal behavior into adulthood. Severity of offending rather than frequency of criminal behavior had the greatest impact on later adult criminality.[61]

These studies indicate that chronic juvenile offenders continue their law-violating careers as adults, a concept referred to as the **continuity of crime.** Kids who are disruptive as early as age five or six are most likely to exhibit disruptive behavior throughout adolescence.[62]

What Causes Chronic Offending?

Research indicates that chronic offenders suffer from a number of personal, environmental, social, and developmental deficits, as shown in Exhibit 2.1.

Other research studies have found that involvement in criminal activity (for example, getting arrested before age fifteen), relatively low intellectual development, and parental drug involvement were key predictive factors for future chronic offending.[63] Measurable problems in learning and motor skills, cognitive abilities, family relations, and other areas also predict chronicity.[64] Youthful offenders who persist are more likely to abuse alcohol, become economically dependent, have lower aspira-

continuity of crime
The idea that chronic juvenile offenders are likely to continue violating the law as adults.

victimization
The number of people who are victims of criminal acts; young teens are fifteen times more likely than older adults (age sixty-five and over) to be victims of crimes.

Checkpoints

✔ Official arrest statistics, victim data, and self-reports indicate that males are significantly more delinquent than females. In recent years, however, the female delinquency rate appears to be increasing faster than that for males.

✔ Although the true association between class and delinquency is still unknown, the official data tell us that delinquency rates are highest in areas with high rates of poverty.

✔ African-American youths are arrested for a disproportionate number of delinquent acts, such as robbery and assault, while White youths are arrested for a disproportionate share of arson and alcohol-related violations.

✔ Some criminologists suggest that institutional racism, such as police profiling, accounts for the racial differences in the delinquency rate. Others believe that high African-American delinquency rates are a function of living in a racially segregated society.

✔ Kids who engage in the most serious forms of delinquency are more likely to be members of the lower class.

✔ Delinquency rates decline with age. As youthful offenders mature, the likelihood that they will commit offenses declines.

✔ Not all juvenile criminals desist as they age; some go on to become chronic adult offenders.

✔ Chronic offenders commit a significant portion of all delinquent acts.

✔ Age of onset has an important effect on a delinquent career: those who demonstrate antisocial tendencies at a very early age are more likely to commit more crimes for a longer duration.

To quiz yourself on this material, go to questions 2.8–2.17 on the Juvenile Delinquency: The Core 2e Web site.

Exhibit 2.1   Childhood Risk Factors for Persistent Delinquency

Individual Factors

- Early antisocial behavior
- Emotional factors such as high behavioral activation and low behavioral inhibition
- Poor cognitive development
- Low intelligence
- Hyperactivity

School and Community Factors

- Failure to bond to school
- Poor academic performance
- Low academic aspirations
- Living in a poor family
- Neighborhood disadvantage
- Disorganized neighborhoods
- Concentration of delinquent peer groups
- Access to weapons

Family Factors

- Parenting
- Maltreatment
- Family violence
- Divorce
- Parental psychopathology
- Familial antisocial behaviors
- Teenage parenthood
- Family structure
- Large family size

Peer Factors

- Association with deviant peers
- Peer rejection

Source: Gail Wasserman, Kate Keenan, Richard Tremblay, John Coie, Todd Herrenkohl, Rolf Loeber, and David Petechuk, "Risk and Protective Factors of Child Delinquency," *Child Delinquency Bulletin Series* (Washington, DC: Office of Juvenile Justice and Delinquency Prevention, 2003).

tions, and have a weak employment record.[65] Apprehension and punishment seem to have little effect on their offending behavior. Youths who have long juvenile records will most likely continue their offending careers into adulthood.

Policy Implications

Efforts to chart the life cycle of crime and delinquency will have a major influence on both theory and policy. Rather than simply asking why youths become delinquent or commit antisocial acts, theorists are charting the onset, escalation, frequency, and cessation of delinquent behavior. Research on delinquent careers has also influenced policy. If relatively few offenders commit a great proportion of all delinquent acts and then persist as adult criminals, it follows that steps should be taken to limit their criminal opportunities.[66] One approach is to identify persistent offenders at the beginning of their offending careers and provide early treatment.[67] This might be facilitated by research aimed at identifying traits (for example, impulsive personalities) that can be used to classify high-risk offenders.[68] Because many of these youths suffer from a variety of problems, treatment must be aimed at a broad range of educational, family, vocational, and psychological problems. Focusing on a single problem, such as a lack of employment, may be ineffective.[69] ✔ Checkpoints

JUVENILE VICTIMIZATION

Juveniles are also victims of crime, and data from victim surveys can help us understand the nature of juvenile **victimization.** One source of juvenile victimization data is the result of an ongoing cooperative effort of the Bureau of Justice Statistics of the U.S. Department of Justice and the U.S. Census Bureau called the National Crime Victimization Survey (NCVS).[70] The NCVS is a household survey of victims of criminal behavior that measures the nature of the crime and the characteristics of victims.

What Does This Mean to Me?

Aging and Wisdom

The research tells us that delinquency declines with age and this book mentions a number of possible reasons for the current "crime drop." Even those of us who did some wild things in our youth behave more responsibly as we get older. But it is difficult, even for us, to understand why this change occurs. The cause might be purely physical: as people age, most become physically weaker. Even professional athletes have to retire in their thirties; the forty-plus athlete is a rare bird. Or it may be social: all of our old friends who use to be "party animals" are now married with children.

1. Have you changed since your high school days? Do you feel responsibility and maturity setting in? In other words, are you slowly turning into your parents?
2. If so, what do you think is the cause: changes in you or changes in your environment?

The total annual sample size of the NCVS has been about forty thousand households, containing about seventy-five thousand individuals. The sample is broken down into subsamples of ten thousand households, and each group is interviewed twice a year. The NCVS has been conducted annually for more than fifteen years.

Victimization in the United States

The NCVS provides estimates of the total number of personal contact crimes (assault, rape, robbery) and household victimizations (burglary, larceny, vehicle theft). The survey indicates that currently about twenty-three million criminal incidents occur each year. Being the target or victim of rape, robbery, or assault is a terrible burden, and one that can have considerable long-term consequences. If we translate the value of pain, emotional trauma, disability, and risk of death into dollar terms, the cost is $450 billion, or $1,800 for every person in the United States.[71] At first glance these figures seem overwhelming, but victimization rates are stable or declining for most crime categories.

Many of the differences between NCVS data and official statistics can be attributed to the fact that victimizations are frequently not reported. During 2002, only 49 percent of all violent victimizations and 40 percent of all property crimes were reported to the police. For example, 71 percent of robberies and 43 percent of simple assaults were reported to the police in 2002.

Young Victims   NCVS data indicate that young people are much more likely to be the victims of crime than adults. The chance of victimization declines with age. The difference is particularly striking when we compare teens under age nineteen with people over age sixty-five—in 2002, teens were more than fifteen times as likely to become victims than their grandparents (see Table 2.5). The data also indicate that male teenagers have a significantly higher chance than females of becoming victims of violent crime, and that African-American youth have a greater chance of becoming victims of violent crimes than Whites of the same age.[72]

Juveniles are much more likely to become crime victims than adults. They have a more dangerous lifestyle, which places them at risk for crime. They spend a great deal of time in one of the most dangerous areas in the community, the local school, and hang out with the most dangerous people, fellow teenagers!

© Michael Newman/PhotoEdit

Table 2.5 Victimization by Age, 2002

Characteristic of Victim	Population	Victimizations per 1,000 Persons Age 12 or Older						
		Violent Crimes						
			Rape/ Sexual Assault	Robbery	Assault			Personal Theft
		All			Total	Aggra- vated	Simple	
Gender								
Male	112,241,930	25.5	0.3	2.9	22.3	5.2	17.1	0.6
Female	119,347,330	20.8	1.8	1.6	17.4	3.4	14.0	0.7
Race								
White	192,956,980	22.8	0.8	1.9	20.0	4.1	15.9	0.7
African American	28,871,440	27.9	2.5	4.1	21.3	6.7	14.6	0.7
Other	9,769,850	14.7	1.2	2.4	11.0	0.9	10.1	0.4
Hispanic origin								
Hispanic	26,991,490	23.6	0.7	3.2	19.7	6.1	13.7	0.4
Non-Hispanic	203,062,880	23.0	1.1	2.1	19.8	4.1	15.8	0.7
Age								
12–15	16,676,560	44.4	2.1	3.0	39.3	5.0	34.3	0.9
16–19	16,171,800	58.2	5.5	4.0	48.6	11.9	36.7	0.6
20–24	19.317,740	47.4	2.9	4.7	39.8	10.1	29.7	1.6
25–34	37,329,720	26.3	0.6	2.8	22.8	5.2	17.6	0.5
35–49	65,263,580	18.1	0.5	1.5	16.1	3.5	12.7	0.7
50–64	43,746,850	10.7	0.2	1.6	8.9	1.7	7.2	0.3
65 or older	33,083,000	3.4	0.1	1.0	2.2	0.7	1.5	0.6

Source: Callie Marie Rennison and Michael Rand, *Current Victimization, 2002* (Washington, DC: Bureau of Justice Statistics, 2003), p. 8.

As part of their Monitoring the Future program, the Institute for Social Research also collects data on teen victimization. The most recent data available (2002) indicate that each year a significant number of adolescents become crime victims (see Table 2.6). This and other self-report surveys reveal that the NCVS seriously *underreports* juvenile victimization, and that the true rate of juvenile victimization may actually be several times higher.[73]

The Victims and Their Criminals

NCVS data can also tell us something about the relationship between victims and offenders. This information is available because victims of violent personal crimes, such as assault and robbery, can identify the age, sex, and race of their attackers.

In general, teens tend to be victimized by their peers. A majority of teens were shown to have been victimized by other teens, whereas victims age twenty and over identified their attackers as being twenty-one or older. However, people in almost all age groups who were victimized by *groups* of offenders identified their attackers as teenagers. Violent crime victims report that a disproportionate number of their attackers are young, ranging in age from sixteen to twenty-five.

The data also tell us that victimization is intraracial (that is, within race). White teenagers tend to be victimized by White teens, and African-American teenagers tend to be victimized by African-American teens.

Most teens are victimized by people with whom they are acquainted, and their victimization is more likely to occur during the day. In contrast, adults are more often

Checkpoints

✔ *The National Crime Victimization Survey (NCVS) samples about seventy-five thousand people annually in order to estimate the total number of criminal incidents, including those not reported to police.*

✔ *Males are more often the victims of delinquency than females.*

✔ *Younger people are more often targets than older people.*

✔ *African-American rates of violent victimization are much higher than White rates. Crime victimization tends to be intraracial.*

✔ *Self-report data show that a significant number of adolescents become crime victims. The NCVS may underreport juvenile victimization.*

 To quiz yourself on this material, go to questions 2.18–2.21 on the Juvenile Delinquency: The Core 2e Web site.

Table 2.6 **Self-Reported Victimization Among High School Seniors, 2002**

	Once (%)	More Than Once (%)
Something stolen (under $50)	26	18
Something stolen (over $50)	18	7
Damaged property	19	13
Injured with a weapon	2	2
Threatened with a weapon	9	6.5

Source: *Monitoring the Future, 2002* (Ann Arbor, MI: Institute for Social Research, 2003).

victimized by strangers, and at night. One explanation for this pattern is that youths are at greatest risk from their own family and relatives. (Chapter 8 deals with the issue of child abuse and neglect.) Another possibility is that many teenage victimizations occur at school, in school buildings, or on school grounds. The issue of teen victimization is discussed further in the following Focus on Delinquency feature.

✔ Checkpoints

Focus on Delinquency

Adolescent Victims of Violence

How many adolescents experience extreme physical and sexual violence and what effect does the experience have on their lives? To answer these critical questions, Dean Kilpatrick, Benjamin Saunders, and Daniel Smith conducted interviews with 4,023 adolescents ages twelve to seventeen to obtain information on their substance use, abuse, delinquency, and Post Traumatic Stress Disorder (PTSD) as well as their experiences with sexual assault, physical assault, physically abusive punishment, and witnessing acts of violence.

Kilpatrick and his colleagues found that rates of interpersonal violence and victimization among adolescents in the United States are extremely high. Approximately 1.8 million adolescents ages twelve to seventeen have been sexually assaulted and 3.9 million have been severely physically assaulted. Another 2.1 million have been punished by physical abuse. The most common form of youth victimization was witnessing violence, with approximately 8.8 million youths indicating that they had seen someone else being shot, stabbed, sexually assaulted, physically assaulted, or threatened with a weapon.

There were distinct racial and ethnic patterns in youth victimization. There is a much higher incidence of all types of victimization among African-American and Native American adolescents; more than half of African-American, Hispanic, and Native American adolescents had witnessed violence in their lifetimes. Native American adolescents had the highest rate for sexual assault victimizations; Whites and Asians reported the lowest. Native Americans, African-

Americans, and Hispanics also reported the highest rate of physical assault victimization—20 to 25 percent of each group reported experiencing at least one physical assault.

Gender also played a role in increasing the exposure to violence. Girls were at greater risk of sexual assault than boys (13.0 percent versus 3.4 percent). Boys were at significantly greater risk of physical assault than girls (21.3 percent versus 13.4 percent). A substantial number of all adolescents (43.6 percent of boys and 35 percent of girls) reported having witnessed violence. Physically abusive punishment was similar for boys (8.5 percent) and girls (10.2 percent).

What Are the Outcomes of Abuse and Violence?

The research discovered a clear relationship exists between youth victimization and mental health problems and delinquent behavior. For example:

- Negative outcomes in victims of sexual assault were three to five times the rates observed in nonvictims.
- The lifetime prevalence of Post Traumatic Stress Disorder (PTSD) is 8.1 percent, indicating that approximately 1.8 million adolescents had met the criteria for PTSD at some point during their lifetime.
- Girls were significantly more likely than boys to have lifetime PTSD (10.1 percent versus 6.2 percent).
- Among boys who had experienced sexual assault, 28.2 percent had PTSD at some point in their lives. The rate of lifetime PTSD among boys who had not been sexually assaulted was 5.4 percent.

- Sexually assaulted girls had a lifetime PTSD rate of 29.8 percent, compared with only 7.1 percent of girls with no sexual assault history.
- Experiencing either a physical assault or physically abusive punishment was associated with a lifetime PTSD rate of 15.2 percent for boys. The rate of lifetime PTSD in boys who had not been physically assaulted or abusively punished was 3.1 percent.
- Approximately 25 percent of physically assaulted or abused adolescents reported lifetime substance abuse or dependence. Rates of substance problems among non-physically assaulted or abused adolescents were roughly 6 percent.
- The percentage of boys who were physically assaulted and had ever committed an index offense was 46.7 percent, compared with 9.8 percent of boys who were not assaulted. Similarly, 29.4 percent of physically assaulted girls reported having engaged in serious delinquent acts at some point in their lives, compared with 3.2 percent of girls who had not been assaulted.

The Kilpatrick research shows that youths ages twelve to seventeen are at great risk for violent acts and that those who experience violent victimizations suffer significant social problems. Protecting adolescents must become a national priority.

CRITICAL THINKING

1. Should people who abuse or harm adolescent children be punished more severely than those who harm adults?
2. Would you advocate the death penalty for someone who rapes an adolescent female?

INFOTRAC COLLEGE EDITION RESEARCH

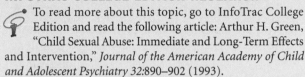 To read more about this topic, go to InfoTrac College Edition and read the following article: Arthur H. Green, "Child Sexual Abuse: Immediate and Long-Term Effects and Intervention," *Journal of the American Academy of Child and Adolescent Psychiatry* 32:890–902 (1993).

Source: Dean Kilpatrick, Benjamin Saunders, and Daniel Smith, *Youth Victimization: Prevalence and Implications* (Washington, DC: National Institute of Justice, 2003).

SUMMARY

- Official delinquency refers to youths who are arrested.
- Arrest data come from the FBI's Uniform Crime Report (UCR), an annual tally of crimes reported to police by citizens.
- The FBI gathers arrest statistics from local police departments. From these, it is possible to determine the number of youths who are arrested each year, along with their age, race, and gender.
- About two million youths are arrested annually.
- After a long increase in juvenile crime, there has been a decade decrease in the number of juveniles arrested for nonviolent and violent crimes.
- Dissatisfaction with the UCR prompted criminologists to develop other means of measuring delinquent behavior. Self-reports are surveys in which subjects are asked to describe their misbehavior. Although self-reports indicate that many more crimes are committed than are known to the police, they also show that the delinquency rate is rather stable.
- The factors that are believed to shape and control teen delinquency rates include gang activity, drug abuse, and teen gun ownership, abortion rates, economy, punishment, and social conditions.
- Delinquents are disproportionately male, although female delinquency rates are rising faster than those for males.
- Minority youth are overrepresented in the delinquency rate, especially for violent crime. Experts are split on the cause of racial differences. Some believe they are a

function of system bias, others see them as representing actual differences in the delinquency rate.
- Disagreement also exists over the relationship between class position and delinquency. Some hold that adolescent crime is a lower-class phenomenon, whereas others see it throughout the social structure. Problems in methodology have obscured the true class-crime relationship. However, official statistics indicate that lower-class youths are responsible for the most serious criminal acts.
- There is general agreement that delinquency rates decline with age. Some experts believe this phenomenon is universal, whereas others believe a small group of offenders persist in crime at a high rate. The age-crime relationship has spurred research on the nature of delinquency over the life course.
- Delinquency data show the existence of a chronic persistent offender who begins his or her offending career early in life and persists as an adult. Wolfgang and his colleagues identified chronic offenders in a series of cohort studies conducted in Philadelphia.
- Ongoing research has identified the characteristics of persistent offenders as they mature, and both personality and social factors help us predict long-term offending patterns.
- The National Crime Victimization Survey (NCVS) is an annual national survey of the victims of crime that is conducted by agencies of the federal government.
- Teenagers are much more likely to become victims of crime than are people in other age groups.

Federal Bureau of Investigation (FBI), p. 23
Uniform Crime Report (UCR), p. 23
Part I offenses, index crimes, p. 23
Part II offenses, p. 24

disaggregated, p. 24
self-reports, p. 29
dark figures of crime, p. 30
aging-out process, desistance, spontaneous remission, p. 37

age of onset, p. 38
chronic delinquent offenders, p. 38
chronic recidivists, p. 38
continuity of crime, p. 40
victimization, p. 40

QUESTIONS FOR DISCUSSION

1. What factors contribute to the aging-out process?

2. Why are males more delinquent than females? Is it a matter of lifestyle, culture, or physical properties?

3. Discuss the racial differences found in the crime rate. What factors account for differences in the African-American and White crime rates?

4. Should kids who have been arrested more than three times be given mandatory incarceration sentences?

5. Do you believe that self-reports are an accurate method of gauging the nature and extent of delinquent behavior?

APPLYING WHAT YOU HAVE LEARNED

As a juvenile court judge you are forced to make a tough decision during a hearing: whether a juvenile should be waived to the adult court. It seems that gang activity has become a way of life for residents living in local public housing projects. The "Bloods" sell crack, and the "Wolfpack" controls the drug market. When the rivalry between the two gangs exploded, sixteen-year-old Shatiek Johnson, a Wolfpack member, shot and killed a member of the Bloods; in retaliation, the Bloods put out a contract on his life. While in hiding, Shatiek was confronted by two undercover detectives who recognized the young fugitive. Fearing for his life, Shatiek pulled a pistol and began firing, fatally wounding one of the officers. During the hearing, you learn that Shatiek's story is not dissimilar from that of many other children raised in tough housing projects. With an absent father and a single mother who could not control her five sons, Shatiek lived in a world of drugs, gangs, and shootouts long before he was old enough to vote. By age thirteen, Shatiek had been involved in the gang-beating death of a homeless man in a dispute over ten dollars, for which he was given a one-year sentence at a youth deten-

tion center and released after six months. Now charged with a crime that could be considered first-degree murder if committed by an adult, Shatiek could—if waived to the adult court—be sentenced to life in prison or even face the death penalty.

At the hearing, Shatiek seems like a lost soul. He claims he thought the police officers were killers out to collect the bounty put on his life by the Bloods. He says that killing the rival gang boy was an act of self-defense. The DA confirms that the victim was in fact a known gang assassin with numerous criminal convictions. Shatiek's mother begs you to consider the fact that her son is only sixteen years old, that he has had a very difficult childhood, and that he is a victim of society's indifference to the poor.

Would you treat Shatiek as a juvenile and see if a prolonged stay in a youth facility could help this troubled young man, or would you transfer (waive) him to the adult justice system? Does a sixteen-year-old like Shatiek deserve a second chance? Is Shatiek's behavior common among adolescent boys or unusual and disturbing?

DOING RESEARCH ON THE WEB

To help you answer these questions and to learn more about gang membership, click on Web Links under the Chapter Resources at http://cj.wadsworth.com/siegel_jdcore2e. to go to the federal site for the National Criminal Justice Reference service, a U.N. site that offers important information, and a site on a private treatment center.

Pro/Con discussions and Viewpoint Essays on some of the topics in this chapter may be found at the Opposing Viewpoints Resource Center: www.gale.com/OpposingViewpoints.

chapter 3

Individual Views of Delinquency: Choice and Trait

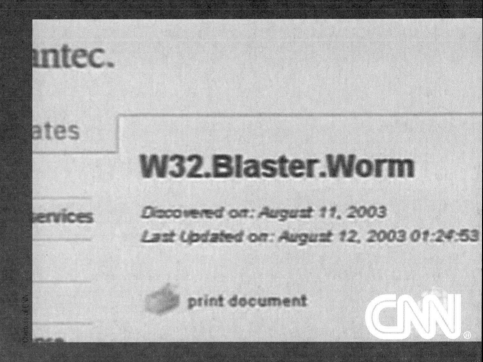

Courtesy of CNN

CHAPTER OBJECTIVES

After reading this chapter you should:

1. Know the difference between choice and trait theories.

2. Understand the concept of criminal choice.

3. Be familiar with the concept of routine activities.

4. Be able to discuss the pros and cons of general deterrence.

5. Recognize what is meant by the term *specific deterrence*.

6. Understand the concept of situational crime prevention.

7. Know the biochemical, neurological, and genetic factors linked to delinquency.

8. Understand the psychodynamic model of delinquency.

9. Understand why, according to the behavioral perspective, watching violent media causes violent behaviors.

10. Be familiar with the term *psychopath*.

11. Recognize the issues linking intelligence to delinquency.

In 2003, a Minnesota high school student, Jeffrey Lee Parsons, was charged in connection with spreading a version of the "Blaster" virus. The virus targeted a flaw in Microsoft's Windows XP and 2000 operating systems, and infected an estimated four hundred thousand computers worldwide. In a twelve-page complaint filed in federal court, Parsons was charged with one count of "intentionally causing and attempting to cause damage to a protected computer."

Described in the media as a heavy-set loner who was depressed and angry, Parsons refuted those assumptions during a *Today Show* interview (accessible on http://msnbc.msn.com/id/3078578/):

Today: In cases like this, there are a lot of quick, simple characterizations of the accused given to the media—for example, he was a loner, he didn't have friends, he was reckless, and so on. How would you describe yourself?

Parsons: I'm the complete opposite of the way I've been portrayed in the press. I'm not a loner. I have a very supportive close group of friends. I'm not reckless, I don't do drugs, smoke, or drink. This is the first time I have ever had a run-in with the law. It's hurtful to see the accounts of me. I'm not depressed, embarrassed about my weight, or a misfit.

CNN. VIEW THE CNN VIDEO CLIP OF THIS STORY AND ANSWER RELATED CRITICAL THINKING QUESTIONS ON YOUR JUVENILE DELINQUENCY: THE CORE 2E CD.

The Parsons case illustrates the view that many youthful offenders are not irrational or angry, but clever, intelligent, and calculating. Some delinquency experts believe that the decision to commit an illegal act is a product of an individual decision-making process that may be shaped by the personal characteristics of the decision maker. They reject the notion that delinquents are a "product of their environment." But if social and economic factors alone determine behavior, how is it that many youths residing in dangerous neighborhoods live law-abiding lives? According to the U.S. Census Bureau, more than thirty-four million Americans live in poverty yet the vast majority do not become delinquents and criminals.[1] Research indicates that relatively few youths in any population, even the most economically disadvantaged, actually become hard-core, chronic delinquents.[2] The quality of neighborhood and family life may have little impact on the choices individuals make.[3]

Considering these data, some delinquency experts believe that the root cause of juvenile misbehavior must be found on the individual, and not the social, level.

Views of delinquency that focus on the individual can be divided into two categories. One position, referred to as **choice theory,** suggests that offenders are rational decision makers who choose to engage in antisocial activity because they believe their actions will be beneficial. Whether they join a gang, steal cars, or sell drugs, their delinquent acts are motivated by the belief that crime can be a relatively risk-free way to better their situation, make money, have fun. They have little fear of getting caught. Some have fantasies of riches, and others may enjoy the excitement produced by criminal acts such as beating up someone or stealing a car.

The second view, referred to as **trait theory,** suggests that delinquent acts, especially violent ones, are not rational choices but uncontrollable, irrational behaviors. Many forms of delinquency, such as substance abuse and violence, appear more impulsive than rational, and these behaviors may be inspired by aberrant physical or

choice theory
Holds that youths will engage in delinquent and criminal behavior after weighing the consequences and benefits of their actions; delinquent behavior is a rational choice made by a motivated offender who perceives that the chances of gain outweigh any possible punishment or loss.

trait theory
Holds that youths engage in delinquent or criminal behavior due to aberrant physical or psychological traits that govern behavioral choices; delinquent actions are impulsive or instinctual rather than rational choices.

psychological traits. Although some youths may choose to commit crime because they desire conventional luxuries and power, others may be driven by abnormalities such as hyperactivity, low intelligence, biochemical imbalance, or genetic defects.

Choice and trait theories are linked because they both focus on an individual's mental processes and behavioral reactions. They suggest that each person reacts to environmental and social circumstances in a unique fashion. Faced with the same set of conditions, one person will live a law-abiding life while another will use antisocial or violent behavior to satisfy his or her needs. Choice theorists suggest that the delinquent freely chooses antisocial behaviors to satisfy needs, while trait theorists argue that the choice of antisocial behavior is shaped by mental and physical traits.

CHOICE THEORY

The first formal explanations of crime held that human behavior is a matter of choice. It was assumed that people had **free will** to choose their behavior and that those who violated the law were motivated by greed, revenge, survival, or hedonism. More than two hundred years ago, **utilitarian** philosophers Cesare Beccaria and Jeremy Bentham argued that people weigh the consequences of their actions before deciding on a course of behavior.[4] Their writings formed the core of what used to be called **classical criminology** and is now referred to as *rational choice theory* (or more simply *choice theory*).

Choice theory holds that the decision to violate the law comes after a careful weighing of the benefits and costs of criminal behaviors. Most potential law violators would cease their actions if the pain associated with a behavior outweighed the gain; conversely, law-violating behavior seems attractive if the rewards seem greater than the punishment.[5]

According to the choice view, youths who decide to become drug dealers compare the benefits, such as cash to buy cars and other luxury items, with the penalties, such as arrest followed by a long stay in a juvenile facility. If they believe that drug dealers are rarely caught, and even when caught avoid severe punishments, they are more likely to choose to become dealers than if they believe dealers are almost always caught and punished by lengthy prison terms. They may know or hear about criminals who make a significant income from their illegal activities and want to follow in their footsteps.[6] Put simply, to prevent crime, the pain of punishment must outweigh the benefit of illegal gain.[7]

free will
The view that youths are in charge of their own destinies and are free to make personal behavior choices unencumbered by environmental factors.

utilitarians
Those who believe that people weigh the benefits and consequences of their future actions before deciding on a course of behavior.

classical criminology
Holds that decisions to violate the law are weighed against possible punishments and to deter crime the pain of punishment must outweigh the benefit of illegal gain; led to graduated punishments based on seriousness of the crime (let the punishment fit the crime).

THE RATIONAL DELINQUENT

The view that delinquents *choose* to violate the law remains a popular approach to the study of delinquency. According to this view, delinquency is not merely a function of social ills, such as lack of economic opportunity or family dysfunction. In reality, many youths from affluent families choose to break the law, and most indigent adolescents are law abiding. For example, at first glance drug abuse appears to be a senseless act motivated by grinding poverty and a sense of desperation. However, economic hopelessness cannot be the motivating force behind the substance abuse of millions of middle-class users, many of whom plan to finish high school and go on to college. These kids are more likely to be motivated by the desire for physical gratification, peer group acceptance, and other social benefits. They choose to break the law because, despite the inherent risks, they believe that taking drugs and drinking provide more pleasure than pain. Their entry into substance abuse is facilitated by their perception that valued friends and family members endorse and encourage drug use and abuse substances themselves.[8] Subscribers to the rational choice model believe the decision to commit a specific type of crime is a matter of personal decision making; hence, the term *rational choice*.

Choosing Delinquent Acts

The focus of choice theory is on the *act,* not on the offender. The concepts of delinquent and delinquency are considered separate: delinquents are youth who maintain the propensity to commit delinquent acts; delinquency is an event during which someone violates the criminal law.[9] Even if youths have a delinquent propensity and are motivated to commit crimes, they may not do so if the opportunity to is restricted or absent. For example, they may want to break into a home but are frightened off by a security system, guard dog, or gun-toting owner. In contrast, the least-motivated adolescent may turn to crime if the rewards are very attractive, the chance of apprehension small, and the punishment tolerable. Why a child has the propensity to commit delinquent acts is an issue quite distinct from the reasons a delinquent decides to break into a particular house one day or to sell narcotics the next.

The decision to "choose" delinquency occurs when an offender decides to take the chance of violating the law after considering his or her situation (that is, need for money, opportunities for conventional success), values (conscience, need for peer approval), and situational factors (the likelihood of getting caught, the punishment if apprehended). Conversely, the decision to forgo law-violating behavior may be based on the perception that the benefits are no longer good or the probability of successfully completing a crime is less than the chance of being caught. For example, aging out may occur because as delinquents mature they begin to realize that the risks of crime are greater than the potential profits. The solution to crime, therefore, may be formulating policies that will cause potential delinquents to choose conventional behaviors.[10] The fact that delinquency can provide benefits to adolescents—and what to do about this—is the subject of the following Focus on Delinquency feature.

Lifestyle and Delinquency

Lifestyle also affects the decision to engage in delinquency. For example, adolescents who are granted a lot of time socializing with peers are more likely to engage in deviant behaviors, especially if their parents are not around to supervise or control their behavior.[11] Teenage boys may have the highest crime rates because they, rather than girls, have the freedom to engage in unsupervised socialization.[12] Girls who are physically mature and have more freedom without parental supervision are the ones most likely to have the opportunity to engage in antisocial acts.[13]

If lifestyle influences choice, can providing kids with "character-building" activities—such as a part-time job after school—reduce their involvement in delinquency? Research shows that adolescent work experience may actually increase antisocial activity rather than limit its occurrence. Kids who get jobs may be looking for an easy opportunity to acquire cash to buy drugs and alcohol; after-school jobs may attract teens who are more impulsive than ambitious.[14] At work, the opportunity to socialize with deviant peers combined with lack of parental supervision increases criminal motivation.[15] While some adults may think that providing teens with a job will reduce their criminal activity ("idle hands are the devil's workshop") many qualities of the work experience—autonomy, increased social status among peers, and increased income—may neutralize the positive effects of working. If providing jobs is to have any positive influence on kids, the jobs must in turn provide a learning experience and support academic achievement.[16]

Gangs and Choice   The emergence of gangs, and their involvement in the drug trade shows how lifestyle can influence choice. Gang members are well-armed entrepreneurs seeking to cash in on a lucrative, albeit illegal, "business enterprise." Gang leaders are surely "rational decision makers," constantly processing information: Who are my enemies? What are the chances of getting caught? Where can I find a good lawyer?[17] Gang members have been found to act like employers, providing

According to choice theory, juvenile offenders are rational decision makers who choose to engage in antisocial activity. Whether they join a gang, steal cars, or smoke pot, as the kids here are doing, their delinquent acts are motivated by the belief that crime can be a relatively risk-free way to better their situation, make money, and have fun.

© Bill Aron/PhotoEdit

their associates with security and the know-how to conduct "business deals." When Steven Levitt and Sudhir Alladi Venkatesh studied the financial rewards of being in a drug gang, they found that despite enormous risks to their health, life, and freedom, the average gang members earned slightly more than what they could in the legitimate labor market (about $6 to $11 per hour).[18] Why did they stay in the gang? They believed that there was a strong potential for future riches if they stayed in the drug business and earned a "management" position (gang leaders earned a lot more than the rank-and-file members). Being in a teenage drug gang was based on the perception of the potential for future gain versus the reality of conventional alternatives and opportunities.[19] Teen gangs will be discussed further in chapter 8.

Routine Activities

If the motivation to commit delinquent acts is a constant, why do delinquency rates rise and fall? Why are some areas more delinquency-ridden than others? To answer these questions, some choice theorists believe that attention must be paid to the *opportunity to commit delinquent acts.*[20]

According to **routine activities theory,** developed by Lawrence Cohen and Marcus Felson, the volume and distribution of **predatory crimes** (violent crimes against persons and crimes in which an offender attempts to steal an object directly from its holder) in a particular area and at a particular time is influenced by the interaction of three variables: the availability of *suitable targets* (such as homes containing easily saleable goods), the absence of *capable guardians* (such as homeowners, police, and security guards), and the presence of *motivated offenders* (such as unemployed teenagers)[21] (see Figure 3.1 on page 54).

This approach gives equal weight to opportunity and propensity: the decision to violate the law is influenced by opportunity and the greater the opportunity, the greater the likelihood of delinquency.[22]

routine activities theory
The view that crime is a "normal" function of the routine activities of modern living; offenses can be expected if there is a motivated offender and a suitable target that is not protected by capable guardians.

predatory crimes
Violent crimes against persons and crimes in which an offender attempts to steal an object directly from its holder.

Lack of Capable Guardians   Kids will commit crimes when they believe their actions will go undetected by guardians such as police, security guards, neighbors, teachers, or homeowners. They choose what they consider safe places to commit crimes and to buy and sell drugs.[23]

Does Delinquency Pay?

The delinquent lifestyle fits well with people who organize their life around risk taking and partying. Delinquent acts provide money for drugs and are an ideal mechanism for displaying courage and fearlessness to one's running mates. What could be a better way for kids to show how tough they are than being able to get into a gang fight with their buddies? Rather than creating overwhelming social problems, a delinquent way of life may be extremely beneficial to some kids, helping them overcome the problems and stresses they face in their daily lives.

According to sociologist Timothy Brezina, crime and delinquency help some achieve a sense of control or mastery over their environment. Adolescents in particular may find themselves feeling "out of control" because society limits their opportunities and resources. Antisocial behavior gives them the opportunity to exert control over their own lives and destinies by helping them to avoid situations they find uncomfortable or repellant (for example, cutting school, running away from an abusive home) or obtain resources for desired activities and commodities (for example, stealing or selling drugs to buy stylish outfits).

Delinquent acts may help them boost their self-esteem by attacking, symbolically or otherwise, perceived enemies (for example, they vandalize the property of an adult who has given them grief). Drinking and drug taking may allow some people to ward off depression and compensate for a lack of positive experiences; they learn how to self-medicate themselves. Some who are angry at their mistreatment may turn to violence to satisfy a desire for revenge or retaliation.

Brezina found a great deal of evidence that people engage in antisocial acts in order to solve problems. The literature on drug and alcohol abuse is replete with examples of research showing how people turn to substance abuse to increase their sense of personal power, to become more assertive, and to reduce tension and anxiety. Some kids embrace deviant lifestyles, such as joining a gang, in order to offend conventional society while at the same time compensating for their feelings of powerlessness or ordinariness. Engaging in risky behavior helps them feel alive and competent. There is also evidence that antisocial acts can provide positive solutions to problems. Violent kids, for example, may have learned that being aggressive with others is a good means to control the situation and get what they want; counterattacks may be one means of controlling people who are treating them poorly.

Why do adolescents age out of crime? Although crime as a short-run problem-solving solution may be appealing to adolescents, it becomes less attractive as they mature and begin to appreciate the dangers of doing so. Going to a drunken frat party may sound appealing to sophomores who want to improve their social life, but the risks involved to safety and reputation make them off-limits to older grads. As people mature their thinking extends further into the future, and risky behavior becomes a threat to long-range plans.

CRITICAL THINKING

According to Brezina, as people mature their thinking extends further into the future and risky behavior threatens long-range plans. Does this vision adequately explain the aging-out process? If so, why do some people continue to commit crime in their adulthood?

INFOTRAC COLLEGE EDITION RESEARCH

Use "rational choice theory" as a key term on InfoTrac College Edition in order to learn more about how kids might use planning to commit delinquent acts.

How do people learn to solve problems? To find out, go to InfoTrac College Edition and use "problem solving" as a subject guide.

Sources: Timothy Brezina, "Delinquent Problem Solving: An Interpretive Framework for Criminological Theory and Research," *Journal of Research in Crime and Delinquency* 37:3–30 (2000); Andy Hochstetler, "Opportunities and Decisions: Interactional Dynamics in Robbery and Burglary Groups," *Criminology* 39:737–763 (2001).

Research does show that crime levels are relatively low in neighborhoods where residents keep a watchful eye on their neighbors' property.[24] Delinquency rates trend upward as the number of adult caretakers (guardians) who are at home during the day decreases. With mothers at work and children in day care, homes are left unguarded, becoming vulnerable targets. In our highly transient society, the traditional neighborhood, in which streets are monitored by familiar guardians such as family members, neighbors, and friends, has been vanishing and replaced by anonymous housing developments.[25] Potential thieves look for these unguarded neighborhoods in order to plan their break-ins and burglaries.[26]

Suitable Targets   The availability of suitable targets, such as DVD and CD players, cell phones, digital cameras, jewelry, and cash, will increase crime rates. Research has generally supported the fact that the more wealth a home contains, the more likely it is to be a crime target.

Why are some areas more crime ridden than others? It may be because of variations in the opportunity to commit crimes. Places that are unguarded may be more vulnerable to criminal activities. Crime may occur not only because a criminal decides to break the law, but also because victims place themselves at risk and no one is around to protect them from harm.

© Nick Lacy/Stock, Boston

Delinquents do not like to travel to commit crimes, and look for suitable targets close to their homes.[27] Familiarity with an area gives kids a ready knowledge of escape routes; this is referred to as their "awareness space."

Motivated Offenders   Routine activities theory also links delinquency rates to the number of kids in the population who are highly motivated to commit crime. If social forces increase the motivated population, then delinquency rates may rise. For example, if the number of teenagers in a given population exceeds the number of available part-time and after-school jobs, the supply of motivated offenders may increase.[28] As the "crack epidemic" of the 1980s waned the delinquency rate dropped, because crack addicts are highly motivated offenders.

CHOICE THEORY AND DELINQUENCY PREVENTION

If delinquency is a rational choice and a routine activity, then delinquency prevention is a matter of convincing potential delinquents that they will be punished for committing delinquent acts, punishing them so severely that they never again commit crimes, or making it so difficult to commit crimes that the potential gain is not worth the risk. The first of these strategies is called *general deterrence,* the second *specific deterrence,* and the third *situational crime prevention.* Let's look at each of these strategies in more detail.

General Deterrence

general deterrence
Crime control policies that depend on the fear of criminal penalties, such as long prison sentences for violent crimes; the aim is to convince law violators that the pain outweighs the benefit of criminal activity.

The **general deterrence** concept holds that the choice to commit delinquent acts can be controlled by the threat of punishment. If people believe illegal behavior will result in severe sanctions, they will choose not to commit crimes.[29] If kids believed that their illegal behavior would result in apprehension and punishment, then only the truly irrational would commit crime.[30]

A guiding principle of deterrence theory is that the more severe, certain, and swift the punishment, the greater the deterrent effect.[31] Even if a particular delinquent act carries a very severe punishment, there will be relatively little deterrent effect if most people do not believe they will be caught. Conversely, even a mild sanction may deter

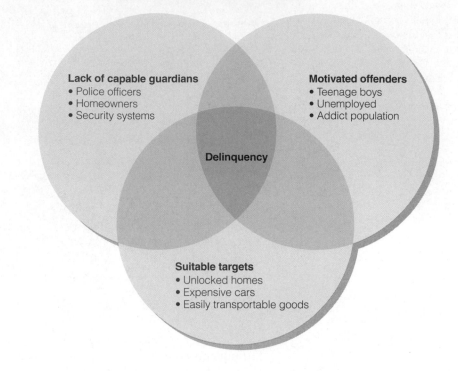

crime if people believe punishment is certain.[32] So if the justice system can convince would-be delinquents that they will be caught—for example, by putting more police officers on the street—these youths may decide that delinquency simply does not pay.[33]

Deterrence and Delinquency Traditionally, juvenile justice authorities have been reluctant to incorporate deterrence-based punishments on the ground that they interfere with the *parens patriae* philosophy. Children are punished less severely than adults, limiting the power of the law to deter juvenile crime. However, during the 1990s the increase in teenage violence, gang activity, and drug abuse prompted a reevaluation of deterrence strategies. Some juvenile courts have shifted from an emphasis on treatment to an emphasis on public safety.[34] Police began to focus on particular problems in their jurisdiction rather than to react after a crime occurred.[35] They began to use aggressive tactics to deter membership in drug-trafficking gangs.[36] Some police officers were sent into high schools undercover to identify and arrest student drug dealers.[37]

Some juvenile court judges became more willing to waive youths to adult courts.[38] The number of offenders under age eighteen admitted to state prison more than doubled from thirty-four hundred in 1985 to seventy-four hundred in 1997, about 2 percent of new admissions in each of the thirteen years.[39] In addition, legislators have passed more restrictive juvenile codes, and the number of incarcerated juveniles continues to increase. Adolescents are not even spared capital punishment; the U.S. Supreme Court has upheld the use of the death penalty for youths sixteen years of age.[40] These efforts seemed to have a beneficial effect: the overall delinquency rate declined as the threat of punishment increased.

Can Delinquency Be Deterred? On the surface, deterrence appears to have benefit, but there is reason to believe that the benefit is limited. Though delinquency rates have declined during a period when deterrence measures are in vogue, that does not necessarily mean that kids were deterred from crime. As you may recall, other social factors in play during the same period may have explained the drop, including lower rates of drug abuse, reduced teen pregnancy, and a strong economy.

Because deterrence strategies are based on the idea of a "rational" offender, they may not be effective when applied to young people. It is possible that punishment may bring defiance rather than deterrence in a teen population not known for its reasonableness. Minors tend to be less capable of making mature judgments, and many younger offenders are unaware of the content of juvenile legal codes. A deterrence policy (for example, mandatory waiver to the adult court for violent crimes) will have little effect on delinquency rates of kids who are not even aware these statutes exist.[41] It seems futile, therefore, to try to deter delinquency through fear of legal punishment. Teens seem more fearful of being punished by their parents or of being the target of disapproval from their friends than they are of the police.[42]

It is also possible that for the highest-risk group of young offenders—teens living in economically depressed neighborhoods—the deterrent threat of formal sanctions may be irrelevant. Inner-city youngsters may not have internalized the norms that hold that getting arrested is wrong. They have less to lose if arrested; they have a limited stake in society and are not worried about their future. They also may not connect their illegal behavior with punishment because they see many people committing crimes and not getting caught or being punished.

Research also shows that many juvenile offenders are under the influence of drugs or alcohol, a condition that might impair their decision-making ability.[43] Similarly, juveniles often commit crimes in groups, a process called **co-offending**, and peer pressure can outweigh the deterrent effect of the law.

In summary, deterring delinquency through the fear of punishment seems to have worked during the past decade but it is also possible that the reduction in the delinquency rate was the result of other social factors. Deterrence may be of limited value in controlling delinquency because children may neither fully comprehend the seriousness of their acts nor appreciate their consequences.[44]

Can delinquency and drug abuse be deterred when so many teens consider it fun and socially acceptable? High school student Cathy, left, parties with other rave fans at an abandoned warehouse in Portland, Oregon. Oregon's rave scene is an escape for teens, a worry for parents, and a worrisome challenge to law enforcement officials.

© 2000 AP/Wide World Photos

co-offending
Committing criminal acts in groups.

Does Punishment Work?

To some experts and pundits, if delinquency is punished severely kids will not risk committing delinquent acts. Consider this statement by Texas congressman Lamar Smith, an advocate of sending juveniles to adult court:

It is commonsense public policy when states pass laws that allow or require violent juveniles to be transferred to adult courts. I strongly believe that we can no longer tolerate young people who commit violent crimes simply because of their age. Young people have the ability to decide between right and wrong, as the vast majority of us do every day. But those youths who choose to prey on other juveniles, senior citizens, merchants, or homeowners will be held responsible. If that choice results in confinement in an adult prison system, perhaps youths who have a propensity to commit violent crimes will think twice before acting.

1. Do you think that sending kids to adult prisons will really deter others from committing crimes?
2. What do you recommend be done to stop or deter delinquency?
3. Do you think kids who commit crime really have the capacity to "think twice" before they act?
4. Can you remember ever being in a situation where you felt forced to break the law because of peer pressure, when being afraid of the consequences had no real effect on your behavior?

Source: Lamar Smith, "Sentencing Youths to Adult Correctional Facilities Increases Public Safety," *Corrections Today 65*:20 (April 2003).

Specific Deterrence

It stands to reason that if delinquents truly are rational and commit crimes because they see them as beneficial, they will stop offending if they are caught and severely punished. What rational person would recidivate after being exposed to an arrest, court appearance, and incarceration in an unpleasant detention facility, with the promise of more to come? According to the concept of **specific deterrence**, if young offenders are punished severely the experience will convince them not to repeat their illegal acts. Juveniles are punished by state authorities with the understanding that their ordeal will deter future misbehavior.

Although the association between punishment and desistance seems logical, there is little evidence that punitive measures alone deter future delinquency. There are research studies that show that arrest and conviction may under some circumstances lower the frequency of reoffending, a finding that supports specific deterrence.[45] However, other studies indicate that punishment has little real effect on reoffending and in some instances may actually increase the likelihood that first-time offenders will commit new crimes (recidivate).[46] Kids who are placed in a juvenile justice facility are just as likely to become adult criminals as those treated with greater leniency.[47] In fact, a history of prior arrests, convictions, and punishments has proven to be the best predictor of rearrest among young offenders released from correctional institutions. Rather than deterring future offending, punishment may encourage it.[48]

Why does punishment encourage rather than reduce delinquency? According to some experts, institutionalization cuts youths off from prosocial supports in the community, making them more reliant on deviant peers. Incarceration may also diminish chances for successful employment, reducing access to legitimate opportunities. This might help explain why delinquency rates are increasing at the same time that incarceration rates are at an all-time high.

The experience of punishment itself may motivate some adolescents to reoffend. For example, the use of mandatory sentences for some crimes means that all youths who are found to have committed those crimes must be institutionalized; first offenders may then be treated the same as chronic recidivists. These novice offenders may be packed into overcrowded facilities with experienced violent juveniles and consequently suffer significant and irrevocable harm from their experience.

Punishment strategies may stigmatize kids and help lock offenders into a delinquent career. Kids who are punished may also believe that the likelihood of getting caught twice for the same type of crime is remote: "Lightning never strikes twice in the same spot," they may reason; no one is that unlucky.[49]

Although some researchers have found that punishment may reduce the frequency of future offending, the weight of the evidence suggests that time served has little impact on recidivism.[50]

Situational Crime Prevention

According to choice theory, rational offenders weigh the potential gains of delinquent acts and balance them with the potential losses (getting arrested, getting punished). It stands to reason that if we can convince these rational decision makers that

specific deterrence
Sending convicted offenders to secure incarceration facilities so that punishment is severe enough to convince them not to repeat their criminal activity.

their illegal activities are risky, the potential gain is minimal, and the opportunity for success is limited, then they will choose not to commit crime. This is the logic behind the measures that have become known collectively as **situational crime prevention.** These strategies are designed to make it so difficult to commit delinquent acts that would-be offenders will be convinced the risks are greater than the rewards.[51] Rather than deterring or punishing individuals, they aim to reduce opportunities to commit delinquent acts. This can be accomplished by:

- Increasing the effort to commit delinquent acts
- Increasing the risks of delinquent activity
- Reducing the rewards attached to delinquent acts
- Increasing the shame of committing a delinquent act

Increasing the effort of delinquency might involve *target-hardening techniques,* such as placing unbreakable glass on storefronts. Some successful target-hardening efforts include installing a locking device on cars that prevents drunken drivers from starting the vehicle (the Breath Analyzed Ignition Interlock Device).[52] Access can be controlled by locking gates and fencing yards.[53] Facilitators of crime can be controlled by banning the sale of spray paint to adolescents in an effort to cut down on graffiti, or putting ID photos on credit cards to reduce their value if stolen.

Increasing the risks of delinquency might involve improving lighting, creating neighborhood watch programs, controlling building exits, installing security systems, or increasing the number of security officers and police patrols. The installation of street lights may convince would-be burglars that their entries will be seen and reported.[54] Closed-circuit TV cameras have been shown to reduce the amount of car theft from parking lots while also reducing the need for higher-cost security personnel.[55]

Reducing the rewards of delinquency could include strategies such as making car radios removable so they can be kept in the home at night, marking property so it is more difficult to sell when stolen, and having gender-neutral phone listings to discourage obscene phone calls. Tracking systems help police locate and return stolen vehicles. Increasing shame might include efforts to publish the names of some offenders in the local papers.

Hot Spots and Crackdowns   One type of situational crime prevention effort targets locales that are known to be the scene of repeated delinquent activity. By focusing on a **hot spot**—for example, a shopping mall, public park, or housing project—law enforcement efforts can be used to crack down on persistent youth crime. For example, a police task force might target gang members who are street-level drug dealers by using undercover agents and surveillance cameras in known drug-dealing locales. Unfortunately, these efforts have not often proven to be successful mechanisms for lowering crime and delinquency rates.[56] **Crackdowns** seem to be an effective short-term strategy, but their effect begins to decay once the initial shock effect wears off.[57] Crackdowns also may displace illegal activity to areas where there are fewer police.

Although these results are discouraging, delinquency rates seem to be reduced when police officers combine the use of aggressive problem solving with community improvement techniques (increased lighting, cleaned vacant lots) to fight particular crimes in selected places.[58] For example, a recent initiative by the Dallas Police Department to aggressively pursue truancy and curfew enforcement resulted in lower rates of gang violence.[59]

These three methods of delinquency prevention and control are summarized in Concept Summary 3.1.

Do Delinquents Choose Crime?

Though the logic of choice theory seems plausible, before we can accept its propositions several important questions need to be addressed. First, why do some poor and

situational crime prevention
A crime prevention method that relies on reducing the opportunity to commit criminal acts by making them more difficult to perform, reducing their reward, and increasing their risks.

hot spot
A particular location or address that is the site of repeated and frequent criminal activity.

crackdown
A law enforcement operation that is designed to reduce or eliminate a particular criminal activity through the application of aggressive police tactics, usually involving a larger than usual contingent of police officers.

Delinquency Prevention Methods

Method	Central Premise	Technique
General deterrence	Kids will avoid delinquency if they fear punishment.	Make punishment swift, severe, and certain.
Specific deterrence	Delinquents who are punished severely will not repeat their offenses.	Use harsh punishments, such as a stay in secure detention.
Situational crime prevention	Make delinquency more difficult and less profitable.	Harden targets, use surveillance, street lighting.

To get detailed information on the **Columbine tragedy**, click on Web Links under the Chapter Resources at http://cj.wadsworth.com/siegel_jdcore2e.

Checkpoints

✔ Choice theory maintains that delinquency is rational and can be prevented by punishment that is sufficiently severe and certain.

✔ Delinquents who choose crime must evaluate the characteristics of a target to determine its suitability.

✔ Routine activities theory suggests that delinquent acts are a function of motivated offenders, lack of capable guardians, and availability of suitable targets.

desperate kids choose to break the law whereas others who live in the same neighborhoods manage to live law-abiding lives? Conversely, why do affluent suburban youths choose to break the law when they have everything to lose and little to gain?

Choice theorists also have difficulty explaining seemingly irrational crimes such as vandalism, arson, and even drug abuse. To say a teenager painted swastikas on a synagogue after making a "rational choice" seems inadequate. Is it possible that violent adolescents—such as Dylan Klebold and Eric Harris, who on April 20, 1999, killed thirteen and wounded twenty-one classmates at Columbine High School—were "rational" decision makers, or was their behavior the product of twisted minds? To assume they made a "rational choice" to kill their classmates seems ill advised.

In summary, choice theory helps us understand criminal events and victim patterns. However, the question remains, why are some adolescents motivated to commit crime whereas others in similar circumstances remain law abiding? Why do some kids choose crime over legal activities? The remaining sections of this chapter present some possible explanations. ✔ Checkpoints

TRAIT THEORIES: BIOSOCIAL AND PSYCHOLOGICAL VIEWS

✔ General deterrence models are based on the fear of punishment. If punishments are severe, swift, and certain, then would-be delinquents would choose not to risk breaking the law.

✔ Specific deterrence aims at reducing crime through the application of severe punishments. Once offenders experience these punishments they will be unwilling to repeat their delinquent activities.

✔ Situational crime prevention efforts are designed to reduce or redirect crime by making it more difficult to profit from illegal acts.

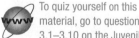

To quiz yourself on this material, go to questions 3.1–3.10 on the Juvenile Delinquency: The Core 2e Web site.

Choice theorists would have us believe that young people select crime after weighing the benefits of delinquent over legal behavior. For example, teens may decide to commit a robbery if they believe they will make a good profit, have a good chance of getting away, and even if caught, stand little chance of being severely punished. Conversely, they will forgo criminal activities if they see a lot of cops around and come to the conclusion they will get caught and punished. Their choice is both rational and logical.

But a number of experts think this model is incomplete. They believe it is simplistic to infer that all youths choose crime simply because the advantages outweigh the risks. If that were the case, how could profitless crimes such as violence or vandalism be explained? These experts argue that behavioral choices are a function of an individual's mental and physical makeup. Most law-abiding youths have traits that keep them within conventional society. In contrast, youths who choose to engage in antisocial behavior manifest abnormal mental and physical traits that influence their choices. When they commit crime, their behavior is shaped by these uncontrollable mental and physical traits.

The *source* of behavioral control, therefore, is one of the main differences between trait and choice theories. Although both views focus on the individual, the choice theorist views delinquents as rational and self-serving decision makers. The trait theorist views their "decisions" as a by-product of uncontrollable personal traits. To a choice theorist, reducing the benefits of crime by increasing the likelihood of

Though choice theory seems logical, it leaves a number of questions unanswered: Why do some poor and desperate kids choose to break the law when others manage to live law-abiding lives? Conversely, why do affluent suburban youths, such as those shown here, choose to break the law when they have everything to lose and little to gain?

© Tony Freeman/PhotoEdit

punishment will lower the crime rate. Because trait theorists question whether delinquents are rational decision makers, they focus more on the treatment of abnormal mental and physical conditions as a method of delinquency reduction. In the next sections, the primary components of trait theory are reviewed.

The Origins of Trait Theory

For a complete list of the crime-producing physical traits identified by Lombroso, click on Web Links under the Chapter Resources at http://cj.wadsworth.com/siegel_jdcore2e.

The first attempts to discover why criminal tendencies develop focused on biological traits present at birth. This school of thought is generally believed to have originated with the Italian physician Cesare Lombroso (1835–1909).[60] Known as the father of criminology, Lombroso developed the theory of **criminal atavism.**[61] He found that delinquents manifest physical anomalies that make them similar to our primitive ancestors. These individuals are throwbacks to an earlier stage of human evolution. Because of this link, the "born criminal" has such traits as enormous jaws, strong canines, a flattened nose, and supernumerary teeth (double rows, as in snakes). Lombroso made statements such as: "[I]t was easy to understand why the span of the arms in criminals so often exceeds the height, for this is a characteristic of apes, whose forelimbs are used in walking and climbing."[62]

Contemporaries of Lombroso refined the notion of a physical basis of crime. Raffaele Garofalo (1851–1934) shared Lombroso's belief that certain physical characteristics indicate a criminal nature.[63] Enrico Ferri (1856–1929), a student of Lombroso, accepted the biological approach to explaining criminal activity, but he attempted to interweave social factors into his explanation.[64] The English criminologist Charles Goring (1870–1919) challenged the validity of Lombroso's research and claimed instead that delinquent behaviors bore a significant relationship to "defective intelligence."[65] Consequently, he advocated that criminality could best be controlled by regulating the reproduction of families exhibiting abnormal traits such as "feeblemindedness."[66]

The early views that portrayed delinquent behavior as a function of a single biological trait had a significant impact on American criminology; biocriminologists helped develop a science of "criminal anthropology."[67] Eventually, these views evoked criticism for their unsound methodology. Many trait studies used captive offender populations and failed to compare experimental subjects with control groups.[68] These methodological flaws make it impossible to determine if biological

criminal atavism
The idea that delinquents manifest physical anomalies that make them biologically and physiologically similar to our primitive ancestors, savage throwbacks to an earlier stage of human evolution.

traits produce delinquency. It is equally plausible that police are more likely to arrest the mentally and physically abnormal. By the middle of the twentieth century, biological theories had fallen out of favor.

Contemporary Trait Theory

For most of the twentieth century, most delinquency research focused on social factors such as poverty and family life. However, a small group of researchers kept alive the biological approach.[69] Some embraced *sociobiology,* a perspective suggesting that behavior will adapt to the environment in which it evolved.[70] Creatures of all species are influenced by their innate need to survive and dominate others. Sociobiology revived interest in a biological basis for crime. If biological (genetic) and psychological (mental) makeup controls all human behavior, it follows that a person's genes should determine whether he or she chooses law-violating or conventional behavior.[71]

Trait theorists argue that a combination of personal traits and environmental influences produce individual behavior patterns. People with pathological traits, such as abnormal personality or a low IQ, may have a heightened risk for crime over the life course.[72] This risk is elevated by environmental stresses such as poor family life, educational failure, and exposure to delinquent peers. The reverse may also apply: a supportive environment may counteract adverse biological and psychological traits.[73]

According to contemporary trait theorists, by themselves individual deficits do not cause delinquency. However, possessing suspect individual traits may make a child more susceptible to the delinquency-producing factors in the environment. For example, an adolescent suffering from a learning disability may have an increased risk of school failure; those who fail at school are at risk to commit delinquent acts. Learning disabilities alone, therefore, are not a cause of delinquency and only present a problem when they produce school failure. Programs to help learning-disabled kids achieve in school will prevent later delinquent involvements.

Today trait theory can be divided into two separate branches: the first, most often called biosocial theory, assumes that the cause of delinquency can be found in a child's physical or biological makeup, and the second points the finger at psychological traits and characteristics.

BIOSOCIAL THEORIES OF DELINQUENCY

The first branch of trait theory—**biosocial theory**—focuses on the association between biological makeup, environmental conditions, and antisocial behaviors. Most research efforts are concentrated in three areas: biochemical factors, neurological dysfunction, and genetic influences.

Biochemical Factors

This area of research concerns the suspected relationship between antisocial behavior and biochemical makeup.[74] One view is that body chemistry can govern behavior and personality, including levels of aggression and depression.[75] For example, exposure to lead in the environment and subsequent lead ingestion has been linked to antisocial behaviors.[76] Exposure to the now banned PCB (polychlorinated biphenyls), a chemical once used in insulation materials, has been shown to negatively influence brain functioning and intelligence levels.[77]

There is evidence that a child's diet may influence his or her behavior through its impact on body chemistry. For example, research shows that persistent abnormality in the way the brain metabolizes glucose can be linked to later involvement with substance abuse.[78] The association between diet and crime is the subject of the following Focus on Delinquency.

biosocial theory
The view that both thought and behavior have biological and social bases.

Are You What You Eat?

Stephen Schoenthaler has conducted a number of studies that indicate a significant association between diet and aggressive behavior patterns. In some cases, the relationship is direct; in others, a poor diet may compromise individual functioning, which in turn produces aggressive behavior responses. For example, a poor diet may inhibit school performance, and children who fail at school are at risk for delinquent behavior and criminality.

In one study of 803 New York City public schools, Schoenthaler found that the academic performance of 1.1 million schoolchildren rose 16 percent after their diets were modified. The number of "learning disabled" children fell from 125,000 to 74,000 in one year. No other changes in school programs for the learning disabled were initiated that year. In a similar experiment conducted in a correctional institution, violent and nonviolent antisocial behavior fell an average of 48 percent among 8,047 offenders after dietary changes were implemented. In both these studies, the improvements in behavior and academic performance were attributed to diets containing more vitamins and minerals compared with the old diets. The greater amounts of these essential nutrients in the new diets were believed to have corrected impaired brain function caused by poor nutrition.

Schoenthaler also conducted three randomized controlled studies in which 66 elementary school children, 62 confined teenage delinquents, and 402 confined adult felons received dietary supplements—the equivalent of a diet providing more fruits, vegetables, and whole grains. In order to remove experimental bias, neither subjects nor researchers knew who received the supplement and who received a placebo. In each study, the subjects receiving the dietary supplement demonstrated significantly less violent and nonviolent antisocial behavior when compared with the control subjects who received placebos. The carefully collected data verified that a very good diet, as defined by the World Health Organization, has significant behavioral benefits beyond its health effects.

And in Phoenix, Arizona, Schoenthaler along with Ian Bier experimented with 468 students ages six to twelve years by giving one group a daily vitamin-mineral supplementation at 50 percent of the U.S. recommended daily allowance (RDA) for four months and another group a placebo. He found that those receiving the vitamin supplement were involved in significantly less antisocial behavior, a finding that convinced him that poor nutritional habits in children that lead to low concentrations of vitamins in the blood impair brain function and subsequently cause violence and other serious antisocial behavior. Correction of nutrient intake, either through a well-balanced diet or low-dose vitamin-mineral supplementation, corrects the low concentrations, improves brain function, and subsequently lowers institutional violence and antisocial behavior by almost half.

Other research findings have backed up Schoenthaler's claims. It is possible that vitamins, minerals, chemicals, and other nutrients from a diet rich in fruits, vegetables, and whole grains can improve brain function, basic intelligence, and academic performance—all variables that have been linked to antisocial behavior.

Still, the relationship between biochemical intake and abnormal behavior is far from settled. A number of controlled experiments have failed to substantiate any link between the two variables. Some research by Marcel Kinsbourne, for example, has found that sugar may actually have a calming effect on children rather than increase their aggressive behaviors. Further research is needed to fully understand the relationship between diet and delinquency.

CRITICAL THINKING

1. If Schoenthaler is correct in his assumptions, should schools be required to provide a proper lunch for all children?
2. How would Schoenthaler explain the aging-out process? (*Hint:* Do people eat better as they mature? What about after they get married?)

INFOTRAC COLLEGE EDITION RESEARCH

To read more about the relationship between nutrition and behavior, use "nutrition and behavior" as a key term on InfoTrac College Edition.

Sources: Stephen Schoenthaler, "Intelligence, Academic Performance, and Brain Function" (Stanislaus: California State University 2000). See also Stephen Schoenthaler and Ian Bier, "The Effect of Vitamin–Mineral Supplementation on Juvenile Delinquency Among American Schoolchildren: A Randomized Double-Blind Placebo-Controlled Trial," *Journal of Alternative and Complementary Medicine: Research on Paradigm, Practice, and Policy 6*:7–18 (2000); C. Bernard Gesch, Sean Hammond, Sarah Hampson, Anita Eves, and Martin Crowder, "Influence of Supplementary Vitamins, Minerals, and Essential Fatty Acids on the Antisocial Behaviour of Young Adult Prisoners: Randomized, Placebo-Controlled Trial," *British Journal of Psychiatry 181*:22–28 (2002); Marcel Kinsbourne, "Sugar and the Hyperactive Child," *New England Journal of Medicine 330*:355–356 (1994).

Hormonal Levels   Antisocial behavior allegedly peaks in the teenage years because hormonal activity is then at its greatest level. It is possible that increased levels of testosterone are responsible for excessive violence among teenage boys. Adolescents who experience more intense moods, anxiety, and restlessness also have the highest crime rates.[79] Research has shown that hormonal sensitivity may begin very early in life if the fetus is exposed to abnormally high levels of testosterone. This may trigger a heightened response to the release of testosterone at puberty. Although testosterone levels may appear normal, the young male is at risk for overly aggressive behavior.[80] Hormonal activity as an explanation of gender differences in delinquency will be discussed further in chapter 6.

Neurological Dysfunction

Another focus of biosocial theory is the neurological—or brain and nervous system— structure of offenders. It has been suggested that children who manifest behaviorial disturbances may have neurological deficits, such as damage to the hemispheres of the brain; this is sometimes referred to as **minimal brain dysfunction (MBD)**.[81] Impairment in brain functioning may be present at birth, produced by factors such as low birthweight, brain injury during pregnancy, birth complications, and inherited abnormalities.[82] Brain injuries can also occur later in life as a result of brutal beatings or sexual abuse by a parent. According to research conducted by Dr. Martin Teicher of the McLean Hospital in Massachusetts, emotional trauma such as child abuse can actually cause adverse physical changes in the brain, and these deformities can lead to depression, anxiety, and other serious emotional conditions.[83]

Children who suffer from measurable neurological deficits at birth are more likely to become criminals as adults.[84] Clinical analysis of death-row inmates found that a significant number had suffered head injuries as children that resulted in neurological impairment.[85] Evidence has also been found linking brain damage to mental disorders such as depression.[86] In an important study by Adrian Raine, researchers looked at the medical histories of 4,269 Danish males born between 1959 and 1961. By age eighteen, boys whose mothers had experienced birth complications and who had also experienced maternal rejection later in life were more than twice as likely to commit a violent crime than boys who did not experience birth trauma and maternal rejection. Raine concluded that birth complications and maternal rejection seemed to predispose offenders to some kinds of criminal offenses.[87]

The form of brain dysfunction most often linked to delinquency is Attention Deficit Hyperactive Disorder, the topic of the following Focus on Delinquency feature.

Early biocriminologists believed that the physical makeup of offenders controlled their behavior. Biological traits present at birth were thought to predetermine whether people would live a life of crime. Here the skull of a criminal is measured in a study to determine if brain size and shape are related to violent behavior.

minimal brain dysfunction (MBD)
Damage to the brain itself that causes antisocial behavior injurious to the individual's lifestyle and social adjustment.

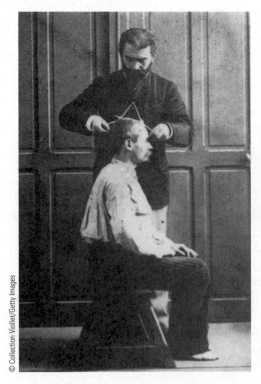

© Collection Viollet/Getty Images

Learning Disabilities   The relationship between **learning disabilities (LD)** and delinquency has been highlighted by studies showing that arrested and incarcerated children have a far higher LD rate than do children in the general population. Although approximately 10 percent of all youths have some form of learning disorder, estimates of LD among adjudicated delinquents range from 26 to 73 percent.[88] There are two possible explanations for the link between learning disabilities and delinquency.[89] One view, known as the *susceptibility rationale,* argues that the link is caused by side effects of learning disabilities, such as impulsiveness and inability to take social cues. In contrast, the *school failure rationale* assumes that the frustration caused by poor school performance will lead to a negative self-image and acting-out behavior.

Psychologist Terrie Moffitt has evaluated the literature on the connection between LD and delinquency and concludes that it is a significant correlate of persistent antisocial behavior (or conduct disorders).[90] She finds that neurological symptoms such as LD and MBD correlate highly with early onset of deviance, hyperactivity, and aggressiveness.[91] And there is new evidence that the factors that cause learning disabilities are also highly related to substance abuse, which may help explain the learning disability–juvenile delinquency connection. The National Center on Addiction and Substance Abuse at Columbia University recently released findings that show how learning disabilities are linked to substance abuse:

- Risk factors for adolescent substance abuse are very similar to the behavioral effects of learning disabilities—reduced self-esteem, academic difficulty, loneliness, depression, and the desire for social acceptance. Thus, learning disabilities may indirectly lead to substance abuse by generating the types of behavior that typically lead adolescents to abuse drugs.

- A child with a learning disability is twice as likely to suffer Attention Deficit Disorder (ADD) as a member of the general population, and there is a high incidence of ADD among individuals who abuse alcohol and drugs. It is known that as many as half of those suffering ADD self-medicate with drugs and alcohol.

- Children who are exposed to alcohol, tobacco, and drugs in the womb are at higher risk for various developmental disorders, including learning disabilities. Furthermore, a mother who uses drugs while pregnant may be a predictor that the child will grow up in a home with a parent who is a substance abuser. This too will increase the risk that the child will abuse drugs or alcohol himself.[92]

Despite this evidence, the learning disability–juvenile delinquency link has always been controversial. It is possible that the LD child may not be more susceptible to delinquent behavior than the non-LD child and that the link may be an artifact of bias in the way LD children are treated at school or by the police. LD youths are more likely to be arrested, and if petitioned to juvenile court, they bring with them a record of school problems that may increase the likelihood of their being sent to juvenile court.

Arousal Theory   It has long been suspected that adolescents may engage in crimes such as shoplifting and vandalism because they offer the thrill of "getting away with it."[93] Is it possible that thrill seekers have some form of abnormal brain functioning? Arousal theorists believe that some people's brains function differently in response to environmental stimuli. We all seek to maintain an optimal level of arousal: too much stimulation leaves us anxious, and too little makes us feel bored. However, there is variation in the way children's brains process sensory input. Some nearly always feel comfortable with little stimulation, whereas others require a high degree of environmental input to feel comfortable. The latter group become "sensation seekers," who seek out stimulating activities that may include aggressive behavior.[94] The factors that determine a person's level of arousal are not fully understood. Suspected sources include brain chemistry and brain structure. Another view is that adolescents with low heart rates are more likely to commit crimes because they seek out stimulation to increase their arousal to normal levels.[95]

learning disabilities (LD)
Neurological dysfunctions that prevent an individual from learning to his or her potential.

Attention Deficit Hyperactivity Disorder

Many parents have noticed that their children do not pay attention to them—they run around and do things in their own way. Sometimes this inattention is a function of age; in other instances it is a symptom of a common learning disability referred to as attention deficit hyperactivity disorder (ADHD), a condition in which a child shows a developmentally inappropriate lack of attention, distractibility, impulsivity, and hyperactivity. The various symptoms of ADHD are listed in the following lists.

Symptoms of ADHD

Lack of Attention

- Frequently fails to finish projects.
- Does not seem to pay attention.
- Does not sustain interest in play activities.
- Cannot sustain concentration on schoolwork or related tasks.
- Is easily distracted.

Impulsivity

- Frequently acts without thinking.
- Often calls out in class.
- Does not want to wait his or her turn.
- Shifts from activity to activity.
- Cannot organize tasks or work.

- Requires constant supervision in school line or while playing games.

Hyperactivity

- Constantly runs around and climbs on things.
- Shows excessive motor activity while asleep.
- Cannot sit still; is constantly fidgeting.
- Does not remain in his or her seat in class.
- Is constantly on the go, like a "motor."
- Has difficulty regulating emotions.
- Has difficulty getting started.
- Has difficulty staying on track.
- Has difficulty adjusting to social demands.

No one is really sure how ADHD develops, but some psychologists believe it is tied to dysfunction in a section of the lower portion of the brain known as the *reticular activating system*. This area keeps the higher brain centers alert and ready for input. There is some evidence that this area is not working properly in ADHD kids and that their behavior is really the brain's attempt to generate new stimulation to maintain alertness. Other suspected origins are neurological damage to the frontal lobes of the brain, prenatal stress, and even food additives and chemical allergies. Some experts suggest that the condition might be traced to the neurological effects of abnormal levels of the chemicals dopamine and norepinephrine.

Children from any background can develop ADHD, but it is five to seven times more common in boys than girls. It does not affect intelligence, and ADHD children often show considerable ability with artistic endeavors. More common

Genetic Influences

It has been hypothesized that some youths inherit a genetic configuration that predisposes them to aggression.[96] In the same way that people inherit genes that control height and eye color, biosocial theorists believe antisocial behavior characteristics and mental disorders also may be passed down. Early theories suggested that proneness to delinquency ran in families. However, most families share a similar lifestyle as well as a similar gene pool, making it difficult to determine whether behavior is a function of heredity or the environment.

Parental Deviance If criminal tendencies are inherited, then the children of criminal parents should be more likely to become law violators than the offspring of conventional parents. A number of studies have found that parental criminality and deviance do, in fact, powerfully influence delinquent behavior.[97] Some of the most important data on parental deviance were gathered by Donald J. West and David P. Farrington as part of the long-term Cambridge Youth Survey. These cohort data indicate that a significant number of delinquent youths have criminal fathers.[98] Whereas 8 percent of the sons of noncriminal fathers eventually became chronic offenders, about 37 percent of boys with criminal fathers were multiple offenders.[99] In another important analysis, Farrington found that one type of parental deviance—schoolyard aggression or bullying—may be both inter- and intragenerational. Bullies have children who bully others, and these second-generation bullies grow up to father children who are also bullies, in a never-ending cycle.[100]

in the United States than elsewhere, ADHD tends to run in families, and there is some suggestion of an association with a family history of alcoholism or depression.

Estimates of ADHD in the general population range from 3 to 12 percent, but it is much more prevalent in adolescents, where some estimates reach as high as one-third of the population. ADHD children are most often treated by giving them doses of stimulants, most commonly Ritalin and Dexedrine (or dextroamphetamine), which, ironically, help these children control their emotional and behavioral outbursts. The antimanic, anticonvulsant drug Tegretol has also been used effectively.

ADHD usually results in poor school performance, including a high dropout rate, bullying, stubbornness, mental disorder, and a lack of response to discipline; these conditions are highly correlated with delinquent behavior. A series of research studies now link ADHD to the onset and continuance of a delinquent career and increased risk for antisocial behavior and substance abuse in adulthood. Children with ADHD are more likely to use illicit drugs, alcohol, and cigarettes in adolescence and are more likely to be arrested, to be charged with a felony, and to have multiple arrests than non-ADHD youths. There is also evidence that ADHD youths who also exhibit early signs of MBD and conduct disorder (for example, fighting) are the most at risk for persistent antisocial behaviors continuing into adulthood. Of course many, if not most, children who are diagnosed with ADHD do not engage in delinquent behavior, and new treatment techniques featuring behavior modification and drug thera-pies are constantly being developed to help children who have attention or hyperactivity problems.

CRITICAL THINKING
Considering that many ADHD kids engage in antisocial behaviors, should those diagnosed with the condition be closely monitored by the school system? Would that be fair to the majority of ADHD kids, who never violate the law? Would paying special attention to the ADHD population stigmatize them and actually encourage their law-violating behaviors?

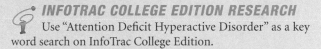

INFOTRAC COLLEGE EDITION RESEARCH
Use "Attention Deficit Hyperactive Disorder" as a key word search on InfoTrac College Edition.

Sources: Molina Pelham, Jr., "Childhood Predictors of Adolescent Substance Use in a Longitudinal Study of Children with ADHD," *Journal of Abnormal Psychology* 112:497–507 (2003); Peter Muris and Cor Meesters, "The Validity of Attention Deficit Hyperactivity and Hyperkinetic Disorder Symptom Domains in Nonclinical Dutch Children," *Journal of Clinical Child & Adolescent Psychology* 32:460–466 (2003); D. R. Blachman and S. P. Hinshaw, "Patterns of Friendship Among Girls with and without Attention Deficit/Hyperactivity Disorder," *Journal of Abnormal Child Psychology* 30:625–640 (2002); Terrie Moffitt and Phil Silva, "Self-Reported Delinquency, Neuropsychological Deficit, and History of Attention Deficit Disorder," *Journal of Abnormal Child Psychology* 16:553–569 (1988); Karen Harding, Richard Judah, and Charles Gant, "Outcome-Based Comparison of Ritalin Versus Food Supplement–Treated Children with AD/HD," *Alternative Medicine Review* 8:319–330 (2003).

To learn more about twin research, go to the Minnesota Twin Family Study, "What's Special About Twins to Science?" by clicking on Web Links under the Chapter Resources at http://cj. wadsworth.com/siegel_jdcore2e.

Farrington's findings are supported by some recent data from the Rochester Youth Development Study (RYDS), a longitudinal analysis that has been monitoring the behavior of a thousand area youths since 1988. RYDS researchers have also found an intergenerational continuity in antisocial behavior: criminal fathers produce delinquent sons who grow up to have delinquent children themselves.[101]

In sum, there is growing evidence that crime is intergenerational: criminal fathers produce criminal sons who then produce criminal grandchildren. It is possible that at least part of the association is genetic.[102]

Twin Studies   One method of studying the genetic basis of delinquency is to compare twins to nontwin siblings. If crime is an inherited trait, identical twins should be quite similar in their behavior because they share a common genetic makeup. Because twins are usually brought up in the same household, however, any similarity in their delinquent behavior might be a function of environmental influences and not genetics. To guard against this, biosocial theorists have compared the behavior of identical, monozygotic (MZ) twins with fraternal, dizygotic (DZ) twins; the former have an identical genetic makeup, whereas the latter share only about 50 percent of their genes. Studies conducted on twin behavior detected a significant relationship between the criminal activities of MZ twins and a much lower association between those of DZ twins.[103] About 60 percent of MZ twins share criminal behavior patterns (if one twin was criminal, so was the other), whereas only 30 percent of DZ twins are similarly related.[104] Although this seems to support a connection between genetic makeup and delinquency, it is also true that MZ twins are more

Arousal theorists believe that, for a variety of genetic and environmental reasons, some people's brains function differently in response to environmental stimuli. All of us seek to maintain a preferred or optimal level of arousal. Too much stimulation may leave us anxious and stressed out; too little may make us bored and weary. Some kids may need the rush that comes from getting into scrapes and conflicts in order to feel relaxed and at ease.

© Frank Siteman/Stock, Boston

likely to look alike and to share physical traits than DZ twins, and they are more likely to be treated similarly. Shared behavior patterns may therefore be a function of socialization and not heredity.

One famous study of twin behavior still under way is the Minnesota Study of Twins Reared Apart, which is part of the Minnesota Twin Family Study. This research compares the behavior of MZ and DZ twin pairs who were raised together with others who were separated at birth and in some cases did not even know of the other's existence. The study shows some striking similarities in behavior and ability for twin pairs raised apart. An MZ twin reared away from a cotwin has about as good a chance of being similar to the cotwin in terms of personality, interests, and attitudes

Exhibit 3.1 **Findings from the Minnesota Study of Twins Reared Apart**

- If you are a DZ twin and your cotwin is divorced, your risk of divorce is 30 percent. If you are an MZ twin and your cotwin is divorced, your risk of divorce rises to 45 percent, which is 25 percent above the rates for the Minnesota population. Since this was not true for DZ twins, we can conclude that genes do influence the likelihood of divorce.

- MZ twins become *more* similar with respect to abilities such as vocabularies and arithmetic scores as they age. As DZ (fraternal) twins get older they become less similar in these traits.

- A P300 is a tiny electrical response (a few millionths of a volt) that occurs in the brain when a person detects something

that is unusual or interesting. For example, if a person were shown nine circles and one square, a P300 brain response would appear after seeing the square because it's different. Identical (MZ) twin children have very similar-looking P300s. By comparison, children who are fraternal (DZ) twins do not show as much similarity in their P300s. These results indicate that the way the brain processes information may be greatly influenced by genes.

- An EEG is a measure of brain activity or brain waves that can be used to monitor a person's state of arousal. MZ twins tend to produce strikingly similar EEG spectra; DZ twins show far less similarity.

Source: University of Minnesota–Twin Cities, Department of Psychology, *Minnesota Study of Twins Reared Apart.* www.psych.umn.edu/psylabs/mtfs/special.htm.

as one who has been reared with the cotwin. The conclusion: similarities between twins are due to genes, not to the environment.[105] (See Exhibit 3.1.)

Adoption Studies   Another way to determine whether delinquency is an inherited trait is to compare the behavior of adopted children with that of their biological parents. If the criminal behavior of children is more like that of their biological parents (whom they have never met) than that of their adoptive parents (who brought them up), it would indicate that the tendency toward delinquency is inherited.

Studies of this kind have generally supported the hypothesis that there is a link between genetics and behavior.[106] Adoptees share many of the behavioral and intellectual characteristics of their biological parents despite the conditions found in their adoptive homes. Genetic makeup is sufficient to counteract even extreme conditions such as malnutrition and abuse.[107] Some of the most influential research in this area has been conducted by Sarnoff Mednick. In one study, Mednick and Bernard Hutchings found that although only 13 percent of the adoptive fathers of a sample of delinquent youths had criminal records, 31 percent of their biological fathers had criminal records.[108] Analysis of a control group's background indicated that about 11 percent of all fathers have criminal records. Hutchings and Mednick were forced to conclude that genetics played at least some role in creating delinquent tendencies.[109]

In sum, twin studies and adoption studies provide some evidence that delinquent-producing traits may be inherited.

The biological basis of delinquency is reviewed in Concept Summary 3.2.

PSYCHOLOGICAL THEORIES OF DELINQUENCY

Some experts view the cause of delinquency as psychological.[110] After all, most behaviors labeled delinquent seem to be symptomatic of some psychological problem. Psychologists point out that many delinquent youths have poor home lives; destructive relationships with neighbors, friends, and teachers; and conflicts with authority figures. These relationships seem to indicate a disturbed personality. Furthermore, studies of incarcerated youths indicate that their personalities are marked by antisocial characteristics. And since delinquent behavior occurs among youths in every

Concept Summary **Biological Views of Delinquency**

Theory	Major Premise	Focus
Biochemical	Delinquency, especially violence, is a function of diet, vitamin intake, hormonal imbalance, or food allergies.	Explains irrational violence. Shows how the environment interacts with personal traits to influence behavior.
Neurological	Delinquents often suffer brain impairment, as measured by the EEG. ADHD and minimal brain dysfunction are related to antisocial behavior.	Explains the relationship between child abuse and delinquency. May be used to clarify the link between school problems and delinquency.
Genetic	Criminal traits and predispositions are inherited. The criminality of parents can predict the delinquency of children.	Explains why only a small percentage of youth in a high-crime area become chronic offenders.

racial, ethnic, and socioeconomic group, psychologists view it as a function of mental disturbance rather than of social factors such as racism and poverty. Many delinquents do not manifest significant psychological problems, but enough do to give clinicians a powerful influence on delinquency theory.

Because psychology is a complex discipline, more than one psychological perspective on crime exists. Three prominent psychological perspectives on delinquency are psychodynamic theory, behavioral theory, and cognitive theory.[111] These are outlined in Figure 3.2.

Psychodynamic Theory

According to the **psychodynamic theory,** which originated with the Austrian physician Sigmund Freud (1856–1939), law violations are a product of an abnormal personality formed early in life.[112] The theory argues that the personality contains three major components. The *id* is the unrestrained, pleasure-seeking component with which each child is born. The *ego* develops through the reality of living in the world and helps restrain the id's need for immediate gratification. The *superego* develops through interactions with parents and others and represents the conscience and the moral rules that are shared by most adults.

All three segments of the personality operate simultaneously. The id dictates needs and desires, the superego counteracts the id by fostering feelings of morality, and the ego evaluates the reality of a position between these two extremes. If these components are balanced, the individual can lead a normal life. If one aspect of the personality becomes dominant at the expense of the others, however, the individual exhibits abnormal personality traits. Furthermore, the theory suggests that an imbalance in personality traits caused by a traumatic early childhood can result in long-term psychological difficulties. For example, if parents fail to help the child develop his or her superego adequately, the child's id may become dominant. The absence of a strong superego results in inability to distinguish clearly between right and wrong. Later, the youth may demand immediate gratification, lack sensitivity for the needs of others, act aggressively and impulsively, or demonstrate psychotic symptoms. Antisocial behavior may result from conflict or trauma occurring early in a child's development, and delinquent activity may become an outlet for these feelings.

Figure 3.2   **Psychological Perspectives of Delinquency**

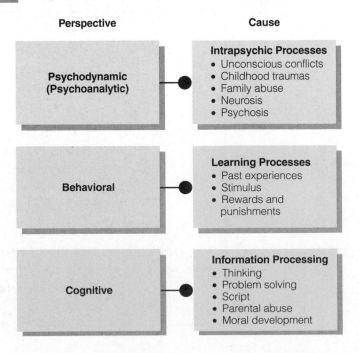

psychodynamic theory
Branch of psychology that holds that the human personality is controlled by unconscious mental processes developed early in childhood.

Disorders and Delinquency   According to Freud's version of psycho-dynamic theory, people who experience anxiety and fear they are losing control are suffering from a form of *neurosis* and are referred to as *neurotics*. People who have lost control and are dominated by their id are known as *psychotics*; their behavior may be marked by hallucinations and inappropriate responses.

Psychosis takes many forms, the most common being *schizophrenia,* a condition marked by illogical thought processes, distorted perceptions, and abnormal emotional expression. According to the classical psychoanalytic view, the most serious types of antisocial behavior might be motivated by psychosis, whereas neurotic feelings would be responsible for less serious delinquent acts and status offenses.[113]

Contemporary psychologists no longer use the term *neuroses* to describe all forms of unconscious conflict. It is more common to refer to specific types of disorders, including *anxiety disorder, mood disorder, sleep disorder,* and so on. Among these is **bipolar disorder,** in which moods alternate between periods of wild elation and deep depression.[114]

The Psychodynamic Tradition and Delinquency   How do psycho-dynamic theorists explain delinquency? Erik Erikson speculated that many adolescents experience a life crisis in which they feel emotional, impulsive, and uncertain of their role and purpose.[115] He coined the phrase **identity crisis** to denote this period of inner turmoil. Erikson's approach might characterize the behavior of youthful drug abusers as an expression of confusion over their place in society, inability to direct their behavior toward useful outlets, and perhaps, dependence on others to offer solutions to their problems.

Some view youth crime as a result of unresolved internal conflict. Some children, especially those who have been abused or mistreated, may experience unconscious feelings of fear and hatred. Others are driven by an unconscious desire to be punished for prior sins, either real or imaginary. They may violate the law to gain attention or punish their parents. If these conflicts cannot be reconciled, regression occurs and the id becomes dominant. This regression accounts for a great number of mental diseases, and in many cases it may be related to criminal behavior.[116]

Another psychodynamic view is that delinquents are unable to control their impulsive drives. Perhaps because they suffered unhappy experiences in childhood or had families that could not provide proper care, they have weak egos and are unable to cope with conventional society.[117] In its most extreme form, delinquency may be viewed as a form of psychosis that prevents delinquent youths from appreciating the feelings of victims or controlling their need for gratification.[118] Research shows that some delinquents exhibit indications of such psychological abnormalities as schizophrenia, paranoia, and obsessive behaviors; female offenders seem to have more serious mental health symptoms and psychological disturbances than male offenders.[119]

It is also possible that antisocial behavior is a consequence of inability to cope with feelings of oppression or depression. In this instance, delinquency actually produces positive psychic results: it helps youths feel independent; gives them the possibility of excitement and the chance to use their skills and imagination; provides the promise of gain; allows them to blame others (the police) for their predicament; and gives them a chance to rationalize their sense of failure ("If I hadn't gotten into trouble, I could have been a success").[120]

The psychodynamic approach places heavy emphasis on the family's role. Antisocial youths frequently come from families in which parents are unable to provide the controls that allow children to develop the personal tools they need to cope with the world.[121] Their destructive behavior may actually be a call for help. In fact, some psychoanalysts view delinquent behaviors as motivated by an unconscious urge to be punished. These children, who feel unloved, assume the reason must be their own inadequacy; hence, they deserve punishment.

bipolar disorder
A psychological condition producing mood swings between wild elation and deep depression.

identity crisis
Psychological state, identified by Erikson, in which youth face inner turmoil and uncertainty about life roles.

Is There a Psychodynamic Link to Delinquency?   The psychodynamic view is supported by research that shows that a number of violent juvenile offenders suffer from some sort of personality disturbance. Violent youths have been clinically diagnosed as "overtly hostile," "explosive or volatile," "anxious," and "depressed."[122] Research efforts have found that juvenile offenders who engage in serious violent crimes often suffer from some sort of mental disturbance, such as depression.[123]

Although this evidence is persuasive, the association between mental disturbance and delinquency is unresolved. It is possible that any link is caused by some intervening variable or factor: troubled youth do poorly in school and school failure leads to delinquency; troubled youth have conflict-ridden social relationships that make them prone to commit delinquent acts.[124] It is also possible that the factors that cause mental turmoil also cause delinquency: kids who suffer child abuse are more likely to have mental anguish and commit violent acts; child abuse is the actual cause of both problems.[125] Further research is needed to clarify this important relationship.

Behavioral Theory

Not all psychologists agree that behavior is controlled by unconscious mental processes determined by relationships early in childhood. Behavioral psychologists argue that personality is learned throughout life during interaction with others. Based primarily on the work of the American psychologist John B. Watson (1878–1958), and popularized by Harvard professor B. F. Skinner (1904–1990), **behaviorism** concerns itself with measurable events rather than unobservable psychic phenomena.

Behaviorists suggest that individuals learn by observing how people react to their behavior. Behavior is triggered initially by a stimulus or change in the environment. If a particular behavior is reinforced by some positive reaction or event, that behavior will be continued and eventually learned. However, behaviors that are not reinforced or are punished will be extinguished. For example, if children are given a reward (dessert) for eating their entire dinner, eventually they will learn to eat successfully. Conversely, if children are punished for some misbehavior, they will associate disapproval with that act and avoid that behavior.

Social Learning Theory   Some behaviorists hold that learning and social experiences, coupled with values and expectations, determine behavior. This is known as **social learning theory.** The most widely read social learning theorists are Albert Bandura, Walter Mischel, and Richard Walters.[126] They hold that children will model their behavior according to the reactions they receive from others; the behavior of adults, especially parents; and the behavior they view on television and in movies. (See Focus on Delinquency, "The Media and Delinquency.") If children observe aggression and see that it is approved or rewarded, they will likely react violently during a similar incident. Eventually, they will master the techniques of aggression and become more confident that their behavior will bring tangible rewards.[127]

Social learning suggests that children who grow up in homes where violence is a way of life may learn to believe that such behavior is acceptable. Even if parents tell children not to be violent and punish them if they are, the children will model their behavior on the observed violence. Thus, children are more likely to heed what parents *do* than what they *say.* By middle childhood, some children have already acquired an association between their use of aggression against others and the physical punishment they receive at home. Often their aggressive responses are directed at other family members. The family may serve as a training ground for violence because the child perceives physical punishment as the norm during conflict situations.[128]

Adolescent aggression is a result of disrupted dependency relations with parents. This refers to the frustration a child feels when parents provide poor role models and hold back affection. Children who lack close ties to their parents may have little

behaviorism
Branch of psychology concerned with the study of observable behavior rather than unconscious processes; focuses on particular stimuli and responses to them.

social learning theory
The view that behavior is modeled through observation either directly through intimate contact with others or indirectly through media; interactions that are rewarded are copied, whereas those that are punished are avoided.

According to cognitive theory, people go through stages during which they develop into mature adults who can use logic and abstract thought. Sometimes they need help along the way. Here in Stark County, Ohio, jail inmates Scott Dishong (left) and John Laughery (right) share their experiences behind bars with a 13-year-old youth. The youth was participating in the Turn-Around Program, a program started by two correctional officers at the jail.

© 2003 AP/Wide World Photos

opportunity or desire to model themselves after them or to internalize their standards. In the absence of such internalized controls, the child's frustration is likely to be expressed in a socially unacceptable fashion such as aggression.

Cognitive Theory

A third area of psychology that has received increasing recognition in recent years is **cognitive theory.** Psychologists with a cognitive perspective focus on mental processes. The pioneers of this school were Wilhelm Wundt (1832–1920), Edward Titchener (1867–1927), and William James (1842–1920). This perspective contains several subgroups. Perhaps the most important of these for delinquency theory is the one that is concerned with how people morally represent and reason about the world.

Jean Piaget (1896–1980), founder of this approach, hypothesized that reasoning processes develop in an orderly fashion, beginning at birth and continuing until age twelve and older.[129] At first, during the *sensorimotor stage,* children respond to the environment in a simple manner, seeking interesting objects and developing their reflexes. By the fourth and final stage, the *formal operations stage,* they have developed into mature adults who can use logic and abstract thought.

Lawrence Kohlberg applied this concept to issues in delinquency.[130] He suggested that there are stages of moral development during which the basis for moral decisions changes. It is possible that serious offenders have a moral orientation that differs from that of law-abiding citizens. Kohlberg classified people according to the stage at which their moral development has ceased to grow. In his studies, the majority of delinquents were revealed as having a lack of respect for the law and a personality marked by self-interest; in contrast, nonoffenders viewed the law as something that benefits all of society and were willing to honor the rights of others.[131] Subsequent research has found that a significant number of nondelinquent youths displayed higher stages of moral reasoning than delinquents.[132]

Information Processing Cognitive theorists who study information processing try to explain antisocial behavior in terms of perception and analysis of data. When people make decisions, they engage in a sequence of thought processes. First, they encode information so it can be interpreted. Then, they search for a proper response and decide on the most appropriate action. Finally, they act on their decision.[133]

cognitive theory
The branch of psychology that studies the perception of reality and the mental processes required to understand the world we live in.

The Media and Delinquency

One aspect of social learning theory that has received a great deal of attention is the belief that children will model their behavior after characters they observe on TV or see in movies. Many parents are concerned about the effects of their children's exposure to violence in the mass media. Often the violence is of a sexual nature, and some experts fear there is a link between sexual violence and viewing pornography.

Children are particularly susceptible to TV imagery. It is believed that many children consider television images to be real, especially if the images are authoritatively presented by an adult (as in a commercial). Some children, especially those considered "emotionally disturbed," may be unable to distinguish between fantasy and reality when watching TV shows. Children begin frequent TV viewing at 2.5 years of age and continue at a high level during the preschool and early school years. But what do they watch? Marketing research indicates that adolescents ages eleven to fourteen rent violent horror movies at a higher rate than any other age group; adolescents also use older peers and siblings or apathetic parents to gain access to R-rated films. More than 40 percent of U.S. households now have cable TV, which features violent films and shows. Even children's programming is saturated with violence. It is estimated that the average child views eight thousand TV murders before finishing elementary school.

TV and Violence

A number of methods have been used to measure the effect of TV viewing on violent behavior. One method is to expose groups of people to violent TV shows in a laboratory setting and compare them to control groups who viewed nonviolent programming; observations have also been made at playgrounds, athletic fields, and residences. Other experiments require individuals to answer attitude surveys after watching violent TV shows. Still another approach is to use aggregate measures of TV viewing; for example, the number of violent TV shows on the air during a given period is compared to crime rates during the same period.

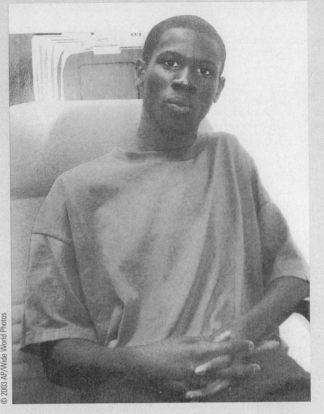

© 2003 AP/Wide World Photos

In 1999, twelve-year-old Lionel Tate killed six-year-old Tiffany Eunick, the daughter of a family friend. Lionel claimed he was practicing wrestling moves he had learned while watching TV. Sentenced to life in prison, he was released in 2004 after he successfully appealed his conviction, and in lieu of a second trial, accepted an agreement where he was sentenced to the three years he had already served, another year of house arrest, and ten years probation. Could the behavior of a young boy like Lionel be controlled by what he sees in the media, or were his actions a matter of free will?

Adolescents who use information properly and can make reasoned decisions when facing emotion-laden events are best able to avoid antisocial behavior.[134] In contrast, delinquency-prone adolescents may have cognitive deficits and use information incorrectly when they make decisions.[135] They may misperceive behavioral cues because their decision making was shaped by traumatic life events such as being the victim of child abuse.[136] These youths view crime as an appropriate means to satisfy their immediate personal needs, which take precedence over more distant social needs such as obedience to the law.[137] They have difficulty making the "right" decision while under stress.

One reason for this may be that they are relying on mental "scripts" learned in early childhood that tell them how to interpret events, what to expect, how they should react, and what the outcome of the interaction should be.[138] Hostile children may have learned improper scripts by observing how others react to events; their own parents' aggressive, inappropriate behavior would have considerable impact.

Most evaluations of experimental data indicate that watching violence on TV is correlated with aggressive behaviors. In one of the most important recent studies, L. Rowell Huesmann and his associates found that children ages six to nine who watched more violent television displayed more aggressive behavior than their peers. Brad Bushman and his colleagues at the University of Michigan contacted 329 of these children fifteen years after they had participated in the Huesmann study. Now as adults, those same children who had viewed violent shows in their adolescence continued to behave in a violent and aggressive manner. Boys who liked violent television shows grew into men who were significantly more likely to have pushed, grabbed, or shoved their wives or others whom they found insulting. They were also much more likely to be convicted of a crime. Ironically, women who watched violent shows as children reported being punched, beaten, or choked as adults at a rate over four times the rate of women who did not watch violent programs.

Rethinking the Media-Violence Link

Though this evidence is persuasive, the relationship between TV viewing and violence is still uncertain. A number of critics say the evidence does not support the claim that TV viewing is related to antisocial behavior. Some assert that experimental results are short-lived. Children may have an immediate reaction to viewing violence on TV, but aggression is extinguished once the viewing ends. Although experiments do show that children act aggressively in a laboratory setting after watching violent TV shows, that does not mean they will commit crimes in the real world such as rape and assault. And while Huesmann showed that kids who watch violent TV grow up to be violent adults, it is also possible that they would have been violent even if they had not watched TV at all. It is possible that violence-prone children like to watch violent TV shows, and not that violent shows turn previously passive children into furious aggressors.

Aggregate data are also inconclusive. Little evidence exists that areas that have high levels of violent TV viewing also have rates of violent crime that are above the norm.

Millions of children watch violence yet fail to become violent criminals. And even if a violent behavior–TV link could be established, it would be difficult to show that antisocial people develop aggressive traits merely from watching TV.

CRITICAL THINKING

1. Should TV shows with a violent theme be prohibited from being aired on commercial TV before 9 P.M.? If you say yes, would you broadcast the national news?
2. Even if a violence-TV link could be established, is it not possible that aggressive, antisocial youths may simply enjoy watching TV shows that support their personal behavioral orientation, in the same way that science fiction fans flock to *Star Wars* and *Star Trek* films?

INFOTRAC COLLEGE EDITION RESEARCH

Use "media violence" as a key term on InfoTrac College Edition in order to learn more about the association between observing violence on TV and in movies and personal involvement in antisocial behaviors.

Sources: L. Rowell Huesmann, Jessica Moise-Titus, Cheryl-Lynn Podolski, and Leonard Eron, "Longitudinal Relations Between Children's Exposure to TV Violence and Their Aggressive and Violent Behavior in Young Adulthood: 1977–1992," *Developmental Psychology* 39:201–221 (2003); Brad Bushman and Craig Anderson, "Media Violence and the American Public," *American Psychologist* 56:477–489 (2001); Edward Donnerstein and Daniel Linz, "The Question of Pornography," *Psychology Today* 20:56–59 (1986); Joyce Sprafkin, Kenneth Gadow, and Monique Dussault, "Reality Perceptions of Television: A Preliminary Comparison of Emotionally Disturbed and Nonhandicapped Children," *American Journal of Orthopsychiatry* 56:147–152 (1986); UCLA Center for Communication Policy, *Television Violence Monitoring Project* (Los Angeles: University of California Press, 1995); Wendy Wood, Frank Wong, and J. Gregory Chachere, "Effects of Media Violence on Viewers' Aggression in Unconstrained Social Interaction," *Psychological Bulletin* 109:371–383 (1991).

Some may have had early, prolonged exposure to violence (such as child abuse), which increases their sensitivity to slights and maltreatment. Oversensitivity to rejection by their peers is a continuation of sensitivity to rejection by their parents.[139] Violence becomes a stable behavior because the scripts that emphasize aggressive responses are repeatedly rehearsed as the child matures. When they attack victims, they may believe they are defending themselves, even though they are misreading the situation.[140] They may have a poor sense of time, leaving them incapable of dealing with social problems in an effective manner.[141]

Cognitive Treatment   Treatment based on information processing acknowledges that people are more likely to respond aggressively to a provocation when thoughts stir feelings of anger. Cognitive therapists attempt to teach people to control aggressive impulses by experiencing provocations as problems demanding a solution rather than as insults requiring retaliation. Programs teach problem-solving skills that may include self-disclosure, listening, following instructions, and using self-control.[142] Areas for improvement include (1) coping and problem-solving skills; (2) relationships with peers, parents, and other adults; (3) conflict resolution and communication skills; (4) decision-making abilities; (5) pro-social behaviors, including cooperation with others and respecting others; and (6) awareness of feelings of others (empathy).[143]

Personality and Delinquency

Personality can be defined as the stable patterns of behavior, including thoughts and emotions, that distinguish one person from another.[144] Personality reflects characteristic ways of adapting to life's demands. The way we behave is a function of how our personality enables us to interpret events and make appropriate choices.

More than fifty years ago, Sheldon and Eleanor Glueck identified a number of personality traits that characterize delinquents:

self-assertiveness	extraversion
defiance	ambivalence
impulsiveness	feeling unappreciated
narcissism	distrust of authority
suspicion	poor personal skills
destructiveness	mental instability
sadism	hostility
lack of concern for others	resentment

This research is representative of the view that delinquents maintain a distinct personality whose characteristics increase the probability that they will be antisocial and that their actions will involve them with agents of social control, ranging from teachers to police.[145]

Following the Glueck effort, researchers have continued to examine the personality traits of delinquents, finding that many are impulsive individuals with short attention spans.[146] Among the most well known efforts was psychologist Hans Eysenck's identification of two traits he closely associates with antisocial behavior: **extraversion** and **neuroticism**.[147] Extraverts are impulsive individuals who lack the ability to examine their own motives; those high in neuroticism are anxious and emotionally unstable.[148] Youths who are both neurotic and extraverted often lack insight and are highly impulsive. They act self-destructively, for example, by abusing drugs, and are the type of offender who will repeat their criminal activity over and over.[149]

The Antisocial Personality   It has also been suggested that delinquency may result from a syndrome interchangeably referred to as the **antisocial, psychopathic,** or **sociopathic personality.** Although no more than 3 percent of male offenders may be classified as antisocial, it is possible that a large segment of persistent offenders share this trait.[150]

Antisocial youths exhibit low levels of guilt and anxiety and persistently violate the rights of others. Although they may exhibit charm and intelligence, these mask a disturbed personality that makes them incapable of forming enduring relationships. Frequently involved in such deviant behaviors as truancy, lying, and substance abuse, antisocial people lack the ability to empathize with others. From an early age, the antisocial person's home life was filled with frustration and quarreling. Consequently, throughout life the antisocial youth is unreliable, unstable, and demanding.

Youths diagnosed as being clinically antisocial are believed to be thrill seekers who engage in destructive behavior. Some become gang members and participate in violent sexual escapades to compensate for a fear of responsibility and an inability to maintain relationships.[151] Delinquents have been described as sensation seekers who desire an extraverted lifestyle, including partying, drinking, and having a variety of sexual partners.[152]

extraversion
Impulsive behavior without the ability to examine motives and behavior.

neuroticism
A personality trait marked by unfounded anxiety, tension, and emotional instability.

psychopathic personality (also known as sociopathic or antisocial personality)
A person lacking in warmth, exhibiting inappropriate behavior responses, and unable to learn from experience; the condition is defined by persistent violations of social norms, including lying, stealing, truancy, inconsistent work behavior, and traffic arrests.

The Origins of Antisocial Personality   A number of factors contribute to the development of antisocial personalities. One source may be family dysfunction and include having an emotionally disturbed parent, parental rejection during childhood, and inconsistent or overly abusive discipline.[153] Another possibility is that psychopaths may have brain-related physical anomalies that cause them to process emotional input differently than nonpsychopaths.[154] Another view is that antisocial youths suffer from lower levels of arousal than the general population. Consequently, they may need greater-than-average stimulation to bring them up to comfortable levels.[155] Psychologists have attempted to treat antisocial youths by giving them adrenaline, which increases their arousal levels.

Intelligence and Delinquency

Early criminologists thought that if they could determine which individuals were less intelligent, they might be able to identify potential delinquents before they committed socially harmful acts.[156] Psychologists began to measure the correlation between IQ and crime by testing adjudicated juvenile delinquents. Delinquent juveniles were believed to be substandard in intelligence and thus inclined to commit more crimes than more intelligent persons. Thus, juvenile delinquents were used as a test group around which numerous theories about intelligence were built.

Nature Theory   When IQ tests were administered to inmates of prisons and juvenile training schools early in the twentieth century, a large proportion of the inmates scored low on the tests. Henry Goddard found in 1920 that many institutionalized persons were "feebleminded" and concluded that at least half of all juvenile delinquents were mental defectives.[157] In 1926, William Healy and Augusta Bronner tested a group of delinquents in Chicago and Boston and found that 37 percent were subnormal in intelligence.[158] They concluded that delinquents were five to ten times more likely to be mentally deficient than nondelinquent boys. These and other early studies were embraced as proof that a correlation existed between innate low intelligence and deviant behavior. IQ tests were believed to measure genetic makeup, and many psychologists accepted the predisposition of substandard individuals toward delinquency. This view is referred to as the **nature theory** of intelligence.

Nurture Theory   In the 1930s, more culturally sensitive explanations of behavior led to the **nurture theory.** Nurture theory argues that intelligence is not inherited and that low-IQ parents do not necessarily produce low-IQ children.[159] This view holds that intelligence must be viewed as partly biological but primarily sociological. Nurture theorists discredit the notion that people commit crimes because they have low IQs. Instead, they postulate that environmental stimulation from parents, schools, peer groups, and others create a child's IQ level and that low IQs result from an environment that also encourages delinquent behavior.[160] For example, if educational environments could be improved, the result might be both an elevation in IQ scores and a decrease in delinquency.[161]

Rethinking IQ and Delinquency   The relationship between IQ and delinquency is controversial because it implies that a condition is present at birth that accounts for delinquent behavior throughout the life cycle and that this condition is not easily changed. Research shows that measurements of intelligence taken in infancy are good predictors of later IQ.[162] By implication, if delinquency is not spread evenly through the social structure, neither is intelligence.

Some social scientists actively dispute that any association actually exists. As early as 1931, Edwin Sutherland evaluated IQ studies of criminals and delinquents and found evidence disputing the association between intelligence and criminality.[163] His findings did much to discredit the notion that a strong relationship exists between

nature theory
The view that intelligence is inherited and is a function of genetic makeup.

nurture theory
The view that intelligence is determined by environmental stimulation and socialization.

✔ According to psychodynamic theory, unconscious motivations developed early in childhood propel some people into destructive or illegal behavior.

✔ Behaviorists view aggression as a learned behavior.

✔ Some learning is direct and experiential while other types are observational, such as watching TV and movies. A link between media and violence has not been proven.

✔ Cognitive theory stresses knowing and perception. Some adolescents have a warped view of the world.

✔ There is evidence that kids with abnormal or antisocial personalities are delinquency-prone.

✔ Although some experts find a link between intelligence and delinquency, others dispute any linkage between IQ level and law-violating behaviors.

To quiz yourself on this material, go to questions 3.11–3.19 on the Juvenile Delinquency: The Core 2e Web site.

IQ and criminality, and for many years the IQ-delinquency link was ignored. Sutherland's research has been substantiated by a number of contemporary studies that find that IQ has a negligible influence on behavior.[164]

Those who still believe in an IQ-delinquency link refer to a study by Travis Hirschi and Michael Hindelang, who, after conducting a statistical analysis of IQ and delinquency data, concluded that "the weight of evidence is that IQ is more important than race and social class" for predicting delinquency.[165] They argued that a low IQ increases the likelihood of delinquent behavior through its effect on school performance. Youths with low IQs do poorly in school, and school failure is highly related to delinquency. Their conclusions have also been supported by a number of research efforts.[166]

Even those experts who believe that IQ influences delinquent behavior are split on the structure of the associations. Some believe IQ has an *indirect influence* on delinquency. For example, children with low IQs are more likely to engage in delinquent behavior because low IQ leads to school failure, and educational underachievement is associated with delinquency.[167] Even high-risk youths are less likely to become delinquents if they have relatively high IQs; low IQ increases the probability of a delinquent career.[168] The relationship between IQ and delinquency has been found to be consistent after controlling for class, race, and personality traits.[169]

Some experts believe IQ may have a *direct influence* on delinquency. The key linkage is the ability to manipulate abstract concepts. Low intelligence limits adolescents' ability to "foresee the consequences of their offending and to appreciate the feelings of victims."[170] Therefore, youths with limited intelligence are more likely to misinterpret events, take risks, and engage in harmful behavior. ✔ **Checkpoints**

CRITIQUING TRAIT THEORY VIEWS

Trait theories have been criticized on a number of grounds. One view is that the research methodologies they employ are invalid. Most research efforts use adjudicated or incarcerated offenders. It is difficult to determine whether findings represent the delinquent population or merely those most likely to be arrested. For example, some critics have described heredity studies as "poorly designed, ambiguously reported, and exceedingly inadequate in addressing the relevant issues."[171] Some critics also fear that trait-theory research can be socially and politically damaging. If an above-average number of indigent youths become delinquent offenders, can it be assumed that the less affluent are genetically inferior? This conclusion is unacceptable to many social scientists in light of what is known about race, gender, and class bias.

Defenders counter that trait theorists do not ignore environmental and social factors.[172] For example, some kids may have emotional and psychological problems that place them at a disadvantage, limit their chances of success, and heighten their feelings of anger and frustration. If their family is affluent, they will have the resources available to treat these problems; a less affluent family would lack the economic means and the institutional support needed to counteract these potentially destructive traits. Delinquency rate differences may then result from differential access to opportunities either to commit crime or to receive the treatment needed to correct developmental problems.

The psychological basis of delinquency is reviewed in Concept Summary 3.3.

TRAIT THEORY AND DELINQUENCY PREVENTION

Trait theory perspectives on delinquency suggest that prevention efforts should be directed at strengthening a youth's home life and relationships. If parents cannot supply proper nurturing, discipline, nutrition, and so on, the child cannot develop

Theory	Major Premise	Focus
Psychodynamic	The development of the unconscious personality early in childhood influences behavior for the rest of a person's life. Criminals have weak egos and damaged personalities.	Explains the onset of delinquency and why crime and drug abuse cut across class lines.
Behavioral	People commit crime when they model their behavior after others they see being rewarded for the same acts. Behavior is reinforced by rewards and extinguished by punishment.	Explains the role of significant others in the delinquency process. Shows how family life and media can influence crime and violence.
Cognitive	Individual reasoning processes influence behavior. Reasoning is influenced by the way people perceive their environment.	Shows why criminal behavior patterns change over time as people mature and develop their reasoning powers. May explain the aging-out process.

properly. Whether we believe that delinquency has a biosocial basis, a psychological basis, or a combination of both, it is evident that prevention efforts should be oriented to reach children early in their development.

County welfare agencies and private treatment centers offer counseling and other mental health services to families referred by schools, welfare agents, and court authorities. In some instances, intervention is focused on a particular family problem that has the potential for producing delinquent behavior—for example, alcohol and drug problems, child abuse, or sexual abuse. In other situations, intervention is oriented toward developing the self-image of parents and children or improving discipline in the family.

Some programs utilize treatment regimens based on specific theories (such as behavioral modification therapies). For example, the Decisions to Actions program in Kincheloe, Michigan, is organized around cognitive-behavioral restructuring of children's personalities. Its main focus is changing attitudes and beliefs associated with improper feelings and behaviors. Youths are taught to identify poor decision making and to explore the thinking behind "bad" decisions. They also are taught relapse prevention techniques that enable them to manage their emotions and behavior better. The ten-week program includes an assessment, meetings between the youths and mentors, victim empathy sessions where convicted felons speak with the youths, and team-building exercises.[173]

In addition, individual approaches have been used to prevent adjudicated youths from engaging in further criminal activities. Incarcerated and court-adjudicated youths are now almost universally given some form of mental and physical evaluation before they begin their correctional treatment. Such rehabilitation methods as

Trait theory suggests that prevention efforts should be directed at strengthening a youth's mental and physical well-being. If parents cannot supply proper nurturing, discipline, nutrition, and so on, the child cannot develop properly; consequently, the juvenile justice system is required to provide assistance. Here Lonnie Kelly climbs the rock wall at Piedmont Wilderness Institute in Clinton, S.C. Looking on are Duprie Owens, 17, Martez Rodgers, 16, and Eddie Outing (no helmet), 15. At the institute the boys learn to trust their ability to overcome limits that they put on themselves. The young men in the program were at various state detention centers for nonviolent felonies before the Juvenile Justice Department assigned them to the institute.

psychological counseling and psychotropic medication (drugs like Ritalin) are often prescribed. In some instances, rehabilitation programs are provided through drop-in centers that service youths who are able to remain in their homes; more intensive programs require residential care. The creation of such programs illustrates that agents of the juvenile justice system believe that many delinquent youths and status offenders have psychological or physical problems and that their treatment can help reduce repeat criminal behavior. Faith in this approach suggests widespread agreement that delinquency can be traced to individual pathology.

The influence of psychological theory on delinquency prevention has been extensive, and programs based on biosocial theory have been dormant for some time. However, institutions are beginning to sponsor projects designed to study the influence of diet on crime and to determine whether regulating metabolism can affect behavior. Such efforts are relatively new and untested. Similarly, schools are making an effort to help youths with learning disabilities and other developmental problems. Delinquency prevention efforts based on biocriminological theory are still in their infancy.

Some questions remain about the effectiveness of individual treatment as a delinquency prevention technique. Little hard evidence exists that clinical treatment alone can prevent delinquency or rehabilitate delinquents. Critics still point to the failure of the Cambridge-Somerville Youth Study as evidence that clinical treatment has little value. In that effort, 325 high-risk youths were given intensive counseling, and their progress was compared with a control group that received no special attention. An evaluation of the project by Joan and William McCord found that the treated youths were more likely to become involved in law violation than the untreated controls.[174] By implication, the danger is that the efforts designed to help youths may actually stigmatize them, hindering their efforts to live conventional lives.

Critics argue that the more we try to help youths, the more likely they will be to see themselves as different, or as troublemakers.[175] Such questions have led to prevention efforts designed to influence the social as well as the psychological world of youths (see chapters 4 and 5).

Both choice and trait theories have been embraced by conservatives because they focus on personal characteristics and traits rather than on the social environment. Both theoretical positions agree that delinquency can be prevented by dealing with the youths who engage in crime, not by transforming the social conditions associated with youth crime. In contrast, more liberal delinquency experts view the environment as the main source of delinquency.

SUMMARY

- Criminological theories that focus on the individual can be classified in two groups: choice theories and trait theories.
- Choice theory holds that people have free will to control their actions. Delinquency is a product of weighing the risks of crime against its benefits. If the risk is greater than the gain, people will choose not to commit crimes.
- One way of creating a greater risk is to make sure that the punishments associated with delinquency are severe, certain, and fast.
- Routine activities theory maintains that a pool of motivated offenders exists and that these offenders will take advantage of suitable targets unless they are heavily guarded.
- General deterrence theory holds that if delinquents are rational, an inverse relationship should exist between punishment and crime. The harsher, more certain, and swifter the punishment, the more likely it will deter delinquency.
- General deterrence assumes that delinquents make a rational choice before committing delinquent acts.
- Research has not indicated that deterrent measures actually reduce the delinquency rate.
- Specific deterrence theory holds that the delinquency rate can be reduced if offenders are punished so severely that they never commit crimes again.
- There is little evidence that harsh punishments reduce the delinquency rate, perhaps because most delinquents are not severely punished.
- Choice theorists agree that if the punishment for delinquency could be increased, the delinquency rate might fall. One method is to transfer youths to the criminal courts or to grant the adult justice system jurisdiction over serious juvenile cases. Similarly, some experts advocate incapacitation for serious juvenile offenders—for example, long-term sentences for chronic delinquents.
- Situational crime prevention strategies aim to reduce opportunities for crime to take place. By imposing obstacles that make it difficult to offend, such strategies strive to dissuade would-be offenders.
- Trait theories hold that delinquents do not choose to commit crimes freely but are influenced by forces beyond their control.
- The two types of current trait theory are biosocial and psychological.
- One of the earliest branches of biosocial theory was biological theory, formulated by Cesare Lombroso, who linked delinquency to inborn traits. Following his lead were theories based on genetic inheritance and body build. Although biological theory was in disrepute for many years, it has recently reemerged.
- Biochemical factors linked to delinquency include diet, hormones, and blood chemistry.
- Neurological factors include brain damage and ADHD.
- Some experts believe that delinquent tendencies may be inherited. Studies use twins and adoptees to test this theory.
- Psychological theories include the psychodynamic model, which links antisocial behaviors to unconscious emotions and feelings developed in early childhood.
- The behavioral perspective emphasizes that children imitate the behavior they observe personally or view on television or in movies. Children who are exposed to violence and see it rewarded may become violent as adults.
- Cognitive psychology is concerned with how people perceive the world. Criminality is viewed as a function of improper information processing or lack of moral development.
- Psychopaths are people with a total lack of concern for others. They may commit the most serious violent crimes.
- Intelligence has also been related to delinquency. Some studies claim to show that delinquents have lower IQs than nondelinquents.
- Many delinquency prevention efforts are based on psychological theory. Judges commonly order delinquent youths to receive counseling. Recently, some delinquent offenders have been given biochemical therapy.

KEY TERMS

choice theory, p. 48
trait theory, p. 48
free will, p. 48
utilitarians, p. 49
classical criminology, p. 49
routine activities theory, p. 51
predatory crimes, p. 51

general deterrence, p. 53
co-offending, p. 55
specific deterrence, p. 56
situational crime prevention, p. 57
hot spot, p. 57
crackdown, p. 57
criminal atavism, p. 59

biosocial theory, p. 60
minimal brain dysfunction (MBD), p. 62
learning disabilities (LD), p. 63
psychodynamic theory, p. 68
bipolar disorder, p. 69
identity crisis, p. 69

QUESTIONS FOR DISCUSSION

1. Are all delinquent acts psychologically abnormal? Can there be "normal" crimes?

2. How would you apply psychodynamic theory to delinquent acts such as shoplifting and breaking-and-entering a house?

3. Can delinquent behavior be deterred by the threat of punishment? If not, how can it be controlled?

4. Do you think that watching violence on TV and in films encourage youths to be aggressive and antisocial?

5. Do beer advertisements that feature attractive, scantily dressed young men and women encourage drinking? If they do not encourage people to drink, why bother advertising? If suggestive advertising works in getting people to buy beer, then why shouldn't suggestive violence encourage kids to be violent?

6. Discuss the characteristics of psychopaths. Do you know anyone who fits the description?

APPLYING WHAT YOU HAVE LEARNED

You are a state legislator who is a member of the subcommittee on juvenile justice. Your committee has been asked to redesign the state's juvenile code because of public outrage over serious juvenile crime.

At an open hearing, a professor from the local university testifies that she has devised a surefire test to predict violence-prone delinquents. The procedure involves brain scans, DNA testing, and blood analysis. Used with samples of incarcerated adolescents, her procedure has been able to distinguish with 90 percent accuracy between youths with a history of violence and those who are exclusively property offenders. The professor testifies that, if each juvenile offender were tested with her techniques, the violence-prone career offender could easily be identified and given special treatment. Their scores could be kept on a registry and law enforcement agencies notified of the offenders' whereabouts.

Opponents argue that this type of testing is unconstitutional because it violates the Fifth Amendment protection against self-incrimination and can unjustly label nonviolent offenders. Any attempt to base policy on biosocial makeup seems inherently wrong and unfair. Those who favor the professor's approach maintain that it is not uncommon to single out the insane or mentally incompetent for special treatment and that these conditions often have a biological basis. It is better that a few delinquents be unfairly labeled than have seriously violent offenders be ignored until it is too late.

- Is it possible that some kids are born to be delinquents? Or do kids "choose" crime?
- Is it fair to test kids to see if they have biological traits related to crime even if they have never committed a single offense?
- Should special laws be created to deal with the "potentially" dangerous offender?
- Should offenders be typed on the basis of their biological characteristics?

DOING RESEARCH ON THE WEB

To get more information on DNA testing, the American Civil Liberties Union's stance on personal privacy rights of Americans in the age of technology, and the DNA registry now operated by Alaska, click on Web Links under the Chapter Resources at **http://cj.wadsworth.com/siegel_jdcore2e** and go to the federal sites for the National Crimi-

nal Justice Reference Service and the Office of Juvenile Justice and Delinquency Prevention.

Pro/Con discussions and Viewpoint Essays on some of the topics in this chapter may be found at the Opposing Viewpoints Resource Center: **www.gale.com/OpposingViewpoints**.

chapter 4

Sociological Views of Delinquency

CHAPTER OUTLINE

CHAPTER OBJECTIVES

After reading this chapter you should:

1. Know what is meant by the term *social disorganization.*
2. Understand the relationship between neighborhood fear, unemployment, social change, and lack of cohesion and delinquent behavior patterns.
3. Be familiar with the concept of strain and anomie.
4. Comprehend the elements of general strain theory and the concept of negative affective states.
5. Understand how cultural deviance creates a breeding ground for gangs and law-violating groups.
6. Know the social processes that have been linked to delinquency.
7. Be able to differentiate between learning and control theories.
8. Identify the elements of labeling and stigma that reinforce delinquency.
9. Recognize the role that social conflict plays in creating an environment that breeds antisocial behaviors.
10. Be familiar with the social programs that have been designed to improve neighborhood conditions, help children be properly socialized, and reduce conflict.

It is difficult to be a teen today. Some kids are being raised in indigent areas that are the sites of poor housing, underfunded schools, and law-violating youth gangs. Others are being raised in dysfunctional families, and some are labeled as "losers" from the day they are born. Kids whose parents are convicted criminals serving prison sentences often face all three of these social problems. The organization No More Victims, founded in 1993 by Marilyn K. Gambrell, an author and former Texas parole officer, works with parents and students to help them cope with the roadblocks in their lives. No More Victims teaches kids to understand their personal pain, and in so doing, learn how to stop hurting themselves and others.

CNN. VIEW THE CNN VIDEO CLIP OF THIS STORY AND ANSWER RELATED CRITICAL THINKING QUESTIONS ON YOUR JUVENILE DELINQUENCY: THE CORE 2E CD.

The kids who are being helped by the No More Victims programs often live in tough urban environments in families torn apart and in stress. Although there may be some factors related to delinquent behavior at the individual level, the majority of delinquency experts believe that the key to understanding delinquent behavior lies in the social environment. Most delinquents are indigent and desperate, not calculating or evil. Most grew up in deteriorated parts of town and lack the social support and economic resources familiar to more affluent members of society. Understanding delinquent behavior, then, requires analyzing the influence of these destructive social forces on human behavior.

Explanations of delinquency as an individual-level phenomenon fail to account for these consistent social patterns in delinquency. If violence is related to biochemical or chromosomal abnormality, then how can we explain the fact that some areas of the city, state, and country have much higher crime and delinquency rates than others? Large cities have more crime problems than rural towns; inner-city areas have higher delinquency rates than suburban areas. It is unlikely that all people with physical or mental problems live in one section of town or in one area of the country. Some individual-level theorists believe that viewing violent TV shows can cause aggression. Yet adolescents in rural and suburban areas watch the same shows and movies as kids who live in the city. If the media causes violence, how can urban-rural delinquency rate differences be explained? If violence has a biological or psychological origin, should it not be distributed more evenly throughout the social structure, as opposed to being concentrated in certain areas?

SOCIAL FACTORS AND DELINQUENCY

What are the critical social factors believed to cause or affect delinquent behaviors?

culture of poverty
View that lower-class people form a separate culture with their own values and norms, which are sometimes in conflict with conventional society.

- *Interpersonal interactions.* The shape of interpersonal relationships may be a source of delinquent behavior. Social relationships with families, peers, schools, jobs, criminal justice agencies, and the like, may play an important role in creating or restraining delinquency.[1] In contemporary American society, there has been a reduction in the influence of the family and an increased emphasis on individuality, independence, and isolation. Weakened family ties have been linked to crime and delinquency.[2]

- *Community ecological conditions.* Residing in a deteriorated inner-city area that is wracked by poverty, decay, fear, and despair influences delinquency. These areas are the home of delinquent gangs and groups.

- *Social change.* Political unrest and mistrust, economic stress, and family disintegration are social changes that have been found to precede sharp increases in crime rates. Conversely, stabilization of traditional social institutions typically precedes crime rate declines.[3]

- *Socioeconomic status.* Socioeconomic status may also affect delinquency. It seems logical that people on the lowest rung of the economic ladder will have the greatest incentive to commit crime: they may be enraged by their lack of economic success or simply financially desperate and disillusioned. In either instance, delinquency, despite its inherent dangers, may appear an attractive alternative to a life of indigence. Economic influences may be heightened by the rapid advance in technology; kids who lack the requisite social and educational training have found the road to success almost impassable. A lack of opportunity for upward mobility may make drug dealing and other crimes an attractive solution for socially deprived but economically enterprising people.[4]

In this chapter we will review the most prominent social theories of delinquency. They are divided into three main groups: (1) *social structure theories* hold that delinquency is a function of a person's place in the economic structure; (2) *social process theories* view delinquency as the result of a person's interaction with critical elements of socialization; and (3) *social conflict theories* consider delinquent behavior to be a result of economic deprivation caused by the inequities of the capitalist system of production.

SOCIAL STRUCTURE THEORIES

In 1966, sociologist Oscar Lewis coined the phrase **culture of poverty** to describe the crushing burden faced by the urban poor.[5] According to Lewis, the culture of poverty is marked by apathy, cynicism, helplessness, and mistrust of institutions such as police and government. Mistrust of authority prevents the impoverished from taking advantage of the few conventional opportunities available to them. The result is a permanent

Social scientists find that stabilization of traditional social institutions usually precedes crime rate declines. Crime rates respond to the ability of social institutions, such as the police, to achieve public acceptance. Here, Officer James R. Clarke hands out his trading cards to students at Hardy Elementary School in Smithfield, Virginia. The cards, paid for through a community policing grant, act as public relations for the Smithfield department, which is trying hard to reach out to children.

© Jeff Greenberg/PhotoEdit

There are more than 13 million kids living in poverty in the United States. Poor children are more likely to receive inadequate health care and as a result they will suffer health problems that will impede their long-term development. Children living in poverty are much more likely than the wealthy to suffer social ills ranging from low birth weight to never earning a college degree. They are at great risk for crime and delinquency.

To read the transcript of an interview with Dr. William Julius Wilson, click on Web Links under the Chapter Resources at http://cj.wadsworth.com/siegel_jdcore2e.

underclass whose members have little chance of upward mobility or improvement. This extreme level of economic and social hardship has been related to psychological maladjustment: people who live in poverty are more likely to suffer low self-esteem, depression, and loneliness.[6]

Nowhere are urban problems more pressing than in the inner-city neighborhoods that experience constant population turnover as their more affluent residents move to stable communities or suburbs. Social conditions have actually worsened in some urban areas during the past decade.[7] As a city becomes *hollowed out*, with a deteriorated inner core surrounded by less devastated communities, delinquency rates spiral upward.[8] Those remaining are forced to live in communities with poorly organized social networks, alienated populations, and high crime.[9] Members of the urban underclass, typically minority group members, are referred to by sociologist William Julius Wilson as the **truly disadvantaged.**[10]

The impoverished are deprived of a standard of living enjoyed by most other citizens, and their children suffer from much more than financial hardship. They attend poor schools, live in substandard housing, and lack good health care. More than half of families in poverty are fatherless and husbandless; many are supported entirely by government aid. Instead of increasing government aid to the needy, however, in the past decade a concerted effort has been made to limit eligibility for public assistance.

Neighborhoods that provide few employment opportunities are the most vulnerable to predatory crime. Unemployment destabilizes households, and unstable families are more likely to produce children who choose aggression as a means of dealing with limited opportunity. Lack of employment opportunity also limits the authority of parents, reducing their ability to influence children. Because adults cannot serve as role models, the local culture is dominated by gangs whose members are both feared and respected. Predatory crime increases to levels that cannot easily be controlled by police. Hundreds of studies have documented the association between family poverty and children's health, achievement, and behavior.[11] Children in poor families suffer many problems, including inadequate education. They are less likely to achieve in school and to complete their schooling than are children with more affluent parents.[12]

Poor children are more likely to suffer from health problems and to receive inadequate health care. Unfortunately, the number of children covered by health insurance has decreased and will continue to do so for the foreseeable future.[13] Lack of coverage almost guarantees that these children will suffer health problems that will impede their long-term development. Children who live in extreme poverty or who remain poor for extended periods exhibit the worst outcomes.[14] Poor children are much more likely than the wealthy to suffer social ills ranging from low birthweight to never earning a college degree. The cycle of poverty can lead to a variety of adverse outcomes, including life- and health-endangering conditions (see Figure 4.1). Providing adequate care to children under these circumstances can be an immense undertaking.

Figure 4.1 Examples of Documented Pathways from Poverty to Adverse Child Outcomes

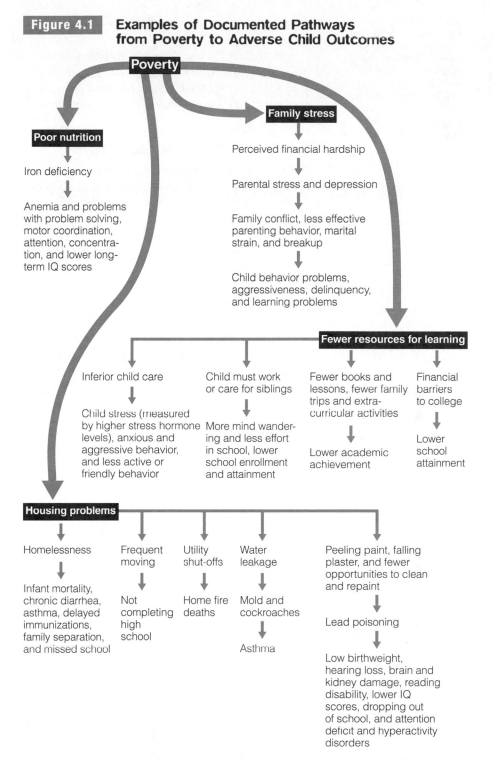

Source: Arloc Sherman, *Poverty Matters* (Washington, DC: Children's Defense Fund, 1997), p. 23.

underclass
Group of urban poor whose members have little chance of upward mobility or improvement.

truly disadvantaged
According to William Julius Wilson, those people who are left out of the economic mainstream and reduced to living in the most deteriorated inner-city areas.

social structure theories
Those theories which suggest that social and economic forces operating in deteriorated lower-class areas, including disorganization, stress, and cultural deviance, push residents into criminal behavior patterns.

This view of delinquency is both *structural* and *cultural.* It holds that delinquency is a consequence of the inequalities built into the social structure and the cultural values that form in inner-city, poverty areas. Even youths who receive the loving support of family members are at risk of delinquency if they suffer from social disadvantage.[15]

The **social structure theories** tie delinquency rates to socioeconomic conditions and cultural values. Areas that experience high levels of poverty and social disorganization will also have high delinquency rates. Residents of such areas view prevailing social values skeptically; they are frustrated by their inability to be part of the American

The Northwestern University/University of Chicago Joint Center for Poverty Research examines what it means to be poor and live in America. Find this Web site by clicking on Web Links under the Chapter Resources at http://cj.wadsworth.com/ siegel_jdcore2e.

Dream. Structural theories are less concerned with why an individual youth becomes delinquent than with why certain areas experience high delinquency rates.

All social structure theorists are linked in their belief that social conditions control behavior choices. However, there are different interpretations of the nature of the interaction between social structure and individual behavior choices. Three prominent views stand out: social disorganization, anomie/strain, and cultural deviance.

Social Disorganization

The concept of **social disorganization** was first recognized early in the twentieth century by sociologists Clifford Shaw and Henry McKay. These Chicago-based scholars found that delinquency rates were high in what they called **transitional neighborhoods**—areas that had changed from affluence to decay. Here, factories and commercial establishments were interspersed with private residences. In such environments, teenage gangs developed as a means of survival, defense, and friendship. Gang leaders recruited younger members, passing on delinquent traditions and ensuring survival of the gang from one generation to the next, a process referred to as **cultural transmission.** While mapping delinquency rates in Chicago, Shaw and McKay noted that distinct ecological areas had developed what could be visualized as a series of concentric zones, each with a stable delinquency rate (see Figure 4.2).[16] The areas of heaviest delinquency concentration appeared to be the poverty-stricken, transitional, inner-city zones. The zones farthest from the city's center were the least prone to delinquency. Analysis of these data indicated a stable pattern of delinquent activity in the ecological zones over a sixty-five-year period.[17]

According to the social disorganization view, a healthy, organized community has the ability to regulate itself so that common goals (such as living in a crime-free area) can be achieved; this is referred to as **social control.**[18] Those neighborhoods that become *disorganized* are incapable of social control because they are wracked by deterioration and economic failure; they are most at risk for delinquency.[19] In areas where social control remains high, children are less likely to become involved with deviant peers and engage in problem behaviors.[20] Social institutions like schools and churches cannot work effectively in the climate of alienation and mistrust that characterizes disorganized areas. The absence of political power limits access to external funding and protection; without outside resources and financial aid, the neighborhood cannot get back on its feet.[21]

Children who reside in disorganized neighborhoods find that involvement with conventional social institutions, such as schools and after-school programs, is either absent or blocked, which puts them at risk for recruitment into gangs.[22]

These problems are stubborn and difficult to overcome. Even when an attempt is made to revitalize a disorganized neighborhood by creating institutional support programs such as community centers and better schools, the effort may be countered by the ongoing drain of deep-rooted economic and social deprivation.[23] Even in relatively crime-free rural areas, areas that are disorganized because of residential instability, family disruption, and changing ethnic composition have relatively high rates of delinquent behavior and youth violence.[24]

A number of concepts define contemporary social disorganization theory.

Relative Deprivation   According to the concept of **relative deprivation,** in communities where the poor and the wealthy live relatively close to one another, kids who feel they are less well off than others begin to form negative self-feelings and hostility, a condition that motivates them to engage in delinquent and antisocial behaviors.[25] This feeling of relative deprivation fuels the frustration that eventually produces high delinquency rates.

Community Change   Some impoverished areas are being rehabilitated or **gentrified,** going from poor, commercial, or transient to stable, residential, and affluent.

---

social disorganization
Neighborhood or area marked by culture conflict, lack of cohesiveness, a transient population, and insufficient social organizations; these problems are reflected in the problems at schools in these areas.

transitional neighborhood
Area undergoing a shift in population and structure, usually from middle-class residential to lower-class mixed use.

cultural transmission
The process of passing on deviant traditions and delinquent values from one generation to the next.

social control
Ability of social institutions to influence human behavior; the justice system is the primary agency of formal social control.

relative deprivation
Condition that exists when people of wealth and poverty live in close proximity to one another; the relatively deprived are apt to have feelings of anger and hostility, which may produce criminal behavior.

gentrified
The process of transforming a lower-class area into a middle-class enclave through property rehabilitation.

Figure 4.2 Concentric Zones Map of Chicago

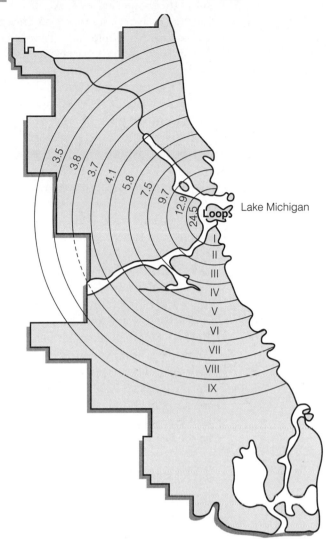

Note: Arabic numerals represent the rate of male delinquency.

Source: Clifford R. Shaw, *Delinquency Areas* (Chicago: University of Chicago Press, 1929), p. 99.

Other formerly affluent communities are becoming rundown. As communities go through these changes, levels of delinquency increase.[26]

Communities on the downswing are likely to experience increases in the number of single-parent families, changes in housing from owner- to renter-occupied units, a loss of semiskilled and unskilled jobs, and the growth in the numbers of discouraged, unemployed workers who are no longer seeking jobs. These communities also tend to develop mixed-use areas in which commercial and residential properties stand side by side, an ecological development that increases the opportunity to commit crime.[27]

Community Fear   Disorganized neighborhoods suffer social incivility—trash and litter, graffiti, burned-out buildings, drunks, vagabonds, loiterers, prostitutes, noise, congestion, angry words. This evidence of incivility convinces residents that their neighborhood is dangerous and in decline.[28] They become fearful and wary and try not to leave their homes at night.

Fear of crime is much higher in disorganized neighborhoods than in affluent suburbs.[29] Residents have little confidence that the government can do anything to counter the drug dealers and gangs that terrorize the neighborhood.[30] They tell others of their experiences, spreading the word that the neighborhood is dangerous. Businesses avoid these areas and neighbors try to move out and relocate to other, safer areas. As people and businesses leave, the neighborhood becomes even more destabilized and crime rates soar. Neighborhood kids may adjust psychologically by taking risks and discounting the future; teenage birthrates soar, and so do violence rates.[31] As crime rates rise, so does fear.[32]

In fear-ridden neighborhoods, social institutions cannot mount an effective social control effort. Because the population is transient, interpersonal relationships tend to be superficial. Neighbors don't know each other and can't help each other out. Social institutions such as schools and religious groups cannot work effectively in a climate of mistrust. When community social control efforts are blunted, crime rates increase, further weakening neighborhood cohesiveness.[33] As cohesiveness declines, fear increases, which reduces community cohesion and thwarts the ability of its institutions to exert social control over its residents.[34] This never-ending cycle is shown in Figure 4.3.

Community Cohesion   In contrast to disorganized areas, cohesive communities have high levels of social control and social integration; people know one another and develop interpersonal ties.[35] Residents of these areas develop a sense of **collective efficacy:** mutual trust and a willingness to intervene in the supervision of children and help maintain public order.[36] Communities that are able to maintain collective efficacy can utilize their local institutions—businesses, stores, schools, churches, and social service and volunteer organizations—to control crime.[37] These institutions can be effective in helping kids avoid gang membership, thereby lowering neighborhood crime rates.[38] Parents in these areas are able to call on neighborhood resources to help control their children; single mothers do not have to face the burden of providing adequate supervision alone.[39]

Anomie/Strain

Inhabitants of a disorganized inner-city area feel isolated, frustrated, ostracized from the economic mainstream, hopeless, and eventually angry. These are all signs of what sociologists call **strain.** How do these feelings affect criminal activities? To relieve strain, indigent people may achieve their goals through deviant methods, such as theft or drug trafficking, or they may reject socially accepted goals and substitute more deviant goals, such as being tough and aggressive.

Strain theorists view crime as a direct result of lower-class frustration and anger. Strain is limited in affluent areas because educational and vocational opportunities

collective efficacy
A process in which mutual trust and a willingness to intervene in the supervision of children and help maintain public order creates a sense of well-being in a neighborhood and helps control antisocial activities.

strain
A condition caused by the failure to achieve one's social goals.

Figure 4.3   **The Cycle of Social Disorganization**

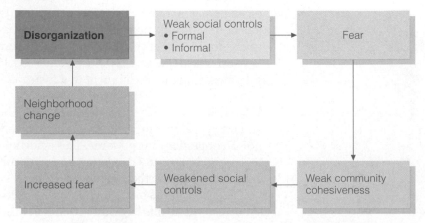

are available. In disorganized areas, strain occurs because legitimate avenues for success are all but closed.

It was Robert Merton (1910–2003), one of America's preeminent sociologists, who adopted the concept of strain to explain crime and delinquency. Merton argued that although most people share common values and goals, the means for legitimate economic and social success are stratified by socioeconomic class. Upper-class kids have ready access to good education and prestigious jobs; kids in the lower class rarely have such opportunities. Without acceptable means for obtaining success, individuals feel social and psychological strain; Merton called this condition **anomie.** Consequently, these youths may either (1) use deviant methods to achieve their goals (for example, stealing money) or (2) reject socially accepted goals and substitute deviant ones (for example, becoming drug users or alcoholics). Feelings of anomie or strain are not typically found in middle- and upper-class communities, where education and prestigious occupations are readily obtainable. In lower-class areas, however, strain occurs because legitimate avenues for success are closed. Considering the economic stratification of U.S. society, anomie predicts that crime will prevail in lower-class culture, which it does.[40]

General Strain Theory Merton's view focuses on the strain that builds up when lower-class kids become frustrated because they lack the means for achieving their personal goals. In his **general strain theory,** sociologist Robert Agnew argues that there are actually more sources of strain than Merton realized (see Figure 4.4).[41]

1. *Strain caused by failure to achieve positively valued goals.* This type of strain will occur when youths aspire to wealth and fame but assume that such goals are impossible to achieve. Also falling within this category is the strain that occurs when individuals compare themselves with peers who seem to be doing a lot better, or when youths believe they are not being treated fairly by a parent or a teacher. Such perceptions may result in reactions ranging from running away from the source of the problem to lowering the benefits of others through physical attacks or vandalism of their property. For example, the student who believes

anomie
Normlessness produced by rapidly shifting moral values; according to Merton, anomie occurs when personal goals cannot be achieved using available means.

general strain theory
Links delinquency to the strain of being locked out of the economic mainstream, which creates the anger and frustration that lead to delinquent acts.

Figure 4.4 **Elements of General Strain Theory**

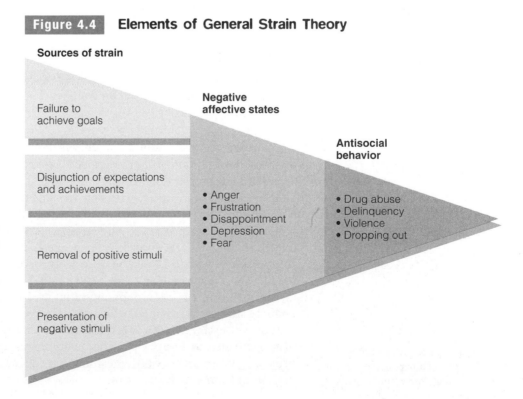

Sources of strain

- Failure to achieve goals
- Disjunction of expectations and achievements
- Removal of positive stimuli
- Presentation of negative stimuli

Negative affective states

- Anger
- Frustration
- Disappointment
- Depression
- Fear

Antisocial behavior

- Drug abuse
- Delinquency
- Violence
- Dropping out

According to Agnew, strain may be caused by the presence of negative pain-inducing interactions within the family, such as child abuse and neglect. Children who are abused at home may take their rage out on younger children at school or become involved in violent delinquency. On the other hand, a warm, supportive family life, such as that shown here, can help kids cope with delinquency-producing environmental strain.

© Michael Newman/PhotoEdit

he is being "picked on" unfairly by a teacher slashes the tires on the teacher's car for revenge.

2. *Strain as the removal of positively valued stimuli.* Strain may occur because of the loss of a positively valued stimulus.[42] For example, the loss of a girlfriend or boyfriend can produce strain, as can the death of a loved one, moving to a new neighborhood, or the divorce or separation of parents.[43] Loss of positive stimuli may lead to delinquency as the adolescent tries to prevent the loss, retrieve what has been lost, obtain substitutes, or seek revenge against those responsible for the loss. For example, a child who experiences parental separation or divorce early in his life may seek out deviant peers to help fill his emotional needs and in so doing increase his chances of delinquency.[44]

3. *Strain as the presentation of negative stimuli.* Strain may also be caused by negative stimuli. Included in this category are such pain-inducing social interactions as child abuse, criminal victimization, school failure, and stressful events, ranging from verbal threats to air pollution. For example, children who are abused at home may take their rage out on younger children at school or become involved in violent delinquency.[45]

According to Agnew, adolescents engage in delinquency as a result of **negative affective states**—the anger, frustration, fear, and other adverse emotions that derive from strain. The greater the intensity and frequency of strain experienced, the greater their impact and the more likely they are to cause delinquency. Research supports many of Agnew's claims: kids who report feelings of stress and anger are more likely to interact with delinquent peers and engage in criminal behaviors;[46] people who fail to meet success goals are more likely to engage in illegal activities.[47]

In sum, kids who feel strain because of stress, disappointment, and anger are more likely to engage in delinquent behaviors.[48] To relieve their feelings of frustration, they may join deviant groups and gangs whose law-violating activities produce even more strain and pressures, which result in even more crime.[49]

Agnew himself has recently found evidence that experiencing violent victimization and anticipating future victimization are associated with antisocial behavior.[50] This finding indicates not only that strain is produced by actual experiences but that it may result from anticipated ones.

negative affective states
Anger, depression, disappointment, fear, and other adverse emotions that derive from strain.

✔ *The social structure view is that position in the socioeconomic structure influences the chances of becoming a delinquent.*

✔ *Poor kids are more likely to commit crimes because they are unable to achieve monetary or social success in any other way.*

✔ *Kids who live in socially disorganized areas commit crime because the forces of social control have broken down.*

✔ *Strain occurs when kids experience anger over their inability to achieve legitimate social and economic success.*

✔ *The best-known strain theory is Robert Merton's theory of anomie, which describes what happens when people have inadequate means to satisfy their goals.*

✔ *Robert Agnew's general strain theory holds that strain has multiple sources.*

✔ *Cultural deviance theories hold that a unique value system develops in lower-class areas; lower-class kids approve of behaviors such as being tough and having street smarts.*

To quiz yourself on this material, go to questions 4.1–4.12 on the Juvenile Delinquency: The Core 2e Web site.

Cultural Deviance

The third structural theory, **cultural deviance theory,** holds that delinquency is a result of youths' desire to conform to lower-class neighborhood cultural values that conflict with those of the larger society. Lower-class values include being tough, never showing fear, living for today, and disrespecting authority. In a socially disorganized neighborhood, conventional values such as honesty, obedience, and hard work make little sense to youths whose role models may include the neighborhood gun runner, drug dealer, or pimp. Those adolescents who share lower-class values and admire criminals, drug dealers, and pimps find it difficult to impress authority figures such as teachers or employers. They experience a form of **culture conflict** and are rendered incapable of achieving success in a legitimate fashion; as a result, they join together in gangs and engage in behavior that is malicious and negativistic.[51]

Both legitimate and illegitimate opportunities are closed to youths in the most disorganized inner-city areas.[52] Consequently, they may join violent gangs to defend their turf, displaying their bravery and fighting prowess.[53] Instead of aspiring to be "preppies" or "yuppies," they want to be considered tough and street-smart.

Youths living in disorganized areas consider themselves part of an urban underclass whose members must use their wits to survive or they will succumb to poverty, alcoholism, and drug addiction.[54] Exploitation of women abounds in a culture wracked by limited opportunity. Sexual conquest is one of the few areas open to lower-class males for achieving self-respect. The absence of male authority figures contributes to the fear that marriage will limit freedom. Peers heap scorn on anyone who allows himself to get "trapped" by a female, fueling the number of single-parent households. Youths who are committed to the norms of this deviant subculture are also more likely to disparage agents of conventional society such as police and teachers.[55] By joining gangs and committing crimes, lower-class youths are rejecting the culture that has already rejected them; they may be failures in conventional society, but they are the kings and queens of the neighborhood.

If the culture of the community helps promote delinquency, then it may be possible to prevent delinquency by reshaping community climate. That approach is the subject of the following Preventing and Treating Delinquency feature. ✔ Checkpoints

SOCIAL PROCESS THEORIES: SOCIALIZATION AND DELINQUENCY

cultural deviance theory
Links delinquent acts to the formation of independent subcultures with a unique set of values that clash with the mainstream culture.

culture conflict
When the values of a subculture clash with those of the dominant culture.

socialization
The process of learning the values and norms of the society or the subculture to which the individual belongs.

Not all sociologists believe that merely living in an impoverished, deteriorated, lower-class area is determinant of a delinquent career. Instead, they argue that the root cause of delinquency may be traced to learning delinquent attitudes from peers, becoming detached from school, or experiencing conflict in the home. Although social position is important, **socialization** is considered to be the key determinant of behavior. If the socialization process is incomplete or negatively focused, it can produce an adolescent with a poor self-image who is alienated from conventional social institutions.

Socialization is the process of guiding people into acceptable behavior patterns through information, approval, rewards, and punishments. It involves learning the techniques needed to function in society. Socialization is a developmental process that is influenced by family and peers, neighbors, teachers, and other authority figures.

Early socialization experiences have a lifelong influence on self-image, values, and behavior. Even children living in the most deteriorated inner-city environments will not get involved in delinquency if their socialization experiences are positive.[56] After all, most inner-city youths do not commit serious crimes, and relatively few of those who do become career criminals.[57] More than fourteen million youths live in poverty, but the majority do not become chronic offenders. Simply living in a violent neighborhood does not produce violent children; research shows that family, peer,

SafeFutures: Using Community Resources to Prevent and Control Youth Crime and Victimization

Youth violence and delinquency are particular problems for communities suffering from economic and social disorganization. In Boston, Massachusetts, the Blue Hill Corridor—consisting of the Grove Hill, Franklin Hill/Franklin Field, and Mattapan neighborhoods—has a history of poor economy, inaccessibility to resources, high unemployment rates, and violence. The SafeFutures program was created to help reduce delinquency in these and other neighborhoods suffering from high delinquency rates and economic problems. The goals of SafeFutures are as follows:

- Create partnerships among all levels of government.
- Develop graduated sanctions to hold youths accountable to their victims and communities.
- Reduce the risk factors of delinquency in the community.
- Provide services for at-risk juveniles and immediate interventions for juvenile offenders.

Program Components

SafeFutures has implemented a set of four services that build on community services, strengths, and supports:

- Treatment and enforcement programs
- Prevention and early intervention programs
- Gang-free schools and community initiatives
- Prevention and early intervention programs for at-risk and delinquent girls

The treatment and enforcement component strengthens relationships between the police department, district attorney, probation department, and city government institutions. This involves a day treatment center for increasing availability of after-care services (services provided after a child gets in trouble with the law), mental health services, counseling, job training, education programs, and enforcement of probation for the juvenile justice system. In addition, this component provides probation officers with funds to work on volunteer programs to help juveniles meet their probation obligations.

The prevention and early intervention component provides age-appropriate violence prevention programs that improve and expand existing mentoring programs. Annual open houses are held for families to meet local social service providers.

The gang-free schools and community initiatives are geared to prevent gang participation in middle schools and high schools. The initiative creates alternative schools for teens who are at a high risk of engaging in gang activity. Finally, there are also prevention and early intervention programs for at-risk and delinquent girls, including a case management system for girls sent to juvenile court, and counseling for girls in need. In a joint effort with local social service agencies, SafeFutures plans to create educational aid, mentoring, team and sport activities, health education, individual treatment help, family counseling, a twenty-four-hour help line, and vocational trade support.

SafeFutures is now being tried as a demonstration project in six communities. In addition to Boston, other sites include Seattle, Washington; St. Louis, Missouri; Contra Costa County and Imperial County, California; and Fort Belknap, Montana. Each of the six communities have received funds from the federal government to provide a group of services that build strength, service, and support in the community.

CRITICAL THINKING

Is it a wise use of scarce public funds to create prevention programs such as SafeFutures, or would society be better served by building more secure juvenile institutions and incarcerating youthful offenders? Would a deterrence strategy be a more effective method of gang control than one based on education, treatment, and counseling?

INFOTRAC COLLEGE EDITION RESEARCH

To read about the use of mentoring to control juvenile violence, go to Delores D. Jones-Brown and Zelma Weston Henriques, "Promises and Pitfalls of Mentoring as a Juvenile Justice Strategy," *Social Justice, 24*:212–234 (1997).

Source: Office of Juvenile Justice and Delinquency Prevention (OJJDP), *SafeFutures.* www.ncjrs.org.

and individual characteristics play a large role in predicting violence in childhood.[58] Only those who experience improper socialization are at risk for crime. This vision has been used to guide many delinquency prevention programs, including the Dare to Be You program discussed in the Preventing and Treating Delinquency box on page 94.

Research consistently shows a relationship between the elements of socialization and delinquency. The primary influence is the family. When parenting is inadequate, a child's maturational processes will be interrupted and damaged. For example, there is now evidence that children who grow up in homes where parents use severe discipline yet lack warmth and involvement in their lives are prone to antisocial behavior.[59] In

What Does This Mean to Me?

Tools That Can Make a Difference

When you think about your community, what organization might you start, or volunteer to assist, that could enhance children's lives and help prevent gang violence and delinquency? Consider, for example, these:

- A peer-support hotline—to address issues and questions about gangs, drugs, crime, and personal problems.
- Preventive education programs—skits and workshops on topics such as suicide, child abuse, teen pregnancy, and AIDS presented at shopping malls, schools, and community centers.
- Improvement projects for neighborhoods—to encourage children and young people to participate in projects to clean up graffiti and improve neighborhoods.
- Learning public life skills—programs might include public speaking, planning, and active listening.
- Organizing young people for social change—volunteers work with children and young people to organize so that their voices can be heard.

Do you think these would work? What others might you suggest?

contrast, parents who are supportive and effectively control their children in a noncoercive fashion are more likely to raise children who refrain from delinquency; this is referred to as **parental efficacy**.[60] Delinquency will be reduced if parents provide the type of structure that integrates children into the family while giving them the ability to assert their individuality and regulate their own behavior.[61]

The family-crime relationship is significant across racial, ethnic, and gender lines and is one of the most replicated findings in the criminological literature.[62]

The literature linking delinquency to poor school performance and inadequate educational facilities is extensive. Youths who feel that teachers do not care, who consider themselves failures, and who drop out of school are more likely to become involved in a delinquent way of life than adolescents who are educationally successful.

Still another suspected element of deviant socialization is peer group relations. Youths who become involved with peers who engage in antisocial behavior and hold antisocial attitudes may be deeply influenced by negative peer pressure. Peers may teach them the "skills" necessary to look and sound "tough."[63]

Even potentially productive activities such as an after-school job can promote crime if it means unsupervised involvement with peers who advocate that money earned be spent on bling bling, drugs, and alcohol rather than saving for a college education![64] Kids who maintain close relations with antisocial peers will sustain their own criminal behavior into their adulthood. When peer influence diminishes, so does delinquent activity.[65]

Sociologists believe that the socialization process affects delinquency in three different ways.

According to social process theories, children's relationships to key societal institutions are a crucial determinant of their development and behavior. It is not surprising, then, that social institutions such as the Redlands, California, Police Department assign officers to bond with teens in an effort to gain their trust and confidence.

© 2000 AP/Wide World Photos

parental efficacy
Parents are said to have parental efficacy when they are supportive and effectively control their children in a noncoercive fashion.

Dare to Be You

Dare to Be You (DTBY) is a multilevel, primary prevention program for children ages two to five and their families. The main goal is to lower the risk of future substance abuse. Program founders believe that a child's future high-risk activities can be curtailed by improving parent- and child-protective factors in the areas of communication, problem solving, self-esteem, and family skills.

How Does It Work?

DTBY is a community-based program. Participants come from every social, racial, and ethnic background. The program targets low parental effectiveness, which causes children to be insufficiently prepared to enter school. The goals include these:

- Improved parental competence
- Increased satisfaction with and positive attitude about being a parent
- Adoption and use of nurturing family management strategies
- Increased and appropriate use of limit setting
- Substantial decreases in parental use of harsh punishment
- Significant increases in child developmental levels

The program has three main components:

- *Family component.* The program offers parent, youth, and family training, with activities teaching self-responsibility, personal and parenting efficacy, communication, and social skills. It seeks to help families suffering from poor communication, unstable family environment, and mental health problems. It consists of a twelve-week (thirty-hour) family workshop series and semiannual twelve-hour reinforcing family workshops.
- *School component.* The program trains and supports teachers and child-care providers who work with the targeted youth.

- *Community component.* The program trains community members who interact with target families: local health departments, social services agencies, probation officers, and counselors. It focuses on community problems such as levels of alcohol and drug use.

Outcomes and Results

The results of this prevention program have been quite good. Families enrolled in the program have experienced an increase in parental effectiveness and satisfaction with their children. Other success indicators are a decrease in parent-child conflict, a reduction in the use of harsh punishment, and an increase in the children's developmental level. Researchers find that the addition of school and community components is necessary for a successful systems approach. Overall, the DTBY program builds on community strengths to establish efficacy.

CRITICAL THINKING

Do you believe it is possible for a government-sponsored program to overcome the negative outcomes of years of personal deprivation suffered by adolescents living in disorganized, deteriorated neighborhoods?

INFOTRAC COLLEGE EDITION RESEARCH

To read about the operations of a similar program, look up Thomas Hanlon, Richard Bateman, Betsy Simon, Kevin O'Grady, and Steven Carswell, "An Early Community-Based Intervention for the Prevention of Substance Abuse and Other Delinquent Behavior," *Journal of Youth and Adolescence* 31:459–471 (2002) on InfoTrac College Edition.

Source: Substance Abuse and Mental Health Services Administration, U.S. Department of Health and Human Services. http://model programs.samhsa.gov/pdfs/FactSheets/Dare.pdf.

- *Learning.* Delinquency may be learned through interaction with other people. By interacting with deviant peers, parents, neighbors, and relatives, kids may learn both the techniques of crime and the attitudes necessary to support delinquency. According to this view, because they learn to commit crimes, children who are born "good" learn to be "bad" from others.
- *Control.* Delinquency may result when life circumstances weaken the attachment a child has to family, peers, school, and society. Because their bonds to these institutions are severed, some adolescents feel free to exercise antisocial behavior. This view assumes that people are born "bad" and then must be taught to control themselves through the efforts of parents and teachers.
- *Reaction.* Some kids are considered winners by others; they are admired and envied. Others are labeled as "troublemakers," "losers," or "punks." They are stigmatized and find themselves locked out of conventional society and into a deviant or delinquent way of life. This view holds that kids are born neither bad nor good but become what they are through the reactions of others.

Each of these views is discussed in the following sections.

Social Learning Theories

Social learning theories hold that children living in even the most deteriorated areas can resist inducements to crime if they have *learned* proper values and behaviors. Delinquency, by contrast, develops by learning the values and behaviors associated with criminal activity. Kids can learn deviant values from their parents, relatives, or peers. Social learning can involve the techniques of crime (how to hot-wire a car) as well as the psychological aspects (how to deal with guilt). The former are needed to commit crimes, whereas the latter are required to cope with the emotional turmoil that follows.

The best-known social learning theory is Edwin Sutherland's **differential association theory.**[66] Sutherland believed that as children are socialized, they are exposed to and learn prosocial and antisocial attitudes and behavior from friends, relatives, parents, and so on. A prodelinquency definition might be "don't get mad, get even" or "only suckers work for a living" (see Figure 4.5). Simply put, if the prodelinquency definitions they have learned outweigh the antidelinquency definitions, kids will be vulnerable to choosing criminal behaviors over conventional ones. The prodelinquency definitions will be particularly influential if they come from significant others such as parents or peers and are frequent and intense. In contrast, if a child is constantly told by her parents to be honest and never harm others, and is brought up in environment in which people "practice what they preach," then she will have learned the necessary attitudes and behaviors to allow her to avoid environmental inducements to delinquency.

Social Control Theories

Social control theories suggest that the cause of delinquency lies in the strength of the relationships a child forms with conventional individuals and groups. Those who are socialized to have close relationships with their parents, friends, and teachers will develop a positive self-image and the ability to resist the lure of deviant behaviors. They develop a strong commitment to conformity that enables them to resist pressures to

social learning theories
Posit that delinquency is learned through close relationships with others; assert that children are born "good" and learn to be "bad" from others.

differential association theory
Asserts that criminal behavior is learned primarily in interpersonal groups and that youths will become delinquent if definitions they learn in those groups that are favorable to violating the law exceed definitions favorable to obeying the law.

social control theories
Posit that delinquency results from a weakened commitment to the major social institutions (family, peers, and school); lack of such commitment allows youths to exercise antisocial behavioral choices.

Figure 4.5 **Social Learning Theory of Delinquency**

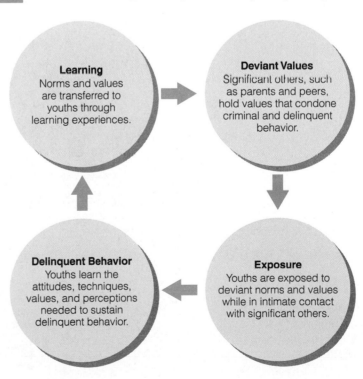

Learning
Norms and values are transferred to youths through learning experiences.

Deviant Values
Significant others, such as parents and peers, hold values that condone criminal and delinquent behavior.

Exposure
Youths are exposed to deviant norms and values while in intimate contact with significant others.

Delinquent Behavior
Youths learn the attitudes, techniques, values, and perceptions needed to sustain delinquent behavior.

violate the law. If, however, their bonds to society become fractured or broken, youths will feel free to violate the law because they are not worried about jeopardizing their social relationships (see Figure 4.6).

The most prominent control theory is the one developed by sociologist Travis Hirschi.[67] In his classic book *Causes of Delinquency,* Hirschi set out the following arguments:

■ All people have the potential to commit crimes—for example, under-age drinking—because they are pleasurable.

■ People are kept in check by their social bonds or attachments to society.

■ If these social bonds are weakened, kids are able to engage in antisocial but personally desirable behaviors.

Hirschi argues that the **social bond** a person maintains with society contains four main elements.

■ *Attachment* to parents, peers, and schools

■ *Commitment* to the pursuit of conventional activities such as getting an education and saving for the future

■ *Involvement* in conventional activities such as school, sports, and religion

■ *Belief* in values such as sensitivity to the rights of others and respect for the legal code

If any or all of these elements of the social bond weaken, kids are free to violate the law. For example, a boy who is not attached to his parents may also lack commitment to his future. It is unlikely that he will be involved in conventional activities such as sports, school, or church. It is also likely that he will not believe in conventional

Figure 4.6   **Elements of the Social Bond**

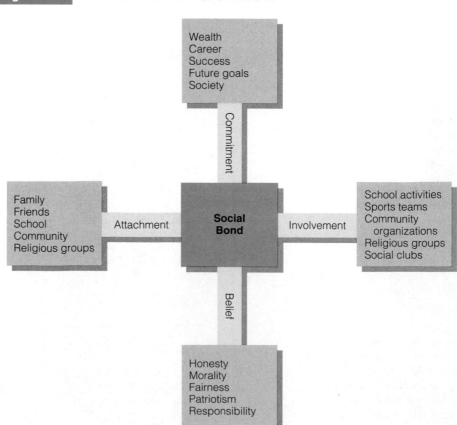

social bond
Ties a person to the institutions and processes of society; elements of the bond include attachment, commitment, involvement, and belief.

values such as "honesty," "hard work," and "discipline." Because he does not have to worry what his parents or teachers think about him or about how his behavior will affect his future, he is free to engage in unconventional activities such as shoplifting, substance abuse, and precocious sex. It really doesn't matter if he gets caught, he has little to lose.

Hirschi's vision of delinquency causation is one of the most influential of recent times. There is a significant amount of research evidence that supports his ideas:

- Positive social attachments help control delinquency.[68]
- Kids who are detached from the educational experience are at risk of criminality.[69]
- Kids who do well and are committed to school are less likely to engage in delinquent acts.[70]
- Kids who are attached to their families are less likely to get involved in a deviant peer group and consequently less likely to engage in criminal activities.[71]

Although many research efforts support Hirschi's ideas, some important questions have been raised about his views. For example, Hirschi argues that commitment to future success, such as an exciting career, reduces delinquent involvement. What about the adolescent who wants to be a success but fails to achieve what he desires; would the resulting strain make him crime-prone?[72] Questions have also been raised about the social relations of delinquents. Hirschi portrays them as "lone wolves," detached from family and friends, while some critics believe that delinquents do maintain close peer group ties.[73] In fact, there is some evidence that drug abusers maintain even more intimate relations with peers than do nonabusers.[74] Hirschi would counter that what appears to be a close friendship is really a relationship of convenience— "Birds of a feather flock together." Do you really believe that gang boys have close relationships and "bond" with one another?

According to Hirschi, kids who are involved in conventional activities, such as the champion athletes shown here, will enhance their social bond and resist delinquent temptations.

Despite these questions, Hirschi's vision of control has remained one of the most influential models of delinquency for the past twenty-five years.

Social Reaction Theories

Another group of sociologists believes that the way *society* reacts to individuals and the way *individuals* react to society determines individual behavior. Becoming **stigmatized,** or labeled, by agents of social control, including official institutions such as the police and the courts, and unofficial institutions, such as parents and neighbors, is what creates and sustains delinquent careers.[75]

According to this view, also known as **labeling theory,** youths may violate the law for a variety of reasons, including poor family relationships, peer pressure, psychological abnormality, and prodelinquent learning experiences. Regardless of the cause, if individuals' delinquent behaviors are detected, the offenders will be given a negative label that can follow them throughout life. These labels include "juvenile delinquent," "mentally ill," "junkie," and many more.

The way labels are applied is likely to have important consequences for the delinquent. The degree to which youngsters are perceived as deviants may affect their treatment at home and at school. Parents may consider them a bad influence on younger brothers and sisters. Neighbors may tell their children to avoid the "troublemaker." Teachers may place them in classes reserved for students with behavior problems, minimizing their chances of obtaining higher education. The delinquency label may also affect the attitudes of society in general, and youthful offenders are subjected to sanctions ranging from mild reprimands to incarceration.

Beyond these results, and depending on the visibility of the label and the manner in which it is applied, youths will have an increasing commitment to delinquent careers. As the negative feedback of law enforcement agencies, teachers, and other figures strengthens their commitment, delinquents may come to see themselves as troublemakers and "screw-ups." Thus, through a process of identification and sanctioning, reidentification, and increased sanctioning, young offenders are transformed. They are no longer children in trouble; they are "delinquents," and they accept that label as a personal identity—a process called **self-labeling** (see Figure 4.7).[76]

When kids who have been rejected by society violate the criminal law, they may be given official labels, applied in "ceremonies"—for example, during juvenile court trials or expulsion hearings in schools—that are designed to redefine the deviant's identity.[77] The effect of this process is a *durable negative label and an accompanying loss of status.* The labeled deviant becomes a social outcast who is prevented from enjoying higher education, well-paying jobs, and other societal benefits. Because this label is "official," few question the accuracy of the assessment. People who may have been merely suspicious now feel justified in their assessments: "I always knew he was a bad kid."

A good example of the labeling ceremony occurs in juvenile courts. Here offenders find (perhaps for the first time) that authority figures consider them incorrigible outcasts who must be separated from the right-thinking members of society. To reach that decision, the judge relies on the testimony of witnesses—parents, teachers, police officers, social workers, and psychologists—who may testify that the offender is unfit to be part of conventional society.[78] As the label *juvenile delinquent* is conferred on offenders, their identities may be transformed from kids who have done something bad to "bad kids."[79] This process has been observed in the United States and abroad, indicating that the labeling process is universal.[80] Kids who perceive that they have been negatively labeled by significant others such as peers and teachers are also more likely to self-report delinquent behavior and adopt a deviant self-concept.[81] The labeling process helps create a **self-fulfilling prophecy.**[82] If children continually receive negative feedback from parents, teachers, and others whose opinion they take to heart, they will interpret this rejection as accurate. Their behavior will begin to conform to the negative expectations; they will become the person that

stigmatized
People who have been negatively labeled because of their participation, or alleged participation, in deviant or outlawed behaviors.

labeling theory
Posits that society creates deviance through a system of social control agencies that designate (or label) certain individuals as delinquent, thereby stigmatizing them and encouraging them to accept this negative personal identity.

self-labeling
The process by which a person who has been negatively labeled accepts the label as a personal role or identity.

self-fulfilling prophecy
Deviant behavior patterns that are a response to an earlier labeling experience; youths act out these social roles even if they were falsely bestowed.

Checkpoints

✔ *Some experts believe that delinquency is a function of socialization.*

✔ *People from all walks of life have the potential to become delinquents if they maintain destructive social relationships with families, schools, peers, and neighbors.*

✔ *Social learning theory stresses that kids learn both how to commit crimes and the attitudes needed to support the behavior.*

✔ *People learn criminal behaviors much as they learn conventional behavior.*

✔ *Social control theory analyzes the failure of society to control anti-social tendencies.*

✔ *All people have the potential to become delinquents, but their bonds to conventional society prevent them from violating the law.*

✔ *Labeling theory (also known as social reaction theory) maintains that negative labels produce delinquent careers.*

✔ *Labels create expectations that the labeled person will act in a certain way; labeled people are always watched and suspected.*

 To quiz yourself on this material, go to questions 4.13–4.19 on the Juvenile Delinquency: The Core 2e Web site.

Figure 4.7 Labeling Theory

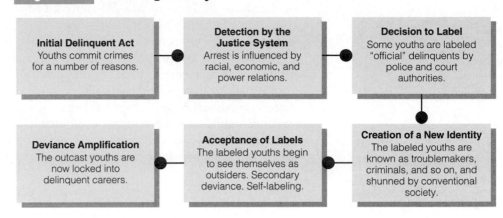

others perceive them to be ("Teachers already think I'm stupid, so why should I bother to study?"). The self-fulfilling prophecy leads to a damaged self-image and an increase in antisocial behaviors.[83]

The labeling perspective can offer important insights:

■ It identifies the role played by social control agents in the process of delinquency causation; delinquent behavior cannot be fully understood if the agencies empowered to control it are ignored.

■ It recognizes that delinquency is not a pathological behavior; it focuses on the social interactions that shape behavior.

■ It distinguishes between delinquent acts and delinquent careers and shows that they must be treated differently.[84]

Labeling theory, then, may help explain the onset and continuation of a delinquent career. It clarifies why some youths continue down the path of antisocial behavior (they are self-labeled), whereas most are able to desist from crime (they are stigma-free).

✔ **Checkpoints**

SOCIAL CONFLICT THEORIES

The conflict view of delinquency is rooted in the political philosophy of Karl Marx. To learn more about Marx's viewpoints, click on Web Links under the Chapter Resources at http://cj.wadsworth.com/siegel_jdcore2e.

According to **social conflict theories,** society is in a constant state of internal conflict, and different groups strive to impose their will on others. Those with money and power succeed in shaping the law to meet their needs and to maintain their interests. Those adolescents whose behavior cannot conform to the needs of the power elite are defined as delinquents and criminals.

According to this view, those in power use the justice system to maintain their status while keeping others subservient: men use their economic power to subjugate women; members of the majority want to stave off the economic advancement of minorities; capitalists want to reduce the power of workers to ensure they are willing to accept low wages. Conflict theory thus centers around a view of society in which an elite class uses the law as a means of meeting threats to its status. The ruling class is a self-interested collective whose primary interest is self-gain.[85]

Law and Justice

social conflict theories
The view that intergroup conflict, born out of the unequal distribution of wealth and power, is the root cause of delinquency.

Social conflict theorists view the law and the justice system as vehicles for controlling the have-not members of society; legal institutions help the powerful and rich to impose their standards of good behavior on the entire society. The law protects the property and physical safety of the haves from attack by the have-nots, and helps control the behavior of those who might otherwise threaten the status quo. The ruling elite draws the lower middle class into this pattern of control, leading it to believe it has a stake in maintaining the status quo. According to social conflict theory, the poor may or may not commit more crimes than the rich, but they certainly are arrested more often. Police may act more forcefully in areas where class conflict creates the perception that extreme forms of social control are needed to maintain order. It is not surprising to conflict theorists that complaints of police brutality are highest in minority neighborhoods.[86] Police misbehavior, which is routine in minority neighborhoods, would never be tolerated in affluent white areas. Consequently, a deep-seated hostility is generated among members of the lower class toward a social order that they may neither shape nor share in.[87]

The Conflict Concept of Delinquency

Conflict theorists view delinquency as a normal response to the conditions created by capitalism.[88] In fact, the creation of the legal category *delinquency* is a function of the class consciousness that occurred around the turn of the century.[89] In *The Child Savers*, Anthony Platt documented the creation of the delinquency concept and the role played by wealthy child savers in forming the philosophy of the juvenile court. Platt believed that the child-saving movement's real goal was to maintain order and control while preserving the existing class system.[90] He and others have concluded that the child savers were powerful citizens who aimed to control the behavior of disenfranchised youths.[91]

Conflict theorists still view delinquent behavior as a function of the capitalist system's inherent inequity. They argue that capitalism accelerates the trend toward replacing human labor with machines so that youths are removed from the labor force.[92] From early childhood, the values of capitalism are reinforced. Social control agencies such as schools prepare youths for placement in the capitalist system by presenting them with behavior models that will help them conform to later job expectations. For example, rewards for good schoolwork correspond to the rewards a manager uses with employees. In fact, most schools are set up to reward youths who show promise in self-discipline and motivation and are therefore judged likely to perform well in the capitalist system. Youths who are judged inferior as potential job prospects wind up in delinquent roles.

Class and Delinquency   The capitalist system affects youths differently at each level of the class structure. In the lowest classes youths form gangs, which can be found in the most desolate ghetto areas. These gangs serve as a means of survival in a system that offers no reasonable alternative. Lower-class youths who live in more stable areas are on the fringe of criminal activity because the economic system excludes them from meaningful opportunity.

Conflict theory also acknowledges middle-class delinquency. The alienation of individuals from one another, the competitive struggle, and the absence of human feeling—all qualities of capitalism—contribute to middle-class delinquency. Because capitalism is dehumanizing, it is not surprising that even middle-class youths turn to drugs, gambling, and illicit sex to find escape.

Controlling Delinquents   Conflict theorists suggest that, rather than inhibiting delinquent behavior, the justice system may help to sustain such behavior. They claim that the capitalist state fails to control delinquents because it is in the state's interest to maintain a large number of outcast deviant youths. These youths can be employed as marginal workers, willing to work for minimum wage in jobs no one else wants. Thus, labeling by the justice system fits in with the capitalist managers' need to maintain an underclass of cheap labor.

Concept Summary 4.1 summarizes the various sociological theories of delinquency.

© 2003 AP/Wide World Photos

According to conflict theory, the alienation of individuals from one another, the competitive struggle, and the absence of human feeling, all qualities of capitalism, contribute to middle-class delinquency. Because capitalism is dehumanizing, it is not surprising that even middle-class youths turn to violence, drugs, gambling, and illicit sex to find escape. Here James Watson, who was raised in a middle-class home, takes a last look at his mother and brother after being fingerprinted. Watson was found delinquent of manslaughter in the beating death of Shane Farrell in New Smyrna Beach, Florida, in 2002, and was sentenced to 9 to 12 months in a high-risk juvenile facility.

Social Structure Theories and Delinquency Prevention

Each of the various branches of social theory has had an impact on delinquency prevention activities and programs. The following sections describe a few of these efforts.

The decade of the 1960s was the heyday of delinquency prevention programs based on social structure theory. The approach seemed compatible with the policies of the Kennedy (New Frontier) and Johnson (Great Society/War on Poverty) administrations. Delinquency prevention programs received copious federal funding. The most ambitious of these was the New York City–based Mobilization for Youth (MOBY). Funded by more than $50 million, MOBY attempted an integrated approach to community development. MOBY created employment opportunities in the community, coordinated social services, and sponsored social action groups such as tenants' committees, legal action services, and voter registration. But MOBY died for lack of funding amid questions about its utility and use of funds. The most prominent contemporary manifestation of a program based on social structure theory is Operation Weed and Seed, the federal multilevel action plan for revitalizing communities.[93] The concept of this program is that no single approach can reduce crime rates and that social service and law enforcement agencies must cooperate to be effective. Therefore, there are four basic elements in this plan: law enforcement; community policing; prevention, intervention, and treatment; and neighborhood restoration. The last element, neighborhood restoration, is the one most closely attached to social structure theory because it is designed to revitalize distressed neighborhoods and improve the quality of life in the target communities. The neighborhood restoration element focuses on economic development activities, such as economic opportunities for residents, improved housing conditions, enhanced social services, and improved public services in the target area. Programs are being developed that will improve living conditions; enhance home security; allow for low-cost physical improvements; develop long-term efforts to renovate and maintain housing; and provide educational, economic, social, recreational, and other vital opportunities. A key feature is the fostering of self-worth and individual responsibility among community members.

Social Process Theories and Delinquency Prevention

Social process theories suggest that delinquency can be prevented by strengthening the socialization process. One approach has been to help social institutions improve their outreach. Educational programs have been improved by expanding preschool programs, developing curricula relevant to students' lives, and stressing teacher development. Counseling and remedial services have been aimed at troubled youth.

Prevention programs have also been aimed at strengthening families in crisis. Because attachment to parents is a cornerstone of all social process theories, developing

Theory	Core Premise	Focus
Social disorganization	Crime is a product of transitional neighborhoods that manifest social disorganization and value conflict. The conflicts and problems of urban social life and communities, including fear, unemployment, deterioration, and siege mentality, influence crime rates.	Identifies why crime rates are highest in lower-class areas. Points out the factors that produce the delinquency.
Strain	People who adopt the goals of society but lack the means to attain them seek alternatives, such as crime.	Points out how competition for success creates conflict and crime. Suggests that social conditions and not personality can account for crime. Can explain middle- and upper-class crime.
Cultural deviance	Obedience to the norms of their lower-class culture puts people in conflict with the norms of the dominant culture.	Identifies the aspects of lower-class life that produce street crime. Creates the concept of culture conflict.
Social learning	People learn to commit delinquent acts through exposure to others who hold deviant values and engage in deviant behaviors.	Explains why some "at-risk" kids do not become delinquents. Accounts for the effects of parental deviance on kids.
Social control	A person's bond to society prevents him or her from violating social rules. If the bond weakens, the person is free to commit delinquent acts.	Explains the onset of delinquency; can apply to both middle- and lower-class crime. Explains its theoretical constructs adequately so it can be measured. Has been empirically tested.
Social reaction	People enter into law-violating careers when they are labeled for their acts and organize their personalities around the labels.	Explains the role of society in creating deviance. Explains why some juvenile offenders do not become adult criminals. Develops concepts of criminal careers.
Social conflict	Crime is a function of class conflict. The law is defined by people who hold social and political power. The capitalist system produces delinquency.	Accounts for class differentials in the delinquency rate. Shows how class conflict influences behavior.

good family relations is an essential element of delinquency prevention. Programs have been developed that encourage families to help children develop the positive self-image necessary to resist the forces promoting delinquency.[94]

Prevention programs have also focused on providing services for youngsters who have been identified as delinquents or predelinquents. Such services usually include counseling, job placement, legal assistance, and more. Their aim is to reach out to troubled youths and provide them with the skills necessary to function in

Social process theories suggest that delinquency can be prevented by strengthening the socialization process and helping social institutions improve their outreach. Educational programs have been improved by developing curricula relevant to students' lives such as job training. Here, Jeanetta Green (right) points to a section of Corrinda Calhoun's practice job application during a training class at Northeast Magnet High School in Wichita, Kansas. The class, Summer Youth B.E.A.T. Employment Program 2003, is part of a program called Hope Street Youth Development, designed to help youth get better trained to find summer jobs.

© 2003 AP/Wide World Photos

their environment before they get into trouble with the law.

In addition to these local efforts, the federal government has sponsored several delinquency-prevention efforts using the principles of social process theory. These include vocational training programs, such as the Comprehensive Employment Training Act, as well as educational enrichment programs, such as Head Start for preschoolers.

Social Reaction Theories and Delinquency Prevention

As the dangers of labeling became known, a massive effort was made to limit the interface of youths with the juvenile justice system. One approach was to divert youths from official processing at the time of their initial contact with police. The usual practice is to have police refer children to treatment facilities rather than to the juvenile court. In a similar vein, children who were petitioned to juvenile court might be eligible for alternative programs rather than traditional juvenile justice processing. For example, restitution allows children to pay back the victims of their crimes for the damage (or inconvenience) they have caused instead of receiving an official delinquency label.

If a youth was found delinquent, efforts were made to reduce stigma by using alternative programs such as boot camp or intensive probation monitoring. Alternative community-based sanctions were substituted for state training schools, a policy known as **deinstitutionalization.** Whenever possible, anything producing stigma was to be avoided, a philosophy referred to as *nonintervention*.

The federal government was a prime mover in the effort to divert children from the justice system. The Office of Juvenile Justice and Delinquency Prevention sponsored numerous diversion and restitution programs. In addition, it made one of its priorities the removal of juveniles from adult jails and the discontinuance of housing status offenders and juvenile delinquents together. These programs were designed to limit juveniles' interaction with the justice system, reduce stigma, and make use of informal treatment modalities. (Diversion and deinstitutionalization are covered in more detail in chapter 14.)[95] Although these programs were initially popular, critics claimed that the nonintervention movement created a new class of juvenile offenders who heretofore might have avoided prolonged contact with

deinstitutionalization
Removing juveniles from adult jails and placing them in community-based programs to avoid the stigma attached to these facilities.

Crime and delinquency are fundamentally a violation of people and interpersonal relationships.	Victims and the community have been harmed and are in need of restoration. Victims include the target of the offense but also include family members, witnesses, and the community at large.
	Victims, offenders, and the affected communities are the key stakeholders in justice. The state must investigate crime and ensure safety, but it is not the center of the justice process. Victims are the key, and they must help in the search for restoration, healing, responsibility, and prevention.
Violations create obligations and liabilities.	Offenders have the obligation to make things right as much as possible. They must understand the harm they have caused. Their participation should be as voluntary as possible; coercion is to be minimized.
	The community's obligations are to both victims and offenders as well as the general welfare of its members. This includes the obligation to reintegrate the offender in the community and to ensure the offender the opportunity to make amends.
Restorative justice seeks to heal and put right the wrongs.	Victims' needs are the focal concern of the justice process. Safety is a top priority, and victims should be empowered to participate in determining their needs and case outcomes.
	The exchange of information between victim and offender should be encouraged; when possible, face-to-face meetings might be undertaken. There should be mutual agreement over imposed outcomes.
	Offenders' needs and competencies need to be addressed. Healing and reintegration are emphasized; isolation and removal from the community are restricted.

juvenile justice agencies; they referred to this phenomenon as *widening the net.*[96] Evaluation of existing programs did not indicate that they could reduce the recidivism rate of clients.[97] While these criticisms proved damaging, many nonintervention programs still operate.

Social Conflict Theories and Delinquency Prevention

If conflict is the source of delinquency, then conflict resolution may be the key to its demise. This is the aim of **restorative justice,** an approach that relies on nonpunitive strategies for delinquency control.[98] Restoration involves turning the justice system into a healing process rather than a distributor of retribution. Most people involved in offender-victim relationships actually know one another or are related. Restorative justice attempts to address the issues that produced conflict between these people rather than to treat one as a victim deserving sympathy and the other as a delinquent deserving punishment. Rather than choose whom to punish, society should try to reconcile the parties.[99]

Restorative justice is based on a social rather than a legal view of delinquency. The relationships damaged by delinquent acts can only be healed in less formal and more cohesive social groups, such as families and communities.[100]

The restorative justice movement has a number of origins. Negotiation, mediation, and peacemaking have been part of the dispute resolution process in European and Asian communities for centuries.[101] Native American and Native Canadian people have long used participation of community members in the adjudication process (sentencing circles, panels of elders).[102] Members of the U.S. peacemaking movement

restorative justice
Nonpunitive strategies for dealing with juvenile offenders that make the justice system a healing process rather than a punishment process.

have also championed the use of nonpunitive alternatives to justice. Gordon Bazemore and other policy experts helped formulate a version of restorative justice known as the *balanced approach,* which emphasizes that victims, offenders, and the community should all benefit from interactions with the justice system.[103] The balanced approach attempts to link community protection and victims' rights. Offenders must take responsibility for their actions, a process that can increase self-esteem and decrease recidivism.[104] In contrast, overreliance on punishment can be counterproductive.[105] To counteract the negative effects of punishment, restorative justice programs for juveniles typically involve diversion from the court process, reconciliation between offenders and victims, victim advocacy, mediation programs, and sentencing circles, in which crime victims and their families are brought together with offenders and their families in an effort to formulate a sanction that addresses the needs of each party. Concept Summary 4.2 summarizes the principles of restorative justice.

To quiz yourself on this material, go to questions 4.20–4.21 on the Juvenile Delinquency: The Core 2e Web site.

SUMMARY

- Social structure theories hold that delinquent behavior is an adaptation to conditions that predominate in lower-class environments.
- The social disorganization view suggests that economically deprived areas lose their ability to control the behavior of residents. Gangs flourish in these areas.
- Delinquency is a product of the socialization mechanisms in a neighborhood: unstable neighborhoods have the greatest chance of producing delinquents. Such factors as fear, unemployment, change, and lack of cohesion help produce delinquent behavior patterns.
- Strain theories hold that lower-class youths may desire legitimate goals but their unavailability causes frustration and deviant behavior.
- Robert Merton linked strain to anomie, a condition caused when there is a disjunction between goals and means.
- In his general strain theory, Robert Agnew identifies two more sources of strain: the removal of positive reinforcements and the addition of negative ones. He shows how strain causes delinquent behavior by creating negative affective states, and he outlines the means adolescents employ to cope with strain.
- Cultural deviance theory maintains that the result of social disorganization and strain is the development of independent subcultures whose members hold values in opposition to mainstream society. These subcultures are the breeding grounds for gangs and law-violating groups.
- Social process theories hold that improper socialization is the key to delinquency.
- One branch, called learning theories, holds that kids learn deviant behaviors and attitudes during interaction with family and peers.
- Control theories suggest that kids are prone to delinquent behavior when they have not been properly socialized and lack a strong bond to society. Without a strong bond they are free to succumb to the lure of delinquent behavior.
- Labeling and stigma may also reinforce delinquency. Kids who receive negative labels may internalize them and engage in self-labeling. This causes a self-fulfilling prophecy, which breeds even more deviant behaviors and locks kids into a delinquent way of life.
- Social conflict theory views delinquency as an inevitable result of the class and racial conflict that pervades society. Delinquents are members of the "have-not" class that is shut out of the mainstream. The law benefits the wealthy over the poor.
- Social views of delinquency have had a great deal of influence on social policy. Programs have been designed to improve neighborhood conditions, help children be properly socialized, and reduce conflict.

KEY TERMS

culture of poverty, p. 82
underclass, p. 85
truly disadvantaged, p. 85
social structure theories, p. 85
social disorganization, p. 86
transitional neighborhood, p. 86

cultural transmission, p. 86
social control, p. 86
relative deprivation, p. 86
gentrified, p. 86
collective efficacy, p. 88
strain, p. 88

anomie, p. 89
general strain theory, p. 89
negative affective states, p. 90
cultural deviance theory, p. 91
culture conflict, p. 91
socialization, p. 91

QUESTIONS FOR DISCUSSION

1. Is there a transitional neighborhood in your town or city?

2. Is it possible that a distinct lower-class culture exists?

3. Have you ever perceived anomie? What causes anomie? Is there more than one cause of strain?

4. How does poverty cause delinquency?

5. Do middle-class youths become delinquent for the same reasons as lower-class youths?

6. Does relative deprivation produce delinquency?

APPLYING WHAT YOU HAVE LEARNED

You have just been appointed as a presidential adviser on urban problems. The president informs you that he wants to initiate a demonstration project in a major city aimed at showing that the government can do something to reduce poverty, crime, and drug abuse. The area he has chosen for development is a large inner-city neighborhood with more than a hundred thousand residents. The neighborhood suffers from disorganized community structure, poverty, and hopelessness. Predatory delinquent gangs run free and terrorize local merchants and citizens. The school system has failed to provide opportunities and education experiences sufficient to dampen enthusiasm for gang recruitment. Stores, homes, and public buildings are deteriorated and decayed. Commercial enterprise has fled the area, and civil servants are reluctant to enter the neighborhood. There is an uneasy truce among the various ethnic and racial groups that populate the area. Residents feel that little can be done to bring the neighborhood back to life.

You are faced with suggesting an urban redevelopment program that can revitalize the area and eventually bring down the crime rate. You can bring any element of the public and private sector to bear on this rather overwhelming problem—including the military! You can also ask private industry to help in the struggle, promising them tax breaks for their participation.

- Do you believe that living in such an area contributes to high delinquency rates? Or is poverty merely an excuse and delinquency a matter of personal choice?
- What programs do you feel could break the cycle of urban poverty?
- Would reducing the poverty rate produce a lowered delinquency rate?
- What role does the family play in creating delinquent behaviors?

DOING RESEARCH ON THE WEB

Before you answer, you may want to learn more about Operation Weed and Seed, the federal office most involved in community development projects designed to reduce delinquency, and on Canada's National Crime Prevention Strategy, which aims to reduce crime and victimization by tackling crime before it happens. Just click on Web Links under the Chapter Resources at http://cj.wadsworth.com/siegel_jdcore2e.

To read about a program in Minneapolis, go to InfoTrac College Edition and read Judith Martin and Paula Pentel,

"What the Neighbors Want: The Neighborhood Revitalization Program's First Decade," *Journal of the American Planning Association* 68:435–449 (2002). To find out more, use "community crime prevention" in a key word search.

Pro/Con discussions and Viewpoint Essays on some of the topics in this chapter may be found at the Opposing Viewpoints Resource Center: www.gale.com/OpposingViewpoints.

Developmental Views of Delinquency

Courtesy of CNN

CHAPTER OBJECTIVES

After reading this chapter you should:

1. Be familiar with the concept of *developmental theory.*

2. Know the factors that influence the life course.

3. Recognize that there are different pathways to delinquency.

4. Be able to discuss the social development model.

5. Describe what is meant by interactional theory.

6. Be familiar with the *turning points in delinquency.*

7. Be able to discuss the influence of social capital on delinquency.

8. Know what is meant by a *latent trait.*

9. Be able to discuss Gottfredson and Hirschi's general theory of crime.

10. Be familiar with the concepts of impulsivity and self-control.

Matthew Lovett was one of those high school kids who seemed at odds with the world. He cared for his younger brother James who, because he was born with a cleft palate, was the target of schoolyard bullies in suburban Oaklyn, New Jersey. Matthew found himself involved in numerous fights and confrontations when kids teased or harassed his brother. Obsessed with the *Matrix* films, Matthew dressed all in black, drew violent pictures, and walked around town with a baseball bat; he kept a list of people who had teased him as far back as grade school. Tired of being a target, Matthew, along with two other, younger boys, ages fourteen and fifteen, hatched a plot to kill three of their tormentors and then kill "as many people as possible" in the streets. On July 6, 2003, they were arrested after a carjacking went awry and the driver alerted police, who went to the scene of the crime and arrested the teens. All three of the boys involved in the would-be massacre were charged with carjacking and conspiracy to commit murder. According to news reports, the allegedly murderous trio "didn't plan on being taken alive."

CNN. VIEW THE CNN VIDEO CLIP OF THIS STORY AND ANSWER RELATED CRITICAL THINKING QUESTIONS ON YOUR JUVENILE DELINQUENCY: THE CORE 2E CD.

Interested in the concept of human development? Access the United Nations' Web site by clicking on Web Links under the Chapter Resources at http://cj.wadsworth.com/siegel_jdcore2e.

developmental theory
The view that criminality is a dynamic process, influenced by social experiences as well as individual characteristics.

life course theory
A developmental theory that focuses on changes in behavior as people travel along the path of life and how these changes affect crime and delinquency.

latent trait theory
The view that delinquent behavior is controlled by a "master trait," present at birth or soon after, that remains stable and unchanging throughout a person's lifetime.

Some criminologists believe that the roots of serious delinquency, such as Matthew Lovett's violent plans, can be traced to much earlier in childhood, and are the culmination of a long history of improper development. They seek the answer to such questions as: Why is it that some kids become delinquents and then abandon the delinquent way of life as they mature, whereas others persist in criminality into their adulthood? Why do some offenders escalate their delinquent activities, while others decrease or limit their law violations? Why do some offenders specialize in a particular delinquency, while others become generalists? Why do some criminals reduce delinquent activity and then resume it once again? Research now shows that some offenders begin their delinquent careers at a very early age, whereas others begin later. How can early- and late-onset criminality be explained? Focusing attention on these questions has produced what is known as the **developmental theory** of crime and delinquency, a view that looks at the onset, continuity, and termination of a delinquent career.

There are actually two distinct developmental views. The first, referred to as the **life course theory,** suggests that delinquent behavior is a dynamic process, influenced by individual characteristics as well as social experiences, and that the factors that cause antisocial behaviors change dramatically over a person's life span.

However, although their position is growing increasingly popular, the life course theorists are challenged by another group of scholars who suggest that human development is controlled by a "master trait" that remains stable, unchanging, throughout a person's lifetime. As people travel through their life course this trait is always there, directing their behavior. Because this master trait is enduring, the ebb and flow of delinquent behavior is shaped less by personal change and more by the impact of external forces such as delinquent opportunity. For example, delinquency may increase when an adolescent joins a gang that provides him with more opportunities to steal, take drugs, and attack others. In other words, the *propensity* to commit delinquent acts is constant, but the *opportunity* to commit them is constantly fluctuating. Concept Summary 5.1 summarizes the main points of the life course and **latent trait theories.**

Life Course Theory	Latent Trait Theory
• People have multiple traits: social, psychological, economic.	• People have a master trait: personality, intelligence, genetic makeup.
• People change over the life course.	• People do not change, criminal opportunities change; maturity brings fewer opportunities.
• Family, job, peers influence behavior.	
• Criminal careers are a passage.	• Early social control and proper parenting can reduce criminal propensity.
• Personal and structural factors influence crime.	• Change affects crime.
	• Unchanging personal factors such as low self-control are more important determinants of behavior than situational factors such as interacting with delinquent peers.

THE LIFE COURSE VIEW

According to the life course view, even as toddlers people begin relationships and behaviors that will determine their entire life course. As children they must learn to conform to social rules and function effectively in society. Later they are expected to begin thinking about careers, leave their parents' home, find permanent relationships, and eventually marry and begin their own families.[1] These transitions are expected to take place in an orderly fashion, beginning with finishing school, entering the workforce, getting married, and having children.

Some kids, however, are incapable of maturing in a reasonable and timely fashion because of family, environmental, or personal problems. In some cases transitions can occur too early—for example, when adolescents engage in precocious sex. In other cases transitions may occur too late, as when a student fails to graduate on time because of bad grades or too many incompletes. Sometimes disruption of one trajectory can harm another. For example, teenage childbirth is likely to disrupt educational and career development. These negative life experiences can become cumulative: as kids acquire more personal deficits, the chances of acquiring additional ones increases.[2] So the boy who experiences significant amounts of anger in early adolescence is the one who is more likely to become involved in antisocial behavior as a teen and to mature into a depressed adult who abuses alcohol.[3]

Disruptions in life's major transitions can be destructive and ultimately promote criminality. Those who are already at risk because of socioeconomic problems or family dysfunction are the most susceptible during these awkward transitions. The cumulative impact of these disruptions sustains criminality from childhood into adulthood.

Because a transition from one stage of life to another can be a bumpy ride, the propensity to commit delinquent acts is neither stable nor constant; it is a *developmental process*. A positive life experience may help some kids desist from delinquency for a while, whereas a negative one may cause them to resume their activities. Delinquent careers are also said to be *interactional* because people are influenced by the behavior of those around them, and in turn, they influence the behavior of others. For example, a girl who is constantly in trouble may be rejected by her friends, which causes her to (a) seek antisocial friends and (b) increase her involvement in antisocial behavior, which causes even more rejection.

Life course theories also recognize that as people mature, the factors that influence their behavior change. At first, family relations may be most influential; in later adolescence, school and peer relations predominate; in adulthood, vocational achievement and marital relations may be the most critical influences. For example, some

According to life course theory, behavior is a dynamic process, influenced by individual characteristics as well as social experiences. Life experiences, such as marrying, having a child, and joining the military, may cause behavior to change dramatically over a person's life span.

antisocial children who are in trouble throughout their adolescence may manage to find stable work and maintain intact marriages as adults; these life events help them desist from delinquency. In contrast, the less fortunate adolescents who develop arrest records and get involved with the wrong crowd may find themselves limited to menial jobs and continue to be at risk for delinquent careers.

The Glueck Research

One of the cornerstones of recent life course theories has been renewed interest in the research efforts of Sheldon and Eleanor Glueck. While at Harvard University in the 1930s, the Gluecks popularized research on the life cycle of delinquent careers. In a series of longitudinal research studies, they followed the careers of known delinquents to determine the factors that predicted persistent offending.[4] The Gluecks made extensive use of interviews and records in their elaborate comparisons of delinquents and non-delinquents.[5]

The Gluecks' research focused on early onset of delinquency as a harbinger of a delinquent career: "The deeper the roots of childhood maladjustment, the smaller the chance of adult adjustment."[6] They also noted the stability of offending careers: children who are antisocial early in life are the most likely to continue their offending careers into adulthood.

The Gluecks identified a number of personal and social factors related to persistent offending. The most important of these factors was family relations, considered in terms of quality of discipline and emotional ties with parents. The adolescent raised in a large, single-parent family of limited economic means and educational achievement was the most vulnerable to delinquency.

The Gluecks did not restrict their analysis to social variables. When they measured such biological and psychological traits as body type, intelligence, and personality, they found that physical and mental factors also played a role in determining behavior. Children with low intelligence, a background of mental disease, and a powerful (mesomorph) physique were the most likely to become persistent offenders.

The Murray Research Center at Radcliffe College sponsors an ongoing "Crime Causation Study: Unraveling Juvenile Delinquency 1940–1963," based on the work of the Gluecks. Find this Web site by clicking on Web Links under the Chapter Resources at http://cj.wadsworth.com/siegel_jdcore2e.

LIFE COURSE CONCEPTS

A number of key concepts help define the life course view. We describe a few of the most critical concepts in this section.[7]

Age of Onset

early onset
The view that kids who begin engaging in antisocial behaviors at a very early age are the ones most at risk for a delinquency career.

The seeds of a delinquent career are planted early in life (preschool); **early onset** of deviance strongly predicts more frequent, varied, and sustained criminality later in life.[8] Most of these early onset delinquents begin their careers with disruptive behavior, truancy, cruelty to animals, lying, and theft.[9] But not all persistent offenders begin at an early age. Some begin their journey at different times.[10] Some stay out of trouble in adolescence and do not violate the law until their teenage years. A few even skip antisocial behavior in their childhood and adolescence altogether and begin their offending career in adulthood.[11]

Why do some kids enter a "path to delinquency" at an early age and why do some wait until late adolescence? Early starters, who begin offending before age four-

In accordance with life course theory, the earlier the age of onset the more likely children will persist in crime as they grow into adulthood.

teen, seem to follow a path that travels from (1) poor parenting to (2) deviant behaviors to (3) involvement with delinquent groups. Late starters, who begin offending after age fourteen, follow a somewhat different path. For them: (1) poor parenting leads to (2) identification with delinquent groups, and then to (3) deviant behaviors. By implication, adolescents who suffer poor parenting and are at risk for deviant careers can avoid criminality if they can bypass involvement with delinquent peers.[12] Although most adolescents eventually reduce their delinquent activity, some persist at a high rate into their twenties.[13]

The earlier the onset, the more likely a kid will engage in serious delinquency and for a longer period of time. Studies of the juvenile justice system show that many incarcerated youth began their offending careers very early in life and that a significant number had engaged in heavy drinking and drug abuse by age ten or younger.[14]

Adolescent-Limiteds Versus Life Course Persisters

According to psychologist Terrie Moffitt, adolescents who repeatedly violate the law can be divided into two groups: **adolescent-limiteds** and **life course persisters.**[15] Adolescent-limited offenders get involved with antisocial activities early in life and then begin to phase out of their delinquent behaviors as they mature. These kids may be considered "typical teenagers" who get into minor scrapes and engage in what might be considered rebellious teenage behavior with their friends, such as recreational drug use.[16] In contrast, life course persisters remain high-rate offenders into young adulthood.[17] They combine family dysfunction with severe neurological problems that predispose them to antisocial behavior patterns. These problems can be the result of maternal drug abuse, poor nutrition, or exposure to toxic agents such as lead. Life course persisters may have lower verbal ability, which inhibits reasoning skills, learning ability, and school achievement. They seem to mature faster and engage in early sexuality and drug use, referred to as **pseudomaturity.**[18]

adolescent-limited
Offender who follows the most common delinquent trajectory, in which antisocial behavior peaks in adolescence and then diminishes.

life course persister
One of the small group of offenders whose delinquent career continues well into adulthood.

pseudomaturity
Characteristic of life course persisters, who tend to engage in early sexuality and drug use.

problem behavior syndrome (PBS)
A cluster of antisocial behaviors that may include family dysfunction, substance abuse, smoking, precocious sexuality and early pregnancy, educational underachievement, suicide attempts, sensation seeking, and unemployment, as well as delinquency.

Problem Behavior Syndrome

The life course view is that delinquency is but one of many social problems faced by at-risk youth. Referred to collectively as **problem behavior syndrome (PBS),** these behaviors include family dysfunction, substance abuse, smoking, precocious sexuality and early pregnancy, educational underachievement, suicide attempts, sensation seeking, and unemployment (see Exhibit 5.1).[19] People who suffer from one of these conditions typically exhibit many symptoms of the others.[20] For example, research has found the following problem behaviors cluster together:

- Youths who drink in the late elementary school years, who are aggressive, and who have attention problems are more likely to be offenders during adolescence.

- Youths who are less attached to their parents and school and have antisocial friends are more likely to be offenders.

- Youths from neighborhoods where drugs are easily available are more likely to be offenders during adolescence.[21]

Exhibit 5.1 Problem Behavior Syndrome

Personal Characteristics
- Substance abuse
- Suicide attempts
- Early sexuality
- Sensation seeking
- Early parenthood
- Accident proneness
- Medical problems
- Mental disease
- Anxiety
- Eating disorders (bulimia, anorexia)

Social Characteristics
- Family dysfunction
- Unemployment
- Educational underachievement
- School misconduct

Environmental Characteristics
- High-delinquency area
- Disorganized area
- Racism
- Exposure to poverty

The Program of Research on the Causes and Correlates of Delinquency, sponsored by the federal government, coordinates longitudinal projects that are often referred to in this text. Find this Web site by clicking on Web Links under the Chapter Resources at http://cj.wadsworth.com/siegel_jdcore2e.

To read highlights of the Pittsburgh Youth Study directed by Rolf Loeber, click on Web Links under the Chapter Resources at http://cj.wadsworth.com/siegel_jdcore2e.

authority conflict pathway
Pathway to delinquent deviance that begins at an early age with stubborn behavior and leads to defiance and then to authority avoidance.

covert pathway
Pathway to a delinquent career that begins with minor underhanded behavior, leads to property damage, and eventually escalates to more serious forms of theft and fraud.

overt pathway
Pathway to a delinquent career that begins with minor aggression, leads to physical fighting, and eventually escalates to violent delinquency.

■ Juvenile delinquents with conduct disorder who have experienced and observed violence, who have been traumatized, and who suffer from a wide spectrum of psychopathology also have high rates of suicidal thoughts and attempts.[22]

People who exhibit one of these conditions typically exhibit many of the others.[23] All varieties of delinquent behavior, including violence, theft, and drug offenses, may be part of a generalized PBS, indicating that all forms of antisocial behavior have similar developmental patterns.[24]

Multiple Pathways

Life course theorists recognize that delinquents may travel more than a single road in their delinquent career. Some are chronic offenders, while others may commit delinquent acts only once or twice; some increase their activities as they age while others de-escalate their antisocial behaviors.[25] Some may specialize in a single type of delinquent act, such as selling drugs, while others may engage in a variety of delinquent acts.

Rolf Loeber and his associates have identified three distinct paths to a delinquent career (see Figure 5.1).[26]

1. The **authority conflict pathway** begins at an early age with stubborn behavior. This leads to defiance (doing things one's own way, disobedience) and then to authority avoidance (staying out late, truancy, running away).
2. The **covert pathway** begins with minor, underhanded behavior (lying, shoplifting) that leads to property damage (setting nuisance fires, damaging property). This behavior eventually escalates to more serious forms of criminality, ranging from joyriding, pocket picking, larceny, and fencing to passing bad checks, using stolen credit cards, stealing cars, dealing drugs, and breaking and entering.
3. The **overt pathway** escalates to aggressive acts beginning with aggression (annoying others, bullying), leading to physical (and gang) fighting and then to violence (attacking someone, forced theft).

Not all youth travel down a single path. Some are stubborn, lie to teachers and parents, are schoolyard bullies, and commit petty thefts. Those who travel more than one path are the most likely to become persistent offenders as they mature.

Continuity of Crime and Delinquency

Another aspect of developmental theory is *continuity of crime and delinquency:* the best predictor of future criminality is past criminality. Children who are repeatedly in trou-

Figure 5.1 Loeber's Pathways to Crime

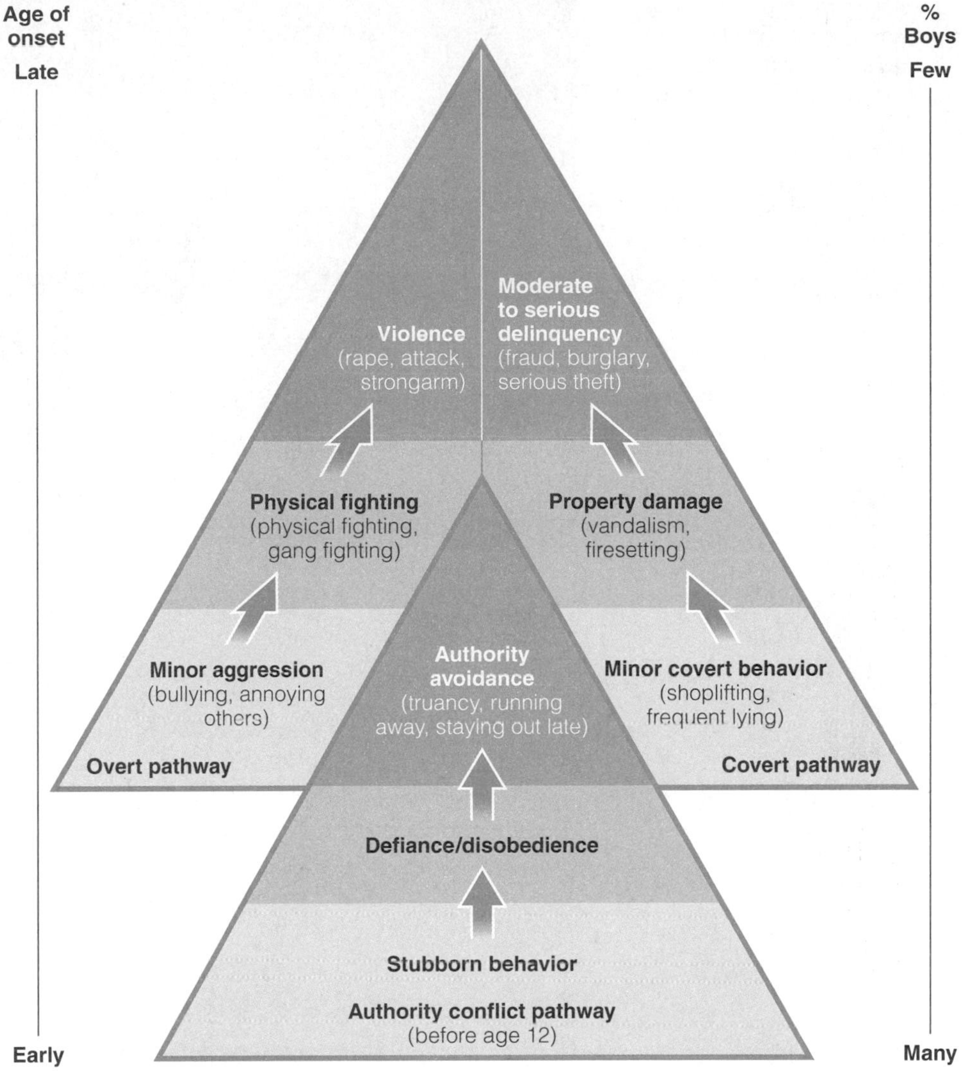

Age of onset: Late → Early

% Boys: Few → Many

Moderate to serious delinquency (fraud, burglary, serious theft)

Violence (rape, attack, strongarm)

Physical fighting (physical fighting, gang fighting)

Property damage (vandalism, firesetting)

Minor aggression (bullying, annoying others)

Authority avoidance (truancy, running away, staying out late)

Minor covert behavior (shoplifting, frequent lying)

Overt pathway

Covert pathway

Defiance/disobedience

Stubborn behavior

Authority conflict pathway (before age 12)

Source: "Serious and Violent Offenders," *Juvenile Justice Bulletin,* May 1998, p. 1.

Checkpoints

✔ Pioneering criminologists Sheldon and Eleanor Glueck tracked the onset and termination of delinquent careers.

✔ Life course theories look at such issues as the onset of delinquency, escalation of offenses, continuity of delinquency, and desistance from delinquency.

✔ The concept of problem behavior syndrome suggests that criminality may be just one of a cluster of social, psychological, and physical problems.

✔ There is more than one pathway to delinquency.

✔ Adolescent-limited offenders begin offending late and age out of delinquency. Life course persisters exhibit early onset of delinquency that persists into adulthood.

www To quiz yourself on this material, go to questions 5.1–5.10 on the Juvenile Delinquency: The Core 2e Web site.

social development model (SDM)
A developmental theory that attributes delinquent behavior patterns to childhood socialization and pro- or antisocial attachments over the life course.

ble during early adolescence will generally still be antisocial in their middle and late teens and as adults.[27] Research shows that kids who persist engage in more aggressive acts and are continually involved in theft offenses and aggression. As they emerge into adulthood, persisters report less emotional support, lower job satisfaction, distant peer relationships, and more psychiatric problems than those who desist.[28]

Early delinquent activity is likely to be sustained because these offenders seem to lack the social survival skills necessary to find work or to develop the interpersonal relationships they need to allow them to drop out of delinquency. Delinquency may be *contagious:* kids at risk for delinquency may be located in families and neighborhoods in which they are constantly exposed to deviant behavior. Having brothers, fathers, neighbors, and friends who engage in and support their activities reinforces their deviance.[29]

As they mature, delinquents may continue to be involved in antisocial behavior. But even if they aren't, they are still at risk for a large variety of adult social behavior problems. There are gender differences in the effect. For males, the path runs from delinquency to problems at work and substance abuse. For females, antisocial behavior in youth leads to relationship problems, depression, tendency to commit suicide, and poor health in adulthood.[30] ✔ **Checkpoints**

There are multiple pathways to crime. The covert pathway begins with minor, underhanded behavior (lying, shoplifting) that leads to property damage (setting nuisance fires, damaging property) and escalates to more serious forms of criminality, ranging from joyriding and passing bad checks to using stolen credit cards and breaking and entering.

© Richard Hutchings/PhotoEdit

LIFE COURSE THEORIES

An ongoing effort has been made to track persistent offenders over their life course.[31] The early data seem to support what is already known about delinquent career patterns: juvenile offenders are likely to become adult criminals; early onset predicts more lasting delinquency; and chronic offenders commit a significant portion of all delinquent acts.[32] Based on these findings, criminologists have formulated a number of systematic theories that account for onset, continuance, and desistance from delinquency.

The Social Development Model

In their **social development model (SDM),** Joseph Weis, Richard Catalano, J. David Hawkins, and their associates focus on the different factors affecting a child's social development over the life course.[33] According to their view, as children mature in their environment, elements of socialization control their developmental process and either insulate them from delinquency or encourage their antisocial activities. The theory has a number of important elements:

- All children face the risk of delinquent behavior, especially those forced to live in the poorest neighborhoods and attend substandard schools. To avoid the risk of antisocial behavior a child must develop and maintain **prosocial bonds.** These are developed in the context of family life, when parents routinely praise children and give them consistent, positive feedback.

- Parental attachment affects a child's behavior for life, determining both school experiences and personal beliefs and values. For those with strong family relationships, the school experience will be meaningful, marked by academic success and commitment to education. Young people growing up in supportive homes are likely to develop conventional beliefs and values, become committed to conventional activities, form attachments to conventional others, and avoid delinquent entanglements.

- Children who cannot form prosocial bonds in their family are at risk for being exposed to deviant attitudes and behaviors. Their ties to conventional institutions such as schools are weakened and they are left unprotected from the lures

prosocial bonds
Socialized attachment to conventional institutions, activities, and beliefs.

of delinquent behavior. These youths will eventually believe that it is easy to get away with antisocial behavior and see such actions as "cool" and rewarding.[34]

■ Adolescents who perceive opportunities and rewards for antisocial behavior will form deep attachments to deviant peers and become committed to a delinquent way of life. In contrast, those who perceive opportunities for prosocial behavior will take a different path, getting involved in conventional activities and forming attachments to others who share their conventional lifestyle (see Figure 5.2).

The SDM holds that commitment and attachment to conventional institutions, activities, and beliefs insulate youths from the delinquency-producing influences in their environment. They may meet peers who promote antisocial behaviors—smoking, drinking, and precocious sex. Without the proper level of bonding, adolescents can succumb to these prodelinquency influences.[35] The following Preventing and Treating Delinquency feature describes a successful delinquency prevention program that relies on the development of prosocial bonds that counteract antisocial influences.

Figure 5.2 **The Social Development Model of Antisocial Behavior**

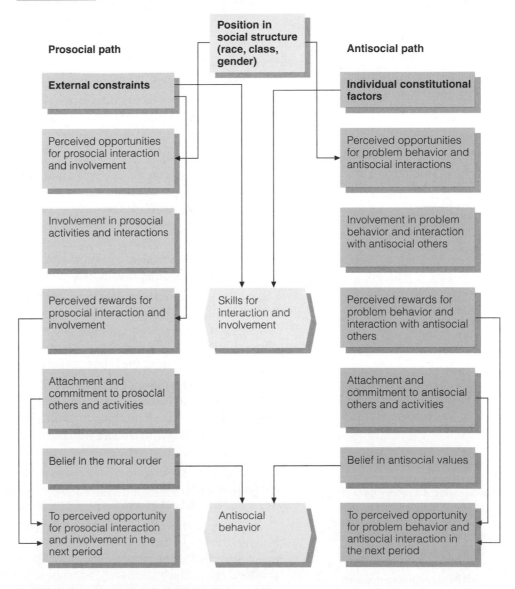

Source: Adapted from Seattle Social Development Project.

According to the Social Development Model (SDM), there are a number of personal, psychological, and community-level "risk factors" that make some children susceptible to the development of antisocial behaviors over the course of their lives. Children with preexisting risk factors find that their antisocial behavior is either reinforced or neutralized through community and individual-level interactions. Actor/Latino activist Edward James Olmos, shown here, is an example of someone who was able to overcome these risk factors and succeed in society. He now helps at-risk youths succeed and reach their potential.

© PhotoEdit

To read more about the social development model, click on Web Links under the Chapter Resources at http://cj.wadsworth.com/siegel_jdcore2e.

Interactional Theory

Like the SDM, Terence Thornberry's **interactional theory** finds that the onset of delinquent behavior can be traced to a deterioration of the social bond during adolescence, marked by weakened attachment to parents, commitment to school, and belief in conventional values (see Figure 5.3).[36] This theory has a number of unique elements:

- *Delinquency is a dynamic developmental process that takes on different meanings and forms as a person matures.*[37] During early adolescence, attachment to the family is the single most important determinant of whether a youth will adjust to conventional society and be shielded from delinquency. By mid-adolescence, the influence of the family is replaced by the "world of friends, school, and youth culture."[38] In adulthood, a person's behavioral choices are shaped by her place in conventional society and her own nuclear family. So interactional theory finds that the root cause of crime and delinquency fluctuates according to a person's place in the life cycle.

- *Delinquency is bidirectional.* Weak bonds lead children to develop friendships with deviant peers and get involved in antisocial behaviors. Frequent delinquent involvement further weakens bonds and makes it difficult to establish conventional relationships. By shutting offenders out of a conventional lifestyle, early criminality helps entrap them in a deviant lifestyle.[39]

- *Delinquency-promoting factors tend to reinforce one another.* Kids who go through stressful life events, such as family financial crises, death of a parent, parents' divorce, physical illness, breaking up with a boyfriend or girlfriend, changing schools, and getting into trouble with classmates, are more likely to later get involved in antisocial behaviors.[40]

- *Early and persistent involvement in antisocial behavior generates consequences that are hard to shake.* Kids who are in trouble with the law find it difficult to establish social bonds and develop positive social relations later on.

- *Delinquency does not terminate in a single generation.* Offenders who are in trouble with the law in their adolescence are unlikely to develop the skills that will make them nurturing parents. The lack of parental efficacy renders their own children susceptible to antisocial behaviors. It is not surprising then, that delinquency seems to be intergenerational: delinquent fathers produce delinquent sons who in turn produce delinquent grandsons.[41]

interactional theory
A developmental theory that attributes delinquent trajectories to mutual reinforcement between delinquents and significant others over the life course—family in early adolescence, school and friends in mid-adolescence, and social peers and one's own nuclear family in adulthood.

Across Ages

Across Ages is a drug prevention program for youths ages nine to thirteen. The program's goal is to strengthen the bonds between adults and children to provide opportunities for positive community involvement. It is unique and highly effective in its pairing of older adult mentors (age fifty-five and above) with young adolescents, mainly those entering middle school.

Designed as a school- and community-based demonstration research project, Across Ages was originally founded in 1991 by the Substance Abuse and Mental Health Services Administration's Center for Substance Abuse Prevention and was replicated in Philadelphia and West Springfield, Massachusetts. Today, there are more than thirty replication sites in seventeen states. Specifically, the program aims to

- Increase knowledge of health and substance abuse and foster healthy attitudes, intentions, and behavior toward drug use among targeted youth.
- Improve school bonding, academic performance, school attendance, and behavior and attitudes toward school.
- Strengthen relationships with adults and peers.
- Enhance problem-solving and decision-making skills.

Target Population

The project was designed for and tested on African-American, Hispanic/Latino, White, and Asian-American middle school students living in a large urban setting. The goal was to assess many risk factors faced by urban youth, including no opportunity for positive free-time activities, few positive role models, and stresses caused by living in extended families when parents are incarcerated or substance abusers.

How It Works

Program materials are offered in English or Spanish so they can be used cross-culturally. A child is matched up with an older adult and participates in activities and interventions that include these:

- Mentoring for a minimum of two hours each week in one-on-one contact
- Community service for one to two hours per week
- Social competence training, which involves the "Social Problem-Solving Module" that is composed of twenty-six weekly lessons at forty-five minutes each
- Activities for the youth and family members and mentors

Benefits and Outcomes

Participating youth learn positive coping skills and have an opportunity to be of service to their community. The program aims to increase prosocial interactions and protective factors and decrease negative ones.

Protective Factors to Increase

- *Individual.* Relationship with significant adult; engagement in positive free-time activities; problem-solving/conflict resolution skills; bonding to school
- *Peer.* Association with peers engaged in positive behavior and activities
- *Family.* Engagement in positive family activities; improved communication between parents and children
- *School.* Improved school attendance, behavior, and performance
- *Community.* Useful role in the community; positive feedback from community members

Risk Factors to Decrease

- *Individual.* School failure; identified behavior problems in school; lack of adult role models; poor decision making and problem-solving skills
- *Peer.* Engagement in risky behavior
- *Family.* Substance-abusing parents and siblings; incarcerated family members; little positive interaction between parents and children
- *School.* Lack of bonding to school
- *Community.* Residence in communities lacking opportunities for positive recreational activities and with high incidence of drug-related delinquency

Results show that participation in the project leads to increased knowledge about the negative effects of drug abuse and decreased use of alcohol and tobacco. Participants improve school attendance, improve grades, and get fewer suspensions. Another positive outcome from the project is seen in the youths' attitudes toward older adults. At the same time, the project helps the older volunteers feel more productive, experience a greater sense of purpose, and regain a central role in their communities.

CRITICAL THINKING

1. Should such issues as early onset and problem behavior syndrome be considered when choosing participants for prevention programs such as Across Ages?
2. Could participation in such programs label or stigmatize participants and thereafter lock them into a deviant role?

INFOTRAC COLLEGE EDITION RESEARCH

To find out more about mentoring programs, go to InfoTrac College Edition and read David DuBois, Bruce Holloway, Jeffrey Valentine, and Harris Cooper, "Effectiveness of Mentoring Programs for Youth: A Meta-analytic Review," *American Journal of Community Psychology,* 30:157–198 (2002).

Source: U.S. Department of Health and Human Services, Substance Abuse and Mental Health Services Administration Center for Substance Abuse Prevention, Across Ages. http://modelprograms.samhsa.gov/pdfs/FactSheets/AcrossAges.pdf.

Figure 5.3 Overview of the Interactional Theory of Delinquency

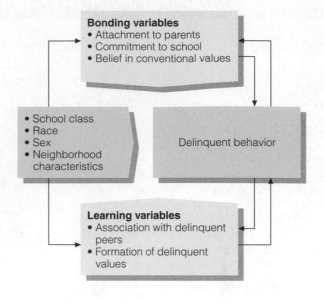

Source: Terence Thornberry, Margaret Farnworth, Alan Lizotte, and Susan Stern, "A Longitudinal Examination of the Causes and Correlates of Delinquency." Working paper no. 1, Rochester Youth Development Study (Albany, NY: Hindelang Criminal Justice Research Center, 1987), p. 11.

In sum, interactional theory suggests that delinquency is part of a dynamic social process and not just an outcome of that process. Although delinquents may be influenced by social forces, their behavior influences those around them in a never-ending cycle.[42]

Age-Graded Theory

If there are various pathways to crime and delinquency, are there various trails back to conformity? In an important 1993 work, *Crime in the Making,* Robert Sampson and John Laub identified **turning points** in a delinquent career.[43] Reanalyzing the original Glueck data, they found that the stability of delinquent behavior can be affected by events that occur later in life, even after a chronic delinquent career has been established. They also believe that formal and informal social controls restrict criminality and that delinquency begins early in life and continues over the life course.

Turning Points   Sampson and Laub's most important contribution is identifying the life events that enable adult offenders to desist from delinquency. Two critical turning points are career and marriage.

■ *Adolescents who are at risk for delinquency can live conventional lives if they can find good jobs or achieve successful careers.* Their success may hinge on a lucky break. Even those who have been in trouble with the law may turn from delinquency if employers are willing to give them a chance despite their records.

■ *Adolescents who have had significant problems with the law are also able to desist from delinquency if, as adults, they become attached to a spouse who supports and sustains them, regardless of their past.[44]* Spending time in marital and family activities reduces exposure to deviant peers, which reduces the opportunity to become involved in delinquent activities.[45] People who cannot sustain secure marital relations are less likely to desist from delinquency.

Social Capital   A cornerstone of age-graded theory is the influence of **social capital** on behavior. Social scientists recognize that people build social capital—

turning points
Critical life events, such as career and marriage, that may enable adult offenders to desist from delinquency.

social capital
Positive relations with individuals and institutions, as in a successful marriage or a successful career, that support conventional behavior and inhibit deviant behavior.

According to criminologist Terence Thornberry, the onset of crime can be traced to a deterioration of the social bond during adolescence, marked by a weakening of attachment to parents, commitment to school, and belief in conventional values. Delinquent youths seek the company of other kids who share their interests and who are likely to reinforce their beliefs about the world and support their delinquent behavior.

© Michael Newman/PhotoEdit

positive relations with individuals and institutions that are life-sustaining. Social capital, which includes the resources accessed through interpersonal connections and relationships, is as critical to individuals (and to social groups, organizations, and communities) in obtaining their objectives as is human capital, or what a person (or organization) actually possesses.[46]

In the same manner that building financial capital improves the chances for economic success, building social capital supports conventional behavior and inhibits deviant behavior (see Figure 5.4).[47]

For example, a successful marriage creates social capital when it improves a person's stature, creates feelings of self-worth, and encourages others to trust the person. A successful career inhibits delinquency by creating a stake in conformity: Why commit delinquency when you are doing well at your job? The relationship is reciprocal. If people are chosen to be employees, they return the favor by doing the best job possible; if they are chosen as spouses, they blossom into devoted partners.

In contrast, losing or wasting social capital increases both personal deficits and the likelihood of getting involved in delinquency. For example, moving to a new city reduces social capital by closing people off from long-term relationships.[48] Losing social capital has a cumulative effect, and as kids develop more and more disadvantages the likelihood of their entering a delinquent and criminal career increases.[49]

Testing Age-Graded Theory   Several indicators support the validity of age-graded theory.[50] Research shows that children who are raised in two-parent families are more likely to grow up to have happier marriages than children whose parents were divorced or never married.[51] This finding suggests that the marriage-delinquency association may be intergenerational: if people with marital problems are more delinquency-prone, their children will also suffer a greater long-term risk of marital failure and antisocial activity.

Evidence now shows that once begun, delinquent career trajectories can be reversed if life conditions improve, an outcome predicted by age-graded theory.[52] Youths who accumulate social capital in childhood (for example, by doing well in school or having a tightly knit family) are also the most likely to maintain steady work as adults. In addition, people who are unemployed or underemployed report higher delinquent participation rates than employed men.[53]

Social scientists recognize that people build social capital in the same manner that they build financial capital. Social capital improves a person's chances for success and inhibits deviant behavior. Here, a young boy is brought to a rally in Boston in which participants demand increased funding for teen parents so that they may become able to have a secure and fulfilling family life.

© 2001 AP/Wide World Photos

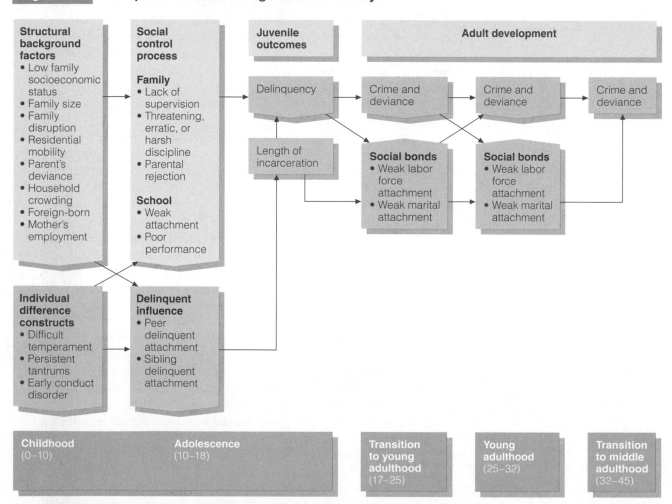

Figure 5.4   **Sampson and Laub's Age-Graded Theory**

Structural background factors
- Low family socioeconomic status
- Family size
- Family disruption
- Residential mobility
- Parent's deviance
- Household crowding
- Foreign-born
- Mother's employment

Social control process

Family
- Lack of supervision
- Threatening, erratic, or harsh discipline
- Parental rejection

School
- Weak attachment
- Poor performance

Juvenile outcomes

Delinquency

Length of incarceration

Adult development

Crime and deviance

Crime and deviance

Crime and deviance

Social bonds
- Weak labor force attachment
- Weak marital attachment

Social bonds
- Weak labor force attachment
- Weak marital attachment

Individual difference constructs
- Difficult temperament
- Persistent tantrums
- Early conduct disorder

Delinquent influence
- Peer delinquent attachment
- Sibling delinquent attachment

Childhood (0–10) **Adolescence** (10–18) **Transition to young adulthood** (17–25) **Young adulthood** (25–32) **Transition to middle adulthood** (32–45)

Source: Robert Sampson and John Laub, *Crime in the Making: Pathways and Turning Points Through Life* (Cambridge, MA: Harvard University Press, 1993), pp. 244–245.

What Does This Mean to Me?

Family Ties

When Bill McCarthy, John Hagan, and Monica Martin studied street kids they found that more than half joined a "street family" for support and emotional connections that their other relationships lacked. One child told the researchers:

My street family gave me more support on the streets and stuff: people loving and caring for you. You know, being there for you. It feels better, you know, than just being, you know, alone when you don't know what to do.

1. Have you ever been involved in a nonfamily group that provided social capital that could not be gained in any other manner? How did it help?
2. Do you believe that it is instinctual for humans to seek out others for support? Would joining a fraternity or sorority fit the model?

Source: Bill McCarthy, John Hagan, and Monica Martin, "In and Out of Harm's Way: Violent Victimization and the Social Capital of Fictive Street Families," *Criminology* 40:831–836 (2002).

Checkpoints

✔ *Life course theories attempt to integrate social, personal, and environmental factors into detailed explanations of the onset and persistence of delinquent careers.*

✔ *The social development model (SDM) integrates social control, social learning, and structural models.*

✔ *According to interactional theory, the causes of crime are bidirectional. Weak bonds lead kids to acquire deviant peer relations and engage in delinquency; delinquency weakens conventional bonds and strengthens relations with deviant peers.*

✔ *According to age-graded theory, building social capital and strong social bonds reduces the likelihood of long-term deviance. As people go through their life course the factors that influence their behavior undergo change.*

 To quiz yourself on this material, go to questions 5.11–5.17 on the Juvenile Delinquency: The Core 2e Web site.

latent trait
A stable feature, characteristic, property, or condition, such as defective intelligence or impulsive personality, that makes some people delinquency-prone over the life course.

As predicted by age-graded theory, delinquent youth who enter the military, serve overseas, and receive veterans' benefits enhance their occupational status (social capital) while reducing delinquent involvement.[54] In contrast, people who are self-centered and present-oriented are less likely to accumulate social capital and more prone to committing delinquent acts.[55]

Laub and Sampson are now conducting an important follow-up to their original research: they are finding and interviewing the survivors from the original Glueck research. These two researchers have located the survivors, the oldest subject being seventy years old and the youngest sixty-two!

The results of their research are examined in the following Focus on Delinquency feature.

✔ Checkpoints

THE LATENT TRAIT VIEW

In a popular 1985 book, *Crime and Human Nature,* two prominent social scientists, James Q. Wilson and Richard Herrnstein, argued that personal traits, such as genetic makeup, intelligence, and body build, operate in tandem with social variables such as poverty and family function. Together these factors influence people to "choose delinquency" over nondelinquent behavioral alternatives.[56]

Following their lead, David Rowe, D. Wayne Osgood, and W. Alan Nicewander proposed the concept of **latent traits.** Their model assumes that a number of people in the population have a personal attribute or characteristic that controls their inclination or propensity to commit delinquent acts.[57] This disposition, or latent trait, is either present at birth or established early in life, and it remains stable over time. Suspected latent traits include defective intelligence, impulsive personality, genetic abnormalities, the physical-chemical functioning of the brain, and environmental influences on brain function such as drugs, chemicals, and injuries.[58] Those who carry one of these latent traits are in danger of becoming career criminals; those who lack the traits have a much lower risk. Latent traits should affect the behavioral choices of all people equally, regardless of their gender or personal characteristics.[59]

According to this latent trait view, the *propensity* or inclination to commit delinquency is stable, but the *opportunity* to commit delinquency fluctuates over time. People age out of delinquency because, as they mature, there are simply fewer opportunities to commit such acts and greater inducements to remain "straight." They may marry, have children, and obtain jobs. The former delinquents' newfound adult responsibilities leave them little time to hang with their friends, abuse substances, and get into scrapes with the law.

Assume, for example, that a stable latent trait such as low IQ causes some people to commit delinquent acts. Teenagers have more opportunity to do so than adults, so at every level of intelligence, adolescent delinquency rates will be higher. As they mature, however, teens with both high and low IQs will commit less delinquency because their adult responsibilities provide them with fewer opportunities to do so. Thus, latent trait theories integrate concepts usually associated with trait theories (such as personality and temperament) and concepts associated with rational choice theories (such as delinquent opportunity and suitable targets).

Although there are a number of latent trait–type theories of crime and delinquency, the most well known is the general theory of crime.

Tracking Down Five Hundred Delinquent Boys in the New Millennium

Why are some delinquents destined to become persistent criminals as adults? John Laub and Robert Sampson are now conducting a follow-up to their reanalysis of Sheldon and Eleanor Glueck's study that matched five hundred delinquent boys with five hundred nondelinquents. The individuals in the original sample were reinterviewed by the Gluecks at ages twenty-five and thirty-two. Now Sampson and Laub have located the survivors of the delinquent sample, the oldest being seventy and the youngest sixty-two, and they are re-interviewing this cohort.

Persistence and Desistance

Laub and Sampson find that delinquency and other forms of antisocial conduct in childhood are strongly related to adult delinquency and drug and alcohol abuse. Former delinquents also suffer consequences in other areas of social life, such as school, work, and family life. For example, delinquents are far less likely to finish high school than are nondelinquents and subsequently more likely to be unemployed, receive welfare, and experience separation or divorce as adults.

In their latest research, Laub and Sampson address one of the key questions posed by life course theories: Is it possible for former delinquents to turn their lives around as adults? They find that most antisocial children do not remain antisocial as adults. For example, of men in the study cohort who survived to age fifty, 24 percent had no arrests for delinquent acts of violence and property after age seventeen (6 percent had no arrests for total delinquency); 48 percent had no arrests for predatory delinquency after age twenty-five (19 percent for total delinquency); 60 percent had no arrests for predatory delinquency after age thirty-one (33 percent for total delinquency); and 79 percent had no arrests for predatory delinquency after age forty (57 per-

cent for total delinquency). They conclude that desistance from delinquency is the norm and that most, if not all, serious delinquents desist from delinquency.

Why Do Delinquents Desist?

Laub and Sampson's earlier research indicated that building social capital through marriage and jobs were key components of desistance from delinquency. However, in this new round of research, they were able to find out more about long-term desistance by interviewing fifty-two men as they approached age seventy. Drawing on the men's own words, they found that one important element for "going straight" is the "knifing off" of individuals from their immediate environment and offering them a new script for the future. Joining the military can provide this knifing-off effect, as does marriage or changing one's residence. One former delinquent (now age sixty-nine) told them:

> I'd say the turning point was, number one, the Army. You get into an outfit, you had a sense of belonging, you made your friends. I think I became a pretty good judge of character. In the Army you met some good ones, you met some foul balls. Then I met the wife. I'd say probably that would be the turning point. Got married, then naturally, kids come. So now you got to get a better job, you got to make more money. And that's how I got to the Navy Yard and tried to improve myself.

Former delinquents who "went straight" were able to put structure into their lives. Structure often led the men to disassociate from delinquent peers, reducing the opportunity to get into trouble. Getting married, for example, may limit the number of nights men can "hang with the guys." As one wife of a former delinquent said, "It is not how many beers you have, it's who you drink with." Even multiple offenders who did time in prison were able to desist with the help of a stabilizing marriage.

Former delinquents who can turn their life around, who have acquired a degree of maturity by taking on family and

General Theory of Crime

Michael Gottfredson and Travis Hirschi's **general theory of crime (GTC)** modifies and redefines some of the principles articulated in Hirschi's social control theory (see chapter 4) by integrating the concepts of control with those of biosocial, psychological, routine activities, and rational choice theories.[60]

The Act and the Offender   In their general theory of crime, Gottfredson and Hirschi consider the delinquent offender and the delinquent act as separate concepts.

general theory of crime (GTC)
A developmental theory that modifies social control theory by integrating concepts from biosocial, psychological, routine activities, and rational choice theories.

- Delinquent acts, such as robberies or burglaries, are illegal events or deeds that people engage in when they perceive them to be advantageous. For example, burglaries are typically committed by young males looking for cash, liquor, and entertainment; the delinquency provides "easy, short-term gratification."[61]

work responsibilities, and who have forged new commitments are the ones most likely to make a fresh start and find new direction and meaning in life. It seems that men who desisted changed their identity as well, and this, in turn, affected their outlook and sense of maturity and responsibility. The ability to change did not reflect delinquency "specialty": violent offenders followed the same path as property offenders.

Early Death

In a follow-up analysis (conducted with George Vaillant), Laub found that while many former delinquents desisted from delinquency, they still faced the risk of an untimely death. Following two matched samples of delinquents and nondelinquents until they reached age sixty-five, Laub found that 13 percent ($N = 62$) of the delinquents as compared to only 6 percent ($N = 28$) of the nondelinquent subjects died unnatural deaths such as through violence, cirrhosis of the liver caused by alcoholism, poor self-care, suicide, and so on. By age sixty-five, 29 percent ($N = 139$) of the delinquents and 21 percent ($N = 95$) of the nondelinquent subjects had died from natural causes. Frequent delinquent involvement in adolescence and alcohol abuse were the strongest predictors of an early and unnatural death. So although many troubled youth are able to reform, their early excesses may haunt them across their life span.

Policy Implications

Laub and Sampson found that youths with problems—delinquency, substance abuse, violence, dropping out, teen pregnancy—often share common risk characteristics. Intervention strategies, therefore, should consider a broad array of antisocial, criminal, and deviant behaviors and not limit the focus to just one subgroup or delinquency type. Because criminality and other social problems are linked, early prevention efforts that reduce delinquency will probably also reduce alcohol abuse, drunk driving, drug abuse, sexual promiscuity, and family violence. The best way to achieve these goals is through four significant life-changing events: marriage, joining the military, getting a job, and changing one's environment or neighborhood. What appears to be important about these processes is that they all involve, to varying degrees, the following items: a "knifing off" of the past from the present; new situations that provide both supervision and monitoring as well as new opportunities of social support and growth; and new situations that provide the opportunity for transforming identity. Prevention of delinquency must be a policy at all times and at all stages of life.

CRITICAL THINKING

Do you believe that the factors that influenced the men in the original Glueck sample are still relevant for change—for example, a military career? Would it be possible for men such as these to join the military today? Do you believe that some sort of universal service program might be beneficial and help people turn their lives around?

INFOTRAC COLLEGE EDITION RESEARCH

Read a review of Laub and Sampson's *Crime in the Making* at Roland Chilton, "Crime in the Making: Pathways and Turning Points Through Life," *Social Forces*, September 1995 v74 n1 p357(2). To learn more about the concept of social capital, use it as a key term on InfoTrac College Edition.

Sources: John Laub and Robert Sampson, "Understanding Desistance from Crime," in Michael Tonry, ed., *Delinquency and Justice: An Annual Review of Research*, vol. 28 (Chicago: University of Chicago Press, 2001), pp. 1–71; John Laub, "Crime Over the Life Course," *Poverty Research News, The Newsletter of the Northwestern University/University of Chicago Joint Center for Poverty Research*, May–June 2000 v4 n3; John Laub and George Vaillant, "Delinquency and Mortality: A 50-Year Follow-Up Study of 1,000 Delinquent and Nondelinquent Boys," *American Journal of Psychiatry 157*:96–102 (2000). Laub and Sampson's new book, *Shared Beginnings, Divergent Lives: Delinquent Boys to Age 70*, is in production at Harvard University Press.

■ Delinquency is rational and predictable. Kids break the law when it promises rewards with minimal threat of pain. Therefore, the threat of punishment can deter delinquency: if targets are well guarded, and guardians are present, delinquency rates will diminish.

■ Delinquent offenders are predisposed to commit crimes. However, they are not robots who commit crimes without restraint; their days are also filled with conventional behaviors, such as going to school, parties, concerts, and church. But given the same set of delinquent opportunities, such as having a lot of free time for mischief and living in a neighborhood with unguarded homes containing valuable merchandise, delinquency-prone kids have a much higher probability of violating the law than do nondelinquents. The propensity to commit delinquent acts remains stable throughout a person's life; change in the frequency of delinquent activity is purely a function of change in opportunity.

By recognizing that there are stable differences in people's propensity to commit delinquent acts, the GTC adds a biosocial element to the concept of social control.

The biological and psychological factors that make people impulsive and delinquency-prone may be inherited or may develop through incompetent or absent parenting.

What Makes People Delinquency-Prone? What, then, causes people to become excessively delinquency-prone? Gottfredson and Hirschi attribute the tendency to commit delinquent acts to a person's level of **self-control.** Low self-control develops early in life and remains stable into and through adulthood.[62] People with limited self-control tend to be **impulsive;** they are insensitive to other people's feelings, physical (rather than mental), risk takers, shortsighted, and non-verbal.[63] They have a "here and now" orientation and refuse to work for distant goals; they lack diligence, tenacity, and persistence. Impulsive people tend to be adventuresome, active, physical, and self-centered. As they mature, they often have unstable marriages, jobs, and friendships.[64] People lacking self-control are less likely to feel shame if they engage in deviant acts and more likely to find them pleasurable.[65] They are also more likely to engage in dangerous behaviors that are associated with criminality[66] (see Figure 5.5).

Because those with low self-control enjoy risky, exciting, or thrilling behaviors with immediate gratification, they are more likely to enjoy delinquent acts, which require stealth, agility, speed, and power, than conventional acts, which demand long-term study and cognitive and verbal skills. And because they enjoy taking risks, they are more likely to get involved in accidents and suffer injuries than people who maintain self-control.[67] As Gottfredson and Hirschi put it, they derive satisfaction from "money

---

Figure 5.5   **The General Theory of Crime**

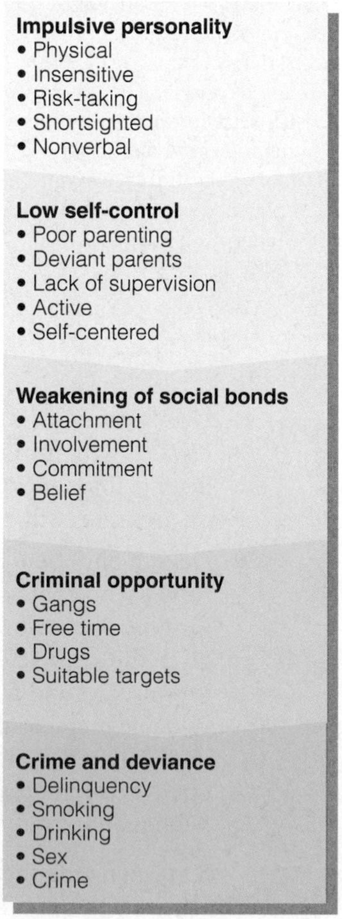

Impulsive personality
• Physical
• Insensitive
• Risk-taking
• Shortsighted
• Nonverbal

Low self-control
• Poor parenting
• Deviant parents
• Lack of supervision
• Active
• Self-centered

Weakening of social bonds
• Attachment
• Involvement
• Commitment
• Belief

Criminal opportunity
• Gangs
• Free time
• Drugs
• Suitable targets

Crime and deviance
• Delinquency
• Smoking
• Drinking
• Sex
• Crime

---

self-control

Refers to a person's ability to exercise restraint and control over his or her feelings, emotions, reactions, and behaviors.

impulsive

Lacking in thought or deliberation in decision making. An impulsive person lacks close attention to details, has organizational problems, is distracted and forgetful.

without work, sex without courtship, revenge without court delays."[68] Many of these individuals who have a propensity for committing delinquent acts also engage in other behaviors, such as smoking, drinking, gambling, reckless driving, and illicit sexuality.[69] Although these acts are not illegal, they too provide immediate, short-term gratification. Exhibit 5.2 lists the elements of impulsivity, or low self-control.

Gottfredson and Hirschi trace the root cause of poor self-control to inadequate child-rearing practices. Parents who are unwilling or unable to monitor a child's behavior, to recognize deviant behavior when it occurs, and to punish that behavior, will produce children who lack self-control. Children who are not attached to their parents, who are poorly supervised, and whose parents are delinquent or deviant themselves are the most likely to develop poor self-control. In a sense, lack of self-control occurs naturally when steps are not taken to stop its development.[70] It comes as no shock to life course theorists when research shows that antisocial behavior runs in families and that having delinquent relatives is a significant predictor of future misbehaviors.[71]

Self-Control and Delinquency   Gottfredson and Hirschi claim that self-control theory can explain all varieties of delinquent behavior and all the social and behavioral correlates of delinquency. That is, such widely disparate delinquent acts as burglary, robbery, embezzlement, drug dealing, murder, rape, and running away from home all stem from a deficiency in self-control. Likewise, gender, racial, and ecological differences in delinquency rates can be explained by discrepancies in self-control: if male delinquency rates are higher than female delinquency rates it is because males have lower levels of self-control than females.

Supporting Evidence for the GTC   Following the publication of *A General Theory of Crime,* dozens of research efforts tested the validity of Gottfredson and Hirschi's theoretical views. One approach involved identifying indicators of impulsiveness and self-control to determine whether scales measuring these factors correlate with measures of delinquent activity. A number of studies conducted both in the United States and abroad have successfully shown this type of association.[72] Some of the most important findings are summarized in Exhibit 5.3.

Analyzing the GTC   By integrating the concepts of socialization and criminality, Gottfredson and Hirschi help explain why some people who lack self-control can escape criminality, and conversely, why some people who have self-control might not escape criminality. People who are at risk because they have impulsive personalities may forgo delinquent careers because there are no opportunities to commit delinquent acts; instead, they may find other outlets for their impulsive personalities. In contrast, if the opportunity is strong enough, even people with relatively strong

---

Exhibit 5.2   **Elements of Impulsivity: Signs That a Person Has Low Self-Control**

- Insensitive
- Physical
- Shortsighted
- Nonverbal
- Here-and-now orientation
- Unstable social relations
- Enjoys deviant behaviors
- Risk taker
- Refuses to work for distant goals

- Lacks diligence
- Lacks tenacity
- Adventuresome
- Self-centered
- Shameless
- Imprudent
- Lacks cognitive and verbal skills
- Enjoys danger and excitement

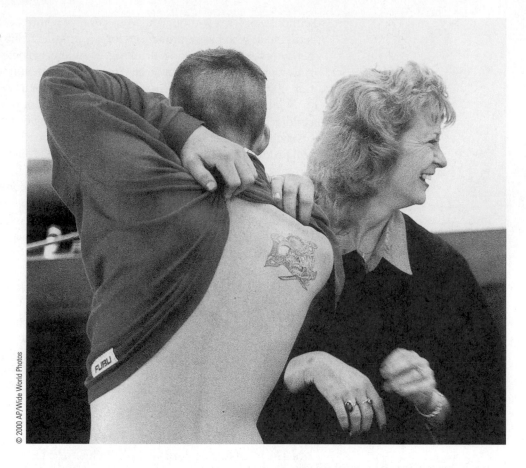

The General Theory of Crime assumes that the opportunity to commit crime constantly fluctuates while delinquent propensity remains the same. Yet treatment programs typically assume that they can help youngsters change. Lorain County, Ohio Judge Paulette Lilly laughs as the first juvenile to graduate from the Lorain County Domestic Relations and Juvenile Drug Court program shows her his new tattoo.

© 2000 AP/Wide World Photos

self-control may be tempted to violate the law; the incentives to commit delinquent acts may overwhelm their self-control.

Integrating delinquent propensity and delinquent opportunity can explain why some children enter into chronic offending while others living in similar environments are able to resist delinquent activity.

The general theory seems persuasive, but several questions and criticisms remain. Among the most important are the following:

1. *Circular reasoning.* Some critics argue that the theory involves circular reasoning. How do we know when people are impulsive? When they commit crime. Are all criminals impulsive? Of course, or else they would not have broken the law![73]

2. *Personality disorder.* It is possible that a lack of self-control is merely a symptom of some broader, underlying personality disorder, such as an antisocial personality, that produces delinquency. Other personality traits such as low self-direction (the tendency not to act in one's long-term benefit) may be a better predictor of criminality than impulsivity or lack of self-control.[74]

3. *Ecological-individual differences.* The GTC also fails to address individual and ecological patterns in the delinquency rate. For example, if delinquency rates are higher in Los Angeles than in Albany, New York, can it be assumed that residents of Los Angeles are more impulsive than residents of Albany? Gottfredson and Hirschi might argue that there are more delinquent opportunities in LA, hence the delinquency rate difference.

4. *Racial and gender differences.* Although distinct gender differences in the delinquency rate exist, there is little evidence that males are more impulsive than females.[75] Similarly, Gottfredson and Hirschi explain racial differences in the delinquency rate as a failure of child-rearing practices in the African-American community.[76] In so doing, they overlook issues of institutional racism, poverty,

Exhibit 5.3   **Empirical Evidence Supporting the General Theory of Crime**

- Offenders lacking in self-control commit a garden variety of delinquent acts.[1]
- More mature and experienced criminals become more specialized in their choice of delinquency (for example, robbers, burglars, drug dealers).[2]
- Male and female drunk drivers are impulsive individuals who manifest low self-control.[3]
- Repeat violent offenders are more impulsive than their less violent peers.[4]
- Incarcerated youth enjoy risk-taking behavior and hold values and attitudes that suggest impulsivity.[5]
- Kids who take drugs and commit delinquency are impulsive and enjoy engaging in risky behaviors.[6]
- Measures of self-control can predict deviant and antisocial behavior across age groups ranging from teens to adults age fifty.[7]
- People who commit white-collar and workplace delinquency have lower levels of self-control than nonoffenders.[8]
- Gang members have lower levels of self-control than the general population; gang members report lower levels of parental management, a factor associated with lower self-control.[9]
- Low self-control shapes perceptions of delinquent opportunity and consequently conditions the decision to commit delinquent acts.[10]
- People who lack self-control expect to commit delinquency in the future.[11]
- Kids whose problems develop early in life are the most resistant to change in treatment and rehabilitation programs.[12]
- Gender differences in self-control are responsible for delinquency rate differences. Females who lack self-control are as delinquency-prone as males with similar personalities.[13]
- Parents who manage their children's behavior increase their self-control, which helps reduce their delinquent activities.[14]
- Having parents (or stepparents) available to control behavior may reduce the opportunity to commit delinquency.[15]
- Victims have lower self-control than nonvictims. Impulsivity predicts both the likelihood that a person will engage in delinquent behavior and the likelihood that the person will become a victim of delinquency.[16]
- Low self-control has been significantly related to antisocial behavior in other cultures and nations.[17]

Notes

1. Xiaogang Deng and Lening Zhang, "Correlates of Self-Control: An Empirical Test of Self-Control Theory," *Journal of Delinquency and Justice 21*:89–103 (1998).

2. Alex Piquero, Raymond Paternoster, Paul Mazeroole, Robert Brame, and Charles Dean, "Onset Age and Offense Specialization," *Journal of Research in Crime and Delinquency 36*:275–299 (1999).

3. Peter Muris and Cor Meesters, "The Validity of Attention Deficit Hyperactivity and Hyperkinetic Disorder Symptom Domains in Nonclinical Dutch Children," *Journal of Clinical Child & Adolescent Psychology 32*:460–466 (2003); Carl Keane, Paul Maxim, and James Teevan, "Drinking and Driving, Self-Control, and Gender: Testing a General Theory of Crime," *Journal of Research in Crime and Delinquency 30*:30–46 (1993).

4. Judith DeJong, Matti Virkkunen, and Marku Linnoila, "Factors Associated with Recidivism in a Delinquent Population," *Journal of Nervous and Mental Disease 180*:543–550 (1992).

5. David Cantor, "Drug Involvement and Offending Among Incarcerated Juveniles." Paper presented at the annual meeting of the American Society of Criminology, Boston, November 1995.

6. David Brownfield and Ann Marie Sorenson, "Self-Control and Juvenile Delinquency: Theoretical Issues and an Empirical Assessment of Selected Elements of a General Theory of Crime," *Deviant Behavior 14*:243–264 (1993); John Cochran, Peter Wood, and Bruce Arneklev, "Is the Religiosity–Delinquency Relationship Spurious? A Test of Arousal and Social Control Theories," *Journal of Research in Crime and Delinquency 31*:92–123 (1994).

7. Velmer Burton, T. David Evans, Francis Cullen, Kathleen Olivares, and R. Gregory Dunaway, "Age, Self-Control, and Adults' Offending Behaviors: A Research Note Assessing a General Theory of Crime," *Journal of Criminal Justice 27*:45–54 (1999); John Gibbs and Dennis Giever, "Self-Control and Its Manifestations Among University Students: An Empirical Test of Gottfredson and Hirschi's General Theory," *Justice Quarterly 12*:231–255 (1995).

8. Carey Herbert, "The Implications of Self-Control Theory for Workplace Offending." Paper presented at the annual meeting of the American Society of Criminology, San Diego, 1997.

9. Dennis Giever, Dana Lynskey, and Danette Monnet, "Gottfredson and Hirschi's General Theory of Crime and Youth Gangs: An Empirical Test on a Sample of Middle School Youth." Paper presented at the annual meeting of the American Society of Criminology, San Diego, 1997.

10. Douglas Longshore, Susan Turner, and Judith Stein, "Self-Control in a Delinquent Sample: An Examination of Construct Validity," *Criminology 34*:209–228 (1996).

11. Deng and Zhang, "Correlates of Self-Control."

12. Linda Pagani, Richard Tremblay, Frank Vitaro, and Sophie Parent, "Does Preschool Help Prevent Delinquency in Boys with a History of Perinatal Complications?" *Criminology 36*:245–268 (1998).

13. Velmer Burton, Francis Cullen, T. David Evans, Leanne Fiftal Alarid, and R. Gregory Dunaway, "Gender, Self-Control, and Delinquency," *Journal of Research in Crime and Delinquency 35*:123–147 (1998).

14. John Gibbs, Dennis Giever, and Jamie Martin, "Parental Management and Self-Control: An Empirical Test of Gottfredson and Hirschi's General Theory," *Journal of Research in Crime and Delinquency 35*:40–70 (1998).

15. Vic Bumphus and James Anderson, "Family Structure and Race in a Sample of Offenders," *Journal of Criminal Justice 27*:309–320 (1999).

16. Christopher Schreck, "Delinquent Victimization and Low Self-Control: An Extension and Test of a General Theory of Crime," *Justice Quarterly 16*:633–654 (1999).

17. Alexander Vazsonyi, Lloyd Pickering, Marianne Junger, and Dick Hessing, "An Empirical Test of a General Theory of Crime: A Four-Nation Comparative Study of Self-Control and the Prediction of Deviance," *Journal of Research in Crime and Delinquency 38*:91–131 (2001).

and relative deprivation, which have been shown to have a significant impact on delinquency rate differentials.

5. *People change.* The general theory assumes that delinquent propensity does not change; opportunities change. A number of research efforts show that factors that help control delinquent behavior, such as peer relations and school performance, vary over time. The social influences that are dominant in early adolescence, such as the peer group, may fade and be replaced by others, such as the nuclear family, in adulthood.[77] Also, as people mature, they may be better able to control their impulsive behavior.[78] These findings contradict the GTC, which assumes that levels of self-control, and therefore delinquent propensity, are constant and independent of personal relationships.

6. *Modest relationship.* Some research results support the proposition that self-control is a causal factor in delinquent and other forms of deviant behavior, but that the association is quite modest.[79] Low self-control alone cannot predict the onset of a delinquent or deviant career.

7. *Cross-cultural differences.* Some evidence shows that law violators in other countries do not lack self-control, indicating that the GTC may be culturally limited.[80] Behavior that may be considered imprudent in one culture may be socially acceptable in another and therefore cannot be viewed as "lack of self-control."[81]

Although questions like these remain, the strength of the general theory lies in its scope and breadth; it attempts to explain all forms of delinquency and deviance, from lower-class gang delinquency to sexual harassment in the business community.[82] By integrating concepts of delinquent choice, delinquent opportunity, socialization, and personality, Gottfredson and Hirschi make a plausible argument that all deviant behaviors may originate at the same source. Continued efforts are needed to test the GTC and establish the validity of its core concepts. It remains one of the key developments of modern criminological theory. **✔ Checkpoints**

Checkpoints

✔ *Latent trait theories assume a physical or psychological trait makes some people delinquency-prone.*

✔ *Opportunity to commit delinquency varies; latent traits remain stable.*

✔ *The general theory of crime says an impulsive personality is key.*

✔ *Impulsive people have low self-control and a weak bond to society.*

✔ *Impulsive people often cannot resist delinquent opportunities.*

 To quiz yourself on this material, go to questions 5.18–5.20 on the Juvenile Delinquency: The Core 2e Web site.

EVALUATING THE DEVELOPMENTAL VIEW

The developmental view is that a delinquent career must be understood as a passage along which people travel, that it has a beginning and an end, and that events and life circumstances influence the journey. The factors that affect a delinquent career may include structural factors, such as income and status; socialization factors, such as family and peer relations; biological factors, such as size and strength; psychological factors, including intelligence and personality; and opportunity factors, such as free time, inadequate police protection, and a supply of easily stolen merchandise.

Life course theories emphasize the influence of changing interpersonal and structural factors—that is, people change along with the world they live in. Latent trait theories assume that an individual's behavior is linked less to personal change than to changes in the surrounding world.

These perspectives differ in their view of human development. Do people constantly change, as life course theories suggest, or are they more stable, constant, and changeless, as the latent trait view indicates? Are the factors that produce criminality different at each stage of life, as the life course view suggests, or does a master trait—for example, impulsivity or self-control—steer the course of human behavior?

It is also possible that these two positions are not mutually exclusive and each may make a notable contribution to understanding the onset and continuity of a delinquent career. For example, recent research by Bradley Entner Wright and his associates found evidence supporting both latent trait and life course theories.[83] Their research, conducted with subjects in New Zealand, indicates that low self-control in childhood predicts disrupted social bonds and delinquent offending later in life, a finding that supports latent trait theory. They also found that maintaining positive social bonds helps reduce criminality and that such bonds could even counteract the effect of low self-control. Latent traits are an important influence on delinquency, but Wright's findings indicate that social relationships that form later in life appear to influence delinquent behavior "above and beyond" individuals' preexisting characteristics.[84] This finding may reflect the fact that there are two classes of criminals: a less serious group who are influenced by life events, and a more chronic group whose latent traits insulate them from any positive prosocial relationships.[85]

SUMMARY

- Life course theories argue that events that take place over the life course influence delinquent choices.
- The cause of delinquency constantly changes as people mature. At first, the nuclear family influences behavior; during adolescence, the peer group dominates; in adulthood, marriage and career are critical.
- There are a variety of pathways to delinquency: some kids are sneaky, others hostile, and still others defiant.
- According to the concept of problem behavior syndrome, delinquency may be just one of a variety of social problems, including health, physical, and interpersonal troubles.
- The social development model theory finds that living in a disorganized neighborhood helps weaken social bonds and sets people off on a delinquent path.
- According to interactional theory, delinquency influences social relations, which in turn influence delinquency; the relationship is interactive. The sources of delinquency evolve over time.

- Sampson and Laub's age-graded theory holds that the social sources of behavior change over the life course. People who develop social capital are best able to avoid antisocial entanglements. Important life events, or turning points, enable adult offenders to desist from delinquency. Among the most important are getting married and serving in the military.
- Latent trait theories hold that some underlying condition present from birth or soon after controls behavior. Suspect traits include low IQ, impulsivity, and personality structure. This underlying trait explains the continuity of offending because, once present, it remains with a person throughout the lifetime.
- The general theory of crime, developed by Gottfredson and Hirschi, integrates rational choice theory concepts. People with latent traits choose delinquency over nondelinquency; the opportunity for delinquency mediates their choice.

KEY TERMS

developmental theory, p. 108
life course theory, p. 108
latent trait theory, p. 108
early onset, p. 110
adolescent-limited, p. 111
life course persister, p. 111
pseudomaturity, p. 111
problem behavior syndrome
   (PBS), p. 111

authority conflict pathway, p. 112
covert pathway, p. 112
overt pathway, p. 112
social development model
   (SDM), p. 113
prosocial bonds, p. 114
interactional theory, p. 116

turning points, p. 118
social capital, p. 118
latent trait, p. 121
general theory of crime
   (GTC), p. 122
self-control, p. 124
impulsive, p. 124

QUESTIONS FOR DISCUSSION

1. Do you consider yourself a holder of "social capital?" If so, what form does it take?

2. A person gets a 1600 on the SAT. Without knowing this person, what personal, family, and social characteristics must he or she have? Another person becomes a serial killer. Without knowing this person, what personal, family, and social characteristics must he or she have? If "bad behavior" is explained by multiple

problems, is "good behavior" explained by multiple strengths?

3. Do you believe there is a "latent trait" that makes a person delinquency-prone, or is delinquency a function of environment and socialization?

4. Do you agree with Loeber's multiple pathways model? Do you know people who have traveled down those paths?

Luis Francisco is the leader of the Almighty Latin Kings and Queens Nation. He was convicted of murder in 1998 and sentenced to life imprisonment plus forty-five years. Luis Francisco's life has been filled with displacement, poverty, and chronic predatory delinquency. The son of a prostitute in Havana, at the age of nine he was sent to prison for robbery. He had trouble in school, and teachers described him as having attention problems; he dropped out in the seventh grade. On his nineteenth birthday in 1980, he emigrated to the United States and soon became a gang member in Chicago, joining the Latin Kings. After moving to the Bronx, he shot and killed his girlfriend in 1981. He fled to Chicago and was not apprehended until 1984. Sentenced to nine years for second-degree manslaughter, Luis Francisco ended up in a New York prison, where he started a prison chapter of the Latin Kings. As King Blood, Inka, First Supreme Crown, Francisco ruled the two thousand Latin Kings in and out of prison. Disciplinary troubles erupted when some Kings were found stealing from the organization. Infuriated, King Blood wrote to his street lieutenants and ordered their termination. Federal authorities, who had been monitoring Francisco's mail, arrested thirty-five Latin Kings. The other thirty-four pled guilty; only Francisco insisted on a trial, where he was found guilty of conspiracy to commit murder.

Explain Luis's behavior patterns from a developmental perspective. How would a latent trait theorist explain his escalating delinquent activities?

Do you think that a repeat offender like Luis Francisco could ever turn his life around and reenter society? It may prove more difficult than you think. To learn about some of the obstacles he would face, go to InfoTrac College Edition and read Devah Pager, "The Mark of a Criminal Record," *American Journal of Sociology* 108:937–977 (2003).

To read more about reentry problems on a Web site maintained by the federal government's Office of Justice Programs, click on Web Links under the Chapter Resources at http://cj.wadsworth.com/siegel_jdcore2e.

Pro/Con discussions and Viewpoint Essays on some of the topics in this chapter may be found at the Opposing Viewpoints Resource Center: www.gale.com/OpposingViewpoints.

Primary Prevention Efforts: Early Childhood

Delinquency prevention refers to intervening in a young person's life prior to engagement in a delinquent act. In some instances, prevention means helping kids develop defenses to help them resist the crime-promoting elements in their immediate environment. In other instances, it can mean helping experienced offenders who have already been involved in antisocial behaviors develop the skills that can enable them to resist delinquency and a delinquent way of life. An understanding of prevention is critical to the field of juvenile delinquency, because efforts to explain and understand why kids commit crime would exist in a vacuum if they could not provide a blueprint for eliminating, controlling, or preventing youth crime.

Traditionally, delinquency prevention efforts are divided into three types: primary prevention, secondary prevention, and tertiary prevention.

- *Primary prevention* focuses on improving the general well-being of individual children through such measures as providing access to health care services and education or modifying conditions in the physical environment, such as removing abandoned vehicles and improving the appearance of neighborhood buildings.
- *Secondary prevention* involves intervening with children and young people who are viewed as being at high risk for becoming juvenile offenders. Secondary programs involve provision of neighborhood youth programs designed to help such kids avoid involvement with gangs, drugs, and delinquency.
- *Tertiary prevention* focuses on intervening with juveniles who have already committed delinquent acts and have been adjudicated delinquent in juvenile court. These youth are placed in substance abuse treatment programs, anger management programs, group counseling, and so on. Here, the goal is to reduce repeat offending or recidivism.

In this section, we will discuss elements of primary prevention—those efforts that are aimed at providing children with an atmosphere in which they can develop and grow in a positive manner and become insulated from delinquency-producing forces in the family and community. Later in the text, secondary and tertiary efforts will be examined independently.

PRIMARY PREVENTION

All of the theoretical models of delinquency we have discussed in the preceding chapters suggest that the seeds of delinquency are planted early in life. While some people may begin their offending career relatively late—in their later teen years or even early adulthood—it appears that the majority experience antisocial episodes much earlier, in their early adolescence or before. Given this finding, primary prevention programs are often aimed at positively influencing the early risk factors or "root causes" of delinquency. Early risk factors may include structural factors such as poverty and residency in a lower-class neighborhood, socialization issues such as inadequate parental supervision and harsh or inconsistent discipline, and individual or trait issues such as a high level of hyperactivity or impulsiveness. Consequently, primary prevention interventions are often multidimensional, targeting more than one risk factor at a time. This approach attacks delinquency on a number of different fronts, including cognitive development, child skills training, and family support. What are some of the directions being explored to deliver primary prevention before the onset of a delinquent career?

HELPING FAMILIES CARE FOR CHILDREN'S HEALTH AND WELL-BEING

Delinquency theorists of all persuasions recognize that a positive home environment is a key element in a child's successful development. Because a supportive and loving home is so important for the successful development of a child, prevention programs are often aimed at improving family well-being. These programs are designed to help parents care for their children's health and general well-being, instill in their children positive values such as honesty and respect for others, and nurture prosocial behaviors.[1]

One of the most important types of family-based programs to prevent juvenile delinquency involves the provision of home visitation by experienced and trained human resource personnel.[2] One of the best-known home visitation programs is the Prenatal/Early Infancy Project (PEIP), which was started in Elmira, New York.[3] This program has three broad objectives:

1. To improve the outcomes of pregnancy.

2. To improve the quality of care that parents provide to their children (and their children's subsequent health and development).

3. To improve the women's own personal life-course development (completing their education, finding work, and planning future pregnancies).[4]

The program targeted first-time mothers-to-be who were under nineteen years of age, unmarried, or poor. In all, four hundred women were enrolled in the program. These mothers-to-be received home visits from nurses during pregnancy and then during the first two years of their child's life. Each home visit lasted about one and a quarter hours, and the mothers were visited on average every two weeks. The home visitors gave advice to the young women about child care, infant development, and the importance of eating properly and avoiding smoking and drinking during pregnancy.

Fifteen years after the program started, the children of the mothers who received home visits had half as many arrests as children of mothers who received no home visits (the control group).[5] It was also found that these children, compared with those in the control group, had fewer convictions and violations of probation, were less likely to run away from home, and were less likely to drink alcohol. In addition to the program's success in preventing juvenile crime and other delinquent activities, it also produced a number of important benefits for the mothers in the program, such as lower rates of child abuse and neglect, less crime in general, and less substance abuse, as well as less reliance on welfare and social services.[6] A Rand study found that these benefits translated into substantial cost savings for government and taxpayers.[7]

There are many other home visitation programs across the United States, such as one very similar to the Elmira program that was implemented in Memphis, Tennessee,[8] and the Hawaii Healthy Start program,[9] but none have been around long enough to test if they are effective in preventing juvenile delinquency. Because of this, it is difficult to say with much certainty how effective home visitation services are in preventing delinquency. The claim can, however, be made that home visitation can be very effective in reducing child abuse and neglect and child injuries and in improving the lives of families, particularly young mothers.[10] These too are very important benefits.

IMPROVING PARENTING SKILLS

Some programs aim to prevent delinquency in the long run by helping parents improve their parenting skills. This is another form of family support that has shown some success in preventing juvenile delinquency. Although the main focus of parent training programs is on the parents, many of these programs also involve children in an effort to improve the parent-child bond. For example, one of the most famous parenting skills programs, the Oregon Social Learning Center (OSLC), is based on the assumption that many parents do not know how to deal effectively with their children, sometimes ignoring their behavior and at other times reacting with explosive rage. Some parents discipline their children for reasons that have little to do with the children's behavior, instead reflecting their own frustrations. The OSLC program uses behavior modification techniques to help parents acquire proper disciplinary methods. Parents are asked to select several behaviors for change and to count the frequency of their occurrence. OSLC personnel teach social skills to reinforce positive behaviors and constructive disciplinary methods to discourage negative ones. Incentive programs are initiated in which a child can earn points for desirable behaviors. Points can be exchanged for allowance, prizes, or privileges. Parents are also taught disciplinary techniques that stress firmness and consistency rather than "nattering" (low-intensity behaviors, such as scowling or scolding) or explosive discipline, such as hitting or screaming. One important technique is the "time-out," in which the child is removed for brief isolation in a quiet room. Parents are taught the importance of setting rules and sticking to them. A number of evaluation studies show that improving parenting skills can lead to reductions in juvenile delinquency.[11] A Rand study found that parent training costs about one-twentieth what a home visit program costs and is more effective in preventing serious crimes.[12]

PROVIDING DAY CARE

Day care services are available to children as young as six weeks old in the United States and other Western countries.[13] In addition to allowing parents to work, day care provides children with a number of important benefits, including social interaction with other children and stimulation of their cognitive, sensory, and motor control skills. Among the best-known early childhood intervention programs that provide high-quality day care services is the Syracuse University Family Development Research Program's Quality Infant and Toddler Caregiving Workshop. This program involves high-risk women during the later stages of their pregnancies. After women have given birth, paraprofessionals are assigned to work with them, encouraging sound parent-child relationships, providing nutrition information, and helping them establish relationships with social service agencies. In addition, their children receive free full-time day care, designed to develop their intellectual abilities, up to age five. A ten-year follow-up compared the children involved in the program with a control group and found that those who received the intervention were less likely to be referred to the juvenile court for delinquency offenses, more likely to express positive feelings about themselves, and more likely to take an active role in dealing with personal problems. Girls seemed especially to benefit, doing better in school, and parents were more likely to express prosocial attitudes.[14]

PROVIDING BETTER NUTRITION

Some trait theorists believe that prevention efforts might best be served by altering the biochemical factors, such as poor nutrition, that have been linked to the onset of delinquent behavior. For example, in one study researchers led by Adrian Raine looked at the long-term effects of a two-year diet enrichment program in which kids were placed at only three years old.[15] One hundred randomly selected children were placed in the program, which provided nutritious lunches, physical exercise, and enhanced education. They were then compared with a control group who did not participate in the program. By age seventeen, kids who had been malnourished before they entered the nutrition program had higher scores on physical and psychological well-being than malnourished kids who had not been in the program. By age twenty-three, the malnourished kids who had been in the program twenty years earlier still did better on personality tests and had lower levels of self-reported crimes than the malnourished children who not been placed in the program. Overall, the results showed that providing children with nutritious diets and enriched environments is associated with greater mental health and reduced antisocial activities later in life.

HELPING KIDS PREPARE FOR SCHOOL

In addition to helping parents become more effective caregivers, primary prevention programs focus on helping kids get ready for the school experience. Preschool is typically provided to children ages three to five years. These are the formative years of brain development; more learning takes place during this developmental stage than at any other stage over the life course. Low

intelligence and school failure are important risk factors for juvenile delinquency.[16] For these reasons, highly structured, cognitive-based preschool programs offer young children an important start in life.

One of the most widely admired preschool programs is the Perry Preschool in Ypsilanti, Michigan. Started in the mid-1960s, it provides disadvantaged children with a program of educational enrichment supplemented with weekly home visits. The Perry formula is that a good preschool program can help children in poverty make a better start in their transition from home to community and thereby set more of them on the path to becoming economically self-sufficient, socially responsible adults.[17] The Perry program provides high-quality, active-learning programming administered by professional teachers who have worked in the field for two years. The educational approach is focused on supporting the development of the children's cognitive and social skills through individualized teaching and learning. Its success is largely due to the following components:

- A developmentally appropriate curriculum that views children as active, self-initiated learners

- Small classrooms of twenty children and at least two staff, which allows a more supervised and supportive learning environment

- Staff who are trained in early childhood development and education, who receive supervision and ongoing instruction, and who actively communicate with parents

- Sensitivity to the non-educational needs of disadvantaged children and their families, which includes providing meals and recommending other social service agencies

- Ongoing monitoring and evaluation of both teachers' activities and children's behaviors and development

Evaluations of the program have demonstrated a wide range of successful outcomes for Perry Preschool children compared with those who do not receive the intervention, including these:

- Less delinquency, including less contact with juvenile justice officials, fewer arrests at age nineteen, and less involvement in serious fights, gang fights, causing injuries, and police contact

- Less antisocial behavior and misconduct during elementary school and at age fifteen

- Higher academic achievement, including higher scores on standardized tests of intellectual ability and higher high school grades

- Fewer school dropouts at age nineteen (33 percent versus 51 percent), and higher rates of high school graduation

- Greater commitment to school and more favorable attitudes about high school
- Higher rates of employment (50 percent versus 32 percent) and pay, and greater job satisfaction
- Greater economic independence and less reliance on public assistance, including welfare
- Fewer pregnancies and births among women at age nineteen[18]

CAN PRIMARY PREVENTION WORK?

The success of these and other primary prevention programs seems to indicate that they can be effective in reducing the incidence of delinquency. However, their effectiveness often rests in their targeting of important individual- and family-level risk factors for delinquency, such as low intelligence, impulsiveness, and inconsistent and poor parenting. Even if these problems can be identified, families may be required to get involved in a package of child- and parent-centered interventions that target multiple risk factors ranging from mental health to educational enrichment.[19] A number of program evaluations, including the Great Smoky Mountains Study of Youth in North Carolina, the Patterns of Care program in San Diego, California, and the Southwestern Pennsylvania Costs of Services in Medicaid Study, have found that the first step toward obtaining effective treatment is to provide families with access to mental health and other social services. Research from these studies shows that the delay between detecting problems and the families' ability to obtain treatment is still extremely low. For primary prevention ultimately to be successful, effective mechanisms must be developed for obtaining timely, specialized help that, although costly, will provide long-term savings by helping children avoid involvement in antisocial behavior and its legal consequences.

Gender and Delinquency

CHAPTER OUTLINE

CHAPTER OBJECTIVES

After reading this chapter you should:

1. Be familiar with the changes in the female delinquency rate.
2. Understand the cognitive differences between males and females.
3. Be able to discuss the differences in socialization between boys and girls and how this may affect their behavior.
4. Understand the psychological differences between the sexes.
5. Be able to discuss the early work on gender, delinquency, and human traits.
6. Know the elements contemporary trait theorists view as the key to understanding gender differences, such as psychological makeup and hormonal differences.
7. Know how socialization is thought to affect delinquency rates.
8. Discuss the views of contemporary socialization theorists.
9. Know to what the term *liberal feminism* refers.
10. Discuss how critical feminists view female delinquency and describe Hagan's power-control theory.
11. Be familiar with how the treatment girls receive by the juvenile justice system differs from the treatment of boys.

On May 4, 2003, girls at a "powder-puff" touch football game in Northbrook, Illinois, went on a rampage that was captured on videotape. Senior girls began the event by chugging beer straight from a keg provided by some parents. Then they began pounding some of the younger girls with their fists and with bats, while pushing them down into the mud. They doused the novice football players with excrement, garbage, and food. The students apparently arranged the event in secret, making sure that school administrators were kept unaware of the time and place. In the aftermath, five girls were hospitalized, including one who broke an ankle and another who suffered a cut that required ten stitches in her head; the attackers were suspended from school and criminal charges filed.

The tape was circulated to the news media and it was shown repeatedly all around the country.

CNN. VIEW THE CNN VIDEO CLIP OF THIS STORY AND ANSWER RELATED CRITICAL THINKING QUESTIONS ON YOUR JUVENILE DELINQUENCY: THE CORE 2E CD.

To find information on the state of adolescent girls and the risks they face, go to the Web site of the Commonwealth Fund by clicking on Web Links under the Chapter Resources at http://cj.wadsworth.com/siegel_jdcore2e.

The Northbrook incident was shocking because it involved young girls in an extremely violent incident, an image that defies the traditional image of females as less aggressive than males. This vision is not new.

To early delinquency experts, the female offender was an aberration who engaged in crimes that usually had a sexual connotation—prostitution, running away (which presumably leads to sexual misadventure), premarital sex, and crimes of sexual passion (killing a boyfriend or a husband).[1] Criminologists often ignored female offenders, assuming that they rarely violated the law, or if they did, that their illegal acts were status-type offenses. Female delinquency was viewed as emotional or family-related, and such problems were not an important concern of criminologists. In fact, the few "true" female delinquents were considered anomalies whose criminal activity was a function of taking on masculine characteristics, a concept referred to as the **masculinity hypothesis.**[2]

Contemporary interest in the association between gender and delinquency has surged, fueled by observations that although the female delinquency rate is still much lower than the male rate, it is growing at a faster pace than male delinquency. Moreover, the types of delinquent acts that young women are engaging in seem quite similar to those of young men. Larceny and aggravated assault, the crimes for which most young men are arrested, are also the most common offenses for which females are arrested. There is evidence that girls are getting more heavily involved in gangs and gang violence.[3] Although girls still commit less crime than boys, members of both sexes are similar in the onset and development of their offending careers.[4] In societies with high rates of male delinquency, there are also high rates of female delinquency. Over time, male and female arrest rates rise and fall in a parallel fashion.[5]

Another reason for the interest in gender studies is that conceptions of gender differences have changed. A feminist approach to understanding crime is now firmly established. The stereotype of the female delinquent as a sexual deviant is no longer taken seriously.[6] The result has been an increased effort to conduct research that would adequately explain differences and similarities in male and female offending patterns.

This chapter provides an overview of gender factors in delinquency. We first discuss some of the gender differences in development and how they may relate to the gender differences in offending rates. Then we turn to some explanations for

masculinity hypothesis
View that women who commit crimes have biological and psychological traits similar to those of men.

these differences: (1) the trait view, (2) the socialization view, (3) the liberal feminist view, and (4) the critical feminist view.

GENDER DIFFERENCES IN DEVELOPMENT

Gender differences in cognition, socialization, and behavior may exist as early as infancy, when boys are able to express emotions at higher rates. Infant girls show greater control over their emotions, whereas boys are more easily angered and depend more on inputs from their mothers.[7] There are indications that gender differences in socialization and development do exist and that they may have an effect on juvenile offending patterns.[8]

Socialization Differences

Psychologists believe that differences in the way females and males are socialized affect their development. Males learn to value independence, whereas females are taught that their self-worth depends on their ability to sustain relationships. Girls, therefore, run the risk of losing themselves in their relationships with others, while boys may experience a chronic sense of alienation. Because so many relationships go sour, females also run the risk of feeling alienated because of the failure to achieve relational success.[9]

Although there are few gender differences in aggression during the first few years of life, girls are socialized to be less aggressive than boys and are supervised more closely.[10] Differences in aggression become noticeable between ages three and six, when children are socialized into organized groups, such as the daycare center. Males are more likely to display physical aggression, whereas females display relational aggression—for example, by excluding disliked peers from play groups.[11]

As they mature, girls learn to respond to provocation by feeling anxious, unlike boys, who are encouraged to retaliate.[12] Overall, women are much more likely to feel distressed than men.[13] Although females get angry as often as males, many have been taught to blame themselves for such feelings. Females are, therefore, much more likely than males to respond to anger with feelings of depression, anxiety, and shame. Females are socialized to fear that anger will harm relationships; males are encouraged to react with "moral outrage," blaming others for their discomfort.[14]

Females are also more likely than males to be targets of sexual and physical abuse. Female victims have been shown to suffer more seriously from these attacks, sustaining damage to their self-image; victims of sexual abuse find it difficult to build autonomy and life skills.

Research shows that males are more likely than females to behave in an aggressive manner. There is evidence that differences in socialization, cognition, and personality may help explain gender-based disparity in rates of antisocial and violent behaviors.

© Dennis MacDonald/PhotoEdit

Cognitive Differences

There are also cognitive differences between males and females starting in childhood. Males excel in tasks that assess the ability to manipulate visual images in working memory, whereas females do better in tasks that require retrieval from long-term memory and the acquisition and use of verbal information.[15] Girls learn to speak earlier and faster, and with better pronunciation, most likely because parents talk more to their infant daughters than to their infant sons. Girls are far less likely than boys to have reading problems, but boys do much better on standardized math tests, which is attributed by some experts to their strategies for approaching math problems. Boys in the United States are more likely than girls to be dyslexic.

In most cases cognitive differences are small, narrowing, and usually attributed to cultural expectations. When given training, girls can increase their visual-spatial skills. However, differences still exert a penalty on young girls. For example, performance on the mathematics portion of the Scholastic Aptitude Test (SAT) still favors males: twice as many boys as girls attain scores over 500 and thirteen times as many boys as girls attain scores over 700.[16]

Personality Differences

Girls are often stereotyped as talkative, but research shows that in many situations boys spend more time talking than girls do. Females are more willing to reveal their feelings and more likely to express concern for others. Females are more concerned about finding the "meaning of life" and less interested in competing for material success.[17] Males are more likely to introduce new topics and to interrupt conversations.

Adolescent females use different knowledge than males and have different ways of interpreting their interactions with others. These gender differences may have an impact on self-esteem and self-concept. Research shows that, as adolescents develop, male self-esteem and self-concept rise whereas female self-confidence is lowered.[18] One reason is that girls are more likely to stress about their weight and be more dissatisfied with the size and shape of their bodies.[19] Young girls are regularly confronted with unrealistically high standards of slimness that make them extremely unhappy with their own bodies; it is not surprising that the incidence of eating disorders such as *anorexia* and *bulimia* have increased markedly in recent years. Psychologist Carol Gilligan uncovered an alternative explanation for this decline in female self-esteem: as girls move into adolescence, they become aware of the conflict between the positive way they see themselves and the negative way society views females. Many girls respond by "losing their voices"—that is, submerging their own feelings and accepting the negative view of women conveyed by adult authorities.[20]

These various gender differences are described in Concept Summary 6.1.

Concept Summary **6.1**   **Gender Differences**

	Females	**Males**
Socialization	Sustain relationships. Be less aggressive. Blame self.	Be independent. Be aggressive. Externalize anger.
Cognitive	Have superior verbal ability. Speak earlier. Have better pronunciation. Read better.	Have superior visual/spatial ability. Are better at math.
Personality	Have lower self-esteem. Are self-aware. Have better attention span.	Have high self-esteem. Are materialistic. Have low attention span.

What Does This Mean to Me?

Sexual Harassment

Can gender differences in perception shape the perception of sexual harassment? For example, research shows that males and females both generally agree that sexual coercion and sexual propositions constitute sexual harassment. Yet males do not think that sex-stereotyped jokes are a form of harassment while females do; females think that repeated requests for dates after a refusal constitute harassment while males think there is nothing wrong with asking girls out again and again. It is not surprising to discover that females perceive that sexual harassment has occurred in situations where males find no wrongdoing.

1. Do you think that these different perceptions are biologically related or a matter of socialization?
2. (For women): Have you ever been in a situation where you felt yourself being sexually harassed by a male who thought he was doing nothing wrong?
3. (For men): Have you ever been accused of sexual harassment by a woman you know even though you personally felt you did nothing wrong?

The mission of the National Council for Research on Women is to enhance the connections among research, policy analysis, advocacy, and innovative programming on behalf of women and girls. Visit their site by clicking on Web Links under the Chapter Resources at http://cj. wadsworth.com/siegel_ jdcore2e.

What Causes Gender Differences?

Why do these gender differences occur? Some experts suggest that gender differences may have a biological origin: males and females are essentially different. They have somewhat different brain organizations; females are more left-brain-oriented and males more right-brain-oriented. (The left brain is believed to control language; the right, spatial relations.) Others point to the hormonal differences between the sexes as the key to understanding their behavior.

Another view is that gender differences are a result of the interaction of socialization, learning, and enculturation. Boys and girls may behave differently because they have been exposed to different styles of socialization, learned different values, and had different cultural experiences. It follows, then, that if members of both sexes were equally exposed to the factors that produce delinquency, their delinquency rates would be equivalent.[21] According to psychologist Sandra Bem's **gender-schema theory,** our culture polarizes males and females by forcing them to obey mutually exclusive gender roles, or "scripts." Girls are expected to be "feminine," exhibiting traits such as being sympathetic and gentle. In contrast, boys are expected to be "masculine," exhibiting assertiveness and dominance. Children internalize these scripts and accept gender polarization as normal. Children's self-esteem becomes wrapped up in how closely their behavior conforms to the proper sex role stereotype. When children begin to perceive themselves as either *boys* or *girls* (which occurs at about age three), they search for information to help them define their role; they begin to learn what behavior is appropriate for their sex.[22] Girls are expected to behave according to the appropriate script and to seek approval of their behavior: Are they acting as girls should at that age? Masculine behavior is to be avoided. In contrast, males look for cues from their peers to define their masculinity; aggressive behavior may be rewarded with peer approval, whereas sensitivity is viewed as nonmasculine.[23]

See the accompanying What Does This Mean to Me feature for an interesting perspective on the issue of sexual harassment.

GENDER DIFFERENCES AND DELINQUENCY

gender-schema theory
A theory of development that holds that children internalize gender scripts that reflect the gender-related social practices of the culture. Once internalized, these gender scripts predispose the kids to construct a self-identity that is consistent with them.

Regardless of their origin, gender distinctions may partly explain the significant gender differences in the delinquency rate. Males seem more aggressive and less likely to form attachments to others, factors that might increase their crime rates. Males view aggression as an appropriate means to gain status. Boys are also more likely than girls to socialize with deviant peers, and when they do, they display personality traits that make them more susceptible to delinquency. Recent research by Jean Bottcher found that young boys perceive their roles as being more dominant than young girls. Male perceptions of power, their ability to have freedom and hang with their friends, helped explain the gender differences in delinquency.[24]

Girls are shielded by their moral sense, which directs them to avoid harming others. Their moral sensitivity may counterbalance the effects of family problems.[25] Females display more self-control than males, a factor that has been related to criminality.[26]

Females are more verbally proficient, a skill that may help them deal with conflict without resorting to violence. They are taught to be less aggressive and view

A youth worker talks with young girls in an after-school program. Are gender differences in personality a matter of experience, or do you believe that males and females are inherently different?

© Gale Zucker/Stock, Boston

A number of institutes at major universities are devoted to the study of women's issues. You can visit the site of the one at the University of Michigan by clicking on Web Links under the Chapter Resources at http://cj.wadsworth.com/ siegel_jdcore2e.

Checkpoints

✔ *Female delinquency was considered unimportant by early delinquency experts because girls rarely committed crime, and when they did it was sexual in nature.*

✔ *Interest in female delinquency has risen because the female crime rate has been increasing, while the male rate is in decline.*

✔ *There are distinct gender patterns in development that may explain crime rate differences.*

✔ *Girls are socialized to be less aggressive than boys.*

✔ *Girls read better and have better verbal skills than boys.*

✔ *Gender differences may have both biological and social origins.*

✔ *The female proportion of the delinquency rate has grown at a faster pace than that of males during the past twenty-five years.*

belligerence as a lack of self-control.[27] When girls are aggressive, they are more likely than boys to hide their behavior from adults; girls who "bully" others are less likely than boys to admit their behavior.[28]

Cognitive and personality differences are magnified when children internalize gender-specific behaviors. Boys who aren't tough are labeled sissies. Girls are expected to form closer bonds with their friends and to share feelings.

Gender Patterns in Delinquency

Over the past decades, females have increased their participation in delinquent behaviors at a faster rate than males. Arrest data indicate that juvenile females make up a greater percentage of the arrest statistics today than they did thirty years ago. In 1967, females constituted 13 percent of all juvenile index-crime arrests; today they make up about 25 percent. The most recent arrest data show that between 1993 and 2002 the total teenage male arrest rate *decreased* by about 16 percent and the female rate *increase*d by 6 percent.[29] Even more striking was the relative change in arrests for serious violent crimes—during a period of falling crime rates (1993 to 2002), teenage male violent crime arrests declined 39 percent, while female arrests declined a more modest 13 percent.

The Monitoring the Future self-report study also shows that patterns of male and female criminality appear to be converging. Self-report data indicate that the rank-ordering of male and female deviant behaviors is similar. The illegal acts most common for boys—petty larceny, using a false ID, and smoking marijuana—are also the ones most frequently committed by girls.[30]

Violent Behavior

Gender differences in the delinquency rate may be narrowing, but males continue to be overrepresented in arrests for violent crimes. For example, almost all homicide offenders are males. In 2002, of the more than 973 juveniles arrested for murder, only 101 were female.[31]

One reason for the gender disparity in lethal violence is that males and females display differences in the victims they target and the weapons they use. The typical male juvenile kills a friend or acquaintance with a handgun during an argument. In contrast, the typical female is as likely to kill a family member as an acquaintance

✔ *Though males still are arrested more often than females, the intergender patterns of delinquency are remarkably similar.*

To quiz yourself on this material, go to questions 6.1–6.5 on the Juvenile Delinquency: The Core 2e Web site.

and is more likely to use a knife. Both males and females tend to kill males—generally their brothers, fathers, or friends.

Why do these differences occur, and why are girls increasing their involvement in delinquent activities at a faster pace than boys? The wide range of opinions on these questions will be presented in the remaining sections of this chapter. ✔ Checkpoints

ARE FEMALE DELINQUENTS BORN THAT WAY?

There is a long tradition of tracing gender differences in delinquency to traits that are uniquely male or female. The argument that biological and psychological differences between males and females can explain differences in crime rates is not a new one. The earliest criminologists focused on physical characteristics believed to be precursors of crime.

Early Biological Explanations

To read more about the chivalry hypothesis and how it relates to gang delinquency, click on Web Links under the Chapter Resources at http://cj.wadsworth.com/siegel_jdcore2e.

With the publication in 1895 of *The Female Offender,* Lombroso (with William Ferrero) extended his work on criminality to females.[32] Lombroso maintained that women were lower on the evolutionary scale than men, more childlike and less intelligent.[33] Women who committed crimes could be distinguished from "normal" women by physical characteristics—excessive body hair, wrinkles, and an abnormal cranium, for example.[34] In appearance, delinquent females appeared closer to men than to other women. The masculinity hypothesis suggested that delinquent girls had excessive male characteristics.[35]

Lombrosian thought had a significant influence for much of the twentieth century. Delinquency rate differentials were explained in terms of gender-based differences. For example, in 1925 Cyril Burt linked female delinquency to menstruation.[36] Similarly, William Healy and Augusta Bronner suggested that males' physical superiority enhanced their criminality. Their research showed that about 70 percent of the delinquent girls they studied had abnormal weight and size, a finding that supported the "masculinity hypothesis."[37]

So-called experts suggested that female delinquency goes unrecorded because the female is the instigator rather than the perpetrator.[38] Females first use their sexual charms to instigate crime and then beguile males in the justice system to obtain deferential treatment. This observation, referred to as the **chivalry hypothesis,** holds that gender differences in the delinquency rate can be explained by the fact that female criminality is overlooked or forgiven by male agents of the justice system. Those who believe in the chivalry hypothesis point to data showing that even though women make up about 20 percent of arrestees, they account for less than 5 percent of inmates. Police and other justice system personnel may be less willing to penalize female offenders than male offenders.[39]

Early Psychological Explanations

chivalry hypothesis (also known as paternalism hypothesis)
The view that low female crime and delinquency rates are a reflection of the leniency with which police treat female offenders.

Psychologists also viewed the physical differences between males and females as a basis for their behavior differentials. Sigmund Freud maintained that girls interpret their lack of a penis as a sign that they have been punished. Boys fear that they can be punished by having their penis cut off, and thus learn to fear women. From this conflict comes *penis envy,* which often produces an inferiority complex in girls, forcing them to make an effort to compensate for their "defect." One way to compensate is to identify with their mothers and accept a maternal role. Also, girls may attempt to compensate for their lack of a penis by dressing well and beautifying themselves.[40] Freud also claimed that "if a little girl persists in her first wish—to grow into a boy—in extreme cases she will end as a manifest homosexual, and otherwise she will exhibit markedly masculine traits in the conduct of her later life, will choose a masculine vocation, and so on."[41]

At midcentury, psychodynamic theorists suggested that girls are socialized to be passive, which helps explain their low crime rate. However, this condition also makes some females susceptible to being manipulated by men; hence, their participation in sex-related crimes such as prostitution. A girl's wayward behavior, psychoanalysts suggested, was restricted to neurotic theft (kleptomania) and overt sexual acts, which were symptoms of personality maladaption.[42]

According to these early versions of the psychoanalytic approach, gender differences in the delinquency rate can be traced to differences in psychological orientation. Male delinquency reflects aggressive traits, whereas female delinquency is a function of repressed sexuality, gender conflict, and abnormal socialization.

Contemporary Trait Views

Contemporary biosocial and psychological theorists have continued the tradition of attributing gender differences in delinquency to physical and emotional traits (see Figure 6.1). These theorists recognize that it is the interaction of biological and psychological traits with the social environment that produces delinquency.

Precocious Sexuality

Early theorists linked female delinquency to early or **precocious sexuality.** According to this view, girls who experience an early onset of physical maturity are most likely to engage in antisocial behavior.[43] Female delinquents were believed to be promiscuous and more sophisticated than male delinquents.[44] Linking female delinquency to sexuality was responsible, in part, for the view that female delinquency is symptomatic of maladjustment.[45]

Equating female delinquency purely with sexual activity is no longer taken seriously, but early sexuality has been linked to other problems, such as a higher risk of teen pregnancy and sexually transmitted diseases.[46] Empirical evidence suggests that girls who reach puberty at an early age are at the highest risk for delinquency.[47] One reason is that "early bloomers" may be more attractive to older adolescent boys, and increased contact with this high-risk group places the girls in jeopardy for antisocial behavior. Girls who are more developed relative to their peers are more likely to socialize at an early age and to get involved in deviant behaviors, especially "party deviance," such as drinking, smoking, and substance abuse. Early puberty is most likely to encourage delinquent activities that occur in the context of socializing with peers and having romantic relationships with boys.[48] The delinquency gap between early and late bloomers narrows when the latter group reaches sexual maturity and increases in exposure to boys.[49] Biological and social factors seem to interact to postpone or accelerate female delinquent activity.

Hormonal Effects

As you may recall from chapter 3, some biosocial theorists link antisocial behavior to hormonal influences.[50] One view is that hormonal imbalance may influence aggressive behavior. For example, changes in the level of the hormone *cortisol,* which is secreted by the adrenal glands in response to any kind of physical or psychological stress, has been linked to conduct problems in young girls.[51]

Another view is that excessive amounts of male hormones (androgens) are related to delinquency. The androgen most often related to antisocial behavior is testosterone.[52] In general, females who test higher for testosterone are more likely to engage in stereotypical male behaviors.[53] Females who have low androgen levels are less aggressive than males, whereas those who have elevated levels will take on characteristically male traits, including aggression.[54]

Some females are overexposed to male hormones in utero. Females affected this way may become "constitutionally masculinized." They may develop abnormal hair growth, large musculature, low voice, irregular menstrual cycle, and hyperaggressiveness; this condition can also develop as a result of steroid use or certain medical dis-

precocious sexuality
Sexual experimentation in early adolescence.

Figure 6.1 **Trait Differences in Male and Female Delinquents**

A longitudinal study that followed children born on the Hawaiian island of Kauai in 1955 for thirty-two years found that the most reliable traits for predicting delinquency in boys included these:

- Disordered care-taking

- Lack of educational stimulation in the home

- Reading problems

- A need for remedial education by age 10

- Late maturation

- An unemployed, criminal, or absent father

In addition, boys appeared to be particularly vulnerable to early childhood learning problems, leading to school failure. A combination of reaching puberty late and lack of a significant male role model also encouraged the persistence of antisocial behavior throughout adolescence.

In the same longitudinal study, researchers found that delinquent girls tend to have the following traits:

- A history of minor congenital defects

- Low development scores by age 2

- A need for mental health services by age 10

- Earlier-than-average onset of puberty

Researchers hypothesize that birth defects and slow early development could lead to poor self-esteem, whereas early sexual development may encourage sexual relationships with older males and conflict with parents.

Source: Felton Earls and Albert Reiss, *Breaking the Cycle: Predicting and Preventing Crime* (Washington, DC: National Institute of Justice, 1994), pp. 24–25.

orders.[55] Author Diana Fishbein has reviewed the literature in this area and finds that, after holding constant a variety of factors (including IQ, age, and environment), females exposed to male hormones in utero are more likely to engage in aggressive behavior later in life.[56]

Premenstrual Syndrome Early biotheorists suspected that premenstrual syndrome (PMS) was a direct cause of the relatively rare instances of female violence: "For several days prior to and during menstruation, the stereotype has been that 'raging hormones' doom women to irritability and poor judgment—two facets of premenstrual syndrome."[57] The link between PMS and delinquency was popularized by Katharina Dalton, whose studies of Englishwomen led her to conclude that females are more likely to commit suicide and be aggressive and otherwise antisocial before or during menstruation.[58]

Today there is conflicting evidence on the relationship between PMS and female delinquency. Diana Fishbein, an expert on biosocial theory, concludes that there is an association between elevated levels of female aggression and menstruation. Research shows that a significant number of incarcerated females committed their crimes during the premenstrual phase, and also that a small percentage of women appear vulnerable to cyclical hormonal changes that make them more prone to anxiety and hostility.[59] Fishbein notes that even though a majority of women do not actually engage in criminal behavior during their menstrual cycle the evidence does show a link.[60] While this evidence is persuasive, the true relationship between crime and the female menstrual cycle still remains unknown.[61] It is possible that the stress associated with menstruation produces crime, and it is also possible that the stress of antisocial behavior produces early menstruation.[62]

Aggression According to some biosocial theorists, gender differences in the delinquency rate can be explained by inborn differences in aggression; males are inherently more likely to be aggressive.[63] Some psychologists have suggested that these differences are present very early in life, appearing before socialization can influence behavior. Males seem to be more aggressive in all societies for which data are available; gender differences in aggression can even be found in nonhuman primates.[64]

Some biosocial theorists argue that gender-based differences in aggression reflect the dissimilarities in the male and female reproductive systems. Males are more aggressive because they wish to possess as many sex partners as possible to increase their chances of producing offspring. Females have learned to control their aggressive impulses because having multiple mates does not increase their chances of conception. Instead, females concentrate on acquiring things that will help them rear their offspring, such as a reliable mate who will supply material resources.[65]

Contemporary Psychological Views

Because girls are socialized to be less aggressive than boys, it is possible that the young women who do get involved in antisocial and violent behavior are suffering from some form of mental anguish or abnormality. Girls are also more likely than boys to be involved in status offenses such as running away and truancy, behaviors that suggest underlying psychological distress.

Research indicates that antisocial adolescent girls do suffer a wide variety of psychiatric problems and have dysfunctional and violent relationships.[66] Incarcerated adolescent female offenders have more acute mental health symptoms and psychological disturbances than male offenders.[67] Female delinquents score high on psychological tests measuring such traits as psychopathic deviation, schizophrenia, paranoia, and psychasthenia (a psychological disorder characterized by phobias, obsessions, compulsions, or excessive anxiety).[68] Clinical interviews indicate that female delinquents are significantly more likely than males to suffer from mood disorders, including any disruptive disorder, major depressive disorder, and separation anxiety disorder.[69] For example, serious female delinquents have been found to have a relatively high incidence of callous-unemotional (CU) traits, an affective disorder described by a lack of remorse or shame, poor judgment, failure to learn by experience, and chronic lying.[70] In sum, there are some experts who believe that female delinquents suffer from psychological deficits ranging from lack of self-control to serious impairments.[71]

SOCIALIZATION VIEWS

Socialization views are based on the idea that a child's social development may be the key to understanding delinquent behavior. If a child experiences impairment, family disruption, and so on, the child will be more susceptible to delinquent associations and criminality.

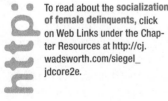

To read about the **socialization of female delinquents**, click on Web Links under the Chapter Resources at http://cj.wadsworth.com/siegel_jdcore2e.

Linking crime rate variations to gender differences in socialization is not a recent phenomenon. In a 1928 work, *The Unadjusted Girl,* W. I. Thomas suggested that some girls who have not been socialized under middle-class family controls can become impulsive thrill seekers. According to Thomas, female delinquency is linked to the "wish" for luxury and excitement.[72] Inequities in social class condemn poor girls from demoralized families to using sex as a means to gain amusement, pretty clothes, and other luxuries. Precocious sexuality makes these girls vulnerable to older men, who lead them down the path to decadence.[73]

Socialization and Delinquency

Scholars concerned with gender differences in crime are interested in the distinction between the lifestyles of males and females. Girls may be supervised more closely than boys. If girls behave in a socially disapproved fashion, their parents may be more likely to notice. Adults may be more tolerant of deviant behavior in boys and expect boys to act tough and take risks.[74] Closer supervision restricts the opportu-

According to contemporary socialization views, if a girl grows up in an atmosphere of sexual tension, where hostility exists between her parents or where the parents are absent, she likely will turn to outside sources for affection and support. In their reaction to loneliness, frustration, and parental hostility, girls begin to engage in the same activities as boys: staying out late at night, drinking, partying, and riding around with their friends.

nity for crime and the time available to mingle with delinquent peers. It follows, then, that the adolescent girl who is growing up in a troubled home and lacks supervision may be more prone to delinquency.[75]

Focus on Socialization In the 1950s, a number of researchers began to focus on gender-specific socialization patterns. They made three assumptions about gender differences in socialization: families exert a more powerful influence on girls than on boys; girls do not form close same-sex friendships but compete with their peers; and female criminals are primarily sexual offenders. First, parents are stricter with girls because they perceive them as needing control. In some families, adolescent girls rebel against strict controls. In others, where parents are absent or unavailable, girls may turn to the streets for companionship. Second, girls rarely form close relationships with female peers because they view them as rivals for males who would make eligible marriage partners.[76] Instead, girls enter into affairs with older men who exploit them, involve them in sexual deviance, and father their illegitimate children.[77] The result is prostitution, drug abuse, and marginal lives. Their daughters repeat this pattern in a never-ending cycle of exploitation.

Broken Homes/Fallen Women A number of experts share emphasis on the family as a primary influence on delinquent behavior. Male delinquents were portrayed as rebels who esteemed "toughness," "excitement," and other lower-class values. Males succumbed to the lure of delinquency when they perceived few legitimate opportunities. In contrast, female delinquents were portrayed as troubled adolescents who suffered inadequate home lives, and more often than not, were victims of sexual and physical abuse. Ruth Morris described delinquent girls as unattractive youths who reside in homes marked by family tensions.[78] In *The Delinquent Girl* (1970), Clyde Vedder and Dora Somerville suggest that female delinquency is usually a problem of adjustment to family pressure; an estimated 75 percent of institutionalized girls have family problems.[79] They also suggest that girls have serious problems in a male-dominated culture with rigid and sometimes unfair social practices.

Other early efforts linked "rebellious" behavior to sexual conflicts in the home.[80] Broken or disrupted homes were found to predict female delinquency.[81] Females petitioned to juvenile court were more likely than males to be charged with ungovernable behavior and sex offenses. They also were more likely to reside in single-parent homes.[82] Studies of incarcerated juveniles found that most of the male delinquents were incarcerated for burglary and other theft-related offenses, but female delinquents tended to be involved in incorrigibility and sex offenses. The conclusion: boys became delinquent to demonstrate their masculinity; girls were delinquent because of hostility toward parents and a consequent need to obtain attention from others.[83]

Contemporary Socialization Views

Investigators continue to support the view that female delinquents have more dysfunctional home lives than male offenders.[84] Institutionalized girls tell of lives filled with severe physical and sexual abuse. In addition to tragic home lives, delinquent girls report social experiences that were frustrating or even degrading.[85]

Preventing Teen Pregnancy

Girls who become pregnant during their teen years often find themselves on a rocky road. Many drop out of school, believing they will not be able to handle being a mother and a student at the same time. Those who do drop out find themselves without the necessary skills and educational degree they need to obtain adequate employment. They may sink into persistent poverty, managing to survive on meager state support. Their plight is often intergenerational: children of teen parents are also more likely to suffer educational deficiencies and be kept back in school, and are more likely to eventually drop out; their daughters are similarly significantly more likely to become teen mothers than the offspring of women who are older, married, and living in two-parent households. For these reasons, juvenile justice experts believe it is critical to help teen moms continue with their high school education while receiving help in developing their parenting skills. A number of programs have been created to reach this objective.

LEAP

One teen parenting program that has been popular is the Ohio-based Learning, Earning, and Parenting program (LEAP). The LEAP program aims at requiring teen moms either to attend high school or to attempt to earn a GED in order to attain financial assistance from the state's Aid to Families with Dependant Children (AFDC). They are also awarded an additional monthly stipend if they attend school and have an equal amount deducted if they drop out. Upon graduation, they are awarded an additional stipend.

The LEAP program strives to help teens continue their high school education, gain employment skills, and also learn effective parenting skills. Evaluations show that the program does in fact increase participants' school enrollment and attendance. However, graduation rates increased only for those teen moms who were already enrolled in school when the program was implemented, not for those who entered after the program was announced. Nonetheless, four-year follow-up tests indicate that the program can be a big help, especially in boosting employment among these teens.

LEAP has proven so successful that it is being adopted in Canada. The Canadian program requires that each teen complete high school credits and take thirty-five hours of parenting classes. Once both these requirements are completed, teens are awarded $500, which can be put away toward further education for themselves or for the child's future education.

GRADS

The Graduation, Reality, and Dual-Role Skills (GRADS) program is a voluntary program for pregnant teenagers or teen parents who are in the seventh through twelfth grades. Also developed in Ohio, GRADS comprises four main areas: pregnancy, parenting, balancing work and family, and security and happiness. Participants attend classes taught by licensed and certified instructors. They are also placed in individual counseling and participate in group sessions with other teen parents. In addition, guest speakers from different organizations, such as Planned Parenthood, come in to enrich the classroom experience.

Girls seem to be more deeply affected than boys by child abuse, and the link between abuse and female delinquency seems stronger than it is for male delinquency.[86] A significant amount of female delinquency can be traced to abuse in the home.[87] Meda Chesney-Lind, a prominent feminist scholar, has described this association: "Young women on the run from homes characterized by sexual abuse and parental neglect are forced, by the very statutes designed to protect them, into the life of an escaped convict."[88] Girls may be forced into a life of sexual promiscuity because their sexual desirability makes them a valuable commodity for families living on the edge. For example, girls may be "lent out" to drug dealers so their parents or partners can get high. Girls on the streets are encouraged to sell their bodies because they have little else of value to trade.[89] Many of these girls may find themselves pregnant at a very young age. A number of programs have been created to help prevent teen pregnancy and to help girls who find themselves pregnant. This is the topic of the above Preventing and Treating Delinquency feature.

There is a significant body of literature linking abusive home lives to gang participation and crime. Joan Moore's analysis of gang girls in East Los Angeles found that many came from troubled homes. Sixty-eight percent of the girls she interviewed were afraid of their fathers, and 55 percent reported fear of their mothers.[90] Many of the girls reported that their parents were overly strict and controlling, despite the fact that they engaged in criminality themselves. Moore also details accounts of sexual abuse; about 30 percent of the girls reported that family members had made sexual advances.[91] Emily

The GRADS program is aimed at strengthening the teens' bond to society. So far, it appears to be a success. Where the national dropout rate for teen mothers is approximately 60 percent, for those involved with the GRADS program it hovers around 14 percent. Repeat pregnancies among teen moms in the program have also dropped; 13 percent of those involved with the GRADS program became pregnant again, whereas 29 percent of those not in the program had additional pregnancies. In fact, the program has proven so successful that it is now implemented in 80 percent of Ohio's school districts and seventeen other states have adopted the program.

ROAD

Reaching Out to Adolescent Dads (ROAD), is a Virginia-based program that targets young fathers between the ages of thirteen and twenty.

The program strives to help these boys continue their education by encouraging high school attendance or participation in a GED program. ROAD helps participants develop job skills and explore career opportunities. Teens are taught to accept responsibility and are educated on preventing further pregnancies. The program teaches participants the importance of father-child relationships and educates them on parenting skills that will benefit them in caring for their child. The program helps them understand the importance of paying child support.

Evaluations suggest that ROAD is successful in increasing paternal levels of responsibility, improves school performance, helps participants gain employment, and also reduces the chances of these teens fathering more children.

CRITICAL THINKING

Do programs that help kids deal with teen pregnancy perhaps encourage them to have even more children while giving others, who are not yet parents, the impression that having children while they are still in school is not such a bad thing? Do you believe that these programs may actually increase the number of kids born to teen parents?

INFOTRAC COLLEGE EDITION RESEARCH

Can spirituality reduce the incidence of precocious sex? Go to InfoTrac College Edition and read Willa Doswell, Malick Kouyate, and Jerome Taylor, "The Role of Spirituality in Preventing Early Sexual Behavior," *American Journal of Health Studies* 18:195–203 (2003).

Sources: Mike Bauer and Lorraine Graham-Watson, "Learning, Earning, and Parenting Program (LEAP)—2001 Progress Report" (Ontario, Canada: Regional Municipality of Niagara, Social Assistance and Employment Opportunities Division, 2001), pp. 1–3; *LEAP Final Report on Ohio's Welfare Initiative to Improve School Attendance Among Teenage Parents* (New York: Manpower Demonstration Research Corporation, 1997); "Learning, Earning, and Parenting Program" (Ontario, Canada: Ministry of Community, Family and Children's Services, 2003), pp. 29–30; U.S. Department of Education, "Compendium of School-Based and School-Linked Programs for Pregnant and Parenting Adolescents." National Institute on Early Childhood Development and Education. Office of Educational Research and Improvement (Washington, DC: U.S. Department of Education, 1999); ROAD Program, "Reaching Out to Adolescent Dads." www.parentingresources.ncjrs.org/familydynamics/teenparent.html, 2002.

Gaarder and Joanne Belknap's interviews with young women sent to adult prisons indicated that most had endured prolonged sexual abuse and violence. For example, Lisa, a young White woman serving time for attempted murder, had used drugs, alcohol, and joined gangs to escape the pain and troubles of her home life. Her mother was an alcoholic, and her father a convicted rapist. She had been sexually and physically abused by her stepfather from the ages of nine to eleven. Soon after, Lisa began skipping school, started using alcohol, and took acid. She joined a gang when she was twelve. "They were like a family to me," she told Gaarder and Belknap. "But I became involved in a lot of stuff. . . . I got high a lot, I robbed people, burglarized homes, stabbed people, and was involved in drive-bys." At age fifteen, she stabbed a woman in a fight. She is serving seven to fifteen years for the crime. She made this statement:

> I had just gotten out of this group home. The lady I stabbed had been messing with my sister's fiancé. This woman [had] a bunch of my sister's stuff, like her stereo and VCR, so me, my sister, her fiancé, and my boyfriend went over to pick up the stuff. We were all getting high beforehand. When we got to the house, my sister and I went in. . . . They [her sister and the victim] started fighting over him, and I started stabbing her with a knife. I always carried a knife with me because I was in a gang.[92]

In summary, the socialization approach holds that family interaction is the key to understanding female delinquency. If a girl grows up in an atmosphere of sexual tension, where hostility exists between her parents, or where her parents are absent, she is likely to turn to outside sources for support. Girls are expected to follow narrowly defined behavioral patterns. In contrast, it is not unusual for boys to stay out late, drive around with friends, or get involved in other unstructured behaviors linked to delinquency. If in reaction to loneliness and parental hostility, girls engage in the same "routine activities" as boys (staying out late, partying, and riding around with friends), they run the risk of engaging in similar types of delinquent behavior.[93]

The socialization approach holds that a poor home life is likely to have an even more damaging effect on females than on males. Because girls are less likely than boys to have close-knit peer associations, they are more likely to need close parental relationships to retain emotional stability. In fact, girls may become sexually involved with boys to receive support from them, a practice that tends to magnify their problems.

LIBERAL FEMINIST VIEWS

The feminist movement has, from its origins, fought to help women break away from their traditional roles and gain economic, educational, and social advancement. There is little question that the women's movement has revised the way women perceive their roles in society, and it has altered the relationships of women to many social institutions.

Liberal feminism has influenced thinking about delinquency. According to liberal feminists, females are less delinquent than males because their social roles provide fewer opportunities to commit crime. As the roles of women become more similar to those of men, so will their crime patterns. Female criminality is motivated by the same influences as male criminality. According to Freda Adler's important book *Sisters in Crime* (1975), by striving for independence women have begun to alter the institutions that had protected males in their traditional positions of power.[94] Adler argued that female delinquency would be affected by the changing role of women. As females entered new occupations and participated in sports, politics, and other traditionally male endeavors, they would also become involved in crimes that had heretofore been male-oriented; delinquency rates would then converge. She noted that girls were becoming increasingly involved in traditionally masculine crimes such as gang activity and fighting.

Adler predicted that the women's movement would produce steeper increases in the rate of female delinquency because it created an environment in which the roles of girls and boys converge. She predicted that the changing female role would produce female criminals who are similar to their male counterparts.[95]

Support for Liberal Feminism

A number of studies support the feminist view of gender differences in delinquency.[96] More than twenty years ago, Rita James Simon explained how the increase in female criminality is a function of the changing role of women. She claimed that as women were empowered economically and socially, they would be less likely to feel dependent and oppressed. Consequently, they would be less likely to attack their traditional targets: their husbands, their lovers, or even their own children.[97] Instead, their new role as breadwinner might encourage women to engage in traditional male crimes, such as larceny and car theft.

Simon's view has been supported in part by research showing a significant correlation between the women's rights movement and the female crime rate.[98] If 1966 is used as a jumping-off point (because the National Organization for Women was founded in that year), there are indications that patterns of serious female crime (robbery and auto theft) correlate with indicators of female emancipation (the divorce rate and participation in the labor force). Although this research does not prove that female crime is related to social change, it identifies behavior patterns that support that hypothesis.

According to liberal feminists, females are less delinquent than males because their social roles provide them with fewer opportunities to commit crime. As the roles of girls and women become more similar to those of males, so too will their crime patterns. Female criminality is actually motivated by the same crime-producing influences as male criminality. The fact that female delinquency is rising at a faster rate than male delinquency reflects the convergence of their social roles.

© Lisa Quinones/Black Star/Stockphoto.com

In addition to these efforts, self-report studies support the liberal feminist view by showing that gender differences in delinquency are fading; that is, the delinquent acts committed most and least often by girls are nearly identical to those reported most and least often by boys.[99] The pattern of female delinquency, if not the extent, is now similar to that of male delinquency,[100] and with few exceptions the factors that seem to motivate both male and female criminality seem similar.[101] For example, research shows that economic disadvantages are felt equally by both male and female residents.[102]

As the sex roles of males and females have become less distinct, their offending patterns have become more similar. Girls may be committing crimes to gain economic advancement and not because they lack parental support. Both of these patterns were predicted by liberal feminists.

Critiques of Liberal Feminism

Not all delinquency experts believe changing sex roles influence crime rates. Some argue that the delinquent behavior patterns of girls have remained static and have not been influenced by the women's movement. Females involved in violent crime more often than not have some connection to a male partner who influences their behavior. One study of women who kill in the course of their involvement in the drug trade found that they kill on behalf of a man or out of fear of a man.[103]

Others dispute that changes in female delinquency rates relate to the feminist movement. Self-report studies show that female participation in most crime has remained stable for the past ten years.[104] It is possible that the women's movement has not influenced crime rates as much as previously thought.[105] Perhaps the greater participation by females in the Uniform Crime Report (UCR) arrest data is more a function of how police are treating females than an actual change in female behavior patterns.

 CRITICAL FEMINIST VIEWS

A number of writers take a more critical view of gender differences in crime. These scholars can be categorized as **critical feminists** (sometimes known as Marxist feminists) who believe gender inequality stems from the unequal power of men and

women in a capitalist society and the exploitation of females by fathers and husbands: under capitalism, women are a "commodity" like land or money.[106] Female delinquency originates with the onset of male supremacy (*patriarchy*), the subordination of women, male aggression, and the efforts of men to control females sexually.[107]

Critical feminists focus on the social forces that shape girls' lives.[108] They attempt to show how the sexual victimization of girls is often a function of male socialization and that young males learn to be exploitive of women. James Messerschmidt, an influential feminist scholar, has formulated a theoretical model to show how misguided concepts of "masculinity" flow from the inequities built into "patriarchal capitalism." Men dominate business in capitalist societies, and males who cannot function well within its parameters are at risk for crime. Women are inherently powerless in such a society, and their crimes reflect their limited access to both legitimate and illegitimate opportunity.[109] It is not surprising that research surveys have found that 90 percent of adolescent girls are sexually harassed in school, with almost 30 percent reporting having been psychologically pressured to "do something sexual," and 10 percent physically forced into sexual behaviors.[110]

According to the critical feminist view, male exploitation acts as a trigger for female delinquent behavior. Female delinquents recount being so severely harassed at school that they were forced to carry knives. Some reported that boyfriends—men sometimes in their thirties—who "knew how to treat a girl" would draw them into criminal activity such as drug trafficking, which eventually entangled them in the justice system.[111]

When female adolescents run away and use drugs, they may be reacting to abuse at home or at school. Their attempts at survival are then labeled delinquent.[112] Research shows that a significant number of girls who are victims of sexual and other forms of abuse later engage in delinquency.[113] All too often, school officials ignore complaints made by female students. Young girls therefore may feel trapped and desperate.

Crime and Patriarchy

A number of theoretical models have attempted to use a critical or Marxist feminist perspective to explain gender differences in delinquency. For example, in *Capitalism, Patriarchy, and Crime,* Marxist James Messerschmidt argues that capitalist society is characterized by both patriarchy and class conflict. Capitalists control workers, and men control women, both economically and biologically.[114] This "double marginality" explains why females in a capitalist society commit fewer crimes than males: they are isolated in the family and have fewer opportunities to engage in elite deviance (white-collar and economic crimes); they are also denied access to male-dominated street crimes. Because capitalism renders women powerless, they are forced to commit less serious crimes such as abusing drugs.

Power-Control Theory

John Hagan and his associates have speculated that gender differences in delinquency are a function of class differences that influence family life. Hagan, who calls his view **power-control theory,** suggests that class influences delinquency by controlling the quality of family life.[115] In paternalistic families, fathers assume the role of breadwinners and mothers have menial jobs or remain at home. Mothers are expected to control the behavior of their daughters while granting greater freedom to sons. The parent-daughter relationship can be viewed as a preparation for the "cult of domesticity," which makes daughters' involvement in delinquency unlikely. Hence, males exhibit a higher degree of delinquent behavior than their sisters.

In **egalitarian families**—in which the husband and wife share similar positions of power at home and in the workplace—daughters gain a kind of freedom that reflects reduced parental control. These families produce daughters whose law-violating behaviors mirror those of their brothers. Ironically, these kinds of relationships also occur in households with absent fathers. Similarly, Hagan and his

power-control theory
Holds that gender differences in the delinquency rate are a function of class differences and economic conditions that influence the structure of family life.

egalitarian families
Husband and wife share power at home; daughters gain a kind of freedom similar to that of sons and their law-violating behaviors mirror those of their brothers.

According to power-control theory, when girls grow up in egalitarian families, where the husband and the wife share similar positions of power at home and in the workplace, they achieve freedom and independence.

© Dwayne Newton/PhotoEdit

Checkpoints

✔ There are a variety of views on why girls become delinquent and why there are gender differences in the crime rate.

✔ At one time it was believed that girls were naturally less aggressive and female criminals were a biological aberration.

✔ Some experts still believe that hormonal differences can explain why males are more aggressive.

✔ Some experts believe that males are more aggressive because they have evolved that way to secure mates.

✔ Under some circumstances females may act more aggressively than males.

✔ Some experts believe that girls have been socialized to be less violent.

✔ Female delinquents may be the product of a destructive home life, rebelling against abusive parents.

✔ The liberal feminist view is that girls did not have the same opportunities to commit crime as boys and that rising female crime rates represent changing life circumstances.

✔ Critical feminists see female delinquency as a function of male domination and abuse.

  To quiz yourself on this material, go to questions 6.6–6.20 on the Juvenile Delinquency: The Core 2e Web site.

associates found that when both fathers and mothers hold equally valued managerial positions the similarity between the rates of their daughters' and sons' delinquency is greatest. Therefore, middle-class girls are most likely to violate the law because they are less closely controlled than lower-class girls.

Research conducted by Hagan and his colleagues has tended to support the core relationship between family structure and gender differences in delinquency.[116] However, some of the basic premises of power-control theory, such as the relationship between social class and delinquency, have been challenged. For example, some critics have questioned the assumption that upper-class youths may engage in more petty delinquency than lower-class youths because they are brought up to be "risk takers" who do not fear the consequences of their misdeeds.[117]

Power-control theory encourages a new approach to the study of delinquency, one that addresses gender differences, class position, and family structure. It also helps explain the relative increase in female delinquency by stressing the significance of changing feminine roles. With the increase in single-parent homes, the patterns Hagan has identified may change. The decline of the patriarchal family may produce looser family ties on girls, changing sex roles, and increased delinquency. Ironically, this raises an interesting dilemma: the daughters of successful and powerful mothers are more at risk for delinquency than the daughters of stay-at-home moms! However, as sociologist Christopher Uggen points out, there may be a bright side to this dilemma: the daughters of independent working mothers may not only be more likely to commit delinquent acts but also be encouraged to take prosocial risks such as engaging in athletic competition and breaking into traditional male-dominated occupations such as policing and the military.[118] ✔ Checkpoints

GENDER AND THE JUVENILE JUSTICE SYSTEM

Gender differences not only have an effect on crime patterns but also may have a significant impact on the way children are treated by the juvenile justice system. Several feminist scholars argue that girls are not only the victims of injustice at home but also risk being victimized by agents of the justice system.

Are girls still "victims" of the juvenile justice system? Meda Chesney-Lind's well-regarded research found that police are more likely to arrest female adolescents for sexual activity and to ignore the same behavior among male delinquents.[119] Girls were also more likely to be sent to a detention facility before trial, and the length of their detention averaged three times that of boys. Girls are far more likely than boys to be picked up by police for status offenses and are more likely to be kept in detention for such offenses.[120]

Girls, more than boys, are still disadvantaged if their behavior is viewed as morally incorrect by government officials or if they are considered beyond parental control.[121] Recent research conducted by John MacDonald and Meda Chesney-Lind found that the juvenile justice system still categorizes female offenders into two distinct groups: girls who momentarily strayed from the "good girl" path and are therefore deserving of solicitous, humanitarian treatment, and dangerously wayward girls who have serious problems and must therefore be kept under strict control lest they stray further.[122]

Girls may also be feeling the brunt of the more punitive policies now being used in the juvenile justice system. For example, when Chesney-Lind and Vickie Paramore analyzed data from the City and County of Honolulu they found that tougher juvenile justice standards meant that more cases were being handled formally in the juvenile justice system.[123] While girls are actually committing fewer violent crimes, they are more likely to become enmeshed in the grasp of the juvenile justice system. Once in the system, they may receive fewer benefits and services than their male counterparts. Institutionalized girls report that they are given fewer privileges and less space, equipment, programs, and treatment than institutionalized boys.[124]

Girls may still be subject to harsh punishments if they are considered dangerously immoral. Girls are significantly more likely to be arrested on status offense charges than boys.[125] However, the arrest rates for girls show that girls are charged with status offenses more often than boys because some of the behaviors they are participating in are considered negative when perpetrated by a female but would not gain official attention if engaged in by a male.[126]

There still appears to be an association between male standards of "beauty" and sexual behavior: criminal justice professionals may look on attractive girls who engage in sexual behavior more harshly, overlooking some of the same behaviors in less attractive girls. In some jurisdictions, girls are still being incarcerated for status offenses because their behavior does not measure up to concepts of "proper" female behavior.[127] Even though girls are still less likely to be arrested than boys, those who fail to measure up to stereotypes of proper female behavior are more likely to be sanctioned than male offenders.[128]

Why do these differences persist? Perhaps because correctional authorities continue to subscribe to stereotyped beliefs about the needs of young girls. Writing in 1998 with Randall Shelden, Meda Chesney-Lind found that court officials and policymakers still show a lack of concern about girls' victimization and instead are more concerned with controlling their behavior than addressing the factors that brought them to the attention of the juvenile justice system in the first place.[129]

SUMMARY

- The relationship between gender and delinquency has become a topic of considerable interest to criminologists.
- At one time, attention was directed solely at male offenders and the rare female delinquent was considered an oddity. The nature and extent of female delinquent activities have changed, and girls are now engaging in more frequent and serious illegal activity.
- Sociologists and psychologists recognize that there are differences in attitudes, values, and behavior between boys and girls.

- There are cognitive differences. Females process information differently than males do and have different cognitive and physical strengths. These differences may, in part, explain gender differences in delinquency.
- Girls are socialized differently, which causes them to internalize rather than externalize anger and aggression.
- There are also psychological differences between the sexes. Girls may actually be at risk for a greater level of mental anguish than boys.

- There are a number of different views of female delinquency.
- Trait views are concerned with biological and psychological differences between the sexes. Early efforts by Cesare Lombroso and his followers placed the blame for delinquency on physical differences between males and females. Girls who were delinquent had inherent masculine characteristics.
- Contemporary trait theorists view girls' psychological makeup and hormonal and physical characteristics as key to their delinquent behavior.
- Socialization has also been identified as a cause of delinquency. Males are socialized to be tough and aggressive, females to be passive and obedient.
- Early socialization views portrayed the adolescent female offender as a troubled girl who lacked love at home and supportive peer relations.
- These theories treated female delinquents as sexual offenders whose criminal activities were linked to destructive relationships with men.
- Contemporary socialization views continue to depict female delinquents as being raised in hellish homes where they are victims of sexual and physical abuse.
- More recent views of gender and delinquency incorporate the changes brought about by the women's movement. Liberal feminists argue that, as the roles of women change, so will their crime patterns. Although a number of studies support this view, some theorists question its validity. The female crime rate has increased, and female delinquency patterns now resemble those of males, but the gender gap has not narrowed after more than two decades.
- Critical feminists view female delinquency as a function of patriarchy and the mistreatment and exploitation of females in a male-dominated society.
- Hagan's power-control theory helps us understand why these differences exist and whether change may be coming.
- The treatment girls receive by the juvenile justice system has also been the subject of debate. Originally, it was thought that police protected girls from the stigma of a delinquency label. Contemporary criminologists charge, however, that girls are discriminated against by agents of the justice system.

KEY TERMS

masculinity hypothesis, p. 136
gender-schema theory, p. 139
chivalry hypothesis, p. 141

precocious sexuality, p. 142
liberal feminism, p. 148
critical feminists, p. 148

power-control theory, p. 150
egalitarian families, p. 150

QUESTIONS FOR DISCUSSION

1. Are girls delinquent for different reasons than boys? Do girls have a unique set of problems?

2. As sex roles become more homogenous, do you believe female delinquency will become identical to male delinquency in rate and type?

3. Does the sexual double standard still exist?

4. Are lower-class girls more strictly supervised than upper- and middle-class girls? Is control stratified across class lines?

5. Are girls the victims of unfairness at the hands of the justice system, or do they benefit from "chivalry?"

APPLYING WHAT YOU HAVE LEARNED

As the principal of a northeastern junior high school, you get a call from a parent who is disturbed because he has heard a rumor that the student literary digest plans to publish a story with a sexual theme. The work is written by a junior high school girl who became pregnant during the year and underwent an abortion. You ask for and receive a copy of the narrative.

The girl's story is actually a cautionary tale of young love that results in an unwanted pregnancy. The author details the abusive home life that led her to engage in an intimate relationship with another student, her pregnancy, her conflict with her parents, her decision to abort, and the emotional turmoil that the incident created. She tells students to use contraception if they are sexually active and recommends appropriate types of birth control. There is nothing provocative or sexually explicit in the work.

Some teachers argue that girls should not be allowed to read this material because it has sexual content from which they must be protected, and that in a sense it advocates defiance of parents. Also, some parents may object to a story about precocious sexuality because they fear it may encourage their children to "experiment." Such behavior is linked to delinquency and drug abuse. Those who advocate publication believe that girls have a right to read about such important issues and decide on their own course of action.

- Should you force the story's deletion because its theme is essentially sexual and controversial?
- Should you allow publication because it deals with the subject matter in a mature fashion?

- Do you think reading and learning about sexual matters encourages or discourages experimentation in sexuality?
- Should young girls be protected from such material? Would it cause them damage?
- Inequalities still exist in the way boys and girls are socialized by their parents and treated by social institutions. Do these gender differences also manifest themselves in the delinquency rate? What effect do gender roles have on behavior choices?

DOING RESEARCH ON THE WEB

To help you answers these questions and to find out more information on the gender of status offenders, click on Web Links under the Chapter Resources at http://cj.wadsworth.com/siegel_jdcore2e. Then go to the Web site for *Hazelwood School District et al. v. Kuhlmeier et al.* and other landmark cases; go also to the National Scholastic Press

Association and the high school journalism Web site to read more about school news and censorship issues.

Pro/Con discussions and Viewpoint Essays on some of the topics in this chapter may be found at the Opposing Viewpoints Resource Center: www.gale.com/OpposingViewpoints.

The Family and Delinquency

Courtesy of CNN

CHAPTER OBJECTIVES

After reading this chapter you should:

1. Be familiar with the link between family relationships and juvenile delinquency.

2. Understand the complex association between family breakup and delinquent behavior.

3. Understand why families in conflict produce more delinquents than those that function harmoniously.

4. Know the association between inconsistent discipline and supervision and juvenile crime.

5. Be able to discuss how parental and sibling misconduct influences delinquent behaviors.

6. Define the concept of child abuse.

7. Know the nature and extent of abuse.

8. Be able to list the factors that are seen as causing child abuse.

9. Be familiar with the complex system of state intervention in abuse cases.

10. Discuss the association between child abuse and delinquent behavior.

Although estimates vary, somewhere from one to three million kids run away from home each year. Most stay with a friend for a few days and then return home. Others stay away longer; some leave home never to return. Many find shelter with other kids living in similar circumstances, sleeping under bridges and in abandoned buildings, forming uneasy alliances for survival. Many abuse drugs and become the victims of predatory criminals. Few remain undamaged by their ordeal.

Why do they run? While some may be evading the law, suffering depression, or dealing with a personal crisis, most are running from a disturbed family or home life. They have problems with their parents' divorce or remarriage; there is conflict over rules and discipline; sibling conflicts have gotten out of control. Many of these kids simply want to remove themselves from a bad situation without any destination in mind or plan for the future. Some teens repeatedly run away from home, only to become an easy target for adult predators who try to lure them into prostitution, drug use, or both.

CNN. VIEW THE CNN VIDEO CLIP OF THIS STORY AND ANSWER RELATED CRITICAL THINKING QUESTIONS ON YOUR JUVENILE DELINQUENCY: THE CORE 2E CD.

A great deal of information on families and children can be found at the Web site of the David and Lucile Packard Foundation by clicking on Web Links under the Chapter Resources at http://cj. wadsworth.com/siegel_jdcore2e.

nuclear family
A family unit composed of parents and their children; this smaller family structure is subject to great stress due to the intense, close contact between parents and children.

The problems faced by runaways illustrate the significant impact that family relationships have on adolescent development. Many experts believe that family dysfunction is a key ingredient in the development of the emotional deficits that eventually lead to long-term social problems.[1] Interactions between parents and children, and between siblings, provide opportunities for children to acquire or inhibit antisocial behavior patterns.[2] Children living in high-crime areas are able to resist the temptation of the streets if they receive fair discipline and support from parents who provide them with positive role models.[3] However, children in affluent families who are being raised in a household characterized by abuse and conflict, or whose parents are absent or separated, will still be at risk for delinquency.[4] Nor is the relationship between family life and delinquency unique to U.S. culture; cross-national data support a significant association between family variables and delinquency.[5]

The assumed relationship between delinquency and family life is critical today because the American family is changing. Extended families, once common, are now for the most part anachronisms. In their place is the **nuclear family,** described as a "dangerous hothouse of emotions" because of the close contact between parents and children; in these families, problems are unrelieved by contact with other kin living nearby.[6]

The nuclear family is showing signs of breakdown. Much of the responsibility for child rearing is delegated to television and daycare providers. Despite these changes, some families are able to continue functioning as healthy units, producing well-adjusted children. Others have crumbled under the stress, severely damaging their children.[7] This is particularly true when child abuse and neglect become part of family life.

Because these issues are critical for understanding delinquency, this chapter is devoted to an analysis of the family's role in producing or inhibiting delinquency. We first cover the changing face of the American family. We then review the way family structure and function influence delinquent behavior. The relationship between child abuse, neglect, and delinquency is covered in some depth.

THE CHANGING AMERICAN FAMILY

The so-called traditional family—with a male breadwinner and a female who cares for the home—is a thing of the past. No longer can this family structure be considered the norm. Changing sex roles have created a family where women play a much greater role in the economic process; this has created a more egalitarian family structure. About three-quarters of all mothers of school-age children are employed, up from 50 percent in 1970 and 40 percent in 1960. The changing economic structure may be reflected in shifting sex roles. Fathers are now spending more time with their children on workdays than they did twenty years ago (2.3 hours versus 1.8), and women are spending somewhat less time (3.0 hours versus 3.3).[8] On their days off, both working men and women spend about an hour more with their children than they did twenty years ago, with women devoting about eight hours, and men six. So although the time spent with children may be less than would be desirable, it has increased over the past twenty years.

Family Makeup

The proportion of American households that have children who live with both parents has declined substantially. Today about 37 percent of African-American children live in families that have two parents; about 74 percent of White children live with two parents.[9] As many as 40 percent of White children and 75 percent of African-American children will experience parental separation or divorce before they reach age sixteen, and many of these children will experience multiple family disruptions over time.[10]

Though there has been a sharp decline in the teen birthrate (dropping 28 percent between 1990 and 2002), a significant number of children are still being born to unmarried women. A total of 4,040,121 births were reported in the United States in 2002, about one-third of them, or 1.3 million, to unmarried women (see Figure 7.1).[11]

Figure 7.1   **Percent of Births to Unmarried Women in the United States, 1990–2001**

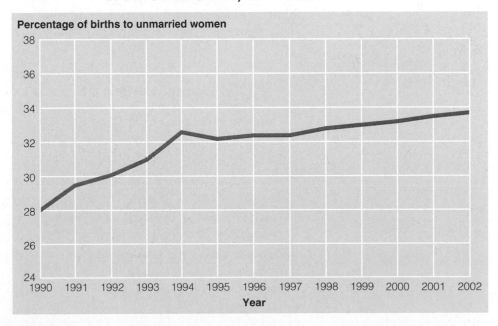

Source: "Birth: Final Data for 2001," *National Vital Statistic Reports,* v51, n2 (Hyattsville, MD: National Center for Health Statistics, 2002), Table C.

Child Care

Charged with caring for children is a daycare system whose workers are often paid the minimum wage. Of special concern are "family daycare homes," in which a single provider takes care of three to nine children. Several states neither license nor monitor these private providers. Even in states that mandate registration and inspection of daycare providers, it is estimated that 90 percent or more of the facilities operate "underground." It is not uncommon for one adult to care for eight infants, an impossible task regardless of training or feelings of concern.

Children from working poor families are most likely to suffer from inadequate child care; these children often spend time in makeshift arrangements that allow their parents to work but lack the stimulating environment children need to thrive.[12] About 3.5 million children under age thirteen spend some time at home alone each week while their parents are at work.

Economic Stress

The family is also undergoing economic stress (see Table 7.1). About 17 percent of all children live in poverty and about 7 percent live in extreme poverty—at least 50 percent below the poverty line. About 30 percent of all children live in families where no parent has full-time, year-round employment.[13] The majority of indigent families live in substandard housing without adequate health care, nutrition, or child care. Those whose incomes place them above the poverty line are deprived of government assistance. Recent political trends suggest that the social "safety net" is under attack and that poor families can expect less government aid in the coming years.

Will this economic pressure be reduced in the future? The number of senior citizens is on the rise. As people retire, there will be fewer workers to cover the costs of Social Security, medical care, and nursing home care. These costs will put greater economic stress on families. Voter sentiment has an impact on the allocation of public funds, and there is concern that an older generation, worried about health care costs, may be reluctant to spend tax dollars on at-risk kids.

THE FAMILY'S INFLUENCE ON DELINQUENCY

Most experts believe a disturbed home environment can have a significant impact on delinquency. The family is the primary unit in which children learn the values and

Table 7.1	Family Well-Being: National Indicators
Median income of families with children	$50,000
Children in extreme poverty (income below 50% of poverty level)	7%
Female-headed families receiving child support or alimony	36%
Households with children receiving Earned Income Tax Credit	15,251,000
Average Earned Income Tax Credit for households with children	$1,968
Households eligible for food stamps, but not receiving them	41%
Children without Internet access at home	52%
Children without a telephone at home	3%
Children without a vehicle at home	7%
Children without health insurance	12%
Two-year-olds who were immunized	79%
Low-income households with children where housing costs exceed 30% of income	59%

Source: *Kids Count 2003 Data Book Online,* www.aecf.org/cgi-bin/kc.cgi?action=profile&area=United+States.

attitudes that guide their actions throughout their lives. Family disruption or change can have a long-lasting impact on children.

Four categories of family dysfunction seem to promote delinquent behavior: families disrupted by spousal conflict or breakup, families involved in interpersonal conflict, negligent parents who are not attuned to their children's behavior and emotional problems, and families that contain deviant parents who may transmit their behavior to their children (see Figure 7.2).[14] These factors may interact; for example, drug-abusing parents may be more likely to experience family conflict, child neglect, and marital breakup. We now turn to the specific types of family problems that have been linked to delinquent behavior.

Family Breakup

One of the most enduring controversies in the study of delinquency is the relationship between a parent absent from the home and the onset of delinquent behavior. Research indicates that parents whose marriage is secure produce children who are secure and independent.[15] In contrast, children growing up in homes with one or both parents absent may be prone to antisocial behavior.

A number of experts contend that a **broken home** is a strong determinant of a child's law-violating behavior. The connection seems self-evident because a child is first socialized at home. Any disjunction in an orderly family structure could be expected to have a negative impact on the child.

The suspected broken home–delinquency relationship is important because, if current trends continue, less than half of all children born today will live continuously with their own mother and father throughout childhood. And because stepfamilies, or so-called **blended families,** are less stable than families consisting of two biological parents, an increasing number of children will experience family breakup two or even three times during childhood.[16]

A number of studies indicate that children who have experienced family breakup are more likely to demonstrate behavior problems and hyperactivity than children in intact families.[17] Family breakup is often associated with conflict, hostility, and aggression; children of divorce are suspected of having lax supervision, weakened

broken home
Home in which one or both parents are absent due to divorce or separation; children in such an environment may be prone to antisocial behavior.

blended families
Nuclear families that are the product of divorce and remarriage, blending one parent from each of two families and their combined children into one family unit.

| Figure 7.2 | **Family Influences on Behavior** |

Each of these four factors has been linked to antisocial behavior and delinquency. Interaction between these factors may escalate delinquent activity.

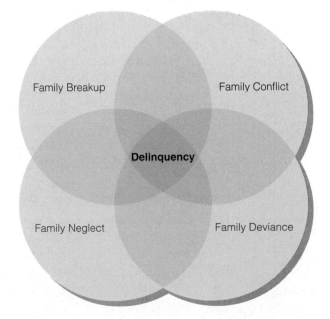

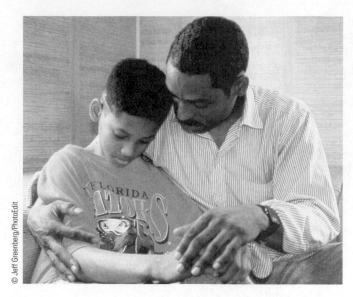

Secure marriages produce children who are protected and learn to become independent. Children growing up in homes with one or both parents absent are more vulnerable to anti-social behavior. Because a child is first socialized at home, any disjunction in an orderly family structure can be expected to have a negative impact on the child.

attachment, and greater susceptibility to peer pressure.[18] And as a recent study of more than four thousand youths in Denver, Pittsburgh, and Rochester found, the more often children are forced to go through family transitions the more likely they are to engage in delinquent activity.[19]

The Effects of Divorce   The relationship between broken homes and delinquency has been controversial, to say the least. It was established in early research, which suggested that a significant association existed between parental absence and youthful misconduct.[20] For many years the link was clear: children growing up in broken homes were much more likely to fall prey to delinquency than those who lived in two-parent households.[21]

Beginning in the late 1950s some researchers began to question the link between broken homes and delinquency. Early studies, they claimed, used the records of police, courts, and correctional institutions.[22] This research may have been tainted by sampling bias: youths from broken homes may get arrested more often than youths from intact families, but this does not necessarily mean they engage in more frequent and serious delinquent behavior. Official statistics may reflect the fact that agents of the justice system treat children from disrupted households more severely because they cannot call on parents for support. The *parens patriae* philosophy of the juvenile courts calls for official intervention when parental supervision is considered inadequate.[23] A number of subsequent studies, using self-report data, have failed to establish any clear-cut relationship between broken homes and delinquent behavior.[24] Boys and girls from intact families seem as likely to self-report delinquency as those whose parents are divorced or separated. Researchers concluded that the absence of parents has a greater effect on agents of the justice system than it does on the behavior of children.[25]

Divorce Reconsidered   Though some researchers still question the divorce-delinquency link, there is growing sentiment that family breakup is traumatic and most likely has a direct influence on factors related to adolescent misbehavior.[26] In her study of the effects of parental absence on children, sociologist Sara McLanahan finds that children who grow up apart from their biological fathers typically do less well than children who grow up with both biological parents. They are less likely to finish high school and attend college, less likely to find and keep a steady job, and more likely to become teen mothers. Although most children who grow up with a single parent do quite well, differences between children in one- and two-parent families are significant, and there is fairly good evidence that father absence per se is responsible for some social problems.[27] The McLanahan research has been supported by other studies showing that divorce is in fact related to delinquency and status offending, especially if a child had a close relationship with the parent who is forced to leave the home.[28] The effects of divorce seem gender-specific:

- Boys seem to be more affected by the postdivorce absence of the father. In postdivorce situations, fathers seem less likely to be around to solve problems, to discuss standards of conduct, or to enforce discipline. A divorced father who remains actively involved in his child's life reduces his son's chances of delinquency.

- Girls are more affected by both the quality of the mother's parenting and postdivorce parental conflict. It is possible that extreme levels of parental conflict may serve as a model to young girls coping with the aftermath of their parents' separation.[29]

intrafamily violence
An environment of discord and conflict within the family; children who grow up in dysfunctional homes often exhibit delinquent behaviors, having learned at a young age that aggression pays off.

Although the prevailing wisdom is that "marriage is better than divorce," research by Sara Jaffee and her associates shows that the quality of marriage may be more important than its makeup. They found that the less time fathers lived with their children, the more conduct problems their children had. However, when fathers engaged in high levels of antisocial behavior, the more time they lived with their children the more conduct problems their children had. Marriage, they conclude, may not be the answer to the problems faced by children living in single-parent families unless their fathers can refrain from deviant behaviors and become reliable sources of emotional and economic support.[30]

Family Conflict

Not all unhappy marriages end in divorce; some continue in an atmosphere of conflict. Intrafamily conflict is a common experience in many American families.[31] The link between parental conflict and delinquency was established almost forty years ago when F. Ivan Nye found that a child's perception of his or her parents' marital happiness was a significant predictor of delinquency.[32] Contemporary studies also find that children who grow up in maladapted homes and witness discord or violence later exhibit emotional disturbance and behavior problems.[33] There seems to be little difference between the behavior of children who merely *witness* **intrafamily violence** and those who are its *victims*.[34] In fact, some research efforts show that observing the abuse of a parent (mother) is a more significant determinant of delinquency than being the target of child abuse.[35]

Research efforts have consistently supported the relationship between family conflict, hostility, and delinquency.[36] Adolescents who are incarcerated report growing up in dysfunctional homes.[37] Parents of beyond-control youngsters have been found to be inconsistent rule-setters, to be less likely to show interest in their children, and to display high levels of hostile detachment.[38]

Although damaged parent-child relationships are associated with delinquency, it is difficult to assess the relationship. It is often assumed that preexisting family problems cause delinquency, but it may also be true that children who act out put enormous stress on a family. Kids who are conflict-prone may actually help to destabilize households. To avoid escalation of a child's aggression, these parents may give in to their children's demands. The children learn that aggression pays off.[39]

Family conflict has been linked to delinquency. Some experts believe that improved parenting skills may be key to reducing the incidence of child abuse. Here, Nicholas, 9 (left), and his brother, Jared, 7, get help with homework from their mom, Wendy Hastie, at their home in Nashville, Tenn. Wendy Hastie and her husband recently completed a Youth Village treatment program so they could learn to cope better with behavioral and health problems experienced by Jared. The program stresses early intervention in an attempt to head off problems before a juvenile breaks the law.

© 2000 AP/Wide World Photos

Parents may feel overwhelmed and shut their child out of their lives. Adolescent misbehavior may be a precursor of family conflict; strife leads to more adolescent misconduct, producing an endless cycle of family stress and delinquency.[40]

Which is worse, growing up in a home marked by conflict or growing up in a broken home? Research shows that children in both broken homes and high-conflict intact homes were worse off than children in low-conflict, intact families.[41] However, even when parents are divorced, kids who maintain attachments to their parents are less likely to engage in delinquency than those who are alienated and detached.[42] See Exhibit 7.1 for other key findings on divorce.

Family Neglect

Parents who are supportive and effectively control their children in a noncoercive fashion—a phenomenon referred to as parental efficacy—are more likely to raise children who refrain from delinquency.[43] Delinquency will be reduced if parents provide the type of structure that integrates children into families while giving them the ability to assert their individuality and regulate their own behavior.[44] In some cultures emotional support from the mother is critical, while in others the father's support remains the key factor.[45]

A number of studies support the link between the quality of family life and delinquency. Children who feel inhibited with their parents and refuse to discuss important issues with them are more likely to engage in deviant activities. Poor child-parent communications have been related to dysfunctional activities such as running away, and in all too many instances these children enter the ranks of homeless street youths who get involved in theft and prostitution to survive.[46] In contrast, even children who appear to be at-risk are better able to resist involvement in delinquent activity when they report a strong attachment to their parents.[47] The importance of close relations with the family may diminish as children reach late adolescence and develop stronger peer-group relations, but most experts believe family influence remains considerable throughout life.[48]

Inconsistent Discipline
Studies show that the parents of delinquent youths tend to be inconsistent disciplinarians, either overly harsh or extremely lenient.[49] But what conclusions can we draw from this observation?

The link between discipline and deviant behavior is uncertain. Most Americans still support the use of corporal punishment in disciplining children. The use of physical punishment cuts across racial, ethnic, and religious groups.[50] There is grow-

---

Exhibit 7.1   The Family Structure–Delinquency Link

- Children growing up in families disrupted by parental death are better adjusted than children of divorce. Parental absence is not per se a cause of antisocial behavior.

- Remarriage does not lessen the effects of divorce on youth: children living with a stepparent exhibit (a) as many problems as youths in divorce situations and (b) considerably more problems than do children living with both biological parents.

- Continued contact with the noncustodial parent has little effect on a child's well-being.

- Evidence that the behavior of children of divorce improves over time is inconclusive.

- Postdivorce conflict between parents is related to child maladjustment.

- Parental divorce raises the likelihood of teenage marriage.

Sources: Nicholas Wolfinger, "Parental Divorce and Offspring Marriage: Early or Late? *Social Forces 82*:337–354 (2003); Paul Amato and Bruce Keith, "Parental Divorce and the Well-Being of Children: A Meta-Analysis," *Psychological Bulletin 110*:26–46 (1991).

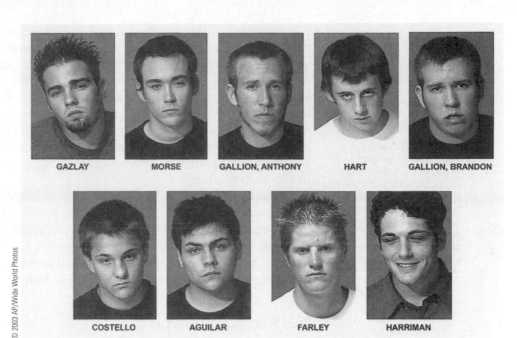

Some kids drift into law-violating gangs and groups when they are raised in families that fail to provide sufficient supervision and care. The teen suspects shown in these police photos are members of a middle-class gang of Nevada boys who were involved in several gruesome attacks during the summer of 2003, leaving victims permanently disfigured. Can their behavior be a result of parental neglect? Can we blame parents for the violent antisocial behavior of their children?

GAZLAY MORSE GALLION, ANTHONY HART GALLION, BRANDON

COSTELLO AGUILAR FARLEY HARRIMAN

ing evidence of a "violence begetting violence" cycle. Children who are subject to even minimal amounts of physical punishment may be more likely to use violence themselves. Sociologist Murray Straus reviewed the concept of discipline in a series of surveys and found a powerful relationship between exposure to physical punishment and later aggression.[51]

Nonviolent societies are also ones in which parents rarely punish their children physically; there is a link between corporal punishment, delinquency, spousal abuse, and adult crime.[52] Research conducted in ten European countries shows that the degree to which parents and teachers approve of corporal punishment is related to the homicide rate.[53]

Physical punishment weakens the bond between parents and children, lowers the children's self-esteem, and undermines their faith in justice. It is not surprising, then, that Straus finds a high correlation between physical discipline and street crime. It is possible that physical punishment encourages children to become more secretive and dishonest.[54] Overly strict discipline may have an even more insidious link to antisocial behaviors: abused children have a higher risk of neurological dysfunction than the nonabused, and brain abnormalities have been linked to violent crime.[55]

Supervision   Evidence also exists that inconsistent supervision can promote delinquency. F. Ivan Nye found that mothers who threatened discipline but failed to carry it out were more likely to have delinquent children than those who were consistent in their discipline.[56] Contemporary research supports this finding with evidence that assaultive boys tend to grow up in homes in which there is inconsistent discipline.[57]

There is ample evidence that effective supervision can reduce children's involvement in delinquency. Youths who believe their parents care little about their activities are more likely to engage in criminal acts than those who believe their actions will be closely monitored.[58] Kids who are not closely supervised spend more time out in the community with their friends and are more likely to get into trouble. In contrast, those who are supervised, especially in disorganized areas, are less likely to succumb to the temptations of the streets. The ability of a family to provide parental supervision seems even more important for children growing up in poor neighborhoods with fewer social ties among adults. In these areas parents cannot call upon neighborhood resources to take up the burden of controlling children; there is, therefore, a greater burden placed on families to provide adequate supervision.[59]

Resource Dilution   Parents may find it hard to control their children because they have such large families that their resources, such as time, are spread too thin (**resource dilution**). It is also possible that the relationship is indirect, caused by the connection of family size to some external factor; for example, resource dilution has been linked to educational underachievement, long considered a correlate of delinquency.[60] Middle children may suffer because they are most likely to be home when large numbers of siblings are also at home and economic resources are most stretched.[61] Larger families are more likely to produce delinquents than smaller ones, and middle children are more likely to engage in delinquent acts than first- or last-born children.

Resource dilution may force some mothers into the workforce in order to support their young children. Critics have suggested that these working mothers are unable to adequately supervise their children, leaving them prone to delinquency. However, recent research by Thomas Vander Ven and his associates found that having a mother who is employed has little if any effect on youthful misbehavior, especially if the children are adequately supervised.[62]

Family Deviance

A number of studies have found that parental deviance has a powerful influence on delinquent behavior.[63] Deviant behavior is intergenerational; the children of deviant parents produce delinquent children themselves.[64]

Some of the most important data on parental deviance was gathered by Donald J. West and David P. Farrington, whose Cambridge Youth Survey found that a significant number of delinquent youths have criminal fathers.[65] About 8 percent of the sons of noncriminal fathers became chronic offenders, compared to 37 percent of youths with criminal fathers.[66] In another analysis, Farrington found that one type of parental deviance, bullying, may be both inter- and intragenerational. Bullies have children who bully others, and these "second-generation bullies" grow up to become the fathers of children who are also bullies (see chapter 9 for more on bullying in the schoolyard).[67]

The cause of intergenerational deviance is uncertain. Genetic, environmental, psychological, and child-rearing factors may all play a role. For example, research shows that fathers of youths who suffer attention deficit hyperactivity disorder (ADHD), a condition linked to delinquency, are five times more likely to suffer antisocial personality disorder (APD) than fathers of non-ADHD youths; this finding indicates that personality problems may be intergenerational.[68] Similarly, research on the sons of alcoholics show that they suffer from neurological impairments related to delinquency.[69] It is possible that parental alcoholism causes genetic problems related to developmental impairment or that the children of substance-abusing parents are more prone to neurological impairment.

The quality of family life may also be key. Criminal parents may be least likely to have close relationships with their offspring; parental neglect has been linked to delinquency. Substance-abusing or criminal parents are more likely to use overly harsh and inconsistent discipline, two factors that have previously been linked to the onset of delinquent behavior.[70]

The association between parental deviance and children's delinquency may be related to labeling and stigma. Social control agents may be quick to fix a delinquent label on the children of known law violators, increasing the likelihood that they will pick up an "official" delinquent label.[71] The resulting stigma increases the chances they may fall into a delinquent career.

Sibling Influences   Some evidence also exists that siblings may influence behavior too; research shows that if one sibling is a delinquent there is a significant likelihood that his brother or sister will engage in delinquent behaviors.[72]

Not surprisingly, siblings who maintain a warm relationship and feel close to one another are also likely to behave in a similar fashion. If one of these siblings

Helping deal with issues of teen pregnancy and other family issues, Planned Parenthood is the world's largest and oldest voluntary family planning organization. Its Web site can be accessed by clicking on Web Links under the Chapter Resources at http://cj.wadsworth.com/siegel_jdcore2e.

resource dilution
A condition that occurs when parents have such large families that their resources, such as time and money, are spread too thin, causing lack of familial support and control.

Checkpoints

✔ *The family today is changing, and an increasing number of children will not live with their birth parents during their entire childhood.*

✔ *Families are experiencing social and economic stresses.*

✔ *A number of factors shape the family's influence on delinquency.*

✔ *Most experts believe that children whose parents have divorced are at risk for delinquency.*

✔ *Kids who grow up in conflict-ridden households are more likely to become delinquent.*

✔ *Poor parent-child relations, including inconsistent discipline, have been linked to delinquency.*

✔ *Parents who commit crimes and use drugs are likely to have children who also do so.*

✔ *If one sibling is delinquent, so are her brothers and sisters.*

To quiz yourself on this material, go to questions 7.1–7.8 on the Juvenile Delinquency: The Core 2e Web site.

takes drugs and engages in delinquent behavior, so too will his brother or sister.[73] A number of interpretations of these data are possible:

■ Siblings who live in the same environment are influenced by similar social and economic factors; it is not surprising that their behavior is similar.

■ Deviance is genetically determined, and the traits that cause one sibling to engage in delinquency are shared by his or her brother or sister.

■ Deviant siblings grow closer because of shared interests. It is possible that the relationship is due to personal interactions: older siblings are imitated by younger siblings.

In summary, the research on delinquency and family relationships offers ample evidence that family life can be a potent force on a child's development. The delinquent child is likely to grow up in a large family with parents who may drink, participate in criminal acts, be harsh and inconsistent disciplinarians, be cold and unaffectionate, have marital conflicts, and be poor role models. Overall, the quality of a child's family life seems to be more important than its structure. **✔ Checkpoints**

CHILD ABUSE AND NEGLECT

Concern about the quality of family life has increased because of reports that many children are physically abused or neglected by their parents and that this treatment has serious consequences for their behavior over the life course. Because of this topic's importance, the remainder of this chapter is devoted to the issue of child abuse and neglect and its relationship with delinquent behavior.

Historical Foundation

Parental abuse and neglect is not a modern phenomenon. Maltreatment of children has occurred throughout history. Some concern for the negative effects of such maltreatment was voiced in the eighteenth century in the United States, but concerted efforts to deal with the problem did not begin until 1874.

In that year, residents of a New York City apartment building reported to public health nurse Etta Wheeler that a child in one of the apartments was being abused by her stepmother. The nurse found a young child named Mary Ellen Wilson who had been repeatedly beaten and was malnourished from a diet of bread and water. Even though the child was seriously ill, the police agreed that the law entitled the parents to raise Mary Ellen as they saw fit. The New York City Department of Charities claimed it had no custody rights over Mary Ellen.

According to legend, Mary Ellen's removal from her parents had to be arranged through the Society for the Prevention of Cruelty to Animals (SPCA) on the ground that she was a member of the animal kingdom. The truth, however, is less sensational: Mary Ellen's case was heard by a judge. Because the child needed protection, she was placed in an orphanage.[74] The SPCA was actually founded the following year.[75]

Little research into the problems of maltreated children occurred before that of C. Henry Kempe, of the University of Colorado. In 1962, Kempe reported the results of a survey of medical and law-enforcement agencies that indicated the child abuse rate was much higher than had been thought. He coined a term, ***battered child syndrome,*** which he applied to cases of nonaccidental injury of children by their parents or guardians.[76]

Defining Abuse and Neglect

battered child syndrome
Nonaccidental physical injury of children by their parents or guardians.

Kempe's pioneering work has been expanded in a more generic expression of child abuse that includes neglect as well as physical abuse. Specifically, it describes any physical or emotional trauma to a child for which no reasonable explanation, such

In 1874 Henry Bugh and Etta Angell Wheeler persuaded a New York court to take a child, Mary Ellen, away from her mother on the grounds of child abuse. This is the first recorded case in which a court was used to protect a child. Mary Ellen is shown at age 9 when she appeared in court showing bruises from a whipping and several gashes from a pair of scissors. The other photograph shows her a year later.

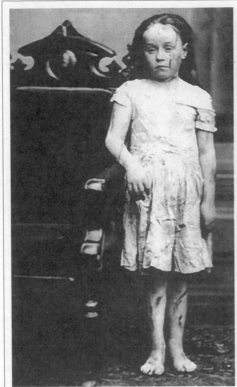

American Humane Society

as an accident, can be found. Child abuse is generally seen as a pattern of behavior rather than a single act. The effects of a pattern of behavior are cumulative. That is, the longer the abuse continues, the more severe the effect will be.[77]

Although the terms **child abuse** and neglect are sometimes used interchangeably, they represent different forms of maltreatment. **Neglect** refers to deprivations children suffer at the hands of their parents (lack of food, shelter, health care, love). *Abuse* is a more overt form of aggression against the child, one that often requires medical attention. The distinction between the terms is often unclear because, in many cases, both abuse and neglect occur simultaneously.

Physical abuse includes throwing, shooting, stabbing, burning, drowning, suffocating, biting, or deliberately disfiguring a child. The greatest number of injuries result from beatings. *Physical neglect* results from parents' failure to provide adequate food, shelter, or medical care for their children, as well as failure to protect them from physical danger.

Emotional abuse or neglect is manifested by constant criticism and rejection of the child.[78] Those who suffer emotional abuse have significantly lower self-esteem as adults.[79] *Emotional neglect* includes inadequate nurturing, inattention to a child's emotional development, and lack of concern about maladaptive behavior.

Sexual abuse refers to the exploitation of children through rape, incest, and molestation by parents, family members, friends, or legal guardians. Finally, **abandonment** refers to the situation in which parents leave their children with the intention of severing the parent-child relationship.[80]

Regardless of how it is defined, the effects of abuse can be devastating. Children who have experienced some form of maltreatment possess mental representations characterized by a devalued sense of self, mistrust of others, a tendency to perceive hostility in others in situations where the intentions of others are ambiguous, a tendency to generate antagonistic solutions to social problems, and a suspicion of close relationships.[81]

child abuse
Any physical, emotional, or sexual trauma to a child, including neglecting to give proper care and attention, for which no reasonable explanation can be found.

neglect
Passive neglect by a parent or guardian, depriving children of food, shelter, health care, and love.

abandonment
Parents physically leave their children with the intention of completely severing the parent-child relationship.

What is the line separating reasonable discipline from child abuse? Kathi Herren, shown here in a Michigan juvenile court, was convicted of a misdemeanor and sentenced to two years probation for slapping her fourteen-year-old daughter after catching her with cigarettes. Should parents have the right to physically punish their children?

Sexual Abuse   Sexual abuse can vary in content and style. It may range from rewarding children for sexual behavior that is inappropriate for their level of development to using force or the threat of force for the purposes of sex. It can involve children who are aware of the sexual content of their actions and others too young to have any idea what their actions mean. It can involve a variety of acts, from inappropriate touching to forcible sexual penetration.

Sexual abuse too can have devastating effects. Abused children suffer disrupted ego and personality development.[82] Guilt and shame are common. The ego of the victim may be overwhelmed by rage and horror over the incident, and the experience can have long-lasting repercussions.

Research indicates a correlation between the severity of abuse and its long-term effects: the less serious the abuse, the more quickly the child can recover.[83] Children who are frequently abused over long periods and suffer actual sexual penetration are most likely to experience long-term trauma, including post-traumatic stress syndrome (PTSD), precocious sexuality, and poor self-esteem.[84] Some victims find themselves sexualizing their own children in ways that lead them to sexual or physical abuse. Several studies have found a close association between sexual abuse and adolescent prostitution.[85] Girls who were sexually and physically abused as children are more often suicidal as adults than the nonabused.[86]

The Extent of Child Abuse

It is almost impossible to estimate the extent of child abuse. Many victims are so young that they have not learned to communicate. Some are too embarrassed or afraid to do so. Many incidents occur behind closed doors, and even when another adult witnesses inappropriate or criminal behavior, the adult may not want to get involved in a "family matter."

Some indications of the severity of the problem came from a groundbreaking 1980 survey conducted by sociologists Richard Gelles and Murray Straus.[87] Gelles and Straus estimated that between 1.4 and 1.9 million children in the United States were subject to physical abuse from their parents. This abuse was rarely a onetime act. The average number of assaults per year was 10.5, and the median was 4.5. Gelles

Every year, millions of children are the victims of abuse and neglect. Some pay with their lives. Sophia Mendoza, shown here, was charged with murder in October 2002, when police entered her home and found one of her children dead and another gravely malnourished. She had given birth to five children by the time she was twenty. What can be done to provide troubled young mothers like Mendoza with the help they need to care for their children properly?

and Straus also found that 16 percent of the couples in their sample reported spousal abuse; 50 percent of the multichild families reported attacks between siblings; 20 percent of the families reported incidents in which children attacked parents.[88]

The Gelles and Straus survey was a milestone in identifying child abuse as a national phenomenon. Surveys conducted in 1985 and 1992 indicated that the incidence of severe violence toward children had declined.[89] One reason was that parental approval of corporal punishment, which stood at 94 percent in 1968, decreased to 68 percent by 1994.[90] Recognition of the problem may have helped moderate cultural values and awakened parents to the dangers of physically disciplining children. Nonetheless, more than one million children were still being subjected to severe violence annually. If the definition of "severe abuse" used in the survey had included hitting with objects such as a stick or a belt, the number of child victims would have been closer to seven million per year.

Monitoring Abuse Not all child abuse and neglect cases are reported to authorities, but those that are become the focus of state action. A number of organizations have been collecting data on reported child abuse. The Department of Health and Human Services conducts an annual survey of child protection services (CPS) agencies to determine the number of reported child abuse victims. In 2001 (the latest data available), an estimated three million referrals concerning the welfare of approximately five million children were made to child protective services agencies throughout the United States. Of these, approximately two-thirds (67 percent) were screened in for further investigation and one-third (33 percent) were screened out. Of the cases that were investigated, more than one-quarter (28 percent) resulted in a finding that the child was maltreated or at risk of maltreatment. In all, approximately 903,000 children were found to be victims of child maltreatment, including neglect, physical abuse, sexual abuse, and psychological maltreatment. As Figure 7.3 shows, the 2001 victimization rate of 12.4 per 1,000 children in the population is quite a bit lower than the abuse rates of a decade earlier. It is uncertain why child abuse rates are in decline. One position is that anti-abuse programs are working and there is simply less abuse. A second vision is that cutbacks in funding have limited the government's ability to investigate and process cases.

Who Are the Victims of Abuse? Younger children are the most likely to be abused and neglected; children in the age group of birth to three years account for 28 percent of all victims. Abuse cuts across racial and gender lines: males and females have almost equal abuse rates; half of all victims were White (50 percent); one-quarter (25 percent) were African American; 15 percent were Hispanic. American Indian/Alaska Natives accounted for 2 percent of victims, and Asian/Pacific Islanders accounted for 1 percent of victims. Approximately 1,300 of these child victims died of abuse or neglect during the year 2001, a rate of 1.81 children per 100,000 children in the population.

Attempts to determine the extent of sexual abuse indicate that perhaps one in ten boys and one in three girls have been the victims of some form of sexual exploita-

http:

Preventing child abuse before it occurs is the aim of **Prevent Child Abuse America.** Visit its site by clicking on Web Links under the Chapter Resources at http://cj.wadsworth.com/ siegel_jdcore2e.

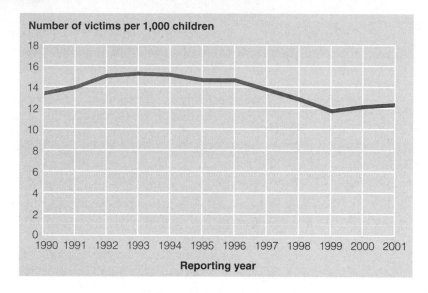

Figure 7.3   Child Abuse Rates, 1990–2001

Number of victims per 1,000 children

Reporting year

Source: U.S. Department of Health & Human Services, Administration for Children & Families. www.acf.hhs.gov/programs/cb/publications/cm00/figure3_2.htm.

tion. Richard J. Estes and Neil Alan Weiner, two researchers at the School of Social Welfare at the University of Pennsylvania, found that the problem of child sexual abuse is much more widespread than was previously believed or documented. Their research indicated that each year in the United States 325,000 children are subjected to some form of sexual exploitation, which includes sexual abuse, prostitution, use in pornography, and molestation by adults. Most are White and middle-class. Equal numbers of boys and girls are involved, but the activities of boys generally receive less attention from authorities. Many of these kids are runaways (more than 120,000) while others have fled mental hospitals and foster homes. More than 50,000 are thrown out of their home by a parent or guardian.[91]

Although sexual abuse is still quite prevalent, the number of reported cases has been in significant decline. After a fifteen-year increase, substantiated child sexual abuse cases in the United States dropped 31 percent between 1992 and 1998.[92] These data may either mean that the actual number of cases is truly in decline or that social service professionals are failing to recognize abuse cases because of overwork and understaffing.

Causes of Child Abuse and Neglect

Maltreatment of children is a complex problem with neither a single cause nor a single solution. It cuts across racial, ethnic, religious, and socioeconomic lines. Abusive parents cannot be categorized by sex, age, or educational level.

Of all factors associated with child abuse, three are discussed most often: (1) parents who themselves suffered abuse tend to abuse their own children; (2) the presence of an unrelated adult increases the risk of abuse; and (3) isolated and alienated families tend to become abusive. A cyclical pattern of violence seems to be perpetuated from one generation to another. Evidence indicates that a large number of abused and neglected children grow into adulthood with a tendency to engage in violent behavior. The behavior of abusive parents can often be traced to negative experiences in their own childhood—physical abuse, emotional neglect, and incest. These parents become unable to separate their own childhood traumas from their relationships with their children. Abusive parents often have unrealistic perceptions of normal development. When their children are unable to act appropriately—when they cry or strike their parents—the parents may react in an abusive manner.[93] Parents may also become abusive if they are isolated from friends, neighbors, or relatives.

Many abusive parents describe themselves as alienated from their extended families, and they lack close relationships with persons who could provide help in stressful situations.[94] The relationship between alienation and abuse may be particularly acute in homes where there has been divorce or separation, or in which parents have never actually married; abusive punishment in single-parent homes has been found to be twice that of two-parent families.[95] Parents who are unable to cope with stressful events—divorce, financial stress, recurring mental illness, drug addiction—are most at risk.[96]

Substance Abuse and Child Abuse   Abusive families suffer from severe stress, and it is therefore not surprising that they frequently harbor members who turn to drugs and alcohol. Studies have found a strong association between child abuse and parental alcoholism.[97]

In addition, evidence exists of a significant relationship between cocaine and heroin abuse and neglect and abuse of children. Because this relationship is so important, it is explored further in the Focus on Delinquency feature, "Relationship Between Substance Abuse and Child Maltreatment."

Stepparents and Abuse   Research indicates that stepchildren share a greater risk for abuse than do biological offspring.[98] Stepparents may have less emotional attachment to the children of another. Often the biological parent has to choose between the new mate and the child, sometimes even becoming an accomplice in the abuse.[99]

Stepchildren are overrepresented in cases of **familicide,** mass murders in which a spouse and one or more children are slain. It is also more common for fathers who kill their biological children to commit suicide than those who kill stepchildren, an indication that the latter act is motivated by hostility and not despair.[100]

Social Class and Abuse   Surveys indicate a high rate of reported abuse and neglect among people in lower economic classes. Children from families with a household income of less than $15,000 per year experience more abuse than children living in more affluent homes. Child care workers indicate that most of their clients either live in poverty or face increased financial stress because of unemployment and economic recession. These findings suggest that parental maltreatment of children is predominantly a lower-class problem. Is this conclusion valid?

One view is that low-income families, especially those headed by a single parent, are often subject to greater environmental stress and have fewer resources to deal with such stress than families with higher incomes.[101] A relationship seems to exist between the burdens of raising a child without adequate resources and the use of excessive force. Self-report surveys do show that indigent parents are more likely than affluent parents to hold attitudes that condone physical chastisement of children.[102]

Higher rates of maltreatment in low-income families reflect the stress caused by the limited resources that lower-class parents have to help them raise their children; in contrast, middle-class parents devote a smaller percentage of their total resources to raising a family.[103]

This burden becomes especially onerous in families with emotionally and physically handicapped children. Stressed-out parents may consider special-needs children a drain on the families' finances with little potential for future success; research finds that children with disabilities are maltreated at a rate almost double that of other children.[104]

familicide
Mass murders in which a spouse and one or more children are slain.

Relationship Between Substance Abuse and Child Maltreatment

The relationship between parental alcohol or other drug problems and child maltreatment is becoming increasingly evident. It is a serious problem because substance abuse is so widespread: an estimated fourteen million adult Americans abuse alcohol, and there may be more than twelve million illicit drug users. With more than six million children under the age of eighteen living in alcoholic households, and an additional number living in households where parents have problems with illicit drugs, it is evident that a significant number of children in this country are being raised by addicted parents.

Do Parental Alcohol or Other Drug Problems Cause Child Maltreatment?

Research clearly indicates a connection between substance abuse and child abuse. Among confirmed cases of child maltreatment, 40 percent involve the use of alcohol or other drugs. This suggests that, of the 1.2 million confirmed victims of child maltreatment each year, an estimated 480,000 children are mistreated by a caretaker with alcohol or other drug problems. In addition, research suggests that alcohol and other drug problems are factors in a majority of cases of emotional abuse and neglect. In fact, neglect is the main reason why children are removed from a home in which parents have alcohol or other drug problems. Children in these homes suffer from a variety of physical, mental, and emotional health problems at a greater rate than do children in the general population. Children of alcoholics suffer more injuries and poisonings than do children in the general population. Alcohol and other substances may act as disinhibitors, lessening impulse control and allowing parents to behave abusively. Children in this environment often demonstrate behavioral problems and are diagnosed as having conduct disorders. This may result in provocative behavior. Increased stress resulting from preoccupation with drugs on the part of the parent combined with behavioral problems exhibited by the child increases the likelihood of maltreatment. Frequently, these parents suffer from depression, anxiety, and low self-esteem. They live in an atmosphere of stress and family conflict. Children raised in such households are themselves more likely to have problems with alcohol and other drugs.

In What Ways Are Children Affected?

Children of alcoholics are more likely than children in the general population to suffer a variety of physical, mental, and emotional health problems. They often have feelings of low self-esteem and failure and suffer from depression and anxiety. It is thought that exposure to violence in both alcohol-abusing and child-maltreating households increases the likelihood that the children will commit, and be recipients of, acts of violence. The effects don't end when these children reach adulthood; they may have difficulty coping with and establishing healthy relationships as adults. In addition to suffering from all the effects of living in a household where alcohol or child-maltreatment problems exist, children whose parents abuse illicit drugs live with the knowledge that their parents' actions are illegal. Although the research is in its infancy, clinical evidence shows that children of parents who have problems with illicit drug use may suffer from an inability to trust legitimate authority because of fear of discovery of a parent's illegal habits.

As they mature, many fall victim to the same patterns exhibited by their parents. Those who have been severely physically abused often have symptoms of post-traumatic disorder and dissociation. Individuals suffering from mental health disorders may use alcohol and illicit drugs to decrease or mitigate their psychological distress. Research suggests that adults who were abused as children may be more likely to abuse their own children than adults who were not abused as children.

Can child maltreatment, when alcohol or other drugs are a problem, be successfully treated? Research has shown that when families exhibit both of these behaviors, the problems must be treated simultaneously in order to ensure a child's safety. Although ending the drug dependency does not automatically end child maltreatment, very little can be done to improve parenting skills until this step is taken. The withdrawal experienced by parents who cease using alcohol or other drugs presents specific risks. The effects of withdrawal often cause a parent to experience intense emotions, which may increase the likelihood of child maltreatment. During this time, lasting as long as two years, it is especially important that resources be available to the family.

CRITICAL THINKING

1. Considering the substance abuse–child abuse association, should the government be proactive in removing kids from homes where parents are known substance abusers?
2. Does the substance abuse–child abuse link support or contradict the view that delinquent behavior is inherited?

INFOTRAC COLLEGE EDITION RESEARCH

To learn more about the problems faced by abused kids and their parents, go to InfoTrac College Edition and read Anna Lau and John Weisz, "Reported Maltreatment Among Clinic-Referred Children: Implications for Presenting Problems, Treatment Attrition, and Long-Term Outcomes," *Journal of the American Academy of Child and Adolescent Psychiatry* 42:1327–1334 (2003).

Source: *The Relationship Between Parental Alcohol or Other Drug Problems and Child Maltreatment* (Chicago: Prevent Child Abuse America, 2000).

The Child Protection System: Philosophy and Practice

For most of our nation's history, courts have assumed that parents have the right to bring up their children as they see fit. In the 2000 case *Troxel v. Granville,* the Supreme Court ruled that the due process clause of the Constitution protects against government interference with certain fundamental rights and liberty interests, including parents' fundamental right to make decisions concerning the care, custody, and control of their children.[105] If the care a child receives falls below reasonable standards, the state may take action to remove a child from the home and place her or him in a less threatening environment. In these extreme circumstances, the rights of both parents and children are constitutionally protected. In the cases of *Lassiter v. Department of Social Services* and *Santosky v. Kramer,* the U.S. Supreme Court recognized the child's right to be free from parental abuse and set down guidelines for a termination-of-custody hearing, including the right to legal representation.[106] States provide a guardian *ad litem* (a lawyer appointed by the court to look after the interests of those who do not have the capacity to assert their own rights). States also ensure confidentiality of reporting.[107]

Though child protection agencies have been dealing with abuse and neglect since the late nineteenth century, recent awareness of the problem has prompted judicial authorities to take increasingly bold steps to ensure the safety of children.[108] The assumption that the parent-child relationship is inviolate has been challenged. In 1974 Congress passed the Child Abuse Prevention and Treatment Act (CAPTA), which provides funds to states to bolster their services for maltreated children and their parents.[109] The act provides federal funding to states in support of prevention, investigation, and treatment. It also provides grants to public agencies and nonprofit organizations for demonstration programs.

The Child Abuse Prevention and Treatment Act has been the impetus for the states to improve the legal frameworks of their child protection systems. Abusive parents are subject to prosecution under statutes against assault, battery, and homicide.

Investigating and Reporting Abuse

Maltreatment of children can easily be hidden from public view. Although state laws require doctors, teachers, and others who work with children to report suspected cases to child protection agencies, many maltreated children are out of the law's reach because they are too young for school or because their parents do not take them to a doctor or a hospital. Parents abuse their children in private, and even when confronted, often accuse their children of lying or blame the children's medical problems on accidents. Social service agencies must find more effective ways to locate abused children and handle such cases once found.

All states have statutes requiring that persons suspected of abuse and neglect be reported. Many have made failure to report child abuse a criminal offense. Though such statutes are rarely enforced, teachers and nurses have been criminally charged for failing to report abuse or neglect cases.[110]

Once reported to a child protection agency, the case is screened by an intake worker and then turned over to an investigative caseworker. In some jurisdictions, if child protective services substantiates a report, the case will likely be referred to a law enforcement agency that will have the responsibility of investigating the case, collecting evidence that can later be used in court proceedings. If the caseworker determines that the child is in imminent danger of severe harm, the caseworker may immediately remove the child from the home. A court hearing must be held shortly after to approve custody. Stories abound of children erroneously taken from their homes, but it is much more likely that these "gatekeepers" will consider cases unfounded and take no action. Among the most common reasons for screening out cases is that the reporting party is involved in a child custody case despite the research showing that the risk of abuse increases significantly in the aftermath of divorce.[111]

Even when there is compelling evidence of abuse, most social service agencies will try to involve the family in voluntary treatment. Case managers will do periodic

The Children's Bureau (CB), the oldest federal agency for children, is located in the U.S. Department of Health and Human Services' Administration for Children and Families, Administration on Children, Youth and Families. It is responsible for assisting states in the delivery of child welfare services, services designed to protect children and strengthen families. The Web site can be accessed by clicking on Web Links under the Chapter Resources at http://cj.wadsworth.com/siegel_jdcore2e.

Should we blame an overworked child protection system for its failures to protect youth? Is it realistic to assume these agencies can effectively monitor the behavior of troubled families? Here, Division of Youth and Family Services union members participate in a rally in Camden, New Jersey, November 3, 2003. The rally was held in response to the firing of seven DYFS workers after a Collingswood couple was accused of allegedly starving their four adopted sons. Union officials said the case has put too much focus on that family's problems and not enough on longstanding problems in the Division of Family and Youth Services.

follow-ups to determine if treatment plans are being followed. If parents are uncooperative, or if the danger to the children is so great that they must be removed from the home, a complaint will be filed in the criminal, family, or juvenile court system. To protect the child, the court could then issue temporary orders placing the child in shelter care during investigation, ordering services, or ordering suspected abusers to have no contact with the child.

The Process of State Intervention

Although procedures vary from state to state, most follow a similar legal process once a social service agency files a court petition alleging abuse or neglect.[112] This process is diagrammed in Figure 7.4.

If the allegation of abuse is confirmed, the child may be placed in protective custody. Most state statutes require that the court be notified "promptly" or "immediately" if the child is removed; some states, including Arkansas, North Carolina, and Pennsylvania, have gone as far as requiring that no more than twelve hours elapse before official action is taken. If the child has not been removed from the home, state authorities are given more time to notify the court of suspected abuse. For example, Louisiana and Maryland set a limit of thirty days to take action, whereas Wisconsin mandates that state action take no more than twenty days once the case has been investigated.

When an abuse or neglect petition is prosecuted, an **advisement hearing** (also called a *preliminary protective hearing* or *emergency custody hearing*) is held. The court will review the facts of the case, determine whether permanent removal of the child is justified, and notify the parents of the charges against them. Parents have the right to counsel in all cases of abuse and neglect, and many states require the court to appoint an attorney for the child as well. If the parents admit the allegations, the court enters a consent decree, and the case is continued for disposition. Approximately one-half of all cases are settled by admission at the advisement hearing. If the parents deny the petition, an attorney is appointed for the child and the case is continued for a **pretrial conference.**

advisement hearing

A preliminary protective or temporary custody hearing in which the court will review the facts and determine whether removal of the child is justified and notify parents of the charges against them.

pretrial conference

The attorney for the social services agency presents an overview of the case, and a plea bargain or negotiated settlement can be agreed to in a consent decree.

At the pretrial conference, the attorney for the social service agency presents an overview of the case and the evidence. Such matters as admissibility of photos and written reports are settled. At this point the attorneys can negotiate a settlement of the case, in which the parents accept a treatment plan detailing:

- The types of services that the child and the child's family will receive, such as parenting classes, mental health or substance abuse treatment, and family counseling

- Reunification goals, including visitation schedules and a target date for a child's return home

- Concurrent plans for alternative permanent placement options should reunification goals not be met

About three-fourths of the cases that go to pretrial conference are settled by a consent decree. About eighty-five out of every one hundred petitions filed are settled at either the advisement hearing or the pretrial conference.

Of the fifteen remaining cases, five are generally settled before trial. Usually no more than ten cases out of every one hundred actually reach the trial stage of the process. This is an adversarial hearing designed to prove the state's allegations.

Figure 7.4 **The Process of State Intervention in Cases of Abuse and Neglect**

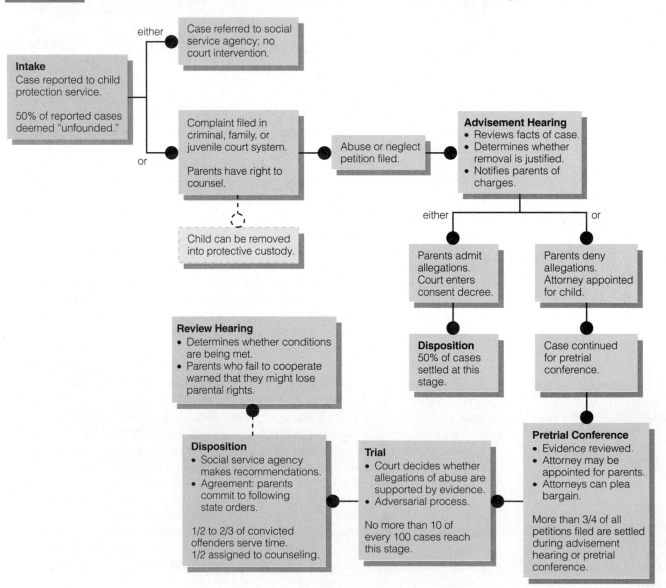

Disposition   The most crucial part of an abuse or neglect proceeding is the **disposition hearing.** The social service agency presents its case plan, which includes recommendations such as conditions for returning the child to the parents, or a visitation plan if the child is to be taken permanently from the parents. An agreement is reached by which the parents commit themselves to following the state orders. Between one-half and two-thirds of all convicted parents will be required to serve time in incarceration; almost half will be assigned to a form of treatment. As far as the children are concerned, some may be placed in temporary care; in other cases, parental rights are terminated and the child is placed in the custody of the child protective service. Legal custody can then be assigned to a relative or some other person. In 2001, approximately 275,000 children were removed from their homes.

In making their decisions, courts are guided by three interests: the role of the parents, protection for the child, and the responsibility of the state. Frequently, these interests conflict. In fact, at times even the interests of the two parents are not in harmony. The state attempts to balance the parents' natural right to control their child's upbringing with the child's right to grow into adulthood free from harm. This is referred to as the **balancing-of-the-interests approach.**

Periodically, **review hearings** are held to determine if the conditions of the case plan are being met. Parents who fail to cooperate are warned that they may lose their parental rights. Most abuse and neglect cases are concluded within a year. Either the parents lose their rights and the child is given a permanent placement, or the child is returned to the parents and the court's jurisdiction ends.

The Abused Child in Court

One of the most significant problems associated with abuse cases is the trauma a child must go through in a court hearing. Children get confused and frightened and may change their testimony. Much controversy has arisen over the accuracy of children's reports of family violence and sexual abuse, resulting in hung juries in some well-known cases, including the McMartin Day Care case in California.[113]

State jurisdictions have instituted procedures to minimize the trauma to the child. Most have enacted legislation allowing videotaped statements, or interviews with child witnesses, taken at a preliminary hearing or at a formal deposition to be admissible in court. Videotaped testimony spares child witnesses the trauma of testifying in open court. States that allow videotaped testimony usually put some restrictions on its use: some prohibit the government from calling the child to testify at trial if the videotape is used; some states require a finding that the child is "medically unavailable" because of the trauma of the case before videotaping can be used; some require that the defendant be present during the videotaping; a few specify that the child not be able to see or hear the defendant.[114]

Most of the states now allow a child's testimony to be given on closed-circuit television (CCTV). The child is able to view the judge and attorneys, and the courtroom participants are able to observe the child. The standards for CCTV testimony vary widely. Some states, such as New Hampshire, assume that any child witness under age twelve would benefit from not having to appear in court. Others require an independent examination by a mental health professional to determine whether there is a "compelling need" for CCTV testimony.

In addition to innovative methods of testimony, children in sexual abuse cases have been allowed to use anatomically correct dolls to demonstrate happenings that they cannot describe verbally. The Victims of Child Abuse Act of 1990 allows children to use these dolls when testifying in federal courts; at least eight states have passed similar legislation.[115] Similarly, states have relaxed their laws of evidence to allow out-of-court statements by the child to a social worker, teacher, or police officer to be used as evidence (such statements would otherwise be considered **hearsay**). Typically, corroboration is required to support these statements if the child does not also testify.

The American Bar Association maintains a Web site with information on legal rights of children in abuse cases. The Web site can be accessed by clicking on Web Links under the Chapter Resources at http://cj.wadsworth.com/ siegel_jdcore2e.

disposition hearing
The social service agency presents its case plan and recommendations for care of the child and treatment of the parents, including incarceration and counseling or other treatment.

balancing-of-the-interests approach
Efforts of the courts to balance the parents' natural right to raise a child with the child's right to grow into adulthood free from physical abuse or emotional harm.

review hearings
Periodic meetings to determine whether the conditions of the case plan for an abused child are being met by the parents or guardians of the child.

hearsay
Out-of-court statements made by one person and recounted in court by another; such statements are generally not allowed as evidence except in child abuse cases wherein a child's statements to social workers, teachers, or police may be admissible.

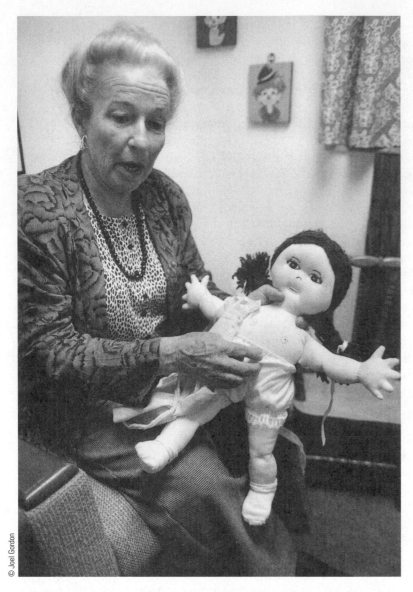

A counselor shows a doll to a victim of child abuse. Children in sexual abuse cases may use anatomically correct dolls to demonstrate happenings that they cannot describe verbally. The Victims of Child Abuse Act of 1990 allows children to use dolls when testifying in federal courts; at least eight states have passed similar legislation.

The prevalence of sexual abuse cases has created new problems for the justice system. Often accusations are made in conjunction with marital disputes. The fear is growing that children may become pawns in custody battles; the mere suggestion of sexual abuse is enough to affect the outcome of a divorce action. The justice system must develop techniques that can get at the truth without creating a lifelong scar on the child's psyche.

Legal Issues   A number of cases have been brought before the Supreme Court testing the right of children to present evidence at trial using nontraditional methods. Two issues stand out. One is the ability of physicians and mental health professionals to testify about statements made to them by children, especially when the children are incapable of testifying. The second concerns the way children testify in court.

In a 1992 case, *White v. Illinois,* the Supreme Court ruled that the state's attorney is required neither to produce young victims at trial nor to demonstrate the reason why they were unavailable to serve as witnesses.[116] *White* involved statements given by the child to the child's baby-sitter and mother, a doctor, a nurse, and a police officer concerning the alleged assailant in a sexual assault case. The prosecutor twice tried to call the child to testify, but both times the four-year-old experienced emotional difficulty and could not appear in court. The outcome hinged solely on the testimony of the five witnesses.

By allowing others to testify as to what the child said, *White* removed the requirement that prosecutors produce child victims in court. This facilitates the prosecution of child abusers in cases where a court appearance by a victim would prove too disturbing or where the victim is too young to understand the court process.[117] The Court noted that statements made to doctors during medical exams or those made when a victim is upset carry more weight than ones made after careful reflection. The Court ruled that such statements can be repeated during trial because the circumstances in which they were made could not be duplicated simply by having the child testify to them in court.

In-Court Statements   Children who are victims of sexual or physical abuse often make poor witnesses. Yet their testimony may be crucial. In a 1988 case, *Coy v. Iowa,* the Supreme Court placed limitations on efforts to protect child witnesses in court. During a sexual assault case, a "one-way" glass screen was set up so that the child victims would not be able to view the defendant (the defendant, however, could view the witnesses).[118] The Iowa statute that allowed the protective screen assumed that children would be traumatized by their courtroom experience. The Court ruled that unless there is a finding that the child witness needs special protection, the Sixth Amendment of the Constitution grants defendants "face-to-face" confrontation with their accusers. In her dissenting opinion, Justice Sandra Day O'Connor suggested that if courts found it necessary, it would be appropriate to allow children to testify via CCTV or videotape.

Justice O'Connor's views became law in *Maryland v. Craig*.[119] In this case a day-care operator was convicted of sexually abusing a six-year-old child; one-way CCTV testimony was used during the trial. The decision was overturned in the Maryland Court of Appeals on the grounds that the procedures used were insufficient to show that the child could only testify in this manner because a trial appearance would be too traumatic. On appeal, the Court ruled that the Maryland statute that allows CCTV testimony is sufficient because it requires a determination that the child will suffer distress if forced to testify. The Court noted that CCTV could serve as the equivalent of in-court testimony and would not interfere with the defendant's right to confront witnesses.

Disposition of Abuse and Neglect Cases

There is considerable controversy over what forms of intervention are helpful in abuse and neglect cases. Today, social service agents avoid removing children from the home whenever possible and instead try to employ techniques to control abusive relationships. In serious cases, the state may remove children from their parents and place them in shelter care or foster homes. Placement of children in foster care is intended to be temporary, but it is not uncommon for children to remain in foster care for three years or more.

Ultimately, the court has the power to terminate the rights of parents over their children, but because the effects of destroying the family unit are far reaching, the court does so only in the most severe cases. Judicial hesitancy is illustrated in a Virginia appellate case in which grandparents contested a father's being awarded custody of his children. Even though he had a history of alcohol abuse, had already been found to be an unfit parent, and was awaiting appeal of his conviction for killing the children's mother, the trial court claimed that he had turned his life around and granted him custody.[120]

Despite such occurrences, efforts have been ongoing to improve the child protection system. Jurisdictions have expedited case processing, instituted procedures designed not to frighten child witnesses, coordinated investigations between social service and law enforcement agencies, and assigned an advocate or guardian *ad litem* to children in need of protection. 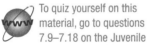 ✔ Checkpoints

Checkpoints

✔ Although the maltreatment of juveniles has occurred throughout history, the concept of child abuse is relatively recent.

✔ C. Henry Kempe first recognized battered child syndrome.

✔ We now recognize sexual, physical, and emotional abuse, as well as neglect.

✔ More than one million confirmed cases of abuse occur each year.

✔ The number of sexual abuse cases has declined.

✔ There are a number of suspected causes of child abuse, including parental substance abuse, isolation, and a history of physical and emotional abuse.

✔ A child protection system has been created to identify and try abuse cases.

✔ The courts have made it easier for children to testify in abuse cases, by using CCTV, for example.

 To quiz yourself on this material, go to questions 7.9–7.18 on the Juvenile Delinquency: The Core 2e Web site.

ABUSE, NEGLECT, AND DELINQUENCY

Because the effects of child abuse are long-term, delinquency experts fear that abused kids will experience mental and social problems across their life span. For example, victims of abuse are prone to suffer mental illness such as dissociative identity disorder (DID), formerly known as multiple personality disorder (MPD); research shows that child abuse is present in the histories of the vast majority of DID subjects.[121]

One particular area of concern is the child's own personal involvement with violence. Psychologists suggest that maltreatment encourages children to use aggression as a means of solving problems and prevents them from feeling empathy for others. It diminishes their ability to cope with stress and makes them vulnerable to the violence in the culture. Abused children have fewer positive interactions with peers, are less well liked, and are more likely to have disturbed social interactions.[122]

The link between maltreatment and delinquency is also supported by a number of criminological theories. For example:

- *Social control theory.* By disrupting normal relationships and impeding socialization, maltreatment reduces the social bond and frees individuals to become involved in deviance.

- *Social learning theory.* Maltreatment leads to delinquency because it teaches children that aggression and violence are justifiable forms of behavior.
- *General strain theory.* Maltreatment creates the "negative affective states" that are related to strain, anger, and aggression.

A significant amount of literature suggests that abuse may have a profound effect on behavior in later years. Exposure to abuse in early life provides a foundation for violent and antisocial behavior.[123] Delinquent behavior is the means by which many abused children act out their hostility toward their parents. Some join gangs, which furnish a sense of belonging and allow pent-up anger to be expressed in group-approved delinquent acts.

Clinical Histories

Studies of juvenile offenders have confirmed that between 70 and 80 percent may have had abusive backgrounds. Many of these juveniles report serious injury, including bruises, lacerations, fractures, and being knocked unconscious by a parent or guardian.[124] Likewise, several studies reveal an association between homicide and maltreatment in early childhood.[125] Among children who kill or who attempt murder, the most common factor is a child's tendency to identify with aggressive parents and imitate their behavior.[126] One study of murder and murderous assault by juveniles indicated that in all cases "one or both parents had fostered and condoned murderous assault."[127]

Cohort Studies

These findings do not necessarily prove that maltreatment causes delinquency. It is possible that child abuse is a reaction to misbehavior and not vice versa. In other words, it is possible that angry parents attack their delinquent and drug-abusing children and that child abuse is a *result* of delinquency, not its cause.

One way of solving this dilemma is to follow a cohort of youths who have been reported as victims of abuse and compare them with a similar cohort of nonabused youths. A classic study conducted by Jose Alfaro in New York found that about half of all children reported to area hospitals as abused children later acquired arrest records. Conversely, a significant number of boys (21 percent) and girls (29 percent) petitioned to juvenile court had prior histories as abuse cases. Children treated for abuse were disproportionately involved in violent offenses.[128]

Cathy Spatz Widom followed the offending careers of 908 youths reported as abused from 1967 to 1971 and compared them with a control group of 667 nonabused youths. Widom found that the abuse involved a variety of perpetrators, including parents, relatives, strangers, and even grandparents. Twenty-six percent of the abused sample had juvenile arrests, compared with 17 percent of the comparison group; 29 percent of those who were abused had adult criminal records, compared with 21 percent of the control group. Race, gender, and age also affected the probability that abuse would lead to delinquency. The highest risk group was composed of older Black males who had suffered abuse; about 67 percent of this group went on to become adult criminals. In contrast, only 4 percent of young, White, nonabused females became adult offenders.[129] Her conclusion: being abused increases the likelihood of arrest both as a juvenile and as an adult.[130]

Widom also tested the hypothesis that victims of childhood violence resort to violence themselves as they mature. The children in her sample who suffered from physical abuse were the most likely to get arrested for violent crimes; their violent crime arrest rate was double that of the control group. More surprising was the discovery that neglected children maintained higher rates of violence than children in the comparison group. Clearly, family trauma of all kinds may influence violence.

Child Victims and Persistent Offending

Widom also interviewed five hundred subjects twenty years after their childhood victimization. Preliminary analysis of this sample indicates that the long-term consequences of childhood victimization continue throughout life. Potential problems include mental health concerns, educational problems, health problems, and occupational difficulties. In a more recent analysis, Widom and Michael Maxfield found that by the time they reached age thirty-two, the abused children had a higher frequency of adult offending than the nonabused. People who began their offending careers as adults were also more likely to have been abused as children. Widom and Maxfield conclude that early intervention may be necessary to stop this cycle of violence.[131]

Sexual Abuse   Cohort research shows that sexually abused youths are much more likely to suffer an arrest than nonabused children. The risk is greatest if the abuse took place when the child was less than seven years of age and the offense was committed by a male.[132] Sexually abused girls share a significant risk of becoming violent over the life course. There is also evidence that sexual abuse victims are more likely to abuse others, especially if they were exposed to other forms of family violence.[133] Self-report studies also confirm that child maltreatment increases the likelihood of delinquency. The most severely abused youths are at the greatest risk for long-term serious delinquency.[134]

The Abuse-Delinquency Link

These findings do not necessarily mean that most abused children become delinquent. Many do not, and many delinquent youths come from what appear to be model homes. Though Widom found that more abused than nonabused children in her cohort became involved in delinquency, the majority of *both* groups did not.[135]

Although these studies suggest an abuse-delinquency link, others find that the association is either nonsignificant or inconsistent (for example, having a greater influence on girls than boys).[136] However, some recent research by Timothy Ireland and his associates indicates that the abuse-delinquency link may be a function of when the abuse occurred: kids who were maltreated solely during their early childhood are less likely to later engage in delinquent acts than (a) those mistreated when they were older or (b) those whose abuse occurred first in childhood and then persisted into later adolescence.[137] Ireland speculates that adolescents who have experienced persistent and long-term maltreatment are more likely to have families suffering an array of other social deficits, including poverty, parental mental illness, and domestic violence, which may make children more likely to engage in antisocial behavior. Persistent maltreatment also gives the victims little opportunity to cope or deal with their ongoing victimization. Because it is suspected that child abuse leads to a cycle of violence, there are programs designed to help abusive parents refrain from repeating their violent episodes.

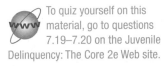 To quiz yourself on this material, go to questions 7.19–7.20 on the Juvenile Delinquency: The Core 2e Web site.

SUMMARY

- Poor family relationships have been linked to juvenile delinquency.
- Early theories viewed the broken home as a cause of youthful misconduct, but subsequent research found that divorce and separation play a smaller role than was previously believed.
- However, contemporary studies now show that parental absence may have a significant influence on delinquency because it is more difficult for one parent to provide the same degree of discipline and support as two.
- The quality of family life also has a great influence on a child's behavior. Families in conflict produce more delinquents than those that function harmoniously.

- Families who neglect their children are at risk for delinquency. Inconsistent discipline and supervision have also been linked to juvenile crime.
- Parental and sibling misconduct is another factor that predicts delinquent behaviors.
- Concern over the relationship between family life and delinquency has been heightened by reports of widespread child abuse.
- Cases of abuse and neglect have been found in every social class and racial group.
- It has been estimated that there are three million reported cases of child abuse each year, of which almost one million are confirmed by child welfare investigators.

- Two factors are seen as causing child abuse. First, parents who themselves suffered abuse as children tend to abuse their own children. Second, isolated and alienated families tend to become abusive.
- Local, state, and federal governments have attempted to alleviate the problem of child abuse. All fifty states have statutes requiring that suspected cases of abuse be reported.
- There is a complex system of state intervention once allegations of child abuse are made. Thousands of youths are removed from their homes every year.

- A number of studies have linked abuse to delinquency. They show that a disproportionate number of court-adjudicated youths had been abused or neglected.
- Although the evidence is not conclusive, the data suggest that a strong relationship exists between child abuse and delinquent behavior.
- To make it easier to prosecute abusers, the Supreme Court has legalized the use of CCTV in some cases. Most states allow children to use anatomically correct dolls when testifying in court.

KEY TERMS

nuclear family, p. 156
broken home, p. 159
blended families, p. 159
intrafamily violence, p. 160
resource dilution, p. 164
battered child syndrome, p. 165

child abuse, p. 166
neglect, p. 166
abandonment, p. 166
familicide, p. 170
advisement hearing, p. 173
pretrial conference, p. 173

disposition hearing, p. 175
balancing-of-the-interests approach, p. 175
review hearings, p. 175
hearsay, p. 175

QUESTIONS FOR DISCUSSION

1. What are the meanings of the terms *child abuse* and *child neglect*?
2. Discuss the association between child abuse and delinquency. Give two different explanations for the positive relationship between abuse and antisocial behavior.
3. What causes parents to abuse their children?
4. What is meant by the child protection system? Do courts act in the best interest of the child when they allow an abused child to remain with the family?

5. Should children be allowed to testify in court via CCTV? Does this approach prevent defendants in child abuse cases from confronting their accusers?
6. Is corporal punishment ever permissible as a disciplinary method?

APPLYING WHAT YOU HAVE LEARNED

You are an investigator with the county bureau of social services. A case has been referred to you by a middle school's head guidance counselor. It seems that a young girl, Emily M., has been showing up to school in a dazed and listless condition. She has had a hard time concentrating in class and seems withdrawn and uncommunicative. The thirteen-year-old has missed more than her normal share of school days and has often been late to class. Last week, she seemed so lethargic that her homeroom teacher sent her to the school nurse. A physical examination revealed that she was malnourished and in poor physical health. She also had evidence of bruising that could only come from a severe beating. Emily told the nurse that she had been punished by her parents for doing poorly at school and failing to do her chores at home.

When her parents were called to school to meet with the principal and guidance counselor, they claimed to be members of a religious order that believes children should be punished severely for their misdeeds. Emily had been placed on a restricted diet as well as beaten with a belt to correct her misbehavior. When the guidance counselor asked them if they would be willing to go into family therapy, they were furious and told her to "mind her own business." It's a sad day, they said, when "God-fearing American citizens cannot bring up their children according to their religious beliefs." The girl is in no immediate danger because her punishment has not been life-threatening.

The case is then referred to your office. When you go to see the parents at home, they refuse to make any change in their behavior, claiming that they are in the right and you represent all that is wrong with society. The "lax" discipline you suggest leads to drugs, sex, and other teenage problems.

- Would you get a court order removing Emily from her house and requiring the parents to go into counseling?
- Would you report the case to the district attorney's office so it could take criminal action against her parents under the state's child protection act?

- Would you take no further action, reasoning that Emily's parents have the right to discipline their child as they see fit?
- Would you talk with Emily and see what she wants to happen?

DOING RESEARCH ON THE WEB

Before you answer these questions, use "child abuse" and "reporting child abuse" in key word searches on InfoTrac College Edition. To further help you answer these questions, click on Web Links under the Chapter Resources at http://cj.wadsworth.com/siegel_jdcore2e. You'll find information from Child USA and the National Clearing-house on Child Abuse and Neglect Information to help you understand the issues surrounding child abuse.

Pro/Con discussions and Viewpoint Essays on some of the topics in this chapter may be found at the Opposing Viewpoints Resource Center: www.gale.com/OpposingViewpoints.

chapter 8

Peers and Delinquency: Juvenile Gangs and Groups

CHAPTER OUTLINE

Courtesy of CNN

CHAPTER OBJECTIVES

After reading this chapter you should:

1. Be familiar with the development of peer relations.

2. Know the various views of peer group cohesiveness.

3. Be able to define the concept of *the gang.*

4. Be familiar with the history of gangs.

5. Know the nature and extent of gang activity.

6. Recognize the various types of gangs.

7. Understand how gangs are structured.

8. Be familiar with the racial and ethnic makeup of gangs.

9. Discuss the various theories of gang development.

10. Know how police departments undertake gang prevention and suppression.

On May 8, 2003 Saul Dos Reis was sentenced to thirty years in prison for killing a young girl—thirteen-year-old Christina Long of Danbury, Connecticut, in 2002. Long and Dos Reis had developed an online relationship, and when they met in person the twenty-five-year-old man strangled the girl and left her body in a stream. Though Long was described by friends and family as a "sweet girl" who was captain of the cheerleading team and an altar girl at her local church, the police found evidence indicating that she regularly visited Internet chat rooms and was using provocative screen names to set up meetings with older men. Some of her peers described her behavior as sexually aggressive. Because of her unusual behavior, Christina was an outsider with few close friends who may have turned to the Internet for companionship.

 VIEW THE CNN VIDEO CLIP OF THIS STORY AND ANSWER RELATED CRITICAL THINKING QUESTIONS ON YOUR JUVENILE DELINQUENCY: THE CORE 2E CD.

For a general overview of gangs in America click on Web Links under the Chapter Resources at http://cj.wadsworth.com/siegel_jdcore2e.

The Long case illustrates the need for teens to bond with a positive peer group. When teens fail to connect they may seek out damaging social relationships. Some, like Christina Long, may get involved with predatory adults. Others may join with deviant peers and form law-violating youth groups and gangs.

Few issues in the study of delinquency are more important today than the problems presented by law-violating gangs and groups.[1] Although some gangs are made up of only a few loosely organized neighborhood youths, others have thousands of members who cooperate in complex illegal enterprises. A significant portion of all drug distribution in the nation's inner cities is believed to be gang-controlled; gang violence accounts for more than a thousand homicides each year. There has been an outcry from politicians to increase punishment for the "little monsters" and to save the "fallen angels," or the victimized youths who are innocent.[2]

The problem of gang control is a difficult one. Gangs flourish in inner-city areas that offer lower-class youths few conventional opportunities, and members are resistant to offers of help that cannot deliver legitimate economic hope. Although gang members may be subject to arrest, prosecution, and incarceration, a new crop of young recruits is always ready to take the place of their fallen comrades. Those sent to prison find that, upon release, their former gangs are only too willing to have them return to action.

We begin this chapter with a discussion of peer relations, showing how they influence delinquent behavior. Then we explore the definition, nature, and structure of delinquent gangs. Finally, the chapter presents theories of gang formation, the extent of gang activity, and gang-control efforts.

ADOLESCENT PEER RELATIONS

Although parents are the primary source of influence and attention in children's early years, between ages eight and fourteen children seek out a stable peer group, and both the number and the variety of friendships increase as children go through adolescence. Friends soon begin to have a greater influence over decision making than parents. By their early teens, children report that their friends give them emotional support when they are feeling bad and that they can confide intimate feelings to peers without worrying about their confidences being betrayed.[3]

As they go through adolescence, children form **cliques,** small groups of friends who share activities and confidences.[4] They also belong to **crowds,** loosely organized groups of children who share interests and activities such as sports, religion, or hobbies. Intimate friends play an important role in social development, but adolescents are also deeply influenced by this wider circle of friends. Adolescent self-image is in part formed by perceptions of one's place in the social world.[5]

In later adolescence, acceptance by peers has a major impact on socialization. Popular youths do well in school and are socially astute. In contrast, children who are rejected by their peers are more likely to display aggressive behavior and to disrupt group activities by bickering or behaving antisocially. Another group of kids—**controversial status youth**—are aggressive kids who are either highly liked or intensely disliked by their peers. These controversial youths are the ones most likely to become engaged in antisocial behavior. When they find themselves in leadership positions among their peers they get them involved in delinquent and problem behaviors.[6]

It is clear that peer status during childhood is an important contributor to a child's social and emotional development that follows the child across the life course.[7] For example, girls who engage in aggressive behavior with childhood peers later have more conflict-ridden relationships with their romantic partners. Boys who are highly aggressive and are therefore rejected by their peers in childhood are also more likely to engage in criminality and delinquency from adolescence into young adulthood.[8] Peer relations, then, are a significant aspect of maturation. Peer influence may be more important than parental nurturance in the development of long-term behavior.[9] Peers guide each other and help each other learn to share and cooperate, to cope with aggressive impulses, and to discuss feelings they would not dare bring up at home. Youths can compare their own experiences with peers and learn that others have similar concerns and problems.[10]

Peer Relations and Delinquency

Research shows that peer group relationships are closely tied to delinquent behaviors: delinquent acts tend to be committed in small groups rather than alone, a process referred to as *co-offending*.[11] Youths who report inadequate or strained peer relations are the ones most likely to become delinquent.[12] Adolescents who maintain delinquent friends are more likely to engage in antisocial behavior and drug abuse.

Some kids are particularly susceptible to peer influence. In one recent study Richard Felson and Dana Haynie found that boys who go through puberty at an early age were more likely to later engage in violence, property crimes, drug use, and precocious sexual behavior. The boys who matured early were the most likely to develop strong attachments to delinquent friends and to be influenced by peer pressure.[13] The conclusion: the earlier youngsters develop relationships with delinquent peers and the closer those relationships get, the more likely they will become delinquent.

Impact of Peer Relations

Does having antisocial peers cause delinquency, or are delinquents antisocial youths who seek out like-minded companions because they can be useful in committing crimes? There are actually four independent viewpoints on this question.

1. According to the control theory approach articulated by Travis Hirschi (chapter 4) delinquents are as detached from their peers as they are from other elements of society.[14] Although they appear to have close friends, delinquents actually lack the social skills to make their peer relations rewarding or fulfilling.[15] Antisocial adolescents seek out like-minded peers for criminal associations. If delinquency is committed in groups, it is because "birds of a feather flock together."

cliques
Small groups of friends who share intimate knowledge and confidences.

crowds
Loosely organized groups who share interests and activities.

controversial status youth
Aggressive kids who are either highly liked or intensely disliked by their peers and who are the ones most likely to become engaged in antisocial behavior.

Although parents are the primary source of influence and attention in a child's early years, peers begin to have a greater influence over decision making in adolescence, and by early adolescence friends give emotional support and are the locus of intimate feelings and emotions.

2. Delinquent friends cause law-abiding youth to "get in trouble." Kids who fall in with a "bad crowd" are at risk for delinquency. Youths who maintain friendships with antisocial peers are more likely to become delinquent regardless of their own personality or the type of supervision they receive at home.[16] Even previously law-abiding youths are more likely to get involved in delinquency if they become associated with friends who initiate them into delinquent careers.[17]

3. Antisocial youths join up with like-minded friends; deviant peers sustain and amplify delinquent careers.[18] As children move through the life course, antisocial friends help them maintain delinquent careers and obstruct the aging-out process.[19] In contrast, nondelinquent friends moderate delinquency.[20] If adulthood brings close and sustaining ties to conventional friends, and marriage and family, the level of deviant behavior will decline.[21]

4. Troubled kids choose delinquent peers out of necessity rather than desire. The social baggage they cart around prevents them from developing associations with conventional peers. Because they are impulsive, they may hook up with friends who are dangerous and get them into trouble.[22] Deviant peers do not cause straight kids to go bad but they amplify the likelihood of a troubled kid getting further involved in antisocial behaviors.[23]

Although each of these scenarios has its advocates, the weight of the empirical evidence clearly indicates that delinquent peers have a significant influence on behavior: youths who are loyal to delinquent friends, belong to gangs, and have "bad companions" are the ones most likely to commit crimes and engage in violence.[24] Furthermore, the friendship patterns of delinquents may not be dissimilar from those of nondelinquents; delinquent youths report that their peer relations contain elements of caring and trust and that they can be open and intimate with their friends.[25] Warm intergroup associations contradict the control theory model, which holds that delinquents are loners, and support the cultural deviance view that delinquents form close-knit groups that sustain their behavior.

YOUTH GANGS

As youths move through adolescence, they gravitate toward cliques that provide them with support, assurance, protection, and direction. In some instances the peer group provides the social and emotional basis for antisocial activity. When this happens, the clique is transformed into a **gang.**

Today, such a powerful mystique has grown up around gangs that mere mention of the word evokes images of black-jacketed youths roaming the streets in groups bearing such names as the Latin Kings, Crips, and Bloods. Films, television shows, novels, and even Broadway musicals have popularized the youth gang.[26]

Considering the suspected role gangs play in violent crime and drug activity, it is not surprising that gangs have recently become the target of a great deal of research interest.[27] Important attempts have been made to gauge their size, location, makeup, and activities.

gang
Group of youths who collectively engage in delinquent behaviors.

What Are Gangs?

Gangs are groups of youths who engage in delinquent behaviors. Yet gang delinquency differs from group delinquency. Whereas group delinquency consists of a short-lived alliance created to commit a particular crime or violent act, gang delinquency involves long-lived institutions that have a distinct structure and organization, including identifiable leadership, division of labor, rules, rituals, and possessions.

Delinquency experts are often at odds over the precise definition of a gang. The term is sometimes used broadly to describe any congregation of youths who have joined together to engage in delinquent acts. However, police departments often use it only to refer to cohesive groups that hold and defend territory, or turf.[28]

Academic experts have also created a variety of definitions. The core elements in the concept of the gang are that it is an **interstitial group**—one falling within the cracks and crevices of society—and that it maintains standard group processes, such as recruiting new members, setting goals, assigning roles, and developing status.[29]

Malcolm Klein argues that two factors stand out in all of these definitions:

- Members have self-recognition of their gang status and use special vocabulary, clothing, signs, colors, graffiti, and names. Members set themselves apart from the community and are viewed as a separate entity by others. Once they get the label of gang, members eventually accept and take pride in their status.

- There is a commitment to criminal activity, although even the most criminal gang members spend the bulk of their time in noncriminal activities.[30]

How Did Gangs Develop?

The youth gang is sometimes viewed as uniquely American, but gangs have also been reported in several other nations.[31] Nor are gangs a recent phenomenon. In the 1600s, London was terrorized by organized gangs that called themselves "Hectors," "Bugles," "Dead Boys," and other colorful names. In the seventeenth and eighteenth centuries, English gang members wore distinctive belts and pins marked with serpents, animals, stars, and the like.[32] The first mention of youth gangs in America occurred in the late 1780s, when prison reformers noted the presence of *gangs* of young people hanging out on Philadelphia's street corners. By the 1820s New York's Bowery and Five Points districts, Boston's North End and Fort Hill, and the outlying Southwark and Moyamensing sections of Philadelphia were the locales of youth gangs with colorful names like the Roach Guards, Chichesters, the Plug Uglies, and the Dead Rabbits.[33]

In the 1920s, Frederick Thrasher initiated the study of the modern gang in his analysis of more than thirteen hundred youth groups in Chicago.[34] He found that the social, economic, and ecological processes that affect the structure of cities create cracks in the normal fabric of society—weak family controls, poverty, and social disorganization—and referred to this as an *interstitial area*. According to Thrasher, groups of youths develop to meet such needs as play, fun, and adventure, activities that sometimes lead to delinquent acts. Impoverished areas present many opportunities for conflict between groups of youths and adult authority. If this conflict continues, the groups become more solidified and their activities become primarily illegal, and the groups develop into gangs.

According to Thrasher, adult society does not meet the needs of lower-class youths, and the gang solves the problem by offering excitement, fun, and opportunity. The gang is not a haven for disturbed youths but an alternative lifestyle for normal boys. Thrasher's work has had an important influence. Recent studies of delinquent gang behavior also view the gang as a means for lower-class boys to achieve advancement and opportunity as well as to defend themselves and to attack rivals. For example, the National Youth Gang Center defines gangs this way:

To view current examples of gang graffiti, click on Web Links under the Chapter Resources at http://cj.wadsworth.com/siegel_jdcore2e.

interstitial group
Delinquent group that fills a crack in the social fabric and maintains standard group practices.

Gang activity by such groups as the Savage Skulls (pictured) reemerged in the 1970s in major cities, including New York, Detroit, El Paso, Los Angeles, and Chicago. In addition, such cities as Cleveland and Columbus, Ohio, and Milwaukee, Wisconsin, which had not experienced serious gang problems before, saw the development of local gangs.

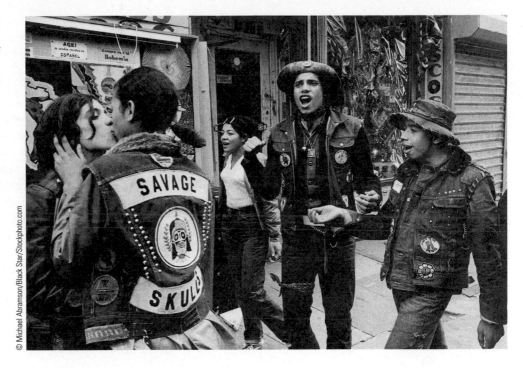

© Michael Abramson/Black Star/Stockphoto.com

A youth gang is commonly thought of as a self-formed association of peers having the following characteristics: three or more members, generally ages twelve to twenty-four; a gang name and some sense of identity, generally indicated by such symbols as style of clothing, graffiti, and hand signs; some degree of permanence and organization; and an elevated level of involvement in delinquent or criminal activity.[35]

Gangs in the 1950s and 1960s   In the 1950s and early 1960s, the threat of gangs and gang violence swept the public consciousness. Newspapers featured stories on the violent behavior of fighting gangs like the Egyptian Kings, the Vice Lords, and the Blackstone Rangers. Movies such as *The Wild Ones* and *Blackboard Jungle* were made about gangs, and the Broadway musical (and later movie) *West Side Story* romanticized violent gangs.

By the mid-1960s, the gang menace seemed to have disappeared. Some experts attribute the decline of gang activity to successful community-based programs.[36] Others believe gangs were eliminated because police gang-control units infiltrated gangs, arrested leaders, and constantly harassed members.[37] Another explanation is the increase in political awareness that developed during the 1960s. Many gang leaders became involved in social or political activities. In addition, many gang members were drafted. Still another explanation is that many gang members became active users of heroin and other drugs, which curtailed their group-related criminal activity.[38]

Gangs Reemerge   Interest in gang activity began anew in the early 1970s. Bearing such names as Savage Skulls and Black Assassins, gangs began to form in New York's South Bronx neighborhoods in the spring of 1971 and quickly spread to other parts of the city. By 1975, there were 275 police-verified gangs with eleven thousand members.[39]

Gang activity also reemerged in other major cities, such as Chicago and Los Angeles. In addition, large urban gangs sent representatives to organize chapters in distant areas or to take over existing gangs. Members of the two largest gangs in Los Angeles, the Crips and the Bloods, began operations in midwestern cities. Even medium-size cities, such as Columbus, Ohio, saw gangs emerge from local dance and "rap" groups and neighborhood street-corner groups.[40]

Why Did Gangs Reemerge?   One reason for the increase in gang activity may be involvement in the sale of illegal drugs.[41] Early gangs relied on group loyalty to encourage membership, but modern gang members are lured by the quest for drug profits. In some areas, gangs have replaced organized crime families as the dominant suppliers of cocaine and crack. The traditional weapons of gangs—chains, knives, and homemade guns—have been replaced by automatic weapons.

Drug trafficking is by no means the only reason for gang activity. Gang formation is the natural consequence of the economic and social dislocation that occurred when the economy shifted from a relatively high-paying manufacturing economy to a low-wage service economy.[42] Some U.S. cities that required a large population base for their manufacturing plants now face economic stress as these plants shut down. In this uneasy economic climate, gangs flourish, while the influence of successful adult role models and stable families declines. The presence of gangs in areas unaccustomed to delinquent group activity can have a devastating effect on community life.

While this social dislocation was occurring the media fell in love with gang images, which appeared in films and music videos. Gangsta rap became a national phenomenon. Because there has been a diffusion of the gang culture through the popular media, in which gang boys are made to appear as successful heroes, urban kids may find the lure of gangs and law-violating peer groups irresistible.

CONTEMPORARY GANGS

The gang cannot be viewed as a uniform or homogeneous social concept. Gangs vary by activity, makeup, location, leadership style, and age. The next sections describe some of the most salient features of contemporary gangs.

Extent

The most recent National Youth Gang Survey (NYGS) sponsored by the federal government illustrates the rise in gang activity over the past twenty years.[43] It is now estimated that youth gangs are active in over twenty-three hundred cities with populations over twenty-five hundred. Gang activity is notably prevalent in the largest cities (over one hundred thousand population): over 90 percent of these cities reported gang activity in each year between 1996 and 2001. As of 2000, an estimated 24,500 gangs containing about 772,500 gang members were active in the United States.[44]

The widespread presence of gangs is not surprising considering that local surveys indicate that a significant number of American youths are now or at one time have been gang members. One survey of nearly six thousand eighth-graders found that 11 percent were currently gang members and 17 percent said they had belonged to a gang at some point in their lives.[45]

Location

While some people think of gangs as a purely urban phenomenon, an estimated fifteen thousand gangs with three hundred thousand members are located in small cities, suburban counties, and even rural areas. Traditionally, gangs have operated in large urban areas experiencing rapid population change. In these transitional neighborhoods, diverse ethnic and racial groups find themselves in competition with one another.[46] Intergang conflict and homicide rates are high in these areas, which house the urban "underclass."[47] However, these neighborhoods eventually evolve into permanently **disorganized neighborhoods,** where population shifts slow down, permitting patterns of behavior and traditions to develop over a number of years. Most typical are the poverty-stricken areas of New York and Chicago and the Mexican American barrios of the southwestern states and California. These

disorganized neighborhood
Inner-city areas of extreme poverty where the critical social control mechanisms have broken down.

areas contain large, structured gang clusters that are resistant to change or control by law enforcement agencies.

The growth of gangs in suburban and rural areas has been attributed to a restructuring of the population. There has been a massive movement of people out of the central city to outlying communities and suburbs. In some cities, once-fashionable neighborhoods have declined, while in others downtown areas have undergone extensive renewal. Previously impoverished inner-city districts of major cities such as New York and Chicago are now quite fashionable and expensive, devoted to finance, retail stores, high-priced condos, and entertainment. Two aspects of this development inhibit urban gang formation: (1) there are few residential areas and thus few adolescent recruits, and (2) there is intensive police patrol.

Migration

Because of redevelopment, gangs in some areas have relocated or migrated. A recent National Gang Survey found that about 20 percent of gang members were migrants from another jurisdiction. In rural areas, about a third of members had come from elsewhere; in suburban counties, 20 percent were outsiders. Larger cities had the smallest percentage of migrants (17 percent), indicating that the flow of gang members was from more to less populated areas, and not vice versa.[48]

About seven hundred U.S. cities have experienced some form of gang migration during the past decade. The most common reason for migrating is personal and social—that is, family relocation causes gang boys to move or stay with relatives. Some migration may have a specific criminal purpose, such as expanding drug sales and markets.

Most migrators are African-American or Hispanic males who maintain close ties with members of their original gangs "back home."[49] Some migrants join local gangs, shedding old ties and gaining new affiliations. Although some experts fear the outcome of migration, it appears the number of migrants is relatively small in proportion to the overall gang population, supporting the contention that most gangs actually are "homegrown."[50]

Types

Gangs have been categorized by activity: some are devoted to violence and to protecting neighborhood boundaries, or turf; others are devoted to theft; some specialize in drug trafficking; others are concerned with recreation rather than crime.[51]

In their early work, Richard Cloward and Lloyd Ohlin recognized that some gangs specialized in violent behavior, others were **retreatists** whose members actively engaged in substance abuse, and a third type were criminal.[52]

It has become increasingly difficult to make these distinctions because so many gang members are now involved in all three behaviors, but experts continue to find that gangs can be characterized according to their dominant activities. For example, Jeffrey Fagan found that most gangs fall into one of these four categories:

1. *Social gang.* Involved in few delinquent activities and little drug use other than alcohol and marijuana. Members are more interested in social activities.
2. Party gang. Concentrates on drug use and sales but forgoes most delinquent behavior. Drug sales are designed to finance members' personal drug use.
3. *Serious delinquent gang.* Engages in serious delinquent behavior while eschewing most drug use. Drugs are used only on social occasions.
4. Organized gang. Heavily involved in criminality. Drug use and sales are related to other criminal acts. For example, violent acts are used to establish control over drug sale territories. This gang is on the verge of becoming a formal criminal organization.[53]

retreatists
Gangs whose members actively engage in substance abuse.

Gangs have been categorized by activity: some are devoted to violence and to protecting their turf, others are devoted to theft, some specialize in drug trafficking. Some gangs are concerned with recreation rather than crime; they are more likely to hang at the beach than engage in a drive-by shooting.

Cohesion

The standard definition of a gang implies that it is a cohesive group. However, some experts refer to gangs as **near-groups,** which have limited cohesion, impermanence, minimal consensus of norms, shifting membership, disturbed leadership, and limited definitions of membership expectations.[54] Gangs maintain a small core of committed members, who work constantly to keep the gang going, and a much larger group of affiliated youths, who participate in gang activity only when the mood suits them. James Diego Vigil found that boys in Latino **barrio** gangs (Hispanic neighborhood gangs) could be separated into regular members and those he describes as "peripheral," "temporary," and "situational."[55]

Current research indicates that, although some gangs remain near-groups, others become quite organized and stable. These gangs resemble traditional organized crime families more than temporary youth groups. Some, such as Chicago's Latin Kings and Gangster Disciples, have members who pay regular dues, are expected to attend gang meetings regularly, and carry out political activities to further gang ambitions.

near-groups
Clusters of youth who, outwardly, seem unified but actually have limited cohesion, impermanence, minimal consensus of norms, shifting membership, disturbed leadership, and limited definitions of membership expectations.

barrio
A Latino word meaning "neighborhood."

Age

The ages of gang members range widely, perhaps from as young as eight to as old as fifty-five.[56] However, members of offending groups are usually no more than a few years apart in age, with a leader who may be a few years older than most other members.[57]

Research indicates that youths first hear about gangs at around nine years of age, get involved in violence at ten or eleven, and join their first gang at twelve. By age thirteen, most members have (a) fired a pistol, (b) seen someone killed or seriously injured, (c) gotten a gang tattoo, and (d) been arrested.[58] Gang experts believe the average age of gang members has been increasing yearly, a phenomenon explained in part by the changing structure of the U.S. economy.[59]

Why Are Gang Members Aging?   Gang members are getting older. Relatively high-paid, low-skilled factory jobs that would entice older gang members to leave the gang have been lost to overseas competition. Replacing them are low-level drug-dealing opportunities that require a gang affiliation. William Julius Wilson found that the inability of inner-city males to obtain adequate jobs means that they cannot afford to marry and raise families. Criminal records acquired at an early age quickly lock these youths out of the job market; remaining in a gang becomes an economic necessity.[60]

John Hagedorn also found that economic change has had an impact on the age structure of gang membership. Whereas in the past older members could easily slip into the economic mainstream, less than one in five founding members of the youth gangs Hagedorn studied were able to find full-time employment by their mid-twenties. "Old heads"—older members with powerful street reputations—were held in high esteem by young gang members. In the past, ex-members helped steer gang members into conventional roles and jobs. Today, young adults continue their relationships with their old gangs and promote hustling, drug use, and sexual promiscuity. As a result, gang affiliations can last indefinitely, and it is not unusual for the children and even grandchildren of gang members to affiliate with the same gang.[61]

Hagedorn and his associates found that there are actually four types of adult gang members:

- *Legits* have left the gang and "hood" behind.
- *Dope fiends* are addicted to cocaine and need drug treatment.
- *New Jacks* have given up on the legitimate economy and see nothing wrong in selling cocaine to anyone.
- *Homeboys* are adult gang members who work regular jobs, but when they cannot make enough money they sell cocaine. They wish to have a "normal" life but believe ganging is the only way to make ends meet.[62]

Gender

Traditionally, gangs were considered a male-dominated enterprise. Of the more than a thousand groups included in Thrasher's original survey, only half a dozen were female gangs. Females were involved in gangs in three ways: as auxiliaries (or branches) of male gangs, as part of sexually mixed gangs, or as autonomous gangs. Auxiliaries are a feminized version of the male gang name, such as the Lady Disciples rather than the Devil's Disciples.

Today the number of female gang members and female gangs is rapidly increasing. An analysis of Denver youths found that approximately 25 percent of the gang members were female.[63] A recent survey of almost six thousand youths in forty-two schools in eleven cities found that almost 40 percent of the gang members were female.[64] It has been estimated that between one-fourth and one-third of all youth gang members are female.[65]

Girls in the Gang   What benefits does gang membership offer to females? According to the "liberation" view, ganging can provide girls with a sense of "sisterhood,"

The number and extent of girl gangs is increasing. In the Grape Street area of Los Angeles, a female gang member is about to kick another young woman. This is not a random or spontaneous attack but part of the "court in" ceremony in which new members are initiated into the gang.

© Nancy Siesel/Corbis-Saba

independence, and solidarity, as well as a chance to earn profit through illegal activities. Although initial female gang participation may be forged by links to male gang members, once in gangs girls form close ties with other female members and engage in group criminal activity.[66]

In contrast, the "social injury" view suggests that female members are still sexually exploited by male gang boys and are sometimes forced to exploit other females. Girls who are members of male gang auxiliaries report that males control them by determining the arenas within which they can operate (for example, the extent to which they may become involved in intergang violence). Males also play a divisive role in the girls' relationships with each other; this manipulation is absent for girls in independent gangs.[67] When criminologist Jody Miller studied female gangs in St. Louis, Missouri, and Columbus, Ohio, she found that girls in mixed gangs expressed little evidence of "sisterhood" and solidarity with other female gang members.[68] Rather, female gang members expressed hostility to other women in the gang, believing, for example, that those who suffered sexual assault by males in the same gang actually deserved what they got. Instead of trying to create a sense of sisterhood, female gang members tried to identify with males and view themselves as thereby becoming "one of the guys" in the gang.

Why then do girls join gangs if they are exploitive and provide little opportunities for "sisterhood?" Miller found that even though being a gang member is not a walk in the park, most girls join gangs in an effort to cope with their turbulent personal lives, which may provide them with an even harsher reality; they see the gang as an institution that can increase their status and improve their lifestyle. The gang provides them with an alternative to a tough urban lifestyle filled with the risk of violence and victimization. Many of the girl gang members had early exposure to neighborhood violence, had encounters with girl gangs while growing up, had experienced severe family problems (violence or abuse), and had close family members who were gang-involved.[69] Did they experience life benefits after they joined the gang? The evidence is mixed. Miller found that female gang members increased their delinquent activities and increased their risk of becoming a crime victim; they were more likely to suffer physical injury than girls who shunned gang membership. The risk of being sexually assaulted by male members of their own gang was also not insignificant. However, female gang membership did have some benefits: it protected female gang members from sexual assault by nongang neighborhood men, which they viewed as a more dangerous and deadly risk.

Formation

Gang formation involves a sense of territoriality. Most gang members live in close proximity to one another, and their sense of belonging extends only to their small area of the city. At first, a gang may form when members of an ethnic minority join together for self-preservation. As the group gains domination over an area, it may view the area as its own territory, or turf, which needs to be defended from outsiders.

Once formed, gangs grow when youths who admire the older gang members "apply" and are accepted for membership. Sometimes the new members will be given a special identity that reflects their apprenticeship status. Joan Moore and her associates found that **klikas,** or youth cliques, in Hispanic gangs remain together as unique groups with separate names, identities, and experiences; they also have more intimate relationships among themselves than among the general gang membership.[70] She likens *klikas* to a particular class in a university, such as the class of '05.

Moore also found that gangs can expand by including members' kin, even if they do not live in the neighborhood, and rival gang members who wish to join because they admire the gang's way of doing things. Adding outsiders gives the gang the ability to take over new territory. However, it also brings with it new problems because it usually results in greater conflicts with rival gangs.

Leadership

Delinquent gangs tend to be small and transitory.[71] Youths often belong to more than a single group or clique and develop an extensive network of delinquent associates. Group roles can vary, and an adolescent who assumes a leadership role in one group may be a follower in another.

Those who assume leadership roles are described as "cool characters" who have earned their position by demonstrating fighting prowess, verbal quickness, or athletic distinction. They emphasize that leadership is held by one person and varies with particular activities, such as fighting, sex, and negotiations. In fact, in some gangs each age level has its own leaders. Older members are not necessarily considered leaders by younger members. In his analysis of Los Angeles gangs, Malcolm Klein observed that many gang leaders deny leadership. He overheard one gang boy claim, "We got no leaders, man. Everybody's a leader, and nobody can talk for nobody else."[72] The most plausible explanation of this ambivalence is the boy's fear that his decisions will conflict with those of other leaders.

There appear, then, to be diverse concepts of leadership, depending on the structure of the gang. Less-organized gangs are marked by diffuse and shifting leadership. More organized gangs have a clear chain of command and leaders who are supposed to plan activities and control members' behavior.[73]

Communications

Gangs seek recognition, both from their rivals and from the community. Image and reputation depend on the ability to communicate to the rest of the world.

One major source of communication is **graffiti** (see Figure 8.1). These wall writings are especially elaborate among Latino gangs, who call them *placasos* or *placa,* meaning *sign* or *plaque.* Latino graffiti usually contain the writer's street name and

http:

To access a site that has a good selection of West Coast gang graffiti, click on Web Links under the Chapter Resources at http://cj.wadsworth.com/siegel_jdcore2e.

klikas
Subgroups of same-aged youths in Hispanic gangs that remain together and have separate names and a unique identity in the gang.

graffiti
Inscriptions or drawings made on a wall or structure and used by delinquents for gang messages and turf definition.

Figure 8.1 **Gang Symbols Used in Graffiti**

Gangster Disciples
(GD)

New Breed Black Gangsters
LLL: Love, Life, Loyalty
III: Third Disciple Nation

Latin Kings
Use 3- or 5-pointed crowns

Latin Disciples

Cobra Stones
putting down
Gangster Disciples

Vice Lords

Ambrose

P R Stones

Source: Illinois State Police, Springfield, 2003. www.isp.state.il.us/docs/gangsym.pdf

the name of the gang. Strength or power is asserted through the terms *rifa,* which means to rule, and *controllo,* indicating that the gang controls the area. Another common inscription is "p/v," for *por vida;* this refers to the fact that the gang expects to control the area "for life." The numeral 13 signifies that the gang is *loco,* or "wild." Crossed-out graffiti indicates that a territory is contested by a rival gang.

Gangs also communicate by means of a secret vocabulary. Members may refer to their *crew, posse, troop,* or *tribe.* Within larger gangs are "sets," who hang in particular neighborhoods, and "tips," small groups formed for particular purposes.

Flashing or tossing gang signs in the presence of rivals often escalates into a verbal or physical confrontation. Chicago gangs call this **representing.** Gang members will proclaim their affiliation and ask victims "Who do you ride?" or "What do you be about?" An incorrect response will provoke an attack. False representing can be used to misinform witnesses and victims.

In some areas, gang members communicate their membership by wearing jackets with the name of their gang on the back. In Boston neighborhoods, certain articles of clothing (for example, sneakers) are worn to identify gang membership. In Los Angeles, the Crips are identified with the color blue and will wear some article of blue clothing to communicate their allegiance; their rivals, the Bloods, identify with the color red.

Ethnic and Racial Composition

The 2001 National Youth Gang Survey found that the race/ethnicity composition of gangs is as follows: nearly half of all gang members are Hispanic/Latino; about one-third are African American/Black; 10 percent are Caucasian/White, 6 percent are Asian, and the remainder are of some other race/ethnicity (Figure 8.2). Racial composition of gangs varies considerably by locality and in some areas there are a larger

representing
Tossing or flashing gang signs in the presence of rivals, often escalating into a verbal or physical confrontation.

Gangs pose a serious problem in inner-city areas. Here Ishan Garrett watches as marchers pass through his neighborhood during a rally to take back the neighborhood in Las Vegas. More than 200 residents joined together in support of the Coalition for Community Peace to voice their opposition to a series of gang slayings.

© 2001 AP/Wide World Photos

proportion of Caucasian/White gang members than any other racial/ethnic group. Most intergang conflict appears to be among groups of the same ethnic and racial background.[74] However, upwards of 40 percent of all gangs are reportedly of mixed race and ethnicity.

The ethnic distribution of gangs corresponds to their geographic location; the racial/ethnic composition of gangs is an extension of the characteristics of the larger community.[75] For example, in Philadelphia and Detroit the overwhelming number of gang members are African American. In New York and Los Angeles, Latino gangs predominate. Newly emerging immigrant groups are making their presence felt in gangs. Authorities in Buffalo, New York, estimate that 10 percent of their gang population is Jamaican. A significant portion of Honolulu's gangs are Filipinos.

African-American Gangs   The first Black youth gangs were organized in the early 1920s.[76] Since they had few rival organizations, they were able to concentrate on criminal activity rather than defending their turf. By the 1930s, the expanding number of rival gangs spawned inner-city gang warfare.

In Los Angeles, the first black youth gang formed in the 1920s was the Boozies. This gang virtually ran the inner city until the 1930s. In the next twenty years, a number of black gangs, including the Businessmen, Home Street, Slauson, and Neighborhood, emerged and met with varying degrees of criminal success. In the 1970s, the dominant Crips gang was formed. Other gangs merged into the Crips or affiliated with it by adding "Crips" to their name, so that the Main Street gang became the Main Street Crips. The dominance of the Crips has since been challenged by its archrivals, the Bloods. Both of these groups, whose total membership exceeds twenty-five thousand youths, are heavily involved in drug trafficking.

In Chicago, the Blackstone Rangers dominated illicit activities for almost twenty-five years, beginning in the 1960s and lasting into the early 1990s, when its leader, Jeff Fort, and many of his associates were indicted and imprisoned.[77] The Rangers, who later evolved into the El Rukn gang, worked with "legitimate" businessmen to import and sell heroin. Earning millions in profits, they established businesses that helped them launder drug money. Though many of the convictions were later overturned, the power of El Rukn was ended.

The Rangers' chief rivals, the Black Gangster Disciples, are now the dominant gang in Chicago. They have a structure, activities, and relationships similar to traditional organized gangs like the Mafia. Members are actively involved in politics. They meet regularly, commit crimes as a group, and maintain ongoing relationships with other street gangs and with prison-based gangs. The Gangster Disciples have extensive

Figure 8.2 Ethnic and Racial Distribution of Youth Gang Members

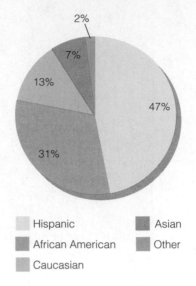

- Hispanic
- African American
- Caucasian
- Asian
- Other

Source: *Highlights of the 1999 National Youth Gang Survey* (Washington, DC: Office of Juvenile Justice and Delinquency Prevention, 2000).

ownership of "legitimate" private businesses. They offer "protection" against rival gangs and supply stolen merchandise to customers and employees.[78]

African-American gang members have some unique characteristics. They frequently use nicknames. "Little 45" might be used by someone whose favorite weapon is a large handgun. Although TV shows portray gangs as wearing distinctive attire, members usually favor nondescript attire to reduce police scrutiny. However, gang members frequently have distinctive hairstyles, such as shaving or braids, that are designed to look like their leaders'. Tattooing is popular, and members often wear colored scarves or "rags" to identify their gang affiliation. It is also common for black gang members to mark their territory with distinctive graffiti: drawings of guns, dollar signs, proclamations of individual power, and profanity.

Hispanic Gangs The popularity of gangs and gang culture is relatively high among youth of Hispanic background, explaining in part their disproportionate participation in gang membership.[79]

Hispanic gangs are made up of youths whose ethnic ancestry can be traced to one of several Spanish-speaking cultures. They are known for their fierce loyalty to their "home" gang. Admission to the gang usually involves an initiation ritual in which boys are required to prove their *machismo*. The most common test requires novices to fight several established members or to commit some crime, such as a robbery. The code of conduct associated with membership means never ratting on a brother, or even a rival.

In some areas, Hispanic gangs have a fixed leadership hierarchy. However, in Southern California, which has the largest concentration of Hispanic youth gangs, leadership is fluid. During times of crisis those with particular skills will assume command.[80] For example, one boy will lead in combat while another negotiates drug deals.

Hispanic gang members are known for their dress codes. Some wear dark-colored caps pulled down over the ears with a small roll at the bottom. Others wear a folded bandana over the forehead and tied in back. Another popular headpiece is the "stingy brim" fedora or a baseball cap with the wearer's nickname and gang affiliation written on the bill. Members favor tank-style T-shirts that give them quick access to weapons.

Members also mark off territory with colorful and intricate graffiti. Hispanic gang graffiti has very stylized lettering and frequently uses three-dimensional designs.

Some Anglo gang members try to be like members of the English punk and skinhead movements of the 1970s. These youths sported wildly dyed hair often shaved into "mohawks," military clothing, and iron-cross earrings. Their creed was antiestablishment, and their anger was directed toward foreigners, who they believed were taking their jobs.

Hispanic gangs have a strong sense of turf, and a great deal of gang violence is directed at warding off any threat to their control. Slights by rivals, including put-downs, stare-downs ("mad-dogging"), defacing gang insignia, and territorial intrusions, can set off a violent confrontation, often with high-powered automatic weapons.

Asian Gangs   Asian gangs are prominent in New York, Los Angeles, San Francisco, Seattle, and Houston. The earliest gangs, the Wah Ching, were formed in the nineteenth century by Chinese youths affiliated with adult crime groups (*tongs*). In the 1960s, two other gangs formed in San Francisco, the Joe Boys and Yu Li, and they now operate, along with the Wah Ching, in many major U.S. cities. National attention focused on the activities of these Chinese gangs in 1977 when a shootout in the Golden Dragon restaurant in San Francisco left five dead and eleven wounded.

Ko-Lin Chin has described the inner workings of Chinese youth gangs.[81] Chin finds that these gangs have unique properties, such as their reliance on raising capital from the Chinese community through extortion and then investing this money in legitimate business enterprises. Chinese gangs recruit new members from the pool of disaffected youths who have problems at school.

In addition to Chinese gangs, Samoan gangs have operated on the West Coast, as have Vietnamese gangs. James Diego Vigil and Steve Chong Yun found that the formation of Vietnamese gangs can be tied to external factors, including racism and economic problems, and to internal problems, including family stress and failure to achieve the success enjoyed by other Asians. Vietnamese gangs are formed when youths feel they need their *ahns,* or brothers, for protection.[82] Asian gangs tend to victimize members of their own ethnic group. Because of group solidarity and distrust of outside authorities, little is known about their activities.

Anglo Gangs   The first American youth gangs were made up of White ethnic youths of European ancestry. During the 1950s, they competed with African-American and Hispanic gangs in the nation's largest cities.

Today, Anglo gang activity is not uncommon, especially in smaller towns.[83] Many are derivatives of the English punk and **skinhead** movement of the 1970s. These youths, generally children of lower-class parents, sported wildly dyed hair often shaved into "mohawks," military clothes, and iron-cross earrings. Their creed was antiestablishment, and their anger was directed toward foreigners, who they believed were taking their jobs.

Today, White gang members are often alienated middle-class youths rather than poor lower-class youths. They include "punkers" or "stoners," who dress in heavy-metal fashions and engage in drug- and violence-related activities. Some espouse religious beliefs involving the occult and satanic worship. Some are obsessed with occult themes, suicide, ritual killings, and animal mutilations. They get involved in devil worship, tattoo themselves with occult symbols, and gouge their bodies to draw blood for satanic rituals.[84] Some skinhead groups are devoted to White supremacist activities and are being actively recruited by adult hate groups.

A recent survey of almost six thousand youths found that about 25 percent of youths who claimed to be gang members were White, a far higher number than that found in national surveys.[85]

skinhead
Member of White supremacist gang, identified by a shaved skull and Nazi or Ku Klux Klan markings.

Criminality and Violence

Regardless of their type, gang members typically commit more crimes than any other youths in the social environment.[86] Members self-report significantly more crime than nonmembers and the more enmeshed a youth is in a gang the more likely he is to report criminal behavior, to have an official record, and to get sent to juvenile court; the gang membership–crime relationship begins as early as middle school.[87]

Gang criminality has numerous patterns.[88] Some gangs specialize in drug dealing. But not all gangs are major players in drug trafficking and those that are tend to distribute small amounts of drugs at the street level. The world of major dealing belongs to adults, not to gang youths.[89] Other gangs engage in a wide variety of criminal activity, ranging from felony assaults to drug dealing.[90] Gang members are most commonly involved in such crimes as larceny/theft, aggravated assault, and burglary/breaking and entering; a significant portion are involved in street drug sales to generate profits for the gang.[91] Drug use is quite common. In one recent survey, Geoffrey Hunt and his associates found that 82 percent of the female gang members they surveyed were multiple-drug users, using drugs such as cocaine, crack, LSD, PCP, methamphetamine, heroin, glue/inhalants, MDMA, and quaaludes.[92]

Do gang kids increase their involvement in criminal activity after they join gangs or do gangs recruit kids who are already high rate offenders? Data from the Rochester Youth Development Study (RYDS), a longitudinal cohort study of one thousand youths in upstate New York, supports the gang–crime association theory. Although only 30 percent of the youths in the sample report being gang members, they account for 65 percent of all reported delinquent acts. The RYDS data show that gang members account for 86 percent of all serious crimes, 63 percent of the alcohol use, and 61 percent of the drug abuse.[93]

Gang Violence   Gang members are heavily armed, dangerous, and more violent than nonmembers. A nationwide survey of arrestees found that half of those who owned or carried guns claimed to be gang members.[94] The 2000 National Youth Gang Survey found that 84 percent of police in areas with a gang problem reported at least one occurrence of firearm use by one or more gang members in an assault crime. Thornberry and his associates found that young gang members in Rochester, New York, were about ten times more likely to carry handguns than nongang juvenile offenders, and gun-toting gang members committed about ten times more violent crimes than nonmembers.[95]

Research indicates that gang violence is impulsive and therefore comes in spurts. It usually involves defense of the gang and gang members' reputations.[96] Once the threat ends, the level of violence may recede, but it remains at a level higher than it was previously. Peaks in gang homicides tend to correspond to a series of escalating confrontations, usually over control of gang turf or a drug market.[97] The most dangerous areas are along disputed boundaries where a drug hot spot intersects with a turf hot spot. There are also "marauder" patterns in which members of rival gangs travel to their enemy's territory in search of victims.[98]

Violence is a core fact of gang formation and life.[99] Gang members feel threatened by other gangs and are wary of encroachments on their turf. It is not surprising that gangs try to recruit youths who are already gun owners; new members are likely to increase gun ownership and possession.[100] Gang members face a far greater chance of death at an early age than do nonmembers.[101]

Revenge, Honor, Courage, and Prestige   When criminologist Scott Decker interviewed gang boys he found that violence is essential to the transformation of a peer group into a gang. When asked why he calls the group he belongs to a gang, one member replied: "There is more violence than a family. With a gang it's like fighting all the time, killing, shooting."[102]

When joining the gang, members may be forced to partake in violent rituals to prove their reliability. Gang members are ready to fight when others attack them or

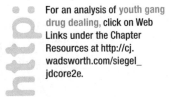

For an analysis of youth gang drug dealing, click on Web Links under the Chapter Resources at http://cj.wadsworth.com/siegel_jdcore2e.

when they believe their territory or turf is being encroached upon. Violence may be directed against rival gang members accused of insults or against those involved in personal disputes. Gang members also expect to fight when they go to certain locations that are "off-limits" or attend events where violence is routine. Girl gang members may fight when they sense that a member of a rival gang is trying to hook up with their boyfriend. Gini Sykes spent two years hanging with girl gangs in New York City in order to develop an understanding of their lives and lifestyle. One girl, Tiny, told her how ferociousness made up for her lack of stature:

Tiny fixed me with a cold stare that wiped away any earlier impression of childish cuteness. "See, we smaller girls, we go for your weak spot." Her gaze moved across my features. "Your face. Your throat. Your eyes, so we can blind you. I don't care if you have more weight on me. I'll still try to kill you because, you know, I have a bad temper—."[103]

Tiny related the story of how she attacked a rival who she caught in a sexual encounter with her boyfriend:

"She was crying and begging, but she'd disrespected me in front of everybody. We started fighting and she pulled that blade out—." Tiny shrugged. "I just wasn't prepared. You can't tell when someone's got a razor in their mouth."

After she was cut, Tiny went into a defensive rage, and

frantically felt for the wound, blood seeping between her fingers. Suddenly, in self-preservation, she grabbed the girl's neck, and blinded by her own blood, began smashing her rival's head into the concrete until Isabel, hearing a siren, dragged her away. The girl had slashed Tiny's face eleven times.

Gang members are sensitive to any rivals who question their honor. Once an insult is perceived, the gang's honor cannot be restored until the "debt" is repaid. Police efforts to cool down gang disputes only delay the revenge, which can be a beating or a drive-by shooting. Random acts of revenge have become so common that physicians now consider them a significant health problem—a major contributor to early morbidity and mortality among adolescents and children in major gang cities.[104]

Violence is used to maintain the gang's internal discipline. If subordinates disobey orders, perhaps by using rather than selling drugs, they may be subject to disciplinary action by other gang members.

Another common gang crime is extortion, called "turf tax," which involves forcing people to pay the gang to be protected from dangerous neighborhood youths. **Prestige crimes** occur when a gang member steals or assaults someone to gain prestige in the gang. These crimes may be part of an initiation rite or an effort to establish a special reputation, a position of responsibility, or a leadership role; to prevail in an internal power struggle; or to respond to a challenge from a rival. ✔ Checkpoints

To quiz yourself on this material, go to questions 8.1–8.18 on the Juvenile Delinquency: The Core 2e Web site.

WHY DO YOUTHS JOIN GANGS?

Though gangs flourish in inner-city areas, gang membership cannot be assumed to be solely a function of lower-class identity. Many lower-class youths do not join gangs, and middle-class youths are found in suburban skinhead groups. Let's look at some of the suspected causes of gang delinquency.

The Anthropological View

prestige crimes
Stealing or assaulting someone to gain prestige in the neighborhood; often part of gang initiation rites.

In the 1950s, Herbert Block and Arthur Niederhoffer suggested that gangs appeal to adolescents' longing for the tribal process that sustained their ancestors.[105] They found that gang processes do seem similar to the puberty rites of some tribal cultures; gang rituals help the child bridge the gap between childhood and adulthood. For example,

According to the anthropological view, gang membership with its signs, writings, and tattoos is similar to joining a tribal cult. Matthew Ricci (left), manager of Skyline Tattoo in Arlington, Va., works on covering up a tattoo—a gang symbol—on Chris Perry's left hand. Perry has many other tattoos on his arms and legs. A large koi fish stretches nearly the length of his right forearm. He also has a half dozen piercings on his head alone: between his eyes, in his nose, tongue, bottom lip, and a couple in each ear.

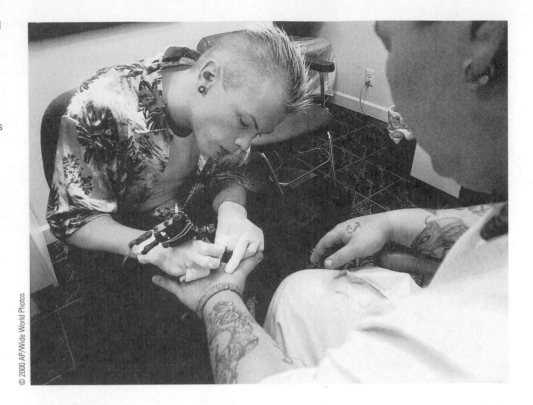

© 2000 AP/Wide World Photos

tattoos and other identifying marks are an integral part of gang culture. Gang initiation ceremonies are similar to the activities of young men in Pacific Island cultures. Many gangs put new members through a hazing to make sure they have "heart," a feature similar to tribal rites. In tribal societies, initiation into a cult is viewed as the death of childhood. By analogy, boys in lower-class urban areas yearn to join the gang and "really start to live." Membership in the gang "means the youth gives up his life as a child and assumes a new way of life."[106] Gang names are suggestive of "totemic ancestors" because they usually are symbolic (Cobras, Jaguars, and Kings, for example).

The Gang Prevention and Intervention Survey found that fully two-thirds of gang members reported having members in their gang whose parents are also active members. These data indicate that ganging is passed on as a rite of passage from one generation to the next.[107] James Diego Vigil has described the rituals of gang initiation, which include pummeling to show that the boy is ready to leave his matricentric (mother-dominated) household; this is reminiscent of tribal initiation rites.[108] These rituals become an important part of gang activities. Hand signs and graffiti have a tribal flavor. Gang members adopt nicknames that reflect personality or physical traits: the more volatile are called "Crazy," "Loco," or "Psycho," and those who wear glasses are dubbed "Professor."[109]

The Social Disorganization/Sociocultural View

Sociologists have commonly viewed the destructive sociocultural forces in poor inner-city areas as the major cause of gang formation. Thrasher introduced this concept, and it is found in the classic studies of Richard Cloward and Lloyd Ohlin and of Albert Cohen.[110] Irving Spergel's study *Racketville, Slumtown, and Haulburg* found that Slumtown—the area with the lowest income and the largest population—had the highest number of violent gangs.[111] According to Spergel, the gang gives lower-class youths a means of attaining status. Malcolm Klein's research of the late 1960s and 1970s also found that typical gang members came from dysfunctional and destitute families and lacked adequate role models.[112]

The social disorganization/sociocultural view retains its prominent position today. In *Barrio Gangs*,[113] Vigil shows that gang members are pushed into membership because of poverty and minority status. Those who join gangs are the most marginal youths in their neighborhoods and families. Vigil finds that barrio dwellers experience psychological, economic, and social "stressors." Gang members usually have more than one of these problems, causing them to suffer from "multiple marginality." Barrio youths join gangs seeking a sense of belonging.[114]

Overall, the sociocultural view assumes that gangs are a natural response to lower-class life and a status-generating medium for boys whose aspirations cannot be realized by legitimate means. Youths who join gangs may hold conventional goals but are either unwilling or unable to accomplish them through conventional means.[115] Gangs are not solely made up of youths who seek deviant peers to compensate for parental brutality or incompetence. They recruit youths from many different kinds of families. The gang thus is a coalition of troubled youths who are socialized mainly by the streets rather than by conventional institutions.[116]

Anomie   Irving Spergel suggests that youths are encouraged to join gangs during periods of social, economic, and cultural turmoil, conditions thought to produce anomie.[117] For example, gangs were present during the Russian Revolution of 1917 and after the crumbling of the Soviet Union in the early 1990s. The rise of right-wing youth gangs in Germany is associated with the unification of East and West Germany. Skinhead groups have formed in Germany in response to immigration from Turkey and North Africa. In the United States, gangs have formed in areas where rapid change has unsettled communities.

Immigration or emigration, rapidly expanding or contracting populations, and the incursion of different racial/ethnic groups, or even different segments or generations of the same racial/ethnic population, can create fragmented communities and gang problems.[118]

The Psychological View

Some believe that gangs serve as an outlet for disturbed youths who suffer a multitude of personal problems and deficits. For example, Lewis Yablonsky found that violent gangs recruit their members from among the more sociopathic youths living in poverty-stricken communities.[119] Yablonsky views the sociopathic youth as one who "has not been trained to have human feelings or compassion or responsibility for another."[120]

Malcolm Klein's analysis of Los Angeles gang members also found that many suffer from a variety of personal deficits, including low self-concept, social deficits, poor impulse control, and limited life skills.[121] In their in-depth study of Rochester youth, Thornberry and his colleagues found that those who joined gangs suffered from a multitude of social problems, including early involvement in delinquency, violence, and drug abuse, dysfunctional family relations, educational deficits, and involvement with deviant peers.[122]

The Rational Choice View

Some youths may make a rational choice to join a gang. Members of the underclass turn to gangs as a method of obtaining desired goods and services, either directly, through theft and extortion, or indirectly, through drug dealing and weapons sales. In this case, joining a gang can be viewed as an "employment decision." Mercer Sullivan's study of Brooklyn gangs found that members call success at crime "getting paid." Gang boys also refer to the rewards of crime as "getting over," which refers to their pride at "beating the system" even though they are far from the economic mainstream.[123] According to this view, the gang boy has long been involved in criminal activity *prior* to his gang membership, and he joins the gang as a means of improving his illegal "productivity."[124]

Gang membership is *not* a necessary precondition for delinquency. Felix Padilla found this when he studied the Diamonds, a Latino gang in Chicago.[125] The decision to join the gang was made after an assessment of legitimate opportunities. The Diamonds made collective business decisions, and individuals who made their own deals were penalized. The gang maintained a distinct structure and carried out other functions similar to those of legitimate enterprises, including recruiting personnel and financing business ventures.

Terence Thornberry and his colleagues at the Rochester Youth Development Study found that before youths join gangs, their substance abuse and delinquency rates are no higher than those of nongang members. When they are in the gang, their crime and drug abuse rates increase, only to decrease when they leave the gang. Thornberry concludes that gangs facilitate criminality rather than provide a haven for youths who are disturbed or already highly delinquent. This research is important because it lends support to the life course model: events that take place during the life cycle, such as joining a gang, have a significant impact on criminal behavior and drug abuse.[126]

Personal Safety View   According to Spergel, some adolescents choose to join gangs from a "rational calculation" to achieve safety.[127] Youths who are new to a community may believe they will be harassed or attacked if they remain "unaffiliated." Girls also join gangs for protection. Though they may be exploited by male gang members, they are protected from assaults by nongang males in the neighborhood.[128]

Motivation may have its roots in interrace or interethnic rivalry; youths who reside in an area dominated by a different racial or ethnic group may be persuaded that gang membership is a means of protection. Ironically, gang members are more likely to be attacked than nonmembers.

Fun and Support View   Some youths join gangs simply to have fun.[129] They enjoy hanging out with others like themselves and want to get involved in exciting experiences. There is evidence that youths learn progang attitudes from their peers and that these attitudes direct them to join gangs.[130]

Some experts suggest that youths join gangs in an effort to obtain a family-like atmosphere. Many gang members report that they have limited contact with their parents, many of whom are unemployed and have substance abuse problems.[131]

These views are summarized in Concept Summary 8.1. ✔ Checkpoints

 # CONTROLLING GANG ACTIVITY

Two methods are used to control gang activity. One involves targeting by criminal justice agencies, and the other involves social service efforts. These methods will be discussed in the next sections.

Concept Summary **8.1**   **Theories of Gang Formation**

Theory	Concept	Evidence
Anthropological	Gangs appeal to adolescents' primitive, tribal instincts.	Use of signs and symbols.
Sociocultural	Gangs appeal to poor kids in disorganized areas.	Gang location and membership.
Psychological	Gangs provide an outlet for psychologically disturbed youth.	Gang violence and substance abuse.
Rational choice	Gangs are a means for survival and profit.	Drug traffickers and organized criminal activities; gang members protect "turf" and one another.

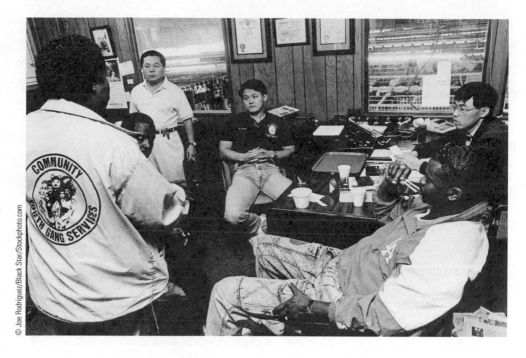

Police departments around the nation maintain specialized units, such as this one in Los Angeles, that focus on gang problems. They maintain intelligence on gang members and train officers to deal with gang problems. Some identify street gang members and enter their names in a computer bank that is programmed to alert the unit if the youths are picked up or arrested. Some departments also sponsor general prevention programs that can help control gang activities.

© Joe Rodriguez/Black Star/Stockphoto.

Law Enforcement Efforts

In recent years gang control has often been left to local police departments. Gang control takes three basic forms:

1. *Youth services programs,* in which traditional police personnel, usually from the youth unit, are given responsibility for gang control
2. *Gang details,* in which one or more police officers, usually from youth or detective units, are assigned exclusively to gang-control work
3. *Gang units,* established solely to deal with gang problems, to which one or more officers are assigned exclusively to gang-control work.[132]

A national assessment found that three-quarters of the departments surveyed maintained separate gang-control units. They are involved in processing information on gangs and gang leaders, prevention efforts, efforts to suppress criminal activity and apprehend those believed to have committed crimes, and follow-up investigations. About 85 percent of these units have special training in gang control for their personnel, 73 percent have specific policies directed at dealing with gang boys, and 62 percent enforce special laws designed to control gang activity.

The Chicago Police Department's gang crime section maintains intelligence on gang problems and trains its more than four hundred officers to deal with gang problems. Officers identify street gang members and enter their names in a computer bank that is programmed to alert the unit if the youths are picked up or arrested. Some departments also sponsor prevention programs such as school-based lectures, police-school liaisons, recreation programs, and street worker programs that offer counseling, assistance to parents, and other services.

Some police departments engage in "gang-breaking" activities. They attempt to arrest, prosecute, convict, and incarcerate gang leaders. For example, Los Angeles police conduct sweeps, in which more than a thousand officers are put on the street to round up gang members. Police say the sweeps let the gangs know "who the streets belong to" and show neighborhood residents that someone cares.[133] Despite such efforts, gang membership and violence remain at all-time highs. Few departments have written policies or procedures on how to deal with youths, and many do not provide gang-control training. The Preventing and Treating Delinquency feature on page 206 discusses one police program in Boston.

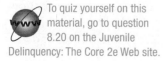

To quiz yourself on this material, go to question 8.20 on the Juvenile Delinquency: The Core 2e Web site.

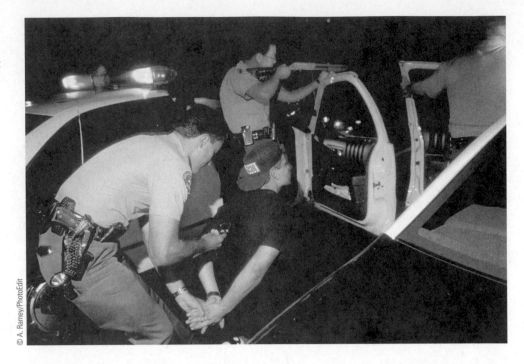

Law enforcement officers arresting gang members during a sweep in California. Can police actions be an effective deterrent to gang activities or would social services be a more effective alternative?

Traditional police tactics may not work on today's drug gangs, which may best be dealt with as organized crime families. In these cases, it might be useful to (1) develop informants through prosecutions, payments, and witness protection programs; (2) rely on electronic surveillance and undercover investigations; and (3) use statutes that create criminal liabilities for conspiracy, extortion, or engaging in criminal enterprises.[134] Of course, these policies are expensive and may be needed only with the most sophisticated gangs. In addition, as new community policing strategies are implemented (see chapter 12), it may be possible to garner sufficient local support and information to counteract gang influences.

Community Control Efforts

During the late nineteenth century, social workers of the YMCA worked with youths in Chicago gangs.[135] During the 1950s, the **detached street worker** program was developed in major centers of gang activity. Social workers went into the community to work with gangs on their own turf. They participated in gang activities and tried to get to know their members. The purpose was to act as advocates for the youths, to provide them with positive role models, and to treat individual problems.

Detached street worker programs are sometimes credited with curbing gang activities in the 1950s and 1960s, although some critics claimed that they turned delinquent groups into legitimate neighborhood organizations.[136] Others believe they helped maintain group solidarity, and as a result, new members were drawn to gangs.

Today, there are numerous community-level programs designed to limit gang activity. Some employ recreation areas open in the evening hours that provide supervised activities.[137] In some areas, citywide coordinating groups help orient gang-control efforts. For example, the Chicago Intervention Network operates field offices around the city in low-income, high-crime areas that provide neighborhood watches, parent patrols, alternative youth programming, and family support efforts. Some community efforts are partnerships with juvenile justice agencies. In Los Angeles County, the Gang Alternative Prevention Program (GAPP) provides prevention services to juveniles before they become entrenched in gangs, including (1) individual and group counseling, (2) bicultural and bilingual services to adolescents and

detached street workers
Social workers who go out into the community and establish close relationships with juvenile gangs with the goal of modifying gang behavior to conform to conventional behaviors and help gang members get jobs and educational opportunities.

Exhibit 8.1 The Elements of Spergel's Community Gang Control Program

1. Community mobilization, including citizens, youth, community groups, and agencies.

2. Provision of academic, economic, and social opportunities. Special school training and job programs are especially critical for older gang members who are not in school but may be ready to leave the gang or decrease participation in criminal gang activity for many reasons, including maturation and the need to provide for family.

3. Social intervention, using street outreach workers to engage gang-involved youth.

4. Gang suppression, including formal and informal social control procedures of the juvenile and criminal justice systems and community agencies and groups. Community-based agencies and local groups must collaborate with juvenile and criminal justice agencies in the surveillance and sharing of information under conditions that protect the community and the civil liberties of youths.

5. Organizational change and development—that is, the appropriate organization and integration of the preceding strategies and potential reallocation of resources.

Sources: Irving Spergel and Candice Kane, *Community-Based Youth Agency Model* (Washington, DC: Office of Juvenile Justice and Delinquency Prevention, 1990); Jim Burch and Candice Kane, *Implementing the OJJDP Comprehensive Gang Model* (Washington, DC: Office of Juvenile Justice and Delinquency Prevention, 1999).

their parents, and (3) special programs such as tutoring, parent training, job development, and recreational and educational experiences.[138]

Still another approach has been to involve schools in gang-control programs. Some invite law enforcement agents to lecture students on the dangers of gang involvement and teach them gang-resistance techniques. Others provide resources that can help parents prevent their children from joining gangs, or if they already are members, get them out.

Sociologist Irving Spergel, a leading expert on gangs, has developed a model for helping communities deal with gang-involved youth that has become the basis for gang-control efforts around the nation. His model includes the five distinct strategies contained in Exhibit 8.1.

Why Gang Control Is Difficult

Experts have charged that to reduce the gang problem, hundreds of thousands of high-paying jobs are needed. Economic opportunities might prove to be particularly effective, because surveys reveal that many gang members might leave gangs if such opportunities existed.[139]

This solution does not, however, seem practical. The more embedded youths become in criminal enterprise, the less likely they are to find meaningful adult work. It is unlikely that gang members can suddenly be transformed into highly paid professionals. A more effective alternative would be to devote more resources to the most deteriorated urban areas, even if it requires pulling funds from other groups that receive government aid, such as the elderly.[140]

Although social solutions to the gang problem seem elusive, the evidence shows that gang involvement is a socioecological phenomenon and must be treated as such. Youths who live in areas where their needs cannot be met by existing institutions join gangs when gang members are there to recruit them.[141] Social causes demand social solutions. Programs that enhance the lives of adolescents are the key to reducing gang delinquency. Exhibit 8.2 illustrates some of the key elements of a successful gang control strategy.

For more on gang prevention efforts, click on Web Links under the Chapter Resources at http://cj.wadsworth.com/siegel_jdcore2e.

Boston's Youth Violence Strike Force (YVSF)

The Youth Violence Strike Force (YVSF) is one of the primary enforcement strategies being pursued by the city of Boston to combat youth gang violence. The YVSF is a multiagency coordinated task force made up of forty-five to fifty full-time Boston police officers and fifteen officers from outside agencies. Members hail from the Massachusetts State Police; the Department of the Treasury's Bureau of Alcohol, Tobacco and Firearms (ATF); police departments from neighboring jurisdictions; Massachusetts Corrections, Probation, Parole, and Division of Youth Service (juvenile corrections) officers; and other agencies, as appropriate. The YVSF works closely with the Suffolk County district attorney's and the state attorney general's offices, and participates in the Department of Justice's AntiViolent Crime Initiative (AVCI) led locally by the United States Attorney. The YVSF investigates youth crimes, arrests those responsible, and breaks up the environment for crime. One important accomplishment of the YVSF has been the creation of a comprehensive computer database, which has allowed tough enforcement efforts against the leaders of gangs and positive interventions in the lives of those who are at risk of becoming hardcore gang members.

In addition, in cooperation with the city of Boston and the Department of Justice, the Youth Violence Strike Force has used criminal and civil forfeiture laws to help secure the safety of the community by taking over drug dens and renovating them as new homes. Drug dens have been closed through joint federal-state-local cooperation. Some former drug houses have been renovated in order to provide low-income elderly housing.

The YVSF takes tough action every day against gangs and gang members across Boston. Yet many of the strike force officers view their work in prevention as equally important, and many help to sponsor numerous prevention activities in the community. For example, YVSF members work in partnership with law enforcement, social service, and private institutions to raise funds for a series of "Kids at Risk" programs, which include camping programs, membership in Boys and Girls Clubs and YMCAs, and attendance at basketball camp or the Boston Police's Teen Summer Academy.

Another program, Operation Night Light, puts the YVSF together with concerned clergy members, youth outreach workers, and social service professionals to prevent youth and gang violence of probationers by regularly visiting their homes.

CRITICAL THINKING

Is it possible to reduce gang membership without providing youths with a reasonable legitimate alternative, including first-rate schools and job opportunities?

INFOTRAC COLLEGE EDITION RESEARCH

To read more about Operation Night Light, go to InfoTrac College Edition and read James T. Jordan, "Boston's Operation Night Light: New Roles, New Rules," *FBI Law Enforcement Bulletin*, August 1998 v67 n8 p1(5).

Source: *Youth Violence: A Community Based Response: One City's Success Story* (Washington, DC: Office of the Attorney General, 1996, updated); personal communication with Boston Police Department, January 5, 2004.

Exhibit 8.2   Essential Ingredients of Effective Gang Control Efforts

- Community leaders must recognize the presence of gangs and seek to understand the nature and extent of the local gang problem through a comprehensive and systematic assessment.

- The combined leadership of the justice system and the community must focus on the mobilization of institutional and community resources to address gang problems.

- Those in principal roles must develop a consensus on definitions (for example, gang, gang incident), specific targets of agency and interagency efforts, and interrelated strategies—based on problem assessment, not assumptions. Coordinated strategies should include those outlined by Irving Spergel: (1) community mobilization; (2) academic, social, and economic opportunities; (3) social intervention; (4) gang suppression; and (5) organizational change and development.

- Any approach must be guided by concern not only for safeguarding the community against youth gang activities but for providing support and supervision to present and potential gang members in a way that contributes to their prosocial development.

SUMMARY

- Peer relations are a critical element of maturation.
- Many experts believe that maintaining delinquent friends is a significant cause of antisocial behaviors.
- Some experts believe that criminal kids seek each other out.
- Gangs are law-violating youth groups that use special vocabulary, clothing, signs, colors, graffiti, and names, and whose members are committed to antisocial behavior.
- Gangs are a serious problem in many cities.
- Gangs have been around since the eighteenth century.
- The gang problem slowed down for a while in the 1960s, then reemerged in the 1970s.
- There are now thousands of gangs containing more than 750,000 members.
- Most gang members are male, ages fourteen to twenty-one, and live in urban areas.
- Gangs can be classified by their structure, behavior, or status. Some are believed to be social groups, others are criminally oriented, and still others are violent.
- Hundreds of thousands of crimes are believed to be committed annually by gangs. Although some gangs specialize in drug dealing, gang kids engage in a wide variety of criminal offenses.
- Violence is an important part of being a gang member.
- Although most gang members are male, the number of females in gangs is growing at a faster pace. African-American and Hispanic gangs predominate, but Anglo and Asian gangs are also quite common.
- We are still not sure what causes gangs. One view is that they serve as a bridge between adolescence and adulthood when adult control is lacking. Another view suggests that gangs serve as an alternative means of advancement for disadvantaged youths. Still another view is that some gangs are havens for disturbed youths.

KEY TERMS

cliques, p. 184
crowds, p. 184
controversial status youth, p. 184
gang, p. 185
interstitial group, p. 186

disorganized neighborhood, p. 188
retreatists, p. 189
near groups, p. 190
barrio, p. 190
klikas, p. 193

graffiti, p. 193
representing, p. 194
skinhead, p. 197
prestige crimes, p. 199
detached street workers, p. 204

QUESTIONS FOR DISCUSSION

1. Do gangs serve a purpose? Differentiate between a gang and a fraternity.
2. Discuss the differences between violent, criminal, and drug-oriented gangs.
3. How do gangs in suburban areas differ from inner-city gangs?
4. Do delinquents have cold and distant relationships with their peers?
5. Can gangs be controlled without changing the economic opportunity structure of society? Are there any truly meaningful alternatives to gangs today for lower-class youths?
6. Can you think of other rituals in society that reflect an affinity or longing for more tribal times? (*Hint:* Have you ever pledged a fraternity or sorority, gone to a wedding, or attended a football game?) Do TV shows like "Survivor" show a longing for more tribal times? After all, they even use tribal names for the competing teams.

APPLYING WHAT YOU HAVE LEARNED

You are a professor at a local state university who teaches courses on delinquent behavior. One day you are approached by the director of the president's National Task Force on Gangs (NTFG). This group has been formed to pool resources from a variety of federal agencies, ranging from the FBI to Health and Human Services, in order to provide local jurisdictions with a comprehensive plan to fight gangs. The director claims that the gang problem is big and becoming bigger. Thousands of gangs are operating around the country, with hundreds of thousands of members. Government sources, he claims, indicate that there has been a significant growth in gang membership over the past twenty years. So far, the government has not been able to do anything at either a state or national level to stem this growing tide of organized criminal activity. The NTFG would like you to be part of the team that provides state and local jurisdictions with a gang control activity model, which, if implemented, would provide a cost-effective means of reducing both gang membership and gang activity.

- Would you recommend that police employ antigang units that use tactics developed in the fight against organized crime families?
- Would you recommend the redevelopment of deteriorated neighborhoods in which gangs flourish?
- Would you try to educate kids about the dangers of gang membership?
- Would you tell the director that gangs have always existed and there is probably not much the government can do to reduce their numbers?

DOING RESEARCH ON THE WEB

To read more about gang prevention efforts, go to InfoTrac College Edition and check out Lonnie Jackson, "Understanding and Responding to Youth Gangs: a Juvenile Corrections Approach," *Corrections Today* 16:62 (August 1999). To do more research on gangs, use "gangs" as a key word.

To read some comprehensive visions of gang prevention, click on Web Links under the Chapter Resources at http://cj.wadsworth.com/siegel_jdcore2e.

Pro/Con discussions and Viewpoint Essays on some of the topics in this chapter may be found at the Opposing Viewpoints Resource Center: www.gale.com/OpposingViewpoints.

Schools and Delinquency

Courtesy of CNN

CHAPTER OBJECTIVES

After reading this chapter you should:

1. Understand the crisis that is facing the education system.
2. Be aware of the association between school failure and delinquency.
3. Be familiar with the factors that cause school failure.
4. Know what is meant by the term *tracking*.
5. Recognize the problem of truancy and what is being done to limit its occurrence.
6. Be familiar with the reasons why kids drop out of school.
7. Understand the nature of school crime and school shootings.
8. Know what school administrators are now doing to prevent delinquency on campus.
9. Be familiar with the various school-based delinquency prevention efforts.
10. Know the legal rights of students.

On March 5, 2001, at Santana High School in Santee, California, Charles "Andy" Williams, a fifteen-year-old student there, opened fire on his classmates. When the shooting stopped, two students were dead and thirteen adults and students were wounded. What caused the shooting? It was reported that Williams was tired of being picked on by bigger, more aggressive kids. He had told friends that he was looking for revenge and at least one adult knew of his threats, but no one took them seriously. No one reported them to the police. During his rampage, Williams fired thirty rounds from an eight-shot revolver, stopping to reload three times before he was cornered and arrested by the police. How did he get the weapon? He took the handgun from his father's locked gun cabinet.

CNN. VIEW THE CNN VIDEO CLIP OF THIS STORY AND ANSWER RELATED CRITICAL THINKING QUESTIONS ON YOUR JUVENILE DELINQUENCY: THE CORE 2E CD.

The U.S. Department of Education seeks to ensure equal access to education and promote educational excellence for all Americans. View its Web site by clicking on Web Links under the Chapter Resources at http://cj.wadsworth.com/siegel_jdcore2e.

School officials must make daily decisions on discipline and crime prevention, something they may not have thought much about when they decided on a career in education!

Because so much of an adolescent's time is spent in school, it would seem logical that some relationship exists between delinquent behavior and what is happening—or not happening—in classrooms.

Numerous studies have confirmed that delinquency is related to **academic achievement,** and experts have concluded that many of the underlying problems of delinquency are related to the nature of the school experience.[1] Most find that school-related factors are as important in contributing to delinquent behavior as the influence of either family or friends; furthermore, the influence of school cuts across racial, ethnic, and gender boundaries.[2]

In this chapter we first explore how educational achievement and delinquency are related and what factors in the school experience appear to contribute to delinquent behavior. Next, we turn to delinquency in the school setting—vandalism, theft, violence, and so on. Finally, we look at the attempts made by schools to prevent delinquency.

THE SCHOOL IN MODERN AMERICAN SOCIETY

The school plays a significant role in shaping the values of children.[3] In contrast to earlier periods, when formal education was a privilege of the upper classes, the U.S. system of compulsory public education has made schooling a legal obligation. Today, more than 90 percent of school-age children attend school, compared with only 7 percent in 1890.[4] As Figures 9.1 and 9.2 show, significantly more American citizens are finishing high school and going to college today than in the past.

In contrast to the earlier, agrarian days of U.S. history, when most adolescents shared in the work of the family, today's young people spend most of their time in school. The school has become the primary instrument of socialization, the "basic conduit through which the community and adult influences enter into the lives of adolescents."[5]

Because young people spend a longer time in school, their adolescence is prolonged. As long as students are still dependent on their families and have not entered

academic achievement
Being successful in a school environment.

Figure 9.1 **Years of School Completed by Persons 25 to 29 Years of Age: 1940–2001**

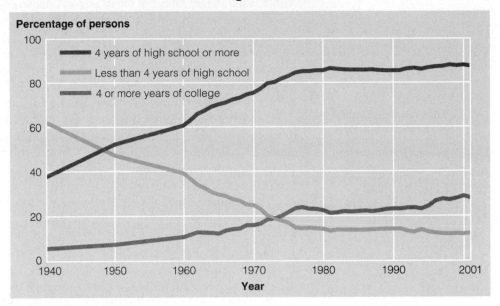

Percentage of persons

- 4 years of high school or more
- Less than 4 years of high school
- 4 or more years of college

Source: *1960 Census of Population,* Volume 1, part 1 (Washington, D.C.: U.S. Department of Commerce, Bureau of the Census); *Current Population Reports, Series P-20* (Washington, D.C.: U.S. Department of Commerce, Bureau of the Census, 2003); *Current Population Survey* (Washington, D.C.: U.S. Department of Labor, Bureau of Labor Statistics, Office of Employment and Unemployment Statistics, unpublished data, 2004).

Figure 9.2 **Highest Level of Education Attained by Persons 25 Years and Older, 2001**

Total persons age 25 and over = 177.0 million

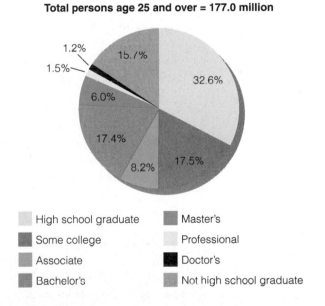

- High school graduate
- Some college
- Associate
- Bachelor's
- Master's
- Professional
- Doctor's
- Not high school graduate

Note: Detail may not sum to totals due to rounding.

Source: *Current Population Reports, Series P-20* (Washington, D.C.: U.S. Department of Commerce, Bureau of the Census, 2003); *Current Population Survey* (Washington, D.C.: U.S. Department of Labor, Bureau of Labor Statistics, Office of Employment and Unemployment Statistics, unpublished data, 2004).

the work world, they are not considered adults. The responsibilities of adulthood come later to modern-day youths than to those in earlier generations, and some experts see this prolonged childhood as one factor contributing to the irresponsible and often irrational behavior of many juveniles who commit delinquent acts.

Socialization and Status

Another significant aspect of the educational experience is that children spend their school hours with their peers, and most of their activities after school take place with school friends. Young people rely increasingly on school friends and become less interested in adult role models. The norms of the peer culture are often at odds with those of adult society, and a pseudoculture with a distinct social system develops. Law-abiding behavior may not be among the values promoted in such an atmosphere. Youth culture may admire bravery, defiance, and having fun much more than adults do.

The school has become a primary determinant of economic and social status. In this technological age, education is the key to a job that will mark its holder as "successful." No longer can parents ensure the status of their children through social class alone. Educational achievement has become of equal, if not greater, importance as a determinant of economic success.

This emphasis on the value of education is fostered by parents, the media, and the schools themselves. Regardless of their social or economic background, most children grow up believing education is the key to success. However, many youths do not meet acceptable standards of school achievement. Whether failure is measured by test scores, not being promoted, or dropping out, the incidence of school failure continues to be a major problem for U.S. society. A single school failure often leads to a pattern of chronic failure. The links between school failure and delinquency will be explored more fully in the next sections.

Education in Crisis

The role schools play in adolescent development is underscored by the problems faced by the U.S. education system.

Cross-national surveys that compare academic achievement show that the United States trails in critical academic areas.[6] There has been some improvement in reading, math, and science achievement during the past decade, but the United States still lags behind many nations in key achievement measures. For example, eighth-graders in the United States lag behind students in some less-affluent nations (Hungary, Slovak Republic, and Bulgaria) in science and math achievement. One reason for the lack of achievement may be that many secondary school math and science teachers did not major in the subjects they teach.[7] Another reason is that the United States, the richest country in the world, devotes less of its resources to education than do many other nations. (See Figure 9.3.) Spending on elementary and secondary education (as a percentage of the U.S. gross domestic product) is less than that of other nations. And budget cutting has reduced educational resources in many communities and curtailed state support for local school systems.

ACADEMIC PERFORMANCE AND DELINQUENCY

Poor academic performance has been directly linked to delinquent behavior; students who are chronic **underachievers** in school are among the most likely to be delinquent.[8] In fact, researchers find that school failure is a stronger predictor of delinquency than variables such as economic class membership, racial or ethnic background, or peer-group relations. Studies that compare the academic records of delinquents and nondelinquents—including their scores on standardized tests, failure rate, and other academic measures—have found that delinquents are often academically deficient, a condition that may lead to their leaving school and becoming involved in antisocial activities.[9] Children who report that they do not like school and do not do well in school are most likely to self-report delinquent acts.[10] In contrast, at-risk youths who do well in school are often able to avoid delinquent involvement.[11]

An association between academic failure and delinquency is commonly found among chronic offenders. Those leaving school without a diploma were more likely to become involved in chronic delinquency than high school graduates.[12] Only 9 percent

To learn more about math and science education, go to the Eisenhower National Clearinghouse for Mathematics and Science Education (ENC) by clicking on Web Links under the Chapter Resources at http://cj.wadsworth.com/siegel_jdcore2e.

underachievers
Those who fail to meet expected levels of school achievement.

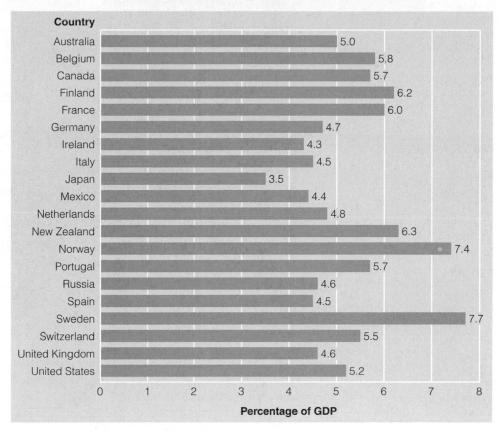

Figure 9.3 Public Direct Expenditures for Education as a Percentage of Gross Domestic Product: Selected Countries

Country	Percentage of GDP
Australia	5.0
Belgium	5.8
Canada	5.7
Finland	6.2
France	6.0
Germany	4.7
Ireland	4.3
Italy	4.5
Japan	3.5
Mexico	4.4
Netherlands	4.8
New Zealand	6.3
Norway	7.4
Portugal	5.7
Russia	4.6
Spain	4.5
Sweden	7.7
Switzerland	5.5
United Kingdom	4.6
United States	5.2

Note: Includes all government expenditures for education institutions.

Source: Organization for Economic Cooperation and Development, *Education at a Glance,* 2002.

of the chronic offenders in Marvin Wolfgang's Philadelphia *Delinquency in a Birth Cohort* study graduated from high school, compared with 74 percent of non-offenders.[13] Chronic offenders also had more disciplinary actions than non-offenders.[14]

The relationship between school achievement and persistent offending is supported by surveys that indicate that only 40 percent of incarcerated felons had twelve or more years of education, compared with about 80 percent of the general population.[15] In sum, the school experience can be a significant factor in shaping the direction of an adolescent's life course.

School Failure and Delinquency

Although there is general agreement that **school failure** and delinquency are related, some questions remain concerning the nature of this relationship (see Figure 9.4). One view is that the school experience is a direct cause of delinquent behavior. Children who fail at school soon feel frustrated and rejected. Believing they will never achieve success through conventional means, they seek out like-minded companions and together engage in antisocial behaviors. Educational failure evokes negative responses from important people in the child's life, including teachers, parents, and prospective employers. These reactions help solidify feelings of inadequacy, and in some cases, lead to a pattern of chronic delinquency.

A second view is that school failure leads to psychological dysfunction, which is the actual cause of antisocial behavior. For example, academic failure reduces self-esteem; studies using a variety of measures of academic competence and self-esteem demonstrate that good students have a better attitude about themselves than poor students; low self-esteem has been found to contribute to delinquent behavior.[16]

school failure
Failing to achieve success in school can result in frustration, anger, and reduced self-esteem, which may contribute to delinquent behavior.

Some students may become alienated from school because they believe that educators have gone overboard in an attempt to maintain school discipline. Here Leonard Lopez and his son, Vincent, sit at home surrounded by folders of newspaper clippings and legal papers in Arlington, Texas. Vincent was removed from his junior high school and placed into an alternative school for five days after one of his drawings was considered to show gang affiliation.

© 2000 AP/Wide World Photos

The association then runs from school failure to low self-concept to delinquency. Schools may mediate these effects by taking steps to improve the self-image of academically challenged children.

A third view is that school failure and delinquency share a common cause. For example, they both may be part of a generalized problem behavior syndrome (PBS). Therefore, it would be erroneous to conclude that school failure *precedes* antisocial behavior. In this view, the correlates of school failure and delinquency are these:

- Delinquents may have lower IQs than nondelinquents, a factor that might also explain their poor academic achievement.
- Delinquent behavior has been associated with a turbulent family life, a condition that most likely leads to academic underachievement.
- Delinquency has been associated with low self-control and impulsivity, traits that also may produce school failure.
- The adolescent who both fails at school and engages in delinquency may be experiencing drug use, depression, abuse, and disease—all symptoms of a troubled lifestyle.[17]

Causes of School Failure

Despite disagreement over the direction the relationship takes, there is little argument that delinquent behavior is influenced by educational experiences. A number of factors have been linked to school failure; the most prominent are discussed in the next sections.

Social Class and School Failure   During the 1950s, research by Albert Cohen indicated that delinquency was a phenomenon of working-class students who were poorly equipped to function in middle-class schools. Cohen referred to this phenomenon as a failure to live up to "middle-class measuring rods."[18] Jackson Toby reinforced this concept, contending that the disadvantages lower-class children have in school (for example, lack of verbal skills) are a result of their position in the social structure and that these disadvantages foster delinquency.[19] These views have been supported by the higher-than-average dropout rates among lower-class children.

Figure 9.4 **Three Views of the School–Delinquency Association**

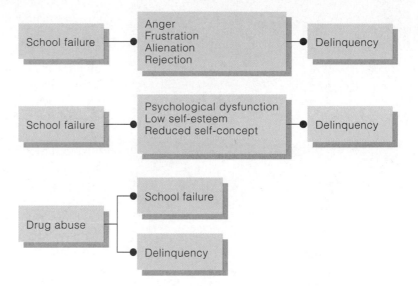

One reason why lower-class children may do poorly in school is that economic problems require them to take part-time jobs. Working while in school seems to lower commitment to educational achievement and is associated with higher levels of delinquent behavior.[20]

Not all experts agree with the social class–school failure–delinquency hypothesis. Early studies found that boys who do poorly in school, regardless of their socioeconomic background, are more likely to be delinquent than those who perform well.[21] There is evidence that affluent students are equally affected by school failure as lower-class youths, and that middle-class youths who do poorly in school are more likely to become delinquent than their lower-class peers who also have academic performance problems.[22] In fact, since expectations are so much higher for affluent youth, their failure to achieve in school may have a more profound effect on their behavior and well-being than it does on lower-class youth, who face so many other social problems. Not surprisingly, middle-class kids who are involved in antisocial behaviors are more likely to experience school failure than lower-class youth who experience similar social problems.[23]

Tracking Most researchers have looked at academic **tracking**—dividing students into groups according to ability and achievement level—as a contributor to school failure. Placement in a noncollege track means consignment to educational oblivion without apparent purpose. Studies indicate that non-college-track students experience greater academic failure and progressive deterioration of achievement, participate less in extracurricular activities, have an increased tendency to drop out, and commit more delinquent acts.

Some school officials begin tracking students in the lowest grade levels. Educators separate youths into groups that have innocuous names ("special enrichment program"), but may carry the taint of academic incompetence. High school students may be tracked within individual subjects based on ability. Classes may be labeled in descending order: advanced placement, academically enriched, average, basic, and remedial. It is common for students to have all their courses in only one or two tracks.[24]

The effects of school labels accumulate over time. If students fail academically, they are often destined to fail again. Repeated instances of failure can help produce the career of the "misfit" or "dropout." Using a tracking system keeps certain students from having any hope of achieving academic success, thereby causing lack of motivation, which may foster delinquent behavior.[25]

tracking
Dividing students into groups according to their ability and achievement levels.

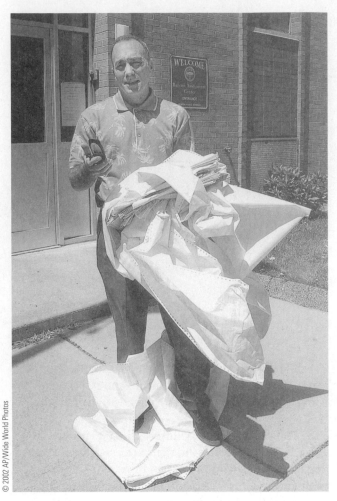

Can technology help reduce truancy? Some school systems believe it can have an effect. Here Elliot Feldman, director of Alternative Education for the Boston school system, holds a new cell phone information device for truancy officers. The device helps keep track of kids found not in school and provides easy access to information regarding where the student is supposed to be. The bundle of paper is what truant officers used to have to refer to when looking up students' records.

Alienation Alienation has also been identified as a link between school failure and delinquency. Students who report they neither like school nor care about their teachers' opinions are more likely to exhibit delinquent behaviors.[26] Youths who like school and report involvement in school activities are less likely to engage in delinquent behaviors.[27] Commitment to school, coupled with the belief that school rules are being consistently applied, helps youths resist criminality.[28] Attachment to teachers also helps insulate high-risk adolescents from delinquency.[29]

Alienation may be a function of students' inability to see the relevance of what they are taught. The gap between their education and the real world leads some students to feel that the school experience is a waste of time.[30]

Many students, particularly those from low-income families, believe schooling has no payoff. Because this legitimate channel appears to be meaningless, delinquent acts become increasingly more attractive. This middle- and upper-class bias is evident in the preeminent role of the college preparatory curriculum in many school systems. Furthermore, both methods of instruction and curriculum materials reflect middle-class language and customs that have little meaning for the disadvantaged child.

Truancy Every day, hundreds of thousands of youth are absent from school; many are absent without an excuse and deemed **truant.** Some large cities report that unexcused absences can number in the thousands on certain days. Truancy can lead to school failure and dropping out. The nature and cause of truancy and what can be done to prevent its occurrence is discussed in the following Preventing and Treating Delinquency feature.

Dropping Out

When kids are alienated from school and become persistent truants they may want to **drop out,** a step that may make them even more prone to antisocial behaviors. Though dropout rates are in decline, more than 10 percent of Americans ages sixteen to twenty-four have left school permanently without a diploma; of these, more than one million withdrew before completing tenth grade.

Dropping out is a serious issue because once kids leave school they are more likely to engage in drug abuse and antisocial behavior and to persist in criminal behavior throughout adulthood.[31] The effects of dropping out may last a lifetime. As Figure 9.5 shows, dropouts are much more likely to be unemployed than graduates, another factor that may increase their involvement in antisocial activities.

Why Do Kids Drop Out?

When surveyed, most dropouts say they left either because they did not like school or because they wanted to get a job. Other risk factors include low academic achievement, poor problem-solving ability, low self-esteem, difficulty getting along with teachers, dissatisfaction with school, substance abuse, and being too old for grade level.[32] Some dropouts could not get along with teachers, had been expelled, or were under suspension. Almost half of all female dropouts left school because they were pregnant or had already given birth.

truant
Being out of school without permission.

drop out
To leave school before completing the required program of education.

© 2002 AP/Wide World Photos

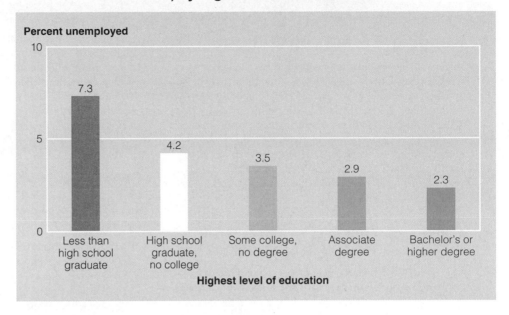

Figure 9.5 **Unemployment Rates of Persons 25 Years Old and Over, by Highest Level of Education**

Percent unemployed

7.3	4.2	3.5	2.9	2.3
Less than high school graduate	High school graduate, no college	Some college, no degree	Associate degree	Bachelor's or higher degree

Highest level of education

Source: U.S. Department of Labor, Bureau of Labor Statistics, Office of Employment and Unemployment Statistics, *Current Population Survey, 2001.*

Poverty and family dysfunction increase the chances of dropping out among all racial and ethnic groups. Dropouts are more likely than graduates to have lived in single-parent families headed by parents who were educational underachievers themselves.

Some youths have no choice but to drop out. They are pushed out of school because they lack attention or have poor attendance records. Teachers label them troublemakers, and school administrators use suspensions, transfers, and other means to "convince" them that leaving school is their only option. Because minority students often come from circumstances that interfere with their attendance, they are more likely to be labeled "disobedient."

Race-based disciplinary practices may help sustain high minority dropout rates. Although the African-American dropout rate has declined faster than the White dropout rate over the past three decades, minority students still drop out at a higher rate than White students. (See Table 9.1.)

In his thoughtful book *Creating the Dropout,* Sherman Dorn shows that graduation rates slowly but steadily rose during the twentieth century while regional, racial, and ethnic differences in graduation rates declined.[33] Nonetheless, Dorn argues that the relatively high dropout rate among minorities is the legacy of disciplinary policies instituted more than forty years ago when educational administrators opposed to school desegregation employed a policy of race-based suspension and expulsion directed at convincing minority students to leave previously all-White high school districts. This legacy still affects contemporary school districts. Dorn

Table 9.1 **Dropout Rates (%), by Race and Ethnicity**

Year	Total	Caucasian	Black	Hispanic
1972	14.6	12.3	21.3	34.3
2001	10.7	7.3	10.9	27.0

Source: National Center for Education Statistics, U.S. Department of Education, *Digest of Education Statistics,* 2002. http://nces.ed.gov/programs/digest/d02/tables/dt108.asp.

Keeping Truants in School

In general, the proportion of truancy cases handled in juvenile court is relatively small. However, the juvenile justice system is increasingly serving as the final stop for truants and as a mechanism for intervening with chronic truants. Recent statistics available on the extent of truancy cases in juvenile court clearly demonstrate how important it is for schools and communities to confront this issue. Truancy accounts for 26 percent of all formally handled status offense cases, representing an 85 percent increase in truancy cases in juvenile court since 1989.

Causes of Truancy

What causes truancy? Among the factors identified are these:

- *Family factors.* These include lack of guidance or parental supervision, domestic violence, poverty, drug or alcohol abuse in the home, lack of awareness of attendance laws, and differing attitudes toward education.
- *School factors.* These include school climate issues—such as school size and attitudes of teachers, other students, and administrators—and inflexibility in meeting the diverse cultural and learning styles of the students.
- *Economic influences.* These include employed students, single-parent homes, high mobility rates, parents who hold multiple jobs, and a lack of affordable transportation and child care.
- *Student variables.* These include drug and alcohol abuse, lack of understanding of attendance laws, lack of social competence, mental health difficulties, and poor physical health.

Costs of Truancy

Truancy places significant burdens on society. Students with the highest truancy rates have the lowest academic achievement rates and have high dropout rates as well. Truancy can also be linked to juvenile delinquency in several ways. Kids who are chronically truant seem at high risk for future criminality and drug abuse. There is also evidence that high rates of truancy can be linked to high rates of daytime burglary and vandalism. In some jurisdictions, a significant portion of all burglaries and aggravated assaults occurring on weekdays between 8 A.M. and 1 P.M. are committed by juveniles.

Combating Truancy

Because of the social cost of truancy, local jurisdictions, with the aid of the federal government, are sponsoring truancy control efforts. A few significant efforts are described here:

1. The State Attorney's Office, Jacksonville, Florida, provides a precourt diversion program for truant youths and their families. The school district refers families to the program when chronic truancy has not been solved by school-based interventions. Following the referral, a hearing is conducted with the parent, youth, school attendance social worker, and volunteer hearing officer. A contract is negotiated that includes plans for reducing truancy and accessing services and community supports. A case manager makes home visits and monitors the family's compliance with the plan. In the fall of 2000, a school-based component was added to address prevention and early intervention at two elementary schools, where an on-site case manager monitors attendance and provides early outreach.

2. The University of Hawaii, Honolulu, is building on a previous program to prevent truancy in the Wai'anae area. Attendance officers in two elementary schools work to provide early outreach to young students and their families when absences become chronic. Community resources are used to address the issues that may prevent youth from attending school regularly. In addition, the

believes that the dropout problem is a function of inequality of educational opportunity rather than the failure of individual students. The proportion of Blacks who fail to graduate from high school remains high compared with the proportion of Whites who fail to graduate because the educational system still fails to provide minority group members with the services and support they need. ✔ Checkpoints

DELINQUENCY IN THE SCHOOL

In its pioneering study of school crime, *Violent Schools–Safe Schools* (1977),[34] the federal government found that, although teenagers spend only 25 percent of their time in school, 40 percent of the robberies and 36 percent of the physical attacks involving this age group occur there. School crime has remained a national concern since the *Safe Schools* study was published.

The School Crime Victimization Survey is a now yearly effort by the U.S. Justice Department and Education Department to measure crime and victimization in the

Checkpoints

✔ *The school is one of the key institutions of socialization in contemporary society.*

schools work with the Honolulu Police Department to provide Saturday truancy workshops for youth with chronic truancy problems and their families.

3. Suffolk County Probation Department's (Yaphank, New York) South Country Truancy Reduction Program, which builds on community policing efforts, targets elementary and middle-school students who have illegal absences. A probation officer monitors attendance in collaboration with school personnel, facilitates access to school and community-based services needed by the student and family to establish regular school attendance, and observes attendance and other school-based indicators to ensure that the student's attendance and engagement at school are improving. A similar model is in existence at the local high school.

4. The Mayor's Anti-Gang Office, Houston, places an experienced case manager in one high school to identify students with chronic truancy patterns. Through home visits and school-based supports, students and their families are provided with services, support, and resources to address truancy. The program also works with community police officers, who provide a "knock and talk" service for youth and their families when truancy continues to be an issue. The officers assess family functioning and deliver information about the law and truancy outcomes; they also issue the official summons to court for a truancy petition.

5. At the King County Superior Court, Seattle, after a truancy petition is filed, families have the option of attending an evening workshop, participating in a community truancy board hearing, or proceeding to court on the charges. The workshop includes education about truancy law and outcomes and facilitates planning between the parent and youth for addressing the cause of truancy. Community truancy boards composed of local community members hear the case, develop a plan for

use with the youth and family, and monitor compliance with the stipulated agreement. In the fall of 2000, a school-based component was added to address prevention and early intervention.

CRITICAL THINKING
Some kids are persistently truant and do not wish to attend school. Should the educational system provide support for these children or simply let them skip classes and then formally drop out once they are of legal age? Is there any purpose to devoting limited resources to kids who simply do not want to learn?

INFOTRAC COLLEGE EDITION RESEARCH
For some children, school attendance is so distressing that they have difficulty attending school, a problem that often results in prolonged absence and truancy. To find out why this phenomenon occurs, go to InfoTrac College Edition and read Neville J. King and Gail A. Bernstein, "School Refusal in Children and Adolescents: A Review of the Past 10 Years," *Journal of the American Academy of Child and Adolescent Psychiatry,* February 2001 v40 i2 p197.

Source: Myriam Baker, Jane Nady Sigmon, and M. Elaine Nugent, *Truancy Reduction: Keeping Students in School* (Washington, DC: Office of Juvenile Justice and Delinquency Prevention, 2001).

✔ Despite its great wealth, the United States lags behind many nations in academic achievement.

✔ Academic performance has been linked to delinquency.

✔ School failure is linked to delinquency.

✔ The causes of school failure include class conflict, alienation, and tracking.

✔ Many kids drop out of school before they graduate, and dropping out has been linked to delinquent behavior.

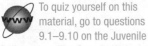 To quiz yourself on this material, go to questions 9.1–9.10 on the Juvenile Delinquency: The Core 2e Web site.

nation's schools.[35] The latest data available show that students ages twelve through eighteen were victims of about 1.9 million total crimes of violence or theft. Included within this number were about 128,000 serious violent crimes at school (that is, rape, sexual assault, robbery, and aggravated assault). Although these numbers seem staggering, the amount and rate of school crime has actually been in decline, mirroring the nation's ongoing crime drop. Between 1992 and 2000, victimization rates dropped from 144 per one thousand students in 1992 to 72 per one thousand students. The percentage of students being victimized at school also has declined over the last few years, from 10 percent in 1995 to 6 percent today.

Although these trends are encouraging, a number of school-based problem behaviors have increased. For example, in 2001, 8 percent of students reported that they had been bullied at school in the last six months, up from 5 percent in 1999. Because this issue of bullying is so important, it is the topic of the following Focus on Delinquency feature. The What Does This Mean to Me? feature offers another perspective.

Bullying in School

Experts define bullying among children as repeated, negative acts committed by one or more children against another. These negative acts may be physical or verbal in nature—for example, hitting or kicking, teasing or taunting—or they may involve indirect actions such as manipulating friendships or purposely excluding other children from activities. Implicit in this definition is an imbalance in real or perceived power between the bully and victim.

Studies of bullying suggest that there are short- and long-term consequences for both the perpetrators and the victims of bullying. Students who are chronic victims of bullying experience more physical and psychological problems than their peers who are not harassed by other children, and they tend not to grow out of the role of victim. Young people mistreated by peers may not want to be in school and may thereby miss out on the benefits of school connectedness as well as educational advancement. Longitudinal studies have found that victims of bullying in early grades also reported being bullied several years later. Studies also suggest that chronically victimized students may, as adults, be at increased risk for depression, poor self-esteem, and other mental health problems, including schizophrenia.

It is not only victims who are at risk for short- and long-term problems; bullies too are at increased risk for negative outcomes. One researcher found that those elementary students who were bullies attended school less frequently and were more likely to drop out than other students. Several studies suggest that bullying in early childhood may be a critical risk factor in the development of future problems with violence and delinquency. For example, bullies are more likely to carry weapons in and out of school. Research conducted in Scandinavia found that, in addition to threatening other children, bullies were several times more likely than their non-bullying peers to commit antisocial acts, including vandalism, fighting, theft, drunkenness, and truancy, and to have an arrest by young adulthood. Another study of more than five hundred children found that aggressive behavior at the age of eight was a powerful predictor of criminality and violent behavior at the age of thirty.

Can Bullying Be Prevented?

The first and best-known intervention to reduce bullying among schoolchildren was launched by Dan Olweus in Norway and Sweden in the early 1980s. Prompted by the suicides of several severely victimized children, Norway supported the development and implementation of a comprehensive program to address bullying among children in school. The program involved interventions at multiple levels:

- *Schoolwide interventions:* A survey of bullying problems at each school, increased supervision, schoolwide assemblies, and teacher in-service training to raise the awareness of children and school staff regarding bullying
- *Classroom-level interventions:* The establishment of classroom rules against bullying, regular class meetings

to discuss bullying at school, and meetings with all parents
- *Individual-level interventions:* Discussions with students to identify bullies and victims

The program was found to be highly effective in reducing bullying and other antisocial behavior among students in primary and junior high schools. Within two years of implementation, both boys' and girls' self-reports indicated that bullying had decreased by half. These changes in behavior were more pronounced the longer the program was in effect. Moreover, students reported significant decreases in rates of truancy, vandalism, and theft, and indicated that their school's climate was significantly more positive as a result of the program. Not surprisingly, those schools that had implemented more of the program's components experienced the most marked changes in behavior. The core components of the Olweus anti-bullying program have been adapted for use in several other cultures, including Canada, England, and the United States. Results of the anti-bullying efforts in these countries have been similar to the results experienced in the Scandinavian countries, with the efforts in Toronto schools showing somewhat more modest results. Again, as in the Scandinavian study, schools that were more active in implementing the program observed the most marked changes in reported behaviors.

Only one U.S. program has been based explicitly on the comprehensive model developed by Olweus. Gary B. Melton, Susan P. Limber, and colleagues at the Institute for Families in Society of the University of South Carolina in Columbia have adapted Olweus's model for use in rural middle schools in that state. Interventions are focused at the levels of the individual, classroom, school, and community at large. A comprehensive evaluation involving sixty-five hundred children currently is under way to measure the effects of the program.

CRITICAL THINKING

Should schoolyard bullies be expelled from school? Would such a measure make a bad situation worse? For example, might expelled bullies shift their aggressive behavior from the schoolyard to the community?

INFOTRAC COLLEGE EDITION RESEARCH

To learn more about the cause and effect of school bullying, use the term in a key word search on InfoTrac College Edition.

Sources: Marla Eisenberg, Dianne Neumark-Sztainer, and Cheryl Perry, "Peer Harassment, School Connectedness, and Academic Achievement," *Journal of School Health* 73:311–316 (2003); Michael Reiff, "Bullying and Violence," *Journal of Developmental & Behavioral Pediatrics* 24:296–297 (2003); Susan Limber and Maury Nation, "Bullying Among Children and Youth," in June Arnette and Marjorie Walsleben, eds., *Combating Fear and Restoring Safety in Schools* (Washington, DC: Office of Juvenile Justice and Delinquency Prevention, 1998); Dan Olweus, "Victimization by Peers: Antecedents and Long-Term Outcomes," in K. H. Rubin and J. B. Asendorf, eds., *Social Withdrawal, Inhibitions, and Shyness* (Hillsdale, NJ: Erlbaum, 1993), pp. 315–341.

School Shootings

Though incidents of school-based crime and violence are not uncommon, it is the highly publicized incidents of fatal school shootings that have helped focus attention on school crime. Upwards of 10 percent of students report bringing weapons to school on a regular basis. Many of these kids have a history of being abused and bullied; many perceive a lack of support from peers, parents, and teachers.[36] Kids who have been the victims of crime themselves and who hang with peers who carry weapons are the ones most likely to bring guns to school.[37] A troubled kid who has little social support but carries deadly weapons makes for an explosive situation.

Nature and Extent of Shootings Social scientists are now conducting studies of these events in order to determine their trends and patterns. One recent study examined all 220 school-related shootings occurring between July 1, 1994 and June 30, 1999.[38] Of the 220 shooting incidents, 172 were homicides, 30 were suicides, 11 were homicide-suicides, 5 were legal intervention deaths, and 2 were unintentional firearm-related deaths. Although highly publicized in the media, this amounted to 0.068 per 100,000 students being affected by these shootings.

The research discovered that most shooting incidents occur around the start of the school day, the lunch period, or the end of the school day. In most of the shootings (55 percent), a note, threat, or other action indicating risk for violence occurred prior to the event. Shooters were also likely to have expressed some form of suicidal behavior prior to the event and to report having been bullied by their peers. These patterns may help school officials one day to identify potential risk factors and respond in a timely fashion.

Not all school bullies are hulking brutes. The ten-year-old girl shown here was the subject of a restraining order brought by a classmate in an effort to stop her taunting. A judge threatened to send both girls to jail if their conflict continued.

Who Is the School Shooter? The United States Secret Service has developed a profile of school shootings and shooters after evaluating forty-one school shooters who participated in thirty-seven incidents.[39] They found that most attacks were neither spontaneous nor impulsive. Shooters typically developed a plan of attack well in advance; more than half had considered the attack for at least two weeks and had a plan for at least two days.

The attackers' mental anguish was well known, and these kids had come to the attention of someone (school officials, police, fellow students) because of their bizarre and disturbing behavior prior to the attack's taking place. One student told more than twenty friends beforehand about his plans, which included killing students and planting bombs. Threats were communicated in more than three-fourths of the cases, and in more than half the incidents the attacker told more than one person. Some people knew detailed information, while others knew "something spectacular" was going to happen on a particular date. In less than one-fourth of the cases did the attacker make a direct threat to the target.

The Secret Service found that the shooters came from such a wide variety of backgrounds that no accurate or useful profile of at-risk kids could be developed. They ranged in age from eleven to twenty-one and came from a wide variety of ethnic and racial backgrounds; about 25 percent of the shooters were minority-group members. Some lived in intact families with strong ties to the community, while

What Does This Mean to Me?

"Bully for You!"

Research indicates that more than 80 percent of school kids say their behavior includes physical aggression, social ridicule, teasing, name calling, and issuing threats over the previous thirty days. Some kids seem proud of being bullies and think their behavior, no matter how destructive, is just fun at another's expense. Many of us have been the targets of bullies but felt unsure of how to cope with the problem. If you told the teacher or your parents you were a wimp; if you did nothing you remained a target.

1. Did you ever find yourself having to confront this dilemma, and if so what did you do to solve the problem?
2. Do you believe there is a link between being the victim of bullying and engaging in school violence? The Columbine shooters were believed to be targets of bullying. Could this have been the spark that caused them to snap?

others were reared in foster homes with histories of neglect. Some were excellent students, while others were poor academic performers. Shooters could not be characterized as isolated and alienated; some had many friends and were considered popular. There was no evidence that shootings were a result of the onset of mental disorder. Drugs and alcohol seemed to have little involvement in school violence.

What the Secret Service did find, however, was that many of the shooters had a history of feeling extremely depressed or desperate because they had been picked on or bullied. About three-fourths either threatened to kill themselves, made suicidal gestures, or tried to kill themselves before the attack; six of the students studied killed themselves during the incident. The most frequent motivation was revenge. More than three-fourths were known to hold a grievance, real or imagined, against the target or others. In most cases, this was the first violent act against the target. Two-thirds of the attackers described feeling persecuted, and in more than three-fourths of the incidents the attackers had difficulty coping with a major change in a significant relationship or a loss of status, such as a lost love or a humiliating failure. Not surprisingly, most shooters had experience with guns and weapons and had access to them at home. Some of the most important factors linked to extreme incidents of school violence are contained in Exhibit 9.1.

Who Commits School Crime?

Schools experiencing drug abuse and crime (other than school shootings such as those just described) are most likely to be found in socially disorganized neighborhoods. Schools with a high proportion of students behind grade level in reading, with many students from families on welfare, and located in a community with high unemployment, crime, and poverty rates, are also at risk for delinquency.[40] In contrast, schools with high-achieving students, a drug-free environment, strong discipline, and involved parents have fewer behavioral problems in the student body.[41]

A number of researchers have observed that school crime is a function of the community in which the school is located. In other words, crime in schools does not occur in isolation from crime in the community.[42] Research shows that the perpetrators and victims of school crime cannot be neatly divided into separate groups and that many offenders have been victims of delinquency themselves.[43] It is possible that school-based crimes have "survival value": striking back against a weaker victim is a method of regaining lost possessions or self-respect.[44] There is also evidence that crime in schools reflects the patterns of antisocial behavior that exist in the surrounding neighborhood. Schools in high-crime areas experience more crime than schools in safer areas; there is less fear in schools in safer neighborhoods than in high-crime ones. Students who report being afraid in school are actually *more afraid* of being in city parks, streets, or subways.[45]

Other research efforts confirm the community influences on school crime. Communities with a high percentage of two-parent families experience fewer school problems; neighborhoods with high population density and transient populations also have problem-prone schools.[46] One study of violent crimes in the schools of Stockholm, Sweden, found that, although only one-fifth of schools were located in areas of social instability and disorganization, almost a third of all school crime happened in these schools.[47] This analysis suggests that it may be futile to attempt to eliminate school crime without considering the impact prevention efforts will have on the community.

Exhibit 9.1   Factors Linked to Children Who Engage in Serious School Violence

- *Social withdrawal.* In some situations, gradual and eventually complete withdrawal from social contacts occurs. The withdrawal often stems from feelings of depression, rejection, persecution, unworthiness, and lack of confidence.

- *Excessive feelings of isolation and being alone.* Research indicates that in some cases feelings of isolation and not having friends are associated with children who behave aggressively and violently.

- *Excessive feelings of rejection.* Children who are troubled often are isolated from their mentally healthy peers. Some aggressive children who are rejected by nonaggressive peers seek out aggressive friends who, in turn, reinforce their violent tendencies.

- *Being a victim of violence.* Children who are victims of violence, including physical or sexual abuse in the community, at school, or at home, are sometimes at risk of becoming violent toward themselves or others.

- *Feelings of being picked on and persecuted.* The youth who feels constantly picked on, teased, bullied, singled out for ridicule, and humiliated at home or at school may initially withdraw socially.

- *Low school interest and poor academic performance.* In some situations—such as when the low achiever feels frustrated, unworthy, chastised, and denigrated—acting out and aggressive behaviors may occur.

- *Expression of violence in writings and drawings.* An overrepresentation of violence in writings and drawings that is consistently directed at specific individuals (family members, peers, other adults) over time may signal emotional problems and the potential for violence.

- *Uncontrolled anger.* Patterns of impulsive and chronic hitting, intimidating, and bullying behaviors, if left unattended, may later escalate into more serious behaviors.

- *History of discipline problems.* Chronic behavior and disciplinary problems, both in school and at home, may suggest that underlying emotional needs are not being met.

- *History of violent and aggressive behavior.* Unless provided with support and counseling, a youth who has a history of aggressive or violent behavior is likely to repeat those behaviors. Similarly, youths who engage in overt behaviors such as bullying, generalized aggression, and defiance, and covert behaviors such as stealing, vandalism, lying, cheating, and fire setting also are at risk for more serious aggressive behavior.

- *Membership in hate groups.* Belonging to a hate group and also the willingness to victimize individuals with disabilities or health problems are seen as precursors to violence.

- *Drug use and alcohol use.* Apart from being unhealthy behaviors, drug use and alcohol use reduce self-control and expose children and youth to violence, either as perpetrators or victims or both.

- *Inappropriate access to, possession of, and use of firearms.* Children and youth who inappropriately possess or have access to firearms can have an increased risk for violence or other emotional problems.

- *Serious threats of violence.* Recent incidents across the country clearly indicate that threats to commit violence against oneself or others should be taken very seriously. Steps must be taken to understand the nature of these threats and to prevent them from being carried out.

Source: Kevin Dwyer, *Early Warning, Timely Response: A Guide to Safe Schools* (Washington, DC: U.S. Department of Education, 1998), Section 3.

Reducing School Crime

Schools around the country have mounted a campaign to reduce the incidence of delinquency on campus. Nearly all states have developed some sort of crime-free, weapon-free, or safe-school zone statute.[48] Most have defined these zones to include school transportation and school-sponsored functions. Schools are also cooperating with court officials and probation officers to share information and monitor students

A police officer uses a handheld metal detector to check for weapons in Hancock (Michigan) Middle School after a threatening letter was found in a boys' bathroom. The use of security measures has become routine in the wake of incidents of school-based violence.

© 2001 AP/Wide World Photos

who have criminal records. School districts are formulating crisis prevention and intervention policies and are directing individual schools to develop safe-school plans.

Some schools have instituted strict controls over student activity—for example, making locker searches, preventing students from having lunch off campus, and using patrols to monitor drug use. According to one national survey, a majority of schools have adopted a **zero tolerance policy** that mandates predetermined punishments for specific offenses, most often possession of drugs, weapons, and tobacco, and also for engaging in violent behaviors.[49]

School Security Efforts

Almost every school attempts to restrict entry of dangerous persons by having visitors sign in before entering, and most close the campus for lunch. Schools have attempted to ensure the physical safety of students and staff by using mechanical security devices such as surveillance cameras, electronic barriers to keep out intruders, and roving security guards.[50] About 4 percent of schools use random metal detectors; metal detectors are much more common in large schools, especially where serious crime has taken place (15 percent).[51] Some districts have gone so far as to infiltrate undercover detectives on school grounds. These detectives attend classes, mingle with students, contact drug dealers, make buys, and arrest campus dealers.[52] Some administrators keep buildings dark at night, believing that brightly illuminated schools give the buildings too high a profile and attract vandals who might have not bothered with the facility, or even noticed it, if the premises were not illuminated.[53]

School security measures have received mixed reviews. Some research finds that they are not really effective in reducing the incidence of school crime or the likelihood of schoolyard victimization.[54] Some critics complain that even when security methods are effective, they reduce staff and student morale. Tighter security may reduce acts of crime and violence in the school, only to displace them to the community. Similarly, expelling or suspending troublemakers puts them on the street with nothing to do, so that in the end, lowering the level of crime in schools may not reduce the total amount of crime committed by young people.

Another approach consists of improving the school climate and increasing educational standards. Programs have been designed to improve the standards of the teaching staff and administrators and the educational climate in the school, increase the relevance of the curriculum, and provide law-related education classes.

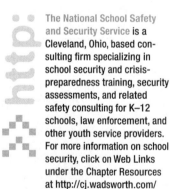

http:

The National School Safety and Security Service is a Cleveland, Ohio, based consulting firm specializing in school security and crisis-preparedness training, security assessments, and related safety consulting for K–12 schools, law enforcement, and other youth service providers. For more information on school security, click on Web Links under the Chapter Resources at http://cj.wadsworth.com/ siegel_jdcore2e.

zero tolerance policy
Mandating specific consequences or punishments for delinquent acts and not allowing anyone to avoid these consequences.

THE ROLE OF THE SCHOOL IN DELINQUENCY PREVENTION

Numerous organizations and groups have called for reforming the educational system to make it more responsive to the needs of students. Educational leaders now recognize that children undergo enormous pressures while in school that can lead to emotional and social problems. At one extreme are the pressures to succeed academically; at the other are the crime and substance abuse students face on school grounds. It is difficult to talk of achieving academic excellence in a deteriorated school dominated by gang members.

The United States is facing an educational crisis. Student dissatisfaction, which begins to increase after elementary school, is accompanied by aversion for teachers and many academic subjects. The rate of student alienation and the social problems that accompany it—absenteeism, dropping out, and substance abuse—all increase as students enter junior high.

Educators have attempted to create programs that will benefit youths and provide them with opportunities for conventional success, but change has been slow in coming. Not until the mid-1980s did concern about the educational system, prompted by the findings of the National Commission on Excellence in Education in *A Nation at Risk,* focus efforts on change.[55]

Skepticism exists over whether the U.S. school system, viewed by critics as overly conservative, can play a significant role in delinquency prevention. Some contend that no significant change in the lives of youths is possible by merely changing the schools; the entire structure of society must be altered.[56] Others suggest that alternative schools, which create a positive learning environment with low student-teacher ratios and individualized learning, may be the answer. Although in theory such programs may promote academic performance and reduce delinquency, evaluations suggest that they have little effect on delinquency rates.[57]

School-Based Prevention Programs

Education officials have instituted numerous programs to make schools more effective instruments of delinquency prevention.[58] Some of the most prevalent strategies are as follows:

- *Cognitive.* Increase students' awareness about the dangers of drug abuse and delinquency.
- *Affective.* Improve students' psychological assets and self-image to give them the resources to resist antisocial behavior.
- *Behavioral.* Train students in techniques to resist peer pressure.
- *Environmental.* Establish school management and disciplinary programs that deter crime, such as locker searches.
- *Therapeutic.* Treat youths who have already manifested problems.

More specific suggestions include creating special classes or schools with individualized programs that foster success for nonadjusting students. Efforts can be made to help students deal constructively with academic failure when it does occur.

More personalized student-teacher relationships have been recommended. This effort to provide young people with a caring, accepting adult role model will, it is hoped, strengthen the controls against delinquency. Counselors acting as liaisons between the family and the school might also be effective in preventing delinquency. These counselors try to ensure cooperation between the parents and the school and to secure needed services for troubled students.

Experiments have been proposed to integrate job training and experience with classroom instruction, allowing students to see education as a relevant prelude to

Schools have adopted a number of different delinquency prevention programs. This school is reaching out to troubled young women and helping them develop life skills that will shield them from delinquency and substance abuse. Ramona High School home economics teacher, Diane Sequine, helps student Lorena Herrera (center) repair a sewing machine as classmate Yulma Chavez watches.

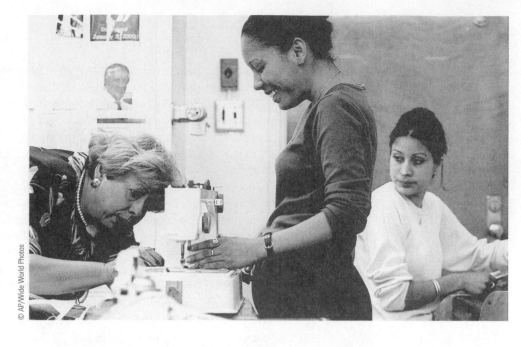

© AP/Wide World Photos

Checkpoints

✔ *A significant number of crimes occur in schools each year.*

✔ *There has been a recent decline in school-based crime that reflects the general crime-rate decline.*

✔ *Almost two million children were victimized between 1994 and 1998.*

✔ *About 5 percent of students are bullied in school.*

✔ *About three-quarters of all students report drugs in their school.*

✔ *A number of efforts are being made to reduce school crime, including enforcing strict security measures through the use of armed guards.*

✔ *Schools have been active in delinquency prevention.*

✔ *After-school programs are becoming popular.*

✔ *The programs that seem most effective focus on a range of social issues, including problem-solving skills, self-control, and stress management.*

 To quiz yourself on this material, go to questions 9.11–9.16 on the Juvenile Delinquency: The Core 2e Web site.

their careers. Job training programs emphasize public service, encouraging students to gain a sense of attachment to their communities.

Because three of four mothers with school-age children are employed, and two-thirds of them work full time, there is a growing need for after-school programs. Today, after-school options include child-care centers, tutoring programs at school, dance groups, basketball leagues, and drop-in clubs. State and federal budgets for education, public safety, crime prevention, and child care provide some funding for after-school programs; in 1999, $200 million in federal grants were made to enable schools to establish after-school programs called Twenty-First Century Community Learning Centers. Research shows that younger children (ages five to nine) and those in low-income neighborhoods gain the most from after-school programs, showing improved work habits, behavior with peers and adults, and performance in school. Young teens who attend after-school activities achieve higher grades in school and engage in less risky behavior. These findings must be interpreted with caution. Because after-school programs are voluntary, participants may be the more motivated youngsters in a given population and the least likely to engage in antisocial behavior.[59]

Schools may not be able to reduce delinquency single-handedly, but a number of alternatives to their present operations could aid a community-wide effort to lessen juvenile crime. And reviews of some of the more successful programs show that the savings in terms of reduced delinquency, school costs, and so on far outweigh the amount of money spent on prevention. ✔ Checkpoints

LEGAL RIGHTS IN THE SCHOOL

The actions of education officials often run into opposition from the courts, which are concerned with maintaining the legal rights of minors. The U.S. Supreme Court has sought to balance the civil liberties of students with the school's mandate to provide a safe environment. Three of the main issues involved are privacy issues, free speech in school, and school discipline.

The Right to Personal Privacy

One major issue is the right of school officials to search students and their possessions on school grounds. Drug abuse, theft, assault and battery, and racial conflicts in schools have increased the need to take action against troublemakers. School administrators have questioned students about their illegal activities, conducted searches of students' persons and possessions, and reported suspicious behavior to the police.

In 1984, in *New Jersey v. T.L.O.*, the Supreme Court helped clarify a vexing problem: whether the Fourth Amendment's prohibition against unreasonable searches and seizures applies to school officials as well as to police officers.[60] In this case, the Court found that students are in fact constitutionally protected from illegal searches but that school officials are not bound by the same restrictions as law enforcement agents. Police need "probable cause" before they can conduct a search, but educators can legally search students when there are reasonable grounds to believe the students have violated the law or broken school rules. In creating this distinction, the Court recognized the needs of school officials to preserve an environment conducive to education and to secure the safety of students.

One question left unanswered by *New Jersey v. T.L.O.* is whether teachers and other school officials can search lockers and desks. Here, the law has been controlled by state decisions, and each jurisdiction may create its own standards. Some allow teachers a free hand in opening lockers and desks.[61]

Drug Testing

Another critical issue involving privacy is the drug testing of students. In 1995, the Supreme Court extended schools' authority to search by legalizing a random drug-testing policy for student athletes. The Supreme Court's decision in *Vernonia School District 47J v. Acton* expanded the power of educators to ensure safe learning environments.[62]

As a result of *Vernonia*, schools may employ safe-school programs such as drug testing procedures as long as the policies satisfy the reasonableness test. *Vernonia* may bring forth a spate of suspicionless searches in public schools across the country. Metal-detection procedures, the use of drug-sniffing dogs, and random locker searches will be easier to justify. In upholding random suspicionless drug testing for student athletes, the Supreme Court extended one step further the schools' authority to search, despite court-imposed constitutional safeguards for children. Underlying this decision, like that of *New Jersey v. T.L.O.*, is a recognition that the use of drugs is a serious threat to public safety and to the rights of children to receive a decent and safe education.

Academic Privacy

Students have the right to expect that their records will be kept private. Although state laws govern the disclosure of information from juvenile court records, a 1974 federal law—the Family Educational Rights and Privacy Act (FERPA)—restricts disclosure of information from a student's education records without parental consent.[63] The act defines an education record to include all records, files, and other materials, such as photographs, containing information related to a student that an education agency maintains. In 1994, Congress passed the Improving America's Schools Act, which allowed educational systems to disclose education records under these circumstances: (1) state law authorizes the disclosure, (2) the disclosure is to a juvenile justice agency, (3) the disclosure relates to the justice system's ability to provide preadjudication services to a student, and (4) state or local officials certify in writing that the institution or individual receiving the information has agreed not to disclose it to a third party other than another juvenile justice system agency.[64]

Free Speech

passive speech
A form of expression protected by the First Amendment but not associated with actually speaking words; examples include wearing symbols or protest messages on buttons or signs.

Freedom of speech is guaranteed in the First Amendment to the U.S. Constitution. This right has been divided into two categories as it affects children in schools. The first category involves **passive speech,** a form of expression not associated with actually speaking words; examples include wearing armbands or political protest buttons. The most important U.S. Supreme Court decision concerning a student's right to

Students in Rochester, New York, are shown protesting a school ruling over the presence of metal detectors. The Supreme Court allows school officials to control student speech while on school premises if it interferes with the school's mission to implant "the shared values of a civilized social order." Student protest off-campus is still an open question. In the future, the courts may be asked to rule whether schools can control such forms of speech or whether they are shielded by the First Amendment.

© AP/Wide World Photos

passive speech was in 1969 in the case of *Tinker v. Des Moines Independent Community School District.*[65] This case involved the right to wear black armbands to protest the war in Vietnam. Three high school students, ages fifteen, sixteen, and thirteen, were suspended for wearing the armbands in school. According to the Court, to justify prohibiting an expression of opinion, the school must be able to show that its action was caused by something more than a desire to avoid the unpleasantness that accompanies the expression of an unpopular view. Unless it can be shown that the forbidden conduct will interfere with the discipline required to operate the school, the prohibition cannot be sustained.[66]

The concept of free speech articulated in *Tinker* was used again in 1986 in *Bethel School District No. 403 v. Fraser.*[67] This case upheld a school system's right to discipline a student who uses obscene or profane language and gestures. The Court found that a school has the right to control offensive speech that undermines the educational mission. In a 1988 case, *Hazelwood School District v. Kuhlmeier,* the Court extended the right of school officials to censor **active speech** when it ruled that the principal could censor articles in a student publication.[68] In this case, students had written about their experiences with pregnancy and parental divorce. The majority ruled that censorship was justified because school-sponsored publications were part of the curriculum and therefore designed to impart knowledge. Control over such activities could be differentiated from the action of the *Tinker* defendants' passive protests. In a dissent, Justice William J. Brennan accused school officials of favoring "thought control."

The Court may now be asked to address off-campus speech issues as well. Students have been suspended for posting messages school officials consider defamatory on Web sites.[69] In the future, the Court may be asked to rule on whether this speech is shielded by the First Amendment.

School Prayer

One of the most divisive issues involving free speech is school prayer. Although some religious-minded administrators, parents, and students want to have prayer sessions in schools or have religious convocations, others view the practice both as a violation of the principle of separation of church and state and as an infringement on the First Amendment right to freedom of religion. The 2000 case of *Santa Fe Independent School District, Petitioner v. Jane Doe* helps clarify the issue.[70]

Prior to 1995, the Santa Fe High School student who occupied the school's elective office of student council chaplain delivered a prayer over the public address system

active speech
Expressing an opinion by speaking or writing; freedom of speech is a protected right under the First Amendment to the U.S. Constitution.

in loco parentis
In the place of the parent; rights given to schools that allow them to assume parental duties in disciplining students.

before each varsity football game for the entire season. After the practice was challenged in federal district court, the school district adopted a different policy that permitted, but did not require, prayer initiated and led by a student at all home games. The district court entered an order modifying that policy to permit only nonsectarian, nonproselytizing prayer. However, a federal appellate court held that, even as modified, the football prayer policy was invalid. This decision was upheld when the case was appealed to the United States Supreme Court. They ruled that prayers led by an "elected" student undermines the protection of minority viewpoints. Such a system encourages divisiveness along religious lines and threatens the imposition of coercion upon those students not desiring to participate in a religious exercise. The Santa Fe case severely limits school-sanctioned prayer at public events.

Despite the Santa Fe decision, the Court has not totally ruled out the role of religion in schools. In its ruling in *Good News Club v. Milford Central School* (2001), the Supreme Court required an upstate New York school district to provide space for an after-school Bible club for elementary students.[71] The Court ruled that it was a violation of the First Amendment's free speech clause to deny the club access to the school space on the ground that the club was religious in nature; the school routinely let secular groups use its space. The Court reasoned that because the club's meetings were to be held after school hours, were not sponsored by the school, and were open to any student who obtained parental consent, it could not be perceived that the school was endorsing the club or that students might feel coerced to participate in its activities.

School Discipline

Most states have statutes permitting teachers to use corporal punishment in public school systems. Under the concept of ***in loco parentis,*** discipline is one of the parental duties given to the school system. In the 1977 case *Ingraham v. Wright,* the Court held that neither the Eighth nor the Fourteenth Amendment was violated by a teacher's use of corporal punishment to discipline students.[72] The Court established the standard that only reasonable discipline is allowed in school systems; today twenty-four states still allow physical punishment. With regard to suspension and expulsion, in 1976, in the case of *Goss v. Lopez,* the Supreme Court ruled that any time a student is to be suspended for up to ten days, he or she is entitled to a hearing.[73]

In summary, schools have the right to discipline students, but students are protected from unreasonable, excessive, and arbitrary discipline.

To quiz yourself on this material, go to questions 9.17–9.20 on the Juvenile Delinquency: The Core 2e Web site.

SUMMARY

- Youths spend much of their time in school because education has become increasingly important as a determinant of social and economic success.
- Educational institutions are among the primary instruments of socialization, and as such they are bound to influence the amount of delinquent behavior by school-age children.
- There is a strong association between school failure and delinquency.
- Those who claim a causal link between school failure and delinquency cite two major factors: (1) academic failure, which arises from lack of aptitude, labeling, or class conflict and results in tracking, and (2) alienation from the educational experience, which is the result of the impersonal nature of schools, the passive role assigned to students, and students' perception of their education as irrelevant to their future lives.

- Student misbehaviors, which may have their roots in the school experience, range from minor infractions of school rules (for example, smoking and loitering in the halls) to serious crimes, such as assault, arson, drug abuse, and vandalism.
- Truancy is a significant educational problem.
- Some dissatisfied students drop out of school, and research has shown a decline in delinquency among those who do drop out.
- The school has also been the setting for important delinquency prevention efforts. Among the measures taken are security squads, electronic surveillance, and teacher training.
- Students do not lose their legal rights at the schoolhouse door. Among the most important legal issues facing students are the right to privacy, free speech, fair discipline, and freedom of religion.

academic achievement, p. 210
underachievers, p. 212
school failure, p. 213
tracking, p. 215

truant, p. 216
drop out, p. 216
zero tolerance policy, p. 224

passive speech, p. 227
active speech, p. 228
in loco parentis, p. 228

QUESTIONS FOR DISCUSSION

1. Was there a delinquency problem in your high school? If so, how was it dealt with?

2. Should disobedient youths be suspended from school? Does this solution hurt or help?

3. What can be done to improve the delinquency prevention capabilities of schools?

4. Is school failure responsible for delinquency, or are delinquents simply school failures?

APPLYING WHAT YOU HAVE LEARNED

You are the principal of a suburban high school. It seems that one of your students, Steve Jones, has had a long-running feud with Mr. Metcalf, an English teacher whom he blames for giving him a low grade unfairly and for being too strict with other students. Steve set up a home-based Web site that posted insulting images of Metcalf and contained messages describing him in unflattering terms ("a slob who doesn't bathe often enough," for example). He posted a photo of the teacher with the caption "Public Enemy Number One." Word of the Web site has gotten out around school. And although students think it's funny and "cool," the faculty are outraged. You bring Steve into your office and ask him to take down the site, explaining that its existence has had a negative effect on school discipline and morale. He refuses, arguing that the site is home-based and you have no right to ask for its removal. Besides, he claims, it is just in fun and not really hurting anyone.

School administrators are asked to make these kinds of decisions every day, and the wrong choice can prove costly. You are aware that a case very similar to this one resulted in a $30,000 settlement in a damage claim against a school system when the principal did suspend a student for posting an insulting Web site and the student later sued for violating his right to free speech.

- Would you suspend Steve if he refuses your request to take down the site?
- Would you allow him to leave it posted and try to placate Mr. Metcalf?
- What would you do if Mr. Metcalf had posted a site ridiculing students and making fun of their academic abilities?

DOING RESEARCH ON THE WEB

There are a number of important resources for educational law on the Internet. Check out the Education Law Association site, the Educational Resource Information Center, and Edlaw by clicking on Web Links under the Chapter Resources at http://cj.wadsworth.com/siegel_jdcore2e.

Pro/Con discussions and Viewpoint Essays on some of the topics in this chapter may be found at the Opposing Viewpoints Resource Center: www.gale.com/OpposingViewpoints.

Drug Use and Delinquency

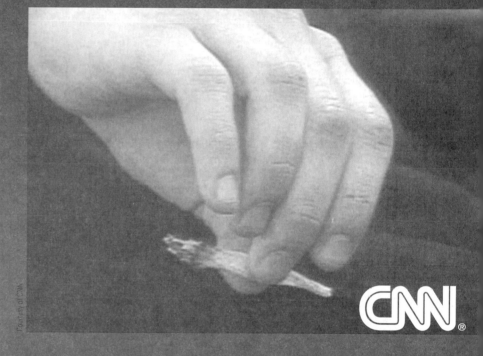

Courtesy of CNN

CHAPTER OBJECTIVES

After reading this chapter you should:

1. Know which are the drugs most frequently abused by American youth.

2. Understand the extent of the drug problem among American youth today.

3. Be able to discuss how teenage drug use in this country has changed over time.

4. Know the main explanations for why youths take drugs.

5. Recognize the different behavior patterns of drug-involved youths.

6. Understand the relationship between drug use and delinquency.

7. Be familiar with the major drug-control strategies.

8. Be able to argue the pros and cons of government using different drug-control strategies.

Surveys indicate that more than half of all high school–age kids have used drugs. Although this is a troubling statistic, these surveys also show that teen drug use is down from five and ten years ago. Many programs have been implemented over the years to help children and teens avoid taking drugs, such as educating them about the dangers of drug use and developing skills to "Just Say No." Some of these programs take place in the school and the community, and some involve police and other juvenile justice agencies. But what role can families play in helping to prevent teen drug use? A study by the Center on Addiction and Substance Abuse suggests that parents can play an important role. The study found that teens whose parents set down rules about what they can watch and listen to, care about how they are doing at school, and generally take an active interest in their lives are the least likely group to use drugs. In contrast, teens with hands-off parents were found to be more likely to try drugs.

CNN. VIEW THE CNN VIDEO CLIP OF THIS STORY AND ANSWER RELATED CRITICAL THINKING QUESTIONS ON YOUR JUVENILE DELINQUENCY: THE CORE 2E CD.

The Lindesmith Center is one of the leading independent drug policy institutes in the United States. View its Web site by clicking on Web Links under the Chapter Resources at http://cj.wadsworth.com/siegel_jdcore2e.

There is little question that adolescent **substance abuse** and its association with delinquency are vexing problems. Almost every town, village, and city in the United States has confronted some type of teenage substance abuse problem. Nor is the United States alone in experiencing this. In the United Kingdom, one out of eight high school students reports having used illicit drugs (other than marijuana) at least once, and in Denmark 85 percent of high school students report using alcohol in the past month. South Africa reports an increase in teen cocaine and heroin abuse, and Thailand has a serious heroin and methamphetamine problem.[1]

Self-report surveys indicate that more than half of high school seniors have tried drugs and almost 80 percent have used alcohol.[2] Adolescents at high risk for drug abuse often come from the most impoverished communities and experience a multitude of problems, including school failure and family conflict.[3] Equally troubling is the association between drug use and crime.[4] Research indicates that 10 percent of all juvenile male arrestees in some cities test positive for cocaine.[5] Self-report surveys show that drug abusers are more likely to become delinquents than are nonabusers.[6] The pattern of drug use and crime makes teenage substance abuse a key national concern.

FREQUENTLY ABUSED DRUGS

A wide variety of substances referred to as drugs are used by teenagers. Some are addicting, others not. Some create hallucinations, others cause a depressed stupor, and a few give an immediate uplift. In this section we will identify the most widely used substances and discuss their effects. All of these drugs can be abused, and because of the danger they present, many have been banned from private use. Others are available legally only with a physician's supervision, and a few are available to adults but prohibited for children.

substance abuse
Using drugs or alcohol in such a way as to cause physical harm to oneself.

hashish
A concentrated form of cannabis made from unadulterated resin from the female cannabis plant.

Marijuana and Hashish

Commonly called "pot" or "grass," marijuana is produced from the leaves of *Cannabis sativa*. **Hashish** (hash) is a concentrated form of cannabis made from unadulterated

Marijuana is the drug most commonly used by teenagers. Surveys suggest that marijuana use among high school students is much lower today than it was during its peak in the mid-1990s.

resin from the female plant. The main active ingredient in both marijuana and hashish is tetrahydrocannabinol (THC), a mild hallucinogen. **Marijuana** is the drug most commonly used by teenagers.

Smoking large amounts of pot or hash can cause distortions in auditory and visual perception, even producing hallucinatory effects. Small doses produce an early excitement ("high") that gives way to drowsiness. Pot use is also related to decreased activity, overestimation of time and space, and increased food consumption. When the user is alone, marijuana produces a dreamy state. In a group, users become giddy and lose perspective.

Marijuana is not physically addicting, but its long-term effects have been the subject of much debate. During the 1970s, it was reported that smoking pot caused a variety of physical and mental problems, including brain damage and mental illness. Although the dangers of pot and hash may have been overstated, use of these drugs does present some health risks, including an increased risk of lung cancer, chronic bronchitis, and other diseases. Prospective parents should avoid smoking marijuana because it lowers sperm counts in male users and females experience disrupted ovulation and a greater chance of miscarriage.[7]

Cocaine

Cocaine is an alkaloid derivative of the coca plant. When first isolated in 1860, it was considered a medicinal breakthrough that could relieve fatigue, depression, and other symptoms, and it quickly became a staple of patent medicines. When its addictive qualities and dangerous side effects became apparent, its use was controlled by the Pure Food and Drug Act of 1906.

Cocaine is the most powerful natural stimulant. Its use produces euphoria, restlessness, and excitement. Overdoses can cause delirium, violent manic behavior, and possible respiratory failure. The drug can be sniffed, or "snorted," into the nostrils, or it can be injected. The immediate feeling of euphoria, or "rush," is short-lived, and heavy users may snort coke as often as every ten minutes. Another dangerous practice is "speedballing"—injecting a mixture of cocaine and heroin.

Crack is processed street cocaine. Its manufacture involves using ammonia or baking soda (sodium bicarbonate) to remove the hydrochlorides and create a crystalline form of cocaine that can be smoked. In fact, crack gets its name from the fact that the sodium bicarbonate often emits a crackling sound when the substance is smoked. Also referred to as "rock," "gravel," and "roxanne," crack gained popularity in the mid-1980s. It is relatively inexpensive, can provide a powerful high, and is highly addictive psychologically.

Heroin

Narcotic drugs have the ability to produce insensibility to pain and to free the mind of anxiety and emotion. Users experience relief from fear and apprehension, release of tension, and elevation of spirits. This short period of euphoria is followed by a period of apathy, during which users become drowsy and may nod off. Heroin, the most commonly used narcotic in the United States, is produced from opium, a drug derived from the opium poppy flower. Dealers cut the drug with neutral substances (sugar or lactose), and street heroin is often only 1 to 4 percent pure.

marijuana
The dried leaves of the cannabis plant.

cocaine
A powerful natural stimulant derived from the coca plant.

crack
A highly addictive crystalline form of cocaine containing remnants of hydrochloride and sodium bicarbonate; it makes a crackling sound when smoked.

What kind of people become addicts? View the Schaffer Library of Drug Policy Web site by clicking on Web Links under the Chapter Resources at http://cj.wadsworth.com/siegel_jdcore2e.

Heroin is probably the most dangerous commonly abused drug. Users rapidly build up a tolerance for it, fueling the need for increased doses to obtain the desired effect. At first heroin is usually sniffed or snorted; as tolerance builds, it is "skin popped" (shot into skin, but not into a vein); and finally it is injected into a vein, or "mainlined."[8] Through this progressive use, the user becomes an **addict**—a person with an overpowering physical and psychological need to continue taking a particular substance by any means possible. If addicts cannot get enough heroin to satisfy their habit, they will suffer withdrawal symptoms, which include irritability, depression, extreme nervousness, and nausea.

Alcohol

Alcohol remains the drug of choice for most teenagers. More than 70 percent of high school seniors reported using alcohol in the past year, and 78 percent say they have tried it at some time during their lifetime; by the twelfth grade just under two-thirds (62 percent) of American youth report that they have "been drunk."[9] More than twenty million Americans are estimated to be problem drinkers, and at least half of these are alcoholics.

Alcohol may be a factor in nearly half of all murders, suicides, and accidental deaths.[10] Alcohol-related deaths number one hundred thousand a year, far more than all other illegal drugs combined. Just over 1.4 million drivers are arrested each year for driving under the influence (including 13,400 teen drivers), and around 1.2 million more are arrested for other alcohol-related violations.[11] The economic cost is staggering. An estimated $185 billion is lost each year, including $36 billion from premature deaths, $88 billion in reduced work effort, and $19 billion arising from short- and long-term medical problems.[12]

Considering these problems, why do so many youths drink to excess? Youths who use alcohol report that it reduces tension, enhances pleasure, improves social skills, and transforms experiences for the better.[13] Although these reactions may follow the limited use of alcohol, alcohol in higher doses acts as a depressant. Long-term use has been linked with depression and physical ailments ranging from heart disease to cirrhosis of the liver. Many teens also think drinking stirs their romantic urges, but scientific evidence indicates that alcohol decreases sexual response.[14]

Other Drug Categories

Other drug categories include anesthetic drugs, inhalants, sedatives and barbiturates, tranquilizers, hallucinogens, stimulants, steroids, designer drugs, and cigarettes.

Anesthetic Drugs   **Anesthetic drugs** are central nervous system (CNS) depressants. Local anesthetics block nervous system transmissions; general anesthetics act on the brain to produce loss of sensation, stupor, or unconsciousness. The most widely abused anesthetic drug is *phencyclidine* (*PCP*), known as "angel dust." Angel dust can be sprayed on marijuana or other leaves and smoked, drunk, or injected. Originally developed as an animal tranquilizer, PCP creates hallucinations and a spaced-out feeling that causes heavy users to engage in violent acts. The effects of PCP can last up to two days, and the danger of overdose is high.

Inhalants   Some youths inhale vapors from lighter fluid, paint thinner, cleaning fluid, or model airplane glue to reach a drowsy, dizzy state that is sometimes accompanied by hallucinations. **Inhalants** produce a short-term euphoria followed by a period of disorientation, slurred speech, and drowsiness. Amyl nitrite ("poppers") is a commonly used volatile liquid packaged in capsule form that is inhaled when the capsule is broken open.

Sedatives and Barbiturates   **Sedatives,** the most commonly used drugs of the barbiturate family, depress the central nervous system into a sleeplike condition.

heroin
A narcotic made from opium and then cut with sugar or some other neutral substance until it is only 1 to 4 percent pure.

addict
A person with an overpowering physical or psychological need to continue taking a particular substance or drug.

alcohol
Fermented or distilled liquids containing ethanol, an intoxicating substance.

anesthetic drugs
Nervous system depressants.

inhalants
Volatile liquids that give off a vapor, which is inhaled, producing short-term excitement and euphoria followed by a period of disorientation.

sedatives
Drugs of the barbiturate family that depress the central nervous system into a sleeplike condition.

On the illegal market sedatives are called "goofballs" or "downers" and are often known by the color of the capsules: "reds" (Scconal), "blue devils" (Amytal), and "rainbows" (Tuinal).

Sedatives can be prescribed by doctors as sleeping pills. Illegal users employ them to create relaxed, sociable feelings; overdoses can cause irritability, repellent behavior, and unconsciousness. Barbiturates are the major cause of drug-overdose deaths.

Tranquilizers   **Tranquilizers** reduce anxiety and promote relaxation. Legally prescribed tranquilizers, such as Ampazine, Thorazine, Pacatal, and Sparine, were originally designed to control the behavior of people suffering from psychoses, aggressiveness, and agitation. Less powerful tranquilizers, such as Valium, Librium, Miltown, and Equanil, are used to combat anxiety, tension, fast heart rate, and headaches. The use of illegally obtained tranquilizers can lead to addiction, and withdrawal can be painful and hazardous.

Hallucinogens   **Hallucinogens,** either natural or synthetic, produce vivid distortions of the senses without greatly disturbing the viewer's consciousness. Some produce hallucinations, and others cause psychotic behavior in otherwise normal people.

One common hallucinogen is mescaline, named after the Mescalero Apaches, who first discovered its potent effect. Mescaline occurs naturally in the peyote, a small cactus that grows in Mexico and the southwestern United States. After initial discomfort, mescaline produces vivid hallucinations and out-of-body sensations.

A second group of hallucinogens are synthetic alkaloid compounds, such as psilocybin. These can be transformed into lysergic acid diethylamide, commonly called LSD. This powerful substance stimulates cerebral sensory centers to produce visual hallucinations, intensify hearing, and increase sensitivity. Users often report a scrambling of sensations; they may "hear colors" and "smell music." Users also report feeling euphoric and mentally superior, although to an observer they appear disoriented. Anxiety and panic may occur, and overdoses can produce psychotic episodes, flashbacks, and even death.

Stimulants   **Stimulants** ("uppers," "speed," "pep pills," "crystal") are synthetic drugs that stimulate action in the central nervous system. They increase blood pressure, breathing rate, and bodily activity, and elevate mood. Commonly used stimulants include Benzedrine ("bennies"), Dexedrine ("dex"), Dexamyl, Bephetamine ("whites"), and Methedrine ("meth," "speed," "crystal meth").

Methedrine is probably the most widely used and most dangerous amphetamine. Some people swallow it; heavy users inject it. Long-term heavy use can result in exhaustion, anxiety, prolonged depression, and hallucinations. A new form of methamphetamine is a crystallized substance with the street name of "ice" or "crystal." Smoking this crystal causes weight loss, kidney damage, heart and respiratory problems, and paranoia.[15]

Steroids   Teenagers use highly dangerous **anabolic steroids** to gain muscle bulk and strength.[16] Black market sales of these drugs approach $1 billion annually. Although not physically addicting, steroids can become a kind of obsession among teens who desire athletic success. Long-term users may spend up to $400 a week on steroids and may support their habit by dealing the drug.

Steroids are dangerous because of the health problems associated with their long-term use: liver ailments, tumors, kidney problems, sexual dysfunction, hypertension, and mental problems such as depression. Steroid use runs in cycles, and other drugs—Clomid, Teslac, and Halotestin, for example—that carry their own dangerous side effects are often used to curb the need for high dosages of steroids. Finally, steroid users often share needles, which puts them at high risk for contracting HIV, the virus that causes AIDS.

tranquilizers
Drugs that reduce anxiety and promote relaxation.

hallucinogens
Natural or synthetic substances that produce vivid distortions of the senses without greatly disturbing consciousness.

stimulants
Synthetic substances that produce an intense physical reaction by stimulating the central nervous system.

anabolic steroids
Drugs used by athletes and bodybuilders to gain muscle bulk and strength.

Designer Drugs   **Designer drugs** are lab-created synthetics that are designed at least temporarily to get around existing drug laws. The most widely used designer drug is Ecstasy, which is actually derived from speed and methamphetamine. After being swallowed, snorted, injected, or smoked, it acts simultaneously as a stimulant and a hallucinogen, producing mood swings, disturbing sleeping and eating habits, altering thinking processes, creating aggressive behavior, interfering with sexual function, and affecting sensitivity to pain. The drug can also increase blood pressure and heart rate. Teenage users taking Ecstasy at raves have died from heat stroke because the drug can cause dehydration.

Cigarettes   Approximately twenty-five countries have established laws to prohibit the sale of cigarettes to minors. The reality, however, is that in many countries children and adolescents have easy access to tobacco products.[17] In the United States, the Synar Amendment, enacted in 1992, requires states to enact and enforce laws restricting the sale of tobacco products to youths under the age of eighteen. States are required to reduce rates of illegal sales to minors to no more than 20 percent within several years. The FDA rules require age verification for anyone under the age of twenty-seven who is purchasing tobacco products. The FDA has also banned vending machines and self-service displays except in adult-only facilities. Despite all of these measures, almost six out of ten high school seniors in America—57 percent of them—report having smoked cigarettes over their lifetime. However, in recent years cigarette use by high school students has been on the decline.[18]

DRUG USE TODAY

Surveys show that alcohol continues to be the most widely used drug and that synthetic drugs such as Ecstasy have become more popular. Some western states report that methamphetamine ("speed," "crank") use is increasing and that its low cost and high potency has encouraged manufacturers ("cookers") to increase production. The use of other synthetics, including PCP and LSD, is focused in particular areas of the country. Synthetics are popular because labs can easily be hidden in rural areas, and traffickers do not have to worry about border searches or payoffs to foreign growers or middlemen. Users like synthetics because they are cheap and produce a powerful, long-lasting high that can be greater than that provided by more expensive natural products such as cocaine.

Crack cocaine use has been in decline in recent years. Heavy criminal penalties, tight enforcement, and social disapproval have helped to lower crack use.[19] Although it was feared that abusers would turn to heroin as a replacement, there has been little indication of a new heroin epidemic. Heroin use has stabilized in most of the country, although there are still hundreds of thousands of regular users in large cities.[20]

Arrest data show that the most frequent heroin users are older offenders who started their habit decades ago. There is reason to believe heroin use is in decline among adolescents, possibly because it has acquired an extremely negative street image. Most youths know that heroin is addictive and destructive to health, and that needle sharing leads to HIV. Research conducted in New York City shows that most youths avoid heroin, shun users and dealers, and wish to avoid becoming addicts.[21]

Despite concern over these "hard drugs," the most persistent teenage substance-abuse problem is alcohol. Teenage alcoholism is sometimes considered less serious than other types of substance abuse, but it actually produces far more problems. Teenage alcohol abusers suffer depression, anxiety, and other symptoms of mental distress. Also, it is well established that alcoholism runs in families; today's teenage abusers may become the parents of the next generation of teenage alcoholics.[22]

What do national surveys tell us about the extent of drug use and the recent trends in teen usage?

designer drugs
Lab-made drugs designed to avoid existing drug laws.

Teenage smoking rates are considerably lower today compared to years past, but millions of teens still smoke cigarettes. Here, police officer Jody Hayes looks on as twelve-year-old smoker Justin Hoover of Des Moines, Iowa, testifies on Capitol Hill before a Democratic hearing on smoking. Hoover said he smoked his first cigarette at age six and by nine was stealing them from convenience stores.

The Monitoring the Future (MTF) Survey

One of the most important and influential surveys of teen substance abuse is the annual Monitoring the Future survey conducted by the Institute for Social Research at the University of Michigan. In all, about forty-five thousand students located in 433 secondary schools participate in the study.

The most recent MTF survey indicates that, with a few exceptions, drug use among American adolescents held steady in 2002, but declined from the recent peak levels reached in 1996 and 1997. As Figure 10.1 shows, drug use peaked in the late 1970s and early 1980s and then began a decade-long decline until showing an uptick in the mid-1990s; usage for most drugs has been stable or in decline since then. Especially encouraging has been a significant drop in the use of crack cocaine among younger kids. As noted earlier, there has also been a continuing decline in cigarette smoking, as well as the use of smokeless tobacco products. More troubling is the use of Ecstasy, which, because of its popularity at dance clubs and raves, rose among older teens (tenth- and twelfth-graders) for much of the late 1990s and up to 2001, but has since dropped sharply. In 2002, just under 5 percent of tenth-graders reported some use of Ecstasy during the previous twelve months (down from 6.2 percent in 2001); slightly over 7 percent of the twelfth-graders also reported some use (down from 9.2 percent in 2001). On the other hand, the use of anabolic steroids by males in their early to mid-teens has increased (4 percent of twelfth-grade boys now take steroids), possibly because of the reported use of similar substances by respected athletes. Heroin use has dropped sharply in the last couple of years (1 percent of twelfth-grade boys are users) after the rates had roughly doubled between 1991 and 1995, when noninjectable forms of heroin use became popular. It is possible that widely publicized overdose deaths of musicians and celebrities may have helped stabilize heroin abuse. Alcohol use among teens has been fairly stable over the past several years. Nonetheless, nearly one-fifth of eighth-graders and almost half of twelfth-graders use alcohol regularly.

The PRIDE Survey

A second source of information on teen drug and alcohol abuse is the National Parents' Resource Institute for Drug Education (PRIDE) survey, which is also conducted

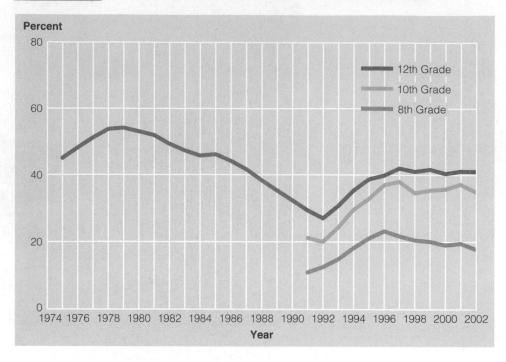

| Figure 10.1 | Trends in Annual Prevalence of Illicit Drug Use |

Source: *Monitoring the Future, 2002* (Ann Arbor, MI: Institute for Social Research, 2003).

annually.[23] Typically, findings from the PRIDE survey correlate highly with the MTF drug survey. The most recent PRIDE survey (for the 2002–03 school year) indicates slight increases in drug activity over the previous school year, but substantial decreases over the last five years. For example, about 24 percent of students in grades six to twelve claimed to have used drugs during the past year, down from 27 percent in the 1998–99 school year (Table 10.1). Cigarette smoking and alcohol use are also down from five years ago. The fact that two surveys generate roughly the same pattern in drug abuse helps bolster their validity and give support to a decline in teenage substance abuse.

Are the Survey Results Accurate?

Student drug surveys must be interpreted with caution. First, it may be overly optimistic to expect that heavy users are going to cooperate with a drug-use survey, especially one conducted by a government agency. Even if they were willing, these students are likely to be absent from school during testing periods. Also, drug abusers are more likely to be forgetful and to give inaccurate accounts of their substance abuse.

Another problem is the likelihood that the most drug-dependent portion of the adolescent population is omitted from the sample. In some cities, almost half of all youths arrested dropped out of school before the twelfth grade, and more than half of these arrestees are drug users (Figure 10.2).[24] Juvenile detainees (those arrested and held in a lockup) test positively for cocaine at a rate many times higher than those reporting recent use in the MTF and PRIDE surveys.[25] The inclusion of eighth-graders in the MTF sample is one way of getting around the dropout problem. Nonetheless, high school surveys may be excluding some of the most drug-prone young people in the population.

Although these problems are serious, they are consistent over time and therefore do not hinder the *measurement of change* or trends in drug usage. That is, prior surveys also omitted dropouts and other high-risk individuals. However, since these problems are built into every wave of the survey, any change recorded in the annual

Checkpoints

✔ *More than half of all high-school-age kids have tried drugs.*

✔ *Use of cocaine and crack is on the decline.*

✔ *Alcohol remains the drug of choice for most teens.*

✔ *Ecstasy has become popular in recent years.*

✔ *Teenage drug use is measured by two national surveys, the Monitoring the Future survey and the PRIDE Survey.*

✔ *Both of these surveys show that drug and alcohol use has declined in recent years.*

 To quiz yourself on this material, go to questions 10.1–10.7 on the Juvenile Delinquency: The Core 2e Web site.

Table 10.1	Annual Drug Use, 1998–99 Versus 2002–03, Grades 6–12		
	1998–99 (%)	*2002–03 (%)*	*Rate of Decrease (%)*
Cigarettes	37.9	27.3	28.0
Any alcohol	56.8	50.1	11.8
Any illicit drug	27.1	24.3	10.3

Source: PRIDE Surveys (Bowling Green, KY: Pride, Inc., 2003).

substance-abuse rate is probably genuine. So, although the *validity* of these surveys may be questioned, they are probably *reliable* indicators of trends in substance abuse.

✔ Checkpoints

WHY DO YOUTHS TAKE DRUGS?

Why do youths engage in an activity that is sure to bring them overwhelming problems? It is hard to imagine that even the youngest drug users are unaware of the problems associated with substance abuse. Although it is easy to understand dealers' desires for quick profits, how can we explain users' disregard for long- and short-term consequences? Concept Summary 10.1 reviews some of the most likely reasons.

Social Disorganization

One explanation ties drug abuse to poverty, social disorganization, and hopelessness. Drug use by young minority group members has been tied to factors such as racial prejudice, low self-esteem, poor socioeconomic status, and the stress of living in a harsh urban environment.[26] The association between drug use, race, and poverty has been linked to the high level of mistrust and defiance found in lower socioeconomic areas.[27]

Despite the long-documented association between social disorganization and drug use, the empirical data on the relationship between class and crime have been inconclusive. For example, the National Youth Survey (NYS), a longitudinal study of delinquent behavior conducted by Delbert Elliott and his associates, found little if any association between drug use and social class. The NYS found that drug use is higher among urban youths, but there was little evidence that minority youths or members of the lower class were more likely to abuse drugs than White youths and the more affluent.[28] Research by the Rand Corporation indicates that many drug-dealing youths had legitimate jobs at the time they were arrested for drug trafficking.[29] Therefore, it would be difficult to describe drug abusers simply as unemployed dropouts.

Concept Summary **Key Reasons Why Youths Take Drugs**

Social disorganization	Poverty, growing up in disorganized urban environment.
Peer pressure	Associating with youths who take drugs.
Family factors	Poor family life, including harsh punishment, neglect.
Genetic factors	Parents abuse drugs.
Emotional problems	Feelings of inadequacy; blame others for failures.
Problem behavior syndrome	Drug use is one of many problem behaviors.
Rational choice	Perceived benefits, including relaxation, greater creativity.

Figure 10.2   Drug Use Among Juvenile Arrestees, by Sex

Phoenix: percent positive for drugs by sex

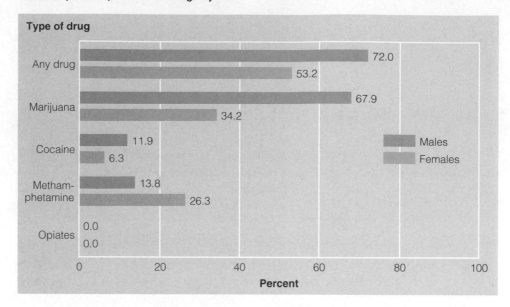

San Diego: percent positive for drugs by sex

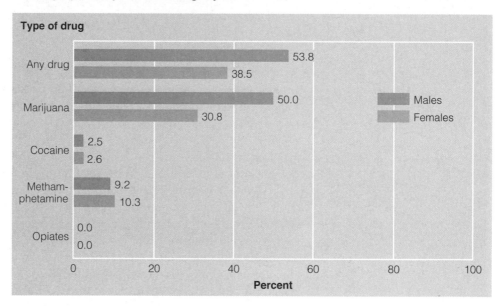

Source: *Preliminary Data on Drug Use & Related Matters Among Adult Arrestees and Juvenile Detainees, 2002* (Washington, DC: National Institute of Justice, Arrestee Drug Abuse Monitoring Program, 2003), Tables 2, 3.

Peer Pressure

Research shows that adolescent drug abuse is highly correlated with the behavior of best friends, especially when parental supervision is weak.[30] Youths in inner-city areas where feelings of alienation run high often come in contact with drug users who teach them that drugs provide an answer to their feelings of inadequacy and stress.[31] Perhaps they join with peers to learn the techniques of drug use; their friendships with other drug-dependent youths give them social support for their habit. Empirical research efforts show that a youth's association with friends who are

Shared feelings and a sense of intimacy lead youths to become fully enmeshed in the "drug-use subculture." Drug users do in fact have intimate and warm relationships with substance-abusing peers, which helps support their habits and behaviors.

substance abusers increases the probability of drug use.[32] The relationship is reciprocal: adolescent substance abusers seek out friends who engage in these behaviors, and associating with drug abusers leads to increased levels of drug abuse.

Peer networks may be the most significant influence on long-term substance abuse. Shared feelings and a sense of intimacy lead youths to become enmeshed in what has been described as the "drug-use subculture."[33] Research indicates that drug users do in fact have warm relationships with substance-abusing peers who help support their behaviors.[34] This lifestyle provides users with a clear role, activities they enjoy, and an opportunity for attaining status among their peers.[35] One reason it is so difficult to treat hard-core users is that quitting drugs means leaving the "fast life" of the streets.

Family Factors

Another explanation is that drug users have a poor family life. Studies have found that the majority of drug users have had an unhappy childhood, which included harsh punishment and parental neglect.[36] The drug abuse and family quality association may involve both racial and gender differences: females and Whites who were abused as children are more likely to have alcohol and drug arrests as adults; abuse was less likely to affect drug use in males and African Americans.[37] It is also common to find substance abusers in large families and with parents who are divorced, separated, or absent.[38]

Social psychologists suggest that drug abuse patterns may also result from observation of parental drug use.[39] Youths who learn that drugs provide pleasurable sensations may be most likely to experiment with illegal substances; a habit may develop if the user experiences lower anxiety and fear.[40] Research shows, for example, that gang members raised in families with a history of drug use were more likely than other gang members to use cocaine and to use it seriously. And even among gang members parental drug abuse was a key factor in the onset of adolescent drug use.[41] Observing drug abuse may be a more important cause of drug abuse than other family-related problems.

Other family factors associated with teen drug abuse include parental conflict over child-rearing practices, failure to set rules, and unrealistic demands followed by harsh punishments. Low parental attachment, rejection, and excessive family conflict have all been linked to adolescent substance abuse.[42]

To read more about the concept of addiction, go to the **Psychedelic Library** by clicking on Web Links under the Chapter Resources at http://cj.wadsworth.com/siegel_jdcore2e.

Genetic Factors

The association between parental drug abuse and adolescent behavior may have a genetic basis. Research has shown that biological children of alcoholics reared by non-alcoholic adoptive parents more often develop alcohol problems than the natural children of the adoptive parents.[43] A number of studies comparing alcoholism among identical and fraternal twins have found that the degree of concordance (that is, both siblings behaving identically) is twice as high among the identical twin groups.[44]

A genetic basis for drug abuse is also supported by evidence showing that future substance abuse problems can be predicted by behavior exhibited as early as six years of age. The traits predicting future abuse are independent from peer relations and environmental influences.[45]

Emotional Problems

As we have seen, not all drug-abusing youths reside in lower-class urban areas. To explain drug abuse across social classes, some experts have linked drug use to emotional problems that can strike youths in any economic class. Psychodynamic explanations of substance abuse suggest that drugs help youths control or express unconscious needs. Some psychoanalysts believe adolescents who internalize their problems may use drugs to reduce their feelings of inadequacy. Introverted people may use drugs as an escape from real or imagined feelings of inferiority.[46] Another view is that adolescents who externalize their problems and blame others for their perceived failures are likely to engage in antisocial behaviors, including substance abuse. Research exists to support each of these positions.[47]

Drug abusers are also believed to exhibit psychopathic or sociopathic behavior characteristics, forming what is called an **addiction-prone personality.**[48] Drinking alcohol may reflect a teen's need to remain dependent on an overprotective mother or an effort to reduce the emotional turmoil of adolescence.[49]

Research on the psychological characteristics of narcotics abusers does, in fact, reveal the presence of a significant degree of pathology. Personality testing of users suggests that a significant percentage suffer from psychotic disorders. Studies have found that addicts suffer personality disorders characterized by a weak ego, low frustration tolerance, and fantasies of omnipotence. Up to half of all drug abusers may also be diagnosed with antisocial personality disorder (ASPD), which is defined as a pervasive pattern of disregard for the rights of others.[50]

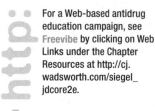
For a Web-based antidrug education campaign, see **Freevibe** by clicking on Web Links under the Chapter Resources at http://cj.wadsworth.com/siegel_jdcore2e.

Problem Behavior Syndrome

For some adolescents, substance abuse is one of many problem behaviors that begin early in life and remain throughout the life course.[51] Longitudinal studies show that youths who abuse drugs are maladjusted, emotionally distressed, and have many social problems.[52] Having a deviant lifestyle means associating with delinquent peers, living in a family in which parents and siblings abuse drugs, being alienated from the dominant values of society, and engaging in delinquent behaviors at an early age.[53] Youths who abuse drugs lack commitment to religious values, disdain education, and spend most of their time in peer activities.[54] Youths who take drugs do poorly in school, have high dropout rates, and maintain their drug use after they leave school.[55] This view of adolescent drug taking is discussed in the Focus on Delinquency feature entitled "Problem Behaviors and Substance Abuse." (Chapter 5 provides an in-depth discussion of problem behavior syndrome.)

Rational Choice

Youths may choose to use drugs because they want to get high, relax, improve their creativity, escape reality, or increase their sexual responsiveness. Research indicates that adolescent alcohol abusers believe getting high will increase their sexual per-

addiction-prone personality The view that the cause of substance abuse can be traced to a personality that has a compulsion for mood-altering drugs.

Most experts believe that drug involvement begins with drinking alcohol at an early age, which progresses to experimentation with marijuana and finally to cocaine and then heroin. Though most recreational users do not progress to addictive drugs, few addicts begin their drug involvement with narcotics.

© Joel Gordon

formance and facilitate their social behavior; they care little about negative consequences.[56] Substance abuse, then, may be a function of the rational, albeit mistaken, belief that substance abuse benefits the user.

PATHWAYS TO DRUG ABUSE

Although there is not a single path to becoming a drug abuser, it is generally believed that most users start at a young age using alcohol as a **gateway drug** to harder substances. That is, drug involvement begins with drinking alcohol at an early age, which progresses to experimentation with marijuana, and finally to using cocaine and even heroin. Research on adolescent drug users in Miami found that youths who began their substance abuse careers early—by experimenting with alcohol at age seven, getting drunk at age eight, having alcohol with an adult present by age nine, and becoming regular drinkers by the time they were eleven years old—later became crack users.[57] Drinking with an adult present was a significant precursor of substance abuse and delinquency.[58]

Although the gateway concept is still being debated, there is little disagreement that serious drug users begin their involvement with alcohol.[59] Though most recreational users do not progress to "hard stuff," most addicts first experiment with recreational alcohol and recreational drugs before progressing to narcotics. By implication, if teen drinking could be reduced, the gateway to hard drugs would be narrowed.

What are the patterns of teenage drug use? Are all abusers similar, or are there different types of drug involvement? Research indicates that drug-involved youths do take on different roles, lifestyles, and behavior patterns, some of which are described in the next sections.[60]

gateway drug
A substance that leads to use of more serious drugs; alcohol use has long been thought to lead to more serious drug abuse.

Problem Behaviors and Substance Abuse

According to the *problem behavior syndrome* model, substance abuse may be one of a constellation of social problems experienced by at-risk youth. There is significant evidence to substantiate the view that kids who abuse substances are also more likely to experience an array of social problems. For example, a recent study of the relationship between adolescent illicit-drug use, physical abuse, and sexual abuse that was based on a sample of Mexican-American and non-Hispanic White youths living in the southwestern United States found that those who report physical or sexual abuse are significantly more likely to report illicit drug use than those who have never been abused. As Figure A shows, 42 percent of youths who have experienced physical abuse

report using marijuana in the last month, while only 28 percent of youths who have never been abused report using the drug during that time. These findings were independent of factors such as academic achievement and family structure, and they suggest that treatment directed at abused adolescents should include drug use prevention, intervention, and education components.

Kids who abuse drugs and alcohol are also more likely to have educational problems. A recent study of substance use among Texas students in grades seven through twelve found that those who were absent ten or more days during the previous school year were more likely to report alcohol, tobacco, and other drug use. For example, twice as many students with high absentee rates reported using marijuana in the past month (29 percent versus 14 percent, respectively) than students who did not miss school.

Figure A **Percent of Youths Reporting Past-Month Marijuana or Past-Year Cocaine Use, by Type of Abuse (*N* = 2,468)**

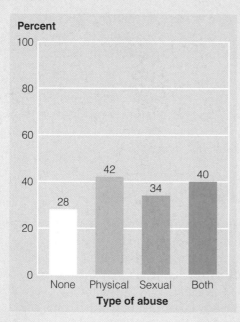

Marijuana

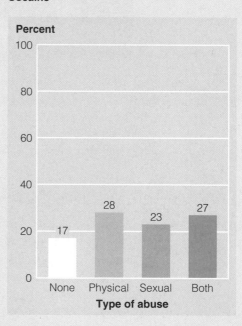

Cocaine

Note: These analyses were based on data collected between 1988 and 1992 for the Mexican-American Drug Use and Dropout Survey, a yearly survey of Mexican-American and non-Hispanic White school dropouts and a comparison group of enrolled students from one school district in each of three communities in the southwestern United States.

Source: D. M. Pérez, "The Relationship Between Physical Abuse, Sexual Victimization, and Adolescent Illicit Drug Use," *Journal of Drug Issues 30*:641–662 (2000).

Adolescents Who Distribute Small Amounts of Drugs

Many adolescents who use and distribute small amounts of drugs do not commit any other serious delinquent acts. They occasionally sell marijuana, crystal, and PCP

There is also a connection between substance abuse and serious behavioral and emotional problems. One national study found that behaviorally troubled youth are seven times more likely than those with less serious problems to report that they were dependent on alcohol or illicit drugs (17.1 percent versus 2.3 percent). In addition, youths with serious emotional problems were nearly four times more likely to report dependence (13.2 percent versus 3.4 percent) (Figure B).

CRITICAL THINKING

These studies provide dramatic evidence that drug abuse is highly associated with other social problems—physical or sexual abuse, school failure, and emotional disorders. They imply that getting young people off drugs may take a lot more effort than relying on some simple solution like "Just Say No." What would it take to get young people to refrain from using drugs?

INFOTRAC COLLEGE EDITION RESEARCH

To find out more about the relationship between problem behaviors and adolescent substance abuse, go to Info-Trac College Edition and read Lisa H. Jaycox, Andrew R. Morral, and Jaana Juvonen, "Mental Health and Medical Problems and Service Use Among Adolescent Substance Users," *Journal of the American Academy of Child & Adolescent Psychiatry* 42(6):701 (June 2003).

Sources: Deanna Pérez, "The Relationship Between Physical Abuse, Sexual Victimization, and Adolescent Illicit Drug Use," *Journal of Drug Issues 30*:641–662 (2000); Texas Commission on Alcohol and Drug Abuse, "Substance Use Among Youths at High Risk of Dropping Out: Grades 7–12 in Texas, 1998," *Texas Commission on Alcohol and Drug Abuse Research Brief,* June 2000; Substance Abuse and Mental Health Services Administration, Office of Applied Studies, "The Relationship Between Mental Health and Substance Abuse among Adolescents," Analytic Series: A-9, 1999. Data and tables supplied by the Center for Substance Abuse Research, University of Maryland, College Park (2001).

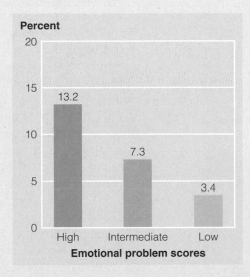

| Figure B | Percent of Youths Ages 12 to 17 Reporting Dependence on Alcohol or Illicit Drugs, by Behavioral and Emotional Problem Scores,* 1994–1996 |

*Severity levels (high, intermediate, and low) for behavioral and emotional problem scale were determined using values set in the Youth Self-Report, an instrument extensively used in adolescent studies to assess psychological difficulties.

Source: Substance Abuse and Mental Health Services Administration, Office of Applied Studies, "The Relationship Between Mental Health and Substance Abuse Among Adolescents," Analytic Series A-9, (1999).

to support their own drug use. Their customers include friends, relatives, and acquaintances. Deals are arranged over the phone, in school, or at public meeting places; however, the actual distribution occurs in more private arenas, such as at home or in cars. Petty dealers do not consider themselves seriously involved in drugs.

Adolescents Who Frequently Sell Drugs

A small number of adolescents are high-rate dealers who bridge the gap between adult drug distributors and the adolescent user. Though many are daily users, they take part in many normal activities, including going to school and socializing with friends.

Frequent dealers often have adults who "front" for them—that is, sell them drugs for cash. The teenagers then distribute the drugs to friends and acquaintances. They return most of the proceeds to the supplier, keeping a commission for themselves. They may also keep drugs for their personal use, and in fact, some consider their dealing as a way of "getting high for free." One young user, Winston, age seventeen, told investigators, "I sell the cracks for money and for cracks. The man, he give me this *much*. I sell most of it and I get the rest for me. I like this much. Every day I do this."[61] James Inciardi and his associates found that about 80 percent of the youths who dealt crack regularly were daily users.[62]

Frequent dealers are more likely to sell drugs in parks, schools, or other public places. Deals occur irregularly, so the chance of apprehension is not significant, nor is the payoff substantial. Robert MacCoun and Peter Reuter found that drug dealers make about $30 per hour when they are working and clear on average about $2,000 per month. These amounts are greater than most dealers could hope to earn in legitimate jobs, but they are not enough to afford a steady stream of luxuries. Most small-time dealers also hold conventional jobs.[63]

Teenage Drug Dealers Who Commit Other Delinquent Acts

A more serious type of drug-involved youth is the one who distributes multiple substances and commits both property and violent crimes. These youngsters make up about 2 percent of the teenage population, but they may commit up to 40 percent of the robberies and assaults and about 60 percent of all teenage felony thefts and drug sales. Few gender or racial differences exist among these youths: girls are as likely as boys to become persistent drug-involved offenders, White youths as likely as Black youths, and middle-class adolescents raised outside cities as likely as lower-class city children.[64]

In cities, these youths frequently are hired by older dealers to act as street-level drug runners. Each member of a crew of three to twelve youths will handle small quantities of drugs; the supplier receives 50 to 70 percent of the drug's street value. The crew members also act as lookouts, recruiters, and guards. Although they may be recreational drug users themselves, crew members refrain from using addictive drugs such as heroin. Between drug sales, the young dealers commit robberies, burglaries, and other thefts.

Some experts question whether gangs are responsible for as much drug dealing as the media would have us believe. Some believe that the tightly organized "super" gangs are being replaced with loosely organized neighborhood groups. The turbulent environment of drug dealing is better handled by flexible organizations than by rigid, vertically organized gangs with a leader who is far removed from the action.[65]

Losers and Burnouts

Some drug-involved youths do not have the savvy to join gangs or groups and instead begin committing unplanned crimes that increase their chances of arrest. Their heavy drug use increases their risk of apprehension and decreases their value for organized drug distribution networks.

Drug-involved "losers" can earn a living by steering customers to a seller in a "copping" area, touting drug availability for a dealer, or acting as a lookout. However, they are not considered trustworthy or deft enough to handle drugs or money.

Checkpoints

✔ Some kids take drugs because they live in disorganized areas in which there is a high degree of hopelessness, poverty, and despair.

✔ There is peer pressure to take drugs and to drink.

✔ Kids whose parents take drugs are more likely to become abusers themselves.

✔ Some experts believe that drug dependency is a genetic condition.

✔ Youngsters with emotional problems may be drug-prone.

✔ Drug use may be part of a general problem behavior syndrome.

✔ Drug use may also be rational: kids take drugs and drink alcohol simply because they enjoy the experience.

✔ There are a number of pathways to drug abuse.

✔ Some users distribute small amounts of drugs, others are frequent dealers, while another group supplements drug dealing with other crimes.

✔ Some users are always in trouble and are considered burnouts.

 To quiz yourself on this material, go to questions 10.8–10.12 on the Juvenile Delinquency: The Core 2e Web site.

Though these offenders get involved in drugs at an early age, they receive little attention from the justice system until they have developed an extensive arrest record. By then they are approaching the end of their minority and will either desist or become so entrapped in the drug-crime subculture that little can be done to deter their illegal activities.

Persistent Offenders

About two-thirds of substance-abusing youths continue to use drugs in adulthood, but about half desist from other criminal activities. Those who persist in both substance abuse and crime maintain these characteristics:

- They come from poor families.
- Their family members include other criminals.
- They do poorly in school.
- They started using drugs and committing other delinquent acts at an early age.
- They use multiple types of drugs and commit crimes frequently.
- They have few opportunities in late adolescence to participate in legitimate and rewarding adult activities.[66]

Some evidence exists that these drug-using persisters have low nonverbal IQs and poor physical coordination. Nonetheless, there is little evidence to explain why some drug-abusing youths drop out of crime while others remain active.

✔ Checkpoints

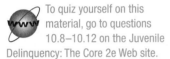

DRUG USE AND DELINQUENCY

An association between drug use and delinquency has been established, and this connection can take a number of forms. Crime may be an instrument of the drug trade: violence erupts when rival gangs use weapons to settle differences and establish territorial monopolies. In New York City, authorities report that crack gangs will burn down their rival's headquarters. It is estimated that between 35 and 40 percent of New York's homicides are drug-related.[67]

Drug users may also commit crimes to pay for their habits.[68] One study conducted in Miami found that 573 narcotics users *annually* committed more than 200,000 crimes to obtain cash. Similar research with a sample of 356 addicts accounted for 118,000 crimes annually.[69] If such proportions hold true, then the nation's estimated 700,000 heroin addicts alone may be committing more than 100 million crimes each year.

Drug users may be more willing to take risks because their inhibitions are lowered by substance abuse. Cities with high rates of cocaine abuse are also more likely to experience higher levels of armed robbery. It is possible that crack and cocaine users are more willing to engage in a risky armed robbery to get immediate cash than a burglary, which requires more planning and effort.[70]

The relationship between alcohol and drug abuse and delinquency has been substantiated by a number of studies. Some have found that youths who abuse alcohol are most likely to engage in violence; as adults, those with long histories of drinking are more likely to report violent offending patterns.[71]

The National Institute of Justice's Arrestee Drug Abuse Monitoring (ADAM) program tracked trends in drug use among arrestees in urban areas. Some, but not all, of its thirty-six sites collected data on juveniles. Due to lack of funding, the Department of Justice ended this program in 2004. The most recent report (2002) found that, among juvenile detainees, almost 60 percent of juvenile males and 30 percent of juvenile females tested positive for marijuana, the most commonly used drug, and its prevalence was ten and six times higher than cocaine use for juvenile males and females, respectively.[72] With the exception of methamphetamines, male detainees were more likely to test positive for the use of any drug than were female detainees. Figure 10.2 shows the ADAM survey results for two cities (Phoenix, Arizona, and San Diego, California) that collect data on juvenile detainees (see again Figure 10.2). Note that in Phoenix more than two-thirds of all juveniles, and in San Diego half, test positively for at least one drug, most commonly marijuana. While males and minority-group members have somewhat higher positive test rates than females and Caucasians, drug use is prevalent among juvenile arrestees, reaffirming the close association between substance abuse and criminality.

There is evidence that incarcerated youths are much more likely to be involved in substance abuse than adolescents in the general population. For example, research by David Cantor on incarcerated youths in Washington, D.C., found their drug involvement more than double that of nonincarcerated area youths.[73]

Drugs and Chronic Offending

It is possible that most delinquents are not drug users but that police are more likely to apprehend muddle-headed substance abusers than clear-thinking abstainers. A second, more plausible, interpretation of the existing data is that the drug abuse–crime connection is so powerful because many criminals are in fact substance abusers. Research by Bruce Johnson and his associates confirms this suspicion. Using data from a national self-report survey, these researchers found that less than 2 percent of the youths who responded to the survey (a) report using cocaine or heroin, and (b) commit two or more index crimes each year. However, these drug-abusing adolescents accounted for 40 to 60 percent of all the index crimes reported in the sample. Less than one-quarter of these delinquents committed crimes solely to support a drug habit. These data suggest that a small core of substance-abusing adolescents commit a significant proportion of all serious crimes. It is also evident that a behavior—drug abuse—that develops late in adolescence influences the extent of delinquent activity through the life course.[74]

Explaining Drug Use and Delinquency

The association between delinquency and drug use has been established in a variety of cultures.[75] It is far from certain, however, whether (a) drug use *causes* delinquency, (b) delinquency *leads* youths to engage in substance abuse, or (c) both drug abuse and delinquency are *functions* of some other factor.[76]

Some of the most sophisticated research on this topic has been conducted by Delbert Elliott and his associates at the Institute of Behavioral Science at the University of Colorado.[77] Using data from the National Youth Survey, the longitudinal study of self-reported delinquency and drug use mentioned earlier in this chapter, Elliott and his colleagues David Huizinga and Scott Menard found a strong association between delinquency and drug use.[78] However, the direction of the relationship is unclear. As a general rule, drug abuse appears to be a *type* of delinquent behavior and not a *cause* of delinquency. Most youths become involved in delinquent acts *before* they are initiated into drugs; it is difficult, therefore, to conclude that drug use causes crime.

According to the Elliott research, both drug use and delinquency seem to reflect developmental problems; they are both part of a disturbed lifestyle. This research reveals some important associations between substance abuse and delinquency:

1. Alcohol abuse seems to be a cause of marijuana and other drug abuse because most drug users started with alcohol, and youths who abstain from alcohol almost never take drugs.

2. Marijuana use is a cause of multiple drug use: about 95 percent of youths who use more serious drugs started on pot; only 5 percent of serious drug users never smoked pot.

What Does This Mean to Me?

Reducing Drug Activity

There is no easy solution to reducing drug-related activities. Some experts argue that less serious drugs like marijuana should be decriminalized, others call for the continued use of police stings and long sentences for drug violations, and some advocate for more education and treatment. Suppose in your community you have witnessed the harms associated with teenage drug use and drug selling, but have also seen the need for some users to get treatment rather than punishment.

1. What do you recommend be done to address the drug problem more effectively? Explain.
2. What are some things you could do in your community to help prevent children and youth from getting involved in drug-related activities?

3. Youths who commit felonies started off with minor delinquent acts. Few delinquents (1 percent) report committing felonies only.

DRUG CONTROL STRATEGIES

Billions of dollars are spent each year to reduce the importation of drugs, deter drug dealers, and treat users. Yet although the overall incidence of drug use has declined, drug use has concentrated in the nation's poorest neighborhoods, with a consequent association between substance abuse and crime.

A number of drug-control strategies have been tried. Some are designed to deter drug use by stopping the flow of drugs into the country, apprehending dealers, and cracking down on street-level drug deals. Another approach is to prevent drug use by educating would-be users and convincing them to "say no" to drugs. A third approach is to treat users so that they can terminate their addictions. Some of these efforts are discussed in the following sections.

Law Enforcement Efforts

Law enforcement strategies are aimed at reducing the supply of drugs and, at the same time, deterring would-be users from drug abuse.

Source Control One approach to drug control is to deter the sale of drugs through apprehension of large-volume drug dealers coupled with enforcement of drug laws that carry heavy penalties. This approach is designed to punish known dealers and users and to deter those who are considering entering the drug trade.

A great effort has been made to cut off supplies of drugs by destroying overseas crops and arresting members of drug cartels; this approach is known as *source control*.

Strategies to control drugs and their use are wide-ranging, and the results of many strategies are disappointing. Here, teens participate in a youth antidrug and antiviolence workshop in Miami, Florida, to learn more about what works and how teens can play a role in preventing drug use and violence.

The federal government has been encouraging exporting nations to step up efforts to destroy drug crops and prosecute dealers. Other less aggressive source control approaches, such as crop substitution and alternative development programs for the largely poor farmers in other countries, have also been tried, and a recent review of international efforts suggests that "some success can be achieved in reduction of narcotic crop production."[79] Three South American nations—Peru, Bolivia, and Colombia—have agreed to coordinate control efforts with the United States. However, translating words into deeds is a formidable task. Drug lords fight back through intimidation, violence, and corruption. The United States was forced to invade Panama with twenty thousand troops in 1989 to stop its leader, General Manuel Noriega, from trafficking in cocaine.

Even when efforts are successful in one area, they may result in a shift in production to another area or in the targeted crop being replaced by another. For example, between 1994 and 1999, enforcement efforts in Peru and Bolivia were so successful that they altered cocaine cultivation patterns. As a consequence, Colombia became the premier coca-cultivating country when the local drug cartels encouraged growers to cultivate coca plants. When the Colombian government mounted an effective eradication campaign in the traditional growing areas, the cartel linked up with rebel groups in remote parts of the country for their drug supply.[80] Leaders in neighboring countries expressed fear when, in August 2000, the United States announced $1.3 billion in military aid to fight Colombia's rural drug dealers/rebels, assuming that success would drive traffickers over the border.[81] Another unintended effect of this campaign has been a recent shift by drug cartels to exploit new crops, from a traditional emphasis on coca to opium poppy, the plant used to make heroin. It is estimated that Latin American countries, including Mexico, now supply upwards of 80 percent of the heroin consumed in the United States.[82]

Border Control   Law enforcement efforts have also been directed at interdicting drug supplies as they enter the country. Border patrols and military personnel have been involved in massive interdiction efforts, and many billion-dollar seizures have been made. It is estimated that between one-quarter and one-third of the annual cocaine supply shipped to the United States is seized by drug enforcement agencies. Yet U.S. borders are so vast and unprotected that meaningful interdiction is impossible. In 2001, U.S. law enforcement agencies seized 233,000 pounds of cocaine and almost 5,500 pounds of heroin.[83] Global rates of interception of cocaine indicate that only one-third of all imports are being seized by law enforcement.[84]

In recent years, another form of border control to interdict drugs entering the country has emerged: targeting Internet drug traffickers in foreign countries. With the increasing popularity of the Internet, some offenders are now turning to this source to obtain designer-type drugs. In 2001, U.S. Customs in Buffalo, New York, discovered that a steady flow of packages containing the drug gamma-butyrolactone or GBL, an ingredient of GBH (gamma hydroxybutyrate), also known as the date-rape drug, were entering the country from Canada; the drug was disguised as a cleaning product. Operation Webslinger, a joint investigation of federal law enforcement agencies in the United States and Canada, was put in place to track down the suppliers. Within a year, Operation Webslinger had shut down four Internet drug rings operating in the United States and Canada, made 115 arrests in eighty-four cities, and seized the equivalent of twenty-five million doses of GBH and other, related drugs.[85] In 2003, another federal task force, known as Operation Gray Lord and involving the Food and Drug Administration and the Drug Enforcement Administration, was set up to combat illegal sales of narcotics on the Internet.[86]

If all importation were ended, homegrown marijuana and lab-made drugs such as Ecstasy could become the drugs of choice. Even now, their easy availability and relatively low cost are increasing their popularity; they are a $10 billion business in the United States today.

Targeting Dealers   Law enforcement agencies have also made a concerted effort to focus on drug trafficking. Efforts have been made to bust large-scale drug rings. The long-term consequence has been to decentralize drug dealing and to encourage teenage gangs to become major suppliers. Ironically, it has proven easier for federal agents to infiltrate traditional organized crime groups than to take on drug-dealing gangs.

Police can also intimidate and arrest street-level dealers and users in an effort to make drug use so much of a hassle that consumption is cut back. Some street-level enforcement efforts have had success, but others are considered failures. "Drug sweeps" have clogged correctional facilities with petty offenders while proving a drain on police resources. These sweeps are also suspected of creating a displacement effect: stepped-up efforts to curb drug dealing in one area or city may encourage dealers to seek out friendlier territory.[87] People arrested on drug-related charges are the fastest growing segment of both the juvenile and adult justice systems. National surveys have found that juvenile court judges are prone to use a get-tough approach on drug-involved offenders. They are more likely to be processed formally by the court and to be detained between referral to court and disposition than other categories of delinquent offenders, including those who commit violent crimes.[88] Despite these efforts, juvenile drug use continues, indicating that a get-tough policy is not sufficient to deter drug use.

Education Strategies

Another approach to reducing teenage substance abuse relies on educational programs. Drug education now begins in kindergarten and extends through the twelfth grade. More than 80 percent of public school districts include these components: teaching students about the causes and effects of alcohol, drug, and tobacco use; teaching students to resist peer pressure; and referring students for counseling and treatment.[89] Education programs such as Project ALERT, based in middle schools in California and Oregon, appear to be successful in training youths to avoid recreational drugs and to resist peer pressure to use cigarettes and alcohol.[90] The most widely used drug prevention program, Drug Abuse Resistance Education (D.A.R.E.), is discussed in the accompanying Preventing and Treating Delinquency feature.

To go to the official site of D.A.R.E., click on Web Links under the Chapter Resources at http://cj.wadsworth.com/siegel_jdcore2e.

The Drug Abuse Resistance Education (D.A.R.E.) program is an elementary school course designed to give students the skills for resisting peer pressure to experiment with tobacco, drugs, and alcohol. It employs uniformed police officers to carry the antidrug message to students before they enter junior high school. While reviews have been mixed, the program continues to be used around the nation.

© Tony Freeman/PhotoEdit

Drug Abuse Resistance Education (D.A.R.E.)

The most widely known drug education program, Drug Abuse Resistance Education (D.A.R.E.), is an elementary school course designed to give students the skills they need to resist peer pressure to experiment with tobacco, drugs, and alcohol. It is unique because it employs uniformed police officers to carry the antidrug message to the children before they enter junior high school. The program focuses on five major areas:

- Providing accurate information about tobacco, alcohol, and drugs
- Teaching students techniques to resist peer pressure
- Teaching students to respect the law and law enforcers
- Giving students ideas for alternatives to drug use
- Building the self-esteem of students

The D.A.R.E. program is based on the concept that the young students need specific analytical and social skills to resist peer pressure and "say no" to drugs. Instructors work with children to raise their self-esteem, provide them with decision-making tools, and help them identify positive alternatives to substance abuse.

The D.A.R.E. approach has been adopted so rapidly since its founding in 1983 that it is now taught in almost 80 percent of school districts nationwide and in fifty-four other countries. In 2002 alone, twenty-six million children in the United States and ten million children in other countries participated in the program. More than 40 percent of all school districts incorporate assistance from local law enforcement agencies in their drug-prevention programming. New community policing strategies commonly incorporate the D.A.R.E. program into their efforts to provide services to local neighborhoods at the grassroots level.

Does D.A.R.E. Work?

Although D.A.R.E. is popular with both schools and police agencies, a number of evaluations have not found it to have an impact on student drug usage. For example, in a highly sophisticated evaluation of the program, Donald Lynam and his colleagues found the program to be ineffective over both the short and long term. They followed a cohort of sixth-grade children who attended a total of thirty-one schools. Twenty-three of the schools were randomly assigned to receive D.A.R.E. in the sixth grade, while the other eight received whatever drug education was routinely provided in their classes. The research team assessed the participants yearly through the tenth grade and then recontacted them when they were twenty years old. They found that D.A.R.E. had no effect on students' drug use at any time through tenth grade. The ten-year follow-up failed to find any hidden or "sleeper" effects that were delayed in developing. At age twenty, there were no differences between those who went through D.A.R.E. and those who did not in their use of cigarettes, alcohol, marijuana, or other drugs; the only difference was that those who had participated in D.A.R.E. reported slightly lower levels of self-esteem at age twenty—an effect that proponents were not aiming for. In the most rigorous and comprehensive review so far on the effectiveness of D.A.R.E, the General Accounting Office (GAO), the research arm of Congress, found that the program neither prevents student drug use nor changes student attitudes toward drugs.

Changing the D.A.R.E. Curriculum

Although national evaluations and independent reviews have questioned the validity of D.A.R.E. and a few communities have discontinued its use, it is still widely employed in school districts around the country. To meet criticism head-on, D.A.R.E. began testing a new curriculum in 2001. The new program is aimed at older students and relies more on having them question their assumptions about drug use than on listening to lectures on the subject. The new program will work largely on changing social norms, teaching students to question whether they really have to use drugs to fit in with their peers. Emphasis will shift from fifth-grade students to those in the seventh grade and a booster program will be added in ninth grade, when kids are more likely to experiment with drugs. Police officers will now serve more as coaches than as lecturers, encouraging students to challenge the social norm of drug use in discussion groups. Students also will do more role-playing in an effort to learn decision-making skills. There will also be an emphasis on the role of media and advertising in shaping behavior. The new curriculum is undergoing tests in 80 high schools and 176 middle schools—half the schools will continue using the curriculum they do now, and the other half will use the new D.A.R.E. program—so that the new curriculum may be scientifically evaluated.

CRITICAL THINKING

1. Do you believe that an education program such as D.A.R.E. can turn kids away from drugs, or are the reasons for teenage drug use so complex that a single school-based program is doomed to fail?
2. If you ran D.A.R.E., what experiences would you give to the children? Do you think it would be effective to have current or ex-addicts address classes about how drugs influenced their lives?

INFOTRAC COLLEGE EDITION RESEARCH

For more information on the enhanced D.A.R.E. program, go to InfoTrac College Edition and read "Enhanced D.A.R.E. Program More Effective for Adolescent Boys," *Brown University Child and Adolescent Behavior Letter* 19:1 (April 2003).

Sources: *Youth Illicit Drug Use Prevention: D.A.R.E. Long-Term Evaluations and Federal Efforts to Identify Effective Programs* (Washington, DC: U.S. General Accounting Office, 2003), p. 2; Brian Vastag, "GAO: DARE Does Not Work," *Journal of the American Medical Association* 289:539 (2003); Kate Zernike, "Antidrug Program Says It Will Adopt a New Strategy," *New York Times,* 15 February 2001, p.1; Donald R. Lynam, Rich Milich, Rick Zimmerman, Scott Novak, T. K. Logan, Catherine Martin, Carl Leukefeld, and Richard Clayton, "Project D.A.R.E.: No Effects at 10-Year Follow-Up," *Journal of Consulting and Clinical Psychology* 67:590–593 (1999).

Love: The Anti-Drug

Staying involved is what you do best
and the best way to keep kids off drugs.
Make dinner together. Catch up on the day.
Hang out and watch their favorite video.

Give them a kiss.
They'll be a lot less likely to get high today.

Do antidrug messages targeted at keeping youths off drugs work? Recent studies report promising findings. The message shown here, "Love: The Anti-Drug," encourages parents to talk to their children and be involved in their lives.

Two recent large-scale studies demonstrate the effectiveness of antidrug messages targeted at youth. An evaluation of the National Youth Anti-Drug Media Campaign, which features ads showing the dangers of marijuana use, reported that almost half of students in grades six to twelve with "high exposure" to the ads said the ads made them less likely to try or use drugs compared with 38 percent of students who had little or no exposure to the ads. Importantly, the study also reported that past-year marijuana use among youth was down 9 percent between 2002 and 2003.[91] The second study, the National Survey on Drug Use and Health, which asked young people ages twelve to seventeen about antidrug messages they had heard or seen outside of school hours, reported that past-month drug use by those exposed to the messages was 15 percent lower than those who had not been exposed to the messages.[92] These are encouraging findings given the limited effectiveness of D.A.R.E.

Community Strategies

Community-based programs reach out to high-risk youths, getting them involved in after-school programs; offering counseling; delivering clothing, food, and medical care when needed; and encouraging school achievement. Community programs also sponsor drug-free activities involving the arts, clubs, and athletics. Evaluations of community programs have shown that they may encourage antidrug attitudes and help insulate participating youths from an environment that encourages drugs.[93]

One of the most successful community-based programs to prevent substance abuse and delinquency is provided by the Boys and Girls Clubs (BGCs) of America. One study examined the effectiveness of BGCs for high-risk youths in public housing developments at five sites across the country. The usual services of BGCs, which include reading classes, sports, and homework assistance, were offered, as well as a program to prevent substance abuse, known as SMART Moves (Self-Management and Resistance Training). This program targets the specific pressures that young people face to try drugs and alcohol and provides education to parents and the community at large to assist youth in learning about the dangers of substance abuse and strategies for resisting the pressures to use drugs and alcohol.[94] Evaluation results showed that housing developments with BGCs, with and without SMART Moves, produced a reduction in substance abuse, drug trafficking, and other drug-related delinquency activity.[95]

Treatment Strategies

Each year more than 131,000 youths ages twelve to seventeen are admitted to treatment facilities in the United States, with over half being referred through the juvenile justice system. Just over 60 percent of all admissions involved marijuana as the primary drug of abuse.[96]

Several approaches are available to treat these users. Some efforts stem from the perspective that users have low self-esteem and employ various techniques to build up their sense of self. Some use psychological counseling, and others, such as the **multisystemic treatment (MST)** technique developed by Scott Henggeler, direct attention to family, peer, and psychological problems by focusing on problem solving and communication skills.[97] In a long-term evaluation of MST, Henggeler found that adolescent substance abusers who went through the program were significantly

multisystemic treatment (MST)
Addresses a variety of family, peer, and psychological problems.

less likely to recidivate than youths who received traditional counseling services. However, mixed treatment effects were reported for future substance abuse by those who received MST compared with those who did not.[98]

Another approach is to involve users in outdoor activities, wilderness training, and after-school community programs.[99] More intensive efforts use group therapy, in which leaders try to give users the skills and support that can help them reject social pressure to use drugs. These programs are based on the Alcoholics Anonymous philosophy that users must find the strength to stay clean and that support from those who understand their experiences can be a successful way to achieve a drug-free life.

Residential programs are used with more heavily involved drug abusers. Some are detoxification units that use medical procedures to wean patients from the more addicting drugs. Others are therapeutic communities that attempt to deal with the psychological causes of drug use. Hypnosis, aversion therapy (getting users to associate drugs with unpleasant sensations, such as nausea), counseling, biofeedback, and other techniques are often used.

There is little evidence that these residential programs can efficiently terminate teenage substance abuse.[100] Many are restricted to families whose health insurance will pay for short-term residential care; when the coverage ends, the children are released. Adolescents do not often enter these programs voluntarily, and most have little motivation to change.[101] A stay can stigmatize residents as "addicts" even though they never used hard drugs; while in treatment, they may be introduced to hard-core users with whom they will associate upon release. One residential program that holds promise for reducing teenage substance abuse is UCLA's Comprehensive Residential Education, Arts, and Substance Abuse Treatment (CREASAT) program, which integrates "enhanced substance abuse services" (group therapy, education, vocational skills) and visual and performing arts programming.[102] ✔ Checkpoints

Checkpoints

✔ There is a strong association between drug use and delinquency.

✔ Juvenile arrestees often test positive for drugs.

✔ Chronic offenders are often drug abusers.

✔ Though drug use and delinquency are associated, it is difficult to show that abusing drugs leads kids into a delinquent way of life.

✔ There are a number of drug-control strategies, some relying on law enforcement efforts and others on treatment.

✔ There are a number of drug education initiatives.

✔ D.A.R.E. is a popular school-based prevention program that has been the target of recent criticism; it is being revamped.

 To quiz yourself on this material, go to questions 10.13–10.20 on the Juvenile Delinquency: The Core 2e Web site.

WHAT DOES THE FUTURE HOLD?

To find out more about the federal government's drug control strategies, click on Web Links under the Chapter Resources at http://cj.wadsworth.com/siegel_jdcore2e.

The United States appears willing to go to great lengths to fight the drug war. Law enforcement efforts, along with prevention programs and treatment projects, have been stepped up. Yet all drug-control strategies are doomed to fail as long as youths want to take drugs and dealers find that their sale is a lucrative source of income. Prevention, deterrence, and treatment strategies ignore the core reasons for the drug problem: poverty, alienation, and family disruption. As the gap between rich and poor widens and the opportunities for legitimate advancement decrease, it should come as no surprise that adolescent drug use continues.

Some commentators have called for the **legalization of drugs.** This approach can have the short-term effect of reducing the association between drug use and crime (since, presumably, the cost of drugs would decrease), but it may have grave consequences. Drug use would most certainly increase, creating an overflow of unproductive people who must be cared for by the rest of society. The problems of teenage alcoholism should serve as a warning of what can happen when controlled substances are made readily available. However, the implications of decriminalization should be further studied: What effect would a policy of partial decriminalization (for example, legalizing small amounts of marijuana) have on drug use rates? Does a get-tough policy on drugs "widen the net?" Are there alternatives to the criminalization of drugs that could help reduce their use?[103] The Rand Corporation study of drug dealing in Washington, D.C., suggests that law enforcement efforts may have little influence on drug-abuse rates as long as dealers can earn more than the minimal salaries they might earn in the legitimate business world. Only by giving youths legitimate future alternatives can hard-core users be made to forgo drug use willingly.[104]

legalization of drugs
Decriminalizing drug use to reduce the association between drug use and crime.

SUMMARY

- Alcohol is the drug most frequently abused by American teens. Other popular drugs include marijuana; cocaine and its derivative, crack; and designer drugs such as Ecstasy.
- Self-report surveys indicate that more than half of all high school–age kids have tried drugs. Surveys of arrestees indicate that a significant proportion of teenagers are drug users and many are high school dropouts. The number of drug users may be even higher than surveys suggest, because these surveys may be missing the most delinquent youths.
- Although the national survey conducted by PRIDE shows that teenage drug use increased slightly in the past year, both it and the Monitoring the Future survey, also national, report that drug and alcohol use are much lower today than five and ten years ago.
- There are many explanations for why youths take drugs, including growing up in disorganized areas in which there is a high degree of hopelessness, poverty, and despair; peer pressure; parental substance abuse; emotional problems; and suffering from general problem behavior syndrome.
- A variety of youths use drugs. Some are occasional users who sell to friends. Others are seriously involved in both drug abuse and delinquency; many of these are gang members. There are also "losers," who filter in and out of the justice system. A small percentage of teenage users remain involved with drugs into adulthood.
- It is not certain whether drug abuse causes delinquency. Some experts believe there is a common cause for both delinquency and drug abuse—perhaps alienation and rage.
- Many attempts have been made to control the drug trade. Some try to inhibit the importation of drugs, others to close down major drug rings, and a few to stop street-level dealing. There are also attempts to treat users through rehabilitation programs and to reduce juvenile use by educational efforts. Some communities have mounted grassroots drives. These efforts have not been totally successful, although overall use of drugs may have declined somewhat.
- It is difficult to eradicate drug abuse because there is so much profit to be made from the sale of drugs. One suggestion: legalize drugs. But critics warn that such a step may produce greater numbers of substance abusers.

KEY TERMS

substance abuse, p. 232
hashish, p. 232
marijuana, p. 233
cocaine, p. 233
crack, p. 233
heroin, p. 234
addict, p. 234

alcohol, p. 234
anesthetic drugs, p. 234
inhalants, p. 234
sedatives, p. 234
tranquilizers, p. 235
hallucinogens, p. 235
stimulants, p. 235

anabolic steroids, p. 235
designer drugs, p. 236
addiction-prone personality, p. 242
gateway drug, p. 243
multisystemic treatment
    (MST), p. 253
legalization of drugs, p. 254

QUESTIONS FOR DISCUSSION

1. Discuss the differences between the various categories and types of substances of abuse. Is the term *drugs* too broad to have real meaning?

2. Why do you think youths take drugs? Do you know anyone with an addiction-prone personality?

3. What policy do you think might be the best strategy to reduce teenage drug use? Source control? Reliance on treatment? National education efforts? Community-level enforcement?

4. Do you consider alcohol a drug? Should greater controls be placed on the sale of alcohol?

5. Do TV shows and films glorify drug usage and encourage youths to enter the drug trade? Should all images of drinking and smoking be banned from TV? What about advertisements that try to convince youths how much fun it is to drink beer or smoke cigarettes?

The president has appointed you the new "drug czar." You have $10 billion under your control with which to wage your campaign. You know that drug use is unacceptably high, especially among poor, inner-city kids, that a great deal of criminal behavior is drug-related, and that drug-dealing gangs are expanding around the United States.

At an open hearing, drug control experts express their policy strategies. One group favors putting the money into hiring new law enforcement agents who will patrol borders, target large dealers, and make drug raids here and abroad. They also call for such get-tough measures as the creation of strict drug laws, the mandatory waiver of young drug dealers to the adult court system, and the death penalty for drug-related gang killings.

A second group believes the best way to deal with drugs is to spend the money on community treatment programs, expanding the number of beds in drug detoxification units, and funding research on how to reduce drug dependency clinically.

A third group argues that neither punishment nor treatment can restrict teenage drug use and that the best course is to educate at-risk kids about the dangers of substance abuse and then legalize all drugs but control their distribution. This course of action will help reduce crime and violence among drug users and also balance the national debt, because drugs could be heavily taxed.

- Do you believe drugs should be legalized? If so, what might be the negative consequences of legalization?
- Can any law enforcement strategies reduce drug consumption?
- Is treatment an effective drug-control technique?

To research this topic, use "youth and drugs" as a key term on InfoTrac College Edition.

The Open Society Institute, Centers for Disease Control and Prevention Health Programs, National Institute on Drug Abuse, National Center on Addiction and Substance Abuse at Columbia University, Partnership for a Drug-Free America, and the U.S. Bureau of Customs and Border Protection provide more information on different approaches to reducing teenage drug use. Before you answer the questions here, check out their Web sites by clicking on Web Links under the Chapter Resources at http://cj.wadsworth.com/siegel_jdcore2e.

Pro/Con discussions and Viewpoint Essays on some of the topics in this chapter may be found at the Opposing Viewpoints Resource Center: www.gale.com/OpposingViewpoints.

Secondary Prevention Efforts: Family and Community

Primary prevention interventions typically take place early in childhood and are based on different views of theories of the onset of delinquency. They aim to stop antisocial activities before they occur. In contrast, secondary prevention efforts take place later, after children show signs that they are involved in antisocial activities. Most are based on the assumption that children's relationship with their environment, their school, neighborhood, family, and peers can either increase their risk of delinquent involvement or help shield them from inducements to commit crime. Therefore, these prevention programs usually target such issues as adjusting to a disrupted home environment, coping with school-related problems, helping kids plan for their future, and providing alternatives to antisocial peers. The following sections review a few prominent examples of secondary delinquency prevention programs.

MENTORING

Mentoring programs usually involve nonprofessional volunteers spending time with young people who are at risk for delinquency, dropping out of school, school failure, and other social problems. They mentor in a supportive, nonjudgmental manner while also acting as role models.[1] In recent years there has been a large increase in the number of mentoring programs, many of them aimed at preventing delinquency.[2]

One of the mentoring programs most successful in preventing juvenile delinquency is the Quantum Opportunities Program (QOP). QOP was implemented in five sites: Milwaukee; Oklahoma City; Philadelphia; Saginaw, Michigan; and San Antonio. The program ran for four years, or up to grade twelve, and was designed around the provision of three "quantum opportunities":

- Educational activities (peer tutoring, computer-based instruction, homework assistance)

- Service activities (volunteering with community projects)

- Development activities (curricula focused on life and family skills, and college and career planning)

Incentives in the form of cash and college scholarships were also offered to students for work carried out in these three areas. These incentives served to provide short-run motivation for school completion and future academic and social achievement. In addition, staff received cash incentives and bonuses for keeping youths involved in the program.[3]

An evaluation of the program six months after it ended found that youths who participated were less likely to be arrested compared to the control group (17 percent versus 58 percent). A number of other significant effects were observed. For example, compared with the control group, QOP group members were

- More likely to have graduated from high school (63 percent versus 42 percent)

- More likely to be enrolled in some form of post-secondary education (42 percent versus 16 percent)

- Less likely to have dropped out of high school (23 percent versus 50 percent)[4]

Despite these findings, the overall evidence of the impact of mentoring on delinquency remains mixed.[5] Other mentoring programs have not had success in academic achievement, school attendance, school dropout rate, and employment.[6]

AFTER-SCHOOL PROGRAMS

Because three out of four mothers of school-age children are employed, and two-thirds of them work full-time, there is a growing need for after-school programs. Today, after-school options include child-care centers, tutoring programs at school, dance groups, basketball leagues, and drop-in clubs. State and federal budgets for education, public safety, delinquency prevention, and child care provide some funding for after-school programs. Research shows that younger children (ages five to nine) and those in low-income neighborhoods gain the most from after-school programs, showing improved work habits, behavior with peers and adults, and performance in school. Young teens who attend after-school activities achieve higher grades in school and engage in less risky behavior. However, these findings must be interpreted with caution. Because after-school programs are voluntary, participants may be the more motivated youngsters in a given population and the least likely to engage in antisocial behavior.[7]

Some of the most successful after-school programs are provided by the Boys and Girls Clubs of America. Founded in 1902, the Boys and Girls Clubs of America is a nonprofit organization with a membership today of more than 1.3 million boys and girls nationwide. Boys and Girls Clubs (BGC) provide programs in six main areas: cultural enrichment, health and physical education, social recreation, personal and educational development, citizenship and leadership development, and environmental education.[8]

Evaluations of the Boys and Girls Club programs show that they are mostly successful and produce reductions in substance abuse, drug trafficking, and other drug-related delinquency activity.[9]

Although the evidence shows that after-school programs can be successful, there is a need for further evaluation.[10] The fact that violent juvenile delinquency is at its peak in the after-school hours underscores the importance of high-quality after-school programs.[11]

JOB TRAINING

As you may recall, the effects of having an after-school job can be problematic. Some research indicates that it may be associated with delinquency and substance abuse. However, helping kids to prepare for the adult workforce is an important aspect of delinquency prevention. Job training programs play an important role in improving the chances of young people obtaining jobs in the legal economy and thereby may reduce delinquency.[12]

The most well known and largest job training program in the United States is the Job Corps, established in 1964 as a federal training program for disadvantaged, unemployed youths. The Department of Labor, which was the designer of the national program, was hopeful that spinoff benefits in the form of reduced dependence on social assistance and a reduction in delinquency would occur as a result of empowering at-risk youth to achieve stable, long-term employment opportunities. The program is still active today, operating out of 119 centers across the nation, and each year it provides services to more than sixty thousand new young people at a cost of over $1 billion.[13]

The main goal of the Job Corps is to improve the employability of participants by offering a comprehensive set of services that largely includes vocational skills training, basic education (the ability to obtain graduate equivalent degrees [GEDs]), and health care. Job Corps is provided to young people between the ages of sixteen and twenty-

four. Most of those enrolled in the program are at high risk of substance abuse, delinquency, and social assistance dependency. Two out of five come from families on social assistance, four out of five have dropped out of school, and the average family income is $6,000 per year.[14] Almost all Job Corps centers require the participants to live in the centers while taking the program.

A large-scale evaluation of Job Corps involving almost twelve thousand young people found that the program was successful in reducing delinquency. Arrest rates were 16 percent lower for those who received the program than a comparison group. Program group members were less likely to be convicted and serve jail time upon conviction. Also, there were higher employment rates and greater earnings for those who received the program.[15] An earlier evaluation of Job Corps found it to be a worthwhile investment of public resources: for each dollar that was spent on the program, $1.45 was saved to government or taxpayers, crime victims, and program participants.[16]

Job training is an important component of an overall strategy to reduce delinquency. The developmental stage of transition to work is very difficult for many young people. Coming from a disadvantaged background, having poor grades in school or perhaps dropping out of school, and having some involvement in delinquency can all pose difficulties in securing a steady, well-paying job in early adulthood.

COMPREHENSIVE COMMUNITY-BASED PROGRAMS

Comprehensive community-based delinquency prevention programs combine many interventions targeted at an array of risk factors for delinquency, and are typically implemented in neighborhoods with high delinquency and crime rates. Experimentation with this type of delinquency prevention program began as early as the 1930s, with Shaw and McKay's Chicago Area Project.[17] The Mobilization for Youth program of the 1960s is another example of a comprehensive community-based initiative to prevent juvenile delinquency. Neither of these programs was found to be overly successful in reducing delinquency. Few of these types of programs have been evaluated.

One contemporary example of a comprehensive community-based delinquency prevention program that has been evaluated is the Children At Risk (CAR) program. CAR was set up to help improve the lives of young people at high risk for delinquency, gang involvement, substance abuse, and other problem behaviors. It was delivered to a large number of young people in poor and high crime neighborhoods in five cities across the country. It involved a wide range of preventive measures, including case management and family counseling, family skills training, tutoring, mentoring, after-school activities, and community policing. The program was different in each neighborhood. A study of all five cities showed that one year after the program ended, the young people who received the program, compared with a control group, were less likely to have committed violent delinquent acts and used or sold drugs. Some of the other beneficial results for those in the program included less association with delinquent peers, less peer pressure to engage in delinquency, and more positive peer support.[18]

Comprehensive community-based delinquency prevention programs are made up of a range of different types of interventions, and typically involve an equally diverse group of community and government agencies that are concerned with the problem of juvenile delinquency, such as the YMCA/YWCA, Boys and Girls Clubs of America, social services, and health. For example, the Communities That Care (CTC) program emphasizes the reduction of risk factors for delinquency and the enhancement of protective factors against delinquency for different developmental stages from birth through adolescence.[19] CTC follows a rigorous, multilevel planning process that includes drawing upon interventions that have previously demonstrated success and tailoring them to the needs of the community.[20]

The CTC and other comprehensive programs rely on a systematic planning model to develop preventive interventions. This includes analysis of the delinquency problem, identification of available resources in the community, development of priority delinquency problems, and identification of successful programs in other communities and tailoring them to local conditions and needs.[21] Not all comprehensive community-based prevention programs follow this model, but there is evidence to suggest that this approach will produce the greatest reductions in juvenile delinquency.[22] One of the main drawbacks to this approach is the difficulty in sustaining the level of resources and the cooperation between agencies that are necessary to lower the rates of juvenile delinquency across a large geographical area such as a city.

FUTURE OF DELINQUENCY PREVENTION

Despite the success of many different types of secondary prevention programs, from mentoring to job training, these programs receive a small fraction of what is spent on the juvenile justice system to deal with young people once they have broken the law.[23] To many juvenile justice officials, policymakers, and politicians, prevention is tantamount to being soft on crime, and delinquency prevention programs are often referred to as "pork barrel," or wasteful, spending.[24] There is also concern about the labeling and stigmatization associated with programs that target high-risk populations: children and families receiving support may be called hurtful names or looked down upon by fellow community members.[25]

Notwithstanding these important issues, the future of secondary delinquency prevention is likely to be very bright. With many local efforts, state initiatives, and a growing list of national programs showing positive results, the prevention of delinquency is proving its worth.

chapter 11

The History and Development of Juvenile Justice

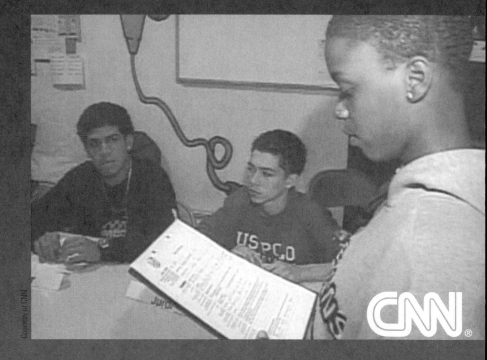

CHAPTER OBJECTIVES

After reading this chapter you should:

1. Understand the major social changes leading to creation of the first modern juvenile court in Chicago in 1899.

2. Be familiar with some of the landmark Supreme Court decisions that have influenced present-day juvenile justice procedures.

3. Be able to comment on the nature of delinquency cases being processed in juvenile court.

4. Know how children are processed by the juvenile justice system, beginning with investigation and arrest and concluding with reentry into society.

5. Understand the conflicting values in contemporary juvenile justice.

6. Recognize key similarities and differences between the adult and juvenile justice systems.

7. Be able to argue the pros and cons of the juvenile justice system's goal to treat rather than punish and assess if this goal is being met today.

8. Understand the need for and be aware of the key elements of a comprehensive juvenile justice strategy to deal with juvenile delinquency.

9. See the difference between prevention and intervention efforts to reduce juvenile delinquency.

10. Be able to identify and comment on pressing issues in the future of juvenile justice.

From the development of the first juvenile court in 1899 to the introduction of graduated sanctions, the history of the juvenile justice system is rife with innovations. One of the more recent innovations is the teen court, also called the youth court. Developed to relieve overcrowding and provide an alternative to traditional forms of juvenile courts, hundreds of jurisdictions across the country have set up these special courts. Teen courts differ from other juvenile justice programs because youths rather than adults determine the disposition in a case. In the South Bronx, New York, one teen court for first-time juvenile offenders includes a sixteen-year-old judge and a prosecutor, defense attorney, and jury who are all teenagers. In addition to being well received by youths, the program claims success in reducing rearrests.

CNN. VIEW THE CNN VIDEO CLIP OF THIS STORY AND ANSWER RELATED CRITICAL THINKING QUESTIONS ON YOUR JUVENILE DELINQUENCY: THE CORE 2E CD.

JUVENILE JUSTICE IN THE NINETEENTH CENTURY

At the beginning of the nineteenth century, delinquent, neglected, and runaway children in the United States were treated in the same way as adult criminal offenders.[1] Like children in England, when convicted of crimes they received harsh sentences similar to those imposed on adults. The adult criminal code applied to children, and no juvenile court existed.

During the early nineteenth century, various pieces of legislation were introduced to humanize criminal procedures for children. The concept of probation, introduced in Massachusetts in 1841, was geared toward helping young people avoid imprisonment. Many books and reports written during this time heightened public interest in juvenile care.

Despite this interest, no special facilities existed for the care of youths in trouble with the law, nor were there separate laws or courts to control their behavior. Youths who committed petty crimes, such as stealing or vandalism, were viewed as wayward children or victims of neglect and were placed in community asylums or homes. Youths who were involved in more serious crimes were subject to the same punishments as adults—imprisonment, whipping, or death.

Several events led to reforms and nourished the eventual development of the juvenile justice system: urbanization, the child-saving movement and growing interest in the concept of *parens patriae,* and development of institutions for the care of delinquent and neglected children.

Urbanization

To learn more about this era, go to the Library of Congress Web site devoted to American history by clicking on Web Links under the Chapter Resources at http://cj.wadsworth.com/siegel_jdcore2e.

Especially during the first half of the nineteenth century, the United States experienced rapid population growth, primarily due to an increased birthrate and expanding immigration. The rural poor and immigrant groups were attracted to urban commercial centers that promised jobs in manufacturing. In 1790, 5 percent of the population lived in cities. By 1850, the share of the urban population had increased to 15 percent; it jumped to 40 percent in 1900, and 51 percent in 1920.[2] New York more than quadrupled its population in the thirty-year stretch between 1825 and 1855—from 166,000 in 1825 to 630,000 in 1855.[3]

Urbanization gave rise to increased numbers of young people at risk, who overwhelmed the existing system of work and training. To accommodate destitute youths, local jurisdictions developed poorhouses (almshouses) and workhouses. The poor, the insane, the diseased, and vagrant and destitute children were all housed there in crowded and unhealthy conditions.

By the late eighteenth century, many began to question the family's ability to exert control over children. Villages developed into urban commercial centers and work began to center around factories, not the home. Children of destitute families left home or were cast loose to make out as best they could; wealthy families could no longer absorb vagrant youth as apprentices or servants.[4] Chronic poverty became an American dilemma. The affluent began to voice concern over the increase in the number of people in what they considered the "dangerous classes"—the poor, single, criminal, mentally ill, and unemployed.

Urbanization and industrialization also generated the belief that certain segments of the population (youths in urban areas, immigrants) were susceptible to the influences of their decaying environment. The children of these classes were considered a group that might be "saved" by a combination of state and community intervention.[5] Intervention in the lives of these so-called dangerous classes became acceptable for wealthy, civic-minded citizens. Such efforts included *settlement houses*, a term used around the turn of the twentieth century to describe shelters, and nonsecure residential facilities for vagrant children.

The Child-Saving Movement

To read more about the child savers, click on Web Links under the Chapter Resources at http://cj.wadsworth.com/siegel_jdcore2e.

The problems generated by urban growth sparked interest in the welfare of the "new" Americans, whose arrival fueled this expansion. In 1817, prominent New Yorkers formed the Society for the Prevention of Pauperism. Although they concerned themselves with attacking taverns, brothels, and gambling parlors, they also were concerned that the moral training of children of the dangerous classes was inadequate. Soon other groups concerned with the plight of poor children began to form. Their focus was on extending government control over youthful activities (drinking, vagrancy, and delinquency) that had previously been left to private or family control.

These activists became known as *child savers*. Prominent among them were penologist Enoch Wines; Judge Richard Tuthill; Lucy Flowers, of the Chicago Women's Association; Sara Cooper, of the National Conference of Charities and Corrections; and Sophia Minton, of the New York Committee on Children.[6] Poor children could become a financial burden, and the child savers believed these children presented a threat to the moral fabric of society. Child-saving organizations influenced state legislatures to enact laws giving courts the power to commit children who were runaways or criminal offenders to specialized institutions.

The most prominent of the care facilities developed by child savers was the **House of Refuge,** which opened in New York in 1825.[7] It was founded on the concept of protecting potential criminal youths by taking them off the streets and reforming them in a family-like environment. When the House of Refuge opened, the majority of children admitted were status offenders placed there because of vagrancy or neglect. Children were placed in the institution by court order, sometimes over their parents' objections. Their length of stay depended on need, age, and skill. Once there, youths were required to do piecework provided by local manufacturers or to work part of the day in the community. The institution was run like a prison, with strict discipline and absolute separation of the sexes. Such a harsh program drove many children to run away, and the House of Refuge was forced to take a more lenient approach.

Despite criticism, the concept enjoyed expanding popularity. In 1826, the Boston City Council founded the House of Reformation for juvenile offenders. Similar institutions were opened elsewhere in Massachusetts and in New York in 1847.[8] The

House of Refuge
A care facility developed by the child savers to protect potential criminal youths by taking them off the street and providing a family-like environment.

Here, young boys are shown working in the machine shop of the Indiana Youth Reformatory, circa 1910.

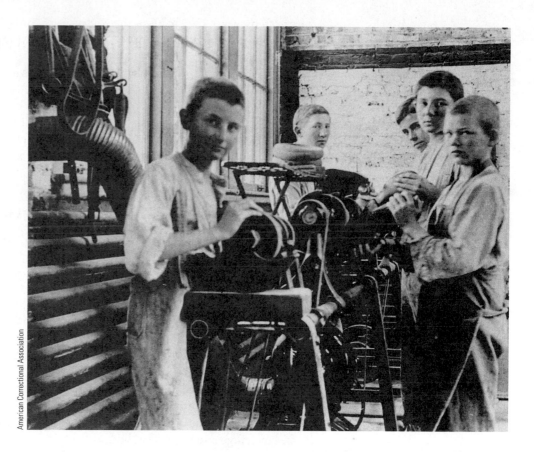

American Correctional Association

courts committed children found guilty of criminal violations, or found to be beyond the control of their parents, to these schools. Because the child savers considered parents of delinquent children to be as guilty as convicted offenders, they sought to have the reform schools establish control over the children. Refuge managers believed they were preventing poverty and crime by separating destitute and delinquent children from their parents and placing them in an institution.[9]

The philosophy of *parens patriae*—that is, the duty of the state to act on behalf of the child and provide care and protection equivalent to that of a parent—was extended to refuge programs, which were given parental control over a committed child. Scholar Robert Mennel summarizes this attitude: "The doctrine of *parens patriae* gave refuge managers the best of two worlds, familial and legal: it separated delinquent children from their natural parents and it circumvented the rigor of criminal law by allowing courts to commit children, under loosely worded statutes, to specially created schools instead of jails."[10]

Were They Really Child Savers?

Debate continues over the true objectives of the early child savers. Some historians conclude that they were what they seemed—concerned citizens motivated by humanitarian ideals.[11] Modern scholars, however, have reappraised the child-saving movement. In *The Child Savers,* Anthony Platt paints a picture of representatives of the ruling class who were galvanized by immigrants and the urban poor to take action to preserve their own way of life.[12]

Other critical thinkers followed Platt in finding that child saving was motivated more by self-interest than by benevolence. For example, Randall Shelden and Lynn Osborne traced the child-saving movement in Memphis, Tennessee, and found that its leaders were a small group of upper-class citizens who desired to control the behavior and lifestyles of lower-class youth. The outcome was ominous. Most cases petitioned to the juvenile court (which opened in 1910) were for petty crimes and status offenses, yet 25 percent of the youths were committed to some form of incarceration; more than 96 percent of the actions with which females were charged were status offenses.[13]

In summary, these scholars believe that the reformers applied the concept of *parens patriae* for their own purposes, including the continuance of middle- and upper-class values and the furtherance of a child labor system consisting of marginal and lower-class skilled workers.

In the course of "saving children" by turning them over to houses of refuge, the basic legal rights of children were violated: children were simply not granted the same constitutional protections as adults.

Development of Juvenile Institutions

State intervention in the lives of children continued well into the twentieth century. The child savers influenced state and local governments to create institutions, called *reform schools,* devoted to the care of vagrant and delinquent youths. State institutions opened in Westboro, Massachusetts, in 1848, and in Rochester, New York, in 1849.[14] Institutional programs began in Ohio in 1850, and in Maine, Rhode Island, and Michigan in 1906. Children spent their days working in the institution, learning a trade where possible, and receiving some basic education. They were racially and sexually segregated, discipline was harsh, and their physical care was poor. Beverly Smith found that girls admitted to the Western House of Refuge in Rochester, during the 1880s were often labeled criminals, but were in reality abused and neglected. They too were subject to harsh working conditions, strict discipline, and intensive labor.[15] Most of these institutions received state support, unlike the privately funded houses of refuge and settlement houses.

Although some viewed reform schools as humanitarian answers to poorhouses and prisons, many were opposed to such programs. As an alternative, New York philanthropist Charles Loring Brace helped develop the **Children's Aid Society** in 1853.[16] Brace's formula for dealing with delinquent youths was to rescue them from the harsh environment of the city and provide them with temporary shelter.

Deciding there were simply too many needy children to care for in New York City, and believing the urban environment was injurious to children, Brace devised what he called his *placing-out plan* to send these children to western farms where they could be cared for and find a home. They were placed on what became known as **orphan trains,** which made preannounced stops in western farming communities. Families wishing to take in children would meet the train, be briefly introduced to the passengers, and leave with one of the children. Brace's plan was activated in 1854 and very soon copied by other child-care organizations. Though the majority of the children benefited from the plan and did find a new life, others were less successful and some were exploited and harmed by the experience. By 1930, political opposition to Brace's plan, coupled with the negative effects of the Great Depression, spelled the end of the orphan trains, but not before 150,000 children were placed in rural homesteads. Concept Summary 11.1 describes those first juvenile institutions and organizations.

Society for the Prevention of Cruelty to Children (SPCC)

In 1874, the first **Society for the Prevention of Cruelty to Children (SPCC)** was established in New York; by 1900 there were three hundred such societies in the United States.[17] Leaders of the SPCCs were concerned that abused boys would become lower-class criminals and that mistreated young girls might become sexually promiscuous women. A growing crime rate and concern about a rapidly changing population served to swell SPCC membership. In addition, these organizations protected children who had been subjected to cruelty and neglect at home and at school.

SPCC groups influenced state legislatures to pass statutes protecting children from parents who did not provide them with adequate food and clothing or made them beg or work in places where liquor was sold.[18] Criminal penalties were created

To read more about the life of **Charles Loring Brace,** click on Web Links under the Chapter Resources at http://cj. wadsworth.com/siegel_ jdcore2e.

Children's Aid Society
Child-saving organization that took children from the streets of large cities and placed them with farm families on the prairie.

orphan train
A practice of the Children's Aid Society in which urban youths were sent West for adoption with local farm couples.

Society for the Prevention of Cruelty to Children (SPCC)
First established in 1874, these organizations protected children subjected to cruelty and neglect at home or at school.

for negligent parents, and provisions were established for removing children from the home. In some states, agents of the SPCC could actually arrest abusive parents; in others, they would inform the police about suspected abuse cases and accompany officers when they made an arrest.[19] See ✔ Checkpoints on page 266.

A CENTURY OF JUVENILE JUSTICE

Although reform groups continued to lobby for government control over children, the committing of children under the doctrine of *parens patriae* without due process of law began to be questioned. Could the state incarcerate children who had not violated the criminal law? Should children be held in facilities that housed adults? Serious problems challenged the effectiveness of the existing system; institutional deficiencies, the absence of due process for poor, ignorant, and noncriminal delinquents, and the treatment of these children by inadequate private organizations all spurred the argument that a juvenile court should be established.

Increasing delinquency rates also hastened the development of a juvenile court. Theodore Ferdinand's analysis of the Boston juvenile court found that in the 1820s and 1830s very few juveniles were charged with serious offenses. By 1850, juvenile delinquency was the fastest growing component of the local crime problem.[20] Ferdinand concluded that the flow of juvenile cases strengthened the argument that juveniles needed their own court.

RESCUED.

HOMELESS.

OFF FOR THE WEST.

THE YOUNG FARMER.

ADOPTED.

Stock Montage, Inc.

This engraving depicts the work of the Children's Aid Society, founded in 1853.

The Illinois Juvenile Court Act and Its Legacy

The child-saving movement culminated in passage of the Illinois Juvenile Court Act of 1899. The principles motivating the Illinois reformers were these:

1. Children should not be held as accountable as adult transgressors.
2. The objective of the juvenile justice system is to treat and rehabilitate rather than punish.
3. Disposition should be predicated on analysis of the youth's special circumstances and needs.
4. The system should avoid the trappings of the adult criminal process with all its confusing rules and procedures.

Reform schools	Devoted to the care of vagrant and delinquent youths.
Children's Aid Society	Designed to protect delinquent youths from the city's dangers through the provision of temporary shelter.
Orphan trains	The practice of using trains to place delinquent urban youths with families in western farming communities.
Society for the Prevention of Cruelty to Children	Designed to protect abused and neglected children by placing them with other families and advocating for criminal penalties for negligent parents.

Checkpoints

✔ *The movement to treat children in trouble with the law as a separate category began in the nineteenth century.*

✔ *Urbanization created a growing number of at-risk youth in the nation's cities.*

✔ *The child savers sought to control children of the lower classes.*

✔ *The House of Refuge was developed to care for unwanted or abandoned youth.*

✔ *Some critics now believe the child savers were motivated by self-interest and not benevolence.*

✔ *Charles Loring Brace created the Children's Aid Society to place urban kids with farm families.*

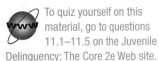 To quiz yourself on this material, go to questions 11.1–11.5 on the Juvenile Delinquency: The Core 2e Web site.

The Illinois Juvenile Court Act was a major event in the juvenile justice movement. Just what were the ramifications of passage of this act? The traditional interpretation is that the reformers were genuinely motivated to pass legislation that would serve the best interests of the child. U.S. Supreme Court Justice Abe Fortas took this position in the landmark 1967 *in re Gault* case:

> *The early reformers were appalled by adult procedures and penalties and by the fact that children could be given long prison sentences and mixed in jails with hardened criminals. They were profoundly convinced that society's duty to the child could not be confined by the concept of justice alone. . . . The child—essentially good, as they saw it—was to be made to feel that he was the object of the state's care and solicitude, not that he was under arrest or on trial. . . . The idea of crime and punishment was to be abandoned. The child was to be treated and rehabilitated, and the procedures from apprehension through institutionalization were to be clinical rather than punitive.*[21]

The child savers believed that children were influenced by their environments. Society was to be concerned with what their problems were and how these problems could be handled in the interests of the children and the state.

Interpretations of its intentions differ, but unquestionably the Illinois Juvenile Court Act established juvenile delinquency as a legal concept. For the first time the distinction was made between children who were neglected and those who were delinquent. Delinquent children were those under the age of sixteen who violated the law. Most important, the act established a court and a probation program specifically for children. In addition, the legislation allowed children to be committed to institutions and reform programs under the control of the state. The key provisions of the act were these:

- A separate court was established for delinquent and neglected children.
- Special procedures were developed to govern the adjudication of juvenile matters.
- Children were to be separated from adults in courts and in institutional programs.
- Probation programs were to be developed to assist the court in making decisions in the best interests of the state and the child.

Following passage of the Illinois Juvenile Court Act, similar legislation was enacted throughout the nation; by 1917, juvenile courts had been established in all but three states. The special courts these laws created maintained jurisdiction over pre-delinquent (neglected and dependent) and delinquent children. Juvenile court jurisdiction was based primarily on a child's noncriminal actions and status, not strictly on a violation of criminal law. The *parens patriae* philosophy predominated, ushering in a form of personalized justice that still did not provide juvenile offenders with the full array of constitutional protections available to adult criminal offenders. The court's process was paternalistic rather than adversarial. Attorneys were not required, and hearsay evidence, inadmissible in criminal trials, was admissible in the adjudication of juvenile offenders. Verdicts were based on a *preponderance of the evidence* instead of the stricter standard used by criminal courts, *beyond a reasonable doubt,* and children were often not granted any right to appeal their convictions.

The major functions of the juvenile justice system were to prevent juvenile crime and to rehabilitate juvenile offenders. The roles of the judge and the probation staff were to diagnose the child's condition and prescribe programs to alleviate it. Until 1967, judgments about children's actions and consideration for their constitutional rights were secondary.

By the 1920s, noncriminal behavior, in the form of incorrigibility and truancy from school, was added to the jurisdiction of many juvenile court systems. Of particular interest was the sexual behavior of young girls, and the juvenile court enforced a strict moral code on working-class girls, not hesitating to incarcerate those who were sexually active.[22] Programs of all kinds, including individualized counseling and institutional care, were used to *cure* juvenile criminality.

By 1925, juvenile courts existed in virtually every jurisdiction in every state. Although the juvenile court concept expanded rapidly, it cannot be said that each state implemented it thoroughly. Some jurisdictions established elaborate juvenile court systems, whereas others passed legislation but provided no services. Some courts had trained juvenile court judges; others had nonlawyers sitting in juvenile cases. Some courts had extensive probation departments; others had untrained probation personnel.

Great diversity also marked juvenile institutions. Some maintained a lenient orientation, but others relied on harsh punishments, including beatings, straitjacket restraints, immersion in cold water, and solitary confinement with a diet of bread and water.

These conditions were exacerbated by the rapid growth in the juvenile institutional population. Between 1890 and 1920, the number of institutionalized youths jumped 112 percent, a rise that far exceeded the increase in the total number of adolescents in the United States.[23] Although social workers and court personnel deplored the increased institutionalization of youth, the growth was due in part to the successful efforts by reformers to close poorhouses, thereby creating a need for institutions to house their displaced populations. In addition, the lack of a coherent national policy on needy children allowed private entrepreneurs to fill the void.[24] Although the increase in institutionalization seemed contrary to the goal of rehabilitation, such an approach was preferable to the poorhouse and the streets.

Reforming the System

Reform of this system was slow in coming. In 1912, the U.S. Children's Bureau was formed as the first federal child welfare agency. By the 1930s, the bureau began to investigate the state of juvenile institutions and tried to expose some of their more repressive aspects.[25] After World War II, critics such as Paul Tappan and Francis Allen began to identify problems in the juvenile justice system, among which were the neglect of procedural rights and the warehousing of youth in ineffective institutions. Status offenders commonly were housed with delinquents and given sentences that were more punitive than those given to delinquents.[26]

From its origin, the juvenile court system denied children procedural rights normally available to adult offenders. Due process rights, such as representation by counsel, a jury trial, freedom from self-incrimination, and freedom from unreasonable search and seizure, were not considered essential for the juvenile court system because its primary purpose was not punishment but rehabilitation. However, the dream of trying to rehabilitate children was not achieved. Individual treatment approaches failed, and delinquency rates soared.

Reform efforts, begun in earnest in the 1960s, changed the face of the juvenile justice system. In 1962, New York passed legislation creating a family court system.[27] The new court assumed responsibility for all matters involving family life, with emphasis on delinquent and neglected children. In addition, the legislation established the PINS classification (person in need of supervision). This category included individuals involved in such actions as truancy and incorrigibility. By using labels like PINS and CHINS (children in need of supervision) to establish jurisdiction over children, juvenile courts expanded their role as social agencies. Because noncriminal children were now involved in the juvenile court system to a greater degree, many juvenile courts had to improve their social services. Efforts were made to personalize the system of justice for children. These reforms were soon followed by a due-process revolution, which ushered in an era of procedural rights for court-adjudicated youth. The next section discusses some key cases that transformed the practice of juvenile justice.

In the 1960s and 1970s, the U.S. Supreme Court radically altered the juvenile justice system when it issued a series of decisions that established the right of juveniles to receive due process of law.[28] The Court established that juveniles had the same rights as adults in important areas of trial process, including the right to confront witnesses, notice of charges, and the right to counsel. Exhibit 11.1 illustrates some of the most important legal cases bringing procedural due process to the juvenile justice process.

Federal Commissions   In addition to the legal revolution brought about by the Supreme Court, a series of national commissions sponsored by the federal government helped change the shape of juvenile justice. In 1967, the *President's Commission on Law Enforcement and the Administration of Justice,* organized by President Lyndon Johnson, suggested that the juvenile justice system must provide underprivileged youths with opportunities for success, including jobs and education. The commission also recognized the need to develop effective law enforcement procedures to control hard-core offenders, while at the same time granting them due process. The commission's report acted as a catalyst for passage of the federal *Juvenile Delinquency Prevention and Control (JDP) Act of 1968.* This law created a Youth Development and Delinquency Prevention Administration, which concentrated on helping states develop new juvenile justice programs, particularly programs involving diversion of youth, decriminalization, and decarceration. In 1968, Congress also passed the *Omnibus Safe Streets and Crime Control Act.*[29] Title I of this law established the **Law Enforcement Assistance Administration (LEAA)** to provide federal funds for improving the adult and juvenile justice systems. In 1972, Congress amended the JDP to allow the LEAA to focus its funding on juvenile justice and delinquency-prevention programs. State and local governments were required to develop and adopt comprehensive plans to obtain federal assistance.

Because crime continued to receive much publicity, a second effort called the *National Advisory Commission on Criminal Justice Standards and Goals* was established in 1973 by the Nixon administration.[30] Its report identified such strategies as preventing delinquent behavior, developing diversion activities, establishing dispositional alternatives, providing due process for all juveniles, and controlling violent and chronic delinquents. This commission's recommendations formed the basis for the *Juvenile Justice and Delinquency Prevention Act of 1974.*[31] This act eliminated the Youth Development and Delinquency Prevention Administration and replaced it with the **Office of Juvenile Justice and Delinquency Prevention (OJJDP)** within the LEAA. In 1980, the LEAA was phased out, and the OJJDP became an independent agency in the Department of Justice. Throughout the 1970s, its two most important goals were removing juveniles from detention in adult jails, and eliminating the incarceration together of delinquents and status offenders. During this period, the OJJDP stressed the creation of formal diversion and restitution programs.

The latest effort has been the *Violent Crime Control and Law Enforcement Act of 1994.*[32] The largest piece of crime legislation in the history of the United States,

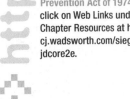

To read about the Juvenile Justice and Delinquency Prevention Act of 1974, click on Web Links under the Chapter Resources at http://cj.wadsworth.com/siegel_jdcore2e.

Law Enforcement Assistance Administration (LEAA)
Unit in the U.S. Department of Justice established by the Omnibus Crime Control and Safe Streets Act of 1968 to administer grants and provide guidance for crime prevention policy and programs.

Office of Juvenile Justice and Delinquency Prevention (OJJDP)
Branch of the U.S. Justice Department charged with shaping national juvenile justice policy through disbursement of federal aid and research funds.

Exhibit 11.1   Leading Constitutional Cases in Juvenile Justice

- *Oklahoma Publishing Co. v. District Court* (1977) ruled that a state court could not prohibit the publication of information obtained in an open juvenile proceeding. When photographs were taken and published of an eleven-year-old boy suspected of homicide and the local court prohibited further disclosure, the publishing company claimed that the court order was a restraint in violation of the First Amendment. The Supreme Court agreed.

- *Smith v. Daily Mail Publishing Co.* (1979) involved the discovery and subsequent publication of the identity of a juvenile suspect in violation of a state statute prohibiting publication. The Supreme Court declared the statute unconstitutional because it believed the state's interest in protecting the child was not of such magnitude as to justify the use of a criminal statute. Criminal trials are open to the public, but juvenile proceedings are meant to be private and confidential, which ordinarily does not violate the First Amendment right to free press discussed in the previous case.

- *Fare v. Michael C.* (1979) held that a child's request to see his probation officer at the time of interrogation did not operate to invoke his Fifth Amendment right to remain silent. According to the Court, the probation officer cannot be expected to offer the type of advice that an accused would expect from an attorney. The landmark *Miranda v. Arizona* case ruled that a request for a lawyer is an immediate revocation of a person's right to silence, but this rule is not applicable for a request to see the probation officer.

- *Eddings v. Oklahoma* (1982) ruled that a defendant's age should be a mitigating factor in deciding whether to apply the death penalty.

- *Schall v. Martin* (1984) upheld a statute allowing for the placement of children in preventive detention before their adjudication. The Court concluded that it was not unreasonable to detain juveniles for their own protection.

- *New Jersey v. T.L.O.* (1985) determined that the Fourth Amendment applies to school searches. The Court adopted a "reasonable suspicion" standard, as opposed to the stricter standard of "probable cause," to evaluate the legality of searches and seizures in a school setting.

- *Thompson v. Oklahoma* (1988) ruled that imposing capital punishment on a juvenile murderer who was fifteen years old at the time of the offense violated the Eighth Amendment's constitutional prohibition against cruel and unusual punishment.

- *Stanford v. Kentucky* and *Wilkins v. Missouri* (1989) concluded that the imposition of the death penalty on a juvenile who committed a crime between the ages of sixteen and eighteen was not unconstitutional and that the Eighth Amendment's cruel and unusual punishment clause did not prohibit capital punishment.

- *Vernonia School District v. Acton* (1995) held that the Fourth Amendment's guarantee against unreasonable searches is not violated by the suspicionless drug testing of all students choosing to participate in interscholastic athletics. The Supreme Court expanded power of public educators to ensure safe learning environments in schools.

- *United States v. Lopez* (1995) ruled that Congress exceeded its authority under the Commerce Clause when it passed the Gun-Free School Zone Act, which made it a federal crime to possess a firearm within one thousand feet of a school.

Sources: *Oklahoma Publishing Co. v. District Court,* 430 U.S. 308, 97 S.Ct. 1045, 51 L.Ed. 2d (1977); *Smith v. Daily Mail Publishing Co.,* 443 U.S. 97, 99 S.Ct. 2667, 61 L.Ed. 2d 399 (1979); *Fare v. Michael C.,* 442 U.S. 707, 99 S.Ct. 2560 (1979); *Eddings v. Oklahoma,* 455 U.S. 104, 102 S.Ct. 869, 71 L.Ed. 2d 1 (1982); *Schall v. Martin,* 467 U.S. 253, 104 S.Ct. 2403 (1984); *New Jersey v. T.L.O.,* 469 U.S. 325, 105 S.Ct. 733 (1985); *Thompson v. Oklahoma,* 487 U.S. 815, 108 S.Ct. 2687, 101 L.Ed. 2d 702 (1988); *Stanford v. Kentucky,* 492 U.S., 109 S.Ct. 2969 (1989); *Vernonia School District v. Acton,* 515 U.S. 646 115 S.Ct. 2386, 132 L.Ed. 2d 564 (1995); *Wilkins v. Missouri,* 492 U.S. 361, 109 S.Ct. 2969 (1909); *United States v. Lopez,* 115 S.Ct. 1624 (1995).

Checkpoints

✔ *The juvenile court movement spread rapidly around the nation.*

✔ *Separate courts and correctional systems were created for youth. However, children were not given the same legal rights as adults.*

✔ *Reformers helped bring due process rights to minors and create specialized family courts.*

✔ *Federal commissions focused attention on juvenile justice and helped revise the system.*

 To quiz yourself on this material, go to questions 11.6–11.13 on the Juvenile Delinquency: The Core 2e Web site.

it provided for a hundred thousand new police officers and billions of dollars for prisons and prevention programs for both adult and juvenile offenders. A revitalized juvenile justice system would need both a comprehensive strategy to prevent and control delinquency and a consistent program of federal funding.[33]   ✔ **Checkpoints**

JUVENILE JUSTICE TODAY

Today the juvenile justice system exercises jurisdiction over two distinct categories of offenders—delinquents and status offenders.[34] *Delinquent children* are those who fall under a jurisdictional age limit, which varies from state to state, and who commit an act in violation of the penal code. *Status offenders* are commonly characterized in state statutes as persons or children in need of supervision (PINS or CHINS). Most states distinguish such behavior from delinquent conduct to lessen the effect of any stigma on children as a result of their involvement with the juvenile court. In addition, juvenile courts generally have jurisdiction over situations involving conduct directed at (rather than committed by) juveniles, such as parental neglect, deprivation, abandonment, and abuse.

The states have also set different maximum ages below which children fall under the jurisdiction of the juvenile court. Most states (and the District of Columbia) include all children under eighteen, others set the upper limit at seventeen, and still others include children under sixteen (Table 11.1).

Today's juvenile justice system exists in all states by statute. Each jurisdiction has a juvenile code and a special court structure to accommodate children in trouble. Nationwide, the juvenile justice system consists of thousands of public and private agencies, with a total budget amounting to hundreds of millions of dollars. Most of the nation's police agencies have juvenile components, and there are more than three thousand juvenile courts and about an equal number of juvenile correctional facilities.

Figure 11.1 depicts the numbers of juvenile offenders removed at various stages of the juvenile justice process. These figures do not take into account the large number of children who are referred to community diversion and mental health programs. There are thousands of these programs throughout the nation. This multitude of agencies and people dealing with juvenile delinquency has led to the development of what professionals view as an incredibly expansive and complex system.

The Juvenile Justice Process

How are children processed by the juvenile justice system?[35] Most children come into the justice system as a result of contact with a police officer. When a juvenile commits a serious crime, the police are empowered to make an arrest. Less serious offenses may also require police action, but in these instances, instead of being arrested, the child may be warned or a referral may be made to a social service program. A little more than 70 percent of all children arrested are referred to the juvenile court. Figure 11.2

Table 11.1	Oldest Age for Juvenile Court Jurisdiction in Delinquency Cases
Age	**State (Total Number)**
15	Connecticut, New York, North Carolina (3)
16	Georgia, Illinois, Louisiana, Massachusetts, Michigan, Missouri, New Hampshire, South Carolina, Texas, Wisconsin (10)
17	Alabama, Alaska, Arizona, Arkansas, California, Colorado, Delaware, Florida, Hawaii, Idaho, Indiana, Iowa, Kansas, Kentucky, Maine, Maryland, Minnesota, Mississippi, Montana, Nebraska, Nevada, New Jersey, New Mexico, North Dakota, Ohio, Oklahoma, Oregon, Pennsylvania, Rhode Island, South Dakota, Tennessee, Utah, Vermont, Virginia, Washington, West Virginia, Wyoming (37 and the District of Columbia)

Source: Melissa Sickmund, *Juveniles in Court* (Washington, DC: Office of Juvenile Justice and Delinquency Prevention, U.S. Department of Justice, 2003), p. 5.

In the 1982 case *Eddings v. Oklahoma,* the U.S. Supreme Court ruled that a defendant's age should be a mitigating factor in deciding whether to apply the death penalty. Should very young killers be eligible for capital punishment, or are juveniles too immature to appreciate the seriousness of their misdeeds? Here, twelve-year-old Tyler King is led into an Allegheny County Coroner's inquest by his Attorney David Shrager. King was ordered held for trial in the shooting death of his best friend, Nick Polowsky, and tried as an adult.

Figure 11.1   **Case Processing of Typical Violent Crimes in the Juvenile Justice System**

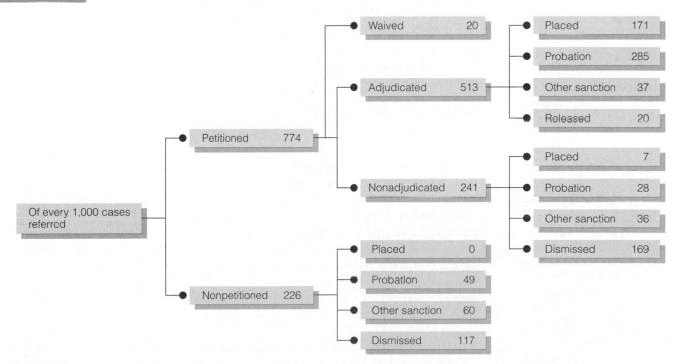

Note: Cases are categorized by their most severe or restrictive sanction. Detail may not add to totals because of rounding.

Source: Charles Puzzanchera, Anne L. Stahl, Terrence A. Finnegan, Nancy Tierney, and Howard N. Snyder, *Juvenile Court Statistics 1999* (Pittsburgh, PA: National Center for Juvenile Justice, 2003).

Figure 11.2   Case Flow Through the Juvenile Justice Process

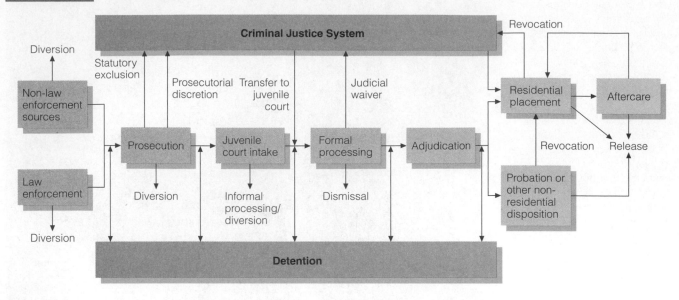

Source: This figure can be accessed online through the Office of Juvenile Justice and Delinquency Prevention at www.ojjdp.ncjrs.org/facts/casejpg.html.

outlines the **juvenile justice process,** and a detailed analysis of this process is presented in the next sections.

Police Investigation

When youths commit a crime, police have the authority to investigate the incident and decide whether to release the youths or commit them to the juvenile court. This is often a discretionary decision, based not only on the nature of the offense but also on conditions existing at the time of the arrest. Such factors as the seriousness of the offense, the child's past contacts with the police, and whether the child denies committing the crime determine whether a petition is filed. As you may recall, juveniles in custody today have constitutional rights similar to those of adult offenders. They are protected against unreasonable search and seizure under the Fourth and Fourteenth Amendments of the Constitution. The Fifth Amendment places limitations on police interrogation procedures.

Detention

If the police decide to file a petition, the child is referred to juvenile court. The primary decision at this point is whether the child should remain in the community or be placed in a detention facility or in shelter care (temporary foster homes, detention boarding homes, programs of neighborhood supervision). In the past, children were routinely held in detention facilities to await court appearances. Normally, a **detention hearing** is held to determine whether to remand the child to a shelter. At this point, the child has a right to counsel and other procedural safeguards. A child who is not detained is usually released to a parent or guardian. Most state juvenile court acts provide for a child to return home to await further court action, except when it is necessary to protect the child, when the child presents a serious danger to the public, or when it is not certain that the child will return to court. In many cases the police will refer the child to a community service program instead of filing a formal charge.

Pretrial Procedures

In most jurisdictions, the adjudication process begins with some sort of hearing. At this hearing, juvenile court rules normally require that juveniles be informed of their right to a trial, that the plea or admission be voluntary, and that they understand the charges and consequences of the plea. The case will often not be further adjudicated if a child admits to the crime at the initial hearing.

juvenile justice process
Under the *parens patriae* philosophy, juvenile justice procedures are informal and nonadversarial, invoked for juvenile offenders rather than against them; a petition instead of a complaint is filed; courts make findings of involvement or adjudication of delinquency instead of convictions; and juvenile offenders receive dispositions instead of sentences.

detention hearing
A hearing by a judicial officer of a juvenile court to determine whether a juvenile is to be detained or released while proceedings are pending in the case.

In some cases, youths may be detained at this stage pending a trial. Juveniles who are detained are eligible for bail in a handful of jurisdictions. Plea bargaining may also occur at any stage of the proceedings. A plea bargain is an agreement between the prosecution and the defense by which the juvenile agrees to plead guilty for certain considerations, such as a lenient sentence. This issue is explored more thoroughly in chapter 13, which discusses pretrial procedures.

If the child denies the allegation of delinquency, an **adjudicatory hearing** or trial is scheduled. Under extraordinary circumstances, a juvenile who commits a serious crime may be waived to adult court. Today, most jurisdictions have laws providing for such transfers. Whether such a transfer occurs depends on the type of offense, the youth's prior record, the availability of treatment services, and the likelihood that the youth will be rehabilitated in the juvenile court system.

Adjudication   Adjudication is the trial stage of the juvenile court process. If the child does not admit guilt at the initial hearing and is not waived to an adult court, the adjudication hearing is held to determine the facts of the case. The court hears evidence on the allegations in the delinquency petition. This is a trial on the merits (dealing with issues of law and facts), and rules of evidence similar to those of criminal proceedings generally apply. At this stage, the juvenile offender is entitled to many of the procedural guarantees given adult offenders. These include the right to counsel, freedom from self-incrimination, the right to confront and cross-examine witnesses, and in certain instances, the right to a jury trial. In addition, many states have their own procedures concerning rules of evidence, competence of witnesses, pleadings, and pretrial motions. At the end of the adjudicatory hearing, the court enters a judgment against the juvenile.

Disposition   If the adjudication process finds the child delinquent, the court must decide what should be done to treat the child. Most juvenile court acts require a dispositional hearing separate from the adjudication. This two-stage decision is often referred to as a **bifurcated process.** The dispositional hearing is less formal than adjudication. Here, the judge imposes a **disposition** on the offender in light of the offense, the youth's prior record, and his or her family background. The judge can prescribe a wide range of dispositions, ranging from a reprimand to probation to institutional commitment. In theory, the judge's decision serves the best interests of the child, the family, and the community.

Treatment   After disposition in juvenile court, delinquent offenders may be placed in some form of correctional treatment. Probation is the most commonly used formal sentence for juvenile offenders, and many states require that a youth fail on probation before being sent to an institution (unless the criminal act is extremely serious). Probation involves placing the child under the supervision of the juvenile probation department for the purpose of community treatment. The most severe of the statutory dispositions available to the juvenile court involves commitment of the child to an institution. The committed child may be sent to a state training school or a private residential treatment facility. These are usually minimum-security facilities with small populations and an emphasis on treatment and education. Some states, however, maintain facilities with populations of over a thousand youths. Currently there are more than one hundred thousand youths in some form of correctional institution in the United States.

Some jurisdictions allow for a program of juvenile aftercare or parole. A youth can be paroled from an institution and placed under the supervision of a parole officer. This means that he or she will complete the period of confinement in the community and receive assistance from the parole officer in the form of counseling, school referral, and vocational training.

Juveniles who are committed to treatment programs or control programs have a legal right to treatment. States are required to provide suitable rehabilitation programs

adjudicatory hearing
The fact-finding process wherein the juvenile court determines whether there is sufficient evidence to sustain the allegations in a petition.

bifurcated process
The procedure of separating adjudicatory and dispositionary hearings so different levels of evidence can be heard at each.

disposition
For juvenile offenders, the equivalent of sentencing for adult offenders; juvenile dispositions should be more rehabilitative than retributive.

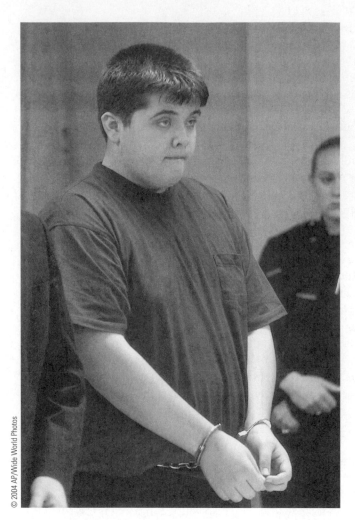

that include counseling, education, and vocational services. Appellate courts have ruled that, if such minimum treatment is not provided, individuals must be released from confinement.

Conflicting Values in Juvenile Justice This overview of the juvenile justice process hints at the often-conflicting values at the heart of the system. Efforts to ensure that juveniles are given appropriate treatment are consistent with the doctrine of *parens patriae* that predominated in the first half of the twentieth century. (See Table 11.2 for a time line of ideologies of juvenile justice during the twentieth century.) Over the past century, the juvenile court has struggled to provide treatment for juvenile offenders while guaranteeing them constitutional due process. But the system has been so overwhelmed by the increase in violent juvenile crime and family breakdown that some judges and politicians have suggested abolishing the juvenile system. Even those experts who want to retain an independent juvenile court have called for its restructuring. Crime-control advocates want to reduce the court's jurisdiction over juveniles charged with serious crimes and liberalize the prosecutor's ability to try them in adult courts. In contrast, child advocates suggest that the court scale back its judicial role and transfer its functions to community groups and social service agencies.[36]

✔ Checkpoints

Are dispositions for juvenile offenders too tough or too lenient? Here, Cody Jackson, fifteen, accused of plotting a killing spree with two friends, appears in Camden County Court in Camden, New Jersey, October 21, 2003, where he pleaded guilty to carjacking. All three teens pleaded guilty in the plot, which prosecutors say could have resulted in a bloodbath in a Philadelphia suburb. The judge ordered Jackson to serve a disposition of five years in a youthful offender facility.

Criminal Justice Versus Juvenile Justice

The components of the adult and juvenile criminal processes are similar. However, the juvenile system has a separate organizational structure. In many communities, juvenile justice is administered by people who bring special skills to the task. Also, more kinds of facilities and services are available to juveniles than to adults.

One concern of the juvenile court reform movement was to make certain that the stigma attached to a convicted offender would not be affixed to young people in juvenile proceedings. Thus, even the language used in the juvenile court differs from that used in the adult criminal court (Exhibit 11.2). Juveniles are not indicted for a crime; they have a **petition** filed against them. Secure pretrial holding facilities are called *detention centers* rather than jails. Similarly, the criminal trial is called a *hearing* in the juvenile justice system. The Focus on Delinquency feature on page 276 compares the two systems.

A COMPREHENSIVE JUVENILE JUSTICE STRATEGY

petition
Document filed in juvenile court alleging that a juvenile is a delinquent, a status offender, or a dependent and asking that the court assume jurisdiction over the juvenile.

At a time when much attention is focused on serious juvenile offenders, a comprehensive strategy has been called for to deal with all aspects of juvenile crime. This strategy focuses on crime prevention and expanding options for handling juvenile offenders. It addresses the links between crime and poverty, child abuse, drugs, weapons, and school behavior. Programs are based on a continuum of care that begins in early childhood and progresses through late adolescence. The components of this strategy include prevention in early childhood; intervention for at-risk teenage youths; graduated sanctions to hold juvenile offenders accountable for crimes;

Table 11.2   Time Line of Juvenile Justice Ideology

Time Line	Activity
Prior to 1899	Juveniles treated similarly to adult offenders. No distinction by age or capacity to commit criminal acts.
1899 to 1950s	Children treated differently, beginning with the Illinois Juvenile Court Act of 1899. By 1925 juvenile court acts are established in virtually every state.
1950s to 1970s	Recognition by experts that the rehabilitation model and the protective nature of *parens patriae* have failed to prevent delinquency.
1960s to 1970s	Constitutional due process is introduced into the juvenile justice system. The concept of punishing children or protecting them under *parens patriae* is under attack by the courts.
1970s to 1980s	Failure of rehabilitation and due process protections to control delinquency leads to a shift to a crime-control and punishment philosophy similar to that of the adult criminal justice system.
Early 1990s	Mixed constitutional protections with some treatment. Uncertain goals and programs; the juvenile justice system relies on punishment and deterrence.
Mid-1990s to present	Attention given to strategy that focuses on reducing the threat of juvenile crime and expanding options for handling juvenile offenders. Emphasis is placed on "what works" and implementing the best intervention and control programs. Effort is made to utilize the restorative justice model, which involves balancing the needs of the victim, the community, and the juvenile.

Checkpoints

✔ *There has been a movement to toughen the juvenile justice system.*

✔ *There are a number of stages in the juvenile justice process, beginning with police investigation.*

✔ *One critical decision is whether a child should be detained prior to trial.*

✔ *The adjudicatory hearing is the trial stage of the process.*

✔ *If a juvenile is found to be delinquent, a proper sentence, or disposition, must be found.*

 To quiz yourself on this material, go to questions 11.14–11.17 on the Juvenile Delinquency: The Core 2e Web site.

proper utilization of detention and confinement; and placement of serious juvenile offenders in adult courts.[37] There are many expected benefits from the use of this comprehensive strategy (Exhibit 11.3).

Prevention

Research has identified certain factors that may suggest future delinquency. For young children, these include abuse and neglect, domestic violence, educational underachieve-

Exhibit 11.2   Comparison of Terms Used in Juvenile and Adult Justice Systems

	Juvenile Terms	Adult Terms
The person and the act	Delinquent child	Criminal
	Delinquent act	Crime
Preadjudicatory stage	Take into custody	Arrest
	Petition	Indictment
	Agree to a finding	Plead guilty
	Deny the petition	Plead not guilty
	Adjustment	Plea bargain
	Detention facility; child care shelter	Jail
Adjudicatory stage	Substitution	Reduction of charges
	Adjudication or fact-finding hearing	Trial
	Adjudication	Conviction
Postadjudicatory stage	Dispositional hearing	Sentencing hearing
	Disposition	Sentence
	Commitment	Incarceration
	Youth development center; treatment; training school	Prison
	Residential child care facility	Halfway house
	Aftercare	Parole

Similarities and Differences Between Juvenile and Adult Justice Systems

Since its creation, the juvenile justice system has sought to maintain its independence from the adult justice system. Yet there are a number of similarities that characterize the institutions, processes, and law of the two systems.

Similarities

Police officers, judges, and correctional personnel use discretion in decision making in both the adult and the juvenile systems.

The right to receive *Miranda* warnings applies to juveniles as well as to adults.

Juveniles and adults are protected from prejudicial lineups or other identification procedures.

Similar procedural safeguards protect juveniles and adults when they make an admission of guilt.

Prosecutors and defense attorneys play equally critical roles in juvenile and adult advocacy.

Juveniles and adults have the right to counsel at most key stages of the court process.

Pretrial motions are available in juvenile and criminal court proceedings.

Negotiations and plea bargaining exist for juvenile and adult offenders.

Juveniles and adults have a right to a hearing and an appeal.

The standard of evidence in juvenile delinquency adjudications, as in adult criminal trials, is proof beyond a reasonable doubt.

Juveniles and adults can be placed on probation by the court.

Both juveniles and adults can be placed in pretrial detention facilities.

Juveniles and adults can be kept in detention without bail if they are considered dangerous.

After trial, both can be placed in community treatment programs.

Juveniles and adults can be required to undergo drug testing.

Differences

The primary purpose of juvenile procedures is protection and treatment. With adults, the aim is to punish the guilty.

Age determines the jurisdiction of the juvenile court. The nature of the offense determines jurisdiction in the adult system. Juveniles can be ordered to the criminal court for trial as adults.

Juveniles can be apprehended for acts that would not be criminal if they were committed by an adult (status offenses).

Juvenile proceedings are not considered criminal; adult proceedings are.

Juvenile court procedures are generally informal and private. Those of adult courts are more formal and are open to the public.

Courts cannot release identifying information about a juvenile to the press, but they must release information about an adult.

Parents are highly involved in the juvenile process but not in the adult process.

The standard of arrest is more stringent for adults than for juveniles.

Juveniles are released into parental custody. Adults are generally given the opportunity for bail.

Juveniles have no constitutional right to a jury trial. Adults have this right. Some state statutes provide juveniles with a jury trial.

Juveniles can be searched in school without probable cause or a warrant.

A juvenile's record is generally sealed when the age of majority is reached. The record of an adult is permanent.

A juvenile court cannot sentence juveniles to county jails or state prisons; these are reserved for adults.

The U.S. Supreme Court has declared that the Eighth Amendment does not prohibit the death penalty for crimes committed by juveniles ages sixteen and seventeen, but it is not a sentence given to children under age sixteen.

CRITICAL THINKING

1. What are some of the key principles of the juvenile justice system that distinguish it from the adult justice system and that have come under increased scrutiny of late?

2. What can be done to ensure that these key principles are protected so that the juvenile justice system remains distinct from the adult system?

INFOTRAC COLLEGE EDITION RESEARCH

For more information on how the juvenile justice system is becoming increasingly like the adult justice system, go to InfoTrac College Edition and read L. Mara Dodge, "Our Juvenile Court Has Become More Like a Criminal Court: A Century of Reform at the Cook County (Chicago) Juvenile Court," *Michigan Historical Review* 26(2):51 (2000); Joseph V. Penn, "Justice for Youth? A History of the Juvenile and Family Court," *Brown University Child and Adolescent Behavior Letter* 17(9):1 (September 2001).

Exhibit 11.3   **Benefits of Using the Comprehensive Strategy**

1. Increased prevention of delinquency (and thus fewer young people entering the juvenile justice system)
2. Enhanced responsiveness from the juvenile justice system
3. Greater accountability on the part of youth
4. Decreased costs of juvenile corrections
5. A more responsible juvenile justice system
6. More effective juvenile justice programs
7. Less delinquency
8. Fewer delinquents becoming serious, violent, and chronic offenders
9. Fewer delinquents becoming adult offenders

Source: James C. Howell, *Preventing and Reducing Juvenile Delinquency: A Comprehensive Framework* (Thousand Oaks, CA: Sage, 2003), p. 245.

ment, and health problems.[38] Early childhood services may prevent delinquency and make a child less vulnerable to future criminality.[39] The federal Head Start program provides children in poverty with, among other things, an enriched educational environment to develop learning and cognitive skills to be better prepared for the early school years. Low intelligence and school failure are important risk factors for juvenile delinquency. Smart Start is designed to make certain children are healthy before starting school. Home-visiting programs target families at risk for child abuse and neglect.

Intervention

Intervention programs are focused on teenage youths considered to be at higher risk for engaging in petty delinquent acts, using drugs or alcohol, or associating with antisocial peers.[40] Interventions at this stage are designed to ward off involvement in more serious delinquency. Many jurisdictions are developing intervention programs for teenage youths. An example is the Big Brother/Big Sister program, which matches a volunteer adult with a youngster. Similarly, in the Office of Juvenile Justice and Delinquency Prevention's Juvenile Mentoring Program (JUMP), responsible and caring adults volunteer their time as mentors to youths at risk for delinquency and dropping out of school. The mentors work one-on-one with the children, offering support and guidance.[41] Job training, through the likes of Job Corps and YouthBuild U.S.A., is another important intervention that receives government funding. These programs improve the chances of young people obtaining jobs in the legal economy and thereby may reduce delinquency. Efforts are also being made to deter them from becoming involved with gangs, because gang members ordinarily have higher rates of serious violent behavior.

Graduated Sanctions

Graduated sanction programs for juveniles are another solution being explored by states across the country. Types of graduated sanctions include immediate sanctions for nonviolent offenders (these consist of community-based diversion and day treatment); intermediate sanctions such as probation and electronic monitoring, which target repeat minor offenders and first-time serious offenders; and secure institutional care, which is reserved for repeat serious offenders and violent offenders. The philosophy behind this approach is to limit the most restrictive sanctions to the most dangerous offenders, while increasing restrictions and intensity of treatment services as offenders move from minor to serious offenses.[42]

Institutional Programs

Another key to a comprehensive strategy is improving institutional programs. Many experts believe that juvenile incarceration is overused, particularly for nonviolent

© 2004 AP/Wide World Photos

Mentoring is one of many types of interventions that have been used with teens considered to be at high risk for engaging in delinquency. These two teens, juniors at North High School in Evansville, Indiana, are part of a mentor program to help incoming freshman.

Checkpoints

✔ *There are conflicting values in juvenile justice. Some experts want to get tough with young criminals, while others want to focus on rehabilitation.*

✔ *There are distinct differences between the juvenile and adult justice system.*

✔ *The terminology used in juvenile justice is designed to shield kids from stigma.*

✔ *Some state jurisdictions are creating comprehensive juvenile care mechanisms using a variety of treatment programs.*

✔ *Some states are experimenting with peer-run teen courts.*

 To quiz yourself on this material, go to questions 11.18–11.20 on the Juvenile Delinquency: The Core 2e Web site.

offenders. That is why the concept of *deinstitutionalization*—removing as many youths from secure confinement as possible—was established by the Juvenile Justice and Delinquency Act of 1974. Considerable research supports the fact that warehousing juveniles without proper treatment does little to deter criminal behavior. The most effective secure corrections programs are those that provide individual services for a small number of participants.[43]

Alternative Courts

New venues of juvenile justice that provide special services to youth while helping to alleviate the case flow problems that plague overcrowded juvenile courts are being implemented across the United States. For example, as of 2003 there were 285 juvenile **drug courts** (another 110 are in the planning process), with 12,500 juveniles enrolled.[44] These special courts have jurisdiction over the burgeoning number of cases involving substance abuse and trafficking. Although juvenile drug courts operate under a number of different frameworks,[45] the aim is to place nonviolent first offenders into intensive treatment programs rather than in a custodial institution. The following Preventing and Treating Delinquency feature discusses the alternative of **teen courts.** ✔ Checkpoints

FUTURE OF JUVENILE JUSTICE

The future of the juvenile court is now being debated. Some experts, including Barry Feld, believe that over the years the juvenile justice system has taken on more of the characteristics of the adult courts, which he refers to as the "criminalizing" of the juvenile court,[46] or in a more stern admonition has said: "Despite juvenile courts' persisting rehabilitative rhetoric, the reality of *treating* juveniles closely resembles *punishing* adult criminals."[47] Robert Dawson suggests that because the legal differences between the juvenile and criminal systems are narrower than they ever have been, it may be time to abolish the juvenile court.[48]

These concerns reflect the changes that have been ongoing in the juvenile justice system. There has been a nationwide effort to modify the system in response to the public's perceived fear of predatory juvenile offenders and the reaction to high-profile cases such as the Columbine tragedy. As a result, states have begun to institute policies that critics believe undermine the true purpose of the juvenile court

drug courts
Courts whose focus is providing treatment for youths accused of drug-related acts.

teen courts
Courts that make use of peer juries to decide nonserious delinquency cases.

movement.[49] Some have made it easier to waive children to the adult courts. During the 1990s, at least four states lowered the age limit for transfer to adult court—today there are twenty-three states and the District of Columbia where no minimum age is specified (Table 11.3)—seven added crimes, and four added or modified prior-record provisions. As a result, more juvenile offenders are being sentenced as adults and incarcerated in adult prisons.[50]

Getting tough on juvenile crime is the primary motivation for moving cases to the adult criminal justice system.[51] Some commentators argue that waiving juveniles is a statement that juvenile crime is taken seriously by society; others believe the fear of being waived serves as a deterrent.[52] Some states, such as Arizona, have initiated legislation that significantly restricts eligibility for juvenile justice processing and criminalizing acts that heretofore would have fallen under the jurisdiction of the juvenile court. For example, the Arizona legislation provides for the statutory exclusion for fifteen-, sixteen-, and seventeen-year-olds charged with violent crimes or if they had two prior felony adjudications and were charged with any third felony. It also added the provision, "once an adult, always an adult," where, if a juvenile was previously tried and convicted in criminal court, any future offenses involving that juvenile will be tried in adult court.[53] Thirty-three other states also have the once an adult, always an adult provision.[54] While there is no mistaking the intention of this provision—to get tough on juvenile crime—some experts point out that inconsistencies that it created between the two justice systems may have inadvertently also produced a number of legal loopholes.[55]

There is other evidence of this get-tough movement. More states are now permitting juvenile court judges to commit a juvenile to the corrections department for a longer period of time than the court's original jurisdiction, typically to age twenty-one. In recent years, at least five states—Florida, Kansas, Kentucky, Montana, Tennessee—increased the age for extended juvenile court jurisdiction for serious and violent juvenile offenders.[56]

These changes concern juvenile justice advocates such as Hunter Hurst, director of the National Center for Juvenile Justice, who warns:

> How could the wholesale criminalization of children possibly be a wise thing? If their vulnerability to predation in jails and prisons does not destroy them, won't the so-called taint of criminality that they carry with them for the rest of their lives be an impossible social burden for them and us? . . . Have our standards of decency devolved to the point where protection of children is no longer a compelling state interest? In many ways the answer is yes.[57]

The National Research Council and Institute of Medicine's Panel on Juvenile Crime also expressed alarm over an increasingly punitive juvenile justice system and called for a number of changes to uphold the importance of treatment for juveniles. One of their recommendations is particularly noteworthy:

> The federal government should assist the states through federal funding and incentives to reduce the use of secure detention and secure confinement, by developing community-based alternatives. The effectiveness of such programs both for the protection of the community and the benefit of the youth in their charge should be monitored.[58]

Although calling for reforms to the juvenile justice system was a key element of this national panel's final report, panel members were equally, and perhaps more, concerned with the need to prevent delinquency before it occurs and intervene with at-risk children and adolescents. Importantly, there is growing public support for prevention and intervention programs designed to reduce delinquency.[59] The panel also called attention to the need for more rigorous experimentation with prevention and intervention programs with demonstrated success in reducing risk factors associated with delinquency.[60] Some states, like Washington, have begun to incorporate a research-based approach to guide juvenile justice programming and policy.[61]

Teen Courts

To relieve overcrowding and provide an alternative to traditional forms of juvenile courts, jurisdictions across the country are now experimenting with teen courts, also called youth courts. These differ from other juvenile justice programs because young people rather than adults determine the disposition in a case. Cases handled in these courts typically involve young juveniles (ages ten to fifteen) with no prior arrest records who are being charged with minor law violations, such as shoplifting, vandalism, and disorderly conduct. Usually, young offenders are asked to volunteer to have their case heard in a teen court instead of the more formal court of the traditional juvenile justice system.

As in a regular juvenile court, teen court defendants may go through an intake process, a preliminary review of charges, a court hearing, and disposition. In a teen court, however, other young people are responsible for much of the process. Charges may be presented to the court by a fifteen-year-old "prosecutor." Defendants may be represented by a sixteen-year-old "defense attorney." Other youths may serve as jurors, court clerks, and bailiffs. In some teen courts, a youth "judge" (or panel of youth judges) may choose the best disposition or sanction for each case. In a few teen courts, teens even determine whether the facts in a case have been proven by the prosecutor (similar to a finding of guilt). Offenders are often ordered to pay restitution or perform community service. Some teen courts require offenders to write formal apologies to their victims; others require offenders to serve on a subsequent teen court jury. Many courts use other innovative dispositions, such as requiring offenders to attend classes designed to improve their decision-making skills, enhance their awareness of victims, and deter them from future theft.

Though decisions are made by juveniles, adults are also involved in teen courts. They often administer the programs, and they are usually responsible for essential functions such as budgeting, planning, and personnel. In many programs, adults supervise the courtroom activities, and they often coordinate the community service placements where the young offenders work to fulfill the terms of their dispositions. In some programs, adults act as the judges while teens serve as attorneys and jurors.

Proponents of teen court argue that the process takes advantage of one of the most powerful forces in the life of an adolescent—the desire for peer approval and the reaction to peer pressure. According to this argument, youth respond better to prosocial peers than to adult authority figures. Thus, teen courts are seen as a potentially effective alternative to traditional juvenile courts that are staffed with paid professionals such as lawyers, judges, and probation officers. Teen court advocates also point out that the benefits extend beyond defendants. Teen courts may benefit the volunteer youth attorneys and judges, who probably learn more about the legal system than they ever could in a classroom. The presence of a teen court may also encourage the entire community to take a more active role in responding to juvenile crime. In sum, teen courts offer at least four potential benefits:

- *Accountability.* Teen courts may help ensure that young offenders are held accountable for their illegal behavior, even when their offenses are relatively minor and would not likely result in sanctions from the traditional juvenile justice system.
- *Timeliness.* An effective teen court can move young offenders from arrest to sanctions within a matter of days rather than the months that may pass with traditional juvenile courts. This rapid response may increase the positive impact of court sanctions, regardless of their severity.
- *Cost savings.* Teen courts usually depend heavily on youth and adult volunteers. If managed properly, they

Table 11.3	**Minimum Age Specified in Statute for Transferring Juveniles to Adult Court**

Age	State (Total Number)
None	Alaska, Arizona, Delaware, Florida, Georgia, Hawaii, Idaho, Indiana, Maine, Maryland, Montana, Nebraska, Oklahoma, Oregon, Pennsylvania, Rhode Island, South Carolina, South Dakota, Tennessee, Texas, Washington, West Virginia, Wisconsin (23 and the District of Columbia)
10	Kansas, Vermont (2)
12	Colorado, Missouri (2)
13	Illinois, Mississippi, New Hampshire, New York, North Carolina, Wyoming (6)
14	Alabama, Arkansas, California, Connecticut, Iowa, Kentucky, Louisiana, Massachusetts, Michigan, Minnesota, Nevada, New Jersey, North Dakota, Ohio, Utah, Virginia (16)
15	New Mexico (1)

Source: Melissa Sickmund, *Juveniles in Court* (Washington, DC: Office of Juvenile Justice and Delinquency Prevention, U.S. Department of Justice, 2003), p. 9.

may handle a substantial number of offenders at relatively little cost to the community.

■ *Community cohesion.* A well-structured and expansive teen court program may affect the entire community by increasing public appreciation of the legal system, enhancing community-court relationships, encouraging greater respect for the law among youth, and promoting volunteerism among both adults and youths.

The teen court movement is one of the fastest-growing delinquency intervention programs in the country, with more than nine hundred of these courts in operation in forty-six states and the District of Columbia. Recent evaluations of teen courts have found that they did not "widen the net" of justice by handling cases that in the absence of the teen court would have been subject to a lesser level of processing. Also, in the OJJDP Evaluation of Teen Courts Project, which covered four states—Alaska, Arizona, Maryland, and Missouri—and compared five hundred first-time offending youths referred to teen court with five hundred similar youths handled by the regular juvenile justice system, it was found that six-month recidivism rates were lower for those who went through the teen court program in three of the four jurisdictions. Importantly, in these three teen courts, the six-month recidivism rates were under 10 percent. A similar finding was reported in another rigorous evaluation of a teen court in Florida. On the other hand, other recent evaluations of teen courts in Kentucky, New Mexico, and Delaware indicate that short-term recidivism rates range from 25 percent to 30 percent. The conclusions from the OJJDP teen court evaluation may be the best guide for future experimentation with teen courts:

> *Teen courts and youth courts may be preferable to the normal juvenile justice process in jurisdictions that do not, or cannot, provide meaningful sanctions for all young, first-time juvenile offenders. In jurisdictions that do not provide meaningful sanctions and services for these offenders, youth court may still perform just as well as a more traditional, adult-run program.*

CRITICAL THINKING

1. Could teen courts be used to try serious criminal acts such as burglary and robbery?
2. Is a conflict of interest created when teens judge the behavior of other teens? Does the fact that they themselves may one day become defendants in a teen court influence their decision making?

INFOTRAC COLLEGE EDITION RESEARCH

To read more about teen courts, go to InfoTrac College Edition and read Kathiann M. Kowalski, "Courtroom Justice for Teens—by Teens," *Current Health 2,* a *Weekly Reader* publication, *25*(8):29 (April 1999).

Sources: Jeffrey A. Butts and Janeen Buck, "Teen Courts: A Focus on Research," *Juvenile Justice Bulletin October 2000* (Washington, DC: Office of Juvenile Justice and Delinquency Prevention, 2000); Jeffrey A. Butts, "Encouraging Findings from the OJJDP Evaluation," *In Session: Newsletter of the National Youth Court Center 2*(3):1, 7 (Summer 2002); Kevin Minor, James Wells, Irinia Soderstrom, Rachel Bingham, and Deborah Williamson, "Sentence Completion and Recidivism Among Juveniles Referred to Teen Courts," *Crime & Delinquency 45*:467–480 (1999); Paige Harrison, James R. Maupin, and G. Larry Mays, "Teen Court: An Examination of Processes and Outcomes," *Crime & Delinquency 47*:243–264 (2001); Arthur H. Garrison, "An Evaluation of a Delaware Teen Court," *Juvenile and Family Court Journal 52*:11–21 (2001); Anthony P. Logalbo and Charlene M. Callahan, "An Evaluation of a Teen Court as a Juvenile Crime Diversion Program," *Juvenile and Family Court Journal 52*:1–11 (2001); Office of Juvenile Justice and Delinquency Prevention, "September Is First National Youth Court Month," *OJJDP News at a Glance 1*(4):1, 3 (July/August 2002).

In teen courts, which are being used across the country as alternatives to traditional forms of juvenile courts, young people rather than adults determine the disposition in a case. Shown here are members of the teen court at the Marinette County Chamber in Marinette, Wisconsin, along with two adults playing the part of parents of the juvenile offender, demonstrating what happens during a real session of the court.

© 2002 AP/Wide World Photos

THE HISTORY AND DEVELOPMENT OF JUVENILE JUSTICE | **281**

Those who support the juvenile justice concept believe that it is too soon to write off the rehabilitative ideal that has always underpinned the separate treatment of juvenile offenders. They note that fears of a juvenile crime wave are misplaced and that the actions of a few violent children should not mask the needs of millions who can benefit from solicitous treatment rather than harsh punishments. Authors Alida Merlo, Peter Benekos, and William Cook note that a child is more likely to be hit by lightning than shot in a school.[62] And while a get-tough approach may be able to reduce the incidence of some crimes, economic analysis indicates that the costs incurred by placing children in more punitive secure facilities outweigh the benefits accrued in crime reduction.[63]

SUMMARY

1. Urbanization created a growing number of at-risk youth in the nation's cities. The juvenile justice system was established at the turn of the twentieth century after decades of efforts by child-saving groups. These reformers sought to create an independent category of delinquent offender and keep their treatment separate from adults.

2. Over the past four decades, the U.S. Supreme Court and lower courts have granted procedural safeguards and the protection of due process in juvenile courts. Major court decisions have laid down the constitutional requirements for juvenile court proceedings. In years past the protections currently afforded to both adults and children were not available to children.

3. For both violent and property offenses, more than half of all formally processed delinquency cases in 1999 resulted in the youth being adjudicated delinquent.

4. The juvenile justice process consists of a series of steps: the police investigation, the intake procedure in the juvenile court, the pretrial procedures used for juvenile offenders, and the adjudication, disposition, and post-dispositional procedures.

5. There are conflicting values in juvenile justice. Some experts want to get tough with young criminals, while others want to focus on rehabilitation.

6. The adult and juvenile justice systems have a number of key similarities and differences. One of the similarities is the right to receive Miranda warnings; this applies to juveniles as well as adults. One of the differences is that juvenile proceedings are not considered criminal, while adult proceedings are.

7. There has been a movement to toughen the juvenile justice system, and because of this many view the importance of treatment as having been greatly diminished. Proponents of treatment argue that it is best suited to the developmental needs of juveniles. Critics contend that treatment simply serves to mollycoddle juveniles and reduces the deterrent value of the juvenile court.

8. A comprehensive juvenile justice strategy has been developed to preserve the need for treatment services for juveniles while at the same time using appropriate sanctions to hold them accountable for their actions. Elements of this strategy include delinquency prevention, intervention programs, graduated sanctions, improvement of institutional programs, and treating juveniles like adults. New courts, such as drug courts and teen courts, are now in place.

9. Prevention efforts are targeted at children and teens in an effort to prevent the onset of delinquency. Intervention efforts are targeted at children and teens considered at higher risk for delinquency and are designed to ward off involvement in more serious delinquent behavior.

10. The future of the juvenile justice system is in doubt. A number of state jurisdictions are now revising their juvenile codes to restrict eligibility in the juvenile justice system and remove the most serious offenders. At the same time there are some promising signs, such as public support for prevention and intervention programs and some states beginning to incorporate research-based initiatives to guide juvenile justice programming and policy.

KEY TERMS

1. What factors precipitated the development of the Illinois Juvenile Court Act of 1899?

2. One of the most significant reforms in dealing with the juvenile offender was the opening of the New York House of Refuge in 1825. What were the social and judicial consequences of this reform on the juvenile justice system?

3. The child savers have been accused of wanting to control the lives of poor and immigrant children for their own benefit. Are there any parallels to the child-saving movement in modern-day America?

4. Should there be a juvenile justice system, or should juveniles who commit serious crimes be treated as adults while the others are handled by social welfare agencies?

5. The Supreme Court has made a number of major decisions in the area of juvenile justice. What are these decisions? What is their impact on the juvenile justice system?

6. What is the meaning of the term *procedural due process of law*? Explain why and how procedural due process has had an impact on juvenile justice.

7. The formal components of the criminal justice system are often considered to be the police, the court, and the correctional agency. How do these components relate to the major areas of the juvenile justice system? Is the operation of justice similar in the juvenile and adult systems?

8. How would the rehabilitation model and the restorative justice model consider the use of capital punishment as a criminal sanction for first-degree murder by a juvenile offender?

9. What role has the federal government played in the juvenile justice system over the last twenty-five years?

Fourteen-year-old Daphne A., a product of the city's best private schools, lives with her wealthy family in a fashionable neighborhood. Her father is an executive at a local financial services conglomerate and earns close to a million dollars per year. Daphne, however, is always in trouble at school, and teachers report she is impulsive and has poor self-control. At times she can be kind and warm, but on other occasions she is obnoxious, unpredictable, insecure, and demanding of attention. She is overly self-conscious about her body and has a drinking problem.

Despite repeated promises to get her life together, Daphne likes to hang out at night in a local park, drinking with neighborhood kids. On more than one occasion she has gone to the park with her friend Chris G., a quiet boy with his own personal problems. His parents have separated and he is prone to severe anxiety attacks. He has been suspended from school and diagnosed with depression, for which he takes two drugs—an antidepressant and a sedative.

One night, the two met up with Michael M., a forty-four-year-old man with a long history of alcoholism. After a night of drinking, a fight broke out and Michael was stabbed, his throat cut, and his body dumped in a pond. Soon after the attack, Daphne called 911, telling police that a friend "jumped in the lake and didn't come out." Police searched the area and found the slashed and stabbed body in the water; the body had been disemboweled in an attempt to sink it. When the authorities traced the call, Daphne was arrested, and she confessed to police that she had helped Chris murder the victim.

During an interview with court psychiatrists, Daphne admits she participated in the killing but cannot articulate what caused her to get involved. She had been drinking and remembers little of the events. She said she was flirting with Michael and Chris stabbed him in a jealous rage. She speaks in a flat, hollow voice and shows little remorse for her actions. It was a spur-of-the-moment thing, she claims, and after all it was Chris who had the knife and not she. Later, Chris claims that Daphne instigated the fight, egged him on, taunting him that he was too scared to kill someone. Chris says that Daphne, while drunk, often talked of killing an adult because she hates older people, especially her parents.

If Daphne is tried as a juvenile she can be kept in institutions until she is seventeen; the sentence could be expanded to age twenty-one, but only if she is a behavior problem in custody and demonstrates conclusive need for further secure treatment.

- Should the case of Daphne A. be dealt with in the juvenile court, even though the maximum possible sentence she can receive is two to six years? If not, over what kind of cases should the juvenile court have jurisdiction?

- How does the concept of *parens patriae* apply in cases such as that of Daphne A?

- If you believe that the juvenile court is not equipped to handle cases of extremely violent youth, then should it be abolished?

- What reforms must be made in the juvenile justice system to rehabilitate adolescents like Daphne? Or should it even try?

Before you answer these questions, you may want to learn more about this topic by checking out the Web sites of the American Youth Policy Forum, Office of Juvenile Justice and Delinquency Prevention, National Center for Juvenile Justice, National Crime Prevention Council, Fight Crime: Invest in Kids, and Office of the Surgeon General. Click on Web Links under the Chapter Resources at http://cj .wadsworth.com/siegel_jdcore2e.

To research the debate on the most effective strategies to address serious and violent juvenile offending, use "juvenile and violence" in a key word search on InfoTrac College Edition.

Pro/Con discussions and Viewpoint Essays on some of the topics in this chapter may be found at the Opposing Viewpoints Resource Center: www.gale.com/OpposingViewpoints.

Police Work with Juveniles

CHAPTER OBJECTIVES

After reading this chapter you
should:

1. Be able to identify key historical
   events that have shaped juvenile
   policing in America today.

2. Understand key roles and
   responsibilities of the police in
   responding to juvenile offenders.

3. Be able to comment on the
   organization and management of
   police services for juveniles.

4. Be aware of major court cases that
   have influenced police practices.

5. Understand key legal aspects of
   police work, including search and
   seizure and custodial interrogation,
   and how they apply to juveniles.

6. Be able to describe police use
   of discretion and factors that
   influence discretion.

7. Understand the importance of
   police use of discretion with
   juveniles and some of the
   associated problems.

8. Be aware of the major policing
   strategies to prevent delinquency.

9. See the pros and cons of police
   using different delinquency
   prevention strategies.

More than 60 percent of the homicides committed by juveniles involve guns. High-profile shootings in schools, such as when Nathaniel Brazill shot and killed his middle-school English teacher in 2001, accidental shootings involving children, and juvenile gang killings have led to numerous proposals to crack down on guns getting into the hands of kids. Some of these proposals include tougher gun laws and gun safety classes in schools. Police are on the front line in an effort to reduce juvenile gun crimes. Problem-oriented policing strategies, often involving other juvenile justice agencies, targeting juvenile gangs and high gun-crime areas in cities have been implemented across the country. In Boston, a comprehensive police-led strategy to reduce the flow of guns to youths substantially reduced juvenile gun homicides and other gun crimes across the city.

CNN. VIEW THE CNN VIDEO CLIP OF THIS STORY AND ANSWER RELATED CRITICAL THINKING QUESTIONS ON YOUR JUVENILE DELINQUENCY: THE CORE 2E CD.

HISTORY OF JUVENILE POLICING

http:

For a comprehensive history of the London Metropolitan Police from 1829 to 2003, click on Web Links under the Chapter Resources at http://cj.wadsworth.com/siegel_jdcore2e.

Providing specialized police services for juveniles is a relatively recent phenomenon. At one time citizens were responsible for protecting themselves and maintaining order.

The origin of police agencies can be traced to early English society.[1] Before the Norman Conquest, the **pledge system** assumed that neighbors would protect each other from thieves and warring groups. Individuals were entrusted with policing themselves and resolving minor problems. By the thirteenth century, however, the **watch system** was created to police larger communities. Men were organized in church parishes to patrol areas at night and guard against disturbances and breaches of the peace. This was followed by establishment of the constable, who was responsible for dealing with more serious crimes. By the seventeenth century, the constable, the justice of the peace, and the night watchman formed the nucleus of the police system in England.

When the Industrial Revolution brought thousands of people from the countryside to work in factories, the need for police protection increased. As a result, the first organized police force was established in London in 1829. The British "bobbies" (so called after their founder, Sir Robert Peel) were not successful at stopping crime and were influenced by the wealthy for personal and political gain.[2]

In the American colonies, the local sheriff became the most important police official. By the mid-1800s, city police departments had formed in Boston, New York, and Philadelphia. Officers patrolled on foot, and conflicts often arose between untrained officers and the public.

When children violated the law they were often treated the same as adult offenders. But even at this stage a belief existed that the enforcement of criminal law should be applied differently to children. (See chapter 1 for more on the development of the concept of a separate status of childhood in America.)

During the late nineteenth century and into the first half of the twentieth, the problems of how to deal with growing numbers of unemployed and homeless youths increased. Groups such as the Wickersham Commission of 1931 and the International Association of Chiefs of Police became the leading voices for police reform.[3] Their efforts resulted in the creation of specialized police units, known as *delinquency control squads.*

pledge system
Early English system in which neighbors protected each other from thieves and warring groups.

watch system
Replaced the pledge system in England; watchmen patrolled urban areas at night to provide protection from harm.

The most famous police reformer of the 1930s was August Vollmer. As the police chief in Berkeley, California, Vollmer instituted numerous reforms, including university training, modern management techniques, and prevention programs, as well as juvenile aid bureaus.[4] These bureaus were the first organized police services for juvenile offenders.

In the 1960s, policing entered a turbulent period.[5] The U.S. Supreme Court handed down decisions designed to restrict police operations and discretion. Civil unrest produced growing tensions between police and the public. Urban police departments were unable to handle the growing crime rate. Federal funding from the Law Enforcement Assistance Administration (LEAA), an agency set up to fund justice-related programs, was a catalyst for developing hundreds of new police programs and enhancing police services for children. By the 1980s, most urban police departments recognized that the problem of juvenile delinquency required special attention.

Today, the role of the juvenile police officer—an officer assigned to juvenile work—has taken on added importance, particularly with the increase in violent juvenile crime. Most of the nation's urban law enforcement agencies now have specialized juvenile police programs. Typically, such programs involve prevention (police athletic leagues, Project D.A.R.E., community outreach), and law enforcement work (juvenile court, school policing, gang control). Other concerns of the programs include child abuse, domestic violence, and missing children.

POLICE AND JUVENILE OFFENDERS

In the minds of most citizens, the primary responsibility of the police is to protect the public. Based on films, books, and TV shows that depict the derring-do of police officers, the public has obtained an image of crime fighters who always get their man. Since the 1960s, however, the public has become increasingly aware that the reality of police work is substantially different from its fictional glorification. When police departments failed to bring the crime rate down despite massive government subsidies, when citizens complained of civil rights violations, and when tales of police corruption became widespread, it was evident that a crisis was imminent in American policing.

Recently, a new view of policing has emerged among the police themselves. Rather than seeing themselves as crime fighters who track down serious criminals or stop armed robberies in progress, many police departments have adopted the concept that the police role should be to maintain order and be a visible and accessible component of the community. The argument is that police efforts can be successful only when conducted in partnership with concerned citizens. This movement is referred to as **community policing.**[6]

Interest in community policing does not mean that the crime-control model of law enforcement is history. An ongoing effort is being made to improve the crime-fighting capability of police agencies and there are some indications that the effort is paying off. Research indicates that aggressive action by police can help reduce the incidence of repeat offending, and innovations such as computerized fingerprinting systems may bring about greater efficiency.[7] Nonetheless, little evidence exists that adding police or improving their skills has had a major impact on crime-fighting success.

Working with juvenile offenders may be especially challenging for police officers because the desire to help young people and to steer them away from crime seems to conflict with the traditional police duties of crime prevention and maintenance of order. In addition, the police are faced with a nationwide adolescent drug problem and renewed gang activity. Although the need to help troubled youths may conflict with traditional police roles, it fits nicely with the newly emerging community policing models. Improving these relationships is critical because many juveniles do not have a high regard for the police; minority teens are especially critical of police performance.[8] A recent large-scale study carried out to investigate juveniles' attitudes toward police confirmed this long-held finding. While minority teens rated the police less

community policing
Police strategy that emphasizes fear reduction, community organization, and order maintenance rather than crime fighting.

One of the main functions of police is to deter juvenile crime. But in recent decades policing has taken on many new functions, including being a visible and accessible component of the community and working with residents to address delinquency problems. This has come to be known as community policing.

© Cleve Bryant/PhotoEdit

favorably than all other racial groups for all questions asked (for example, "Are police friendly? Are police courteous?"), the most striking racial differences pertained to the question about police honesty: only 15 percent of African-American youths said the police were honest. In contrast, 57 percent of Whites, 51 percent of Asians, 31 percent of Hispanics, and 30 percent of Native Americans said they were.[9]

Police Roles

Juvenile officers operate either as specialists in a police department or as part of the juvenile unit of a police department. Their role is similar to that of officers working with adult offenders: to intervene if the actions of a citizen produce public danger or disorder. Most juvenile officers are appointed after having had some general patrol experience. A desire to work with juveniles as well as an aptitude for the work are considered essential for the job. Officers must also have a thorough knowledge of the law, especially the constitutional protections available to juveniles. Some officers undergo special training in the handling of aggressive or potentially aggressive juveniles.[10]

Most officers regard the violations of juveniles as nonserious unless they are committed by chronic troublemakers or involve significant damage to persons or property. Police encounters with juveniles are generally the result of reports made by citizens, and the bulk of such encounters pertain to matters of minor legal consequence.[11]

Of course, police must also deal with serious juvenile offenders whose criminal acts are similar to those of adults, but these are a small minority of the offender population. Thus, police who deal with delinquency must concentrate on being peacekeepers and crime preventers.[12]

Handling juvenile offenders can produce major **role conflicts** for police. They may experience a tension between their desire to perform what they consider their primary duty, law enforcement, and the need to aid in the rehabilitation of youthful offenders. Police officers' actions in cases involving adults are usually controlled by the law and their own judgment or discretion. (The concept of *discretion* is discussed later in this chapter.) In contrast, a case involving a juvenile often demands that the officer consider the "best interests of the child" and how the officer's actions will influence the child's future well-being. However, in recent years police have become more likely to refer juvenile offenders to courts. It is estimated that 73 percent of all juvenile arrests are referred to juvenile court, while around 20 percent of all juvenile

juvenile officers
Police officers who specialize in dealing with juvenile offenders; they may operate alone or as part of a juvenile police unit in the department.

role conflicts
Conflicts police officers face that revolve around the requirement to perform their primary duty of law enforcement and a desire to aid in rehabilitating youthful offenders.

Juvenile officers operate either as specialists in a police department or as part of the juvenile unit of a police department. Here, officers of the Los Angeles Police Department's Youth Gang Services Unit respond to problems reported in the area.

© Les Stone/Corbis Sygma

arrests are handled informally within the police department or are referred to a community-service agency (Figure 12.1). These informal dispositions are the result of the police officer's discretionary authority.[13]

Police intervention in situations involving juveniles can be difficult and emotional. The officer often encounters hostile behavior from the juvenile offender, as well as agitated witnesses. Overreaction by the officer can result in a violent incident. Even if the officer succeeds in quieting or dispersing the witnesses, they will probably reappear the next day, often in the same place.[14]

Role conflicts are common, because most encounters between police and juveniles are brought about by loitering and rowdiness rather than by serious law violations. Public concern has risen about out-of-control youth. Yet, because of legal constraints and family interference, the police are often limited in the ways in which they can respond to such offenders.[15]

What role should the police play in mediating problems with youths: law enforcer or delinquency prevention worker? The answer may lie somewhere between the two. Most police departments operate juvenile programs that combine law enforcement and delinquency prevention, and the police work with the juvenile court to determine a role most suitable for their community.[16] Police officers may even act as prosecutors in some rural courts when attorneys are not available. Thus, the police role with juveniles extends from the on-the-street encounter to the station house to the courtroom. For juvenile matters involving minor criminal conduct or incorrigible behavior, the police ordinarily select the least restrictive alternative, which includes such measures as temporary assistance or referral to community agencies. In contrast, violent juvenile crime requires that the police arrest youths while providing constitutional safeguards similar to those available for adult offenders.

Police and Violent Juvenile Crime

Violent juvenile offenders are defined as those adjudicated delinquent for crimes of homicide, rape, robbery, aggravated assault, and kidnapping. Juveniles typically account for nearly 20 percent of all violent crime arrests. Though the juvenile violence rate has recently declined, the future is still uncertain. Some experts believe that a surge of violence will occur as the children of baby boomers enter their "prime crime" years. Some experts predict that juvenile arrests for violent crime will double by the year 2010.[17] (See chapter 2 for more on juvenile crime rates).

Figure 12.1   The Police Response to Juvenile Crime

To understand how police deal with juvenile crime, picture a funnel, with the result shown here. For every five hundred juveniles taken into custody, a little more than 70 percent are sent to juvenile court, and around 20 percent are released.

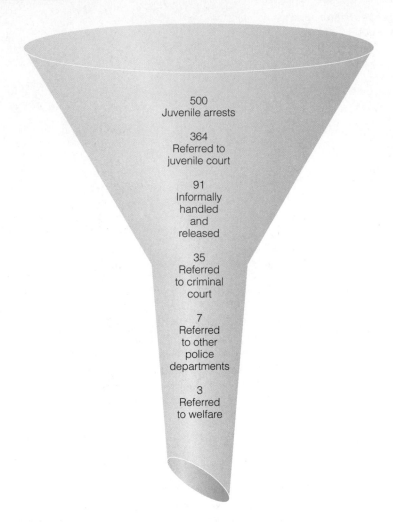

500
Juvenile arrests

364
Referred to
juvenile court

91
Informally
handled
and
released

35
Referred
to criminal
court

7
Referred
to other
police
departments

3
Referred
to welfare

Source: FBI, *Crime in the United States, 2002* (Washington, DC: U.S. Government Printing Office, 2003), Table 68.

Checkpoints

✔ *Modern policing developed in England at the beginning of the nineteenth century.*

✔ *Most modern police agencies have specialized units or officers who interface with teens.*

✔ *Many juvenile cases are handled informally.*

✔ *Police who work with juvenile offenders usually have skills and talents that go beyond those associated with regular police work.*

✔ *The number of police officers assigned to juvenile work has increased in recent years.*

✔ *Most juvenile officers are appointed after they have had some general patrol experience.*

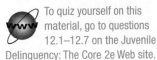 To quiz yourself on this material, go to questions 12.1–12.7 on the Juvenile Delinquency: The Core 2e Web site.

problem-oriented policing
Law enforcement that focuses on addressing the problems underlying incidents of juvenile delinquency rather than the incidents alone.

As a result of these predictions, police and other justice agencies are experimenting with different methods of controlling violent youth. Some of these methods, such as placing more officers on the beat, have existed for decades; others rely on state-of-the-art technology to pinpoint the locations of violent crimes and develop immediate countermeasures. Research shows that there are a number of effective policing practices, including increased directed patrols in street-corner hot spots of crime, proactive arrests of serious repeat offenders, and **problem-oriented policing**.[18] (See Exhibit 12.1 for a complete list of policing practices that work, do not work, or are promising.) These strategies address problems of community disorganization and can be effective deterrents when combined with other laws and policies, such as restricting the possession of firearms.[19] Although many of these policing strategies are not new, implementing them as one element of an overall police plan may have an impact on preventing juvenile violence.

Finally, one key component of any innovative police program dealing with violent juvenile crime is improved communications between the police and the community. Community policing is discussed in more detail at the conclusion of this chapter.

✔ Checkpoints

Exhibit 12.1   Policing Programs That Work

What Works

- Increased directed patrols in street-corner hot spots of crime
- Proactive arrests of serious repeat offenders
- Proactive arrests of drunk drivers
- Arrests of employed suspects for domestic assault

What Does Not Work

- Neighborhood block watch
- Arrests of juveniles for minor offenses
- Arrests of unemployed suspects for domestic assault
- Drug market arrests

- Community policing that is not targeted at risk factors
- Adding extra police in cities with no regard to assignment or activity

What Is Promising

- Police traffic enforcement patrols targeting illegally carried handguns
- Community policing when the community is involved in setting priorities
- Community policing focused on improving police legitimacy
- Warrants for arrest of suspects absent when police respond to domestic violence

Source: Lawrence W. Sherman and John E. Eck, "Policing for Crime Prevention," in Lawrence W. Sherman, David P. Farrington, Brandon C. Welsh, and Doris Layton MacKenzie, eds., *Evidence-Based Crime Prevention* (New York: Routledge, 2002), pp. 321–322.

POLICE AND THE RULE OF LAW

When police are involved with the criminal activity of juvenile offenders, their actions are controlled by statute, constitutional case law, and judicial review. Police methods of investigation and control include the arrest procedure, search and seizure, and custodial interrogation.

The Arrest Procedure

When a juvenile is apprehended, the police must decide whether to release him or her or make a referral to the juvenile court. Cases involving serious crimes against property or persons are often referred to court. Less serious cases, such as disputes between juveniles, petty shoplifting, runaways, and assaults of minors, are often diverted from court action.

Most states require that the law of **arrest** be the same for both adults and juveniles. To make a legal arrest, an officer must have probable cause to believe that an offense took place and that the suspect is the guilty party. **Probable cause** is usually defined as falling somewhere between a mere suspicion and absolute certainty. In misdemeanor cases the police officer must personally observe the crime to place a suspect in custody. For a felony, the police officer may make the arrest without having observed the crime if the officer has probable cause to believe the crime occurred and the person being arrested committed it. A felony is a serious offense; a misdemeanor is a minor or petty crime. Crimes such as murder, rape, and robbery are felonies; crimes such as petty larceny and disturbing the peace are misdemeanors.

The main difference between arrests of adult and juvenile offenders is the broader latitude police have to control youthful behavior. Most juvenile codes, for instance, provide broad authority for the police to take juveniles into custody.[20] Such statutes are designed to give the police the authority to act *in loco parentis* (Latin for "in place of the parent"). Accordingly, the broad power granted to police is consistent with the notion that a juvenile is not arrested but rather taken into custody—which implies a protective rather than a punitive form of detention.[21] Once a juvenile is arrested, however, the constitutional safeguards of the Fourth and Fifth Amendments available to adults are applicable to the juvenile as well.

arrest
Taking a person into the custody of the law to restrain the accused until he or she can be held accountable for the offense in court proceedings.

probable cause
Reasonable ground to believe the existence of facts that an offense was committed and that the accused committed that offense.

Police officers must deal with serious offenders whose violent acts are similar to those of adults, but these are a small minority of the offender population. Here, San Diego Sheriff's deputies lead three of the seven teenage defendants from Juvenile Court in San Diego. The seven San Diego area youths were convicted of attacking several migrant workers. The victims, all men in their 60s, told police that a group of eight to ten young men fired at them with a BB gun, beat them with pipes, and stole money from them at a migrant workers' camp in northern San Diego.

As you may recall, there is currently a trend toward treating juvenile offenders more like adults. Related to this trend are efforts by the police to provide a more legalistic and less informal approach to the arrest process, and a more balanced approach to case disposition.[22]

Search and Seizure

Do juveniles have the same right to be free from unreasonable **search and seizure** as adults? In general, a citizen's privacy is protected by the Fourth Amendment of the Constitution, which states:

> The right of the people to be secure in their persons, houses, papers, and effects, against unreasonable searches and seizures, shall not be violated, and no warrants shall issue, but upon probable cause, supported by oaths or affirmation, and particularly describing the place to be searched, and the persons or things to be seized.[23]

Most courts have held that the Fourth Amendment ban against unreasonable search and seizure applies to juveniles and that illegally seized evidence is inadmissible in a juvenile trial. To exclude incriminating evidence, a juvenile's attorney makes a pretrial motion to suppress the evidence, the same procedure used in the adult criminal process.

A full discussion of search and seizure is beyond the scope of this text, but it is important to note that the Supreme Court has ruled that police may stop a suspect and search for evidence without a warrant under certain circumstances. A person may be searched after a legal arrest, but then only in the immediate area of the suspect's control. For example, after an arrest for possession of drugs, the pockets of a suspect's jacket may be searched;[24] an automobile may be searched if there is probable cause to believe a crime has taken place;[25] a suspect's outer garments may be frisked if police are suspicious of his or her activities;[26] and a search may be conducted if a person volunteers for the search.[27] These rules are usually applied to juveniles as well as to adults. Concept Summary 12.1 reviews when warrantless searches are allowed.

Custodial Interrogation

In years past, police often questioned juveniles without their parents or even an attorney present. Any incriminating statements arising from such **custodial interrogation** could be used at trial. However, in the 1966 *Miranda* case, the Supreme Court placed constitutional limitations on police interrogation procedures with adult offenders. *Miranda* held that persons in police custody must be told the following:

- They have the right to remain silent.
- Any statements they make can be used against them.
- They have the right to counsel.
- If they cannot afford counsel, it will be furnished at public expense.[28]

search and seizure
The U.S. Constitution protects citizens from any search and seizure by police without a lawfully obtained search warrant; such warrants are issued when there is probable cause to believe that an offense has been committed.

custodial interrogation
Questions posed by the police to a suspect held in custody in the prejudicial stage of the juvenile justice process; juveniles have the same rights as adults against self-incrimination when being questioned.

Action	Scope of Search
Stop-and-frisk	Pat-down of a suspect's outer garments.
Search incident to arrest	Full body search after a legal arrest.
Automobile search	If probable cause exists, full search of car, including driver, passengers, and closed containers found in trunk. Search must be reasonable.
Consent search	Warrantless search of person or place is justified if suspect knowingly and voluntarily consents to search.
Plain view	Suspicious objects seen in plain view can be seized without a warrant.
Electronic surveillance	Material can be seized electronically without a warrant if suspect has no expectation of privacy.

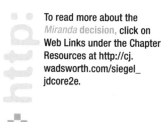

To read more about the *Miranda* decision, **click on Web Links under the Chapter Resources at http://cj.wadsworth.com/siegel_jdcore2e.**

The ***Miranda* warning** has been made applicable to children taken into custody. The Supreme Court case of *in re Gault* stated that constitutional privileges against self-incrimination are applicable in juvenile cases too. Because *in re Gault* implies that *Miranda* applies to custodial interrogation in criminal procedure, state court jurisdictions apply the requirements of *Miranda* to juvenile proceedings as well. Since the *Gault* decision in 1967, virtually all courts that have ruled on the question of the *Miranda* warning have concluded that the warning does apply to the juvenile process.

One problem associated with custodial interrogation of juveniles has to do with waiver of *Miranda* rights: Under what circumstances can juveniles knowingly and willingly waive the rights given them by *Miranda v. Arizona*? Does a youngster, acting alone, have sufficient maturity to appreciate the right to remain silent?

Most courts have concluded that parents or attorneys need not be present for children effectively to waive their rights.[29] In a frequently cited California case, *People v. Lara*, the court said that the question of a child's waiver is to be determined by the *totality of the circumstances doctrine*.[30] This means that the validity of the waiver rests

A teen in Los Angeles in police custody hopes that the officers will release him with a warning. His friends are also concerned about their futures. Police have discretion to take formal action against youthful offenders or to release them with a warning or take some other informal action.

Miranda warning
Supreme Court decisions require police officers to inform individuals under arrest of their constitutional rights; warnings must also be given when suspicion begins to focus on an individual in the accusatory stage.

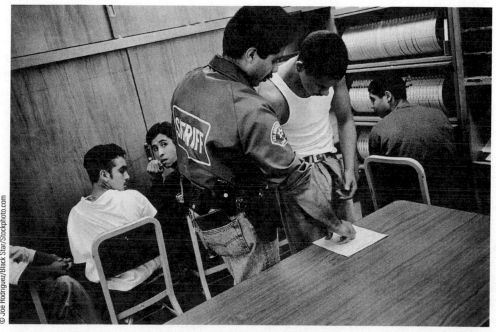

© Joe Rodriguez/Black Star/Stockphoto.com

not only on the age of the child but also on a combination of other factors, including the child's education, the child's knowledge of the charge, whether the child was allowed to consult with family or friends, and the method of interrogation.[31]

The waiver of *Miranda* rights by a juvenile is one of the most controversial legal issues addressed in the state courts. It has also been the subject of federal constitutional review. In two cases, *Fare v. Michael C.* and *California v. Prysock,* the Supreme Court has attempted to clarify children's rights when they are interrogated by the police. In *Fare v. Michael C.,* the Court ruled that a child's asking to speak to his probation officer was not the equivalent of asking for an attorney; consequently, statements he made to the police absent legal counsel were admissible in court.[32] In *California v. Prysock,* the Court was asked to rule on the adequacy of a *Miranda* warning given Randall Prysock, a young murder suspect.[33] After reviewing the taped exchange between the police interrogator and the boy, the Court upheld Prysock's conviction when it ruled that even though the *Miranda* warning was given in slightly different language and out of exact context, its meaning was easily understandable, even to a juvenile.

Taken together, *Fare* and *Prysock* make it seem indisputable that juveniles are at least entitled to receive the same *Miranda* rights as adults. *Miranda v. Arizona* is a historic decision that continues to protect the rights of all suspects placed in custody.[34]

DISCRETIONARY JUSTICE

To read about trends in juvenile arrests, click on Web Links under the Chapter Resources at http://cj. wadsworth.com/siegel_ jdcore2e.

Today, juvenile offenders receive nearly as much procedural protection as adult offenders. However, the police have broader authority in dealing with juveniles than with adults. Granting such **discretion** to juvenile officers raises some important questions: Under what circumstances should an officer arrest status offenders? Should a summons be used in lieu of arrest? Under what conditions should a juvenile be taken into protective custody?

When police confront a case involving a juvenile offender, they rely on their discretion to choose an appropriate course of action. *Police discretion* is selective enforcement of the law by authorized police agents. Discretion gives officers a choice among possible courses of action within the limits on their power.[35] It is a prime example of low-visibility decision making, or decisions by public officials that the public is not in a position to regulate or criticize.[36]

Much discretion is exercised in juvenile work because of the informality that has been built into the system in an attempt to individualize justice.[37] Furthermore, officials in the juvenile justice system make decisions about children that often are without oversight or review. The daily procedures of juvenile personnel are rarely subject to judicial review, except when they clearly violate a youth's constitutional rights. As a result, discretion sometimes deteriorates into discrimination and other abuses on the part of the police. The real danger in discretion is that it allows the law to discriminate against precisely those elements in the population—the poor, the ignorant, the unpopular—who are least able to draw attention to their plight.[38]

The problem of discretion in juvenile justice is one of extremes. Too little discretion provides insufficient flexibility to treat juvenile offenders as individuals. Too much discretion can lead to injustice. Guidelines and controls are needed to structure the use of discretion.

Generally, the first contact a youth has with the juvenile justice system is with the police. Research indicates that most police decisions arising from this initial contact involve discretion.[39] These studies show that many juvenile offenders are never referred to juvenile court.

In a classic 1963 study, Nathan Goldman examined the arrest records of more than a thousand juveniles from four communities in Pennsylvania.[40] He concluded that more than 64 percent of police contacts with juveniles were handled informally. Subsequent research offered additional evidence of informal disposition of juvenile cases.[41] For example, in the 1970s, Paul Strasburg found that about 50 percent of all

discretion
Use of personal decision making and choice in carrying out operations in the criminal justice system, such as deciding whether to make an arrest or accept a plea bargain.

children who come in contact with the police do not get past the initial stage of the juvenile justice process.[42]

A recent study analyzed juvenile data collected as part of the Project on Policing Neighborhoods—a comprehensive study of police patrols in Indianapolis, Indiana, and St. Petersburg, Florida. This study indicated that police still use discretion.[43] It found that 13 percent of police encounters with juveniles resulted in arrest.[44] As shown in Table 12.1, the most likely disposition of police encounters with juveniles is a command or threat to arrest (38 percent), and the second most likely is search or interrogation of the suspects (24 percent).

After arrest, the most current data show an increase in the number of cases referred to the juvenile court. The FBI estimates that almost three-quarters of all juvenile arrests are referred to juvenile court.[45] Despite the variations between the estimates, these studies indicate that the police use significant discretion in their decisions regarding juvenile offenders. Research shows that differential decision making goes on without clear guidance.

If all police officers acted in a fair and just manner, the seriousness of the crime, the situation in which it occurred, and the legal record of the juvenile would be the factors that affected their decision making. Research does show that police are much more likely to take formal action if the crime is serious and has been reported by a victim who is a respected member of the community, and if the offender is well known to them.[46] However, there are other factors that are believed to shape police discretion; they are discussed next.

Environmental Factors

How does a police officer decide what to do with a juvenile offender? The norms of the community affect the decision. Some officers work in communities that tolerate a fair amount of personal freedom. In liberal environments, the police may be inclined to release juveniles rather than arrest them. Other officers work in conservative communities that expect a no-nonsense approach to police enforcement. Here, police may be more inclined to arrest a juvenile.

Police officers may be influenced by their perception of community alternatives to police intervention. Some officers may make an arrest because they believe nothing else can be done.[47] Others may favor referring juveniles to social service agencies, particularly if they believe the community has a variety of good resources. These referrals save time and effort, records do not have to be filled out, and court appearances can be avoided. The availability of such options allows for greater latitude in police decision making.[48]

Police Policy

The policies and customs of the local police department also influence decisions. Juvenile officers may be pressured to make more arrests or to refrain from making

Table 12.1 Disposition of Police Encounters with Juveniles

Disposition	Juveniles (%)
Release	14
Advise	11
Search/interrogate	24
Command/threaten	38
Arrest	13

Source: Robert E. Worden and Stephanie M. Myers, *Police Encounters with Juvenile Suspects* (Albany: Hindelang Criminal Justice Research Center and School of Criminal Justice, State University of New York, 2001), Table 3.

arrests under certain circumstances. Directives instruct officers to be alert to certain types of juvenile violations. The chief of police might initiate policies governing the arrest practices of the juvenile department. For example, if local merchants complain that youths congregating in a shopping center parking lot are inhibiting business, police may be called on to make arrests. Under other circumstances, an informal warning might be given. Similarly, a rash of deaths caused by teenage drunk driving may galvanize the local media to demand police action. The mayor and the police chief, sensitive to possible voter dissatisfaction, may then demand that formal police action be taken in cases of drunk driving.

Another source of influence is pressure from supervisors. Some supervising officers may believe it is important to curtail disorderly conduct or drug use. In addition, officers may be influenced by the discretionary decisions made by their peers.

Situational Factors

In addition to the environment, a variety of situational factors affect a police officer's decisions. Situational factors are those attached to a particular crime, such as specific traits of offenders. Traditionally, it was believed that police officers relied heavily on the demeanor and appearance of the juvenile in making decisions. Some research shows that the decision to arrest is often based on factors such as dress, attitude, speech, and level of hostility toward the police.[49] Kids who displayed "attitude" were believed to be the ones more likely to be arrested than those who were respectful and contrite.[50] However, more recent research has challenged the influence of demeanor on police decision making, suggesting that it is delinquent behavior and actions that occur during police detention that influence the police decision to take formal action.[51] For example, a person who struggles or touches police during a confrontation is a likely candidate for arrest, but those who merely sport a bad attitude or negative demeanor are as likely to suffer an arrest as the polite and contrite.[52] It is possible that the earlier research reflected a time when police officers demanded absolute respect and were quick to take action when their authority was challenged. The more recent research may indicate that police, through training or experience, are now less sensitive to slights and confrontational behavior and view them as just part of the job. Most studies conclude that the following variables are important in the police discretionary process:

- The attitude of the complainant
- The type and seriousness of the offense
- The race, sex, and age of the offender
- The attitude of the offender
- The offender's prior contacts with the police
- The perceived willingness of the parents to assist in solving the problem (in the case of a child)
- The setting or location in which the incident occurs
- Whether the offender denies the actions or insists on a court hearing (in the case of a child)
- The likelihood that a child can be served by an agency in the community[53]

Bias and Police Discretion

Do police allow bias to affect their decisions on whether to arrest youths? Do they routinely use "racial profiling" when they decide to make an arrest? A great deal of debate has been generated over this issue. Some experts believe that police decision making is deeply influenced by the offender's personal characteristics, whereas others maintain that crime-related variables are more significant.

When a juvenile commits a crime, police have the authority to investigate the incident and decide whether to release the child or place him under arrest. This is often a discretionary decision based not only on the nature of the offense but also on such factors as the seriousness of the crime, the child's past record, and whether the victim wishes to press charges, as well as the behavior of the juvenile. Those who struggle or fight the police during a confrontation are likely to be arrested; those who merely have bad or negative attitudes are as likely to be arrested as the polite and contrite.

© Michael A. Dwyer/Stock, Boston

To read about what is being done to reduce racial profiling, click on Web Links under the Chapter Resources at http://cj.wadsworth.com/siegel_jdcore2e.

Racial Bias   It has long been charged that police are more likely to act formally with African-American suspects and use their discretion to benefit Whites.[54] In the context of traffic stops by police, the phrase "Driving While Black" has been coined to refer to the repeated findings of many studies that African-American drivers are disproportionately stopped by police and that race is the primary reason for this practice.[55] African-American youth are arrested at a rate disproportionate to their representation in the population (compare Table 12.2 to the data on page 34). Research on this issue has yielded mixed conclusions. One view is that, although discrimination may have existed in the past, there is no longer a need to worry about racial discrimination because minorities now possess sufficient political status to protect them within the justice system.[56] As Harvard University law professor Randall Kennedy forcefully argues, even if a law enforcement policy exists that disproportionately affects African-American suspects, it might be justified as a "public good" because law-abiding African Americans are statistically more often victims of crimes committed by other African Americans.[57]

Table 12.2   **African-American Representation in Arrest Statistics**

Most Serious Offense	African-American Juvenile Arrests in 2002 (%)
Murder	50
Forcible rape	34
Robbery	54
Aggravated assault	34
Burglary	28
Larceny/theft	29
Motor vehicle theft	37
Weapons	36
Drug abuse violations	33
Curfew and loitering	29
Runaways	18

Note: Percentage is of all juvenile arrests.

Source: FBI, *Crime in the United States, 2002* (Washington, DC: U.S. Government Printing Office, 2003), Table 43.

In contrast to these views, several research efforts do show evidence of police discrimination against African-American youths.[58] Donna Bishop and Charles Frazier found that race can have a direct effect on decisions made at several junctures of the juvenile justice process.[59] According to Bishop and Frazier, African Americans are more likely than Whites to be recommended for formal processing, referred to court, adjudicated delinquent, and given harsher dispositions for comparable offenses. In the arrest category, specifically, being African American increases the probability of formal police action.[60]

Similarly, a study by the National Council on Crime and Delinquency revealed significant overrepresentation by Black youths at every point in the California juvenile justice system. Although they make up less than 9 percent of the state youth population, Black youths accounted for 19 percent of juvenile arrests. According to the study, the causes for the disparity included institutional racism, environmental factors, family dysfunction, cultural barriers, and school failure.[61] (For more on racial bias, see chapter 2.)

Gender Bias   Is there a difference between police treatment of male and female offenders? Some experts favor the *chivalry hypothesis,* which holds that police are likely to act paternally toward young girls and not arrest them. Others believe that police may be more likely to arrest female offenders because their actions violate officers' stereotypes of the female.

There is some research support for various forms of gender bias. The nature of this bias may vary according to the seriousness of the offense and the age of the offender. Studies offer a variety of conclusions, but there seems to be general agreement that police are less likely to process females for delinquent acts and that they discriminate against them by arresting them for status offenses. Examples of the conclusions reached by some of these studies follow:

- Police tend to be more lenient toward females than males with regard to acts of delinquency. Merry Morash found that boys who engage in "typical male" delinquent activities are much more likely to develop police records than females.[62]
- Females who have committed minor or status offenses seem to be referred to juvenile court more often than males. Meda Chesney-Lind has found that adolescent female status offenders are arrested for less serious offenses than boys.[63]
- Recent evidence has confirmed earlier studies showing that the police, and most likely the courts, apply a double standard in dealing with male and female juvenile offenders. Bishop and Frazier found that both female status offenders and male delinquents are differently disadvantaged in the juvenile justice system.[64]

In sum, there appears to be general agreement that police are less likely to process females for delinquent acts and that they discriminate against them by arresting them for status offenses. (Gender bias is discussed in more detail in chapter 6.)

Organizational Bias   The policies of some police departments may result in biased practices. Research has found that police departments can be characterized by their professionalism (skills and knowledge) and bureaucratization.[65] Departments that are highly bureaucratized (with a high emphasis on rules and regulations) and at the same time unprofessional are most likely to be insulated from the communities they serve. Organizational policy may be influenced by the perceptions of police decision makers. A number of experts have found that law enforcement administrators have a stereotyped view of the urban poor as troublemakers who must be kept under control.[66] Consequently, lower-class neighborhoods experience much greater police scrutiny than middle-class areas, and their residents face a proportionately greater chance of arrest. For example, there is a significant body of literature that shows that police are more likely to "hassle" or arrest African-American males in

Checkpoints

✔ *Most states require that the law of arrest be the same for both adults and juveniles.*

✔ *The main difference between arrests of adult and juvenile offenders is the broader latitude police have to control youthful behavior.*

✔ *Most courts have held that the Fourth Amendment ban against unreasonable search and seizure applies to juveniles.*

✔ *Most courts have concluded that parents or attorneys need not be present for children effectively to waive their right to remain silent.*

✔ *The police have broader authority in dealing with juveniles than in dealing with adults.*

✔ *A great deal of discretion is exercised in juvenile work because of the informality that has been built into the system.*

✔ *It has long been charged that police are more likely to act formally with African-American youth and use their discretion to benefit White adolescents.*

✔ *Police tend to be more lenient toward females than males with regard to acts of delinquency, but more restrictive with status offenses.*

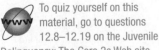 To quiz yourself on this material, go to questions 12.8–12.19 on the Juvenile Delinquency: The Core 2e Web site.

poor neighborhoods.[67] It is therefore not surprising, as criminologist Robert Sampson has found, that teenage residents of neighborhoods with low socioeconomic status have a significantly greater chance of acquiring police records than youths living in higher socioeconomic areas, regardless of the actual crime rates in these areas.[68] Sampson's research indicates that, although police officers may not discriminate on an individual level, departmental policy that focuses on lower-class areas may result in class and racial bias in the police processing of delinquent youth.

Not all experts believe there is rampant police organizational bias. For example, when Ronald Weitzer surveyed people in three Washington, D.C., neighborhoods, he found that residents in primarily African-American neighborhoods value racially integrated police services.[69] Similarly, Thomas Priest and Deborah Brown Carter have found that the African-American community is supportive of the local police, especially when they respond quickly to calls for service. It is unlikely that African Americans would appreciate rapid service, or the presence of White officers, if police routinely practiced racial discrimination.[70]

In summary, the policies, practices, and customs of the local police department influence discretion. Conditions vary from department to department and depend on the judgment of the chief and others in the organizational hierarchy. Because the police retain a large degree of discretionary power, the ideal of nondiscrimination is often difficult to achieve in practice. However, policies to limit police discretion can help eliminate bias. ✔ Checkpoints

POLICE WORK AND DELINQUENCY PREVENTION

Police have taken the lead in delinquency prevention. They have used a number of strategies: some rely on their deterrent powers; others rely on their relationship with schools, the community, and other juvenile justice agencies; and others rely on a problem-solving model. Concept Summary 12.2 lists the main police strategies to prevent delinquency.

Aggressive Law Enforcement

One method of contemporary delinquency prevention relies on aggressive patrolling targeted at specific patterns of delinquency. Police departments in Chicago and Los Angeles have at one time used *saturation patrol*, targeting gang areas and arresting members for any law violations. These tactics have not proven to be effective against gangs. For example, in 1996 the Dallas Police Department initiated a successful gang-control effort that employed such tactics as saturating known gang areas with anti-gang units as well as making aggressive enforcement of curfew and truancy laws. Targeting truancy and curfew laws led to a significant reduction in gang activity, but the saturation patrols proved ineffective.[71]

Concept Summary **Police Strategies to Prevent Delinquency**

Strategy	Scope
Aggressive law enforcement	High visibility; make arrests for minor and serious infractions.
Police in schools	Collaborate with school staff to create a safer school environment and develop programs.
Community policing	Engage citizens and community-based organizations.
Problem-oriented policing	Focus on problems underlying criminal incidents; often engage community and other juvenile justice agencies.

In response to youth gang violence and other serious juvenile crimes, police departments in many large and medium-size cities across the country have experimented with what has come to be known as aggressive law enforcement tactics. This can include targeting gang areas and arresting members for any law violations. Here, an officer of the Des Moines (Iowa) Police Department's Gang Unit questions two suspected gang members after pulling them over for not wearing seat belts.

You can visit G.R.E.A.T.'s Web site by clicking on Web Links under the Chapter Resources at http://cj.wadsworth.com/siegel_jdcore2e.

Police in Schools

One of the most important institutions playing a role in delinquency prevention is the school (see chapter 9). In schools cross the country, there are almost fourteen thousand full-time police working as school resource officers. In addition to helping to make the school environment safe for students and teachers, school resource officers work closely with staff and administrators in developing delinquency prevention programs.[72] For example, these officers and liaison officers from schools and police departments have played a leadership role in developing recreational programs for juveniles. In some instances, police have actually operated such programs. In others, they have encouraged community support for recreational activities, including Little League baseball, athletic clubs, camping outings, and police athletic and scouting programs.

The Gang Resistance Education and Training (G.R.E.A.T.) program is one example of a police and school partnership to prevent delinquency. Modeled after D.A.R.E. (Drug Abuse and Resistance Education; see chapter 10), G.R.E.A.T. was developed among a number of Arizona police departments in an effort to reduce adolescent involvement in criminal behavior. Today the program is in school curricula in all fifty states and the District of Columbia.[73] The program has two main objectives: to reduce gang activity and to teach students about the negative consequences of becoming involved in a gang. Trained police officers administer the program in school classrooms about once a week. The program, which is designed for middle-school students, comprises eight main lessons that help students to learn about the impact of crime on victims, cultural sensitivity, responsibility, and establishing prosocial goals.

Evaluations of G.R.E.A.T. show mixed results in reducing delinquency and gang involvement. One evaluation found that students who complete the curriculum develop more prosocial attitudes and have lower rates of gang membership and delinquency than those in a comparison group who were not exposed to G.R.E.A.T.[74] A more recent evaluation of the program, four years after students completed the curriculum, did not find any significant differences for gang membership or delinquency compared with a control group. The evaluation did find that those who took the program held more prosocial attitudes than those who did not.[75]

Another example of police working in close collaboration with schools is the Community Outreach Through Police in Schools Program. This program brings together Yale University's Child Study Center and the New Haven Police Department to address the mental health and emotional needs of middle-school students who have been exposed to violence in the community. Specifically, the program aims to help these students:

- Better understand the way their feelings affect their behavior.
- Develop constructive means of responding to violence and trauma.
- Change their attitudes toward police and how to seek help in their community.[76]

An evaluation of the program found that students benefited from it in a number of ways, including improved emotional and psychological functioning (for example, feeling less nervous, having fewer thoughts of death), as well as improved attitudes toward and relationships with the police.[77] The accompanying What Does This Mean to Me? feature offers another perspective on police in schools.

Community Policing

One of the most important changes in U.S. law enforcement is the emergence of the community policing model of delinquency prevention. This concept is based on the premise that the police can carry out their duties more effectively if they gain the trust and assistance of concerned citizens. Under this model, the main police role should be to increase feelings of community safety and encourage area residents to cooperate with their local police agencies.[78]

The community policing model has been translated into a number of policy initiatives. It has encouraged police departments to get officers out of patrol cars, where they were insulated from the community, and onto the streets via foot or bicycle patrol.[79] A recent survey of policing in the United States—the Law Enforcement Management and Administrative Statistics (LEMAS) survey—reports that two-thirds (66 percent) of local police departments, employing 86 percent of all officers, had full-time community policing officers. Across the country, local police departments employ about 103,000 community policing officers.[80]

One community policing program, the Youth Firearms Violence Initiative (YFVI) of the federal Office of Community Oriented Policing Services (COPS), which is running in ten cities across the United States, aims to reduce juvenile gun violence. Each city was provided with up to $1 million to pay for interventions that incorporated community policing strategies. The strategies include these:

- Working in partnership with other city agencies to promote education, prevention, and intervention programs related to handguns and their safety
- Developing community-based programs focused on youth handgun violence
- Developing programs involving and assisting families in addressing youth handgun problems[81]

To learn about other community policing programs, click on Web Links under the Chapter Resources at http://cj.wadsworth.com/siegel_jdcore2e.

The YFVI programs also include some traditional law enforcement measures, such as the setup of new enforcement units within the police department and standard surveillance and intelligence-gathering techniques. An evaluation of the YFVI was conducted in all ten cities, but in only five cities (Baltimore; Cleveland; Inglewood, California; Salinas, California; and San Antonio) was program effectiveness in reducing gun violence measured. Police-reported gun crimes were reduced in each of the five cities and in every target area of the cities with the exception of one area in Baltimore.[82]

Problem-Oriented Policing

Also referred to as *problem-solving policing,* problem-oriented policing involves a systematic analysis and response to the problems or conditions underlying criminal incidents rather than the incidents themselves.[83] The theory is that by attending to the underlying problems that cause criminal incidents, the police will have a greater chance of preventing the crimes from recurring—the main problem with reactive or "incident-driving policing."[84] However, as noted by Harvard criminologist Mark Moore, "This is not the same as seeking out the root causes of the crime problem in general. It is a much shallower, more situational approach."[85]

The systematic nature of problem-oriented policing is characterized by its adherence to a four-step model, often referred to as S.A.R.A., which stands for *S*canning, *A*nalysis, *R*esponse, and *A*ssessment. Descriptions of the four steps are as follows:

1. *Scanning* involves identifying a specific crime problem through various data sources (for example, victim surveys, 911 calls).

2. *Analysis* involves carrying out an in-depth analysis of the crime problem and its underlying causes.

3. *Response* brings together the police and other partners to develop and implement a response to the problem based on the results produced in the analysis stage.

4. *Assessment* is the stage in which the response to the problem is evaluated.[86]

Like community policing, problem-oriented policing is viewed as a proactive delinquency prevention strategy. Unlike community policing, however, the engagement of the community in problem-oriented policing is not imperative, but more often than not these operations involve close collaborations with the community. Collaborations with other juvenile justice agencies are also common in problem-oriented policing operations.

As you may recall, problem-oriented policing has been shown to be effective in reducing juvenile delinquency in some circumstances. One of the most successful applications of this policing strategy is Boston's Operation Ceasefire, which is the subject of this chapter's Preventing and Treating Delinquency feature.

Following on the success of the Boston program, the Office of Juvenile Justice and Delinquency Prevention (OJJDP) launched a comprehensive initiative to reduce juvenile gun violence in four other cities (Baton Rouge and Shreveport, Louisiana; Oakland, California; and Syracuse, New York). Called the Partnerships to Reduce Juvenile Gun Violence Program, problem-oriented policing strategies are at the center of the program, but other intervention strategies are also important. These include specific delinquency prevention strategies (job training and mentoring), juvenile justice sanctions, and a public information campaign designed to communicate the dangers and consequences of gun violence to juveniles, families, and community residents.[87] An evaluation of the implementation of the program found that three of the four cities were successful in developing comprehensive strategies.[88] An evaluation of the effectiveness of the program in reducing juvenile gun violence is under way.[89] With successful implementation and inclusion of many of the components of the Boston program, this program offers promise.

Around the same time in the late 1990s, the federal COPS office initiated a national Problem-Solving Partnerships (PSP) program with the objective of assisting police agencies to "solve recurrent crime and disorder problems by helping them form community partnerships and engage in problem-solving activities."[90] Various case studies to emerge out of a national evaluation of this program by the Police Executive Research Forum identify a wide range of successful efforts to reduce delinquency.[91]

Today, many experts consider delinquency prevention efforts to be crucial to the development of a comprehensive approach to youth crime. Although such efforts cut across the entire juvenile justice system, police programs have become increasingly popular. ✔ Checkpoints

Checkpoints

✔ Police departments have used aggressive saturation patrol, targeting gang areas and arresting members for any law violations.

✔ Prevention programs between the police and the schools have been implemented in many communities.

✔ Police are now identifying the needs of youth in the community and helping the community meet those needs.

✔ Problem-oriented or problem-solving policing, which very often involves community groups and other juvenile justice agencies, is an innovative and successful approach to preventing delinquency.

✔ Many experts consider police-based delinquency prevention efforts to be crucial to the development of a comprehensive approach to youth crime.

 To quiz yourself on this material, go to question 12.20 on the Juvenile Delinquency: The Core 2e Web site.

Boston's Operation Ceasefire

One of the most successful examples of problem-oriented policing focused on reducing juvenile crime and violence is the program known as Operation Ceasefire. Implemented in Boston, this program aims to reduce youth homicide victimization and youth gun violence. Although it is a police-led program, Operation Ceasefire involves many other juvenile and criminal justice and social agencies, including probation and parole, the Bureau of Alcohol, Tobacco and Firearms (ATF), gang outreach and prevention streetworkers, and the Drug Enforcement Administration (DEA). This group of agencies has become known as the Ceasefire Working Group.

The program has two main elements:

1. A direct law enforcement focus on illicit gun traffickers who supply youth with guns
2. An attempt to generate a strong deterrent to gang violence

A wide range of measures have been used to reduce the flow of guns to youth, including pooling the resources of local, state, and federal justice authorities to track and seize illegal guns and targeting traffickers of the types of guns most used by gang members. The response to gang violence has been to pull every deterrence "lever" available, including shutting down drug markets, serving warrants, enforcing probation restrictions, and making disorder arrests. The Ceasefire Working Group delivered its message clearly to gang members: "We're ready, we're watching, we're waiting: Who wants to be next?"

An evaluation from before the program started to the time it ended showed a 63 percent reduction in the mean monthly number of youth homicide victims across the city. The program was also associated with significant decreases in the mean monthly number of gun assaults and overall gang violence across the city. In a comparison with other New England cities and large cities across the United States, most of which also experienced a reduction in youth homicides over the same period, it was found that the significant reduction in youth homicides in Boston was due to Operation Ceasefire.

Maintaining the level of intensity of this program and the cooperation of the many agencies involved, which are essential ingredients of its success, has not been easy. In recent years, there have been cutbacks in local policing, fewer federal criminal justice resources made available to the program, and a perception that the deterrence strategy is no longer focused on the most dangerous suspects. Recent research suggests that in order for the program to maintain its success it will also have to adapt to changes in the nature of gang and youth violence across the city.

While the city of Boston works to improve its program, similar problem-oriented policing programs have been established in cities across the country. Of great interest is the replication of this program in an area of Los Angeles that suffers from exceptionally high rates of juvenile violence. The implementation of this program shows much promise, and an evaluation of the program is planned.

CRITICAL THINKING

1. What is the importance of having a multidisciplinary team as part of the program?
2. With comprehensive programs it is often difficult to assess the independent effects of the different program elements. In your opinion, what is the most important element of this program? Why?

INFOTRAC COLLEGE EDITION RESEARCH

For more information on problem-oriented policing and juvenile delinquency, go to InfoTrac College Edition and read Terry Eisenberg and Bruce Glasscock, "Looking Inward with Problem-Oriented Policing," *FBI Law Enforcement Bulletin 70*:1 (July 2001).

Sources: Anthony A. Braga, *Problem-Oriented Policing and Crime Prevention* (Monsey, NY: Criminal Justice Press, 2002); Anthony A. Braga, David M. Kennedy, Elin J. Waring, and Anne Morrison Piehl, "Problem-Oriented Policing, Deterrence, and Youth Violence: An Evaluation of Boston's Operation Ceasefire," *Journal of Research in Crime and Delinquency 38*:195–225 (2001); Fox Butterfield, "Killing of Girl, 10, and Increase in Homicides Challenge Boston's Crime Fighting Model," *New York Times,* 14 July 2002; David M. Kennedy, Anthony A. Braga, and Anne Morrison Piehl, "Developing and Implementing Operation Ceasefire," in *Reducing Gun Violence: The Boston Gun Project's Operation Ceasefire.* Research report (Washington, DC: National Institute of Justice, 2001); David M. Kennedy, "Pulling Levers: Chronic Offenders, High-Crime Settings, and a Theory of Prevention," *Valparaiso University Law Review 31*:449–484 (1997); David M. Kennedy, "Pulling Levers: Getting Deterrence Right," *National Institute of Justice Journal,* July 1998, pp. 2–8; Jack McDevitt, Anthony A. Braga, Dana Nurge, and Michael Buerger, "Boston's Youth Violence Prevention Program: A Comprehensive Community-Wide Approach," in Scott H. Decker, ed., *Policing Gangs and Youth Violence* (Belmont, CA: Wadsworth, 2003); George Tita, K. Jack Riley, and Peter Greenwood, "From Boston to Boyle Heights: The Process and Prospects of a 'Pulling Levers' Strategy in a Los Angeles Barrio," in Scott H. Decker, ed., *Policing Gangs and Youth Violence* (Belmont, CA: Wadsworth, 2003).

SUMMARY

- Modern policing developed in England at the beginning of the nineteenth century. The Industrial Revolution, recognition of the need to treat children as a distinguishable group, and growing numbers of unemployed and homeless youths were among some of the key events that helped shape juvenile policing in America.
- The role of juvenile officers is similar to that of officers working with adult offenders: to intervene if the

actions of a citizen produce public danger or disorder. Juvenile officers must also have a thorough knowledge of the law, especially the constitutional protections available to juveniles.

- Juvenile officers operate either as specialists in a police department or as part of the juvenile unit of a police department.
- Through the *Miranda v. Arizona* decision, the U.S. Supreme Court established a clearly defined procedure for custodial interrogation.
- Most courts have held that the Fourth Amendment ban against unreasonable search and seizure applies to juveniles and that illegally seized evidence is inadmissible in a juvenile trial. Most courts have concluded that parents or attorneys need not be present for children effectively to waive their right to remain silent.
- Discretion is a low-visibility decision made in the administration of adult and juvenile justice. Discretionary decisions are made without guidelines from the police administrator. Numerous factors influence the decisions police make about juvenile offenders, including the seriousness of the offense, the harm inflicted on the victim, and the likelihood that the juvenile will break the law again.

- Discretion is essential in providing individualized justice but problems such as discrimination, unfairness, and bias toward particular groups of juveniles must be controlled.
- Police have taken the lead in delinquency prevention. Major policing strategies to prevent delinquency include aggressive law enforcement, police in schools, community policing, and problem-oriented policing.
- The ever-changing nature of juvenile delinquency calls for further experimentation and innovation in policing strategies to prevent delinquency. Tailoring policing activities to local conditions and engaging the community and other stakeholders are important first steps.

KEY TERMS

pledge system, p. 286
watch system, p. 286
community policing, p. 287
juvenile officers, p. 288

role conflicts, p. 288
problem-oriented policing, p. 290
arrest, p. 291
probable cause, p. 291

search and seizure, p. 292
custodial interrogation, p. 292
Miranda warning, p. 293
discretion, p. 294

QUESTIONS FOR DISCUSSION

1. The term *discretion* is often defined as selective decision making by police and others in the juvenile justice system who are faced with alternative modes of action. Discuss some of the factors affecting the discretion of the police when dealing with juvenile offenders.

2. What role should police organizations play in delinquency prevention and control? Is it feasible to expect police departments to provide social services to children and families? How could police departments be better organized to provide for the control of juvenile delinquency?

3. What qualities should a police juvenile officer have? Should a college education be a requirement?

4. In light of the traditional and protective roles assumed by law enforcement personnel in juvenile justice, is there any reason to require a *Miranda* warning for youths taken into custody?

5. Can the police and community be truly effective in forming a partnership to reduce juvenile delinquency? Discuss the role of the juvenile police officer in preventing and investigating juvenile crime.

6. The experience of Boston's successful Operation Ceasefire program suggests that it may be difficult to sustain the needed intensity and problem-solving partnerships to keep violent juvenile crime under control over the long term. What other innovative problem-oriented policing measures could be employed to achieve this?

APPLYING WHAT YOU HAVE LEARNED

You are a newly appointed police officer assigned to a juvenile unit of a medium-size urban police department. Wayne G. is an eighteen-year-old White male who was caught shoplifting with two male friends of the same age. Wayne attempted to leave a large department store with a $25 shirt and was apprehended by a police officer in front of the store.

Wayne seemed quite remorseful about the offense. He said several times that he didn't know why he did it and that he had not planned to do it. He seemed upset and scared, and while admitting the offense, did not want to go to court. Wayne had three previous contacts with the police as a juvenile: one for malicious mischief when he destroyed some property, another involving a minor assault on a boy, and a third involving another shoplifting charge. In all three cases, Wayne promised to refrain from ever committing such acts again, and as a result was not required to go to court. The other shoplifting incident involved a baseball worth only $3.

Wayne appeared at the police department with his mother. His parents are divorced. The mother did not seem overly concerned about the case and felt that her son was not really to blame. She argued that he was always getting in trouble and she was not sure how to control him. She blamed most of his troubles with the law on his being in the wrong crowd. Besides, a $25 shirt was "no big deal" and she offered to pay back the store. The store had left matters in the hands of the police and would support any decision you make.

Deciding what to do in a case like Wayne's is a routine activity for most police officers. When dealing with juveniles, they must consider not only the nature of the offense but also the needs of the juvenile. Police officers realize that actions they take can have a long-term effect on an adolescent's future.

- Would you submit Wayne's case for prosecution, release him with a warning, or use some other tactic?
- Should police officers be forced to act as counselors for troubled youth?

DOING RESEARCH ON THE WEB

Before you answer, you may want to learn more about this topic by checking out the Web sites of the International Association of Chiefs of Police, the Police Foundation, COPS on Community Policing, and the Police Executive Research Forum. Just click on Web Links under the Chapter Resources at http://cj.wadsworth.com/siegel_jdcore2e.

To research police handling of juveniles suspected of committing crimes, use "police and discretion" in a key word search on InfoTrac College Edition.

Pro/Con discussions and Viewpoint Essays on some of the topics in this chapter may be found at the Opposing Viewpoints Resource Center: www.gale.com/OpposingViewpoints.

chapter 13

Juvenile Court Process: Pretrial, Trial, and Sentencing

Courtesy of CNN

CHAPTER OBJECTIVES

**After reading this chapter you
should:**

1. Understand the roles and responsibilities of the main players in the
   juvenile court.

2. Be able to discuss key issues of the
   preadjudicatory stage of juvenile
   justice, including detention, intake,
   diversion, pretrial release, plea
   bargaining, and waiver.

3. Be able to argue the pros and cons
   of waiving youths to adult court.

4. Understand key issues of the trial
   stage of juvenile justice, including
   constitutional rights of youths
   and disposition.

5. Be familiar with major U.S. Supreme
   Court decisions that have influenced
   the handling of juveniles at the
   preadjudicatory and trial stages.

6. Know the most common dispositions for juvenile offenders.

7. Know the major arguments
   opposed to and in favor of the
   death penalty for juveniles.

8. Be able to argue the pros and
   cons of confidentiality in juvenile
   proceedings and privacy of juvenile
   records.

On December 23, 2003, a Virginia jury rejected the death penalty sentence for Lee Boyd Malvo, the teenage D.C.-area sniper who, one week earlier, had been convicted of terrorism, capital murder, and weapons charges by the same jury. The jury decided instead that Malvo should be sentenced to life in prison without possibility of parole. Although the case met both aggravating factors required to put the offender to death—that his conduct was depraved and that he still presented a danger to society—the jurors exercised the other option available to them.

This case once again put the controversial issue of the death penalty for juveniles in the national spotlight, with many pundits believing that if there ever was a case for the juvenile death penalty it was this one. One month later, on January 26, 2004, the Supreme Court agreed to decide whether the death penalty for sixteen- and seventeen-year-olds violates the Constitution. In 1988, the Supreme Court struck down the death penalty for those age fifteen and younger. **CNN.** VIEW THE CNN VIDEO CLIP OF THIS STORY AND ANSWER RELATED CRITICAL THINKING QUESTIONS ON YOUR JUVENILE DELINQUENCY: THE CORE 2E CD.

THE JUVENILE COURT AND ITS JURISDICTION

Today's juvenile delinquency cases are sometimes handled as part of a criminal trial court jurisdiction, or even within the probate court. Also called surrogate court in some states, probate court is a court of special jurisdiction that handles wills, administration of estates, and guardianship of minors and incompetents. However, in most jurisdictions they are treated in the structure of a family court or an independent juvenile court (fourteen states use more than one method to process juvenile cases).[1] The independent juvenile court is a specialized court for children, designed to promote rehabilitation of youth in a framework of procedural due process. It is concerned with acting both in the best interest of the child and in the best interest of public protection, two often incompatible goals. Family courts, in contrast, have broad jurisdiction over a wide range of personal and household problems, including delinquency, paternity, child support, and custody issues. The major advantages of such a system are that it can serve sparsely populated areas, permits judicial personnel and others to deal exclusively with children's matters, and can obtain legislative funding more readily than other court systems.

Court Case Flow

Today, more than 1.6 million delinquency cases are adjudicated annually. Between 1990 and 1999 (the last data available), case flow increased 27 percent. The increasing numbers of cases were the product of a significant rise in the number of drug law violation cases (up 169 percent), public order offense cases (up 74 percent), and cases involving personal offenses (up 55 percent); property offense cases, in contrast, decreased 19 percent.[2]

There were distinct gender- and race-based differences in the juvenile court population. In 1999, 76 percent of delinquency cases involved a male and 24 percent involved a female. However, the number of females processed by juvenile courts has increased from 1990, when less than 20 percent of the cases involved females. Similarly, 28 percent of the juvenile court population was made up of African-American

© Shelley Gazin/Corbis

youth, although African Americans make up only about 15 percent of the general population.[3]

The Actors in the Juvenile Courtroom

The key players in the juvenile court are the defense attorneys, prosecutors, and judges.

The Defense Attorney As the result of a series of Supreme Court decisions, the right of a delinquent youth to have counsel at state trials has become a fundamental part of the juvenile justice system.[4] Today, courts must provide counsel to indigent defendants who face the possibility of incarceration. Over the past three decades, the rules of juvenile justice administration have become extremely complex. Preparation of a case for juvenile court often involves detailed investigation of a crime, knowledge of court procedures, use of rules of evidence, and skills in trial advocacy. The right to counsel is essential if children are to have a fair chance of presenting their cases in court.

In many respects, the role of the **juvenile defense attorney** is similar to that in the criminal and civil areas. Defense attorneys representing children in the juvenile court play an active and important part in virtually all stages of the proceedings. For example, the defense attorney helps to clarify jurisdictional problems and to decide whether there is sufficient evidence to warrant filing a formal petition. The defense attorney helps outline the child's position regarding detention hearings and bail, and explores the opportunities for informal adjustment of the case. If no adjustment or diversion occurs, the defense attorney represents the child at adjudication, presenting evidence and cross-examining witnesses to see that the child's position is made clear to the court. Defense attorneys also play a critical role in the disposition hearing. They present evidence bearing on the treatment decision and help the court formulate alternative plans for the child's care. Finally, defense attorneys pursue any appeals from the trial, represent the child in probation revocation proceedings, and generally protect the child's right to treatment.

Important to these roles is the attorney-juvenile relationship and the competence of the attorney. Some studies report that many juvenile offenders do not trust their attorney,[5] but juvenile offenders represented by private attorneys are more trusting in their attorney than those represented by court-appointed attorneys.[6] One

juvenile defense attorneys
Represent children in juvenile court and play an active role at all stages of the proceedings.

possible reason for this difference may be the belief among juveniles that because court-appointed attorneys work for the "system" they might share information with the judge, police, or others.[7] Another important dimension of the attorney-juvenile relationship is effective participation of the juvenile as a defendant, which "requires a personally relevant understanding of the lawyer's advocacy role and the confidential nature of the attorney-client relationship."[8] A recent study investigating effective participation among juvenile and adult defendants concluded that juveniles are in need of extra procedural safeguards, such as training for lawyers on how to be more effective counselors.[9] There may also be a need to improve the competency of juvenile defense attorneys, as well as to overcome some of the time constraints they face in case preparation. In a study of legal representation of juveniles charged with felonies in three juvenile courts in Missouri, it was found that they were more likely to receive an out-of-home placement disposition (instead of a less punitive disposition) if they had an attorney, even after controlling for other legal and individual factors.[10] (See the following section for other problems specific to public defenders.)

In some cases, a **guardian *ad litem*** may be appointed by the court.[11] The guardian *ad litem*—ordinarily seen in abuse, neglect, and dependency cases—may be appointed in delinquency cases when there is a question of a need for a particular treatment (for example, placement in a mental health center) and offenders and their attorneys resist placement. The guardian *ad litem* may advocate for the commitment on the ground that it is in the child's best interests. The guardian *ad litem* fulfills many roles, ranging from legal advocate to concerned individual who works with parents and human service professionals in developing a proper treatment plan that best serves the interests of the minor child.[12]

Court-Appointed Special Advocates (CASA)   Court-Appointed Special Advocates (CASA) are volunteers who advise the juvenile court about child placement. The CASA programs (*casa* is Spanish for "home") have demonstrated that volunteers can investigate the needs of children and provide a vital link between the judge, the attorneys, and the child in protecting the juvenile's right to a safe placement.[13]

Public Defender Services for Children   To satisfy the requirement that indigent children be provided with counsel, the federal government and the states have expanded **public defender** services. Three alternatives exist for providing children with legal counsel: (1) an all-public defender program; (2) an appointed private-counsel system; and (3) a combination system of public defenders and appointed private attorneys.

The public defender program is a statewide program established by legislation and funded by the state government to provide counsel to children at public expense. This program allows access to the expertise of lawyers who spend a considerable amount of time representing juvenile offenders every day. Defender programs generally provide separate office space for juvenile court personnel, as well as support staff and training programs for new lawyers.

In many rural areas where individual public defender programs are not available, defense services are offered through appointed private counsel. Private lawyers are assigned to individual juvenile court cases and receive compensation for the time and services they provide. When private attorneys are used in large urban areas, they are generally selected from a list established by the court, and they often operate in conjunction with a public defender program. The weaknesses of a system of assigned private counsel include assignment to cases for which the lawyers are unqualified, inadequate compensation, and lack of support or supervisory services.

Though efforts have been made to supply juveniles with adequate legal representation, many juveniles still go to court unrepresented, or with an overworked lawyer who provides inadequate representation. Many juvenile court defense lawyers work on more than five hundred cases per year, and more than half leave their jobs in under

Volunteer Court-Appointed Special Advocates (CASA) are people who are appointed by judges to advocate for the best interests of abused and neglected children. To read more about the CASA program, click on Web Links under the Chapter Resources at http://cj. wadsworth.com/siegel_ jdcore2e.

guardian *ad litem*
A court-appointed attorney who protects the interests of the child in cases involving the child's welfare.

public defender
An attorney who works in a public agency or under private contractual agreement as defense counsel to indigent defendants.

two years.[14] Other problems facing juvenile public defenders include lack of resources for independent evaluations, expert witnesses, and investigatory support; lack of computers, telephones, files, and adequate office space; inexperience, lack of training, low morale, and salaries lower than those of their counterparts who defend adults or serve as prosecutors; and inability to keep up with rapidly changing juvenile codes.[15] In a six-state study of access to counsel and quality of legal representation for indigent juveniles, the American Bar Association found these and many other problems,[16] as shown in Exhibit 13.1. With juvenile offenders facing the prospect of much longer sentences, mandatory minimum sentences, and time in adult prisons, the need for quality defense attorneys for juveniles has never been greater.

The Prosecutor

The **juvenile prosecutor** is the attorney responsible for bringing the state's case against the accused juvenile. Depending on the level of government and the jurisdiction, the prosecutor can be called a *district attorney, county attorney, state attorney,* or *United States attorney.* Prosecutors are members of the bar selected for their positions by political appointment or popular election.

For the first sixty years of its existence, the juvenile court did not include a prosecutor, because the concept of an adversary process was seen as inconsistent with the philosophy of treatment. The court followed a social-service helping model, and informal proceedings were believed to be in the best interests of the child. Today, in a more legalistic juvenile court, almost all jurisdictions require by law that a prosecutor be present in the juvenile court.

A number of states have passed legislation giving prosecutors control over intake and waiver decisions. Some have passed concurrent-jurisdiction laws that allow prosecutors to decide in which court to bring serious juvenile cases. In some jurisdictions, it is the prosecutor and not the juvenile court judge who is entrusted with the decision of whether to waive a case to adult court.

The prosecutor has the power either to initiate or to discontinue delinquency or status-offense allegations. Like police officers, prosecutors have broad discretion in the exercise of their duties. Because due process rights have been extended to juveniles, the prosecutor's role in the juvenile court has in some ways become similar to the prosecutor's role in the adult court.

Because children are committing more serious crimes today and because the courts have granted juveniles constitutional safeguards, the prosecutor is likely to play an increasingly significant role in the juvenile court system. According to authors James Shine and Dwight Price, the prosecutor's involvement will promote a due process model that should result in a fairer, more just system for all parties. But they also point out that, to meet current and future challenges, prosecutors need more information on such issues as how to identify repeat offenders, how to determine which programs are most effective, how early-childhood experiences relate to delinquency, and what measures can be used in place of secure placements without reducing public safety.[17]

Today, prosecutors are addressing the problems associated with juvenile crime. A balanced approach has been recommended—one that emphasizes enforcement, prosecution, and detention of serious offenders and the use of proven prevention and intervention programs.[18]

The Juvenile Court Judge

Even with the elevation of the prosecutor's role, the **juvenile court judge** is still the central character in a court of juvenile or family law. The responsibilities of this judge have become far more extensive and complex in recent years. Juvenile or family court judges perform the functions listed in Exhibit 13.2.

In addition, judges often have extensive influence over other agencies of the court: probation, the court clerk, the law enforcement officer, and the office of the juvenile prosecutor. Juvenile court judges exercise considerable leadership in developing solutions to juvenile justice problems. In this role they must respond to the pressures the community places on juvenile court resources. According to the *parens*

juvenile prosecutor
Government attorney responsible for representing the interests of the state and bringing the case against the accused juvenile.

juvenile court judge
A judge elected or appointed to preside over juvenile cases whose decisions can only be reviewed by a judge of a higher court.

Exhibit 13.1 Selected Problems in Public Defender Services for Indigent Juveniles in Six States

Maine

- Juvenile defenders are paid $50 per hour, with a cap of $315; therefore, defenders are expected to spend only a little over six hours on each case.
- In 2002, only two hours of juvenile-justice-related training were available to defenders.

Maryland

- In one jurisdiction, juvenile public defenders handle about 360 cases each year; this is almost double the ABA standard's recommended maximum of 200.
- In ten of the jurisdictions studied, more than a third of juveniles waived their right to counsel.

Montana

- Nearly all the interviewed youth revealed that their attorneys had done no investigation into their cases.
- There are no minimum requirements for attorneys seeking appointment to defend children and youth in the justice system.

North Carolina

- Some 44 percent of juvenile defense attorneys surveyed reported that they rarely or never see the police report or other investigative material prior to their first meeting with a client.
- Some 44 percent also said they had no or inadequate access to investigators.

Pennsylvania

- About 94 percent of juvenile defense attorneys do not have access to independent investigators or social workers.
- Of the forty public defender offices that confirmed representing youth at dispositional reviews, only 9 percent usually interview the youth before hearings.

Washington

- In some counties, up to 30 percent of children appear without counsel.
- Juvenile defenders working full-time reported that they are assigned an average of close to four hundred cases annually.

Sources: *Statistics: Juvenile Indigent Defense Reports by the Numbers* (Chicago: Juvenile Justice Center, 2003); *Montana: An Assessment of Access to Counsel and Quality of Representation in Delinquency Proceedings* (Chicago: American Bar Association, 2003), p. 5.

Exhibit 13.2 Duties of the Juvenile Court Judge

- Rule on pretrial motions involving such legal issues as arrest, search and seizure, interrogation, and lineup identification.
- Make decisions about the continued detention of children prior to trial.
- Make decisions about plea-bargaining agreements and the informal adjustment of juvenile cases.
- Handle trials, rule on the appropriateness of conduct, settle questions of evidence and procedure, and guide the questioning of witnesses.
- Assume responsibility for holding disposition hearings and deciding on the treatment accorded the child.
- Handle waiver proceedings.
- Handle appeals where allowed by statute.

The **American Judicature Society** is a nonpartisan organization with a membership of judges, lawyers, and nonlegally trained citizens interested in the administration of justice. Visit this organization's Web site by clicking on Web Links under the Chapter Resources at http://cj.wadsworth.com/siegel_jdcore2e

patriae philosophy, the juvenile judge must ensure that the necessary community resources are available so that the children and families who come before the court can receive the proper care and help.[19] This may be the most untraditional role for the juvenile court judge, but it may also be the most important.

In some jurisdictions, juvenile court judges handle family-related cases exclusively. In others they preside over criminal and civil cases as well. Traditionally, juvenile court judges have been relegated to a lower status than other judges. Judges assigned to juvenile courts have not ordinarily been chosen from the highest levels of

Checkpoints

✔ In most jurisdictions, kids are adjudicated within the structure of either a family court or an independent juvenile court.

✔ More than 1.6 million delinquency cases are adjudicated annually.

✔ All juveniles must be provided with legal counsel if they face the possibility of incarceration.

✔ A guardian ad litem is an attorney who represents the child during special legal proceedings, including abuse, neglect, and dependency cases.

✔ Court-Appointed Special Advocates (CASA) are volunteers who advise the juvenile court about child placement.

✔ The juvenile prosecutor is the attorney responsible for bringing the state's case against the accused juvenile.

✔ The juvenile judge must ensure that the children and families who come before the court can receive the proper care and help.

 To quiz yourself on this material, go to questions 13.1–13.10 on the Juvenile Delinquency: The Core 2e Web site.

the legal profession. Such groups as the American Judicature Society have noted that the field of juvenile justice has often been shortchanged by the appointment of unqualified judges. In some jurisdictions, particularly major urban areas, juvenile court judges may be of the highest caliber, but many courts continue to function with mediocre judges. ✔ Checkpoints

JUVENILE COURT PROCESS

Now that we have briefly described the setting of the juvenile court and the major players who control its operations, we turn to a discussion of the procedures that shape the contours of juvenile justice: the pretrial process and the juvenile trial and disposition. Many critical decisions are made at this stage of the juvenile justice system: whether to detain or release the youth to the community; whether to waive youths to the adult court or retain them in the juvenile justice system; whether to treat them in the community or send them to a secure treatment center. Each of these can have a profound influence on the child, with effects lasting throughout the life course. What are these critical stages, and how are decisions made within them?

Release or Detain?

After a child has been taken into custody and a decision is made to treat the case formally (that is, with a juvenile court hearing), a decision must be made either to release the child into the custody of parents or to detain the child in the temporary care of the state, in physically restrictive facilities pending court disposition or transfer to another agency.[20] Nationally, about 70 percent of all states have detention centers administered at the county level, about 34 percent have state-level facilities, 16 percent have court-administered facilities, and 11 percent contracted with private vendors to operate facilities.[21]

Detention can be a traumatic experience because many facilities are prison-like, with locked doors and barred windows. Consequently, most experts in juvenile justice advocate that detention be limited to alleged offenders who require secure custody for the protection of themselves and others. However, children who are neglected and dependent, runaways, or homeless may under some circumstances be placed in secure detention facilities along with violent and dangerous youth until more suitable placements can be found.[22] Others have had a trial but have not been sentenced, or are awaiting the imposition of their sentence. Some may have violated probation and are awaiting a hearing while being kept alongside a severely mentally ill adolescent for whom no appropriate placement can be found. Another group are adjudicated delinquents awaiting admittance to a correctional training school.[23] Consequently, it is possible for nonviolent status offenders to be housed in the same facility with delinquents who have committed felony-type offenses.

To remedy this situation, an ongoing effort has been made to remove status offenders and neglected or abused children from detention facilities that also house juvenile delinquents. In addition, alternatives to detention centers—temporary foster homes, detention boarding homes, and programs of neighborhood supervision—have been developed. These alternatives, referred to as **shelter care,** enable youths to live in a more homelike setting while the courts dispose of their cases.

National Detention Trends Despite an ongoing effort to limit detention, juveniles are still being detained in 20 percent of all delinquency cases, with some variation across the major offense categories: violent (23 percent), property (16 percent), drugs (23 percent), and public order (23 percent). Although the detention rate for delinquency cases is down from 23 percent in 1990, over the ten-year period of 1990 to 1999, the total number of juveniles held in short-term detention facilities increased 11 percent, from 302,800 to 336,200.[24]

shelter care
A place for temporary care of children in physically unrestricting facilities.

The typical delinquent detainee is male, over fifteen years of age, and charged with a violent crime,[25] whereas the typical status offense detainee is female, under sixteen years of age, and a runaway.[26] Racial minorities are heavily overrepresented in detention, especially those who are indigent and whose families may be receiving public assistance. Minority overrepresentation is particularly vexing, considering that detention may increase the risk of a youth's being adjudicated and eventually confined.[27]

The Decision to Detain Most children taken into custody by the police are released to their parents or guardians. Some are held overnight until their parents can be notified. Police officers normally take a child to a place of detention only after other alternatives have been exhausted. Many juvenile courts in urban areas have staff members, such as intake probation officers, on duty twenty-four hours a day to screen detention admissions.

Ordinarily, delinquent children are detained if the police believe they are inclined to run away while awaiting trial, or if they are likely to commit an offense dangerous to the parent. There is evidence that some decision makers are more likely to detain minority youth, especially if they dwell in dangerous lower-class areas.[28]

Generally, children should not be held in a detention facility or shelter-care unit for more than twenty-four hours without a formal petition (a written request to the court) being filed to extend the detention period. To detain a juvenile, there must be clear evidence of probable cause that the child has committed the offense and will flee if not detained. Although the requirements for detention hearings vary, most jurisdictions require that they occur almost immediately after the child's admission to a detention facility and provide the youth with notice and counsel.

The juvenile court judge is the central character in a court of juvenile or family law. The duties of the juvenile court judge are wide-ranging. The most important of these duties may be the need to ensure that the necessary community resources are available so that the children and families that come before the court can receive the proper care and help.

To find out more about the needs of detention, go to the *Juvenile Detention Training Needs Assessment Research Report,* by David W. Roush. You can find it by clicking on Web Links under the Chapter Resources at http://cj. wadsworth.com/siegel_jdcore2e.

New Approaches to Detention Efforts have been ongoing to improve the process and conditions of detention. Experts maintain that detention facilities should provide youth with education, visitation, private communications, counseling, continuous supervision, medical and health care, nutrition, recreation, and reading. Detention should also include, or provide, a system for clinical observation and diagnosis that complements the wide range of helpful services.[29]

The consensus today is that juvenile detention centers should be reserved for youths who present a clear threat to the community. In some states, nonsecure facilities are being used to service juveniles for a limited period. Alternatives to secure detention include in-home monitoring, home detention, day-center electronic monitoring, high-intensity community supervision, and comprehensive case management programs. The successful Detention Diversion Advocacy Program (DDAP) relies on a case management strategy. Because this is an important development, it is covered in more detail in the accompanying Preventing and Treating Delinquency feature.

Undoubtedly, juveniles pose special detention problems, but some efforts are being made to improve programs and to reduce pretrial detention use, especially in secure settings. Of all the problems associated with detention, however, none is as critical as the issue of placing youths in adult jails.

Many critical decisions are made before the juvenile trial begins: whether to detain youths or release them to the community; whether to waive them to the adult court or retain them in the juvenile justice system; whether to treat them in the community or send them to a secure treatment center. These teens are waiting during the intake process in the juvenile court in Orlando, Florida. The intake process refers to the screening of cases by the juvenile court system. Intake officers, who are often probation staff members, determine whether the services of the juvenile court are needed.

© Joel Gordon

Restricting Detention in Adult Jails   A significant problem in juvenile justice is placing youths in adult jails. This is usually done in rural areas where no other facility exists. Almost all experts agree that placing children under the age of eighteen in any type of jail facility should be prohibited because youngsters can easily be victimized by other inmates and staff, be forced to live in squalid conditions, and be subject to physical and sexual abuse.

Until a few years ago, placing juveniles in adult facilities was common, but efforts have been made to change this situation. In 1989, the Juvenile Justice and Delinquency Prevention Act (JJDPA) of 1974 was amended to require that states remove all juveniles from adult jails and lockups. According to federal guidelines, all juveniles in state custody must be separated from adult offenders or the state could lose federal juvenile justice funds. The Office of Juvenile Justice and Delinquency Prevention (OJJDP) defines separation as the condition in which juvenile detainees have either totally independent facilities or shared facilities that are designed so that juveniles and adults neither have contact nor share programs or staff.[30]

Much debate has arisen over whether the initiative to remove juveniles from adult jails has succeeded. Most indications are that the number of youths being held in adult facilities has declined significantly from the almost five hundred thousand a year recorded in 1979.[31] Today, fewer than one hundred thousand juveniles are detained annually in adult jails. These figures may be misleading, however, because they do not include youths held in urban jails for under six hours, or in rural ones for under twenty-four hours; youths transferred to adult courts; or youths in states that consider anyone over sixteen or seventeen to be an adult.

With federal help, some progress appears to have been made in removing juveniles from adult facilities, but thousands each year continue to be held in close contact with adults, and thousands more are held in facilities that, although physically separate, put them in close proximity to adults. To the youths held within their walls, there may appear to be little difference between the juvenile detention facilities and the adult jail.

Removing Status Offenders   Along with removing all juveniles from adult jails, the OJJDP has made deinstitutionalization of status offenders a cornerstone of its policy. The Juvenile Justice and Delinquency Prevention Act of 1974 prohibits the placement of status offenders in secure detention facilities.

The Detention Diversion Advocacy Program

The Detention Diversion Advocacy Program (DDAP) employs the efforts of a staff of laypersons or nonlegal experts to advocate for youthful offenders at disposition hearings. It relies on a case-management strategy coordinating human services, opportunities, or benefits. Case-management efforts are designed to integrate services across a cluster of organizations, to ensure continuity of care, and to facilitate development of client skills (for example, job interviewing, or reading and writing skills) by involving a variety of social networks and service providers (social agencies that provide specific services to youth, like drug counseling and crisis intervention).

Detention advocacy involves identifying youths likely to be detained pending their adjudication. DDAP clients are identified primarily through referrals from the public defender's office, the probation department, community agencies, and parents. Admission to DDAP is restricted to youth currently held, or likely to be held, in secure detention. Once a potential client is identified, DDAP case managers present a release plan to the judge that includes a list of appropriate community services (tutoring, drug counseling, family counseling) that will be made available on the youth's behalf. The plan also includes specified objectives (improved grades, victim restitution, drug-free status) as a means of evaluating the youth's progress in the program. Emphasis is placed on allowing the youth to live at home while going through the program. If this is not a viable option, program staff will identify and secure a suitable alternative. If the judge deems the release plan acceptable, the youth is released to DDAP supervision.

The DDAP case-management model provides frequent and consistent support and supervision to the children and their families. Case managers link youths to community-based services and closely monitor their progress. The DDAP program requires the case manager to have daily contact with the youth, the family, and significant others, including a minimum of three in-person meetings with the youth each week. The youth's family members, particularly parents and guardians, are provided with additional services that usually include assistance in securing employment, day care, drug treatment services, and income support (for example, food stamps).

Evaluations of the DDAP program indicated that it is very successful:

- The overall recidivism rate of the DDAP group was 34 percent, compared with 60 percent for the comparison group.
- Only 14 percent of the DDAP group had two or more subsequent referrals, compared with 50 percent of the comparison group.
- Only 9 percent of the DDAP group returned to court on a violent crime charge, compared with 25 percent of the comparison group.
- Only 5 percent of the DDAP group had two or more subsequent petitions, compared with 22 percent of the comparison group.

CRITICAL THINKING

1. Should adolescents be detained for nonviolent offenses such as substance abuse or theft?
2. Do you believe that the decision to detain children should be based on an evaluation of their behavior or their parents' behavior and ability to provide care and supervision? If the latter, is that a violation of due process? In other words, why should children be punished for their parents' shortcomings?

INFOTRAC COLLEGE EDITION RESEARCH

To learn more about the concept of *juvenile detention,* use the term as a subject guide on InfoTrac College Edition.

Source: Randall G. Shelden, "Detention Diversion Advocacy: An Evaluation," *Juvenile Justice Bulletin* (Washington, DC: Office of Juvenile Justice and Delinquency Prevention, 1999).

Removing status offenders from secure facilities serves two purposes: it reduces interaction with serious offenders, and it insulates status offenders from the stigma associated with being a detainee in a locked facility. Efforts appear to be working, and the number of status offenders being held in some sort of secure confinement has been on a two-decade decline. Nonetheless, the debate over the most effective way to handle juvenile status offenders continues, and some critics have argued that if the juvenile court is unable to take effective action in status offender cases it should be stripped of jurisdiction over these youths. Most judges would prefer to retain jurisdiction so they can help children and families resolve problems that cause runaways, truancy, and other status offense behaviors.[32]

Bail for Children One critical detention issue is whether juveniles can be released on **bail.** Adults retain the right, via the Eighth Amendment to the Constitution, to reasonable bail in noncapital cases. Most states, however, refuse juveniles the

bail
Amount of money that must be paid as a condition of pretrial release to ensure that the accused will return for subsequent proceedings; bail is normally set by the judge at the initial appearance, and if unable to make bail the accused is detained in jail.

right to bail. They argue that juvenile proceedings are civil, not criminal, and that detention is rehabilitative, not punitive. In addition, they argue that juveniles do not need a constitutional right to bail because statutory provisions allow children to be released into parental custody.

State juvenile bail statutes fall into three categories: those guaranteeing the right to bail, those that grant the court discretion to give bail, and those that deny a juvenile the right to bail.[33] This disparity may be a function of the lack of legal guidance on the matter. The U.S. Supreme Court has never decided the issue of juvenile bail. Some courts have stated that bail provisions do not apply to juveniles. Others rely on the Eighth Amendment against cruel and unusual punishment, or on state constitutional provisions or statutes, and conclude that juveniles do have a right to bail.

Preventive Detention   Although the U.S. Supreme Court has not yet decided whether juveniles have a right to traditional money bail, it has concluded that the state has a right to detain dangerous youth until their trial, a practice called **preventive detention.** On June 4, 1984, the U.S. Supreme Court dealt with this issue in *Schall v. Martin,* when it upheld the state of New York's preventive detention statute.[34] Because this is a key case in juvenile justice, it is the subject of the accompanying Juvenile Law in Review feature. Today, most states allow "dangerous" youths to be held indefinitely before trial. Because preventive detention may attach a stigma of guilt to a child presumed innocent, the practice remains a highly controversial one, and the efficacy of such laws remains unknown.[35]

The Intake Process

The term *intake* refers to the screening of cases by the juvenile court system. The child and the child's family are screened by intake officers to determine whether the services of the juvenile court are needed. Intake officers may send the youth home with no further action, divert the youth to a social agency, petition the youth to the juvenile court, or file a petition and hold the youth in detention. The intake process reduces demands on court resources, screens out cases that are not in the court's jurisdiction, and enables assistance to be obtained from community agencies without court intervention. Juvenile court intake is provided for by statute in almost all the states.

About 17 percent (279,100) of all delinquency cases in 1999 were dismissed at intake, often because they were not legally sufficient. Another 26 percent (432,000) were processed informally, with the juvenile voluntarily agreeing to the recommended disposition (for example, voluntary treatment).[36] Intake screening allows juvenile courts to enter into consent decrees with juveniles without filing petitions and without formal adjudication. The *consent decree* is a court order authorizing disposition of the case without a formal label of delinquency. It is based on an agreement between the intake department of the court and the juvenile who is the subject of the complaint.

But intake also suffers from some problems. Although almost all state juvenile court systems provide intake and diversion programs, there are few formal criteria for selecting children for such alternatives. There are also legal problems associated with the intake process. Among them are whether the child has a right to counsel, whether the child is protected against self-incrimination, and to what degree the child needs to consent to nonjudicial disposition as recommended by the intake officer. Finally, intake dispositions are often determined by the prior record rather than by the seriousness of the offense or the social background of the child. This practice departs from the philosophy of *parens patriae.*[37]

Diversion

One of the most important alternatives chosen at intake is *nonjudicial disposition,* or as it is variously called, *nonjudicial adjustment, handling or processing, informal disposition, adjustment,* or (most commonly) **diversion.** Juvenile diversion is the process

preventive detention
Keeping the accused in custody prior to trial because the accused is suspected of being a danger to the community.

intake
Process during which a juvenile referral is received and a decision made to file a petition in juvenile court to release the juvenile, to place the juvenile under supervision, or to refer the juvenile elsewhere.

diversion
Officially halting or suspending a formal criminal or juvenile justice proceeding at any legally prescribed processing point after a recorded justice system entry, and referral of that person to a treatment or care program or a recommendation that the person be released.

Schall v. Martin

Facts

Gregory Martin was arrested in New York City on December 13, 1977, on charges of robbery, assault, and criminal possession of a weapon. Because he was arrested at 11:30 P.M. and lied about his residence, Martin was kept overnight in detention and brought to juvenile court the next day for an "initial appearance" accompanied by his grandmother. The family court judge, citing possession of a loaded weapon, the false address given to police, and the fact that Martin was left unsupervised late in the evening, ordered him detained before trial under section 320.5(3)(6) of the New York State code, which authorizes pretrial detention of an accused juvenile delinquent if "there is a substantial probability that he will not appear in court on the return date or there is a serious risk that he may before the return date commit an act which if committed by an adult would constitute a crime." Later, at trial, Martin was found to be a delinquent and sentenced to two years' probation.

While he was in pretrial detention, Martin's attorneys filed a class action on behalf of all youths subject to preventive detention in New York, charging that this form of detention was a denial of due process rights under the Fifth and Fourteenth Amendments. The New York appellate courts upheld Martin's claim on the ground that because, at adjudication, most delinquents are released or placed on probation it was unfair to incarcerate them before trial. The prosecution brought the case to the U.S. Supreme Court for final judgment.

Decision

The U.S. Supreme Court upheld the state's right to place juveniles in preventive detention, holding that the practice serves the legitimate objective of protecting both the juvenile and society from pretrial crime. Pretrial detention need not be considered punishment merely because the juvenile is eventually released or put on probation. In addition, there are procedural safeguards, such as notice and a hearing, and a statement of facts that must be given to juveniles before they are placed in detention. The Court also found that detention based on prediction of future behavior was not a violation of due process. Many decisions are made in the justice system, such as the decision to sentence or grant parole, that are based in part on a prediction of future behavior, and these have all been accepted by the courts as legitimate exercises of state power.

Significance of the Case

Schall v. Martin established the right of juvenile court judges to deny youths pretrial release if they perceive them to be dangerous. However, the case also established a due process standard for detention hearings that includes notice and a statement of substantial reasons for the detention. Despite these measures, opponents hold that preventive detention deprives offenders of their freedom because guilt has not been proven. It is also unfair, they claim, to punish people for what judicial authorities believe they may do in the future, because it is impossible to predict who will be a danger to the community. Moreover, because judges are able to use discretion in their detention decisions, an offender could unfairly be deprived of freedom without legal recourse.

CRITICAL THINKING

1. Is the use of pretrial detention warranted for all juveniles charged with violent crimes? Explain
2. Should judicial discretion be limited in decisions on pretrial release or detention?

INFOTRAC COLLEGE EDITION RESEARCH

To learn about innovations in pretrial detention for juveniles, read Amanda Paulson, "Chicago's Alternative to Locking Up Youth," *Christian Science Monitor*, January 21, 2004, p. 1.

Source: *Schall v. Martin*, 104 S.Ct. 2403 (1984).

---

of placing youths suspected of law-violating behavior into treatment programs prior to formal trial and disposition to minimize their penetration into the justice system and thereby avoid stigma and labeling.

Diversion implies more than simply screening out cases for which no additional treatment is needed. Screening involves abandoning efforts to apply coercive measures to a defendant. In contrast, diversion encourages an individual to participate in some specific program or activity to avoid further prosecution.

Most court-based diversion programs employ a particular formula for choosing youths. Criteria such as being a first offender, a nonviolent offender, or a status offender, or being drug- or alcohol-dependent, are used to select clients. In some programs, youths will be asked to partake of services voluntarily in lieu of a court appearance. In other programs, prosecutors will agree to defer, and then dismiss, a case once a youth has completed a treatment program. Finally, some programs can be initiated by the juvenile court judge after an initial hearing. Concept Summary 13.1 lists the factors considered in diversion decisions.

The intake process involves the screening of cases by the juvenile justice system, which can produce a number of results, from releasing the youth to placing the youth under supervision. Here, juvenile offenders begin the intake process by being searched by a correctional officer at the Department of Youth Services Detention Center in Rathbone, Ohio.

© 2002 AP/Wide World Photos

In sum, diversion programs have been created to remove nonserious offenders from the justice system, provide them with nonpunitive treatment services, and help them avoid the stigma of a delinquent label.

Issues in Diversion: Widening the Net   Diversion has been viewed as a promising alternative to official procedures, but over the years its basic premises have been questioned.[38] The most damaging criticism has been that diversion programs are involving children in the juvenile justice system who previously would have been released without official notice. This is referred to as **widening the net.** Various studies indicate that police and court personnel are likely to use diversion programs for youths who ordinarily would have been turned loose at the intake or arrest stage.[39] Why does this "net widening" occur? One explanation is that police and prosecutors find diversion a more attractive alternative than either official processing or outright release—diversion helps them resolve the conflict between doing too much and doing too little.

Diversion has also been criticized as ineffective; that is, youths being diverted make no better adjustment in the community than those who go through official channels. However, not all experts are critical of diversion. Some challenge the net-widening concept as naive: How do we know that diverted youths would have had less interface with the justice system if diversion didn't exist?[40] Even if juveniles escaped official labels for their current offense, might they not eventually fall into the hands of the police? The rehabilitative potential of diversion should not be overlooked.[41] Juvenile diversion programs represent one alternative to the traditional process.

The Petition

A **complaint** is the report made by the police or some other agency to the court to initiate the intake process. Once the agency makes a decision that judicial disposition is required, a petition is filed. The petition is the formal complaint that initiates judicial action against a juvenile charged with delinquency or a status offense. The petition includes basic information such as the name, age, and residence of the child; the parents' names; and the facts alleging the child's delinquency. The police officer, a family member, or a social service agency can file a petition.

If after being given the right to counsel, the child admits the allegation in the petition, an initial hearing is scheduled for the child to make the admission before the court and information is gathered to develop a treatment plan. If the child does not

widening the net
Phenomenon that occurs when programs created to divert youths from the justice system actually involve them more deeply in the official process.

complaint
Report made by the police or some other agency to the court that initiates the intake process.

Factors Considered	Criteria for Eligibility
Past criminal record	It is the juvenile's first offense.
Type of offense	It is a nonviolent or status offense.
Other circumstances	The juvenile abuses drugs or alcohol.

Checkpoints

✔ Detention is the temporary care of children by the state in physically restrictive facilities pending court disposition or transfer to another agency.

✔ The federal government has encouraged the removal of status offenders from detention facilities that also house juvenile delinquents; it has encouraged the removal of delinquents from adult jails.

✔ Racial minorities are overrepresented in detention.

✔ Experts maintain that detention facilities should provide youth with treatment, such as education, counseling, and health care.

✔ Intake refers to the screening of cases by the juvenile court system to determine whether the services of the juvenile court are needed.

✔ One of the most important alternatives chosen at intake is nonjudicial disposition, or as it is most commonly called, diversion.

✔ The petition is the formal complaint that initiates judicial action against a juvenile charged with delinquency or a status offense.

 To quiz yourself on this material, go to questions 13.11–13.15 on the Juvenile Delinquency: The Core 2e Web site.

plea bargaining
The exchange of prosecutorial and judicial concessions for a guilty plea by the accused; plea bargaining usually results in a reduced charge or a more lenient sentence.

admit to any of the facts in the petition, a date is set for a hearing on the petition. This hearing, whose purpose is to determine the merits of the petition, is similar to the adult trial. Once a hearing date has been set, the probation department is normally asked to prepare a social study report. This predisposition report contains relevant information about the child, along with recommendations for treatment and service.

When a date has been set for the hearing on the petition, parents or guardians and other persons associated with the petition (witnesses, the arresting police officer, and victims) are notified. On occasion, the court may issue a summons—a court order requiring the juvenile or others involved in the case to appear for the hearing. The statutes in a given jurisdiction govern the contents of the petition. Some jurisdictions, for instance, allow for a petition to be filed based on the information of the complainant alone. Others require that the petition be filed under oath or that an affidavit accompany the petition. Some jurisdictions authorize only one official, such as a probation officer or prosecutor, to file the petition. Others allow numerous officials, including family and social service agencies, to set forth facts in the petition.

✔ Checkpoints

The Plea and Plea Bargaining

In the adult criminal justice system, the defendant normally enters a plea of guilty or not guilty. More than 90 percent of all adult defendants plead guilty. A large proportion of those pleas involve **plea bargaining,** the exchange of prosecutorial and judicial concessions for guilty pleas.[42] Plea bargaining permits a defendant to plead guilty to a less-serious charge in exchange for an agreement by the prosecutor to recommend a reduced sentence to the court. It involves a discussion between the child's attorney and the prosecutor by which the child agrees to plead guilty to obtain a reduced charge or a lenient sentence.

Few juvenile codes require a guilty or not-guilty plea when a petition is filed against a child. In most jurisdictions an initial hearing is held at which the child either submits to a finding of the facts or denies the petition.[43] If the child admits to the facts, the court determines an appropriate disposition. If the child denies the allegations, the case normally proceeds to trial. When a child enters no plea, the court ordinarily imposes a denial of the charges. This may occur when a juvenile doesn't understand the nature of the complaint or isn't represented by an attorney.

A high percentage of juvenile offenders enter guilty pleas—that is, they admit to the facts of the petition. How many of these pleas involve plea bargaining is unknown. In the past it was believed that plea bargaining was unnecessary in the juvenile justice system because there was little incentive to bargain in a system that does not have jury trials or long sentences. In addition, because the court must dispose of cases in the best interests of the child, plea negotiation seemed unnecessary. Consequently, there has long been a debate over the appropriateness of plea bargaining in juvenile justice. The arguments in favor of plea bargaining include lower court costs and efficiency. Counterarguments hold that plea bargaining with juveniles is an unregulated and unethical process. When used, experts believe the process requires the highest standards of good faith by the prosecutor.[44]

Growing concern about violent juvenile crime has spurred attorneys increasingly to seek to negotiate a plea rather than accept the so-called good interests of the court judgment—a judgment that might result in harsher sanctions.

Plea bargaining negotiations generally involve one or more of the following: reduction of a charge, change in the proceedings from that of delinquency to a status offense, elimination of possible waiver to the criminal court, and agreements regarding dispositional programs for the child. In states where youths are subject to long mandatory sentences, reduction of the charges may have a significant impact on the outcome of the case. In states where youths may be waived to the adult court for committing certain serious crimes, a plea reduction may result in the juvenile court's maintaining jurisdiction.

There is little clear evidence on how much plea bargaining occurs in the juvenile justice system, but it is apparent that such negotiations do take place and seem to be increasing. Joseph Sanborn found that about 20 percent of the cases processed in Philadelphia resulted in a negotiated plea. Most were for reduced sentences, typically probation in lieu of incarceration. Sanborn found that plea bargaining was a complex process, depending in large measure on the philosophy of the judge and the court staff. In general, he found it to have greater benefit for the defendants than for the court.[45]

In summary, the majority of juvenile cases that are not adjudicated seem to be the result of admissions to the facts rather than actual plea bargaining. Plea bargaining is less common in juvenile courts than in adult courts because incentives such as dropping multiple charges or substituting a misdemeanor for a felony are unlikely. Nonetheless, plea bargaining is firmly entrenched in the juvenile process. Any plea bargain, however, must be entered into voluntarily and knowingly; otherwise, the conviction may be overturned on appeal.

TRANSFER TO THE ADULT COURT

One of the most significant actions that can occur in the early court processing of a juvenile offender is the **transfer process.** Otherwise known as *waiver, bindover,* or *removal,* this process involves transferring a juvenile from the juvenile court to the criminal court. Virtually all state statutes allow for this kind of transfer.

The number of delinquency cases judicially waived to criminal court peaked in 1994 at 12,100 cases, an increase of almost 50 percent over the number of cases waived in 1990 (8,300). From 1994 to 1999 (the latest data available), however, the number of cases waived to criminal court has actually declined 38 percent to 7,500 cases, representing less than 1 percent of the formally processed delinquency caseload.[46] A 2003 federal study of juveniles waived to criminal court in the nation's forty largest counties found that 7,100 juvenile felony defendants were adjudicated in adult criminal court.[47] Figure 13.1 shows numbers of delinquency cases waived to criminal court during the 1990s.

Waiver Procedures

Today, all states allow juveniles to be tried as adults in criminal courts in one of three ways:

1. *Concurrent jurisdiction.* In about fifteen states, the prosecutor has the discretion of filing charges for certain offenses in either juvenile or criminal court.

2. *Statutory exclusion policies.* In about twenty-nine states, certain offenses are automatically excluded from juvenile court. These offenses can be minor, such as traffic violations, or serious, such as murder or rape. Statutory exclusion accounts for the largest number of juveniles tried as adults.

3. *Judicial waiver.* In the waiver (or bindover or removal) of juvenile cases to criminal court, a hearing is held before a juvenile court judge, who then decides whether jurisdiction should be waived and the case transferred to criminal

transfer process
Transferring a juvenile offender from the jurisdiction of juvenile court to adult criminal court.

Figure 13.1 **Delinquency Cases Waived to Criminal Court, 1990–1999**

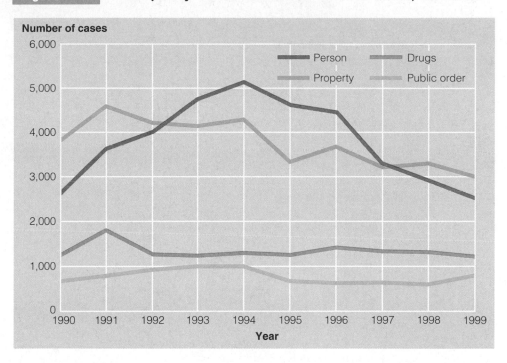

Source: Charles Puzzanchera, Anne L. Stahl, Terrence A. Finnegan, Nancy Tierney, and Howard N. Snyder, *Juvenile Court Statistics 1999* (Pittsburgh, PA: National Center for Juvenile Justice, 2003).

court. All but four states (Massachusetts, Nebraska, New Mexico, and New York) offer provisions for juvenile waivers.[48]

Due Process in Transfer Proceedings

The standards for transfer procedures are set by state statute. Some jurisdictions allow for transfer between the ages of fourteen and seventeen. Others restrict waiver proceedings to mature juveniles and specify particular offenses. In a few jurisdictions, any child can be sentenced to the criminal court system, regardless of age.

Those states that have amended their waiver policies with statutory exclusion policies now exclude certain serious offenses from juvenile court jurisdiction. For example, Indiana excludes cases involving sixteen- and seventeen-year-olds charged with kidnapping, rape, and robbery. In Illinois, youths ages fifteen and sixteen who are charged with murder, assault, or robbery with a firearm are automatically sent to criminal court; in Pennsylvania, any child accused of murder, regardless of age, is tried before the criminal court.[49] Other jurisdictions use exclusion to remove traffic offenses and public ordinance violations.

The trend toward excluding serious violent offenses from juvenile court jurisdictions is growing in response to the current demand to get tough on crime. In addition, large numbers of youth under age eighteen are tried as adults in states where the upper age of juvenile court jurisdiction is fifteen or sixteen.

In a minority of states, statutes allow prosecutors to file particularly serious cases in either the juvenile court or the adult court.[50] Prosecutor discretion may occasionally be a more effective transfer mechanism than the waiver process, because the prosecutor can file a petition in criminal or juvenile court without judicial approval.

Since 1966, the U.S. Supreme Court and other federal and state courts have attempted to ensure fairness in the waiver process by handing down decisions that spell out the need for due process. Two Supreme Court decisions, *Kent v. United States* (1966) and *Breed v. Jones* (1975), are relevant.[51] The *Kent* case declared a District of

Kent v. United States and Breed v. Jones

Kent v. United States: Facts

Morris Kent was arrested at age sixteen in connection with charges of housebreaking, robbery, and rape. As a juvenile, he was subject to the exclusive jurisdiction of the District of Columbia Juvenile Court. The District of Columbia statute declared that the court could transfer the petitioner "after full investigation" and remit him to trial in the U.S. District Court. Kent admitted his involvement in the offenses and was placed in a receiving home for children. Subsequently, his mother obtained counsel, and they discussed with the social service director the possibility that the juvenile court might waive its jurisdiction.

Kent was detained at the receiving home for almost a week. There was no arraignment, no hearing, and no hearing for petitioner's apprehension. Kent's counsel arranged for a psychiatric examination, and a motion requesting a hearing on the waiver was filed. The juvenile court judge did not rule on the motion and entered an order that stated: "After full investigation, the court waives its jurisdiction and directs that a trial be held under the regular proceedings of the criminal court." The judge made no finding and gave no reasons for his waiver decision. It appeared that the judge denied motions for a hearing, recommendations for hospitalization for psychiatric observation, requests for access to the social service file, and offers to prove that the petitioner was a fit subject for rehabilitation under the juvenile court.

After the juvenile court waived its jurisdiction, Kent was indicted by the grand jury and was subsequently found guilty of housebreaking and robbery and not guilty by reason of insanity on the charge of rape. Kent was sentenced to serve a period of thirty to ninety years on his conviction.

Decision

The petitioner's lawyer appealed the decision on the basis of the infirmity of the proceedings by which the juvenile court waived its jurisdiction. He further attacked the waiver on statutory and constitutional grounds, stating: "(1) no hearing occurred, (2) no findings were made, (3) no reasons were stated before the waiver, and (4) counsel was denied access to the social service file." The U.S. Supreme Court found that the juvenile court order waiving jurisdiction and remitting the child to trial in the district court was invalid. Its arguments were based on the following criteria:

- The theory of the juvenile court act is rooted in social welfare procedures and treatments.
- The philosophy of the juvenile court, namely *parens patriae*, is not supposed to allow procedural unfairness.
- Waiver proceedings are critically important actions in the juvenile court.
- The juvenile court act requiring full investigation in the District of Columbia should be read in the context of constitutional principles relating to due process of law. These principles require at a minimum that the petitioner be entitled to a hearing, access to counsel, access by counsel to social service records, and a statement of the reason for the juvenile court decision.

Significance of the Case

This case examined for the first time the substantial degree of discretion associated with a transfer proceeding in the District of Columbia. Thus, the Supreme Court significantly limited its holding to the statute involved but justified its reference to constitutional principles relating to due process and the assistance of counsel. In addition, it said that the juvenile court waiver hearings need to measure up to the essentials of due process and fair treatment. Furthermore, in an appendix to its opinion, the Court set up criteria concerning waiver of the jurisdictions. These are:

Columbia transfer statute unconstitutional and attacked the subsequent conviction of the child by granting him the specific due process rights of having an attorney present at the hearing and access to the evidence that would be used in the case. In *Breed v. Jones*, the U.S. Supreme Court declared that the child was to be granted the protection of the double-jeopardy clause of the Fifth Amendment after he was tried as a delinquent in the juvenile court: once found to be a delinquent, the youth could no longer be tried as an adult. The accompanying Juvenile Law in Review feature discusses these two important cases in more detail.

Today, as a result of *Kent* and *Breed*, states that have transfer hearings provide a legitimate transfer hearing, sufficient notice to the child's family and defense attorney, the right to counsel, and a statement of the reason for the court order regarding transfer. These procedures recognize that the transfer process is critical in determining the statutory rights of the juvenile offender.

- The seriousness of the alleged offense to the community
- Whether the alleged offense was committed in an aggressive, violent, or willful manner
- Whether the alleged offense was committed against persons or against property
- The prosecutive merit of the complaint
- The sophistication and maturity of the juvenile
- The record and previous history of the juvenile
- Prospects for adequate protection of the public and the likelihood of reasonable rehabilitation

Breed v. Jones: Facts

In 1971, a petition in the juvenile court of California was filed against Jones, who was then seventeen, alleging that he had committed an offense that, if committed by an adult, would constitute robbery. The petitioner was detained pending a hearing. At the hearing the juvenile court took testimony, found that the allegations were true, and sustained the petition. The proceedings were continued for a disposition hearing, at which point Jones was found unfit for treatment in the juvenile court. It was ordered that he be prosecuted as an adult offender. At a subsequent preliminary hearing, the petitioner was held for criminal trial, an information was filed against him for robbery, and he was tried and found guilty. He was committed to the California Youth Authority over objections that he was being subjected to double jeopardy.

Petitioner Jones sought an appeal in the federal district court on the basis of the double-jeopardy argument that jeopardy attaches at the juvenile delinquency proceedings. The writ of habeas corpus was denied.

Decision

The U.S. Supreme Court held that the prosecution of Jones as an adult in the California Superior Court, after an adjudicatory finding in the juvenile court that he had violated a criminal statute and a subsequent finding that he was unfit for treatment as a juvenile, violated the double-jeopardy clause of the Fifth Amendment to the U.S. Constitution as applied to the states through the Fourteenth Amendment. Thus, Jones's trial in the California Superior Court for the same offense as that for which he was tried in the juvenile court violated the policy of the double-jeopardy clause, even if he never faced the risk of more than one punishment. *Double jeopardy* refers to the risk or potential risk of trial and conviction, not punishment.

Significance of the Case

The *Breed* case provided answers on several important transfer issues: (1) it prohibits trying a child in an adult court when there has been a prior adjudicatory juvenile proceeding; (2) probable cause may exist at a transfer hearing, and this does not violate subsequent jeopardy if the child is transferred to the adult court; (3) because the same evidence is often used in both the transfer hearing and subsequent trial in either the juvenile or adult court, a different judge is often required for each hearing.

CRITICAL THINKING

Do you believe that some cases should be automatically waived to the adult system, or should all juvenile offenders be evaluated for the possibility of treatment in the juvenile court before a waiver decision is made?

INFOTRAC COLLEGE EDITION RESEARCH

Use "juvenile waiver" as a subject guide on InfoTrac College Edition to find out more about this issue.

Sources: *Kent v. United States,* 383 U.S. 541, 86 S.Ct. 1045, 16 L.Ed.2d 84 (1966); *Breed v. Jones,* 421 U.S. 519, 95 S.Ct. 1779 (1975).

Should Youths Be Transferred to Adult Court?

Most juvenile justice experts oppose waiver because it clashes with the rehabilitative ideal. Basing waiver decisions on type and seriousness of offense rather than on the rehabilitative needs of the child has advanced the *criminalization* of the juvenile court and interfered with its traditional mission of treatment and rehabilitation.[52] And despite this sacrifice, there is little evidence that strict waiver policies can lower crime rates.[53]

Waiver can also create long-term harm. Waived children may be stigmatized by a conviction in the criminal court. Labeling children as adult offenders early in life may seriously impair their future educational, employment, and other opportunities. Youthful offenders convicted in adult courts are more likely to be incarcerated and to receive longer sentences than if they remained in the juvenile court. And these children

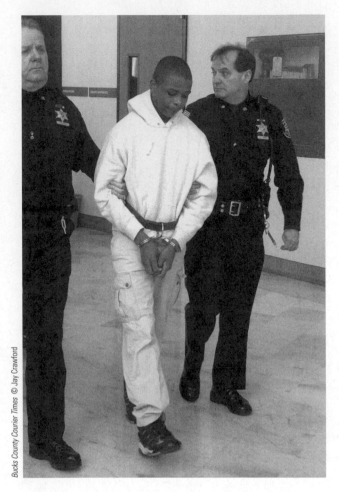

Some kids who commit the most serious crimes are routinely waived to adult court. Here, 14-year-old Kareem Watts is led from court in Doylestown, Pennsylvania, where he was tried as an adult for the murder of a neighbor, Darlyne Jules. A troubled young man, Watts started hearing voices in his head at age 8 and began to self-medicate by smoking pot and snorting household chemicals at age 11. When he stabbed his neighbor, Jules, he was high on pot laced with embalming fluid. After his conviction, Watts was sent to a special unit within the juvenile justice system that houses young convicted offenders who need special psychiatric care. He will be released on his 21st birthday, following an evaluation of his mental condition.

may be incarcerated under conditions so extreme, and in institutions where they may be physically and sexually exploited, that they will become permanently damaged.[54] In a small-scale study of female youths transferred to criminal court and subsequently placed in a prison for adult women, it was found that the prison was severely limited in its ability to care for and provide needed treatment services for these youths compared with the adults.[55]

Waivers don't always support the goal of increased public protection. Because juveniles may only serve a fraction of the prison sentence imposed by the criminal court, the actual treatment of delinquents in adult court is similar to what they might have received had they remained in the custody of juvenile authorities.[56] Also, transferred juveniles convicted of felonies are not more likely to be sentenced to prison than similarly charged felons who are under the age of eighteen but considered adults by the state.[57] Once they are released, waived juveniles have a higher recidivism rate than those kept in juvenile court.[58] This has prompted some critics to ask: Why bother transferring these children?

Sometimes waiver can add an undue burden to youthful offenders. Studies have found that, although transfer to criminal court was intended for the most serious juvenile offenders, many transferred juveniles were not violent offenders but repeat property offenders.[59] Cases involving waiver take significantly longer than comparable juvenile court cases, during which time the waived youth is more likely to be held in a detention center. This finding is vexing, considering that some research shows that many waived youths are no more dangerous than youths who remain in juvenile courts.[60]

Transfer decisions are not always carried out fairly or equitably and there is evidence that minorities are waived at a rate that is greater than their representation in the population.[61] Just over two-fifths (44 percent) of all waived youth are African Americans, even though they represent 28 percent of the juvenile court population.[62] The federal study of transfer in the nation's forty largest counties found that 62 percent of waived youth were African American.[63] However, between 1990 and 1999, the number of judicially waived cases involving African-American youth decreased 24 percent compared with a 9 percent increase for White youth.[64]

In Support of Waiver   Not all experts challenge the waiver concept. Waiver is attractive to conservatives because it jibes with the get tough policy that is currently popular. Some have argued that the increased use of waiver can help get violent offenders off the streets and should be mandatory for juveniles committing serious violent crimes.[65] Others point to studies that show that, for the most part, transfer is reserved for the most serious cases and the most serious juvenile offenders. Kids are most likely to be transferred to criminal court if they have injured someone with a weapon or if they have a long juvenile court record.[66] The most recent federal study of waiver found that 27 percent of juveniles tried in criminal court were sent to prison. This outcome might be expected because those waived to criminal court were more likely (64 percent) than adults (24 percent) to be charged with a violent felony. These juvenile defendants were generally regarded as serious offenders, because 52 percent did not receive pretrial release, 63 percent were con-

Bucks County Courier Times © Jay Crawford

victed of a felony, and 43 percent of those convicted received a prison sentence.[67] Clearly, many waived juveniles might be considered serious offenders.

Author Franklin Zimring argues that, despite its faults, waiver is superior to alternative methods for handling the most serious juvenile offenders.[68] Some cases involving serious offenses, he argues, require a minimum criminal penalty greater than that available to the juvenile court. It is also possible that some juveniles take advantage of decisions to transfer them to the adult court. Although the charge against a child may be considered serious in the juvenile court, the adult criminal court will not find it so; consequently, a child may have a better chance for dismissal of the charges, or acquittal, after a jury trial.

In sum, though the use of waiver has leveled off somewhat, it is still being used today as an important strategy for attacking serious youth crime.[69] Its continued use can be attributed to the get-tough attitude toward the serious juvenile offender.

JUVENILE COURT TRIAL

If the case cannot be decided during the pretrial stage, it will be brought for trial in the juvenile court. An adjudication hearing is held to determine the merits of the petition claiming that a child is either a delinquent youth or in need of court supervision. The judge is required to make a finding based on the evidence and arrive at a judgment. The adjudication hearing is comparable to an adult trial. Rules of evidence in adult criminal proceedings are generally applicable in juvenile court, and the standard of proof used—*beyond a reasonable doubt*—is similar to that used in adult trials.

State juvenile codes vary with regard to the basic requirements of due process and fairness. Most juvenile courts have bifurcated hearings—that is, separate hearings for adjudication and disposition (sentencing). At disposition hearings, evidence can be submitted that reflects nonlegal factors, such as the child's home life.

Most state juvenile codes provide specific rules of procedure. These rules require that a written petition be submitted to the court, ensure the right of a child to have an attorney, provide that the adjudication proceedings be recorded, allow the petition to be amended, and provide that a child's plea be accepted. Where the child admits to the facts of the petition, the court generally seeks assurance that the plea is voluntary. If plea bargaining is used, prosecutors, defense counsel, and trial judges take steps to ensure the fairness of such negotiations.

At the end of the adjudication hearing, most juvenile court statutes require the judge to make a factual finding on the legal issues and evidence. In the criminal court, this finding is normally a prelude to reaching a verdict. In the juvenile court, however, the finding itself is the verdict—the case is resolved in one of three ways:

1. The juvenile court judge makes a finding of fact that the child or juvenile is not delinquent or in need of supervision.

2. The juvenile court judge makes a finding of fact that the juvenile is delinquent or in need of supervision.

3. The juvenile court judge dismisses the case because of insufficient or faulty evidence.

To get information on juvenile courts, go to the Web site of the National Center for State Courts by clicking on Web Links under the Chapter Resources at http://cj. wadsworth.com/siegel_ jdcore2e.

In some jurisdictions, informal alternatives are used, such as filing the case with no further consequences or continuing the case without a finding for a period of time such as six months. If the juvenile does not get into further difficulty during that time, the case is dismissed. These alternatives involve no determination of delinquency or noncriminal behavior. Because of the philosophy of the juvenile court that emphasizes rehabilitation over punishment, a delinquency finding is not the same thing as a criminal conviction. The disabilities associated with conviction, such as disqualifications for employment or being barred from military service, do not apply in an adjudication of delinquency.

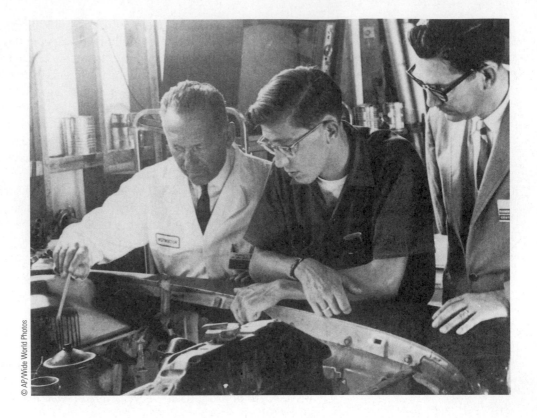

The appeal of Gerald Gault (center) heralded in the due process revolution in juvenile justice.

© AP/Wide World Photos

There are other differences between adult and juvenile proceedings. For instance, while adults are entitled to public trials by a jury of their peers, these rights are not extended to juveniles.[70] Because juvenile courts are treating some defendants in a similar way as adult criminals, an argument can be made that the courts should extend to these youths the Sixth Amendment right to a public jury trial.[71] For the most part, however, state juvenile courts operate without recognizing a juvenile's constitutional right to a jury trial.

Constitutional Rights at Trial

In addition to mandating state juvenile code requirements, the U.S. Supreme Court has mandated the application of constitutional due process standards to the juvenile trial. **Due process** is addressed in the Fifth and Fourteenth Amendments to the U.S. Constitution. It refers to the need for rules and procedures that protect individual rights. Having the right to due process means that no person can be deprived of life, liberty, or property without such protections as legal counsel, an open and fair hearing, and an opportunity to confront those making accusations against him or her.

For many years, children were deprived of their due process rights because the *parens patriae* philosophy governed their relationship to the juvenile justice system. Such rights as having counsel and confronting one's accusers were deemed unnecessary. After all, why should children need protection from the state when the state was seen as acting in their interest? As we have seen, this view changed in the 1960s, when the U.S. Supreme Court began to grant due process rights and procedures to minors. The key case was that of Gerald Gault; it articulated the basic requirements of due process that must be satisfied in juvenile court proceedings. Because *Gault* remains the key constitutional case in the juvenile justice system, it is discussed in depth in the accompanying Juvenile Law in Review feature.

The *Gault* decision reshaped the constitutional and philosophical nature of the juvenile court system, and with the addition of legal representation, made it more similar to the adult system.[72] Following the *Gault* case, the U.S. Supreme Court decided in *in re Winship* that the amount of proof required in juvenile delinquency

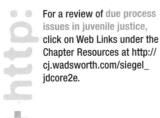

For a review of due process issues in juvenile justice, click on Web Links under the Chapter Resources at http://cj.wadsworth.com/siegel_jdcore2e.

due process
Basic constitutional principle based on the concept of the primacy of the individual and the complementary concept of limitation on governmental power; safeguards the individual from unfair state procedures in judicial or administrative proceedings; due process rights have been extended to juvenile trials.

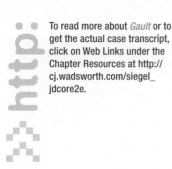

To read more about *Gault* or to get the actual case transcript, click on Web Links under the Chapter Resources at http://cj.wadsworth.com/siegel_jdcore2e.

adjudications is "beyond a reasonable doubt," a level equal to the requirements in the adult system.[73]

Although the ways in which the juvenile court operates were altered by *Gault* and *Winship,* the trend toward increased rights for juveniles was somewhat curtailed by the U.S. Supreme Court's decision in *McKeiver v. Pennsylvania* (1971), which held that trial by jury in a juvenile court's adjudicative stage is not a constitutional requirement.[74] This decision does not prevent states from giving the juvenile a trial by jury, but in most states a child has no such right.

Once an adjudicatory hearing has been completed, the court is normally required to enter a judgment or finding against the child. This may take the form of declaring the child delinquent, adjudging the child to be a ward of the court, or possibly even suspending judgment so as to avoid the stigma of a juvenile record. After a judgment has been entered, the court can begin its determination of possible dispositions.

Disposition

The sentencing step of the juvenile justice process is called *disposition.* At this point the court orders treatment for the juvenile.[75] According to prevailing juvenile justice philosophy, dispositions should be in the *best interest of the child,* which in this context means providing the help necessary to resolve or meet the adolescent's personal needs, while at the same time meeting society's needs for protection.

As already noted, in most jurisdictions, adjudication and disposition hearings are bifurcated, so that evidence that could not be entered during the juvenile trial can be considered at the dispositional hearing. At the hearing, the defense counsel represents the child, helps the parents understand the court's decision, and influences the direction of the disposition. Others involved at the dispositional stage include representatives of social service agencies, psychologists, social workers, and probation personnel.

The Predisposition Report   After the child has admitted to the allegations, or the allegations have been proved in a trial, the judge normally orders the probation department to complete a predisposition report. The predisposition report, which is similar to the presentence report of the adult justice system, has a number of purposes:

- It helps the judge decide which disposition is best for the child.
- It aids the juvenile probation officer in developing treatment programs where the child is in need of counseling or community supervision.
- It helps the court develop a body of knowledge about the child that can aid others in treating the child.[76]

Some state statutes make the predisposition report mandatory. Other jurisdictions require the report only when there is a probability that the child will be institutionalized. Some appellate courts have reversed orders institutionalizing children where the juvenile court did not use a predisposition report in reaching its decision. Access to predisposition reports is an important legal issue.

In the final section of the predisposition report, the probation department recommends a disposition to the presiding judge. This is a critical aspect of the report because it has been estimated that the court follows more than 90 percent of all probation-department recommendations.

Juvenile Court Dispositions   Historically, the juvenile court has had broad discretionary power to make dispositional decisions. The major categories of dispositional choices are community release, out-of-home placement, fines or restitution, community service, and institutionalization. A more detailed list of the dispositions open to the juvenile court judge appears in Exhibit 13.3.[77]

Most state statutes allow the juvenile court judge to select whatever disposition seems best suited to the child's needs, including institutionalization. In some states

In re Gault

Facts

Gerald Gault, fifteen years of age, was taken into custody by the sheriff of Gila County, Arizona, because a woman complained that he and another boy had made an obscene telephone call to her. At the time, Gault was under a six-month probation disposition after being found delinquent for stealing a wallet. As a result of the woman's complaint, the boy was taken to a children's home. His parents were not informed that he was being taken into custody. His mother appeared in the evening and was told by the superintendent of detention that a hearing would be held in the juvenile court the following day. On the day in question, the police officer who had taken him into custody filed a petition alleging his delinquency. Gault, his mother, and the police officer appeared before the judge in his chambers. Mrs. Cook, the complainant, was not at the hearing. The boy was questioned about the telephone calls and sent back to the detention home and subsequently released a few days later.

On the day of his release, Mrs. Gault received a letter indicating that a hearing would be held on his delinquency a few days later. A hearing was held, and the complainant again was not present. There was no transcript or recording of the proceedings, and the juvenile officer stated that Gault had admitted making the lewd telephone calls. Neither the boy nor his parents were advised of any right to remain silent, right to be represented by counsel, or any other constitutional rights. At the conclusion of the hearing, the juvenile court committed Gault as a juvenile delinquent to the state industrial school for the period of his minority.

This meant that, at age fifteen, Gerald Gault was sentenced to remain in the state school until he reached the age of twenty-one, unless he was discharged sooner. An adult charged with the same crime would have received a maximum punishment of no more than a $50 fine or two months in prison.

Decision

Gault's attorneys filed a writ of habeas corpus, which was denied by the Superior Court of the State of Arizona. That decision was subsequently affirmed by the Arizona Supreme Court. On appeal to the U.S. Supreme Court, Gault's counsel argued that the juvenile code of Arizona under which the boy was found delinquent was invalid because it was contrary to the due process clause of the Fourteenth Amendment. In addition, Gault was denied the following basic due process rights: (1) notice of the charges with respect to their timeliness and specificity, (2) right to counsel, (3) right to confrontation and cross-examination, (4) privilege against self-incrimination, (5) right to a transcript of the trial record, and (6) right to appellate review. In deciding the case, the U.S. Supreme Court had to determine whether procedural due process of law in the context of fundamental fairness under the Fourteenth Amendment applied to juvenile delinquency proceedings in which a child is committed to a state industrial school.

The Court, in a far-reaching opinion, agreed that Gerald Gault's constitutional rights had been violated. Notice of charges was an essential ingredient of due process of law, as was the right to counsel, the right to cross-examine and to confront witnesses, and the privilege against self-incrimination. The questions of appellate review and a right to a transcript were not answered by the Court in this case.

Significance of the Case

The *Gault* case established that a child has the due process constitutional rights listed here in delinquency adjudication proceedings, where the consequences were that the child could be committed to a state institution. It was confined to rulings at the adjudication state of the juvenile process.

This decision was significant not only because of the procedural reforms it initiated but also because of its far-reaching impact throughout the entire juvenile justice system. *Gault* instilled in juvenile proceedings the development of due process standards at the pretrial, trial, and posttrial stages of the juvenile process. While recognizing the history and development of the juvenile court, it sought to accommodate the motives of rehabilitation and treatment with children's rights. It recognized the principle of fundamental fairness of the law for children as well as for adults. Judged in the context of today's juvenile justice system, *Gault* redefined the relationships between juveniles, their parents, and the state. It remains the single most significant constitutional case in the area of juvenile justice.

CRITICAL THINKING

The *Gault* case is hailed as a milestone for giving juveniles due process rights. Does the provision of those rights actually harm juveniles? In other words, would it have been advisable to keep attorneys and legal process out of the juvenile court? Is it too late to transform the system so that it reflects its original ideals?

INFOTRAC COLLEGE EDITION RESEARCH

How has the *Gault* case shaped the philosophy of the juvenile court? To find out, read Lise A. Young, "Suffer the Children: The Basic Principle of Juvenile Justice Is to Treat the Child, Not Punish the Offense," *America* 185(12):19 (October 22, 2001).

Source: *In re Gault*, 387 U.S. 1; 87 S.Ct. 1248 (1967).

the court determines commitment to a specific institution; in other states the youth corrections agency determines where the child will be placed. In addition to the dispositions shown in Exhibit 13.3, some states grant the court the power to order parents into treatment or suspend a youth's driver's license.

Exhibit 13.3 **Common Juvenile Dispositions**

Disposition	Action Taken
Informal consent decree	In minor or first offenses, an informal hearing is held, and the judge will ask the youth and his or her guardian to agree to a treatment program, such as counseling. No formal trial or disposition hearing is held.
Probation	A youth is placed under the control of the county probation department and required to obey a set of probation rules and participate in a treatment program.
Home detention	A child is restricted to his or her home in lieu of a secure placement. Rules include regular school attendance, curfew observance, avoidance of alcohol and drugs, and notification of parents and the youth worker of the child's whereabouts.
Court-ordered school attendance	If truancy was the problem that brought the youth to court, a judge may order mandatory school attendance. Some courts have established court-operated day schools and court-based tutorial programs staffed by community volunteers.
Financial restitution	A judge can order the juvenile offender to make financial restitution to the victim. In most jurisdictions, restitution is part of probation (see chapter 14), but in a few states, such as Maryland, restitution can be a sole order.
Fines	Some states allow fines to be levied against juveniles age sixteen and over.
Community service	Courts in many jurisdictions require juveniles to spend time in the community working off their debt to society. Community service orders are usually reserved for victimless crimes, such as possession of drugs, or crimes against public order, such as vandalism of school property. Community service orders are usually carried out in schools, hospitals, or nursing homes.
Outpatient psychotherapy	Youths who are diagnosed with psychological disorders may be required to undergo therapy at a local mental health clinic.
Drug and alcohol treatment	Youths with drug- or alcohol-related problems may be allowed to remain in the community if they agree to undergo drug or alcohol therapy.
Commitment to secure treatment	In the most serious cases a judge may order an offender admitted to a long-term treatment center, such as a training school, camp, ranch, or group home. These may be either state-run or privately run institutions, and are usually located in remote regions. Training schools provide educational, vocational, and rehabilitation programs in a secure environment (see chapter 14).
Commitment to a residential community	Youths who commit crimes of a less serious nature but who still need to be removed from their homes can be placed in community-based group homes or halfway houses. They attend school or work during the day and live in a controlled, therapeutic environment at night.
Foster home placement	Foster homes are usually sought for dependent or neglected children and status offenders. Today judges are placing delinquents with insurmountable problems at home in state-licensed foster care homes.

Today it is common for juvenile court judges to employ a graduated sanction program for juveniles: immediate sanctions for nonviolent offenders, which consist of community-based diversion and day treatment imposed on first-time nonviolent offenders; intermediate sanctions, which target repeat minor offenders and first-time serious offenders; and secure care, which is reserved for repeat serious offenders and violent offenders.[78]

In 1999, juveniles were adjudicated delinquent in two-thirds (66 percent) of the 962,000 cases brought before a judge. Once adjudicated, the majority of these juveniles (62 percent or 398,200 cases) were placed on formal probation, one-quarter (24 percent or 155,200 cases) were placed in a residential facility, and 10 percent (or 64,000 cases) were given another disposition, such as referral to an outside agency, community service, or restitution.[79]

Although the juvenile court has been under pressure to get tough on youth crime, these figures show that probation is the disposition of choice, even in the most serious cases,[80] and its use has grown in recent years. Between 1990 and 1999, the number of cases in which the court ordered an adjudicated delinquent to be placed on formal probation increased 80 percent, while the number of cases involving placement in a residential facility increased 24 percent.[81]

Juvenile Sentencing Structures

For most of the juvenile court's history, disposition was based on the presumed needs of the child. Although critics have challenged the motivations of early reformers in championing rehabilitation, there is little question that the rhetoric of the juvenile court has promoted that ideal.[82] For example, in their classic work *Beyond the Best Interest of the Child,* Joseph Goldstein, Anna Freud, and Albert Solnit said that placement of children should be based on the **least detrimental alternative** available in order to foster the child's development.[83] Most states have adopted this ideal in their sentencing efforts, and state courts usually insist that the purpose of disposition must be rehabilitation and not punishment.[84] Consequently, it is common for state courts to require judges to justify their sentencing decisions if it means that juveniles are to be incarcerated in a residential treatment center: they must set forth in writing the reasons for the placement, address the danger the child poses to society, and explain why a less restrictive alternative has not been used.[85]

Traditionally, states have used the **indeterminate sentence** in juvenile court. In about half the states, this means having the judge place the offender with the state department of juvenile corrections until correctional authorities consider the youth ready to return to society or until the youth reaches legal majority. A preponderance of states consider eighteen to be the age of release; others peg the termination age at nineteen; a few can retain minority status until the twenty-first birthday. In practice, few youths remain in custody for the entire statutory period, but juveniles are usually released if their rehabilitation has been judged to have progressed satisfactorily. This practice is referred to as the individualized treatment model.

Another form of the indeterminate sentence allows judges to specify a maximum term. Under this form of sentencing, youths may be released if the corrections department considers them to be rehabilitated or they reach the automatic age of termination (usually eighteen or twenty-one). In states that stipulate a maximum sentence, the court may extend the sentence, depending on the youth's progress in the institutional facility.

A number of states have changed from an indeterminate to a **determinate sentence.** This means sentencing juvenile offenders to a fixed term of incarceration that must be served in its entirety. Other states have passed laws creating **mandatory sentences** for serious juvenile offenders. Juveniles receiving mandatory sentences are usually institutionalized for the full sentence and are not eligible for early parole. The difference between mandatory and determinate sentences is that the mandatory sentence carries a statutory requirement that a certain penalty be set in all cases on conviction for a specified offense.

Sentencing Reform

During the past decade there have been a number of attempts to create rational sentencing in juvenile justice. In some instances the goal has been to reduce judicial discretion, in others to toughen sentencing practices and create mandatory periods of

least detrimental alternative
Choosing a program that will best foster a child's growth and development.

indeterminate sentence
Does not specify the length of time the juvenile must be held; rather, correctional authorities decide when the juvenile is ready to return to society.

determinate sentence
Specifies a fixed term of detention that must be served.

mandatory sentences
Sentences are defined by a statutory requirement that states the penalty to be set for all cases of a specific offense.

When making disposition decisions, juvenile court judges may select programs that will enhance life skills and help youths form a positive bond with society. Here, juvenile offenders work with severely disabled kids at El Camino School as part of their jail time and rehabilitation.

© Tony Savino/The Image Works

incarceration for juveniles who commit serious crimes. However, not all statutory changes have had the desired effect. For instance, New York State has implemented a juvenile offender law requiring that juveniles accused of violent offenses be tried in criminal court as a get-tough-on-crime measure; evaluations found that many youths ended up receiving lighter sentences than they would have in the family court.[86]

Probably the best-known effort to reform sentencing in the juvenile court is the state of Washington's Juvenile Justice Reform Act of 1977. This act created a mandatory sentencing policy requiring juveniles ages eight to seventeen who are adjudicated delinquent to be confined to an institution for a minimum time.[87] The intent of the act was to make juveniles accountable for criminal behavior and to provide for punishment commensurate with the age, crime, and prior history of the offender. Washington's approach is based on the principle of *proportionality*. How much time a youth must spend in confinement is established by the Juvenile Dispositions Standards Commission, based on the three stated criteria. The introduction of such mandatory sentencing procedures reduces disparity in the length of sentences, according to advocates of a get-tough juvenile justice system.

Blended Sentences State sentencing trends indicate that punishment and accountability, in addition to rehabilitation, have become equally important in juvenile justice policy. As a result, many states have created blended sentencing structures for cases involving serious offenders. Blended sentencing allows the imposition of juvenile and adult sanctions for juvenile offenders adjudicated in juvenile court or convicted in criminal court. In other words, this expanded sentencing authority allows criminal and juvenile courts to impose either a juvenile or an adult sentence, or both, in cases involving juvenile offenders. When both sentences are imposed simultaneously, the court suspends the adult sanction. If the youth follows the conditions of the juvenile sentence and commits no further violation, the adult sentence is revoked. This type of statute has become popular in recent years, with Connecticut, Kentucky, and Minnesota among the states adopting it since 1994.[88]

The Death Penalty for Juveniles

Juveniles who have been waived to adult court can receive the death penalty. The execution of minor children has not been uncommon in our nation's history; at least 366 juvenile offenders have been executed since 1642.[89] This represents about 2 percent of the total of more than eighteen thousand executions carried out since colonial times.

During the past twenty years, 196 juvenile death sentences have been imposed (about 3 percent of the almost sixty-nine hundred total U.S. death sentences). Approximately two-thirds of these have been imposed on seventeen-year-olds and nearly one-third on fifteen- and sixteen-year-olds.[90] As of 2003, twenty-one states permitted the juvenile death penalty[91] and seventy-eight juvenile offenders were on death row. Since the death penalty was reinstated in 1976, twenty-two juvenile offenders have been executed in seven states, with Texas accounting for thirteen of these twenty-two executions (Table 13.1). All twenty-two of the executed juvenile offenders were male, twenty-one committed their crimes at age seventeen, and just over half (twelve of them) were minorities.[92]

Legal Issues In *Thompson v. Oklahoma* (1988), the U.S. Supreme Court prohibited the execution of persons *under age sixteen* but left open the age at which execution would be legally appropriate.[93] They then answered this question in two 1989 cases, *Wilkins v. Missouri* and *Stanford v. Kentucky,* in which they ruled that states were free to impose the death penalty for murderers who committed their crimes after they reached age sixteen or seventeen.[94] According to the majority opinion, society has not formed a consensus that the execution of such minors constitutes cruel and unusual punishment.

Those who oppose the death penalty for children find that it has little deterrent effect on youngsters who are impulsive and do not have a realistic view of the destructiveness of their misdeeds or their consequences. Victor Streib, the leading critic of the death penalty for children, argues that such a practice is cruel and unusual punishment for four primary reasons: the condemnation of children makes no measurable contribution to the legitimate goals of punishment; condemning any minor to death violates contemporary standards of decency; the capacity of the young for change, growth, and rehabilitation makes the death penalty particularly harsh and inappropriate; and both legislative attitudes and public opinion reject juvenile executions.[95] Those who oppose the death penalty for children also refer to a growing body of research that shows that the brain continues to develop through the late teen years, in addition to important mental functions, such as planning, judgment, and emotional control.[96] Supporters of the death penalty hold that, regardless of their age, people can form criminal intent and therefore should be responsible for their actions. If the death penalty is legal for adults, they assert, then it can also be used for children who commit serious crimes.

The fact that the United States is not alone in executing criminals appears to support retention of the death penalty. However, the fact that many countries have abolished capital punishment encourages those who want it to be abandoned here.

✔ Checkpoints

The Child's Right to Appeal

Regardless of the sentence imposed, juveniles may want to appeal the decision made by the juvenile court judge. Juvenile court statutes normally restrict appeals to cases where the juvenile seeks review of a **final order,** one that ends the litigation between two parties by determining all their rights and disposing of all the issues.[97] The **appellate process** gives the juvenile the opportunity to have the case brought before a reviewing court after it has been heard in the juvenile or family court. Today, the law does not recognize a federal constitutional right of appeal. In other words, the U.S. Constitution does not require any state to furnish an appeal to a juvenile charged and found to be delinquent in a juvenile or family court. Consequently, appellate

final order
Order that ends litigation between two parties by determining all their rights and disposing of all the issues.

appellate process
Allows the juvenile an opportunity to have the case brought before a reviewing court after it has been heard in juvenile or family court.

Table 13.1

Juveniles Executed or Facing Execution, by State, 1976–2003

State	Juvenile Offenders on Death Row	Juvenile Offenders Executed
Alabama	13	0
Arizona	5	0
Arkansas	0	0
Delaware	0	0
Florida	2	0
Georgia	2	1
Idaho	0	0
Kentucky	1	0
Louisiana	7	1
Mississippi	5	0
Missouri*	2	1
Nevada	1	0
New Hampshire	0	0
North Carolina	5	0
Oklahoma	0	2
Pennsylvania	3	0
South Carolina	3	1
South Dakota	0	0
Texas	28	13
Utah	0	0
Virginia	1	3
Wyoming	0	0
Total	78	22

*In August 2003, the Supreme Court of Missouri declared the death penalty to be unconstitutional for offenders under the age of eighteen. The state petitioned the U.S. Supreme Court to take up this matter.

Source: *Fact Sheet: The Juvenile Death Penalty* (Chicago: American Bar Association Juvenile Justice Center, 2003), p. 2.

review of a juvenile case is a matter of statutory right in each jurisdiction. However, the majority of states do provide juveniles with some method of statutory appeal.

The appeal process was not always part of the juvenile law system. In 1965, few states extended the right of appeal to juveniles.[98] Even in the *Gault* case in 1967, the U.S. Supreme Court refused to review the Arizona juvenile code, which provided no appellate review in juvenile matters. It further rejected the right of a juvenile to a transcript of the original trial record.[99] Today, however, most jurisdictions that provide a child with some form of appeal also provide for counsel and for securing a record and transcript, which are crucial to the success of any appeal.

Because juvenile appellate review is defined by individual statutes, each jurisdiction determines for itself what method of review will be used. There are two basic methods of appeal: the direct appeal and the collateral attack.

The *direct appeal* normally involves an appellate court review to determine whether, based on the evidence presented at the trial, the rulings of law and the judgment of the court were correct. The second major area of review involves the collateral attack of a case. The term *collateral* implies a secondary or indirect method of attacking a final judgment. Instead of appealing the juvenile trial because of errors, prejudice, or lack of evidence, *collateral review* uses extraordinary legal writs to challenge the lower-court position. One such procedural device is the writ of habeas corpus. Known as the *Great Writ,* the **writ of habeas corpus** refers to a procedure for

writ of habeus corpus
Judicial order requesting that a person detaining another produce the body of the prisoner and give reasons for his or her capture and detention.

determining the validity of a person's custody. In the context of the juvenile court, it is used to challenge the custody of a child in detention or in an institution. This writ is often the method by which the Supreme Court exercises its discretionary authority to hear cases involving constitutional issues. Even though there is no constitutional right to appeal a juvenile case and each jurisdiction provides for appeals differently, juveniles have a far greater opportunity for appellate review today than in years past.

Confidentiality in Juvenile Proceedings

Along with the rights of juveniles at adjudication and disposition, the issue of **confidentiality** in juvenile proceedings has also received attention in recent years. The debate on confidentiality in the juvenile court deals with two areas: open versus closed hearings, and privacy of juvenile records. Confidentiality has become moot in some respects, because many legislatures have broadened access to juvenile records.

Open Versus Closed Hearings   Generally, juvenile trials are closed to the public and the press, and the names of the offenders are kept secret. The U.S. Supreme Court has ruled on the issue of privacy in three important decisions. In *Davis v. Alaska,* the Court concluded that any injury resulting from the disclosure of a juvenile's record is outweighed by the right to completely cross-examine an adverse witness.[100] The *Davis* case involved an effort to obtain testimony from a juvenile probationer who was a witness in a criminal trial. After the prosecutor was granted a court order preventing the defense from making any reference to the juvenile's record, the Supreme Court reversed the state court, claiming that a juvenile's interest in confidentiality was secondary to the constitutional right to confront adverse witnesses.

The decisions in two subsequent cases, *Oklahoma Publishing Co. v. District Court* and *Smith v. Daily Mail Publishing Co.,* sought to balance juvenile privacy with freedom of the press. In the *Oklahoma* case, the Supreme Court ruled that a state court was not allowed to prohibit the publication of information obtained in an open juvenile proceeding.[101] The case involved an eleven-year-old boy suspected of homicide, who appeared at a detention hearing where photographs were taken and published in local newspapers. When the local district court prohibited further disclosure, the publishing company claimed that the court order was a restraint in violation of the First Amendment, and the Supreme Court agreed.

The *Smith* case involved the discovery and publication of the identity of a juvenile suspect in violation of a state statute prohibiting publication. The Supreme Court, however, declared the statute unconstitutional because it believed the state's interest in protecting the child's identity was not of such a magnitude as to justify the use of such a statute.[102] Therefore, if newspapers lawfully obtain pictures or names of juveniles, they may publish them. Based on these decisions, it appears that the Supreme Court favors the constitutional rights of the press over the right to privacy of the juvenile offender.

Privacy of Juvenile Records   For most of the twentieth century, juvenile records were kept confidential.[103] Today, however, the record itself, or information contained in it, can be opened by court order in many jurisdictions on the basis of statutory exception. The following groups can ordinarily gain access to juvenile records: law enforcement personnel, the child's attorney, parents or guardians, military personnel, and public agencies such as schools, court-related organizations, and correctional institutions.

Today, most states recognize the importance of juvenile records in sentencing. Many first-time adult offenders committed numerous crimes as juveniles, and evidence of these crimes may not be available to sentencing for the adult offenses unless states pass statutes allowing access. Knowledge of a defendant's juvenile record may help prosecutors and judges determine appropriate sentencing for offenders ages eighteen to twenty-four, the age group most likely to be involved in violent crime.

According to experts such as Ira Schwartz, the need for confidentiality to protect juveniles is far less than the need to open up the courts to public scrutiny.[104] The

confidentiality
Restricting information in juvenile court proceedings in the interest of protecting the privacy of the juvenile.

problem of maintaining confidentiality of juvenile records will become more acute in the future as electronic information storage makes these records both more durable and more accessible.

In conclusion, virtually every state provides prosecutors and judges with access to the juvenile records of adult offenders. There is great diversity, however, regarding provisions for the collection and retention of juvenile records.[105]

SUMMARY

- Prosecutors, judges, and defense attorneys are the key players in the juvenile court. The juvenile prosecutor is the attorney responsible for bringing the state's case against the accused juvenile. The juvenile judge must ensure that the children and families who come before the court receive the proper help. Defense attorneys representing children in the juvenile court play an active part in virtually all stages of the proceedings.

- Many decisions about what happens to a child may occur prior to adjudication. Key issues include detention, intake, diversion, pretrial release, plea bargaining, and waiver. Because the juvenile justice system is not able to try every child accused of a crime or a status offense due to personnel limitations, diversion programs seem to hold greater hope for the control of delinquency. As a result, such subsystems as statutory intake proceedings, plea bargaining, and other informal adjustments are essential ingredients in the administration of the juvenile justice system.

- Each year, thousands of youths are transferred to adult courts because of the seriousness of their crimes. This process, known as *waiver,* is an effort to remove serious offenders from the juvenile process and into the more punitive adult system. Most juvenile experts oppose waiver because it clashes with the rehabilitative ideal. Supporters argue that its increased use can help get violent juvenile offenders off the street, and they point to studies that show that, for the most part, transfer is reserved for the most serious cases and the most serious juvenile offenders.

- Most jurisdictions have a bifurcated juvenile code system that separates the adjudication hearing from the dispositional hearing. Juveniles alleged to be delin-

quent have virtually all the rights given a criminal defendant at trial—except possibly the right to a trial by jury. In addition, juvenile proceedings are generally closed to the public.

- *In re Gault* is the key legal case that set out the basic requirements of due process that must be satisfied in juvenile court proceedings. In *Wilkins v. Missouri* and *Stanford v. Kentucky,* the U.S. Supreme Court ruled that states were free to impose the death penalty for murderers who committed their crimes after they reached age sixteen or seventeen.

- The major categories of dispositional choice in juvenile cases are community release, out-of-home placements, fines or restitution, community service, and institutionalization. Although the traditional notion of rehabilitation and treatment as the proper goals for disposition is being questioned, many juvenile codes do require that the court consider the *least restrictive alternative.*

- Juveniles who have been waived to adult court can receive the death penalty. Those who oppose the death penalty for juveniles find that it has little deterrent effect on youngsters who are impulsive and do not have a realistic view of the destructiveness of their misdeeds or their consequences. Supporters of the death penalty hold that people, regardless of their age, can form criminal intent and therefore should be responsible for their actions.

- Many state statutes require that juvenile hearings be closed and that the privacy of juvenile records be maintained to protect the child from public scrutiny and to provide a greater opportunity for rehabilitation. This approach may be inconsistent with the public's interest in taking a closer look at the juvenile justice system.

1. Discuss and identify the major participants in the juvenile adjudication process. What are each person's role and responsibilities in the course of a juvenile trial?

2. The criminal justice system in the United States is based on the adversarial process. Does the same principle apply in the juvenile justice system?

3. Children have certain constitutional rights at adjudication, such as the right to an attorney and the right to confront and cross-examine witnesses. But they do not have the right to a trial by jury. Should juvenile offenders have a constitutional right to a jury trial? Should each state make that determination? Discuss the legal decision that addresses this issue.

4. What is the point of obtaining a predisposition report in the juvenile court? Is it of any value in cases where the child is released to the community? Does it have a significant value in serious juvenile crime cases?

5. The standard of proof in juvenile adjudication is to show that the child is guilty beyond a reasonable doubt. Explain the meaning of this standard of proof in the U.S. judicial system.

6. Should states adopt get-tough sentences in juvenile justice or adhere to the individualized treatment model?

7. What are blended sentences?

8. Do you agree with the principle of imposing the death penalty on juveniles found to have committed certain capital crimes?

9. Should individuals who committed murder while under age sixteen be legally executed?

APPLYING WHAT YOU HAVE LEARNED

As an experienced family court judge, you are often faced with difficult decisions, but few are more difficult than the case of John M., arrested at age fourteen for robbery and rape. His victim, a young neighborhood girl, was badly injured in the attack and needed extensive hospitalization; she is now in counseling. Even though the charges are serious, because of his age John can still be subject to the jurisdiction of the juvenile division of the state family court. However, the prosecutor has filed a petition to waive jurisdiction to the adult court. Under existing state law, a hearing must be held to determine whether there is sufficient evidence that John cannot be successfully treated in the juvenile justice system and therefore warrants transfer to the adult system; the final decision on the matter is yours alone.

At the waiver hearing, you discover that John is the oldest of three siblings living in a single-parent home. He has had no contact with his father for more than ten years. His psychological evaluation showed hostility, anger toward females, and great feelings of frustration. His intelligence is below average, and his behavioral and academic records are poor. In addition, he seems to be involved with a local youth gang, although he denies any formal association with them. This is his first formal involvement with the juvenile court. Previous contact was limited to an informal complaint for disorderly conduct at age thirteen, which was dismissed by the court's intake department. During the hearing, John verbalizes what you interpret to be superficial remorse for his offenses.

To the prosecutor, John seems to be a youth with poor controls who is likely to commit future crimes. The defense attorney argues that there are effective treatment opportunities within the juvenile justice system that can meet John's needs. Her views are supported by an evaluation of the case conducted by the court's probation staff, which concludes that the case can be dealt with in the confines of juvenile corrections.

If the case remains in the juvenile court, John can be kept in custody in a juvenile facility until age eighteen; if transferred to felony court, he could be sentenced to up to twenty years in a maximum-security prison. As judge, you recognize the seriousness of the crimes committed by John and realize that it is very difficult to predict or assess his future behavior and potential dangerousness.

- Would you authorize a waiver to adult court or keep the case in the juvenile justice system?
- Can fourteen-year-olds truly understand the seriousness of their behavior?
- Should a juvenile court judge consider the victim in making a disposition decision?

DOING RESEARCH ON THE WEB

Before you answer these questions, research waivers to adult court by using "juveniles and waivers" in a key word search on InfoTrac College Edition. To get further information on this topic, click on Web Links under the Chapter Resources at **http://cj.wadsworth.com/siegel_jdcore2e** and go to the Web sites of the American Bar Association Juvenile Justice Center; OJJDP Statistical Briefing Book; American Youth Policy Forum on Juvenile Justice; the Juvenile Justice Division of the Child Welfare League of America; and the National Council on Crime and Delinquency and Children's Research Center.

Pro/Con discussions and Viewpoint Essays on some of the topics in this chapter may be found at the Opposing Viewpoints Resource Center: **www.gale.com/OpposingViewpoints**.

chapter 14

Juvenile Corrections: Probation, Community Treatment, and Institutionalization

CHAPTER OUTLINE

CHAPTER OBJECTIVES

After reading this chapter you
should:

1. Be able to distinguish between community treatment and institutional treatment for juvenile offenders.

2. Be familiar with the disposition of probation, including how it is administered and by whom and recent trends in its use compared with other dispositions.

3. Be aware of new approaches for providing probation services to juvenile offenders and comment on their effectiveness in reducing recidivism.

4. Understand key historical developments of secure juvenile corrections in this country, including the principle of *least restrictive alternative*.

5. Be familiar with recent trends in the use of juvenile institutions for juvenile offenders and how their use differs across states.

6. Understand key issues facing the institutionalized juvenile offender.

7. Be able to identify the various juvenile correctional treatment approaches that are in use today and comment on their effectiveness in reducing recidivism.

8. Know the nature of aftercare for juvenile offenders.

Started in the late 1980s, juvenile boot camps were introduced as a way to get tough on youthful offenders through rigorous military-style training, while at the same time providing them with treatment programs. In theory, a successful boot camp program should rehabilitate juvenile offenders, reduce the number of beds needed in secure institutional programs, and thus reduce the overall cost of care. However, evaluations of these programs across the country found this not to be the case, and some found juveniles in boot camps to have higher recidivism rates than similar youths in other institutional settings. Research shows that one of the main reasons for their ineffectiveness is that the treatment component is often left out. In New Jersey, juvenile justice administrators are trying to change this trend. Here, juvenile boot camps combine rigorous physical training with a strong emphasis on education, drug counseling, job skills training, and other treatment programs to help them prepare for their return to the community. One other change that administrators point to as promising is that boot camp leaders are trained to act as mentors or role models to the juvenile offenders.

CNN. VIEW THE CNN VIDEO CLIP OF THIS STORY AND ANSWER RELATED CRITICAL THINKING QUESTIONS ON YOUR JUVENILE DELINQUENCY: THE CORE 2E CD.

There is a wide choice of correctional treatments available for juveniles, which can be subdivided into two major categories: community treatment and institutional treatment. **Community treatment** refers to efforts to provide care, protection, and treatment for juveniles in need. These efforts include probation; treatment services (such as individual and group counseling); restitution; and other programs. The term *community treatment* also refers to the use of privately maintained residences, such as foster homes, small-group homes, and boarding schools, which are located in the community. Nonresidential programs, where youths remain in their own homes but are required to receive counseling, vocational training, and other services, also fall under the rubric of community treatment.

Institutional treatment facilities are correctional centers operated by federal, state, and county governments; these facilities restrict the movement of residents through staff monitoring, locked exits, and interior fence controls. There are several types of institutional facilities in juvenile corrections, including reception centers that screen juveniles and assign them to an appropriate facility; specialized facilities that provide specific types of care, such as drug treatment; training schools or reformatories for youths needing a long-term secure setting; ranch or forestry camps that provide long-term residential care; and boot camps, which seek to rehabilitate youth through the application of rigorous physical training.

Choosing the proper mode of juvenile corrections can be difficult. Some experts believe that any hope for rehabilitating juvenile offenders and resolving the problems of juvenile crime lies in community treatment programs. Such programs are smaller than secure facilities for juveniles, operate in a community setting, and offer creative approaches to treating the offender. In contrast, institutionalizing young offenders may do more harm than good. It exposes them to prisonlike conditions and to more experienced delinquents without giving them the benefit of constructive treatment programs.

Those who favor secure treatment are concerned about the threat that violent young offenders present to the community and believe that a stay in a juvenile institu-

community treatment
Using nonsecure and noninstitutional residences, counseling services, victim restitution programs, and other community services to treat juveniles in their own communities.

tion may have a long-term deterrent effect. They point to the findings of Charles Murray and Louis B. Cox, who uncovered what they call a **suppression effect,** a reduction in the number of arrests per year following release from a secure facility, which is not achieved when juveniles are placed in less punitive programs.[1] Murray and Cox concluded that the justice system must choose which outcome its programs are aimed at achieving: prevention of delinquency, or the care and protection of needy youths. If the former is a proper goal, institutionalization or the threat of institutionalization is desirable. Not surprisingly, secure treatment is still being used extensively, and the populations of these facilities continue to grow as state legislators pass more stringent and punitive sentencing packages aimed at repeat juvenile offenders.

JUVENILE PROBATION

Probation and other forms of community treatment generally refer to nonpunitive legal dispositions for delinquent youths, emphasizing treatment without incarceration. Probation is the primary form of community treatment used by the juvenile justice system. A juvenile who is on probation is maintained in the community under the supervision of an officer of the court. Probation also encompasses a set of rules and conditions that must be met for the offender to remain in the community. Juveniles on probation may be placed in a wide variety of community-based treatment programs that provide services ranging from group counseling to drug treatment.

Community treatment is based on the idea that the juvenile offender is not a danger to the community and has a better chance of being rehabilitated in the community. It provides offenders with the opportunity to be supervised by trained personnel who can help them reestablish forms of acceptable behavior in a community setting. When applied correctly, community treatment maximizes the liberty of the individual while at the same time vindicating the authority of the law and protecting the public; promotes rehabilitation by maintaining normal community contacts; avoids the negative effects of confinement, which often severely complicate the reintegration of the offender into the community; and greatly reduces the financial cost to the public.[2]

Historical Development

Although the major developments in community treatment have occurred in the twentieth century, its roots go back much further. In England, specialized procedures for dealing with youthful offenders were recorded as early as 1820, when the magistrates of the Warwickshire quarter sessions (periodic court hearings held in a county, or shire, of England) adopted the practice of sentencing youthful criminals to prison terms of one day, then releasing them conditionally under the supervision of their parents or masters.[3]

In the United States, juvenile probation developed as part of the wave of social reform characterizing the latter half of the nineteenth century. Massachusetts took the first step. Under an act passed in 1869, an agent of the state board of charities was authorized to appear in criminal trials involving juveniles, to find them suitable homes, and to visit them periodically. These services were soon broadened, so that by 1890 probation had become a mandatory part of the court structure.[4]

Probation was a cornerstone in the development of the juvenile court system. In fact, in some states, supporters of the juvenile court movement viewed probation as the first step toward achieving the benefits that the new court was intended to provide. The rapid spread of juvenile courts during the first decades of the twentieth century encouraged the further development of probation. The two were closely related, and to a large degree, both sprang from the conviction that the young could be rehabilitated and that the public was responsible for protecting them.

suppression effect
A reduction of the number of arrests per year for youths who have been incarcerated or otherwise punished.

probation
Nonpunitive, legal disposition of juveniles emphasizing community treatment in which the juvenile is closely supervised by an officer of the court and must adhere to a strict set of rules to avoid incarceration.

Probation is the most widely used legal disposition for juvenile offenders. It emphasizes community treatment without incarceration and requires juveniles to be closely supervised and adhere to a number of conditions. Here, Chance Copp, fifteen, with his mother, heads back to juvenile detention following a hearing in Ross County Juvenile Court in Chillicothe, Ohio, on November 26, 2003. Copp, already on probation for arson, acknowledged that he was afraid of getting caught for smoking marijuana so he submitted a male relative's urine. To add to his problems the sample tested positive for cocaine.

© 2004 AP/Wide World Photos

Expanding Community Treatment

By the mid-1960s, juvenile probation had become a complex institution that touched the lives of an enormous number of children. To many experts, institutionalization of even the most serious delinquent youths was a mistake. Reformers believed that confinement in a high-security institution could not solve the problems that brought a youth into a delinquent way of life, and that the experience could actually help amplify delinquency once the youth returned to the community.[5] Surveys indicating that 30 to 40 percent of adult prison inmates had prior experience with the juvenile court, and that many had been institutionalized as youths, gave little support to the argument that an institutional experience can be beneficial or reduce recidivism.[6]

Contemporary Juvenile Probation

Traditional probation is still the backbone of community-based corrections. As Figure 14.1 shows, almost 400,000 juveniles were placed on formal probation in 1999, which amounts to more than 60 percent of all juvenile dispositions. The use of probation has increased significantly since 1990, when around 220,000 adjudicated youths were placed on probation.[7] These figures show that, regardless of public sentiment, probation continues to be a popular dispositional alternative for judges. Here are the arguments in favor of probation:

1. For youths who can be supervised in the community, probation represents an appropriate disposition.

2. Probation allows the court to tailor a program to each juvenile offender, including those involved in interpersonal offenses.

3. The justice system continues to have confidence in rehabilitation, while accommodating demands for legal controls and public protection, even when caseloads may include many more serious offenders than in the past.

4. Probation is often the disposition of choice, particularly for status offenders.[8]

Figure 14.1   Probation and Correctional Population Trends, 1990–1999

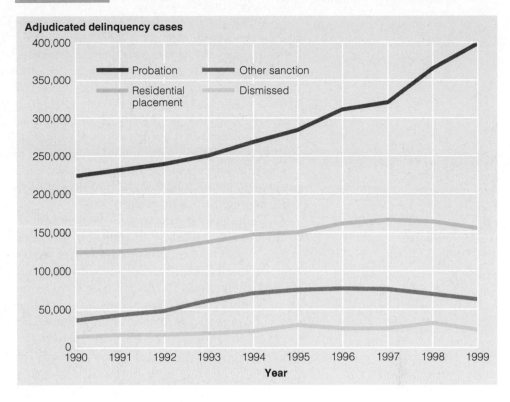

Note: There was a substantial increase in the number of cases in which adjudicated juveniles were placed on probation or ordered to a residential facility between 1990 and 1999.

Source: Charles Puzzanchera, Anne L. Stahl, Terrence A. Finnegan, Nancy Tierney, and Howard N. Snyder, *Juvenile Court Statistics 1999* (Pittsburgh, PA: National Center for Juvenile Justice, 2003).

The Nature of Probation   In most jurisdictions, probation is a direct judicial order that allows a youth who is found to be a delinquent or status offender to remain in the community under court-ordered supervision. A probation sentence implies a contract between the court and the juvenile. The court promises to hold a period of institutionalization in abeyance; the juvenile promises to adhere to a set of rules mandated by the court. The rules of probation vary, but they typically involve conditions such as attending school or work, keeping regular hours, remaining in the jurisdiction, and staying out of trouble.

In the juvenile court, probation is often ordered for an indefinite period. Depending on the statutes of the jurisdiction, the seriousness of the offense, and the juvenile's adjustment on probation, youths can remain under supervision until the court no longer has jurisdiction over them (that is, when they reach the age of majority). State statutes determine if a judge can specify how long a juvenile may be placed under an order of probation. In most jurisdictions, the status of probation is reviewed regularly to ensure that a juvenile is not kept on probation needlessly. Generally, discretion lies with the probation officer to discharge youths who are adjusting to the treatment plan.

Conditions of Probation   Probation conditions are rules mandating that a juvenile on probation behave in a particular way. They can include restitution or reparation, intensive supervision, intensive counseling, participation in a therapeutic program, or participation in an educational or vocational training program. In addition to these specific conditions, state statutes generally allow courts to insist that probationers lead law-abiding lives, maintain a residence in a family setting, refrain from associating with certain types of people, and remain in a particular area unless they have permission to leave.

Although probation conditions vary, they are never supposed to be capricious, cruel, or beyond the capacity of the juvenile to satisfy. Furthermore, conditions of probation should relate to the crime that was committed and to the conduct of the child.

Courts have invalidated probation conditions that were harmful or that violated the juvenile's due process rights. Restricting a child's movement, insisting on a mandatory program of treatment, ordering indefinite terms of probation, and demanding financial reparation where this is impossible are all grounds for appellate court review. For example, it would not be appropriate for a probation order to bar a youth from visiting his girlfriend (unless he had threatened or harmed her) merely because her parents objected to the relationship.[9] However, courts have ruled that it is permissible to bar juveniles from such sources of danger as a "known gang area" in order to protect them from harm.[10]

If a youth violates the conditions of probation—and especially if the juvenile commits another offense—the court can revoke probation. In this case, the contract is terminated and the original commitment order may be enforced. The juvenile court ordinarily handles a decision to revoke probation upon recommendation of the probation officer. Today, as a result of Supreme Court decisions dealing with the rights of adult probationers, a juvenile is normally entitled to legal representation and a hearing when a violation of probation occurs.[11]

Organization and Administration

Probation services are administered by the local juvenile court, or by the state administrative office of courts, in twenty-three states and the District of Columbia. In another fourteen states, juvenile probation services are split, with the juvenile court having control in urban counties and a state executive serving in smaller counties. About ten states have a statewide office of juvenile probation located in the executive branch. In three states, county executives administer probation.[12] These agencies employ an estimated eighteen thousand probation officers throughout the United States.

In the typical juvenile probation department, the chief probation officer is central to its effective operation. In addition, large probation departments include one or more assistant chiefs, each of whom is responsible for one aspect of probation service. One assistant chief might oversee training, another might supervise special offender groups, and still another might act as liaison with police or community-service agencies.

Duties of Juvenile Probation Officers

The **juvenile probation officer** plays an important role in the justice process, beginning with intake and continuing throughout the period in which a juvenile is under court supervision. Probation officers are involved at four stages of the court process. At *intake,* they screen complaints by deciding to adjust the matter, refer the child to an agency for service, or refer the case to the court for judicial action. During the *predisposition* stage, they participate in release or detention decisions. At the *postadjudication* stage, they assist the court in reaching its dispositional decision. During *postdisposition,* they supervise juveniles placed on probation.

At intake, the probation staff has preliminary discussions with the child and the family to determine whether court intervention is necessary or whether the matter can be better resolved by some form of social service. If the child is placed in a detention facility, the probation officer helps the court decide whether the child should continue to be held or be released pending the adjudication and disposition of the case.

The probation officer exercises tremendous influence over the child and the family by developing a **social investigation,** or **predisposition, report** and submitting it to the court. This report is a clinical diagnosis of the child's problems and the need for

juvenile probation officer
Officer of the court involved in all four stages of the court process—intake, predisposition, postadjudication, and postdisposition—who assists the court and supervises juveniles placed on probation.

social investigation report (also known as predisposition report)
Developed by the juvenile probation officer, this report includes clinical diagnosis of the juvenile and the need for court assistance, relevant environmental and personality factors, and other information to assist the court in developing a treatment plan.

conditions of probation
Rules and regulations mandating that a juvenile on probation behave in a particular way.

Juvenile probation officers provide supervision and treatment in the community. The treatment plan is a product of the intake, diagnostic, and investigative aspects of probation. Treatment plans vary in terms of approach and structure. Some juveniles simply report to the probation officer and follow the conditions of probation. In other cases, juvenile probation officers will supervise young people more intensely, monitor their daily activities, and work with them in directed treatment programs. Here, a juvenile probation officer and police officer talk with Crips gang members in California.

© A. Ramey/PhotoEdit

Checkpoints

✔ *Community treatment refers to efforts to provide care, protection, and treatment for juveniles in need.*

✔ *Institutional treatment facilities restrict the movement of residents through staff monitoring, locked exits, and interior fence controls.*

✔ *Probation is the primary form of community treatment used by the juvenile justice system.*

✔ *First developed in Massachusetts, probation had become a cornerstone of the court structure by 1890.*

✔ *Massachusetts has closed most of its secure juvenile facilities and relies almost entirely on community treatment.*

✔ *Probation is a direct judicial order that allows a youth to remain in the community under court-ordered supervision.*

✔ *Probation conditions are rules mandating that a juvenile on probation behave in a particular way.*

✔ *The juvenile probation officer plays an important role in the justice process, beginning with intake and continuing throughout the period in which a juvenile is under court supervision.*

 To quiz yourself on this material, go to questions 14.1–14.9 on the Juvenile Delinquency: The Core 2e Web site.

court assistance based on an evaluation of social functioning, personality, and environmental issues. The report includes an analysis of the child's feelings about the violations and the child's capacity for change. It also examines the influence of family members, peers, and other environmental influences in producing and possibly resolving the problems. All of this information is brought together in a complex but meaningful picture of the offender's personality, problems, and environment.

Juvenile probation officers also provide the child with supervision and treatment in the community. Treatment plans vary in approach and structure. Some juveniles simply report to the probation officer and follow the **conditions of probation.** In other cases, the probation officer may need to provide extensive counseling to the child and family, or more often, refer them to other social service agencies, such as a drug treatment center. Exhibit 14.1 summarizes the probation officer's role. Performance of such a broad range of functions requires good training. Today, juvenile probation officers have legal or social work backgrounds or special counseling skills.

✔ **Checkpoints**

Exhibit 14.1   **Duties of the Juvenile Probation Officer**

- Provide direct counseling and casework services.
- Interview and collect social service data.
- Make diagnostic recommendations.
- Maintain working relationships with law enforcement agencies.
- Use community resources and services.
- Direct volunteer case aides.
- Write predisposition or social investigation reports.

- Work with families of children under supervision.
- Provide specialized services, such as group therapy.
- Supervise specialized caseloads involving children with special problems.
- Make decisions about revocation of probation and its termination.

PROBATION INNOVATIONS

Community corrections have traditionally emphasized offender rehabilitation. The probation officer has been viewed as a caseworker or counselor whose primary job is to help the offender adjust to society. Offender surveillance and control have seemed more appropriate for law enforcement, jails, and prisons than for community corrections.[13] Since 1980, a more conservative justice system has reoriented toward social control. Although the rehabilitative ideals of probation have not been abandoned, new programs have been developed that add a control dimension to community corrections. In some cases this has involved the use of police officers, working in collaboration with probation officers, to enhance the supervision of juvenile probationers.[14] These programs can be viewed as "probation plus," because they add restrictive penalties and conditions to community-service orders. More punitive than probation, this kind of intermediate sanction can be politically attractive to conservatives, while still appealing to liberals as alternatives to incarceration. What are some of these new alternative sanctions (see Concept Summary 14.1 below)?

Intensive Supervision

Juvenile intensive probation supervision (JIPS) involves treating offenders who would normally have been sent to a secure treatment facility as part of a very small probation caseload that receives almost daily scrutiny.[15] The primary goal of JIPS is *decarceration;* without intensive supervision, youngsters would normally be sent to secure juvenile facilities that are already overcrowded. The second goal is control; high-risk juvenile offenders can be maintained in the community under much closer security than traditional probation efforts can provide. A third goal is maintaining community ties and reintegration; offenders can remain in the community and complete their education while avoiding the pains of imprisonment.

Intensive probation programs get mixed reviews. Some jurisdictions find that they are more successful than traditional probation supervision and come at a much cheaper cost than incarceration.[16] However, most research indicates that the failure rate is high and that younger offenders who commit petty crimes are the most likely to fail when placed in intensive supervision programs.[17] It is not surprising that intensive probation clients fail more often because, after all, they are more serious offenders who might otherwise have been incarcerated and are now being watched and supervised more closely than probationers.

Concept Summary **Community-Based Corrections**

Although correctional treatment in the community generally refers to nonpunitive legal dispositions, in most cases there are still restrictions designed to protect the public and hold juvenile offenders accountable for their actions.

Type	Main Restrictions
Probation	Regular supervision by a probation officer; youth must adhere to conditions such as attend school or work, stay out of trouble.
Intensive supervision	Almost daily supervision by a probation officer; adhere to similar conditions as regular probation.
House arrest	Remain at home during specified periods; often there is monitoring through random phone calls, visits, or electronic devices.
Balanced probation	Restrictions are tailored to the risk the juvenile offender presents to the community.
Restitution	None.
Residential programs	Placement in a residential, nonsecure facility such as group home or foster home; adhere to conditions; close monitoring.

juvenile intensive probation supervision (JIPS)
A true alternative to incarceration that involves almost daily supervision of the juvenile by the probation officer assigned to the case.

A number of probation innovations have been experimented with to keep juvenile offenders from being sent to secure juvenile facilities. One of these is juvenile intensive probation supervision, which, in addition to having to follow strict conditions, requires the juvenile to report to a probation officer as often as every day. Here, a juvenile probation officer discusses court papers with a juvenile offender.

© James Shaffer/PhotoEdit

An innovative experiment in three Mississippi counties examined the differential effects on juvenile justice costs for intensive supervision and monitoring, regular probation, and cognitive behavioral treatment, which involved sessions on problem solving, social skills, negotiation skills, the management of emotion, and values enhancement, to improve the thinking and reasoning ability of juvenile offenders. After one year of the program, the intensive supervision treatment was found to be less cost-effective than the other two treatments, with the cognitive behavioral treatment imposing the fewest costs on the juvenile justice system.[18]

Electronic Monitoring

Another program, which has been used with adult offenders and is finding its way into the juvenile justice system, is **house arrest,** which is often coupled with **electronic monitoring.** This program allows offenders sentenced to probation to remain in the community on condition that they stay at home during specific periods (for example, after school or work, on weekends, and in the evenings). Offenders may be monitored through random phone calls, visits, or in some jurisdictions, electronic devices.

Most systems employ radio transmitters that receive a signal from a device worn by the offender and relay it back to the computer via telephone lines. Probationers are fitted with an unremovable monitoring device that alerts the probation department's computers if they leave their place of confinement.[19]

Recent indications are that electronic monitoring can be effective. Evaluations show that recidivism rates are no higher than in traditional programs, costs are lower, and institutional overcrowding is reduced. Also, electronic monitoring seems to work better with some individuals than others: serious felony offenders, substance abusers, repeat offenders, and people serving the longest sentences are the most likely to fail.[20]

Electronic monitoring combined with house arrest is being hailed as one of the most important developments in correctional policy. Its supporters claim that it has the benefits of relatively low cost and high security, while at the same time it helps offenders avoid imprisonment in overcrowded, dangerous state facilities. Furthermore, fewer supervisory officers are needed to handle large numbers of offenders. Despite these strengths, electronic monitoring has its drawbacks: existing systems can be affected by faulty telephone equipment, most electronic monitoring/house arrest programs do not provide rehabilitation services, and some believe electronic monitoring is contrary to a citizen's right to privacy.[21]

house arrest
Offender is required to stay home during specific periods of time; monitoring is done by random phone calls and visits or by electronic devices.

electronic monitoring
Active monitoring systems consist of a radio transmitter worn by the offender that sends a continuous signal to the probation department computer; passive systems employ computer-generated random phone calls that must be answered in a certain period of time from a particular phone.

Balanced Probation

In recent years some jurisdictions have turned to a **balanced probation** approach in an effort to enhance the success of probation.[22] Balanced probation systems integrate community protection, the accountability of the juvenile offender, and individualized attention to the offender. These programs are based on the view that juveniles are responsible for their actions and have an obligation to society whenever they commit an offense. The probation officer establishes a program tailored to the offender while helping the offender accept responsibility for his or her actions. The balanced approach is promising because it specifies a distinctive role for the juvenile probation system.[23]

One promising program that adheres to a balanced probation approach is the California 8% Solution, which is run by the Orange County Probation Department. The "8 percent" refers to the percentage of juvenile offenders who are responsible for the majority of crime: in the case of Orange County, 8 percent of first-time offenders were responsible for 55 percent of repeat cases over a three-year period. This 8 percent problem has become the 8 percent solution thanks to the probation department initiating a comprehensive, multiagency program targeting this group of offenders.[24]

Once the probation officer identifies an offender for the program—the 8% Early Intervention Program—the youth is referred to the Youth and Family Resource Center. Here the youth's needs are assessed and an appropriate treatment plan is developed. Some of the services provided to youths include these:

- An outside school for students in junior and senior high school
- Transportation to and from home
- Counseling for drug and alcohol abuse
- Employment preparation and job placement services
- At-home, intensive family counseling for families[25]

Although balanced probation programs are still in their infancy and their effectiveness remains to be tested, they have generated great interest because of their potential for relieving overcrowded correctional facilities and reducing the pain and stigma of incarceration. There seems to be little question that the use of these innovations, and juvenile probation in general, will increase in the years ahead. Given the $40,000 cost of a year's commitment to a typical residential facility, it should not be a great burden to develop additional probation services.

Restitution

Victim restitution is another widely used method of community treatment. In most jurisdictions, restitution is part of a probationary sentence and is administered by the county probation staff. In many jurisdictions, independent restitution programs have been set up by local governments; in others, restitution is administered by a private nonprofit organization.[26]

Restitution can take several forms. A juvenile can reimburse the victim of the crime or donate money to a charity or public cause; this is referred to as **monetary restitution.** In other instances, a juvenile may be required to provide some service directly to the victim (**victim service restitution**) or to assist a community organization (**community service restitution**).

Requiring youths to reimburse the victims of their crimes is the most widely used method of restitution in the United States. Less widely used, but more common in Europe, is restitution to a charity. In the past few years numerous programs have been set up to enable juvenile offenders to provide a service to the victim or participate in community programs—for example, working in schools for mentally challenged children. In some cases, juveniles are required to contribute both money and community service. Other programs emphasize employment.[27]

balanced probation
Programs that integrate community protection, accountability of the juvenile offender, competency, and individualized attention to the juvenile offender; based on the principle that juvenile offenders must accept responsibility for their behavior.

monetary restitution
Offenders compensate crime victims for out-of-pocket losses caused by the crime, including property damage, lost wages, and medical expenses.

victim service restitution
Offenders provide some service directly to the crime victim.

community service restitution
Offenders assist some worthwhile community organization for a period of time.

Restitution programs can be employed at various stages of the juvenile justice process. They can be part of a diversion program prior to conviction, a method of informal adjustment at intake, or a condition of probation. Restitution has a number of advantages: it provides alternative sentencing options; it offers monetary compensation or service to crime victims; it allows the juvenile the opportunity to compensate the victim and take a step toward becoming a productive member of society; it helps relieve overcrowded juvenile courts, probation caseloads, and detention facilities. Finally, like other alternatives to incarceration, restitution has the potential for allowing vast savings in the operation of the juvenile justice system. Monetary restitution programs in particular may improve the public's attitude toward juvenile justice by offering equity to the victims of crime and ensuring that offenders take responsibility for their actions.

The use of restitution is increasing. In 1977 there were fewer than fifteen formal restitution programs around the United States. By 1985, formal programs existed in four hundred jurisdictions, and thirty-five states had statutory provisions that gave courts the authority to order juvenile restitution.[28] Today, all fifty states, as well as the District of Columbia, have statutory restitution programs.

Does Restitution Work?   How successful is restitution as a treatment alternative? Most evaluations have shown that it is reasonably effective, and should be expanded.[29] In an analysis of federally sponsored restitution programs, Peter Schneider and his associates found that about 95 percent of youths who received restitution as a condition of probation successfully completed their orders.[30] Factors related to success were family income, good school attendance, few prior offenses, minor current offense, and size of restitution order. Schneider found that the youths who received restitution as a sole sanction (without probation) were those originally viewed by juvenile court judges as the better risks, and consequently they had lower failure and recidivism rates than youths ordered to make restitution after being placed on probation.

Anne Schneider conducted a thorough analysis of restitution programs in four different states and found that participants had lower recidivism rates than youths in control groups (regular probation caseloads).[31] Although Schneider's data indicate that restitution may reduce recidivism, the number of youths who had subsequent involvement in the justice system still seemed high. In short, there is evidence that most restitution orders are successfully completed and that youths who make restitution are less likely to become recidivists; however, the number of repeat offenses committed by juveniles who made restitution suggests that, by itself, restitution is not the answer to the delinquency problem.

Restitution programs may be difficult to implement in some circumstances. Offenders may find it difficult to make monetary restitution without securing new employment, which can be difficult during periods of high unemployment. Problems also arise when offenders who need jobs suffer from drug abuse or emotional problems. Public and private agencies are likely sites for community-service restitution, but their directors are sometimes reluctant to allow delinquent youths access to their organizations. In addition to these problems, some juvenile probation officers view restitution programs as a threat to their authority and to the autonomy of their organizations.

Another criticism of restitution programs is that they foster involuntary servitude. Indigent clients may be unfairly punished when they are unable to make restitution payments or face probation violations. To avoid such bias, probation officers should first determine why payment has stopped and then suggest appropriate action, rather than simply treating nonpayment as a matter of law enforcement.

Residential Community Treatment

Many experts believe that institutionalization of even the most serious delinquent youths is a mistake. Confinement in a high-security institution usually cannot solve the problems that brought a youth into a delinquent way of life, and the experience may actually amplify delinquency once the youth returns to the community. Many agree that warehousing juveniles without attention to their treatment needs does little to prevent their return to criminal behavior. Research has shown that the most effective secure-corrections programs provided individualized services for a small number of participants. Large training schools have not proved to be effective.[32] This realization has produced a wide variety of residential community-treatment programs to service youths who need a more secure environment than can be provided by probation services, but who do not require a placement in a state-run juvenile correctional facility.

How are community corrections implemented? In some cases, youths are placed under probation supervision, and the probation department maintains a residential treatment facility. Placement can also be made to the department of social services or juvenile corrections with the direction that the youth be placed in a residential facility. **Residential programs** are generally divided into four major categories: group homes, including boarding schools and apartment-type settings; foster homes; family group homes; and rural programs.

Group homes are nonsecure residences that provide counseling, education, job training, and family living. They are staffed by a small number of qualified persons, and generally house twelve to fifteen youngsters. The institutional quality of the environment is minimized, and the kids are given the opportunity to build a close relationship with the staff. They reside in the home, attend public schools, and participate in community activities.

Foster care programs involve one or two juveniles who live with a family—usually a husband and wife who serve as surrogate parents. The juveniles enter into a close relationship with the foster parents and receive the attention and care they did not receive in their own homes. The quality of the foster home experience depends on the foster parents. Foster care for adjudicated juvenile offenders has not been extensive in the United States. Welfare departments generally handle foster placements, and funding of this treatment option has been a problem for the juvenile justice system. However, foster home services have expanded as a community treatment approach.

One example of a successful foster care program is the multidimensional treatment foster care (MTFC) program, developed by social scientists at the Oregon Social Learning Center. Designed for the most serious and chronic male young offenders, this program combines individual therapy such as skill building in problem solving for the youths, and family therapy for the biological or adoptive parents. The foster care families receive training by program staff so they can provide the young people with close supervision, fair and consistent limits and consequences, and a supportive relationship with an adult.[33] Foster care families also receive close supervision and are consulted regularly on the progress of the youth by program staff. An experiment of MTFC found that one year after the completion of the program, participating youths were significantly less likely to be arrested than a control group.[34]

Family group homes combine elements of foster care and group home placements. Juveniles are placed in a group home that is run by a family rather than by a professional staff. Troubled youths have an opportunity to learn to get along in a family-like situation, and at the same time the state avoids the start-up costs and neighborhood opposition often associated with establishing a public institution.

Rural programs include forestry camps, ranches, and farms that provide recreational activities or work for juveniles. Programs usually handle from thirty to fifty youths. Such programs have the disadvantage of isolating juveniles from the community, but reintegration can be achieved if a youth's stay is short and if family and friends are allowed to visit.

Most residential programs use group counseling as the main treatment tool. Although group facilities have been used less often than institutional placements, there is a trend toward developing community-based residential facilities; see the accompanying What Does This Mean to Me? feature.

residential programs
Residential, nonsecure facilities such as a group home, foster home, family group home, or rural home where the juvenile can be closely monitored and develop close relationships with staff members.

group homes
Nonsecured, structured residences that provide counseling, education, job training, and family living.

foster care programs
Placement with families who provide attention, guidance, and care.

family group homes
A combination of foster care and group home; they are run by a single family rather than by professional staff.

rural programs
Specific recreational and work opportunities provided for juveniles in a rural setting such as a forestry camp, a farm, or a ranch.

reform schools
Institutions in which educational and psychological services are used in an effort to improve the conduct of juveniles who are forcibly detained.

cottage system
Housing in a compound of small cottages, each of which accommodates twenty to forty children.

Checkpoints

✔ There are new programs being developed that are "probation plus," because they add restrictive penalties and conditions to community service orders.

✔ Juvenile intensive probation supervision (JIPS) involves treatment as part of a very small probation caseload that receives almost daily scrutiny.

✔ Electronic monitoring combined with house arrest is being implemented in juvenile correction policy.

✔ Balanced probation systems integrate community protection, accountability of the juvenile offender, and individualized attention to the offender.

✔ Monetary restitution allows a juvenile to reimburse the victim of the crime or donate money to a charity or public cause.

✔ Community service restitution allows juveniles to engage in public works as part of their disposition.

✔ Residential community programs are usually divided into four major categories: group homes, foster homes, family group homes, and rural programs.

To quiz yourself on this material, go to questions 14.10–14.13 on the Juvenile Delinquency: The Core 2e Web site.

As jurisdictions continue to face ever-increasing costs for juvenile justice services, community-based programs will play an important role in providing rehabilitation of juvenile offenders and ensuring public safety. ✔ Checkpoints

SECURE CORRECTIONS

When the court determines that community treatment can't meet the special needs of a delinquent youth, a judge may refer the juvenile to a secure treatment program. Today, correctional institutions operated by federal, state, and county governments are generally classified as secure or open facilities. *Secure facilities* restrict the movement of residents through staff monitoring, locked exits, and interior fence controls. *Open institutions* generally do not restrict the movement of the residents and allow much greater freedom of access to the facility.[35] In the following sections, we analyze the state of secure juvenile corrections, beginning with some historical background. This is followed by a discussion of life in institutions, the juvenile client, treatment issues, legal rights, and aftercare programs.

History of Juvenile Institutions

Until the early 1800s, juvenile offenders, as well as neglected and dependent children, were confined in adult prisons. The inhumane conditions in these institutions were among the factors that led social reformers to create a separate children's court system in 1899.[36] Early juvenile institutions were industrial schools modeled after adult prisons but designed to protect children from the evil influences in adult facilities. The first was the New York House of Refuge, established in 1825. Not long after this, states began to establish **reform schools** for juveniles. Massachusetts was the first, opening the Lyman School for Boys in Westborough in 1846. New York opened the State Agricultural and Industrial School in 1849, and Maine opened the Maine Boys' Training School in 1853. By 1900, thirty-six states had reform schools.[37] Although it is difficult to determine exact population of these institutions, by 1880 there were approximately eleven thousand youths in correctional facilities, a number that more than quadrupled by 1980.[38] Early reform schools were generally punitive in nature and were based on the concept of rehabilitation (or reform) through hard work and discipline.

In the second half of the nineteenth century, emphasis shifted to the **cottage system.** Juvenile offenders were housed in compounds of cottages, each of which could accommodate twenty to forty children. A set of "parents" ran each cottage, creating a homelike atmosphere. This setup was believed to be more conducive to rehabilitation.

The first cottage system was established in Massachusetts in 1855, the second in Ohio in 1858.[39] The system was held to be a great improvement over reform schools. The belief was that, by moving away from punishment and toward rehabilitation, not only could offenders be rehabilitated but also crime among unruly children could be prevented.[40]

Twentieth-Century Developments The early twentieth century witnessed important changes in juvenile corrections. Because of the influence of World War I, reform schools began to adopt a militaristic style. Living units became barracks, cottage groups became companies, house fathers became captains, and superintendents became majors or colonels. Military-style uniforms were standard wear.

In addition, the establishment of the first juvenile court in 1899 reflected the expanded use of confinement for delinquent children. As the number of juvenile offenders increased, the forms of juvenile institutions varied to include forestry camps, ranches, and vocational schools. Beginning in the 1930s, camps modeled after the camps run by the Civilian Conservation Corps became a part of the juvenile correctional system. These camps centered on conservation activities and work as a means of rehabilitation.

Los Angeles County was the first to use camps during this period.[41] Southern California was experiencing problems with transient youths who came to California with no money and then got into trouble with the law. Rather than filling up the jails, the county placed these offenders in conservation camps, paid them low wages, and released them when they had earned enough money to return home. The camps proved more rehabilitative than training schools, and by 1935 California had established a network of forestry camps for delinquent boys. The idea soon spread to other states.[42]

Also during the 1930s, the U.S. Children's Bureau sought to reform juvenile corrections. The bureau conducted studies to determine the effectiveness of the training school concept. Little was learned from these programs because of limited funding and bureaucratic ineptitude, and the Children's Bureau failed to achieve any significant change. But such efforts recognized the important role of positive institutional care.[43]

Another innovation came in the 1940s with passage of the American Law Institute's Model Youth Correction Authority Act. This act emphasized reception/classification centers. California was the first to try out this idea, opening the Northern Reception Center and Clinic in Sacramento in 1947. Today, there are many such centers scattered around the United States.

Since the 1970s, a major change in institutionalization has been the effort to remove status offenders from institutions housing juvenile delinquents. This includes removing status offenders from detention centers and removing all juveniles from contact with adults in jails. This *decarceration* policy mandates that courts use the **least restrictive alternative** in providing services for status offenders. A non-criminal youth should not be put in a secure facility if a community-based program is available. In addition, the federal government prohibits states from placing status offenders in separate facilities that are similar in form and function to those used for delinquent offenders. This is to prevent states from merely shifting their institutionalized population around so that one training school houses all delinquents and another houses all status offenders, but actual conditions remain the same.

Throughout the 1980s and into the 1990s, admissions to juvenile correctional facilities grew substantially.[44] Capacities of juvenile facilities also increased, but not enough to avoid overcrowding. Training schools became seriously overcrowded in some states, causing private facilities to play an increased role in juvenile corrections. Reliance on incarceration became costly to states: inflation-controlled juvenile corrections expenditures for public facilities grew to more than $2 billion in 1995, an increase of 20 percent from 1982.[45] A 1994 report issued by the Office of Juvenile Justice and Delinquency Prevention (OJJDP) said that crowding, inadequate health care, lack of security, and poor control of suicidal behavior was widespread in juvenile corrections facilities. Despite new construction, crowding persisted in more than half the states.[46]

JUVENILE INSTITUTIONS TODAY: PUBLIC AND PRIVATE

Most juveniles are housed in public institutions that are administered by state agencies: child and youth services, health and social services, corrections, or child welfare.[47] In some states these institutions fall under a centralized system that covers adults as well as juveniles. Recently, a number of states have removed juvenile corrections from an existing adult corrections department or mental health agency. However, the majority of states still place responsibility for the administration of juvenile corrections within social service departments.

Supplementing publicly funded institutions are private facilities that are maintained and operated by private agencies funded or chartered by state authorities.

least restrictive alternative
A program with the least restrictive or secure setting that will benefit the child.

Most of today's private institutions are relatively small facilities holding fewer than thirty youths. Many have a specific mission or focus (for example, treating females who display serious emotional problems). Although about 80 percent of public institutions can be characterized as secure, only 20 percent of private institutions are high-security facilities.

Population Trends

Whereas most delinquents are held in public facilities, most status offenders are held in private facilities. At last count, there were slightly less than 109,000 juvenile offenders being held in public (70 percent) and private (30 percent) facilities in the United States.[48] Between 1997 and 1999, the number of juveniles held in custody increased 3 percent.[49] The juvenile custody rate varies widely among states: South Dakota makes the greatest use of custodial treatment, incarcerating around 630 delinquents in juvenile facilities per 100,000 juveniles in the population, while Vermont and Hawaii have the lowest juvenile custody rates (less than 100). Although not a state, the District of Columbia actually has the highest juvenile custody rate in the nation, at over 700 per 100,000 juveniles. This is almost twice the national average (see Table 14.1).[50] Some states rely heavily on privately run facilities, while others place many youths in out-of-state facilities.

Although the number of institutionalized youths appears to have stabilized in the last few years, the data may reveal only the tip of the iceberg. The data do not include many minors who are incarcerated after they are waived to adult courts or who have been tried as adults because of exclusion statutes. Most states place under-age juveniles convicted of adult charges in youth centers until they reach the age of majority, whereupon they are transferred to an adult facility. In addition, there may be a hidden, or subterranean, correctional system that places wayward youths in private mental hospitals and substance-abuse clinics for behaviors that might otherwise have brought them a stay in a correctional facility or community-based program.[51] These data suggest that the number of institutionalized children may be far greater than reported in the official statistics.[52]

Physical Conditions

The physical plans of juvenile institutions vary in size and quality. Many of the older training schools still place all offenders in a single building, regardless of the offense. More acceptable structures include a reception unit with an infirmary, a security unit, and dormitory units or cottages. Planners have concluded that the most effective design for training schools is to have facilities located around a community square. The facilities generally include a dining hall and kitchen area, a storage warehouse, academic and vocational training rooms, a library, an auditorium, a gymnasium, an administration building, and other basic facilities.

The individual living areas also vary, depending on the type of facility and the progressiveness of its administration. Most traditional training school conditions were appalling. Today, however, most institutions provide toilet and bath facilities, beds, desks, lamps, and tables. New facilities usually try to provide a single room for each individual. However, the Juvenile Residential Facility Census, which collects information about the facilities in which juvenile offenders are held, found that 39 percent of the 2,875 facilities that reported information were overcrowded—that is, they had more residents than available standard beds.[53] Some states, like Massachusetts and Rhode Island, report that upwards of 75 percent of all of their facilities for juvenile offenders are overcrowded. It was also found that overcrowded facilities were significantly more likely than other facilities (45 percent versus 38 percent) to report having transported juveniles to emergency rooms because of injuries sustained in fights.[54]

The physical conditions of secure facilities for juveniles have come a long way from the training schools of the turn of the twentieth century. However, many administrators realize that more modernization is necessary to comply with national

Table 14.1 State Comparison of Numbers and Rates of Juvenile Offenders in Custody, 1999

State of offense	Number	Rate	State of offense	Number	Rate
U.S. total	**108,931**	**371**	Oklahoma	1,123	273
Upper age 17			Oregon	1,549	404
Alabama	1,589	333	Pennsylvania	3,819	285
Alaska	382	419	Rhode Island	310	284
Arizona	1,901	334	South Dakota	603	632
Arkansas	705	234	Tennessee	1,534	256
California	19,072	514	Utah	985	320
Colorado	1,979	407	Vermont	67	*96*
Delaware	347	431	Virginia	3,085	415
Dist. of Columbia	259	*704*	Washington	2,094	307
Florida	6,813	427	West Virginia	388	202
Hawaii	118	*96*	Wyoming	310	488
Idaho	360	220	**Upper age 16**		
Indiana	2,650	384	Georgia	3,729	475
Iowa	1,017	296	Illinois	3,885	322
Kansas	1,254	383	Louisiana	2,745	580
Kentucky	1,188	270	Massachusetts	1,188	206
Maine	242	167	Michigan	4,324	417
Maryland	1,579	269	Missouri	1,161	205
Minnesota	1,760	290	New Hampshire	216	167
Mississippi	784	229	South Carolina	1,650	441
Montana	246	220	Texas	7,954	370
Nebraska	720	342	Wisconsin	1,924	338
Nevada	789	378	**Upper age 15**		
New Jersey	2,386	273	Connecticut	1,466	513
New Mexico	855	378	New York	4,813	334
North Dakota	235	297	North Carolina	1,429	221
Ohio	4,531	345			

Note: The rate is the number of juvenile offenders in residential placement in 1999 per 100,000 juveniles age ten through the upper age of original juvenile court jurisdiction in each state. The U.S. total includes 2,645 juvenile offenders in private facilities for whom state of offense was not reported and 174 juvenile offenders in tribal facilities.

Source: Melissa Sickmund, *Juveniles in Corrections* (Washington, DC: Office of Juvenile Justice and Delinquency Prevention, 2004).

standards for juvenile institutions. Correctional administrators have described conditions as horrendous, and health officials have cited institutions for violations such as pollution by vermin and asbestos.[55] Although some improvements have been made, there are still enormous problems to overcome.

THE INSTITUTIONALIZED JUVENILE

The typical resident of a juvenile facility is a fifteen- to sixteen-year-old White male incarcerated for an average stay of five months in a public facility or six months in a private facility. Private facilities tend to house younger youths, while public institutions provide custodial care for older ones, including a small percentage between eighteen and twenty-one years of age. Most incarcerated youths are person, property, or drug offenders.

Although the physical conditions of secure facilities for juveniles have greatly improved over the years, one of the arguments in opposition to sending juveniles to these facilities is that many are overcrowded and expose juveniles to serious health problems. Shown here is the Connecticut Juvenile Training School located in Middletown, Connecticut. Its fifteen-foot-high security fence surrounds a modern, $15 million facility.

© 2001 AP/Wide World Photos

To read about life in a secure Canadian facility, go to the Web site maintained by the **Prince George Youth Custody Center** in British Columbia that provides a range of programs to allow youths to make maximal constructive use of their time while in custody. Click on Web Links under the Chapter Resources at http://cj.wadsworth.com/siegel_jdcore2e.

Minority youths are incarcerated at a rate two to five times that of White youths. The difference is greatest for African-American youths, with a custody rate of 1,004 per 100,000 juveniles; for White youths the rate is 212.[56] In a number of states such as Illinois, New Jersey, and Wisconsin the difference in custody rates between African-American and White youths is considerably greater (Table 14.2). Research has found that this overrepresentation is not a result of differentials in arrest rates, but often stems from disparity at early stages of case processing.[57] Of equal importance, minorities are more likely to be confined in secure public facilities rather than in open, private facilities that might provide more costly and effective treatment,[58] and among minority groups African-American youths are more likely to receive more punitive treatment—throughout the juvenile justice system—compared with others.[59]

Minority youths accused of delinquent acts are less likely than White youths to be diverted from the court system into informal sanctions and are more likely to receive sentences involving incarceration. Racial disparity in juvenile disposition is a growing problem that demands immediate public scrutiny.[60] In response, some jurisdictions have initiated studies of racial disproportion in their juvenile justice systems.[61] Today, more than six in ten juveniles in custody belong to racial or ethnic minorities, and seven in ten youths held in custody for a violent crime are minorities.[62]

For more than two decades, shocking exposés, sometimes resulting from investigations by the U.S. Department of Justice's civil rights division, continue to focus public attention on the problems of juvenile corrections.[63] Today, more so than in years past, some critics believe public scrutiny has improved conditions in training schools. There is greater professionalism among the staff, and staff brutality seems to have diminished. Status offenders and delinquents are, for the most part, held in separate facilities. Confinement length is shorter, and rehabilitative programming has increased. However, there are significant differences in the experiences of male and female delinquents in institutions.

Male Inmates

Males make up the great bulk of institutionalized youth, accounting for six out of every seven juvenile offenders in residential placement,[64] and most programs are directed toward their needs. In many ways their experiences mirror those of adult offenders. In an important paper, Clement Bartollas and his associates identified an inmate value system that they believed was common in juvenile institutions:

Table 14.2 State Comparison of Custody Rates Between White and African-American Juvenile Offenders, 1999

State of offense	White	African American	State of offense	White	African American
U.S average	*212*	*1,004*	Missouri	146	554
Alabama	208	588	Montana	148	1,463
Alaska	281	612	Nebraska	220	1,552
Arizona	234	957	Nevada	305	1,019
Arkansas	139	575	New Hampshire	150	1,278
California	269	1,666	New Jersey	70	1,108
Colorado	257	1,436	New Mexico	211	1,011
Connecticut	160	2,143	New York	169	1,119
Delaware	203	1,143	North Carolina	123	466
Dist. of Columbia	173	855	North Dakota	204	1,136
Florida	306	964	Ohio	221	1,038
Georgia	273	878	Oklahoma	194	821
Hawaii	39	87	Oregon	353	1,689
Idaho	203	871	Pennsylvania	123	1,230
Illinois	152	1,005	Rhode Island	155	1,363
Indiana	280	1,260	South Carolina	244	772
Iowa	240	1,726	South Dakota	436	2,908
Kansas	239	1,691	Tennessee	170	576
Kentucky	192	1,030	Texas	204	965
Louisiana	223	1,127	Utah	267	1,043
Maine	166	390	Vermont	93	698
Maryland	136	575	Virginia	225	1,024
Massachusetts	93	648	Washington	232	1,507
Michigan	243	1,058	West Virginia	166	1,060
Minnesota	183	1,504	Wisconsin	164	1,965
Mississippi	118	300	Wyoming	396	2,752

Note: Custody rate (per 100,000).

Note: The custody rate is the number of juvenile offenders in residential placement on October 27, 1999, per 100,000 juveniles age ten through the upper age of original juvenile court jurisdiction in each state. The U.S. total includes 2,645 juvenile offenders in private facilities for whom state of offense was not reported and 174 juvenile offenders in tribal facilities.

Source: Melissa Sickmund, *Juveniles in Corrections* (Washington, DC: Office of Juvenile Justice and Delinquency Prevention, 2004).

"Exploit whomever you can.

Don't play up to staff.

Don't rat on your peers.

Don't give in to others."[65]

In addition to these general rules, the researchers found that there were separate norms for African-American inmates ("exploit Whites"; "no forcing sex on Blacks"; "defend your brother") and for Whites ("don't trust anyone"; "everybody for himself").

Other research efforts confirm the notion that residents do in fact form cohesive groups and adhere to an informal inmate culture.[66] The more serious the youth's record and the more secure the institution, the greater the adherence to the inmate social code. Male delinquents are more likely to form allegiances with members of their own racial group and attempt to exploit those outside the group. They also scheme to manipulate staff and take advantage of weaker peers. However, in institutions that are treatment-oriented, and where staff-inmate relationships are more intimate, residents are less likely to adhere to a negativistic inmate code.

Female Inmates

The growing involvement of girls in criminal behavior and the influence of the feminist movement have drawn more attention to the female juvenile offender. This attention has revealed a double standard of justice. For example, girls are more likely than boys to be incarcerated for status offenses. Institutions for girls are generally more restrictive than those for boys, and they have fewer educational and vocational programs and fewer services. Institutions for girls also do a less-than-adequate job of rehabilitation. It has been suggested that this double standard operates because of a male-dominated justice system that seeks to "protect" young girls from their own sexuality.[67]

Over the years, the number of females held in public institutions has declined. This represents the continuation of a long-term trend to remove girls, many of whom are nonserious offenders, from closed institutions and place them in private or community-based facilities. So although a majority of males are housed in public facilities today, most female delinquents reside in private facilities.[68]

The same double standard that brings a girl into an institution continues to exist once she is in custody. Females tend to be incarcerated for longer terms than males. In addition, institutional programs for girls tend to be oriented toward reinforcing traditional roles for women. How well these programs rehabilitate girls is questionable.

Many of the characteristics of juvenile female offenders are similar to those of their male counterparts, including poor social skills and low self-esteem. Other problems are more specific to the female juvenile offender (sexual abuse issues, victimization histories, lack of placement options).[69] In addition, there have been numerous allegations of emotional and sexual abuse by correctional workers, who either exploit vulnerable young women or callously disregard their emotional needs. A recent (1998) interview survey conducted by the National Council on Crime and Delinquency uncovered

Girls in a Marlin, Texas, juvenile facility. While the trend has been to remove female juvenile inmates from closed institutions and place them in private or community-based facilities, female inmates continue to face numerous obstacles, including being placed in institutions far from family members and receiving inadequate educational and recreational services.

© David Woo/Stock, Boston

Checkpoints

✔ *Massachusetts opened the first juvenile correctional facility, the Lyman School for Boys in Westborough, in 1846.*

✔ *Since the 1970s, a major change in institutionalization has been the effort to remove status offenders from institutions housing juvenile delinquents.*

✔ *Throughout the 1980s and into the 1990s, admissions to juvenile correctional facilities grew substantially.*

✔ *Today, there are slightly less than 109,000 juveniles being held in public and private facilities.*

✔ *There may be a hidden juvenile correctional system that places wayward youths in private mental hospitals and substance abuse clinics.*

✔ *The typical resident of a juvenile facility is a fifteen- to sixteen-year-old White male incarcerated for an average stay of five months in a public facility or six months in a private facility.*

✔ *Minority youths are incarcerated at a rate two to five times that of Whites.*

numerous incidents of abuse, and bitter resentment by the young women over the brutality of their custodial treatment.[70]

Although there are more coed institutions for juveniles than in the past, most girls remain incarcerated in single-sex institutions that are isolated in rural areas and rarely offer adequate rehabilitative services. Several factors account for the different treatment of girls. One is sexual stereotyping by administrators, who believe that teaching girls "appropriate" sex roles will help them function effectively in society. These beliefs are often held by the staff as well, many of whom have highly sexist ideas of what is appropriate behavior for adolescent girls. Another factor that accounts for the different treatment of girls is that staff are often not adequately trained to understand and address the unique needs of this population.[71] Girls' institutions tend to be smaller than boys' institutions and lack the money to offer as many programs and services as the larger male institutions.[72]

It appears that although society is more concerned about protecting girls who act out, it is less concerned about rehabilitating them because the crimes they commit are not serious. These attitudes translate into fewer staff, older facilities, and poorer educational and recreational programs than those found in boys' institutions.[73] To help address these and other problems facing female juveniles in institutions, the American Bar Association and the National Bar Association recommend a number of important changes, including these:

- Identify, promote, and support effective gender-specific, developmentally sound, culturally sensitive practices with girls.
- Promote an integrated system of care for at-risk and delinquent girls and their families based on their competencies and needs.
- Assess the adequacy of services to meet the needs of at-risk or delinquent girls and address gaps in service.
- Collect and review state and local practices to assess the gender impact of decision making and system structure.[74] ✔ **Checkpoints**

CORRECTIONAL TREATMENT FOR JUVENILES

✔ *Males make up the bulk of institutionalized youth, and most programs are directed toward their needs.*

✔ *Female inmates are believed to be the target of sexual abuse and are denied the same treatment options as males.*

 To quiz yourself on this material, go to questions 14.14–14.16 on the Juvenile Delinquency: The Core 2e Web site.

Nearly all juvenile institutions implement some form of treatment program: counseling, vocational and educational training, recreational programs, and religious counseling. In addition, most institutions provide medical programs as well as occasional legal service programs. Generally, the larger the institution, the greater the number of programs and services offered.

The purpose of these programs is to rehabilitate youths to become well-adjusted individuals and send them back into the community to be productive citizens. Despite good intentions, however, the goal of rehabilitation is rarely attained because in large part the programs are poorly implemented.[75] A significant number of juvenile offenders commit more crimes after release and some experts believe that correctional treatment has little effect on recidivism.[76] However, a careful evaluation of both community-based and institutional treatment services found that juveniles who receive treatment have recidivism rates about 10 percent lower than untreated juveniles, and that the best programs reduced recidivism between 20 and 30 percent.[77] The most successful programs provide training to improve interpersonal skills, self-control, and school achievement. These programs also tend to be the most intensive in amount and duration of attention to youths. Programs of a more psychological orientation, such as individual, family, and group counseling, showed only moderate positive effects on delinquents. Education, vocational training, and specific counseling strategies can be effective if they are intensive, relate to program goals, and meet the youth's individual needs.[78]

What are the drawbacks to correctional rehabilitation? One of the most common problems is the lack of well-trained staff members. Budgetary limitations are a primary

If you want to learn more about improving the conditions of children in custody, click on Web Links under the Chapter Resources at http://cj.wadsworth.com/siegel_jdcore2e.

concern. It costs a substantial amount of money per year to keep a child in an institution, which explains why institutions generally do not employ large professional staffs.

The most glaring problem with treatment programs is that they are not administered as intended. Although the official goals of many may be treatment and rehabilitation, the actual programs may center around security and punishment. The next sections describe some treatment approaches that aim to rehabilitate offenders.

Individual Treatment Techniques: Past and Present

In general, effective individual treatment programs are built around combinations of psychotherapy, reality therapy, and behavior modification. **Individual counseling** is one of the most common treatment approaches, and virtually all juvenile institutions use it to some extent. This is not surprising, because psychological problems such as depression are prevalent in juvenile institutions.[79] Individual counseling does not attempt to change a youth's personality. Rather, it attempts to help individuals understand and solve their current adjustment problems. Some institutions employ counselors who are not professionally qualified, which subjects offenders to a superficial form of counseling.

To learn more about reality therapy, go to William Glasser's Web site by clicking on Web Links under the Chapter Resources at http://cj.wadsworth.com/siegel_jdcore2e.

Professional counseling may be based on **psychotherapy.** Psychotherapy requires extensive analysis of the individual's childhood experiences. A skilled therapist attempts to help the individual make a more positive adjustment to society by altering negative behavior patterns learned in childhood. Another frequently used treatment is **reality therapy.**[80] This approach, developed by William Glasser during the 1970s, emphasizes current, rather than past, behavior by stressing that offenders are completely responsible for their own actions. The object of reality therapy is to make individuals more responsible people. This is accomplished by giving them confidence through developing their ability to follow a set of expectations as closely as possible. The success of reality therapy depends greatly on the warmth and concern of the counselor. Many institutions rely heavily on this type of therapy because they believe trained professionals aren't needed to administer it. In fact, a skilled therapist is essential to the success of this form of treatment.

Behavior modification is used in many institutions.[81] It is based on the theory that all behavior is learned and that current behavior can be shaped through rewards and punishments. This type of program is easily used in an institutional setting that offers privileges as rewards for behaviors such as work, study, or the development of skills. It is reasonably effective, especially when a contract is formed with the youth to modify certain behaviors. When youths are aware of what is expected of them, they plan their actions to meet these expectations and then experience the anticipated consequences. In this way, youths can be motivated to change. Behavior modification is effective in controlled settings where a counselor can manipulate the situation, but once the youth is back in the real world it becomes difficult to use.

Group Treatment Techniques

Group therapy is more economical than individual therapy because one therapist can counsel more than one individual at a time. Also, the support of the group is often valuable to individuals in the group, and individuals derive hope from other members of the group who have survived similar experiences. Another advantage of group therapy is that a group can often solve a problem more effectively than an individual.

One disadvantage of group therapy is that it provides little individual attention. Everyone is different, and some group members may need more individualized treatment. Others may be afraid to speak up in the group and thus fail to receive the benefits of the experience. Conversely, some individuals may dominate group interaction, making it difficult for the leader to conduct an effective session. In addition, group condemnation may seriously hurt a participant. Finally, there is also the concern that

individual counseling
Counselors help juveniles understand and solve their current adjustment problems.

psychotherapy
Highly structured counseling in which a therapist helps a juvenile solve conflicts and make a more positive adjustment to society.

reality therapy
A form of counseling that emphasizes current behavior and requires the individual to accept responsibility for all of his or her actions.

behavior modification
A technique for shaping desired behaviors through a system of rewards and punishments.

group therapy
Counseling several individuals together in a group session.

To see how positive peer culture can be used effectively, click on Web Links under the Chapter Resources at http://cj.wadsworth.com/siegel_jdcore2e.

by providing therapy in a group format, those who are more chronically involved in delinquency may negatively affect those who are marginally involved.[82]

Guided group interaction (GGI) is a fairly common method of group treatment. It is based on the theory that, through group interactions a delinquent can acknowledge and solve personal problems. A leader facilitates interaction, and a group culture develops. Individual members can be mutually supportive and reinforce acceptable behavior. In the 1980s, a version of GGI called **positive peer culture (PPC)** became popular. These programs used groups in which peer leaders encourage other youths to conform to conventional behaviors. The rationale is that if negative peer influence can encourage youths to engage in delinquent behavior, then positive peer influence can help them conform.[83] Though research results are inconclusive, there is evidence that PPC may facilitate communication ability for incarcerated youth.[84]

Another common group treatment approach, **milieu therapy,** seeks to make all aspects of the inmates' environment part of their treatment and to minimize differences between custodial staff and treatment personnel. Milieu therapy, based on psychoanalytic theory, was developed during the late 1940s and early 1950s by Bruno Bettelheim.[85] This therapy attempted to create a conscience, or superego, in delinquent youths by getting them to depend on their therapists to a great extent and then threatening them with loss of the caring relationship if they failed to control their behavior. Today, milieu therapy more often makes use of peer interactions and attempts to create an environment that encourages meaningful change, growth, and satisfactory adjustment. This is often accomplished through peer pressure to conform to group norms.

Today, group counseling often focuses on drug and alcohol issues, self-esteem development, or role-model support. In addition, because more violent juveniles are entering the system than in years past, group sessions often deal with appropriate expressions of anger and methods for controlling such behavior.

Educational, Vocational, and Recreational Programs

Because educational programs are an important part of social development and have therapeutic as well as instructional value, they are an essential part of most treatment programs. What takes place through education is related to all other aspects of the institutional program—work activities, cottage life, recreation, and clinical services.

Educational programs are probably the best-staffed programs in training schools, but even at their best, most of them are inadequate. Educational programs contend with myriad problems. Many of the youths coming into these institutions are mentally challenged, have learning disabilities, and are far behind their grade levels in basic academics. Most have become frustrated with the educational experience, dislike school, and become bored with any type of educational program. Their sense of frustration often leads to disciplinary problems.

Ideally, institutions should allow the inmates to attend a school in the community or offer programs that lead to a high school diploma or GED certificate. Unfortunately, not all institutions offer these types of programs. Secure institutions, because of their large size, are more likely than group homes or day treatment centers to offer programs such as remedial reading, physical education, and tutoring. Some offer computer-based learning and programmed learning modules.

Vocational training has long been used as a treatment technique for juveniles. Early institutions were even referred to as "industrial schools." Today, vocational programs in institutions include auto repair, printing, woodworking, computer training, foodservice, cosmetology, secretarial training, and data processing. A common drawback of vocational training programs is sex-typing. The recent trend has been to allow equal access to all programs offered in institutions that house girls and boys. Sex-typing is more difficult to avoid in single-sex institutions, because funds aren't usually available for all types of training.

guided group interaction (GGI)
Through group interactions a delinquent can acknowledge and solve personal problems with support from other group members.

positive peer culture (PPC)
Counseling program in which peer leaders encourage other group members to modify their behavior and peers help reinforce acceptable behaviors.

milieu therapy
All aspects of the environment are part of the treatment, and meaningful change, increased growth, and satisfactory adjustment are encouraged.

© 2004 AP/Wide World Photos

Most juvenile facilities have ongoing vocational and educational programs. Here, a detention caseworker looks in on juvenile inmates in a classroom at the Northern Maine Juvenile Detention Facility in Charleston, Maine.

These programs alone are not panaceas. Youths need to acquire the kinds of skills that will give them hope for advancement. The Ventura School for Female Juvenile Offenders, established under the California Youth Authority, has been a pioneer in the work placement concept. Private industry contracts with this organization to establish businesses on the institution's grounds. The businesses hire, train, and pay for work. Wages are divided into a victim's restitution fund, room and board fees, and forced savings, with a portion given to the juvenile to purchase canteen items.[86] A study by the National Youth Employment Coalition (NYEC) finds that employment and career-focused programs can do a great deal to prepare youth involved in the juvenile justice system for a successful transition to the workforce as long as they are comprehensive, last for a relatively long period of time, and are connected to further education or long-term career opportunities.[87]

Recreational activity is also important in helping relieve adolescent aggressions, as evidenced by the many programs that focus on recreation as the primary treatment technique.

In summary, the treatment programs that seem to be most effective for rehabilitating juvenile offenders are those that use a combination of techniques. Programs that are comprehensive, build on a juvenile's strengths, and adopt a socially grounded position have a much greater chance for success. Successful programs address issues relating to school, peers, work, and community.

Wilderness Programs

Wilderness probation programs involve troubled youths in outdoor activities as a mechanism to improve their social skills, self-concept, and self-control. Typically, wilderness programs maintain exposure to a wholesome environment; where the concepts of education and the work ethic are taught and embodied in adult role models, troubled youth can regain a measure of self-worth.

A few wilderness programs for juvenile offenders have been evaluated for their effects on recidivism. In a detailed review of the effects of wilderness programs on recidivism, Doris MacKenzie concludes that these programs do not work.[88] Although some of the programs show success, such as the Spectrum Wilderness Program in Illinois,[89] others had negative effects; that is, the group that received the program had higher arrest rates than the comparison group that did not. Taken together, the programs suffered from poor implementation, weak evaluation designs or problems with too few subjects or large dropout rates, and failure to adhere to principles of successful rehabilitation, such as targeting high-risk youths and lasting for a moderate period of time.[90]

Juvenile Boot Camps

Correctional **boot camps** combine the get-tough elements of adult programs with education, substance-abuse treatment, and social skills training. In theory, a successful boot camp program should rehabilitate juvenile offenders, reduce the number of beds needed in secure institutional programs, and thus reduce the overall cost of care. The Alabama boot camp program for youthful offenders estimated savings of $1 million annually when compared with traditional institutional sentences.[91] However, no one seems convinced that participants in these programs have lower recidivism rates than

wilderness probation
Programs involving outdoor expeditions that provide opportunities for juveniles to confront the difficulties of their lives while achieving positive personal satisfaction.

boot camps
Programs that combine get-tough elements with education, substance abuse treatment, and social skills training.

Juvenile boot camps use strict discipline regimes, which some critics find demeaning to inmates. Here at the Prison Boot Camp in Illinois, one correctional officer bangs a metal wastebasket against the cement floor. Both officers yell at the new inmate, demanding that he hurry and gather his newly cut hair into the basket. They hurl a barrage of nonprofane insults at him. Profanity by correctional officers as well as inmates is forbidden at the boot camp.

© Jacksonville Courier/Zuzana Killian/The Image Works

To read more about **boot camps,** click on Web Links under the Chapter Resources at http://cj.wadsworth.com/siegel_jdcore2e.

those who serve normal sentences. Ronald Corbett and Joan Petersilia do note, however, that boot camp participants seem to be less antisocial upon returning to society.[92]

Other successes of juvenile boot camps were revealed in a national study comparing the environments of boot camps with more traditional secure correctional facilities for juveniles. Some of the main findings include these:

- Boot camp youths report more positive attitudes to their environment.
- Initial levels of depression are lower for boot camp youths but initial levels of anxiety are higher; both of these declined over time for youths in both traditional and boot camp facilities.
- Staff at boot camps report more favorable working conditions, such as less stress and better communication among staff.[93]

However, the bottom line for juvenile boot camps, like other correctional sanctions, is whether or not they reduce recidivism. A recent **metanalysis** of the effects of juvenile boot camps on recidivism found this to be an ineffective correctional approach to reducing it; from the sixteen different program samples, the control groups had, on average, lower recidivism rates than the treatment groups (boot camps).[94] Interestingly, when compared with the effects of twenty-eight program samples of boot camps for adults, the juvenile boot camps had a higher average recidivism rate, although the difference was not significant.[95]

Why do boot camps for juveniles fail to reduce future offending? The main reason is that they provide little in the way of therapy or treatment to correct offending behavior. Experts have also suggested that part of the reason for not finding differences in recidivism between boot camps and other correctional alternatives (the control groups) may be due to juveniles in the control groups receiving enhanced treatment while juveniles in the boot camps are spending more time on physical activities.[96]

The ineffectiveness of boot camps to reduce reoffending in the community by juvenile offenders (and adult offenders) appears to have resulted in this approach falling into disfavor with some correctional administrators. At the height of its popularity in the mid-1990s, more than seventy-five state-run boot camps were in operation in more than thirty states across the country; today, fifty-one remain.[97] Despite

metanalysis
An analysis technique that synthesizes results across many programs over time.

this, boot camps appear to still have a place among the array of sentencing options, if for no other reason than to appease the public with the promise of tougher sentences and lower costs.[98] If boot camps are to become a viable alternative for juvenile corrections they must be seen not as a panacea that provides an easy solution to the problems of delinquency, but merely part of a comprehensive approach to juvenile care that is appropriate to a select group of adolescents.[99] ✔ Checkpoints

THE LEGAL RIGHT TO TREATMENT

Checkpoints

✔ *Nearly all juvenile institutions implement some form of treatment program.*

✔ *Reality therapy, a commonly used individual approach, emphasizes current, rather than past, behavior by stressing that offenders are completely responsible for their own actions.*

✔ *Group therapy is more commonly used with kids than individual therapy.*

✔ *Guided group interaction and positive peer culture are popular group treatment techniques.*

✔ *Many but not all institutions either allow juveniles to attend a school in the community or offer programs that lead to a high school diploma or GED certificate.*

✔ *Wilderness programs involve troubled youth using outdoor activities as a mechanism to improve their social skills, self-concepts, and self-control.*

✔ *Correctional boot camps combine the get-tough elements of adult programs with education, substance abuse treatment, and social skills training.*

To quiz yourself on this material, go to questions 14.17–14.19 on the Juvenile Delinquency: The Core 2e Web site.

The primary goal of placing juveniles in institutions is to help them reenter the community successfully. Therefore, lawyers claim that children in state-run institutions have a legal right to treatment.

The concept of a **right to treatment** was introduced to the mental health field in 1960 by Morton Birnbaum, who argued that individuals who are deprived of their liberty because of a mental illness are entitled to treatment to correct that condition.[100] The right to treatment has expanded to include the juvenile justice system, an expansion bolstered by court rulings that mandate that rehabilitation and not punishment or retribution be the basis of juvenile court dispositions.[101] It stands to reason then that, if incarcerated, juveniles are entitled to the appropriate social services that will promote their rehabilitation.

One of the first cases to highlight this issue was *Inmates of the Boys' Training School v. Affleck* in 1972.[102] In its decision, a federal court argued that rehabilitation is the true purpose of the juvenile court and that, without that goal, due process guarantees are violated. It condemned such devices as solitary confinement, strip cells, and lack of educational opportunities, and held that juveniles have a statutory right to treatment. The court also established the following minimum standards for all juveniles confined in training schools:

- A room equipped with lighting sufficient for an inmate to read until 10 P.M.
- Sufficient clothing to meet seasonal needs
- Bedding, including blankets, sheets, pillows, and pillow cases, to be changed once a week
- Personal hygiene supplies, including soap, toothpaste, towels, toilet paper, and toothbrush
- A change of undergarments and socks every day
- Minimum writing materials: pen, pencil, paper, and envelopes
- Prescription eyeglasses, if needed
- Equal access to all books, periodicals, and other reading materials located in the training school
- Daily showers
- Daily access to medical facilities, including provision of a twenty-four-hour nursing service
- General correspondence privileges[103]

In 1974, in the case of *Nelson v. Heyne,* the First Federal Appellate Court affirmed that juveniles have a right to treatment and condemned the use of corporal punishment in juvenile institutions.[104] In *Morales v. Turman,* the court held that all juveniles confined in training schools in Texas have a right to treatment, including development of education skills, delivery of vocational education, medical and psychiatric treatment, and adequate living conditions.[105] In a more recent case, *Pena v. New York State Division for Youth,* the court held that the use of isolation, hand restraints, and tranquilizing drugs at Goshen Annex Center violated the Fourteenth Amendment right to due process and the Eighth Amendment right to protection against cruel and unusual punishment.[106]

right to treatment
Philosophy espoused by many courts that juvenile offenders have a statutory right to treatment while under the jurisdiction of the courts.

To learn more about the right to treatment, read "Meeting the Needs of the Mentally Ill—A Case Study of the 'Right to Treatment' as Legal Rights Discourse in the USA," by Michael McCubbin and David N. Weisstub. Click on Web Links under the Chapter Resources at http://cj. wadsworth.com/siegel_ jdcore2e.

The right to treatment has also been limited. For example, in *Ralston v. Robinson*, the Supreme Court rejected a youth's claim that he should continue to be given treatment after he was sentenced to a consecutive term in an adult prison for crimes committed while in a juvenile institution.[107] In the *Ralston* case, the offender's proven dangerousness outweighed the possible effects of rehabilitation. Similarly, in *Santana v. Callazo*, the U.S. First Circuit Court of Appeals rejected a suit brought by residents at the Maricao Juvenile Camp in Puerto Rico on the ground that the administration had failed to provide them with an individualized rehabilitation plan or adequate treatment. The circuit court concluded that it was a legitimate exercise of state authority to incarcerate juveniles solely to protect society if they are dangerous.

The Struggle for Basic Civil Rights

Several court cases have led federal, state, and private groups—for example, the American Bar Association, the American Correctional Association, and the National Council on Crime and Delinquency—to develop standards for the juvenile justice system. These standards provide guidelines for conditions and practices in juvenile institutions and call on administrators to maintain a safe and healthy environment for incarcerated youths.

For the most part, state-sponsored brutality has been outlawed, although the use of restraints, solitary confinement, and even medication for unruly residents has not been eliminated. The courts have ruled that corporal punishment in any form violates standards of decency and human dignity.

There are a number of mechanisms for enforcing these standards. For example, the federal government's Civil Rights of Institutionalized Persons Act (CRIPA) gives the Civil Rights Division of the U.S. Department of Justice (DOJ) the power to bring actions against state or local governments for violating the civil rights of persons institutionalized in publicly operated facilities.[108] CRIPA does not create any new substantive rights; it simply confers power on the U.S. Attorney General to bring action to enforce previously established constitutional or statutory rights of institutionalized persons; about 25 percent of cases involve juvenile detention and correctional facilities. There are many examples in which CRIPA-based litigation has helped ensure that incarcerated adolescents obtain their basic civil rights. For example, in November 1995 a federal court in Kentucky ordered state officials to remedy serious deficiencies in the state's thirteen juvenile treatment facilities. The decree required the state to take a number of steps to protect juveniles from abuse, mistreatment, and injury; to ensure adequate medical and mental health care; and to provide adequate educational, vocational, and aftercare services. Another CRIPA consent decree, ordered by a federal court in Puerto Rico in October 1994, addressed life-threatening conditions at eight juvenile detention and correction facilities. These dire conditions included juveniles committing and attempting suicide without staff intervention or treatment, widespread infection-control problems caused by rats and other vermin, and defective plumbing that forced juveniles to drink from their toilet bowls.

What provisions does the juvenile justice system make to help institutionalized offenders return to society? The remainder of this chapter is devoted to this topic.

JUVENILE AFTERCARE

aftercare
Transitional assistance to juveniles equivalent to adult parole to help youths adjust to community life.

Aftercare in the juvenile justice system is the equivalent of parole in the adult criminal justice system. When juveniles are released from an institution, they may be placed in an aftercare program of some kind, so that those who have been institutionalized are not simply returned to the community without some transitional assistance. Whether individuals who are in aftercare as part of an indeterminate sentence remain in the community or return to the institution for further rehabilitation depends on their actions during the aftercare period. Aftercare is an extremely important stage in the juvenile justice process because few juveniles age out of custody.[109]

Aftercare—the equivalent of parole in the adult criminal justice system—includes a range of services designed to help juveniles adjust to community life upon release from an institution. Here, Tristan Cassidy, seventeen, *top,* and Scott Epperley, fifteen, work on a project for their geography class at the Northwest Regional Learning Center (NRLC) in Everett, Washington. The NRLC is a detention school for juveniles on probation or in aftercare that serves as a last chance for some to earn their high school diploma if their former schools will not accept them back.

© 2004 AP/Wide World Photos

In a number of jurisdictions, a paroling authority, which may be an independent body or part of the corrections department or some other branch of state services, makes the release decision. Juvenile aftercare authorities, like adult parole officers, review the youth's adjustment inside the institution, whether there is chemical dependence, what the crime was, and other specifics of the case. Some juvenile authorities are even making use of **parole guidelines** first developed with adult parolees. Each youth who enters a secure facility is given a recommended length of confinement that is explained at the initial interview with parole authorities. The stay is computed on the basis of the offense record, influenced by aggravating and mitigating factors. The parole authority is not required to follow the recommended sentence but uses it as a tool in making parole decisions.[110] Whatever approach is used, several primary factors are considered by virtually all jurisdictions when recommending a juvenile for release: institutional adjustment, length of stay and general attitude, and likelihood of success in the community.

Risk classifications have also been designed to help parole officers make decisions about which juveniles should receive aftercare services.[111] The risk-based system uses an empirically derived risk scale to classify youths. Juveniles are identified as most likely or least likely to commit a new offense based on factors such as prior record, type of offense, and degree of institutional adjustment.

Supervision

One purpose of aftercare is to provide support during the readjustment period following release. First, individuals whose activities have been regimented for some time may not find it easy to make independent decisions. Second, offenders may perceive themselves as scapegoats, cast out by society. Finally, the community may view the returning minor with a good deal of prejudice; adjustment problems may reinforce a preexisting need to engage in deviant behavior.

Juveniles in aftercare programs are supervised by parole caseworkers or counselors whose job is to maintain contact with the juvenile, make sure that a corrections plan is followed, and show interest and caring. The counselor also keeps the youth informed of services that may assist in reintegration and counsels the youth and his or her family. Unfortunately, aftercare caseworkers, like probation officers, often carry such large caseloads that their jobs are next to impossible to do adequately.

parole guidelines
Recommended length of confinement and kinds of aftercare assistance most effective for a juvenile who committed a specific offense.

The Intensive Aftercare Program (IAP) Model New models of aftercare have been aimed at the chronic or violent offender. The **Intensive Aftercare Program (IAP)** model developed by David Altschuler and Troy Armstrong offers a continuum of intervention for serious juvenile offenders returning to the community following placement.[112] The IAP model begins by drawing attention to five basic principles, which collectively establish a set of fundamental operational goals:

1. Preparing youth for progressively increased responsibility and freedom in the community

2. Facilitating youth-community interaction and involvement

3. Working with both the offender and targeted community support systems (families, peers, schools, employers) on qualities needed for constructive interaction and the youths' successful community adjustment

4. Developing new resources and supports where needed

5. Monitoring and testing the youths and the community on their ability to deal with each other productively

These basic goals are then translated into practice, which incorporates individual case planning with a family and community perspective. The program stresses a mix of intensive surveillance and services and a balance of incentives and graduated consequences coupled with the imposition of realistic, enforceable conditions. There is also "service brokerage," in which community resources are used and linkage with social networks established.[113]

The IAP initiative was designed to help correctional agencies implement effective aftercare programs for chronic and serious juvenile offenders. After more than twelve years of testing, the program is now being aimed at determining how juveniles are prepared for reentry into their communities, how the transition is handled, and how the aftercare in the community is provided.[114] The Focus on Preventing and Treating Delinquency feature, "Using the Intensive Aftercare Program (IAP) Model," illustrates how it is being used in three state jurisdictions.

Aftercare Revocation Procedures

Juvenile parolees are required to meet set standards of behavior, which generally include but are not limited to the following:

- Adhere to a reasonable curfew set by youth worker or parent.
- Refrain from associating with persons whose influence would be detrimental.
- Attend school in accordance with the law.
- Abstain from drugs and alcohol.
- Report to the youth worker when required.
- Refrain from acts that would be crimes if committed by an adult.
- Refrain from operating an automobile without permission of the youth worker or parent.
- Refrain from being habitually disobedient and beyond the lawful control of parent or other legal authority.
- Refrain from running away from the lawful custody of parent or other lawful authority.

If these rules are violated, the juvenile may have his parole revoked and be returned to the institution. Most states have extended the same legal rights enjoyed by adults at parole revocation hearings to juveniles who are in danger of losing their aftercare privileges, as follows:

- Juveniles must be informed of the conditions of parole and receive notice of any obligations.

Intensive Aftercare Program (IAP)
A balanced, highly structured, comprehensive continuum of intervention for serious and violent juvenile offenders returning to the community.

Using the Intensive Aftercare Program (IAP) Model

How has the IAP model been used around the nation?

Colorado

Although adolescents are still institutionalized, community-based providers begin weekly services (including multifamily counseling and life-skills services) that continue during aftercare. Sixty days prior to release, IAP youths begin a series of step-down measures, including supervised trips to the community, and thirty days before release, there are overnight or weekend home passes. Upon release to parole, most program youths go through several months of day treatment that, in addition to services, provides a high level of structure during the day. Trackers provide evening and weekend monitoring during this period of reentry. As a youth's progress warrants, the frequency of supervision decreases. The planned frequency of contact is once a week during the first few months of supervision, with gradual reductions to once a month in later stages of supervision.

Nevada

Once the parole plan is finalized, all IAP youth begin a thirty-day prerelease phase, during which IAP staff provide a series of services that continue through the early months of parole. These consist primarily of two structured curricula on life skills (Jettstream) and substance abuse (Rational Recovery). In addition, a money management program (The Money Program) is initiated. Youths are provided with mock checking accounts from which "bills" must be paid for rent, food, insurance, and other necessities. They can also use their accounts to purchase recreation and other privileges, but each must have a balance of at least $50 at the end of the thirty days to purchase his bus ticket home. The initial thirty days of release are considered an institutional furlough (that is, the kids are still on the institutional rolls) that involves intensive supervision and service, any time during which they may be returned to the institution for significant program infractions. During furlough, they are involved in day programming and are subject to frequent drug testing and evening and weekend surveillance. Upon successful comple-

tion of the furlough, the IAP transition continues through the use of phased levels of supervision. During the first three months, three contacts per week with the case manager or field agent are required. This level of supervision is reduced to two contacts per week for the next two months, and then to once a week during the last month of parole.

Virginia

Virginia's transition differs from the other two sites in that its central feature is the use of group home placements as a bridge between the institution and the community. Immediately after release from the institution, youths enter one of two group homes for a thirty- to sixty-day period. The programs and services in which they will be involved in the community are initiated shortly after placement in the home. Virginia uses a formal step-down system to ease the intensity of parole supervision gradually. In the two months following the youth's release from the group home, staff are required to contact him five to seven times per week. This is reduced to three to five times per week during the next two months, and again to three times per week during the final thirty days.

CRITICAL THINKING

1. What is the importance of reducing the number of supervision contacts with the juvenile offender toward the end of the aftercare program?
2. Should juvenile offenders who have committed less serious offenses also have to go through intensive aftercare programs?

INFOTRAC COLLEGE EDITION RESEARCH

To learn more about aftercare programs for juvenile offenders, read Kit Glover and Kurt Bumby, "Re-Entry at the Point of Entry," *Corrections Today* 63:68 (December 2001) on InfoTrac College Edition. Use "juvenile corrections" as a key term to find out more about this topic.

Source: Richard G. Wiebush, Betsie McNulty, and Thao Le, *Implementation of the Intensive Community-Based Aftercare Program* (Washington, DC: Office of Juvenile Justice and Delinquency Prevention, Juvenile Justice Bulletin, 2000).

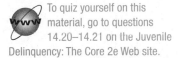 To quiz yourself on this material, go to questions 14.20–14.21 on the Juvenile Delinquency: The Core 2e Web site.

- Juveniles have the right to legal counsel at state expense if necessary.
- They maintain the right to confront and cross-examine witnesses against them.
- They have the right to introduce documentary evidence and witnesses.
- They have the right to a hearing before an officer who shall be an attorney but not an employee of the revoking agency.[115]

SUMMARY

- Community treatment encompasses efforts to keep offenders in the community and spare them the stigma of incarceration. The primary purpose is to provide a nonrestrictive or home setting, employing educational, vocational, counseling, and employment services. Institutional treatment encompasses provision of these services but in more restrictive and sometimes secure facilities.
- The most widely used community treatment method is probation. Behavior is monitored by probation officers. If rules are violated, youths may have their probation revoked.
- It is now common to enhance probation with more restrictive forms of treatment, such as intensive supervision and house arrest with electronic monitoring. Restitution programs involve having juvenile offenders either reimburse their victims or do community service.
- Residential community treatment programs allow youths to live at home while receiving treatment. There are also residential programs that require that youths reside in group homes while receiving treatment.
- The secure juvenile institution was developed in the mid-nineteenth century as an alternative to placing youths in adult prisons. Youth institutions evolved from large, closed institutions to cottage-based education- and rehabilitation-oriented institutions.
- The juvenile institutional population appears to have stabilized in recent years, but an increasing number of youths are "hidden" in private medical centers and drug treatment clinics.
- A disproportionate number of minorities are incarcerated in more secure, state-run youth facilities.
- Most juvenile institutions maintain intensive treatment programs featuring individual or group therapy. Little evidence has been found that any single method is effective in reducing recidivism, yet rehabilitation remains an important goal of juvenile practitioners.
- The right to treatment is an important issue in juvenile justice. Legal decisions have mandated that a juvenile cannot simply be warehoused in a correctional center but must receive proper care and treatment to aid rehabilitation. What constitutes proper care is still being debated, however.
- Juveniles released from institutions are often placed on parole, or aftercare. There is little evidence that community supervision is more beneficial than simply releasing youths. Many jurisdictions are experiencing success with halfway houses and reintegration centers.

KEY TERMS

community treatment, p. 338
suppression effect, p. 339
probation, p. 339
juvenile probation officer, p. 342
social investigation report,
   predisposition report, p. 342
conditions of probation, p. 342
juvenile intensive probation
   supervision (JIPS), p. 344
house arrest, p. 345
electronic monitoring, p. 345
balanced probation, p. 346
monetary restitution, p. 346
victim service restitution, p. 346

community service restitution,
   p. 346
residential programs, p. 348
group homes, p. 348
foster care programs, p. 348
family group homes, p. 348
rural programs, p. 348
reform schools, p. 348
cottage system, p. 348
least restrictive alternative, p. 350
individual counseling, p. 357
psychotherapy, p. 357
reality therapy, p. 357
behavior modification, p. 357

group therapy, p. 357
guided group interaction (GGI),
   p. 358
positive peer culture (PPC), p. 358
milieu therapy, p. 358
wilderness probation, p. 359
boot camps, p. 359
metanalysis, p. 360
right to treatment, p. 361
aftercare, p. 362
parole guidelines, p. 362
Intensive Aftercare Program (IAP),
   p. 364

QUESTIONS FOR DISCUSSION

1. Would you want a community treatment program in your neighborhood? Why or why not?
2. Is widening the net a real danger, or are treatment-oriented programs simply a method of helping troubled youths?
3. If youths violate the rules of probation, should they be placed in a secure institution?
4. Is juvenile restitution fair? Should a poor child have to pay back a wealthy victim, such as a store owner?

5. What are the most important advantages to community treatment for juvenile offenders?
6. What is the purpose of juvenile probation? Identify some conditions of probation and discuss the responsibilities of the juvenile probation officer.
7. Has community treatment generally proven successful?
8. Why have juvenile boot camps not been effective in reducing recidivism?

APPLYING WHAT YOU HAVE LEARNED

As a local juvenile court judge you have been assigned the case of Jim Butler, a thirteen-year-old so short he can barely see over the bench. On trial for armed robbery, the boy has been accused of threatening a woman with a knife and stealing her purse. Barely a teenager, he has already had a long history of involvement with the law. At age eleven he was arrested for drug possession and placed on probation; soon after, he stole a car. At age twelve he was arrested for shoplifting. Jim is accompanied by his legal guardian, his maternal grandmother. His parents are unavailable because his father abandoned the family years ago and his mother is currently undergoing inpatient treatment at a local drug clinic. After talking with his attorney, Jim decides to admit to the armed robbery. At a dispositional hearing, his court-appointed attorney tells you of the tough life Jim has been forced to endure. His grandmother states that, although she loves the boy, her advanced age makes it impossible for her to provide the care he needs to stay out of trouble. She says that Jim is a good boy who has developed a set of bad companions; his current scrape was precipitated by his friends. A representative of the school system testifies that Jim has above-average intelligence and is actually respectful of teachers. He has potential but his life circumstances have short-circuited his academic success. Jim himself shows remorse and appears to be a sensitive youngster who is easily led astray by older youths.

You must now make a decision. You can place Jim on probation and allow him to live with his grandmother while being monitored by county probation staff. You can place him in a secure incarceration facility for up to three years. You can also put him into an intermediate program such as a community-based facility, which would allow him to attend school during the day while residing in a halfway house and receiving group treatment in the evenings. Although Jim appears salvageable, his crime was serious and involved the use of a weapon. If he remains in the community he may offend again; if he is sent to a correctional facility he will interact with older, tougher kids. What mode of correctional treatment would you choose?

- Would you place Jim on probation and allow him to live with his grandmother while being monitored?
- Would you send him to a secure incarceration facility for up to three years?
- Would you put him into an intermediate program such as a community-based facility?

DOING RESEARCH ON THE WEB

Before you answer these questions, you may want to research the effectiveness of different types of correctional treatment for juvenile offenders. Use "juvenile correctional treatment" in a key word search on InfoTrac College Edition. To learn more about juvenile treatment options, click on Web Links under the Chapter Resources at http://cj. wadsworth.com/siegel_jdcore2e to go to the California Department of the Youth Authority, Center for the Study and Prevention of Violence, Washington State Institute for Public Policy on Juvenile Justice, the National Council on Crime and Delinquency and Children's Research Center, and the Urban Institute.

Pro/Con discussions and Viewpoint Essays on some of the topics in this chapter may be found at the Opposing Viewpoints Resource Center: www.gale.com/OpposingViewpoints.

Tertiary Prevention Efforts:
The Role of the Juvenile Justice System

Juvenile justice measures designed to prevent delinquency can include the police making an arrest as part of an operation to crack down on gang problems, a juvenile court sanction to a secure correctional facility, or in the extreme case, a death penalty sentence. Although these measures have as an objective the prevention of future delinquent activities (or repeat offending, or recidivism), they can also be referred to as measures of delinquency control or delinquency repression. This is because, unlike with the other strategies to prevent delinquency—the primary prevention and secondary prevention efforts discussed in the two earlier preventing delinquency essays—juvenile justice measures also have as an objective the protection of the public. For this to happen there also needs to be some type of formal control exercised over offenders.

From a public health perspective, juvenile justice measures are a form of tertiary-level delinquency prevention. Tertiary prevention focuses on intervening with offenders once a delinquent activity or crime has been committed. This form of delinquency prevention is considered reactive—there is a response only after (for the most part) a crime has taken place. It can also be considered the measure of last resort.

Many experts argue that there is an overreliance on police, courts, and corrections to prevent juvenile crime. Many are also of the opinion that this approach has become increasingly harsh or punitive in recent years. Juvenile courts have delivered harsher sentences, more juvenile offenders have been transferred to adult court, there has been a greater reliance on the use of confinement than rehabilitation, and a growing number of juvenile offenders are serving time in prison. This increased punitiveness has led many scholars to argue that the treatment and protection aims of the juvenile system have become more a matter of the abstract than of reality. According to University of Minnesota law professor Barry Feld:

> Evaluations of juvenile court sentencing practices, treatment effectiveness, and conditions of confinement reveal increasingly punitive juvenile court and corrections systems. These various indicators

strongly suggest that despite juvenile courts' persisting rehabilitative rhetoric, the reality of *treating* juveniles closely resembles *punishing* adult criminals.[1]

For some, this increased punitiveness in dealing with juvenile offenders makes the juvenile justice system seem less appealing as a vehicle for preventing delinquency. It may be that more checks and balances are needed for tertiary prevention measures. It may also be that a greater balance needs to be struck among this approach and primary and secondary delinquency prevention strategies. But the juvenile system plays an integral role in addressing juvenile delinquency, and there are many promising delinquency prevention programs operated by the police, courts, and corrections.

POLICE

The police are the first contact that juvenile offenders have with the juvenile justice system. Working with juvenile offenders presents special challenges for police, such as role conflicts arising from traditional policing practices and wanting to steer youths away from crime, the use of discretion, and the low regard held by youths toward police. But police have taken the lead in delinquency prevention. They have used a number of strategies: some rely on their deterrent powers whereas others rely on their relationship with schools, the community, and other juvenile justice agencies, or another on a problem-solving model.

These policing innovations have produced results. Boston's Operation Ceasefire, which brought together the police, juvenile probation, social services, and other key local, state, and federal agencies, more than halved the number of juvenile homicide victims and greatly reduced gang activity across the city.[2] Another promising example of police taking the lead in preventing delinquency is the Partnerships to Reduce Juvenile Gun Violence Program. This involves problem-oriented policing strategies and other interventions, including a public information campaign to communicate the dangers and consequences of gun violence to juveniles, families, and community residents.[3]

COURTS

Many critical decisions are made at this stage of the juvenile justice system that have implications for preventing delinquency in the short or long term. Some of these are whether to detain a youth or release the youth to the community, whether to waive youths to the adult court or retain them in the juvenile system, or whether to treat them in the community or send them to a secure treatment center.

In recent years, the juvenile court has introduced a number of innovations to foster more effective delinquency prevention for specific types of juvenile offenders. One of these is the juvenile drug court. Although these courts operate under a number of different frameworks, the aim is to place nonviolent first offenders into intensive treatment programs rather than into a custodial institution. Teen or youth court is another alternative to the traditional juvenile court in which young people rather than adults determine the disposition in a case. Cases handled in these courts typically involve young juveniles with no prior arrest records who have been charged with minor law violations. A recent evaluation of teen courts in four states found promising results in reducing recidivism.[4]

CORRECTIONS

At this stage of the juvenile system, measures to prevent delinquency can be organized into two main categories: community treatment and institutional treatment. Community treatment covers a wide range of modalities, including probation, treatment services (such as individual and group counseling), and restitution. There are also a wide variety of institutional treatments for juvenile offenders, ranging from training schools or reformatories to boot camps.

There exists much debate about the effectiveness of community versus institutional treatment. Considerable research shows that warehousing juveniles without proper treatment does little to prevent future delinquent activities. The most effective secure corrections programs are those that provide individual services for a small number of participants.[5] Evaluations of community treatment provide evidence of a number of successful ways to prevent delinquency without jeopardizing the safety of community residents.

There is also a long-standing debate about the effectiveness of correctional treatments compared with other delinquency prevention measures. In their assessment of the full range of interventions to prevent serious and violent juvenile offending, Rolf Loeber and David Farrington found that it is never too early and never too late to make a difference.[6]

Concluding Notes: American Delinquency

We have reviewed in this text the current knowledge of the nature, cause, and correlates of juvenile delinquency and society's efforts to bring about its elimination and control. We have analyzed research programs, theoretical models, governmental policies, and legal cases. Taken in sum, this information presents a rather broad and complex picture of the youth crime problem and the most critical issues confronting the juvenile justice system. Delinquents come from a broad spectrum of society; kids of every race, gender, class, region, family type, and culture are involved in delinquent behaviors. To combat youthful law violations, society has tried a garden variety of intervention and control strategies: tough law enforcement; counseling, treatment and rehabilitation; provision of legal rights; community action; educational programs; family change strategies. Yet, despite decades of intense effort and study, it is still unclear why delinquency occurs and what, if anything, can be done to control its occurrence. One thing is certain, juvenile crime is one of the most serious domestic problems faced by Americans.

Though uncertainty prevails, it is possible to draw some inferences about youth crime and its control. After reviewing the material contained in this volume, certain conclusions seem self-evident. Some involve social facts; that is, particular empirical relationships and associations have been established that have withstood multiple testing and verification efforts. Other conclusions involve social questions; there are issues that need clarification, and the uncertainty surrounding them has hampered progress in combating delinquency and treating known delinquents.

In sum, we have reviewed some of the most important social facts concerning delinquent behavior and posed some of the critical questions that still remain to be answered.

The statutory concept of juvenile delinquency is in need of review and modification.

Today, the legal definition of a juvenile delinquent is a minor child, usually under the age of 17, who has been found to have violated the criminal law (juvenile code). The concept of juvenile delinquency still occupies a legal position falling somewhere between criminal and civil law; juveniles still enjoy more rights, protections, and privileges than adults. Nonetheless, concerns about teen violence may eventually put an end to the separate juvenile justice system. If kids are equally or even more violent as adults, why should they be given a special legal status consideration? If the teen violence rate, which has been in a decline, begins to rise again, so too may calls for the abolition of a separate juvenile justice system.

The concept of the status offender (PINS, CHINS, and MINS) may be in for revision.

Special treatment for the status offender conforms with the *parens patriae* roots of the juvenile justice system. Granting the state authority to institutionalize noncriminal youth in order "to protect the best interest of the child" cannot be considered an abuse of state authority. While it is likely that the current system of control will remain in place for the near future, it is not beyond the realm of possibility to see the eventual restructuring of the definition of status offenders, with jurisdiction of "pure" noncriminal first offenders turned over to a department of social services, and chronic status offenders and those with prior records of delinquency petitioned to juvenile court as delinquency cases.

Juvenile offenders are becoming less violent.

Official delinquency data suggests that there has been a decade-long decrease in the juvenile violence rate. After a long-term increase in juvenile violence, juvenile offenders are now decreasing their involvement in murder and other serious felony offenses. While this news is welcome, some forecasters suggest that this respite will be a short-term phenomenon and predict a long-term increase in the violence rate.

Easy availability of guns is a significant contributor to teen violence.

Research indicates a close tie between gun use, control of drug markets, and teen violence. Efforts to control the spread of handguns and/or devise programs to deter handgun use have resulted in reduced violence rates.

The chronic violent juvenile offender is a serious social problem for society and the juvenile justice system.

Official crime data indicate that the juvenile violence rate is at an all-time high. Chronic male delinquent offenders commit a disproportionate amount of violent behavior, including a significant amount of the most serious juvenile crimes, such as homicides, rapes, robberies, and aggravated assaults. Many chronic offenders become adult criminals and eventually end up in the criminal court system. How to effectively deal with chronic juvenile offenders and drug users remains a high priority for the juvenile justice system.

The best approach to dealing with chronic offenders remains uncertain, but concern about such offenders has shifted juvenile justice policy toward a punishment-oriented philosophy.

Female delinquency has been increasing at a faster pace than male delinquency.

The nature and extent of female delinquent activities changed in the late 1980s, and it now appears that girls are engaging in more frequent and serious illegal activity than ever before. While male delinquency rates have actually declined during the past decade female rates have continued the trend upward. While gender differences in the rate of the most serious crimes such as murder still persist, it is possible that further convergence will occur in the near future.

There are distinct racial patterns in the delinquency rate.

African-American youths are arrested for a disproportionate number of murders, rapes, robberies, and assaults, while White youths are arrested for a disproportionate share of arsons. Some experts believe that racial differences can be explained by institutional racism: police are more likely to arrest African-American youths than they are White offenders. Others argue that structural disparity in society is responsible for racial differences: minority youth are more likely to be poor and live in disorganized areas.

There is little question that family environment affects patterns of juvenile behavior.

Family relationships have been linked to the problem of juvenile delinquency by many experts. While divorce may not be a per se cause of delinquency, there is evidence that children being raised in single-parent households are more inclined to behavioral problems than those who reside in two-parent homes. Limited resource allocations limit the single parent's ability to control and supervise children.

There is a strong association between abuse and delinquency.

There seems to be a strong association in family relationships between child abuse and delinquency. Cases of abuse and neglect have been found in every level of the economic strata, and a number of studies have linked child abuse and neglect to juvenile delinquency. While the evidence is not conclusive, it does suggest that a strong relationship exists between child abuse and subsequent delinquent behavior.

Juvenile gangs have become a serious and growing problem in many major metropolitan areas throughout the United States.

Ethnic youth gangs, mostly males aged 14 to 21, appear to be increasing in such areas as Los Angeles, Chicago, Boston, and New York. National surveys of gang activity now estimate that there are more than 750,000 members in the United States, up sharply over the previous twenty years. One view of gang development is that such groups serve as a bridge between adolescence and adulthood in communities where adult social control is not available. Another view suggests that gangs are a product of lower-class social disorganization and that they serve as an alternative means of economic advancement for poorly motivated and uneducated youth. Today's gangs are more often commercially than culturally oriented, and the profit motive may be behind increasing memberships. It is unlikely that gang control strategies can be successful as long as legitimate economic alternatives are lacking. Look for rapid growth in ganging when the current adolescent population matures and limited job opportunities encourage gang members to prolong their involvement in illegal activities.

Many of the underlying problems of youth crime and delinquency are directly related to education.

Numerous empirical studies have confirmed that lack of educational success is an important contributing factor in delinquency; experts generally agree chronic offenders have had a long history of school failure. Dropping out of school is now being associated with long-term anti-social behavior. About 10 percent of all victimizations occur on school grounds. Though some school-based delinquency control projects have been very successful, a great deal more effort is needed in this critical area of school-delinquency prevention control.

Substance abuse is closely associated with juvenile crime and delinquency.

Self-report surveys indicate that more than half of all high school-age kids have tried drugs. Surveys of arrestees indicate that a significant proportion of teenagers are drug users and many are high school dropouts. While one national survey shows that teenage drug use increased slightly in the past year, both national surveys report that drug and alcohol use are much lower today than 5 and 10 years ago. Traditional prevention efforts and education programs have not had encouraging results.

Prevention is a key component of an overall strategy to address the problem of juvenile delinquency.

In recent years, many different types of delinquency prevention programs have been targeted at children, young people, and families, and many of these programs show positive results in reducing delinquency as well as other problem behaviors, such as substance abuse and truancy. They have also been shown to lead to improvements in other areas of life, such as educational achievement, health, and employment. These benefits often translate into substantial cost savings.

An analysis of the history of juvenile justice over the past 100 years shows how our policy regarding delinquency has gone through cycles of reform.

Many years ago, society primarily focused on the treatment of youths who committed criminal behavior, often through no fault of their own. Early in the nineteenth century, juveniles were tried in criminal courts, like everyone else. Reformers developed the idea of establishing separate institutions for juvenile offenders in which the rehabilitation idea could proceed without involvement with criminal adults. As a result, the House of Refuge Movement was born. By the late 1890s the system proved unworkable, because delinquent juveniles, minor offenders, and neglected children weren't benefiting from institutional placement. The 1899 Illinois Juvenile Court

Act was an effort to regulate the treatment of children and secure institutional reform. *Parens patriae* was the justification to ignore legal formalities in the juvenile courts up until the early twentieth century. In the 1960s, the *Gault* decision heralded the promise of legal rights for children and interrupted the goal of individualized rehabilitation. The 1970s yielded progress in the form of the Juvenile Justice and Delinquency Prevention Act. Throughout the 1980s and 1990s, the juvenile justice system seemed suspended between the assurance of due process and efforts to provide services for delinquent children and their families. Today, society is concerned with the control of serious juvenile offenders and the development of firm sentencing provisions in the juvenile courts. These cycles represent the shifting philosophies of the juvenile justice system.

Today no single ideology or view dominates the direction, programs, and policies of the juvenile justice system.

Throughout the past decade, numerous competing positions regarding juvenile justice have emerged. As the liberal program of the 1970s has faltered, more restrictive sanctions have been imposed. The "crime control" position seems most formidable in this new millennium. However, there remains a great deal of confusion over what the juvenile justice system does, what it should do, and how it should deal with youthful antisocial behavior. The juvenile justice system operates on distinctly different yet parallel tracks. On the one hand, significant funding is available for prevention and treatment strategies. At the same time, states are responding to anxiety about youth crime by devising more punitive measures.

Today's problems in the juvenile justice system can often be traced to the uncertainty of its founders, the "child savers."

Such early twentieth-century groups formed the juvenile justice system on the misguided principle of reforming wayward youth and remodeling their behavior. The "best interest of the child" standard has long been the guiding light in juvenile proceedings, calling for the strongest available rehabilitative services. Today's juvenile justice system is often torn between playing the role of social versus crime control agent.

In recent years, the juvenile justice system has become more legalistic by virtue of U.S. Supreme Court decisions that have granted children procedural safeguards in various court proceedings.

The case of *In re Gault* of the 1960s motivated state legislators to revamp their juvenile court legal procedures. Today, the Supreme Court is continuing to struggle with making distinctions between the legal rights of adults and those of minors. Recent Court decisions that allowed children to be searched by teachers and denied their right to a jury trial showed that the Court continues to recognize a legal separation between adult and juvenile offenders.

Despite some dramatic distinctions, juveniles have gained many of the legal due process rights enjoyed by adults.

Among the more significant elements of due process are the right to counsel, evidence efficiency, protection from double jeopardy and self-incrimination, and the right to appeal. While the public continues to favor providing juveniles with the same due process and procedural guarantees accorded to adults, it is likely that constitutional protections that adults receive are not actually provided to juvenile offenders. High caseloads, poor pretrial preparation and trial performance, and the lack of dispositional representation are issues where juveniles are being denied due process of law. More resources are needed to implement constitutional procedures so that legal protections are not discarded.

The key area in which due process is required by *Gault* is the right to counsel. While progress has been made in improving the availability and quality of legal counsel afforded youths in delinquency proceedings in over four decades since *Gault*, much remains to be done.

States are increasingly taking legislative action to ensure that juvenile arrest and disposition records are available to prosecutors and judges.

Knowledge of defendants' juvenile records may help determine appropriate sentencing for offenders aged 18 to 24, the age group most likely to be involved in violent crime. Laws that are being passed include (1) police fingerprinting of juveniles charged with crimes that are felonies if committed by an adult; (2) centralized juvenile arrest and disposition record-holding and dissemination statutes; (3) prosecutor and court access to juvenile disposition records; and (4) limitations on expungement of juvenile records when there are subsequent adult convictions.

The Juvenile Court is the focal point of the contemporary juvenile justice system.

Created at the turn of the century, it was adopted as an innovative solution to the problem of wayward youth. In the first half of the century, these courts (organized by the states and based on the historic notion of *parens patriae*) were committed to the treatment of the child. They functioned without procedures employed in the adult criminal courts. When the system was reviewed by the U.S. Supreme Court in 1966, due process was imposed on the juvenile court system. Almost 40 years have since passed,

and numerous reform efforts have been undertaken. But the statement of Judge Abe Fortas "that the child receives the worst of both worlds—neither the protection afforded adults nor the treatment needed for children," still rings true. Reform efforts have been disappointing.

What are the remedies for the current juvenile court system?

Some suggest abolishing the delinquency-status jurisdiction of the courts. This is difficult to do because the organization of the courts is governed by state law. Others want to strengthen the legal rights of juveniles by improving the quality of services of legal counsel. The majority of experts believe there is an urgent need to develop meaningful dispositional programs and expand treatment services. Over the last fifty years, the juvenile court system has been transformed from a rehabilitative to a quasi-criminal court. With limited resources and procedural deficiencies, there is little likelihood of much change in the near future. One area of change has been the development of specialized courts, such as drug courts, which focus attention on specific problems, and teen or youth courts, which use peer jurors and other officers of the court to settle less serious matters.

The death penalty for children has been upheld by the Supreme Court.

According to the *Wilkens v. Missouri* and *Standford v. Kentucky* cases in 1989, the Supreme Court concluded that states are free to impose the death penalty for murderers who commit their crimes while age 16 or 17. According to the majority decision written by Justice Antonin Scalia, society has not formed a consensus that such executions are a violation of the cruel and unusual punishment clause of the Eighth Amendment. In August 2003, the Supreme Court of Missouri declared the death penalty to be unconstitutional for offenders under the age of 18, and petitioned the U.S. Supreme Court to take up this matter. In January 2004, the Supreme Court agreed to decide whether the death penalty for 16- and 17-year-olds violates the Constitution.

New approaches to policing juvenile delinquency show promising results in reducing serious offenses, such as gang activity and gun crimes.

Some of these new approaches include aggressive law enforcement, community-based policing services, and police in schools. One of the most successful approaches has involved the police working closely with other juvenile justice agencies and the community. Operation Ceasefire in Boston, which brought together a broad range of juvenile justice and social agencies and community groups, produced substantial reductions in youth homicide victims, youth gun assaults, and gang violence across the city. Versions of this successful program are now being replicated in other cities across the country.

The use of detention in the juvenile justice system continues to be a widespread problem.

After almost three decades of work, virtually all jurisdictions have passed laws requiring that status offenders be placed in shelter care programs rather than detention facilities. Another serious problem related to the use of juvenile detention is the need to remove young people from lockups in adult jails. The Office of Juvenile Justice and Delinquency Prevention continues to give millions of dollars in aid to encourage the removal of juveniles from such adult lockups. But eliminating the confinement of children in adult institutions remains an enormously difficult task in the juvenile justice system. Although most delinquency cases do not involve detention, its use is more common for cases involving males, minorities, and older juveniles. Juvenile detention is one of the most important elements of the justice system and one of the most difficult to administer. It is experiencing a renewed emphasis on programs linked to short-term confinement.

The use of waiver, bind-over, and transfer provisions in juvenile court statutes is now more common.

This trend has led toward a criminalization of the juvenile system. Because there are major differences between the adult and juvenile court systems, transfer to an adult court exposes youths to more serious consequences of their antisocial behavior and is a strong recommendation of those favoring a crime control model. Waiver of serious offenders is one of the most significant developments in the trend to criminalize the juvenile court. According to the National Conference of State Legislatures, every state has transfer proceedings. Many states are considering legislation that makes it easier to transfer juveniles into adult courts. States continue to modify age and offense criteria, allowing more serious offenders to be tried as criminals; some are considering new transfer laws, such as mandatory and presumptive waiver provisions.

The role of the attorney in the juvenile justice process requires further research and analysis.

Most attorneys appear to be uncertain whether they should act as adversaries or advocates in the juvenile process. In addition, the role of the juvenile prosecutor has become more significant as a result of new and more serious statutory sentencing provisions, as well as legal standards promulgated by such organizations as the American Bar Association and the National District Attorneys Association. Juvenile defendants also need and are entitled to effective legal representation. Through creative and resourceful strategies, many more states are providing comprehensive representation for delinquent youth. These programs include law internships, attorney mentoring, and neighborhood defender services.

Juvenile sentencing procedures now reflect the desire to create uniformity and limited discretion in the juvenile court, and this trend is likely to continue.

Many states have now developed programs such as mandatory sentences, sentencing guidelines, and limited-discretion sentencing to bring uniformity into the juvenile justice system. As a result of the public's fear about serious juvenile crime, legislators have amended juvenile codes to tighten up juvenile sentencing provisions. Graduated sanctions are the latest type of sentencing solution being explored by states. The most popular piece of juvenile crime legislation in the near future will be tougher sentences for violent and repeat offenders. Perhaps the most dramatic impact on sentencing will be felt by the imposition of "blended sentences" that combine juvenile and adult sentences. Today, more than a dozen states now use blended sentencing statutes, which allow courts to impose juvenile and/or adult correctional sanctions on certain young offenders.

In the area of community sentencing, new forms of probation supervision have received greater attention in recent years.

Intensive probation supervision, balanced probation, wilderness probation, and electronic monitoring have become important community-based alternatives over the last few years. Some studies report mixed results for these new forms of probation, but more experimentation is needed. Probation continues to be the single most significant intermediate sanction available to the juvenile court system.

Restorative community juvenile justice is a new designation that refers to a preference for neighborhood-based, more accessible, and less formal juvenile services.

The restorative justice idea focuses on the relationship between the victim, the community, and the offender. For the victim, restorative justice offers the hope of restitution or other forms of reparation, information about the case, support for healing, the opportunity to be heard, and input into the case, as well as expanded opportunities for involvement and influence. For the community, there is the promise of reduced fear and safer neighborhoods, a more accessible justice process, and accountability, as well as the obligation for involvement and participation in sanctioning crime, supporting victim restoration, reintegrating offenders, and crime prevention and control. For the offender, restorative justice requires accountability in the form of obligations to repair the harm to individual victims and victimized communities, and the opportunity to develop new competencies, social skills, and the capacity to avoid future crime.

Deinstitutionalization has become an important goal of the juvenile justice system.

The Office of Juvenile Justice and Delinquency Prevention has provided funds to encourage this process. In the early 1980s, the deinstitutionalization movement seemed to be partially successful. Admissions to public juvenile correctional facilities declined in the late 1970s and early 1980s. In addition, the number of status offenders being held within the juvenile justice system was reduced. However, the number of institutionalized children in the 1990s and in the early part of the 2000s has increased, and the deinstitutionalization movement has failed to meet all of its optimistic goals. Nonetheless, the majority of states have achieved compliance with the DSO mandate (Deinstitutionalizing Status Offenders). Because juvenile crime is a high priority, the challenge to the states will be to retain a focus on prevention despite societal pressures for more punitive approaches. If that can be achieved, then deinstitutionalization will remain a central theme in the juvenile justice system.

The number of incarcerated youths remains high.

The juvenile institutional population appears to have stabilized in recent years (there are slightly less than 109,000 youths in some type of correctional institution). The juvenile courts, however, seem to be using the most severe of the statutory dispositions, that is, commitment to the juvenile institution, rather than the "least restrictive statutory alternative." There is also a wide variation in juvenile custody rates across the nation. The District of Columbia has the highest juvenile incarceration rate at over 700 per 100,000 juveniles, which is almost twice the national average.

Minority youths have higher incarceration rates.

A disproportionate number of minority youths are incarcerated in youth facilities. The difference is greatest for black youths, with the incarceration rate being almost five times greater than that for whites. Of equal importance, minorities are more likely to be placed in secure public facilities rather than in open private facilities that might provide more costly and effective treatment. The OJJDP is committed to ensuring that the country address situations where there is disproportionate confinement of minority offenders in the nation's juvenile justice system.

Juvenile boot camps don't work.

Correctional boot camps, which combine get-tough elements of adult programs with education, substance-abuse treatment, and social-skills training, are used to shock the offender into going straight. Systematic reviews and meta-analyses of the research evidence show that juvenile boot camps fail to reduce future offending. Despite their poor results, many states continue to use boot camps as a correctional option for juvenile offenders.

The future of the legal right to treatment for juveniles remains uncertain.

The appellate courts have established minimum standards of care and treatment on a case-by-case basis, but it does not appear that the courts can be persuaded today to expand this constitutional theory to mandate that incarcerated children receive adequate treatment. Eventually, this issue must be clarified by the Supreme Court. Reforms in state juvenile institutions often result from class-action lawsuits filed on behalf of incarcerated youth.

A serious crisis exists in the U.S. juvenile justice system.

How to cope with the needs of large numbers of children in trouble remains one of the most controversial and frustrating issues in our society. The magnitude of the problem is such that around 2 million youths are arrested each year; over 1.6 million delinquency dispositions and 150,000 status offense cases are heard in court. Today, the system and the process seem more concerned with crime control and more willing to ignore the rehabilitative ideal. Perhaps the answer lies outside the courtroom in the form of greater job opportunities, improved family relationships, and more effective education. Much needs to be done in delinquency prevention. One fact is also certain: according to many experts, the problem of violent juvenile crime is a national crisis. While the good news is that the juvenile crime rate declined in recent years, violence by juveniles is still too prevalent and remains an issue of great concern. Developing programs to address juvenile violence seems to overshadow all other juvenile justice objectives.

Federal funding for juvenile delinquency is essential to improving state practices and programs.

The Juvenile Justice and Delinquency Prevention Act of 1974 has had a tremendous impact on America's juvenile justice systems. Its mandates to deinstitutionalize status offenders and remove juveniles from adult jails have spurred change for over two decades. The survival of many state programs will likely depend on this federal legislation. Because the Act has contributed to a wide range of improvements, Congress will most likely approve future financial incentives.

Today, the juvenile justice system and court of 100 years is under attack more than ever before.

Yet the system has weathered criticism for failing to control and rehabilitate juveniles. It is a unique American institution duplicated in many other countries as being the best model for handling juveniles who commit crime. The major recommendations of such important organizations as the national Council of Juvenile Court Judges, the American Bar Association, and the Office of Juvenile Justice and Delinquency prevention for the new century are (1) the court should be a leader for juvenile justice in the community; (2) people (judges, attorneys, and probation officers) are the key to the health of the juvenile justice system; (3) public safety and rehabilitation are the goals of the juvenile justice system; (4) juvenile court workloads are shaped today and in the future by the increase of substance abuse cases that must be resolved; and (5) the greatest future needs of the juvenile court in particular are resources and funding for more services, more staff, and more facilities.

Appendix: Excerpts from the U.S. Constitution

Amendment I (1791)

Congress shall make no law respecting an establishment of religion, or prohibiting the free exercise thereof; or abridging the freedom of speech, or of the press; or the right of the people peaceably to assemble, and to petition the government for a redress of grievances.

Amendment II (1791)

A well regulated militia, being necessary to the security of a free state, the right of the people to keep and bear arms, shall not be infringed.

Amendment III (1791)

No soldier shall, in time of peace, be quartered in any house, without the consent of the owner, nor in time of war, but in a manner to be prescribed by law.

Amendment IV (1791)

The right of the people to be secure in their persons, houses, papers, and effects, against unreasonable searches and seizures, shall not be violated, and no warrants shall issue, but upon probable cause, supported by oath or affirmation, and particularly describing the place to be searched, and the persons or things to be seized.

Amendment V (1791)

No person shall be held to answer for a capital, or otherwise infamous, crime unless on a presentment or indictment of a grand jury, except in cases arising in the land or naval forces, or in the militia, when in actual service in time of war or public danger; nor shall any person be subject for the same offense to be twice put in jeopardy of life or limb; nor shall be compelled in any criminal case to be a witness against himself, nor be deprived of life, liberty, or property; without due process of law; nor shall private property be taken for public use without just compensation.

Amendment VI (1791)

In all criminal prosecutions, the accused shall enjoy the right to a speedy and public trial, by an impartial jury of the state and district wherein the crime shall have been committed, which district shall have been previously ascertained by law, and to be informed of the nature and cause of the accusation; to be confronted with the witnesses against him; to have compulsory process for obtaining witnesses in his favor, and to have the assistance of counsel for his defense.

Amendment VII (1791)

In suits at common law, where the value in controversy shall exceed twenty dollars, the right of trial by jury shall be preserved, and no fact tried by a jury shall be otherwise reexamined in any court of the United States, than according to the rules of common law.

Amendment VIII (1791)

Excessive bail shall not be required, nor excessive fines imposed, nor cruel and unusual punishment inflicted.

Amendment IX (1791)

The enumeration in the Constitution of certain rights shall not be construed to deny or disparage others retained by the people.

Amendment X (1791)

The powers not delegated to the United States by the Constitution, nor prohibited by it to the states, are reserved to the states respectively, or to the people.

Amendment XIV (1868)

Section I. All persons born or naturalized in the United States, and subject to the jurisdiction thereof, are citizens of the United States and of the state wherein they reside. No state shall make or enforce any laws which abridge the privilege or immunities of citizens of the United States; nor shall any state deprive any person of life, liberty, or property, without due process of law; nor deny to any person within its jurisdiction the equal protection of the laws.

NOTES

Chapter 1

1. *Current Population Reports, Series P-20* (Washington, D.C.: U.S. Department of Commerce, Bureau of the Census, 2003).
2. *America's Children: Key National Indicators of Well-Being* (Washington, DC: Interagency Forum on Child and Family Statistics, 2003).
3. Nanette Davis, *Youth Crisis: Growing Up in the High-Risk Society* (New York: Praeger/Greenwood, 1998).
4. Erik Erikson, *Childhood and Society* (New York: Norton, 1963).
5. Roger Gould, "Adult Life Stages: Growth Toward Self-Tolerance," *Psychology Today* 8:74–78 (1975).
6. Kevin Thompson, David Brownfield, and Ann Marie Sorenson, "At-Risk Behavior and Gang Involvement: A Latent Structure Analysis," *Journal of Gang Research* 5:1–15 (1998).
7. Anthony Jackson and Gayle Davis, *Turning Points 2000: Educating Adolescents in the 21st Century* (New York: Carnegie Council on Adolescent Development, Task Force on Education of Young Adolescents, 2000), p. 27.
8. Greg Duncan, W. Jean Yeung, Jeanne Brooks-Gunn, and Judith Smith, "How Much Does Childhood Poverty Affect the Life Chances of Children?" *American Sociological Review* 63:406–423 (1998).
9. Children's Defense Fund, *Number of Black Children in Extreme Poverty Hits Record High* (Washington, DC: Children's Defense Fund, May 28, 2003).
10. Jeanne Brooks-Gunn and Greg J. Duncan, "The Effects of Poverty on Children," *Future of Children* 7: 34–39 (1997).
11. *America's Children.*
12. "Children's Defense Fund Analysis Shows Percentage of Uninsured Children Varies by State." Press release (Washington, DC: Children's Defense Fund, October 24, 2003).
13. *America's Children.*
14. David Eggebeen and Daniel Lichter, "Race, Family Structure, and Changing Poverty Among American Children," *American Sociological Review* 56:801–817 (1991).
15. Tami Videon, "The Effects of Parent-Adolescent Relationships and Parental Separation on Adolescent Well-Being," *Journal of Marriage & the Family* 64:489–504 (2002).
16. Gary Evans, Nancy Wells, and Annie Moch, "Housing and Mental Health: A Review of the Evidence and a Methodological and Conceptual Critique," *Journal of Social Issues* 59:475–501 (2003).
17. *America's Children.*
18. *Current Population Survey (CPS)* (Washington, DC: U.S. Department of Commerce, U.S. Census Bureau, October 2000).
19. *America's Children.*
20. Ibid.
21. National Education Goals Panel, *The National Education Goals Report, Building a Nation of Learners* (Washington, DC: United States Government Printing Office, 1997), pp. iii–iv.
22. Bruce Johnson, George Thomas, and Andrew Golub, "Trends in Heroin Use Among Manhattan Arrestees from the Heroin and Crack Era," in James Inciardi and Lana Harrison, eds., *Heroin in the Age of Crack Cocaine* (Thousand Oaks, CA: Sage, 1998), pp. 08–130.
23. Federal Bureau of Investigation, *Crime in the United States, 2002* (Washington, DC: U.S. Government Printing Office, 2003), p. 244.
24. John Whitehead and Steven Lab, "A Meta-Analysis of Juvenile Correctional Treatment," *Journal of Research in Crime and Delinquency* 26:276–295 (1989).
25. Francis Cullen, Sandra Evans Skovron, Joseph Scott, and Velmer Burton, "Public Support for Correctional Treatment: The Tenacity of Rehabilitative Ideology," *Criminal Justice and Behavior* 17:6–18 (1990).
26. Rhena Izzo and Robert Ross, "Meta-Analysis of Rehabilitation Programs for Juvenile Delinquents," *Criminal Justice and Behavior* 17:134–142 (1990).
27. Gordon Bazemore and Lynette Feder, "Judges in the Punitive Juvenile Court: Organizational, Career, and Ideological Influences on Sanctioning Orientation," *Justice Quarterly* 14:87–114 (1997).
28. *Stanford v. Kentucky* and *Wilkins v. Missouri,* 492 US 361, 109 S. Ct. 2969, 106 L. Ed. 2d 306 (1989).
29. See Lawrence Stone, *The Family, Sex, and Marriage in England: 1500–1800* (New York: Harper & Row, 1977).
30. This section relies on Jackson Spielvogel, *Western Civilization* (St. Paul, MN: West, 1991), pp. 279–286.
31. Ibid.
32. Philippe Aries, *Centuries of Childhood: A Social History of Family Life* (New York: Vintage Books, 1962).
33. Nicholas Orme, *Medieval Children* (New Haven: Yale University Press, 2003).
34. See Aries, *Centuries of Childhood.*
35. See Douglas R. Rendleman, "*Parens Patriae:* From Chancery to the Juvenile Court," *South Carolina Law Review* 23:205 (1971).
36. See Stone, *The Family, Sex, and Marriage in England;* and Lawrence Stone, ed., *Schooling and Society: Studies in the History of Education* (Baltimore: Johns Hopkins University Press, 1970).
37. Ibid.
38. See Wiley B. Sanders, *Some Early Beginnings of the Children's Court Movement in England, National Probation Association Yearbook* (New York: National Council on Crime and Delinquency, 1945).
39. Rendleman, "*Parens Patriae,*" p. 205.
40. Douglas Besharov, *Juvenile Justice Advocacy—Practice in a Unique Court* (New York: Practicing Law Institute, 1974), p. 2.
41. *Wellesley v. Wellesley,* 4 Eng. Rep. 1078 (1827).
42. Rendleman, "*Parens Patriae,*" p. 209.
43. Anthony Platt, "The Rise of the Child Saving Movement: A Study in Social Policy and Correctional Reform," *Annals of the American Academy of Political and Social Science* 381:21–38 (1969).
44. Robert Bremner, ed., and John Barnard, Hareven Tamara, and Robert Mennel, asst. eds., *Children and Youth in America* (Cambridge, MA: Harvard University Press, 1970), p. 64.
45. Elizabeth Pleck, "Criminal Approaches to Family Violence: 640–1980," in Lloyd Ohlin and Michael Tonry, eds., *Family Violence* (Chicago: University of Chicago Press, 1989), pp. 19–58.
46. Ibid.
47. John R. Sutton, *Stubborn Children: Controlling Delinquency in the United States, 1640–1981* (Berkeley: University of California Press, 1988).
48. Pleck, "Criminal Approaches to Family Violence," p. 29.
49. John Demos, *Past, Present, and Personal* (New York: Oxford University Press, 1986), pp. 80–88.
50. Elizabeth Pleck, *Domestic Tyranny: The Making of Social Policy Against Family Violence from Colonial Times to the Present* (New York: Oxford University Press, 1987), pp. 28–30.
51. Graeme Newman, *The Punishment Response* (Philadelphia: Lippincott, 1978), pp. 53–79; Aries, *Centuries of Childhood.* The history of childhood juvenile justice is discussed in detail in chapter 12.
52. Stephen J. Morse, "Immaturity and Irresponsibility," *Journal of Criminal Law and Criminology* 88:15–67 (1997).
53. Shay Bilchik, "Sentencing Juveniles to Adult Facilities Fails Youths and Society," *Corrections Today* 65:21 (2003).
54. Ibid.
55. John L. Hutzler, *Juvenile Court Jurisdiction over Children's Conduct: 1982 Comparative Analysis of Juvenile and Family Codes and National Standards* (Pittsburgh: National Center for Juvenile Justice, 1982), p. 2.

56. See, generally, David Rothman, *The Discovery of the Asylum* (Boston: Little, Brown, 1971).

57. Reports of the Chicago Bar Association Committee, 1899, cited in Anthony Platt, *The Child Savers: The Invention of Delinquency* (Chicago: University of Chicago Press, 1969), p. 119.

58. Susan Datesman and Mikel Aickin, "Offense Specialization and Escalation Among Status Offenders," *Journal of Criminal Law and Criminology* 75:1246–1275 (1985).

59. Ibid.

60. *Juvenile Justice and Delinquency Prevention Act (JJDPA)* of 1974, as amended (42 U.S.C. 5601 *et seq.*).

61. Runaway and Homeless Youth Act (RHYA) of 1974 (42 U.S.C. § 5701 *et seq.*).

62. 42 U.S.C.A. 5601B5751 (1983 and Supp. 1987).

63. Office of Juvenile Justice and Delinquency Prevention, *State Compliance Based on 1998 Reports: Deinstitutionalization of Status Offenders* (Washington, DC: Office of Juvenile Justice and Delinquency Prevention, 2000).

64. National Council on Crime and Delinquency, "Juvenile Curfews— A Policy Statement," *Crime and Delinquency* 18:132–133 (1972).

65. National Advisory Commission on Criminal Justice Standards and Goals, *Juvenile Justice and Delinquency Prevention* (Washington, DC: U.S. Government Printing Office, 1977), p. 311.

66. Gail Robinson and Tim Arnold, "Changes in Laws Impacting Juveniles—An Overview," *The Advocate* 22: 14–15 (2000).

67. Barry Feld, "Criminalizing the American Juvenile Court," in Michael Tonry, ed., *Crime and Justice: A Review of Research* (Chicago: University of Chicago Press, 1993), p. 232.

68. Kimberly Tyler, Les Whitbeck, Dan Hoyt, and Kurt Johnson, "Self-Mutilation and Homeless Youth: The Role of Family Abuse, Street Experiences, and Mental Disorders," *Journal of Research on Adolescence*, 13:457–474, 2003.

69. Carolyn Smith, "Factors Associated with Early Sexual Activity Among Urban Adolescents," *Social Work* 42:334–346 (1997).

Chapter 2

1. Howard Snyder and Melissa Sickmund, *Juvenile Offenders and Victims: A National Report* (Washington, DC: National Center for Juvenile Justice, 1995).

2. Federal Bureau of Investigation, *Crime in the United States, 2002* (Washington, DC: United States Government Printing Office, 2003). Text cites refer to this publication as the Uniform Crime Report.

3. Thomas Bernard, "Juvenile Crime and the Transformation of Juvenile Justice: Is There a Juvenile Crime Wave?" *Justice Quarterly* 16:336–356 (1999).

4. James A. Fox, *Trends in Juvenile Violence: A Report to the United States Attorney General on Current and Future Rates of Juvenile Offending* (Boston: Northeastern University, 1996).

5. Steven Levitt, "The Limited Role of Changing Age Structure in Explaining Aggregate Crime Rates," *Criminology* 37:581–599 (1999).

6. Steven Levitt, "Understanding Why Crime Fell in the 1990s: Four Factors That Explain the Decline and Six That Do Not," *Journal of Economic Perspectives* (in press, 2004).

7. Fox Butterfield, "Possible Manipulation of Crime Data Worries Top Police," *New York Times*, 3 August 1998, p. 1.

8. A pioneering effort of self-report research is A. L. Porterfield's *Youth in Trouble* (Fort Worth, TX: Leo Potishman Foundation, 1946); for a review, see Robert Hardt and George Bodine, *Development of Self-Report Instruments in Delinquency Research: A Conference Report* (Syracuse, NY: Syracuse University Youth Development Center, 1965); see also Fred Murphy, Mary Shirley, and Helen Witmer, "The Incidence of Hidden Delinquency," *American Journal of Orthopsychiatry* 16:686–696 (1946).

9. For example, the following studies have noted the great discrepancy between official statistics and self-report studies: Maynard Erickson and LaMar Empey, "Court Records, Undetected Delinquency, and Decision Making," *Journal of Criminal Law, Criminology, and Police Science* 54:456–469 (1963); Martin Gold, "Undetected Delinquent Behavior," *Journal of Research in Crime and Delinquency* 3:27–46 (1966); James Short and F. Ivan Nye, "Extent of Unrecorded Delinquency, Tentative Conclusions," *Journal of Criminal Law, Criminology, and Police Science* 49:296–302 (1958).

10. Jerald Bachman, Lloyd Johnston, and Patrick O'Malley, *Monitoring the Future: Questionnaire Responses from the Nation's High School Seniors, 2002* (Ann Arbor, MI: Institute for Social Research, 2003).

11. Julia Yun Soo Kim, Michael Fendrich, and Joseph S. Wislar, "The Validity of Juvenile Arrestees' Drug Use Reporting: A Gender Comparison," *Journal of Research in Crime and Delinquency* 37:419–432 (2000).

12. Michael Hindelang, Travis Hirschi, and Joseph Weis, *Measuring Delinquency* (Beverly Hills, CA: Sage, 1981); Gary Jensen and Raymond Eve, "Sex Differences in Delinquency: An Examination of Popular Sociological Explanation," *Criminology* 13:427–448 (1976); Michael Hindelang, "Age, Sex, and the Versatility of Delinquent Involvements," *Social Problems* 18:522–535 (1979); James Short and F. Ivan Nye, "Extent of Unrecorded Juvenile Delinquency, Tentative Conclusions," *Journal of Criminal Law, Criminology, and Police Science* 49:296–302 (1958).

13. For a review, see Meda Chesney-Lind and Randall Shelden, *Girls, Delinquency, and Juvenile Justice* (Pacific Grove, CA: Brooks/Cole, 1992), pp. 7–14.

14. Leroy Gould, "Who Defines Delinquency? A Comparison of Self-Report and Officially Reported Indices of Delinquency for Three Racial Groups," *Social Problems* 16:325–336 (1969); Harwin Voss, "Ethnic Differentials in Delinquency in Honolulu," *Journal of Criminal Law, Criminology, and Police Science* 54:322–327 (1963); Ronald Akers, Marvin Krohn, Marcia Radosevich, and Lonn Lanza-Kaduce, "Social Characteristics and Self-Reported Delinquency," in Gary Jensen, ed., *Sociology of Delinquency* (Beverly Hills, CA: Sage, 1981), pp. 48–62.

15. David Huizinga and Delbert Elliott, "Juvenile Offenders: Prevalence, Offender Incidence, and Arrest Rates by Race," *Crime and Delinquency* 33:206–223 (1987); see also Dale Dannefer and Russell Schutt, "Race and Juvenile Justice Processing in Court and Police Agencies," *American Journal of Sociology* 87:1113–1132 (1982).

16. Paul Tracy, "Race and Class Differences in Official and Self-Reported Delinquency," in Marvin Wolfgang, Terrence Thornberry, and Robert Figlio, eds., *From Boy to Man, from Delinquency to Crime* (Chicago: University of Chicago Press, 1987), p. 120.

17. Bachman, Johnston, and O'Malley, *Monitoring the Future*, pp. 102–104.

18. Samuel Walker, Cassia Spohn, and Miriam DeLone, *The Color of Justice: Race, Ethnicity, and Crime in America* (Belmont, CA: Brooks/Cole, 1992), pp. 46–47.

19. Miriam Sealock and Sally Simpson, "Unraveling Bias in Arrest Decisions: The Role of Juvenile Offender Typescripts," *Justice Quarterly* 15:427–457 (1998).

20. Rodney Engen, Sara Steen, and George Bridges, "Racial Disparities in the Punishment of Youth: A Theoretical and Empirical Assessment of the Literature." *Social Problems* 49:194–221 (2002).

21. Christina DeJong and Kenneth Jackson, "Putting Race into Context: Race, Juvenile Justice Processing, and Urbanization," *Justice Quarterly* 15:487–504 (1998).

22. Engen, Steen, and Bridges, "Racial Disparities in the Punishment of Youth."

23. David Eitle, Stewart D'Alessio, Lisa Stolzenberg, "Racial Threat and Social Control: A Test of the Political, Economic, and Threat of Black Crime Hypotheses," *Social Forces* 81:557–576 (2002). Michael Leiber and Jayne Stairs, "Race, Contexts, and the Use of Intake Diversion," *Journal of Research in Crime and Delinquency* 36:56–86 (1999); Darrell Steffensmeier, Jeffery Ulmer, and John Kramer, "The Interaction of Race, Gender, and Age in Criminal Sentencing: The Punishment Cost of Being Young, Black, and Male," *Criminology* 36:763–98 (1998).

24. For a general review, see William Wilbanks, The Myth of a Racist Criminal Justice System (Pacific Grove, CA: Brooks/Cole, 1987).

25. Walker, Spohn, and DeLone, The Color of Justice, pp. 47–48.

26. Mallie Paschall, Robert Flewelling, and Susan Ennett, "Racial Differences in Violent Behavior Among Young Adults: Moderating and Confounding Effects," Journal of Research in Crime and Delinquency 35:148–165 (1998).

27. Julie Phillips, "Variation in African-American Homicide Rates: An Assessment of Potential Explanations," *Criminology* 35:527–559 (1997).

28. Melvin Thomas, "Race, Class, and Personal Income: An Empirical Test of the Declining Significance of Race Thesis, 1968–1988," *Social Problems* 40:328–339 (1993).

29. Thomas McNulty and Paul Bellair, "Explaining Racial and Ethnic Differences in Adolescent Violence: Structural Disadvantage, Family Well-Being, and Social Capital," *Justice Quarterly* 20:1–32 (2003).

30. Julie Phillips, "White, Black, and Latino Homicide Rates: Why the Difference?" *Social Problems* 49:349–374 (2002).

31. Carl Pope and William Feyerherm, "Minority Status and Juvenile Processing: An Assessment of the Research Literature." Paper presented at the American Society of Criminology Meeting, Reno, Nevada, November 1989.

32. Robert Agnew, "A General Strain Theory of Community Differences in Crime Rates," *Journal of Research in Crime and Delinquency* 36:123–155 (1999).

33. Bonita Veysey and Steven Messner, "Further Testing of Social Disorganization Theory: An Elaboration of Sampson and Groves's 'Community Structure and Crime,'" *Journal of Research in Crime and Delinquency* 36:156–174 (1999).

34. James Short and Ivan Nye, "Reported Behavior as a Criterion of Deviant Behavior," *Social Problems* 5:207–213 (1958).

35. Classic studies include Ivan Nye, James Short, and Virgil Olsen, "Socio-economic Status and Delinquent Behavior," *American Journal of Sociology* 63:381–389 (1958); Robert Dentler and Lawrence Monroe, "Social Correlates of Early Adolescent Theft," *American Sociological Review* 26:733–743 (1961); Charles Tittle, Wayne Villemez, and Douglas Smith, "The Myth of Social Class and Criminality: An Empirical Assessment of the Empirical Evidence," *American Sociological Review* 43:643–656 (1978).

36. R. Gregory Dunaway, Francis Cullen, Velmer Burton, and T. David Evans, "The Myth of Social Class and Crime Revisited: An Examination of Class and Adult Criminality," *Criminology* 38:589–632 (2000).

37. Margaret Farnworth, Terence Thornberry, Marvin Krohn, and Alan Lizotte, *Measurement in the Study of Class and Delinquency: Integrating Theory and Research.* Working paper no. 4, rev. (Albany, NY: Rochester Youth Development Survey, 1992), p. 19.

38. G. Roger Jarjoura and Ruth Triplett, "Delinquency and Class: A Test of the Proximity Principle," *Justice Quarterly* 14:765–792 (1997).

39. See, generally, David Farrington, "Age and Crime," in Michael Tonry and Norval Morris, eds., *Crime and Justice: An Annual Review,* vol. 7 (Chicago: University of Chicago Press, 1986), pp. 189–250.

40. Travis Hirschi and Michael Gottfredson, "Age and the Explanation of Crime," *American Journal of Sociology* 89:552–584 (1983).

41. Michael Gottfredson and Travis Hirschi, "The True Value of Lambda Would Appear to Be Zero: An Essay on Career Criminals, Criminal Careers, Selective Incapacitation, Cohort Studies, and Related Topics," *Criminology* 24:213–234 (1986); further support for their position can be found in Lawrence Cohen and Kenneth Land, "Age Structure and Crime," *American Sociological Review* 52:170–183 (1987).

42. David Greenberg, "Age, Crime, and Social Explanation," *American Journal of Sociology* 91:1–21 (1985).

43. Robert Sampson and John Laub, *Crime in the Making: Pathways and Turning Points Through Life* (Cambridge, MA: Harvard University Press, 1993).

44. Marvin Wolfgang, Robert Figlio, and Thorsten Sellin, *Delinquency in a Birth Cohort* (Chicago: University of Chicago Press, 1972); Lyle Shannon, *Assessing the Relationship of Adult Criminal Careers to Juvenile Careers: A Summary* (Washington, DC: U.S. Department of Justice, 1982); D. J. West and David P. Farrington, *The Delinquent Way of Life* (London: Heinemann, 1977); Donna Hamparian, Richard Schuster, Simon Dinitz, and John Conrad, *The Violent Few* (Lexington, MA: Lexington Books, 1978).

45. Rolf Loeber and Howard Snyder, "Rate of Offending in Juvenile Careers: Findings of Constancy and Change in Lambda," *Criminology* 28:97–109 (1990).

46. Margo Wilson and Martin Daly, "Life Expectancy, Economic Inequality, Homicide, and Reproductive Timing in Chicago Neighbourhoods," *British Journal of Medicine* 31:1271–1274 (1997).

47. Edward Mulvey and John LaRosa, "Delinquency Cessation and Adolescent Development: Preliminary Data," *American Journal of Orthopsychiatry* 56:212–224 (1986).

48. Timothy Brezina, "Delinquent Problem-Solving: An Interpretive Framework for Criminological Theory and Research," *Journal of Research in Crime and Delinquency* 37:3–30 (2000).

49. Gordon Trasler, "Cautions for a Biological Approach to Crime," in Sarnoff Mednick, Terrie Moffitt, and Susan Stack, eds., *The Causes of Crime, New Biological Approaches* (Cambridge: Cambridge University Press, 1987), pp. 7–25.

50. Alicia Rand, "Transitional Life Events and Desistance from Delinquency and Crime," in Wolfgang, Thornberry, and Figlio, eds., *From Boy to Man,* pp. 134–163.

51. Marc LeBlanc, "Late Adolescence Deceleration of Criminal Activity and Development of Self- and Social-Control," *Studies on Crime and Crime Prevention* 2:51–68 (1993).

52. Barry Glassner, Margaret Ksander, Bruce Berg, and Bruce Johnson, "Note on the Deterrent Effect of Juvenile vs. Adult Jurisdiction," *Social Problems* 31:219–221 (1983).

53. Neal Shover and Carol Thompson, "Age, Differential Expectations, and Crime Desistance," *Criminology* 30:89–104 (1992).

54. D. Wayne Osgood, "The Covariation Among Adolescent Problem Behaviors." Paper presented at the American Society of Criminology Meeting, Baltimore, November 1990.

55. Stephen Tibbetts, "Low Birth Weight, Disadvantaged Environment, and Early Onset: A Test of Moffitt's Interactional Hypothesis." Paper presented at the American Society of Criminology Meeting, Boston, November 1995.

56. Arnold Barnett, Alfred Blumstein, and David Farrington, "A Prospective Test of a Criminal Career Model," *Criminology* 27:373–388 (1989).

57. Wolfgang, Figlio, and Sellin, *Delinquency in a Birth Cohort.*

58. Paul Tracy, Marvin Wolfgang, and Robert Figlio, *Delinquency in Two Birth Cohorts, Executive Summary* (Washington, DC: U.S. Department of Justice, 1985).

59. Shannon, *Assessing the Relationship of Adult Criminal Careers to Juvenile Careers;* Howard Snyder, *Court Careers of Juvenile Offenders* (Washington, DC: Office of Juvenile Justice and Delinquency Prevention, 1988); Donald J. West and David P. Farrington, *The Delinquent Way of Life* (London: Heinemann, 1977); Donna Hamparian, Richard Schuster, Simon Dinitz, and John Conrad, *The Violent Few* (Lexington, MA: Lexington Books, 1978).

60. See, generally, Wolfgang, Thornberry, and Figlio, *From Boy to Man.*

61. Paul Tracy and Kimberly Kempf-Leonard, *Continuity and Discontinuity in Criminal Careers* (New York: Plenum, 1996).

62. R. Tremblay, R. Loeber, C. Gagnon, P. Charlebois, S. Larivee, and M. LeBlanc, "Disruptive Boys with Stable and Unstable High Fighting Behavior Patterns During Junior Elementary School," *Journal of Abnormal Child Psychology* 19:285–300 (1991).

63. Peter Jones, Philip Harris, James Fader, and Lori Grubstein, "Identifying Chronic Juvenile Offenders," *Justice Quarterly* 18:478–507 (2001).

64. Jennifer White, Terrie Moffitt, Felton Earls, Lee Robins, and Phil Silva, "How Early Can We Tell? Predictors of Childhood Conduct Disorder and Adolescent Delinquency," *Criminology* 28:507–535 (1990).

65. Kimberly Kempf-Leonard, Paul Tracy, and James Howell, "Serious, Violent, and Chronic Juvenile Offenders: The Relationship of Delinquency Career Types to Adult Criminality," *Justice Quarterly* 18:449–478 (2001).

66. Kimberly Kempf, "Crime Severity and Criminal Career Progression," *Journal of Criminal Law and Criminology* 79:524–540 (1988).

67. Jeffrey Fagan, "Social and Legal Policy Dimensions of Violent Juvenile Crime," *Criminal Justice and Behavior* 17:93–133 (1990).

68. Peter Greenwood, *Selective Incapacitation* (Santa Monica, CA: Rand, 1982).

69. Terence Thornberry, David Huizinga, and Rolf Loeber, "The Prevention of Serious Delinquency and Violence," in James Howell, Barry Krisberg, J. David Hawkins, and John Wilson, eds., *Sourcebook on Serious, Violent, and Chronic Juvenile Offenders* (Thousand Oaks, CA: Sage, 1995).

70. Callie Marie Rennison and Michael Rand, *Criminal Victimization, 2002* (Washington, DC: Bureau of Justice Statistics, 2003).

71. Ted Miller, Mark Cohen, and Brian Wiersema, *The Extent and Costs of Crime Victimization: A New Look* (Washington, DC: National Institute of Justice, 1995).

72. Craig A. Perkins, *Age Patterns of Victims of Serious Violent Crime* (Washington, DC: Bureau of Justice Statistics, 1997).

73. L. Edward Wells and Joseph Rankin, "Juvenile Victimization: Convergent Validation of Alternative Measurements," *Journal of Research in Crime and Delinquency* 32:301–304 (1995).

Chapter 3

1. U.S. Census Bureau, *Current Population Survey (CPS), 2003 Annual Social & Economic Supplement* (ASEC), 2003. http://www.census.gov/hhes/poverty/poverty02/pov02hi.html.

2. Marvin Wolfgang, Robert Figlio, and Thorsten Sellin, *Delinquency in a Birth Cohort* (Chicago: University of Chicago Press, 1972).

3. Alan Lizotte, Terence Thornberry, Marvin Krohn, Deborah Chard-Wierschem, and David McDowall, "Neighborhood Context and Delinquency: A Longitudinal Analysis," in H. J. Kerner and E. Weitekamp, eds., *Cross-National Longitudinal Research on Human Development and Criminal Behavior* (Dordrecht, The Netherlands: Kluwer Academic Publishers, 1993), pp. 11–15.

4. Jeremy Bentham, in Wilfrid Harrison, ed., *A Fragment on Government and an Introduction to the Principles of Morals and Legislation,* (Oxford, England: Basil Blackwell, 1948).

5. See, generally, Ernest Van den Haag, *Punishing Criminals* (New York: Basic Books, 1975).

6. Pierre Tremblay and Carlo Morselli, "Patterns in Criminal Achievement: Wilson and Abrahamsen Revisited," *Criminology* 38:633–660 (2000).

7. See, generally, James Q. Wilson, *Thinking About Crime* (New York: Basic Books, 1975).

8. John Petraitis, Brian Flay, and Todd Miller, "Reviewing Theories of Adolescent Substance Use: Organizing Pieces in the Puzzle," *Psychological Bulletin* 117:67–86 (1995).

9. Travis Hirschi, "Rational Choice and Social Control Theories of Crime," in D. Cornish and R. Clarke, eds., *The Reasoning Criminal* (New York: Springer-Verlag, 1986), p. 114.

10. See, generally, Derek Cornish and Ronald Clarke, eds., *The Reasoning Criminal* (New York: Springer-Verlag, 1986); see also Philip Cook, "The Demand and Supply of Criminal Opportunities," in Michael Tonry and Norval Morris, eds., *Crime and Justice,* vol. 7 (Chicago: University of Chicago Press, 1986), pp. 1–28; Ronald Clarke and Derek Cornish, "Modeling Offenders' Decisions: A Framework for Research and Policy," in Michael Tonry and Norval Morris, eds., *Crime and Justice,* vol. 6 (Chicago: University of Chicago Press, 1985), pp. 147–187; Morgan Reynolds, *Crime by Choice: An Economic Analysis* (Dallas: Fisher Institute, 1985).

11. D. Wayne Osgood, Janet Wilson, Patrick O'Malley, Jerald Bachman, and Lloyd Johnston, "Routine Activities and Individual Deviant Behavior," *American Sociological Review* 61:635–55 (1996).

12. Brenda Sims Blackwell, "Perceived Sanction Threats, Gender, and Crime: A Test and Elaboration of Power-Control Theory," *Criminology* 38:439–488 (2000).

13. Dana Haynie, "Contexts of Risk? Explaining the Link Between Girls' Pubertal Development and Their Delinquency Involvement," *Social Forces* 82:355–397 (2003).

14. Raymond Paternoster, Shawn Bushway, Robert Brame, and Robert Apel, "The Effect of Teenage Employment on Delinquency and Problem Behaviors," *Social Forces* 82:297–336 (2003).

15. Matthew Ploeger, "Youth Employment and Delinquency: Reconsidering a Problematic Relationship," *Criminology* 35:659–675 (1997).

16. Jeremy Staff and Christopher Uggen, "The fruits of good work: early work experiences and adolescent deviance," *Journal of Research in Crime and Delinquency* 40:263–290 (2003).

17. Mary Tuck and David Riley, "The Theory of Reasoned Action: A Decision Theory of Crime," in D. Cornish and R. Clarke, eds., *The Reasoning Criminal* (New York: Springer-Verlag, 1986), pp. 156–169.

18. Steven Levitt and Sudhir Alladi Venkatesh, "An Economic Analysis of a Drug-Selling Gang's Finances." NBER working paper 6592 (Cambridge, MA: National Bureau of Economic Research, Inc., 1998).

19. Bill McCarthy, "New Economics of Sociological Criminology," *Annual Review of Sociology* 28:417–442 (2002).

20. Michael Hindelang, Michael Gottfredson, and James Garofalo, *Victims of Personal Crime: An Empirical Foundation for a Theory of Personal Victimization* (Cambridge, MA: Ballinger, 1978).

21. Lawrence Cohen and Marcus Felson, "Social Change and Crime Rate Trends: A Routine Activities Approach," *American Sociological Review* 44:588–608 (1979).

22. David Maume, "Inequality and Metropolitan Rape Rates: A Routine Activity Approach," *Justice Quarterly* 6:513–527 (1989).

23. Gordon Knowles, "Deception, Detection, and Evasion: A Trade Craft Analysis of Honolulu, Hawaii's, Street Crack Cocaine Traffickers," *Journal of Criminal Justice* 27:443–455 (1999).

24. Paul Bellair, "Informal Surveillance and Street Crime: A Complex Relationship," *Criminology* 38:137–67 (2000).

25. Denise Osborn, Alan Trickett, and Rob Elder, "Area Characteristics and Regional Variates as Determinants of Area Property Crime Levels," *Journal of Quantitative Criminology* 8:265–282 (1992).

26. Matthew Robinson, "Lifestyles, Routine Activities, and Residential Burglary Victimization," *Journal of Criminal Justice* 22:37–52 (1999).

27. William Smith, Sharon Glave Frazee, and Elizabeth Davison, "Furthering the Integration of Routine Activity and Social Disorganization Theories: Small Units of Analysis and the Study of Street Robbery as a Diffusion Process," *Criminology* 38:489–521 (2000).

28. Robert O'Brien, "Relative Cohort Sex and Age-Specific Crime Rates: An Age-Period-Relative-Cohort-Size Model," *Criminology* 27:57–78 (1989).

29. Daniel Nagin and Greg Pogarsky, "Integrating Celerity, Impulsivity, and Extralegal Sanction Threats into a Model of General Deterrence: Theory and Evidence," *Criminology* 39:865–892 (2001); R. Steven Daniels, Lorin Baumhover, William Formby, and Carolyn Clark-Daniels, "Police Discretion and Elder Mistreatment: A Nested Model of Observation, Reporting, and Satisfaction," *Journal of Criminal Justice* 27:209–225 (1999).

30. Nagin and Pogarsky, "Integrating Celerity, Impulsivity, and Extralegal Sanction Threats into a Model of General Deterrence."

31. Cesare Beccaria, *On Crimes and Punishments and Other Writings,* Richard Bellamy, ed., Richard Davies, trans. (London: Cambridge University Press, 1995)

32. Daniel Nagin and Greg Pogarsky, "An Experimental Investigation of Deterrence: Cheating, Self-Serving Bias, and Impulsivity," *Criminology* 41:167–195 (2003).

33. Tomislav V. Kovandzic and John J. Sloan, "Police Levels and Crime Rates Revisited: A County-Level Analysis from Florida (1980–1998)," *Journal of Criminal Justice* 30:65–76 (2002).

34. Gordon Bazemore and Mark Umbreit, "Rethinking the Sanctioning Function in Juvenile Court: Retributive or Restorative Responses to Youth Crime," *Crime and Delinquency* 41:296–316 (1995).

35. Michael White, James Fyfe, Suzanne Campbell, and John Goldkamp, "The Police Role in Preventing Homicide: Considering the Impact of Problem-Oriented Policing on the Prevalence of Murder," *Journal of Research in Crime and Delinquency* 40:194–226 (2003).

36. Eric Fritsch, Tory Caeti, and Robert Taylor, "Gang Suppression Through Saturation Patrol, Aggressive Curfew, and Truancy Enforcement: A Quasi-Experimental Test of the Dallas Anti-Gang Initiative," *Crime and Delinquency* 45:122–139 (1999).

37. Bruce Jacobs, "Anticipatory Undercover Targeting in High Schools," *Journal of Criminal Justice* 22:445–457 (1994).

38. Leona Lee, "Factors Determining Waiver in a Juvenile Court," *Journal of Criminal Justice* 22:329–339 (1994).

39. Kevin Strom, *Profile of State Prisoners under Age 18, 1985–1997* (Washington, DC: Bureau of Justice Statistics, 2000).

40. *Wilkins v. Missouri, Stanford v. Kentucky,* 109 S.Ct. 2969 (1989).

41. Eric Jensen and Linda Metsger, "A Test of the Deterrent Effect of Legislative Waiver on Violent Juvenile Crime," *Crime and Delinquency* 40:96–104 (1994).

42. Wanda Foglia, "Perceptual Deterrence and the Mediating Effect of Internalized Norms Among Inner-City Teenagers," *Journal of Research in Crime and Delinquency* 34:414–42 (1997); Donald Green, "Measures of Illegal Behavior in Individual-Level Deter-

rence Research," *Journal of Research in Crime and Delinquency* 26:253–275 (1989); Charles Tittle, *Sanctions and Social Deviance: The Question of Deterrence* (New York: Praeger, 1980).

43. Bureau of Justice Statistics, *Prisoners and Drugs* (Washington, DC: U.S. Government Printing Office, 1983); idem, *Prisoners and Alcohol* (Washington, DC: U.S. Government Printing Office, 1983).

44. Maynard Erickson and Jack Gibbs, "Punishment, Deterrence, and Juvenile Justice," in D. Shichor and D. Kelly, eds., *Critical Issues in Juvenile Justice* (Lexington, MA: Lexington Books, 1980), pp. 183–202.

45. Doris Layton MacKenzie and Spencer De Li, "The Impact of Formal and Informal Social Controls on the Criminal Activities of Probationers," *Journal of Research in Crime and Delinquency* 39:243–276 (2002).

46. Christina Dejong, "Survival Analysis and Specific Deterrence: Integrating Theoretical and Empirical Models of Recidivism," *Criminology* 35:561–576 (1997).

47. Paul Tracy and Kimberly Kempf-Leonard, *Continuity and Discontinuity in Criminal Careers* (New York: Plenum, 1996).

48. Pamela Lattimore, Christy Visher, and Richard Linster, "Predicting Rearrest for Violence Among Serious Youthful Offenders," *Journal of Research in Crime and Delinquency* 32:54–83 (1995).

49. Greg Pogarsky and Alex R. Piquero, "Can Punishment Encourage Offending? Investigating the 'Resetting' Effect," *Journal of Research in Crime and Delinquency* 40:92–117 (2003).

50. David Altschuler, "Juveniles and Violence: Is There an Epidemic and What Can Be Done?" Paper presented at the American Society of Criminology Meeting, Boston, November 1995; Charles Murray and Louis B. Cox, *Beyond Probation* (Beverly Hills, CA: Sage, 1979).

51. Marcus Felson, "Routine Activities and Crime Prevention," in National Council for Crime Prevention, *Studies on Crime and Crime Prevention, Annual Review,* vol. 1 (Stockholm: Scandinavian University Press, 1992), pp. 30–34.

52. Andrew Fulkerson, "Blow and Go: the Breath-Analyzed Ignition Interlock Device as a Technological Response to DWI," *American Journal of Drug and Alcohol Abuse* 29:219–235 (2003).

53. Barry Webb, "Steering Column Locks and Motor Vehicle Theft: Evaluations for Three Countries," in Ronald Clarke, ed., *Crime Prevention Studies* (Monsey, NY: Criminal Justice Press, 1994), pp. 71–89.

54. David Farrington and Brandon Welsh, "Improved Street Lighting and Crime Prevention," *Justice Quarterly* 19:313–343 (2002).

55. Brandon Welsh and David Farrington, "Effects of Closed-Circuit Television on Crime" *Annals of the American Academy of Political and Social Science* 587:110–136 (2003).

56. Kenneth Novak, Jennifer Hartman, Alexander Holsinger, and Michael Turner, "The Effects of Aggressive Policing of Disorder on Serious Crime," *Policing* 22:171–190 (1999).

57. Lawrence Sherman, "Police Crackdowns: Initial and Residual Deterrence," in Michael Tonry and Norval Morris, eds., *Crime and Justice: A Review of Research,* vol. 12 (Chicago: University of Chicago Press, 1990), pp. 1–48.

58. Anthony Braga, David Weisburd, Elin Waring, Lorraine Green Mazerolle, William Spelman, and Francis Gajewski, "Problem-Oriented Policing in Violent Crime Places: A Randomized Controlled Experiment," *Criminology* 39:541–580 (1999).

59. Eric Fritsch, Tory Caeti, and Robert Taylor, "Gang Suppression Through Saturation Patrol, Aggressive Curfew, and Truancy Enforcement: A Quasi-Experimental Test of the Dallas Anti-Gang Initiative," *Crime and Delinquency* 45:122–139 (1999).

60. For an excellent review of Lombroso's work, as well as that of other well-known theorists, see Randy Martin, Robert Mutchnick, and W. Timothy Austin, *Criminological Thought: Pioneers Past and Present* (New York: Macmillan, 1990).

61. Marvin Wolfgang, "Cesare Lombroso," in Herman Mannheim, ed., *Pioneers in Criminology* (Montclair, NJ: Patterson Smith, 1970), pp. 232–271.

62. Gina Lombroso-Ferrero, *Criminal Man According to the Classification of Cesare Lombroso* (1911; reprint, Montclair, NJ: Patterson Smith, 1972), p. 7.

63. Edwin Driver, "Charles Buckman Goring," in Herman Mannheim, ed., *Pioneers in Criminology* (Montclair, NJ: Patterson Smith, 1970), pp. 429–442.

64. See, generally, Thorsten Sellin, "Enrico Ferri," in Herman Mannheim, ed., *Pioneers in Criminology* (Montclair, NJ: Patterson Smith, 1970), pp. 361–384.

65. Driver, "Charles Buckman Goring," pp. 434–435.

66. Ibid., p. 440.

67. Nicole Hahn Rafter, "Criminal Anthropology in the United States," *Criminology* 30:525–547 (1992).

68. B. R. McCandless, W. S. Persons, and A. Roberts, "Perceived Opportunity, Delinquency, Race, and Body Build Among Delinquent Youth," *Journal of Consulting and Clinical Psychology* 38:281–383 (1972).

69. Edmond O. Wilson, *Sociobiology: The New Synthesis* (Cambridge, MA: Harvard University Press, 1975).

70. For a general review, see John Archer, "Human Sociobiology: Basic Concepts and Limitations," *Journal of Social Issues* 47:11–26 (1991).

71. Arthur Caplan, *The Sociobiology Debate: Readings on Ethical and Scientific Issues* (New York: Harper & Row, 1978).

72. Dalton Conley and Neil Bennett, "Is Biology Destiny? Birth Weight and Life Chances," *American Sociological Review* 654:458–467 (2000).

73. Diana Fishbein, "Selected Studies on the Biology of Crime," in John Conklin, ed., *New Perspectives in Criminology* (Needham Heights, MA: Allyn & Bacon, 1996), pp. 26–38.

74. See, generally, Adrian Raine, *The Psychopathology of Crime* (San Diego: Academic Press, 1993); see also Leonard Hippchen, *The Ecologic-Biochemical Approaches to Treatment of Delinquents and Criminals* (New York: Van Nostrand Reinhold, 1978).

75. Paul Marshall, "Allergy and Depression: A Neurochemical Threshold Model of the Relation Between the Illnesses," *Psychological Bulletin* 113:23–43 (1993); Elizabeth McNeal and Peter Cimbolic, "Antidepressants and Biochemical Theories of Depression," *Psychological Bulletin* 99:361–374 (1986); for an opposing view, see "Adverse Reactions to Food in Young Children," *Nutrition Reviews* 46:120–121 (1988).

76. Jeff Evans, "Asymptomatic, High Lead Levels Tied to Delinquency," *Pediatric News* 37:13 (2003); Herbert Needleman, Christine McFarland, Roberta Ness, Stephen Fienberg, and Michael Tobin, "Bone Lead Levels in Adjudicated Delinquents: A Case Control Study," *Neurotoxicology and Teratology* 24:711–717 (2002).

77. Jens Walkowiak, Jörg A. Wiener, Annemarie Fastabend, Birger Heinzow, Ursula Krämer, Eberhard Schmidt, Hans J. Steingürber, Sabine Wundram, and Gerhard Winneke, "Environmental Exposure to Polychlorinated Biphenyls and Quality of the Home Environment: Effects on Psychodevelopment in Early Childhood," *The Lancet* 358:92–93 (2001).

78. Diana Fishbein, "Neuropsychological Function, Drug Abuse, and Violence: A Conceptual Framework," *Criminal Justice and Behavior* 27:139–159 (2000).

79. Christy Miller Buchanan, Jacquelynne Eccles, and Jill Becker, "Are Adolescents the Victims of Raging Hormones? Evidence for Activational Effects of Hormones on Moods and Behavior at Adolescence," *Psychological Bulletin* 111:62–107 (1992).

80. Diana Fishbein, "Selected Studies on the Biology of Crime."

81. Kytja Voeller, "Right-Hemisphere Deficit Syndrome in Children," *American Journal of Psychiatry* 143:1004–1009 (1986).

82. Terrie Moffitt, "Adolescence-Limited and Life-Course-Persistent Antisocial Behavior: A Developmental Taxonomy," *Psychological Review* 100:674–701 (1993).

83. "McLean Researchers Document Brain Damage Linked to Child Abuse and Neglect." Information provided by newsletter of McLean's Hospital, Belmont, MA, December 14, 2000.

84. Adrian Raine, Patricia Brennan, Brigitte Mednick, and Sarnoff Mednick, "High Rates of Violence, Crime, Academic Problems, and Behavioral Problems in Males with Both Early Neuromotor Deficits and Unstable Family Environments," *Archives of General Psychiatry* 53:544–549 (1966).

85. Dorothy Otnow Lewis, Jonathan Pincus, Marilyn Feldman, Lori Jackson, and Barbara Bard, "Psychiatric, Neurological, and Psychoeducational Characteristics of 15 Death Row Inmates in the United States," *American Journal of Psychiatry* 143:838–845 (1986).

86. Adrian Raine, H. Andrews, C. Sheard, C. Walder, and D. Manders, "Interhemispheric Transfer in Schizophrenics, Depressives, and

Normals with Schizoid Tendencies," *Journal of Abnormal Psychology* 98:35–41 (1989).

87. Adrian Raine, P. Brennan, and S. Mednick, "Interaction Between Birth Complications and Early Maternal Rejection in Predisposing to Adult Violence: Specificity to Serious, Early Onset Violence," *American Journal of Psychiatry* 154:1265–1271 (1997).

88. Joel Zimmerman, William Rich, Ingo Keilitz, and Paul Broder, "Some Observations on the Link Between Learning Disabilities and Juvenile Delinquency," *Journal of Criminal Justice* 9:9–17 (1981); J. W. Podboy and W. A. Mallory, "The Diagnosis of Specific Learning Disabilities in a Juvenile Delinquent Population," *Juvenile and Family Court Journal* 30:11–13 (1978).

89. Charles Murray, "The Link Between Learning Disabilities and Juvenile Delinquency: Current Theory and Knowledge" (Washington, DC: U.S. Government Printing Office, 1976).

90. Terrie Moffitt, "The Neuropsychology of Conduct Disorder." Mimeo (Madison: University of Wisconsin, 1992).

91. Ibid.

92. National Center for Addiction and Substance Abuse (CASA) at Columbia University, *Substance Abuse and Learning Disabilities: Peas in a Pod or Apples and Oranges?* (New York: CASA, 2000).

93. Jack Katz, *Seduction of Crime: Moral and Sensual Attractions of Doing Evil* (New York: Basic Books, 1988), pp. 12–15.

94. Lee Ellis, "Arousal Theory and the Religiosity-Criminality Relationship," in Peter Cordella and Larry Siegel, eds., *Contemporary Criminological Theory* (Boston: Northeastern University, 1996), pp. 65–84.

95. Adrian Raine, Peter Venables, and Sarnoff Mednick, "Low Resting Heart Rate at Age 3 Years Predisposes to Aggression at Age 11 Years: Evidence from the Mauritius Child Health Project," *Journal of the American Academy of Adolescent Psychiatry* 36:1457–1464 (1997).

96. For a review, see Lisabeth Fisher DiLalla and Irving Gottesman, "Biological and Genetic Contributors to Violence—Widom's Untold Tale," *Psychological Bulletin* 109:125–129 (1991).

97. For an early review, see Barbara Wooton, *Social Science and Social Pathology* (London: Allen and Unwin, 1959); John Laub and Robert Sampson, "Unraveling Families and Delinquency: A Re-analysis of the Gluecks' Data," *Criminology* 26:355–380 (1988).

98. Donald J. West and David P. Farrington, "Who Becomes Delinquent?" in Donald J. West and David P. Farrington, eds., *The Delinquent Way of Life* (London: Heinemann, 1977), pp. 1–28; D. J. West, *Delinquency: Its Roots, Careers, and Prospects* (Cambridge, MA: Harvard University Press, 1982).

99. West, *Delinquency,* p. 114.

100. David Farrington, "Understanding and Preventing Bullying," in Michael Tonry, ed., *Crime and Justice,* vol. 17 (Chicago: University of Chicago Press, 1993), pp. 381–457.

101. Terence Thornberry, Adrienne Freeman-Gallant, Alan Lizotte, Marvin Krohn, and Carolyn Smith, "Linked Lives: The Intergenerational Transmission of Antisocial Behavior," *Journal of Abnormal Child Psychology* 31:171–185 (2003).

102. David Rowe and David Farrington, "The Familial Transmission of Criminal Convictions," *Criminology* 35:177–201 (1997).

103. Edwin J. C. G. van den Oord, Frank Verhulst, and Dorret Boomsma, "A Genetic Study of Maternal and Paternal Ratings of Problem Behaviors in 3-Year-Old Twins," *Journal of Abnormal Psychology* 105:349–357 (1996).

104. Ibid., p. 95.

105. Thomas Bouchard, "Genetic and Environmental Influences on Intelligence and Special Mental Abilities," *American Journal of Human Biology,* 70:253–275 (1998).

106. Remi Cadoret, Colleen Cain, and Raymond Crowe, "Evidence for a Gene-Environment Interaction in the Development of Adolescent Antisocial Behavior," *Behavior Genetics* 13:301–310 (1983).

107. David Rowe, *The Limits of Family Influence: Genes, Experiences, and Behavior* (New York: Guilford Press, 1995); Cadoret, Cain, and Crowe, "Evidence for a Gene-Environment Interaction."

108. Bernard Hutchings and Sarnoff Mednick, "Criminality in Adoptees and Their Adoptive and Biological Parents: A Pilot Study," in Sarnoff A. Mednick and Karl O. Christiansen, eds., *Biosocial Bases of Criminal Behavior* (New York: Gardner, 1977).

109. For similar findings, see William Gabrielli and Sarnoff Mednick, "Urban Environment, Genetics, and Crime," *Criminology* 22:645–653 (1984).

110. For a thorough review of this issue, see David Brandt and S. Jack Zlotnick, *The Psychology and Treatment of the Youthful Offender* (Springfield, IL: Charles C. Thomas, 1988).

111. Spencer Rathus, *Psychology* (New York: Holt, Rinehart & Winston, 1996), pp. 11–21.

112. See, generally, Sigmund Freud, *An Outline of Psychoanalysis,* James Strachey, trans. (New York: Norton, 1963).

113. Seymour Halleck, *Psychiatry and the Dilemmas of Crime* (Berkeley: University of California Press, 1971).

114. Robert Krueger, Avshalom Caspi, Phil Silva, and Rob McGee, "Personality Traits Are Differentially Linked to Mental Disorders: A Multitrait-Multidiagnosis Study of an Adolescent Birth Cohort," *Journal of Abnormal Psychology* 105:299–312 (1996).

115. See, generally, Erik Erikson, *Identity, Youth, and Crisis* (New York: Norton, 1968).

116. David Abrahamsen, *Crime and the Human Mind* (New York: Columbia University Press, 1944), p. 137.

117. See, generally, Fritz Redl and Hans Toch, "The Psychoanalytic Perspective," in Hans Toch, ed., *Psychology of Crime and Criminal Justice* (New York: Holt, Rinehart & Winston, 1979), pp. 193–195.

118. August Aichorn, *Wayward Youth* (New York: Viking Press, 1935).

119. Dorothy Espelage, Elizabeth Cauffman, Lisa Broidy, Alex Piquero, Paul Mazerolle, and Hans Steiner, "A Cluster-Analytic Investigation of MMPI Profiles of Serious Male and Female Juvenile Offenders," *Journal of the American Academy of Child & Adolescent Psychiatry* 42:770–777 (2003).

120. Jennifer Beyers and Rolf Loeber, "Untangling Developmental Relations Between Depressed Mood and Delinquency in Male Adolescents," *Journal of Abnormal Child Psychology* 31:247–267 (2003).

121. Brandt and Zlotnick, *The Psychology and Treatment of the Youthful Offender,* pp. 72–73.

122. James Sorrells, "Kids Who Kill," *Crime and Delinquency* 23:312–320 (1977).

123. Beyers and Loeber, "Untangling Developmental Relations."

124. Eric Silver, "Mental Disorder and Violent Victimization: The Mediating Role of Involvement in Conflicted Social Relationships," *Criminology* 40:191–212 (2002).

125. Stacy De Coster and Karen Heimer, "The Relationship Between Law Violation and Depression: An Interactionist Analysis," *Criminology* 39:799–836 (2001).

126. Walter Mischel, Yuichi Shoda, and Philip Peake, "The Nature of Adolescent Competencies Predicted by Preschool Delay of Gratification," *Journal of Personality and Social Psychology* 54:687–696 (1988). Albert Bandura and Richard Walters, *Social Learning and Personality Development* (New York: Holt, Rinehart & Winston, 1963).

127. David Perry, Louise Perry, and Paul Rasmussen, "Cognitive Social Learning Mediators of Aggression," *Child Development* 57:700–711 (1986).

128. Bonnie Carlson, "Children's Beliefs About Punishment," *American Journal of Orthopsychiatry* 56:308–312 (1986).

129. See, generally, Jean Piaget, *The Moral Judgment of the Child* (London: Kegan Paul, 1932).

130. Lawrence Kohlberg, *Stages in the Development of Moral Thought and Action* (New York: Holt, Rinehart & Winston, 1969).

131. L. Kohlberg, K. Kauffman, P. Scharf, and J. Hickey, *The Just Community Approach in Corrections: A Manual* (Niantic: Connecticut Department of Corrections, 1973).

132. Scott Henggeler, *Delinquency in Adolescence* (Newbury Park, CA: Sage, 1989), p. 26.

133. K. A. Dodge, "A Social Information Processing Model of Social Competence in Children," in M. Perlmutter, ed., *Minnesota Symposium in Child Psychology,* vol. 18 (Hillsdale, NJ: Erlbaum, 1986), pp. 77–125.

134. Adrian Raine, Peter Venables, and Mark Williams, "Better Autonomic Conditioning and Faster Electrodermal Half-Recovery Time at Age 15 Years as Possible Protective Factors against Crime at Age 29 Years," *Developmental Psychology* 32:624–630 (1996).

135. Jean Marie McGloin and Travis Pratt, "Cognitive Ability and Delinquent Behavior Among Inner-City Youth: A Life-Course Analysis of Main, Mediating, and Interaction Effects," *International Journal of Offender Therapy & Comparative Criminology* 47:253–271 (2003).

136. Judith Baer and Tina Maschi, "Random Acts of Delinquency: Trauma and Self-Destructiveness in Juvenile Offenders," *Child & Adolescent Social Work Journal* 20:85–99 (2003).

137. Tony Ward and Claire Stewart, "The Relationship Between Human Needs and Criminogenic Needs," *Psychology, Crime & Law* 9:219–225 (2003).

138. L. Huesmann and L. Eron, "Individual Differences and the Trait of Aggression," *European Journal of Personality* 3:95–106 (1989).

139. Rolf Loeber and Dale Hay, "Key Issues in the Development of Aggression and Violence from Childhood to Early Adulthood," *Annual Review of Psychology* 48:371–410 (1997).

140. Kathleen Cirillo, B. E. Pruitt, Brian Colwell, Paul M. Kingery, Robert S. Hurley, and Danny Ballard, "School Violence: Prevalence and Intervention Strategies for At-Risk Adolescents," *Adolescence* 33:319–331 (1998).

141. Leilani Greening, "Adolescent Stealers' and Nonstealers' Social Problem-Solving Skills," *Adolescence* 32:51–56 (1997).

142. Graeme Newman, *Understanding Violence* (New York: Lippincott, 1979), pp. 145–146.

143. Kathleen Cirillo, B. E. Pruitt, Brian Colwell, Paul Kingery, Robert Hurley, and Danny Ballard, "School Violence: Prevalence and Intervention Strategies for At-Risk Adolescents," *Adolescence* 33:319–331 (1998).

144. See, generally, Walter Mischel, *Introduction to Personality,* 4th ed. (New York: Holt, Rinehart & Winston, 1986).

145. Sheldon Glueck and Eleanor Glueck, *Unraveling Juvenile Delinquency* (Cambridge, MA: Harvard University Press, 1950).

146. Edelyn Verona and Joyce Carbonell, "Female Violence and Personality," *Criminal Justice and Behavior* 27:176–195 (2000); David Farrington, "Psychobiological Factors in the Explanation and Reduction of Delinquency," *Today's Delinquent* 7:37–51 (1988).

147. See, generally, Hans Eysenck, *Personality and Crime* (London: Routledge and Kegan Paul, 1977).

148. Hans Eysenck and M. W. Eysenck, *Personality and Individual Differences* (New York: Plenum, 1985).

149. Catrien Bijleveld and Jan Hendriks, "Juvenile Sex Offenders: Differences Between Group and Solo Offenders," *Psychology, Crime & Law* 9:237–246 (2003).

150. Linda Mealey, "The Sociobiology of Sociopathy: An Integrated Evolutionary Model," *Behavioral and Brain Sciences* 18:523–540 (1995).

151. Lewis Yablonsky, *The Violent Gang* (New York: Penguin Books, 1971), pp. 195–205.

152. Helene Raskin White, Erich Labouvie, and Marsha Bates, "The Relationship Between Sensation Seeking and Delinquency: A Longitudinal Analysis," *Journal of Research in Crime and Delinquency* 2:197–211 (1985).

153. Rathus, *Psychology,* p. 452.

154. Kent. Kiehl, Andra Smith, Robert Hare, Adrianna Mendrek, Bruce Forster, Johann Brink, and Peter F. Liddle, *Biological Psychiatry* 5:677–684 (2001).

155. David Lykken, "Psychopathy, Sociopathy, and Crime," *Society* 34:30–38 (1996).

156. L. M. Terman, "Research on the Diagnosis of Predelinquent Tendencies," *Journal of Delinquency* 9:124–30 (1925); L. M. Terman, *Measurement of Intelligence* (Boston: Houghton-Mifflin, 1916); for example, see M. G. Caldwell, "The Intelligence of Delinquent Boys Committed to Wisconsin Industrial School," *Journal of Criminal Law and Criminology* 20:421–28 (1929); and C. Murcheson, *Criminal Intelligence* (Worcester, MA: Clark University, 1926), pp. 41–44.

157. Henry Goddard, *Efficiency and Levels of Intelligence* (Princeton, NJ: Princeton University Press, 1920).

158. William Healy and Augusta Bronner, *Delinquency and Criminals: Their Making and Unmaking* (New York: Macmillan, 1926).

159. Joseph Lee Rogers, H. Harrington Cleveland, Edwin van den Oord, and David Rowe, "Resolving the Debate Over Birth Order, Family Size, and Intelligence," *American Psychologist* 55:599–612 (2000).

160. Kenneth Eels, *Intelligence and Cultural Differences* (Chicago: University of Chicago Press, 1951), p. 181.

161. Sorel Cahahn and Nora Cohen, "Age Versus Schooling Effects on Intelligence Development," *Child Development* 60:1239–1249 (1989).

162. Robert McCall and Michael Carriger, "A Meta-Analysis of Infant Habituation and Recognition Memory Performance as Predictors of Later IQ," *Child Development* 64:57–79 (1993).

163. Edwin Sutherland, "Mental Deficiency and Crime," in Kimball Young, ed., *Social Attitudes* (New York: Henry Holt, 1973), ch. 15.

164. H. D. Day, J. M. Franklin, and D. D. Marshall, "Predictors of Aggression in Hospitalized Adolescents," *Journal of Psychology* 132:427–435 (1998); Scott Menard and Barbara Morse, "A Structuralist Critique of the IQ-Delinquency Hypothesis: Theory and Evidence," *American Journal of Sociology* 89:1347–1378 (1984).

165. Travis Hirschi and Michael Hindelang, "Intelligence and Delinquency: A Revisionist Review," *American Sociological Review* 42:471–586 (1977).

166. Terrie Moffitt and Phil Silva, "IQ and Delinquency: A Direct Test of the Differential Detection Hypothesis," *Journal of Abnormal Psychology* 97:1–4 (1988); E. Kandel, S. Mednick, L. Sorenson-Kirkegaard, B. Hutchings, J. Knop, R. Rosenberg, and F. Schulsinger, "IQ as a Protective Factor for Subjects at a High Risk for Antisocial Behavior," *Journal of Consulting and Clinical Psychology* 56:224–226 (1988); Christine Ward and Richard McFall, "Further Validation of the Problem Inventory for Adolescent Girls: Comparing Caucasian and Black Delinquents and Nondelinquents," *Journal of Consulting and Clinical Psychology* 54:732–733 (1986).

167. Terri Moffitt, William Gabrielli, Sarnoff Mednick, and Fini Schulsinger, "Socioeconomic Status, IQ, and Delinquency," *Journal of Abnormal Psychology* 90:152–56 (1981); for a similar finding, see L. Hubble and M. Groff, "Magnitude and Direction of WISC-R Verbal Performance IQ Discrepancies among Adjudicated Male Delinquents," *Journal of Youth and Adolescence* 10:179–83 (1981).

168. Jennifer White, Terrie Moffitt, and Phil Silva, "A Prospective Replication of the Protective Effects of IQ in Subjects at High Risk for Juvenile Delinquency," *Journal of Consulting and Clinical Psychology* 37:719–24 (1989).

169. Donald Lynam, Terrie Moffitt, and Magda Stouthamer-Loeber, "Explaining the Relations Between IQ and Delinquency: Class, Race, Test Motivation, School Failure, or Self-Control," *Journal of Abnormal Psychology* 102:187–96 (1993).

170. David Farrington, "Juvenile Delinquency," in John C. Coleman, ed., *The School Years* (London: Routledge, 1992), p. 137.

171. Glenn Walters and Thomas White, "Heredity and Crime: Bad Genes or Bad Research," *Justice Quarterly* 27:455–485 (1989), p. 478.

172. Lee Ellis, "Genetics and Criminal Behavior," *Criminology* 10:58 (1982).

173. Sheryl Ellis, "It Does Take a Village: A Youth Violence Program in Kincheloe, Michigan, Galvanizes the Community," *Corrections Today* 60:100–103 (1998).

174. Joan McCord and William McCord, "A Follow-Up Report on the Cambridge-Somerville Youth Study," *Annals* 322:89–98 (1959).

175. Edwin Schur, *Radical Nonintervention: Rethinking the Delinquency Problem* (Englewood Cliffs, NJ: Prentice-Hall, 1973).

Chapter 4

1. Edwin Lemert, *Human Deviance, Social Problems, and Social Control* (Englewood Cliffs, NJ: Prentice-Hall, 1967).

2. See, generally, Stephen Cernkovich and Peggy Giordano, "Family Relationships and Delinquency," *Criminology* 25:295–321 (1987); Paul Howes and Howard Markman, "Marital Quality and Child Functioning: A Longitudinal Investigation," *Child Development* 60:1044–1051 (1989).

3. Gary LaFree, *Losing Legitimacy: Street Crime and the Decline of Social Institutions in America* (Boulder, CO: Westview, 1998).

4. Emilie Andersen Allan and Darrell Steffensmeier, "Youth, Underemployment, and Property Crime: Differential Effects of Job Availability and Job Quality on Juvenile and Young Adult Arrest Rates," *American Sociological Review* 54:107–123 (1989).

5. Oscar Lewis, "The Culture of Poverty," *Scientific American* 215:19–25 (1966).

6. Laura G. De Haan and Shelley MacDermid, "The Relationship of Individual and Family Factors to the Psychological Well-Being of Junior High School Students Living in Urban Poverty," *Adolescence* 33:73–90 (1998).

7. Julian Chow and Claudia Coulton, "Was There a Social Transformation of Urban Neighborhoods in the 1980s?" *Urban Studies* 35:135–175 (1998).

8. Rodrick Wallace, "Expanding Coupled Shock Fronts of Urban Decay and Criminal Behavior: How U.S. Cities Are Becoming 'Hollowed Out,'" *Journal of Quantitative Criminology* 7:333–355 (1991).

9. Ken Auletta, *The Under Class* (New York: Random House, 1982).

10. William Julius Wilson, *The Truly Disadvantaged* (Chicago: University of Chicago Press, 1987).

11. Jeanne Brooks-Gunn and Greg J. Duncan, "The Effects of Poverty on Children," *The Future of Children* 7:34–39 (1997).

12. Greg Duncan, W. Jean Yeung, Jeanne Brooks-Gunn, and Judith Smith, "How Much Does Childhood Poverty Affect the Life Chances of Children?" *American Sociological Review* 63:406–423 (1998).

13. Ibid., p. 29.

14. Brooks-Gunn and Duncan, "The Effects of Poverty on Children."

15. G. R. Patterson, L. Crosby, and S. Vuchnich, "Predicting Risk for Early Police Arrest," *Journal of Quantitative Criminology* 8:335–353 (1992).

16. Clifford R. Shaw and Henry D. McKay, *Juvenile Delinquency and Urban Areas,* rev. ed. (Chicago: University of Chicago Press, 1972).

17. Ibid.

18. Robert Bursik and Harold Grasmick, "The Multiple Layers of Social Disorganization." Paper presented at the annual meeting of the American Society of Criminology, New Orleans, November 1992; Robert Bursik and Harold Grasmick, "Longitudinal Neighborhood Profiles in Delinquency: The Decomposition of Change," *Journal of Quantitative Criminology* 8:247–256 (1992).

19. Delber Elliott, William Julius Wilson, David Huizinga, Robert Sampson, Amanda Elliott, and Bruce Rankin, "The Effects of Neighborhood Disadvantage on Adolescent Development," *Journal of Research in Crime and Delinquency* 33:414 (1996).

20. Robert Bursik and Harold Grasmick, "Economic Deprivation and Neighborhood Crime Rates, 1960–1980," *Law and Society Review* 27:263–278 (1993).

21. Robert Sampson and W. Byron Groves, "Community Structure and Crime: Testing Social Disorganization Theory," *American Journal of Sociology* 94:774–802 (1989); Denise Gottfredson, Richard McNeill, and Gary Gottfredson, "Social Area Influences on Delinquency: A Multilevel Analysis," *Journal of Research in Crime and Delinquency* 28:197–206 (1991).

22. For a classic look, see Frederick Thrasher, *The Gang* (Chicago: University of Chicago Press, 1927).

23. Ruth Peterson, Lauren Krivo, and Mark Harris, "Disadvantage and Neighborhood Violent Crime: Do Local Institutions Matter?" *Journal of Research in Crime and Delinquency* 37:31–63 (2000).

24. D. Wayne Osgood and Jeff Chambers, "Social Disorganization Outside the Metropolis: An Analysis of Rural Youth Violence," *Criminology* 38:81–117 (2000).

25. Beverly Stiles, Xiaoru Liu, and Howard Kaplan, "Relative Deprivation and Deviant Adaptations: The Mediating Effects of Negative Self-Feelings," *Journal of Research in Crime and Delinquency* 37:64–90 (2000).

26. Ora Simcha-Fagan and Joseph Schwartz, "Neighborhood and Delinquency: An Assessment of Contextual Effects," *Criminology* 24:667–703 (1986).

27. Ellen Kurtz, Barbara Koons, and Ralph Taylor, "Land Use, Physical Deterioration, Resident-Based Control, and Calls for Service on Urban Street Blocks," *Justice Quarterly* 15:121–149 (1998).

28. Pamela Wilcox Rountree and Kenneth Land, "Burglary Victimization, Perceptions of Crime Risk, and Routine Activities: A Multilevel Analysis Across Seattle Neighborhoods and Census Tracts," *Journal of Research in Crime and Delinquency* 33:147–180 (1996).

29. See, generally, Wesley Skogan, "Fear of Crime and Neighborhood Change," in Albert Reiss and Michael Tonry, eds., *Communities and Crime* (Chicago: University of Chicago Press, 1986), pp. 191–232.

30. Jeffery Will and John McGrath, "Crime, Neighborhood Perceptions, and the Underclass: The Relationship Between Fear of Crime and Class Position," *Journal of Criminal Justice* 23:163–176 (1995).

31. Margo Wilson and Martin Daly, "Life Expectancy, Economic Inequality, Homicide, and Reproductive Timing in Chicago Neighborhoods," *British Medical Journal,* 314:1271–1275 (1997)

32. Randy LaGrange, Kenneth Ferraro, and Michael Supancic, "Perceived Risk and Fear of Crime: Role of Social and Physical Incivilities," *Journal of Research in Crime and Delinquency* 29:311–334 (1992).

33. Robert Sampson, Jeffrey Morenoff, and Felton Earls, "Beyond Social Capital: Spatial Dynamics of Collective Efficacy for Children," *American Sociological Review* 64:633–660 (1999).

34. Fred Markowitz, Paul Bellair, Allen Liska, and Jianhong Liu, "Extending Social Disorganization Theory: Modeling the Relationships Between Cohesion, Disorder, and Fear," *Criminology* 39:293–320 (2001).

35. Robert J. Sampson and Stephen W. Raudenbush, *Disorder in Urban Neighborhoods: Does It Lead to Crime?* (Washington, DC: National Institute of Justice, 2001).

36. Chris Gibson, Jihong Zhao, Nicholas Lovrich, Michael Gaffney, "Social Integration, Individual Perceptions of Collective Efficacy, and Fear of Crime in Three Cities." *Justice Quarterly* 19:537–564 (2002); Felton Earls, *Linking Community Factors and Individual Development* (Washington, DC: National Institute of Justice, 1998).

37. Bursik and Grasmick, "The Multiple Layers of Social Disorganization." Paper presented at the annual meeting of the American Society of Criminology, New Orleans, November 1992.

38. George Capowich, "The Conditioning Effects of Neighborhood Ecology on Burglary Victimization," *Criminal Justice and Behavior* 30:39–62 (2003); Ruth Peterson, Lauren Krivo, and Mark Harris, "Disadvantage and Neighborhood Violent Crime: Do Local Institutions Matter?" *Journal of Research in Crime and Delinquency* 37:31–63 (2000).

39. Jennifer Beyers, John Bates, Gregory Pettit, Kenneth Dodge, "Neighborhood Structure, Parenting Processes, and the Development of Youths' Externalizing Behaviors: A Multilevel Analysis," *American Journal of Community Psychology* 31:35–53 (2003).

40. See, for example, Robert Merton, *Social Theory and Social Structure* (Glencoe, IL: Free Press, 1957).

41. Robert Agnew, "Foundation for a General Strain Theory of Crime and Delinquency," *Criminology* 30: 47–87 (1992).

42. Ibid., p. 57.

43. Tami Videon, " The Effects of Parent-Adolescent Relationships and Parental Separation on Adolescent Well-Being," *Journal of Marriage & the Family* 64:489–504 (2002).

44. Cesar Rebellon, "Reconsidering the Broken Homes/Delinquency Relationship and Exploring Its Mediating Mechanism(s)," *Criminology* 40:103–135 (2002).

45. Timothy Brezina, "Adolescent Maltreatment and Delinquency: The Question of Intervening Processes," *Journal of Research in Crime and Delinquency* 35:71–99 (1998).

46. Paul Mazerolle, Velmer Burton, Francis Cullen, T. David Evans, and Gary Payne, "Strain, Anger, and Delinquent Adaptations Specifying General Strain Theory," *Journal of Criminal Justice* 28:89–101 (2000).

47. Stephen Cernkovich, Peggy Giordano, and Jennifer Rudolph, "Race, Crime, and the American Dream," *Journal of Research in Crime and Delinquency* 37:131–170 (2000).

48. Paul Mazerolle, Velmer Burton, Francis Cullen, T. David Evans, and Gary Payne, "Strain, Anger, and Delinquent Adaptations: Specifying General Strain Theory," *Journal of Criminal Justice* 28:89–101 (2000); Paul Mazerolle and Alex Piquero, "Violent Responses to Strain: An Examination of Conditioning Influences," *Violence and Victimization* 12:323–345 (1997).

49. George E. Capowich, Paul Mazerolle, and Alex Piquero, "General Strain Theory, Situational Anger, and Social Networks: An Assessment of Conditioning Influences," *Journal of Criminal Justice* 29:445–461 (2001).

50. Robert Agnew, "Experienced, Vicarious, and Anticipated Strain: An Exploratory Study on Physical Victimization and Delinquency," *Justice Quarterly* 19:603–633 (2002).

51. Albert Cohen, *Delinquent Boys* (New York: Free Press, 1955).

52. Richard Cloward and Lloyd Ohlin, *Delinquency and Opportunity* (New York: Free Press, 1960).

53. See, for example, Irving Spergel, *Racketville, Slumtown, and Haulburg* (Chicago: University of Chicago Press, 1964).

54. James Short, "Gangs, Neighborhoods, and Youth Crime," *Criminal Justice Research Bulletin* 5:1–11 (1990).

55. Michael Leiber, Mahesh Nalla, and Margaret Farnworth, "Explaining Juveniles' Attitudes Toward the Police," *Justice Quarterly* 15:151–173 (1998).

56. A. Leigh Ingram, "Type of Place, Urbanism, and Delinquency: Further Testing of the Determinist Theory," *Journal of Research in Crime and Delinquency* 30:192–212 (1993).

57. Alan Lizotte, Terence Thornberry, Marvin Krohn, Deborah Chard-Wierschem, and David McDowall, "Neighborhood Context and Delinquency: A Longitudinal Analysis," in H. J. Kerner and E. Weitekamp, eds., *Cross-National Longitudinal Research on Human Development and Criminal Behavior* (Dordrecht, The Netherlands: Kluwer Academic Publishers, 1993), pp. 1–11.

58. Eric Stewart, Ronald Simons, and Rand Conger, "Assessing Neighborhood and Social Psychological Influences on Childhood Violence in an African-American Sample," *Criminology* 40:801–830 (2002).

59. Ronald Simons, Chyi-In Wu, Kuei-Hsiu Lin, Leslie Gordon, and Rand Conger, "A Cross-Cultural Examination of the Link Between Corporal Punishment and Adolescent Antisocial Behavior," *Criminology* 38:47–79 (2000).

60. John Paul Wright and Francis Cullen, "Parental Efficacy and Delinquent Behavior: Do Control and Support Matter?" *Criminology* 39:677–706 (2001).

61. Karol Kumpfer and Rose Alvarado, "Strengthening Approaches for the Prevention of Youth Problem Behaviors," *American Psychologist* 58:457–465 (2003); Carter Hay, "Parenting, Self-Control, and Delinquency: A Test of Self-Control Theory," *Criminology* 39:707–736 (2001).

62. Alexander Vazsonyi and Lloyd Pickering, "The Importance of Family and School Domains in Adolescent Deviance: African-American and Caucasian Youth," *Journal of Youth and Adolescence* 32:115–129 (2003).

63. Isabela Granic and Thomas Dishion, "Deviant Talk in Adolescent Friendships: A Step Toward Measuring a Pathogenic Attractor Process," *Social Development* 12:314–334 (2003).

64. Jeremy Staff and Christopher Uggen, "The Fruits of Good Work: Early Work Experiences and Adolescent Deviance," *Journal of Research in Crime and Delinquency* 40:263–290 (2003).

65. David Fergusson, L. John Horwood, and Daniel Nagin, "Offending Trajectories in a New Zealand Birth Cohort," *Criminology* 38:525–551 (2000).

66. Edwin Sutherland, *Principles of Criminology* (Philadelphia: Lippincott, 1939).

67. Travis Hirschi, *Causes of Delinquency* (Berkeley: University of California Press, 1969).

68. Bobbi Jo Anderson, Malcolm Holmes, and Erik Ostresh, "Male and Female Delinquents' Attachments and Effects of Attachments on Severity of Self-Reported Delinquency," *Criminal Justice and Behavior* 26:425–452 (1999).

69. Patricia Jenkins, "School Delinquency and the School Social Bond," *Journal of Research in Crime and Delinquency* 34:337–367 (1997).

70. Thomas Vander Ven, Francis Cullen, Mark Carrozza, and John Paul Wright, "Home Alone: The Impact of Maternal Employment on Delinquency," *Social Problems* 48:236–257 (2001).

71. Helen Garnier and Judith Stein, "An 18-Year Model of Family and Peer Effects on Adolescent Drug Use and Delinquency," *Journal of Youth and Adolescence* 31:45–56 (2002).

72. Cernkovich, Giordano, and Rudolph, "Race, Crime, and the American Dream."

73. Peggy Giordano, Stephen Cernkovich, and M. D. Pugh, "Friendships and Delinquency," *American Journal of Sociology* 91:1170–1202 (1986).

74. Denise Kandel and Mark Davies, "Friendship Networks, Intimacy, and Illicit Drug Use in Young Adulthood: A Comparison of Two Competing Theories," *Criminology* 29:441–467 (1991).

75. For a review of this position, see Anne R. Mahoney, "The Effect of Labeling Upon Youths in the Juvenile Justice System: A Review of the Evidence," *Law and Society Review* 8.583–614 (1974); see also David Matza, *Becoming Deviant* (Englewood Cliffs, NJ: Prentice-Hall, 1974).

76. The self-labeling concept originated in Edwin Lemert, *Social Pathology* (New York: McGraw-Hill, 1951); see also Frank Tannenbaum, *Crime and the Community* (Boston: Ginn, 1936).

77. Harold Garfinkel, "Conditions of Successful Degradation Ceremonies," in Jerome Manis and Bernard Meltzer, eds., *Symbolic Interactionism* (New York: Allyn & Bacon, 1972), pp. 201–208.

78. M. A. Bortner, *Inside a Juvenile Court: The Tarnished Ideal of Individualized Justice* (New York: NYU Press, 1982).

79. Edwin Lemert, *Human Deviance, Social Problems, and Social Control* (Englewood Cliffs, NJ: Prentice-Hall, 1967), p. 15.

80. Lening Zhang, "Official Offense Status and Self-Esteem Among Chinese Youths," *Journal of Criminal Justice*, 31:99–105 (2003).

81. Mike Adams, Craig Robertson, Phyllis Gray-Ray, and Melvin Ray, "Labeling and Delinquency," *Adolescence* 38:171–186 (2003).

82. Charles H. Cooley, *Human Nature and the Social Order* (New York: Scribner's, 1902).

83. Ross Matsueda, "Reflected Appraisals, Parental Labeling, and Delinquency: Specifying a Symbolic Interactionist Theory," *American Journal of Sociology* 97:1577–1611 (1992).

84. Raymond Paternoster and Leeann Iovanni, "The Labeling Perspective and Delinquency: An Elaboration of the Theory and an Assessment of the Evidence," *Justice Quarterly* 6:358–394 (1989).

85. Robert Meier, "The New Criminology: Continuity in Criminological Theory," *Journal of Criminal Law and Criminology* 67:463 (1977).

86. Malcolm Holmes, "Minority Threat and Police Brutality: Determinants of Civil Rights Criminal Complaints in U.S. Municipalities," *Criminology* 38:343–368 (2000).

87. Ibid.

88. Robert Gordon, "Capitalism, Class, and Crime in America," *Crime and Delinquency* 19:174 (1973).

89. Richard Quinney, *Class, State, and Crime* (New York: Longman, 1977), p. 52.

90. Anthony Platt, "The Triumph of Benevolence: The Origins of the Juvenile Justice System in the United States," in Richard Quinney, ed., *Criminal Justice in America: A Critical Understanding* (Boston: Little, Brown, 1974), p. 367; see also Anthony Platt, *The Child Savers: The Invention of Delinquency* (Chicago: University of Chicago Press, 1969).

91. Barry Krisberg and James Austin, *Children of Ishmael* (Palo Alto, CA: Mayfield, 1978), p. 2.

92. Herman Schwendinger and Julia Schwendinger, "Delinquency and Social Reform: A Radical Perspective," in Lamar Empey, ed., *Juvenile Justice* (Charlottesville: University of Virginia Press, 1979), p. 250.

93. Operation Weed and Seed Executive Offices, U.S. Department of Justice, Washington, DC, 1998; *Weed and Seed In-sites*, vol. I, no. 5, August-September 1998.

94. Terence Thornberry, David Huizinga, and Rolf Loeber, "The Prevention of Serious Delinquency and Violence," in James Howell, Barry Krisberg, J. David Hawkins, and John Wilson, eds., *Sourcebook on Serious, Violent, and Chronic Juvenile Offenders* (Thousand Oaks, CA: Sage, 1995).

95. Malcolm Klein, "Deinstitutionalization and Diversion of Juvenile Offenders: A Litany of Impediments," in Norval Morris and Michael Tonry, eds., *Crime and Justice*, vol. 1 (Chicago: University of Chicago Press, 1979).

96. James Austin and Barry Krisberg, "The Unmet Promise of Alternatives to Incarceration," *Crime and Delinquency* 28:3–19 (1982).

97. William Selke, "Diversion and Crime Prevention," *Criminology* 20:395–406 (1982).

98. Kathleen Daly and Russ Immarigeon, "The Past, Present, and Future of Restorative Justice: Some Critical Reflections," *Contemporary Justice Review* 1:21–45 (1998).

99. Gene Stephens, "The Future of Policing: From a War Model to a Peace Model," in Brendan Maguire and Polly Radosh, eds., *The Past, Present, and Future of American Criminal Justice* (Dix Hills, NY: General Hall, 1996), pp. 77–93.

100. Peter Cordella, "Justice." Unpublished paper, St. Anselm College, Manchester, NH, 1997; see also Herbert Bianchi, *Justice as Sanctuary*

(Bloomington: Indiana University Press, 1994); Nils Christie, "Conflicts as Property," *British Journal of Criminology* 17:1–15 (1977); L. Hulsman, "Critical Criminology and the Concept of Crime," *Contemporary Crises* 10:63–80 (1986).

101. Kay Pranis, "Peacemaking Circles: Restorative Justice in Practice Allows Victims and Offenders to Begin Repairing the Harm," *Corrections Today* 59:72–76 (1997).

102. Carol LaPrairie, "The 'New' Justice: Some Implications for Aboriginal Communities," *Canadian Journal of Criminology* 40:61–79 (1998).

103. Gordon Bazemore, "What's New About the Balanced Approach?" *Juvenile and Family Court Journal* 48:1–23 (1997); Gordon Bazemore and Mara Schiff, "Community Justice/Restorative Justice: Prospects for a New Social Ecology for Community Corrections," *International Journal of Comparative and Applied Criminal Justice* 20:311–335 (1996).

104. Jay Zaslaw and George Ballance, "The Socio-Legal Response: A New Approach to Juvenile Justice in the '90s," *Corrections Today* 58:72–75 (1996).

105. Gordon Bazemore, "Restorative Justice and Earned Redemption: Communities, Victims, and Offender Reintegration," *American Behavioral Scientist* 41:768–814 (1998).

Chapter 5

1. Marvin Krohn, Alan Lizotte, and Cynthia Perez, "The Interrelationship Between Substance Use and Precocious Transitions to Adult Sexuality," *Journal of Health and Social Behavior* 38:88 (1997).

2. Peggy Giordano, Stephen Cernkovich, and Jennifer Rudolph, "Gender, Crime, and Desistance: Toward a Theory of Cognitive Transformation?" *American Journal of Sociology* 107:990–1064 (2002).

3. John Hagan and Holly Foster, "S/He's a Rebel: Toward a Sequential Stress Theory of Delinquency and Gendered Pathways to Disadvantage in Emerging Adulthood," *Social Forces* 82:53–86 (2003).

4. See, generally, Sheldon Glueck and Eleanor Glueck, *500 Delinquent Careers* (New York: Knopf, 1930); Sheldon Glueck and Eleanor Glueck, *One Thousand Juvenile Delinquents* (Cambridge, MA: Harvard University Press, 1934); Sheldon Glueck and Eleanor Glueck, *Predicting Delinquency* (Cambridge, MA: Harvard University Press, 1967), pp. 82–83.

5. Sheldon Glueck and Eleanor Glueck, *Unraveling Juvenile Delinquency* (Cambridge, MA: Harvard University Press, 1950).

6. Ibid., p. 48.

7. Rolf Loeber and Marc LeBlanc, "Toward a Developmental Criminology," in Norval Morris and Michael Tonry, eds., *Delinquency and Justice,* vol. 12 (Chicago: University of Chicago Press, 1990), pp. 375–473; Rolf Loeber and Marc LeBlanc, "Developmental Criminology Updated," in Michael Tonry, ed., *Delinquency and Justice,* vol. 23 (Chicago: University of Chicago Press, 1998), pp. 115–198.

8. Alex R. Piquero and He Len Chung, "On the Relationships Between Gender, Early Onset, and the Seriousness of Offending," *Journal of Delinquent Justice* 29:189–206 (2001).

9. Rolf Loeber and David Farrington, "Young Children Who Commit Delinquency: Epidemiology, Developmental Origins, Risk Factors, Early Interventions, and Policy Implications," *Development and Psychopathology* 12:737–762 (2000).

10. Ick-Joong Chung, Karl G Hill, J. David Hawkins, Lewayne Gilchrist, and Daniel Nagin, "Childhood Predictors of Offense Trajectories," *Journal of Research in Crime and Delinquency* 39:60–91 (2002).

11. Elaine Eggleston and John Laub, "The Onset of Adult Offending: A Neglected Dimension of the Criminal Career," *Journal of Criminal Justice* 30:603–622 (2002).

12. Ronald Simons, Chyi-In Wu, Rand Conger, and Frederick Lorenz, "Two Routes to Delinquency: Differences Between Early and Later Starters in the Impact of Parenting and Deviant Careers," *Criminology* 32:247–275 (1994).

13. Alex R. Piquero, Robert Brame, Paul Mazerolle, and Rudy Haapanen, "Crime in Emerging Adulthood," *Criminology* 40:137–169 (2002).

14. Ronald Prinz and Suzanne Kerns, "Early Substance Use by Juvenile Offenders," *Child Psychiatry & Human Development* 33:263–268 (2003).

15. Terrie Moffitt, "Natural Histories of Delinquency," in Elmar Weitekamp and Hans-Jurgen Kerner, eds., *Cross-National Longitudinal Research on Human Development and Delinquent Behavio*r (Dordrecht, Netherlands: Kluwer, 1994), pp. 3–65.

16. Alex Piquero and Timothy Brezina, "Testing Moffitt's Account of Adolescent-Limited Delinquency," *Criminology* 39:353–370 (2001).

17. Amy D'Unger, Kenneth Land, Patricia McCall, and Daniel Nagin, "How Many Latent Classes of Delinquent/Criminal t Careers Results from Mixed Poisson Regression Analyses?" *American Journal of Sociology* 103:1593–1630 (1998).

18. Michael Newcomb, "Pseudomaturity Among Adolescents: Construct Validation, Sex Differences, and Associations in Adulthood," *Journal of Drug Issues* 26:477–504 (1996).

19. Magda Stouthamer-Loeber and Evelyn Wei, "The Precursors of Young Fatherhood and Its Effect on Delinquency of Teenage Males," *Journal of Adolescent Health* 22:56–65 (1998); Richard Jessor, John Donovan, and Francis Costa, *Beyond Adolescence: Problem Behavior and Young Adult Development* (New York: Cambridge University Press, 1991).

20. Marvin Krohn, Alan Lizotte, and Cynthia Perez, "The Interrelationship Between Substance Use and Precocious Transitions to Adult Sexuality," *Journal of Health and Social Behavior* 38:88 (1997); Richard Jessor, "Risk Behavior in Adolescence: A Psychosocial Framework for Understanding and Action," in D. E. Rogers and E. Ginzburg, eds., *Adolescents at Risk: Medical and Social Perspectives* (Boulder, CO: Westview, 1992).

21. Ick-Joong Chung, J. David Hawkins, Lewayne Gilchrist, Karl Hill, and Daniel Nagin, "Identifying and Predicting Offending Trajectories Among Poor Children," *Social Service Review* 76:663–687 (2002).

22. Vladislav Ruchkin, Mary Schwab-Stone, Roman Koposov, Robert Vermeiren, and Robert King, "Suicidal Ideations and Attempts in Juvenile Delinquents," *Child Psychology & Psychiatry & Allied Disciplines* 44:1058–1067 (2003).

23. Marvin Krohn, Alan Lizotte, and Cynthia Perez, "The Interrelationship Between Substance Use and Precocious Transitions to Adult Sexuality," *Journal of Health and Social Behavior* 38:88 (1997); Jessor, "Risk Behavior in Adolescence."

24. Deborah Capaldi and Gerald Patterson, "Can Violent Offenders Be Distinguished from Frequent Offenders? Prediction from Childhood to Adolescence," *Journal of Research in Crime and Delinquency* 33:206–231 (1996).

25. Margit Wiesner and Deborah Capaldi, "Relations of Childhood and Adolescent Factors to Offending Trajectories of Young Men," *Journal of Research in Crime and Delinquency* 40:231–262 (2003).

26. Rolf Loeber, Phen Wung, Kate Keenan, Bruce Giroux, Magda Stouthamer-Loeber, Wemoet Van Kammen, and Barbara Maughan, "Developmental Pathways in Disruptive Behavior," *Development and Psychopathology* 11:12–48 (1993).

27. Mark Lipsey and James Derzon, "Predictors of Violent or Serious Delinquency in Adolescence and Early Adulthood: A Synthesis of Longitudinal Research," in Rolf Loeber and David Farrington, eds., *Serious and Violent Juvenile Offenders: Risk Factors and Successful Interventions* (Thousand Oaks, CA: Sage, 1998).

28. Glenn Clingempeel and Scott Henggeler, "Aggressive Juvenile Offenders Transitioning into Emerging Adulthood: Factors Discriminating Persistors and Desistors," *American Journal of Orthopsychiatry* 73:310–323 (2003).

29. Marshall Jones and Donald Jones, "The Contagious Nature of Antisocial Behavior," *Criminology* 38:25–46 (2000).

30. Terrie Moffitt, Avshalom Caspi, Michael Rutter, and Phil Silva, *Sex Differences in Antisocial Behavior: Conduct Disorder, Delinquency, and Violence in the Dunedin Longitudinal Study* (London: Cambridge University Press, 2001).

31. See, for example, the *Rochester Youth Development Study* (Albany, NY: Hindelang Delinquent Justice Research Center, 2003).

32. David Farrington, "The Development of Offending and Antisocial Behavior from Childhood to Adulthood." Paper presented at the Congress on Rethinking Delinquency, University of Minho, Braga, Portugal, July 1992.

33. Joseph Weis and J. David Hawkins, *Reports of the National Juvenile Assessment Centers: Preventing Delinquency* (Washington, DC: U.S.

Department of Justice, 1981); Richard Catalano and J. D. Hawkins, "The Social Development Model: A Theory of Antisocial Behavior," in J. D. Hawkins, ed., *Delinquency and Crime: Current Theories* (New York: Cambridge University Press, 1996), pp. 149–197.

34. Bu Huang, Rick Kosterman, Richard Catalano, J. David Hawkins, and Robert Abbott, "Modeling Mediation in the Etiology of Violent Behavior in Adolescence: A Test of the Social Development Model," *Criminology* 39:75–107 (2001).

35. Todd Herrenkohl, Bu Huang, Rick Kosterman, J. David Hawkins, Richard Catalano, and Brian Smith, "A Comparison of Social Development Processes Leading to Violent Behavior in Late Adolescence for Childhood Initiators and Adolescent Initiators of Violence," *Journal of Research in Crime and Delinquency* 38:45–63 (2001).

36. Terence Thornberry, "Toward an Interactional Theory of Delinquency," *Criminology* 25:863–891 (1987).

37. Thornberry, "Toward an Interactional Theory of Delinquency."

38. Ibid., p. 863.

39. Terence Thornberry and Marvin Krohn, "The Development of Delinquency: An Interactional Perspective," in Susan White, ed., *Handbook of Youth and Justice* (New York: Plenum, 2001), pp. 289–305.

40. Kee Jeong Kim, Rand Conger, Glen Elder Jr., and Frederick Lorenz, "Reciprocal Influences Between Stressful Life Events and Adolescent Internalizing and Externalizing Problems," *Child Development* 74:127–143 (2003).

41. Terence Thornberry, Adrienne Freeman-Gallant, Alan Lizotte, Marvin Krohn, and Carolyn Smith, "Linked Lives: The Intergenerational Transmission of Antisocial Behavior," *Journal of Abnormal Child Psychology* 31:171–185 (2003).

42. Terrence Thornberry, Alan Lizotte, Marvin Krohn, Margaret Farnworth, and Sung Joon Jang, *Delinquent Peers, Beliefs, and Delinquent Behavior: A Longitudinal Test of Interactional Theory*. Working paper no. 6, rev., Rochester Youth Development Study (Albany, NY: Hindelang Delinquent Justice Research Center, 1992), pp. 628–629.

43. Robert Sampson and John Laub, *Crime in the Making: Pathways and Turning Points Through Life* (Cambridge, MA: Harvard University Press, 1993); John Laub and Robert Sampson, "Turning Points in the Life Course: Why Change Matters to the Study of Crime." Paper presented at the annual meeting of the American Society of Criminology, New Orleans, November 1992.

44. Terri Orbuch, James House, Richard Mero, and Pamela Webster, "Marital Quality Over the Life Course," *Social Psychology Quarterly* 59:162–171 (1996); Lee Lillard and Linda Waite, "'Til Death Do Us Part: Marital Disruption and Mortality," *American Journal of Sociology* 100:1131–1156 (1995).

45. Mark Warr, "Life-Course Transitions and Desistance from Crime," *Criminology* 36:183–216 (1998).

46. Nan Lin, *Social Capital: A Theory of Social Structure and Action* (Cambridge, UK: Cambridge University Press, 2002).

47. Sampson and Laub, *Crime in the Making*, p. 249.

48. John Hagan, Ross MacMillan, and Blair Wheaton, "New Kid in Town: Social Capital and the Life Course Effects of Family Migration on Children," *American Sociological Review* 61:368–385 (1996).

49. Robert Sampson and John Laub, "A Life-Course Theory of Cumulative Disadvantage and the Stability of Delinquency," in Terence Thornberry, ed., *Developmental Theories of Crime and Delinquency* (Somerset, NJ: Transaction Publishing, 1997), pp. 138–162.

50. Raymond Paternoster and Robert Brame, "Multiple Routes to Delinquency? A Test of Developmental and General Theories of Crime," *Criminology* 35:49–84 (1997).

51. Pamela Webster, Terri Orbuch, and James House, "Effects of Childhood Family Background on Adult Marital Quality and Perceived Stability," *American Journal of Sociology* 101:404–432 (1995).

52. Robert Hoge, D. A. Andrews, and Alan Leschied, "An Investigation of Risk and Protective Factors in a Sample of Youthful Offenders," *Journal of Child Psychology and Psychiatry* 37:419–424 (1996).

53. Avshalom Caspi, Terrie Moffitt, Bradley Entner Wright, and Phil Silva, "Early Failure in the Labor Market: Childhood and Adolescent Predictors of Unemployment in the Transition to Adulthood," *American Sociological Review* 63:424–451 (1998).

54. Robert Sampson and John Laub, "Socioeconomic Achievement in the Life Course of Disadvantaged Men: Military Service as a Turn-

ing Point, circa 1940–1965," *American Sociological Review* 61:347–367 (1996).

55. Daniel Nagin and Raymond Paternoster, "Personal Capital and Social Control: The Deterrence Implications of a Theory of Offending," *Criminology* 32:581–606 (1994).

56. James Q. Wilson and Richard Herrnstein, *Crime and Human Nature* (New York: Simon & Schuster, 1985).

57. David Rowe, D. Wayne Osgood, and W. Alan Nicewander, "A Latent Trait Approach to Unifying Criminal Careers," *Criminology* 28:237–270 (1990).

58. Lee Ellis, "Neurohormonal Bases of Varying Tendencies to Learn Delinquent and Criminal Behavior," in E. Morris and C. Braukmann, eds., *Behavioral Approaches to Crime and Delinquency* (New York: Plenum, 1988), pp. 499–518.

59. David Rowe, Alexander Vazsonyi, and Daniel Flannery, "Sex Differences in Crime: Do Means and Within-Sex Variation Have Similar Causes?" *Journal of Research in Crime and Delinquency* 32:84–100 (1995).

60. Michael Gottfredson and Travis Hirschi, *A General Theory of Crime* (Stanford, CA: Stanford University Press, 1990).

61. Ibid., p. 27.

62. Robert Agnew, "The Contribution of Social-Psychological Strain Theory to the Explanation of Crime and Delinquency," *Advances in Criminological Theory* 6:211–213 (1994).

63. Ibid., p. 90.

64. Ibid., p. 89.

65. Alex Piquero and Stephen Tibbetts, "Specifying the Direct and Indirect Effects of Low Self-Control and Situational Factors in Offenders' Decision Making: Toward a More Complete Model of Rational Offending," *Justice Quarterly* 13:481–508 (1996).

66. David Forde and Leslie Kennedy, "Risky Lifestyles, Routine Activities, and the General Theory of Crime," *Justice Quarterly* 14:265–294 (1997).

67. Marianne Junger and Richard Tremblay, "Self-Control, Accidents, and Delinquency," *Criminal Justice and Behavior* 26:485–501 (1999).

68. Gottfredson and Hirschi, *A General Theory of Crime*, p. 112.

69. Ibid.

70. Dennis Giever, "An Empirical Assessment of the Core Elements of Gottfredson and Hirschi's General Theory of Crime." Paper presented at the annual meeting of the American Society of Criminology, Boston, November 1995.

71. David Farrington, Darrick Jolliffe, Rolf Loeber, Magda Southamer-Loeber, and Larry Kalb, "The Concentration of Offenders in Families, and Family Criminality in the Prediction of Boy's Delinquency," *Journal of Adolescence* 24:579–596 (2001).

72. Peter Muris and Cor Meesters, "The Validity of Attention Deficit Hyperactivity and Hyperkinetic Disorder Symptom Domains in Nonclinical Dutch Children," *Journal of Clinical Child & Adolescent Psychology* 32:460–466 (2003); David Brownfield and Ann Marie Sorenson, "Self-Control and Juvenile Delinquency: Theoretical Issues and an Empirical Assessment of Selected Elements of a General Theory of Crime," *Deviant Behavior* 14:243–264 (1993); Harold Grasmick, Charles Tittle, Robert Bursik, and Bruce Arneklev, "Testing the Core Empirical Implications of Gottfredson and Hirschi's General Theory of Crime," *Journal of Research in Crime and Delinquency* 30:5–29 (1993).

73. Ronald Akers, "Self-Control as a General Theory of Crime," *Journal of Quantitative Criminology* 7:201–211 (1991).

74. Richard Wiebe, "Reconciling Psychopathy and Low Self-Control," *Justice Quarterly* 20:297–336 (2003).

75. Alan Feingold, "Gender Differences in Personality: A Meta-Analysis," *Psychological Bulletin* 116:429–456 (1994).

76. Gottfredson and Hirschi, *A General Theory of Crime*, p. 153.

77. Scott Menard, Delbert Elliott, and Sharon Wofford, "Social Control Theories in Developmental Perspective," *Studies on Crime and Delinquency Prevention* 2:69–87 (1993).

78. Charles R. Tittle and Harold G. Grasmick, "Delinquent Behavior and Age: A Test of Three Provocative Hypotheses," *Journal of Criminal Law and Criminology* 88:309–342 (1997).

79. Travis Pratt and Frank Cullen, "The Empirical Status of Gottfredson and Hirschi's General Theory of Crime: A Meta-Analysis," *Criminology* 38:938–964 (2000); Douglas Longshore, "Self-Control and

Delinquent Opportunity: A Prospective Test of the General Theory of Delinquency," *Social Problems* 45:102–114 (1998).

80. Otwin Marenin and Michael Resig, "A General Theory of Crime and Patterns of Crime in Nigeria: An Exploration of Methodological Assumptions," *Journal of Crime and Justice* 23:501–518 (1995).

81. Bruce Arneklev, Harold Grasmick, Charles Tittle, and Robert Bursik, "Low Self-Control and Imprudent Behavior," *Journal of Quantitative Criminology* 9:225–246 (1993).

82. Kevin Thompson, "Sexual Harassment and Low Self-Control: An Application of Gottfredson and Hirschi's General Theory of Crime." Paper presented at the annual meeting of the American Society of Criminology, Phoenix, November 1993.

83. Bradley Entner Wright, Avshalom Caspi, Terrie Moffitt, and Phil Silva, "Low Self-Control, Social Bonds, and Delinquency: Social Causation, Social Selection, or Both?" *Criminology* 37:479–514 (1999).

84. Ibid., p. 504.

85. Stephen Cernkovich and Peggy Giordano, "Stability and Change in Antisocial Behavior: The Transition from Adolescence to Early Adulthood," *Criminology* 39:371–410 (2001).

New Directions in Preventing Delinquency: Primary Prevention Efforts: Early Childhood

1. Deanna S. Gomby, Patti L. Culross, and Richard E. Behrman, "Home Visiting: Recent Program Evaluations—Analysis and Recommendations," *The Future of Children*, vol. 9 (Los Altos, CA: David and Lucile Packard Foundation, 1999), pp. 4–26.

2. Ibid.

3. David L. Olds, Charles R. Henderson, Robert Chamberlin, Robert Tatelbaum, "Preventing Child Abuse and Neglect: A Randomized Trial of Nurse Home Visitation," *Pediatrics* 78:65–78 (1986).

4. David L. Olds, Charles R. Henderson, Charles Phelps, Harriet Kitzman, and Carole Hanks, "Effects of Prenatal and Infancy Nurse Home Visitation on Government Spending," *Medical Care* 31:158 (1993).

5. David L. Olds, Charles R. Henderson, Robert Cole, John Eckenrode, Harriet Kitzman, Dennis Luckey, Lisa Pettitt, Kimberly Sidora, Pamela Morris, and Jane Powers, "Long-Term Effects of Nurse Home Visitation on Children's Criminal and Antisocial Behavior: 15-Year Follow-Up of a Randomized Controlled Trial," *Journal of the American Medical Association* 280:1238–1244 (1998).

6. David L. Olds, John Eckenrode, Charles R. Henderson, Harriet Kitzman, Jane Powers, Robert Cole, Kimberly Sidora, Pamela Morris, Lisa M. Pettitt, and Dennis Luckey, "Long-Term Effects of Home Visitation on Maternal Life Course and Child Abuse and Neglect: Fifteen-Year Follow-Up of a Randomized Trial," *Journal of the American Medical Association* 278:637–643 (1997).

7. Lynn A. Karoly, Peter W. Greenwood, Susan S. Everingham, Jill Houbé, M. Rebecca Kilburn, C. Peter Rydell, Matthew Sanders, and James Chiesa, *Investing in Our Children: What We Know and Don't Know About the Costs and Benefits of Early Childhood Interventions* (Santa Monica, CA: Rand, 1998).

8. Harriet Kitzman, David L. Olds, Charles R. Henderson, Carole Hanks, Robert Cole, Robert Tatelbaum, Kenneth M. McConnochie, Kimberly Sidora, Dennis W. Luckey, David Shaver, Kay Engelhardt, David James, and Kathryn Barnard, "Effect of Prenatal and Infancy Home Visitation by Nurses on Pregnancy Outcomes, Childhood Injuries, and Repeated Childbearing: A Randomized Controlled Trial," *Journal of the American Medical Association* 278:644–652 (1997).

9. Anne K. Duggan, Elizabeth C. McFarlane, Amy M. Windham, Charles A. Rohde, David S. Salkever, Loretta Fuddy, Leon A. Rosenberg, Sharon B. Buchbinder, and Calvin C. J. Sia, "Evaluation of Hawaii's Healthy Start Program," *The Future of Children* 9(1):66–90 (1999).

10. David P. Farrington and Brandon C. Welsh, "Delinquency Prevention Using Family-Based Interventions," *Children and Society* 13:287–303 (1999); David P. Farrington and Brandon C. Welsh, "Family-Based Crime Prevention," in Lawrence W. Sherman, David P. Farrington, Brandon C. Welsh, and Doris Layton MacKenzie, eds., *Evidence-Based Crime Prevention* (London, England: Routledge, 2002).

11. Gerald R. Patterson, Patricia Chamberlain, and John B. Reid, "A Comparative Evaluation of a Parent-Training Program," *Behavior Therapy* 13:638–650 (1982); Gerald R. Patterson, John B. Reid, and Thomas J. Dishion, *Antisocial Boys* (Eugene, OR: Castalia, 1992).

12. Peter W. Greenwood, Karyn E. Model, C. Peter Rydell, and James Chiesa, *Diverting Children from a Life of Crime: Measuring Costs and Benefits* (Santa Monica, CA: Rand, 1996).

13. Sonya Michel, *Children's Interests/Mother's Rights: The Shaping of America's Child Care Policy* (New Haven, CT: Yale University Press, 1999).

14. J. Ronald Lally, Peter L. Mangione, and Alice S. Honig, "The Syracuse University Family Development Research Program: Long-Range Impact of an Early Intervention with Low-Income Children and their Families," in D. R. Powell, ed., *Parent Education as Early Childhood Intervention: Emerging Directions in Theory, Research and Practice* (Norwood, NJ: Ablex, 1988).

15. Adrian Raine, Kjetil Mellingen, Jianghong Liu, Peter Venables, and Sarnoff Mednick, "Effects of Environmental Enrichment at Age Three to Five Years on Schizotypal Personality and Antisocial Behavior at Ages Seventeen and Twenty-Three Years," *American Journal of Psychiatry* 160:1–9 (2003).

16. David P. Farrington, "Early Developmental Prevention of Juvenile Delinquency," *Criminal Behavior and Mental Health* 4:216–217.

17. Lawrence J. Schweinhart, Helen V. Barnes, and David P. Weikart, *Significant Benefits: The High/Scope Perry Preschool Study Through Age 27* (Ypsilanti, MI: High/Scope Press, 1993), p. 3.

18. Blueprints Promising Programs Fact Sheets (Boulder, CO: Center for the Study and Prevention of Violence, 2004). http://www.colorado.edu/cspv/publications/factsheets/blueprints/FS-BPP06.html.

19. Richard E. Tremblay and Wendy M. Craig, "Developmental Crime Prevention," in Michael Tonry and David P. Farrington, eds., *Building a Safer Society: Strategic Approaches to Crime Prevention. Crime and Justice: A Review of Research*, vol. 19 (Chicago: University of Chicago Press, 1995), pp. 151–236.

Chapter 6

1. Cesare Lombroso, *The Female Offender* (New York: Appleton, 1920); W. I. Thomas, *The Unadjusted Girl* (New York: Harper & Row, 1923).

2. Cesare Lombroso and William Ferrero, *The Female Offender* (New York: Philosophical Library, 1895).

3. Cheryl Maxson and Monica Whitlock, "Joining the Gang: Gender Differences in Risk Factors for Gang Membership," in C. Ronald Huff, ed., *Gangs in America III* (Thousand Oaks, CA: Sage, 2002), pp. 19–35.

4. Paul Mazerolle, Robert Brame, Ray Paternoster, Alex Piquero, and Charles Dean, "Onset Age, Persistence, and Offending Versatility: Comparisons Across Sex." Paper presented at the annual American Society of Criminology meeting, San Diego, November 1997.

5. Kathleen Daly, "From Gender Ratios to Gendered Lives: Women's Gender in Crime and Criminological Theory," in Michael Tonry, ed., *Handbook of Crime and Punishment* (New York: Oxford University Press, 1998).

6. Rita James Simon, *The Contemporary Woman and Crime* (Washington, DC: U.S. Government Printing Office, 1975).

7. Rolf Loeber and Dale Hay, "Key Issues in the Development of Aggression and Violence from Childhood to Early Adulthood," *Annual Review of Psychology* 48:371–410 (1997).

8. This section relies on Spencer Rathus, *Psychology in the New Millennium* (Fort Worth, TX: Harcourt, Brace, 1996); see also Darcy Miller, Catherine Trapani, Kathy Fejes-Mendoza, Carolyn Eggleston, and Donna Dwiggins, "Adolescent Female Offenders: Unique Considerations," *Adolescence* 30:429–435 (1995).

9. Allison Morris, *Women, Crime, and Criminal Justice* (Oxford, England: Basil Blackwell, 1987).

10. Dennis Giever, "An Empirical Assessment of the Core Elements of Gottfredson and Hirschi's General Theory of Crime." Paper presented to the American Society of Criminology meeting, Boston, November 1995.

11. Loeber and Hay, "Key Issues in the Development of Aggression and Violence," p. 378.

12. John Mirowsky and Catherine Ross, "Sex Differences in Distress: Real or Artifact?" *American Sociological Review* 60:449–468 (1995).

13. Ibid., pp. 460–465.

14. For a review of this issue, see Anne Campbell, *Men, Women, and Aggression* (New York: Basic Books, 1993).

15. Diane Halpern and Mary LaMay, "The Smarter Sex: A Critical Review of Sex Differences in Intelligence," *Educational Psychology Review,* 12:229–246 (2000).

16. Camilla Benbow, David Lubinski, Daniel Shea, and Hossain Eftekhari-Sanjani, "Sex Differences in Mathematical Reasoning Ability at Age 13: Their Status 20 Years Later," *Psychological Science* 11:474–480 (2000).

17. Ann Beutel and Margaret Mooney Marini, "Gender and Values," *American Sociological Review* 60:436–448 (1995).

18. American Association of University Women, *Shortchanging Girls, Shortchanging America: Executive Summary* (Washington, DC: American Association of University Women, 1991).

19. Spencer Rathus, *Voyages in Childhood* (Belmont, CA: Wadsworth, 2004).

20. Carol Gilligan, *In a Different Voice* (Cambridge, MA: Harvard University Press, 1982).

21. David Rowe, Alexander Vazsonyi, and Daniel Flannery, "Sex Differences in Crime: Do Means and Within-Sex Variation Have Similar Causes?" *Journal of Research in Crime and Delinquency* 32:84–100 (1995).

22. Sandra Bem, *The Lenses of Gender* (New Haven: Yale University Press, 1993).

23. Walter DeKeseredy and Martin Schwartz, "Male Peer Support and Woman Abuse," *Sociological Spectrum* 13:393–413 (1993).

24. Jean Bottcher, "Social Practices of Gender: How Gender Relates to Delinquency in the Everyday Lives of High-Risk Youths," *Criminology* 39:893–932 (2001).

25. Daniel Mears, Matthew Ploeger, and Mark Warr, "Explaining the Gender Gap in Delinquency: Peer Influence and Moral Evaluations of Behavior," *Journal of Research in Crime and Delinquency* 35:251–266 (1998).

26. John Gibbs, Dennis Giever, and Jamie Martin, "Parental Management and Self-Control: An Empirical Test of Gottfredson and Hirschi's General Theory," *Journal of Research in Crime and Delinquency* 35:40–70 (1998); Velmer Burton, Francis Cullen, T. David Evans, Leanne Fiftal Alarid, and R. Gregory Dunaway, "Gender, Self-Control, and Crime," *Journal of Research in Crime and Delinquency* 35:123–147 (1998).

27. James Messerschmidt, *Masculinities and Crime: Critique and Reconceptualization of Theory* (Lanham, MD: Rowman and Littlefield, 1993).

28. D. J. Pepler and W. M. Craig, "A Peek Behind the Fence: Naturalistic Observations of Aggressive Children with Remote Audiovisual Recording," *Developmental Psychology* 31:548–553 (1995).

29. Federal Bureau of Investigation, *Crime in the United States, 2002* (Washington, DC: U.S. Government Printing Office, 2003), p. 239.

30. *Monitoring the Future, 2002* (Ann Arbor, MI: Institute for Social Research, 2003).

31. Federal Bureau of Investigation, *Crime in the United States, 2002,* p. 248.

32. Lombroso and Ferrero, *The Female Offender.*

33. Ibid., p. 122.

34. Ibid., pp. 51–52.

35. For a review, see Anne Campbell, *Girl Delinquents* (Oxford, England: Basil Blackwell, 1981), pp. 41–48.

36. Cyril Burt, *The Young Delinquent* (New York: Appleton, 1925); see also Warren Middleton, "Is There a Relation Between Kleptomania and Female Periodicity in Neurotic Individuals?" *Psychology Clinic* (December 1933), pp. 232–247.

37. William Healy and Augusta Bronner, *Delinquents and Criminals: Their Making and Unmaking* (New York: Macmillan, 1926).

38. Ibid., p. 10.

39. Miriam Sealock and Sally Simpson, "Unraveling Bias in Arrest Decisions: The Role of Juvenile Offender Typescripts," *Justice Quarterly* 15:427–457 (1998); Christina Polsenberg and Kenneth Jackson, "Putting Race into Context: Race, Juvenile Justice Processing, and Urbanization." Paper presented at the American Society of Criminology meeting, Boston, November 1995 (rev. version, January 1996); for a general review, see Carl Pope and William Feyerherm, "Minority Status and Juvenile Justice Processing (Part I)," *Criminal Justice Abstracts* 22:327–335 (1990); see also Douglas Smith and Jody Klein, "Police Control of Interpersonal Disputes," *Social Problems* 31:468–481 (1984).

40. Sigmund Freud, *An Outline of Psychoanalysis,* trans. James Strachey (New York: Norton, 1949), p. 278.

41. Dorie Klein, "The Etiology of Female Crime: A Review of the Literature," in Freda Adler and Rita Simon, eds., *The Criminology of Deviant Women* (Boston: Houghton Mifflin, 1979), pp. 69–71.

42. Peter Blos, "Pre-Oedipal Factors in the Etiology of Female Delinquency," *Psychoanalytic Studies of the Child* 12:229–242 (1957).

43. Sheldon Glueck and Eleanor Glueck, *Five Hundred Delinquent Women* (New York: Knopf, 1934).

44. J. Cowie, V. Cowie, and E. Slater, *Delinquency in Girls* (London: Heinemann, 1968).

45. Anne Campbell, "On the Invisibility of the Female Delinquent Peer Group," *Women and Criminal Justice* 2:41–62 (1990).

46. Carolyn Smith, "Factors Associated with Early Sexual Activity Among Urban Adolescents," *Social Work* 42:334–346 (1997).

47. For a review, see Christy Miller Buchanan, Jacquelynne Eccles, and Jill Becker, "Are Adolescents the Victims of Raging Hormones? Evidence for Activational Effects of Hormones on Moods and Behavior at Adolescence," *Psychological Bulletin* 111:63–107 (1992).

48. Dana Haynie, "Contexts of Risk? Explaining the Link Between Girls' Pubertal Development and Their Delinquency Involvement," *Social Forces* 82:355–397 (2003).

49. Avshalom Caspi, Donald Lyman, Terrie Moffitt, and Phil Silva, "Unraveling Girls' Delinquency: Biological, Dispositional, and Contextual Contributions to Adolescent Misbehavior," *Developmental Psychology* 29:283–289 (1993).

50. Eleanor Maccoby and Carol Jacklin, *The Psychology of Sex Differences* (Stanford, CA: Stanford University Press, 1974).

51. Kathleen Pajer, William Gardner, Robert Rubin, James Perel, and Stephen Neal, "Decreased Cortisol Levels in Adolescent Girls with Conduct Disorder," *Archives of General Psychiatry* 58:297–302 (2001).

52. Alan Booth and D. Wayne Osgood, "The Influence of Testosterone on Deviance in Adulthood: Assessing and Explaining the Relationship," *Criminology* 31:93–118 (1993).

53. D. H. Baucom, P. K. Besch, and S. Callahan, "Relationship Between Testosterone Concentration, Sex Role Identity, and Personality Among Females," *Journal of Personality and Social Psychology* 48:1218–1226 (1985).

54. Lee Ellis, "Evidence of Neuroandrogenic Etiology of Sex Roles from a Combined Analysis of Human, Nonhuman Primate, and Nonprimate Mammalian Studies," *Personality and Individual Differences* 7:519–552 (1986).

55. Diana Fishbein, "Selected Studies on the Biology of Antisocial Behavior," in John Conklin, ed., *New Perspectives in Criminology* (Needham Heights, MA: Allyn & Bacon, 1996), pp. 26–38.

56. Diana Fishbein, "The Psychobiology of Female Aggression," *Criminal Justice and Behavior* 19:99–126 (1992).

57. Spencer Rathus, *Psychology,* 3rd ed. (New York: Holt, Rinehart & Winston, 1987), p. 88.

58. See, generally, Katharina Dalton, *The Premenstrual Syndrome* (Springfield, IL: Charles C. Thomas, 1971).

59. Fishbein, "Selected Studies on the Biology of Antisocial Behavior."

60. Fishbein, "Selected Studies on the Biology of Antisocial Behavior"; Karen Paige, "Effects of Oral Contraceptives on Affective Fluctuations Associated with the Menstrual Cycle," *Psychosomatic Medicine* 33:515–537 (1971).

61. B. Harry and C. Balcer, "Menstruation and Crime: A Critical Review of the Literature from the Clinical Criminology Perspective," *Behavioral Sciences and the Law* 5:307–322 (1987).

62. Julie Horney, "Menstrual Cycles and Criminal Responsibility," *Law and Human Nature* 2:25–36 (1978).

63. Lee Ellis, "The Victimful-Victimless Crime Distinction and Seven Universal Demographic Correlates of Victimful Criminal Behavior," *Personality and Individual Differences* 9:525–548 (1988).

64. Maccoby and Jacklin, *The Psychology of Sex Differences.*

65. Lee Ellis, "Evolutionary and Neurochemical Causes of Sex Differences in Victimizing Behavior: Toward a Unified Theory of Criminal Behavior and Social Stratification," *Social Science Information* 28:605–636 (1989).

66. Kathleen Pajer, "What Happens to 'Bad' Girls? A Review of the Adult Outcomes of Antisocial Adolescent Girls," *American Journal of Psychiatry* 155:862–870 (1998).

67. Jan ter Laak, Martijn de Goede, Liesbeth Aleva, Gerard Brugman, Miranda van Leuven, and Judith Hussmann, "Incarcerated Adolescent Girls: Personality, Social Competence, and Delinquency," *Adolescence* 38:251–265 (2003).

68. Dorothy Espelage, Elizabeth Cauffman, Lisa Broidy, Alex Piquero, Paul Mazerolle, and Hans Steiner, "A Cluster-Analytic Investigation of MMPI Profiles of Serious Male and Female Juvenile Offenders," *Journal of the American Academy of Child and Adolescent Psychiatry* 42:770–777 (2003).

69. Kristen McCabe, Amy Lansing, Ann Garland, and Richard Hough, "Gender Differences in Psychopathology, Functional Impairment, and Familial Risk Factors Among Adjudicated Delinquents," *Journal of the American Academy of Child and Adolescent Psychiatry* 41:860–867 (2002).

70. Paul Frick, Amy Cornell, Christopher Barry, Doug Bodin, and Heather Dane, "Callous-Unemotional Traits and Conduct Problems in the Prediction of Conduct Problem Severity, Aggression, and Self-Report of Delinquency," *Journal of Abnormal Child Psychology* 31:457–470 (2003).

71. Alex Mason and Michael Windle, "Gender, Self-Control, and Informal Social Control in Adolescence: A Test of Three Models of the Continuity of Delinquent Behavior," *Youth & Society* 33:479–514 (2002).

72. Thomas, *The Unadjusted Girl.*

73. Ibid., p. 109.

74. David Farrington, "Juvenile Delinquency," in John Coleman, ed., *The School Years* (London: Routledge, 1992), p. 133.

75. Ibid.

76. Ruth Morris, "Female Delinquents and Relational Problems," *Social Forces* 43:82–89 (1964).

77. Cowie, Cowie, and Slater, *Delinquency in Girls*, p. 27.

78. Morris, "Female Delinquency and Relational Problems."

79. Clyde Vedder and Dora Somerville, *The Delinquent Girl* (Springfield, IL: Charles C. Thomas, 1970).

80. Ames Robey, Richard Rosenwal, John Small, and Ruth Lee, "The Runaway Girl: A Reaction to Family Stress," *American Journal of Orthopsychiatry* 34:763–767 (1964).

81. William Wattenberg and Frank Saunders, "Sex Differences Among Juvenile Court Offenders," *Sociology and Social Research* 39:24–31 (1954).

82. Don Gibbons and Manzer Griswold, "Sex Differences Among Juvenile Court Referrals," *Sociology and Social Research* 42:106–110 (1957).

83. Gordon Barker and William Adams, "Comparison of the Delinquencies of Boys and Girls," *Journal of Criminal Law, Criminology, and Police Science* 53:470–475 (1962).

84. George Calhoun, Janelle Jurgens, and Fengling Chen, "The Neophyte Female Delinquent: A Review of the Literature," *Adolescence* 28:461–471 (1993).

85. Joanne Belknap, Kristi Holsinger, and Melissa Dunn, "Understanding Incarcerated Girls: The Results of a Focus Group Study," *Prison Journal* 77:381–405 (1997).

86. Kimberly Barletto, "Who's at Risk: Delinquent Trajectories of Children with Attention and Conduct Problems." Paper presented at the American Society of Criminology meeting, San Diego, November 1997; Veronica Herrera, "Equals in Risk? The Differential Impact of Family Violence on Male and Female Delinquency." Paper presented at the American Society of Criminology meeting, San Diego, November 1997.

87. Meda Chesney-Lind, "Girls' Crime and Women's Place: Toward a Feminist Model of Female Delinquency." Paper presented at the American Society of Criminology meeting, Montreal, November 1987.

88. Ibid., p. 20.

89. Emily Gaarder and Joanne Belknap, "Tenuous Borders: Girls Transferred to Adult Court," *Criminology* 40:481–518 (2002).

90. Joan Moore, *Going Down to the Barrio: Homeboys and Homegirls in Change* (Philadelphia: Temple University Press, 1991), p. 93.

91. Ibid., p. 101.

92. Gaarder and Belknap, "Tenuous Borders."

93. D. Wayne Osgood, Janet Wilson, Patrick O'Malley, Jerald Bachman, and Lloyd Johnston, "Routine Activities and Individual Deviant Behaviors," *American Sociological Review* 61:635–655 (1996).

94. Freda Adler, *Sisters in Crime* (New York: McGraw-Hill, 1975).

95. Ibid., pp. 10–11.

96. Rita James Simon, "Women and Crime Revisited," *Social Science Quarterly* 56:658–663 (1976).

97. Ibid., pp. 660–661.

98. Roy Austin, "Women's Liberation and Increase in Minor, Major, and Occupational Offenses," *Criminology* 20:407–430 (1982).

99. "Delinquency Involvements," *Social Forces* 14:525–534 (1971).

100. Martin Gold, *Delinquent Behavior in an American City* (Pacific Grove, CA: Brooks/Cole, 1970), p. 118; John Clark and Edward Haurek, "Age and Sex Roles of Adolescents and Their Involvement in Misconduct: A Reappraisal," *Sociology and Social Research* 50:495–508 (1966); Nancy Wise, "Juvenile Delinquency in Middle-Class Girls," in E. Vaz, ed., *Middle Class Delinquency* (New York: Harper & Row, 1967), pp. 179–88; Gary Jensen and Raymond Eve, "Sex Differences in Delinquency: An Examination of Popular Sociological Explanations," *Criminology* 13:427–448 (1976).

101. Beth Bjerregaard and Carolyn Smith, "Gender Differences in Gang Participation and Delinquency," *Journal of Quantitative Criminology* 9:329–350 (1993).

102. Darrell Steffensmeier and Dana Haynie, "Gender, Structural Disadvantage, and Urban Crime: Do Macrosocial Variables Also Explain Female Offending Rates?" *Criminology* 38:403–438 (2000).

103. Henry Brownstein, Barry Spunt, Susan Crimmins, and Sandra Langley, "Women Who Kill in Drug Market Situations," *Justice Quarterly* 12:472–498 (1995).

104. Darrell Steffensmeier and Renee Hoffman Steffensmeier, "Trends in Female Delinquency," *Criminology* 18:62–85 (1980); see also, idem, "Crime and the Contemporary Woman: An Analysis of Changing Levels of Female Property Crime, 1960–1975," *Social Forces* 57:566–584 (1978); Darrell Steffensmeier and Michael Cobb, "Sex Differences in Urban Arrest Patterns, 1934–1979," *Social Problems* 29:37–49 (1981).

105. Darrell Steffensmeier, "National Trends in Female Arrests, 1960–1990: Assessment and Recommendations for Research," *Journal of Quantitative Criminology* 9:411–437 (1993).

106. Julia Schwendinger and Herman Schwendinger, *Rape and Inequality* (Beverly Hills, CA: Sage, 1983).

107. For a review of feminist theory, see Sally Simpson, "Feminist Theory, Crime and Justice," *Criminology* 27:605–632 (1989).

108. Ibid., p. 611.

109. Messerschmidt, *Masculinities and Crime.*

110. Center for Research on Women, *Secrets in Public: Sexual Harassment in Our Schools* (Wellesley, MA: Wellesley College, 1993).

111. Belknap, Holsinger, and Dunn, "Understanding Incarcerated Girls."

112. Kathleen Daly and Meda Chesney-Lind, "Feminism and Criminology," *Justice Quarterly* 5:497–538 (1988).

113. Jane Siegel and Linda Williams, "The Relationship Between Child Sexual Abuse and Female Delinquency and Crime: A Prospective Study," *Journal of Research in Crime & Delinquency* 40:71–94 (2003).

114. James Messerschmidt, *Capitalism, Patriarchy, and Crime* (Totowa, NJ: Rowman and Littlefield, 1986); for a critique of this work, see Herman Schwendinger and Julia Schwendinger, "The World According to James Messerschmidt," *Social Justice* 15:123–145 (1988).

115. John Hagan, A. R. Gillis, and John Simpson, "The Class Structure and Delinquency: Toward a Power-Control Theory of Common Delinquent Behavior," *American Journal of Sociology* 90:1151–1178 (1985); John Hagan, John Simpson, and A. R. Gillis, "Class in the Household: A Power-Control Theory of Gender and Delinquency," *American Journal of Sociology* 92:788–816 (1987).

116. John Hagan, A. R. Gillis, and John Simpson, "Clarifying and Extending Power-Control Theory," *American Journal of Sociology* 95:1024–1037 (1990).

117. Gary Jensen and Kevin Thompson, "What's Class Got to Do with It? A Further Examination of Power-Control Theory," *American Jour-*

nal of Sociology 95:1009–1023 (1990); Kevin Thompson, "Gender and Adolescent Drinking Problems: The Effects of Occupational Structure," *Social Problems* 36:30–44 (1989); for some critical research, see Simon Singer and Murray Levine, "Power-Control Theory, Gender, and Delinquency: A Partial Replication with Additional Evidence on the Effects of Peers," *Criminology* 26:627–648 (1988).

118. Christopher Uggen, "Class, Gender, and Arrest: An Intergenerational Analysis of Workplace Power and Control," *Criminology* 38:835–862 (2001).

119. Meda Chesney-Lind, "Judicial Enforcement of the Female Sex Role: The Family Court and the Female Delinquent," *Issues in Criminology* 8:51–59 (1973).

120. Thomas J. Gamble, Sherrie Sonnenberg, John Haltigan, and Amy Cuzzola-Kern, "Detention Screening: Prospects for Population Management and the Examination of Disproportionality by Race, Age, and Gender," *Criminal Justice Policy Review* 13:380–395 (2002); Kimberly Kempf-Leonard and Lisa Sample, "Disparity Based on Sex: Is Gender-Specific Treatment Warranted?" *Justice Quarterly* 17:89–128 (2000).

121. Meda Chesney-Lind and Randall Shelden, *Girls, Delinquency, and Juvenile Justice* (Belmont, CA: West/Wadsworth, 1998).

122. John MacDonald and Meda Chesney-Lind, "Gender Bias and Juvenile Justice Revisited: A Multiyear Analysis," *Crime and Delinquency* 47:173–195 (2001).

123. Meda Chesney-Lind and Vickie Paramore, "Are Girls Getting More Violent? Exploring Juvenile Robbery Trends," *Journal of Contemporary Criminal Justice* 17:142–166 (2001).

124. Belknap, Holsinger, and Dunn, "Understanding Incarcerated Girls."

125. Carol Pepi, "Children Without Childhoods: A Feminist Intervention Strategy Utilizing Systems Theory and Restorative Justice in Treating Female Adolescent Offenders," *Women and Therapy* 20:85–101 (1997).

126. Holly Hartwig and Jane Myers, "A Different Approach: Applying a Wellness Paradigm to Adolescent Female Delinquents and Offenders," *Journal of Mental Health Counseling* 25:57–75 (2003).

127. Jill Leslie Rosenbaum and Meda Chesney-Lind, "Appearance and Delinquency: A Research Note," *Crime and Delinquency* 40:250–261 (1994).

128. Sealock and Simpson, "Unraveling Bias in Arrest Decisions."

129. Chesney-Lind and Shelden, *Girls, Delinquency, and Juvenile Justice,* p. 243.

Chapter 7

1. Paul Amato and Bruce Keith, "Parental Divorce and the Well-Being of Children: A Meta-Analysis," *Psychological Bulletin* 110:26–46 (1991).

2. Rolf Loeber and Magda Stouthamer-Loeber, "Development of Juvenile Aggression and Violence," *American Psychologist* 53:250 (1998).

3. Joan McCord, "Family Relationships, Juvenile Delinquency, and Adult Criminality," *Criminology* 29:397–417 (1991); Scott Henggeler, ed., *Delinquency and Adolescent Psychopathology: A Family Ecological Systems Approach* (Littleton, MA: Wright–PSG, 1982).

4. For a general review of the relationship between families and delinquency, see Alan Jay Lincoln and Murray Straus, *Crime and the Family* (Springfield, IL: Charles C. Thomas, 1985); Rolf Loeber and Magda Stouthamer-Loeber, "Family Factors as Correlates and Predictors of Juvenile Conduct Problems and Delinquency," in Michael Tonry and Norval Morris, eds., *Crime and Justice,* vol. 7 (Chicago: University of Chicago Press, 1986), pp. 29–151.

5. David Farrington, "Juvenile Delinquency," in John Coleman, ed., *The School Years* (London: Routledge, 1992), pp. 139–140.

6. Ruth Inglis, *Sins of the Fathers: A Study of the Physical and Emotional Abuse of Children* (New York: St. Martin's Press, 1978), p. 131.

7. See Joseph J. Costa and Gordon K. Nelson, *Child Abuse and Neglect: Legislation, Reporting, and Prevention* (Lexington, MA: Heath, 1978), p. xiii.

8. Tamar Lewin, "Men Assuming Bigger Role at Home, New Survey Shows," *New York Times,* 15 April 1998, p. A18.

9. U.S. Census Bureau, *Children's Living Arrangements and Characteristics: March 2002,* Detailed Tables for Current Population Report, P20-547. http://www.census.gov/population/www/socdemo/hh-fam/cps2002.html.

10. Terence P. Thornberry, Carolyn A. Smith, Craig Rivera, David Huizinga, and Magda Stouthamer-Loeber, *Family Disruption and Delinquency, Juvenile Justice Bulletin* (Washington, DC: Office of Juvenile Justice and Delinquency Prevention, September 1999).

11. *U.S. Pregnancy Rate Down from Peak; Births and Abortions on the Decline.* Press release (Washington, D.C. Department of Health and Human Services, October 31, 2003); *HHS Report Shows Teen Birth Rate Falls to New Record Low in 2001.* Press release (Washington, DC: Department of Health and Human Services, June 6, 2002).

12. *Kids Count Survey 1998.* News release. (Baltimore: Annie E. Casey Foundation, May 5, 1998).

13. *Kids Count Survey 2003* (Baltimore: Annie E. Casey Foundation, 2003), p. 59.

14. Loeber and Stouthamer-Loeber, "Family Factors," pp. 39–41.

15. Paul Howes and Howard Markman, "Marital Quality and Child Functioning: A Longitudinal Investigation," *Child Development* 60:1044–1051 (1989).

16. Barbara Dafoe Whitehead, "Dan Quayle Was Right," *Atlantic Monthly* 271:47–84 (1993).

17. C. Patrick Brady, James Bray, and Linda Zeeb, "Behavior Problems of Clinic Children: Relation to Parental Marital Status, Age, and Sex of Child," *American Journal of Orthopsychiatry* 56:399–412 (1986).

18. Scott Henggeler, *Delinquency in Adolescence* (Newbury Park, CA: Sage, 1989), p. 48.

19. Thornberry, Smith, Rivera, Huizinga, and Stouthamer-Loeber, *Family Disruption and Delinquency.*

20. Sheldon Glueck and Eleanor Glueck, *Unraveling Juvenile Delinquency* (Cambridge, MA: Harvard University Press, 1950); Ashley Weeks, "Predicting Juvenile Delinquency," *American Sociological Review* 8:40–46 (1943).

21. Jackson Toby, "The Differential Impact of Family Disorganization," *American Sociological Review* 22:505–512 (1957); Ruth Morris, "Female Delinquency and Relation Problems," *Social Forces* 43:82–89 (1964); Roland Chilton and Gerald Markle, "Family Disruption, Delinquent Conduct, and the Effects of Sub-Classification," *American Sociological Review* 37:93–99 (1972).

22. For a review of these early studies, see Thomas Monahan, "Family Status and the Delinquent Child: A Reappraisal and Some New Findings," *Social Forces* 35:250–258 (1957).

23. Clifford Shaw and Henry McKay, *Report on the Causes of Crime: Social Factors in Juvenile Delinquency,* vol. 2 (Washington, DC: U.S. Government Printing Office, 1931), p. 392.

24. John Laub and Robert Sampson, "Unraveling Families and Delinquency: A Reanalysis of the Gluecks' Data," *Criminology* 26:355–380 (1988); Lawrence Rosen, "The Broken Home and Male Delinquency," in M. Wolfgang, L. Savitz and N. Johnston, eds., *The Sociology of Crime and Delinquency* (New York: Wiley, 1970), pp. 489–495.

25. Christina DeJong and Kenneth Jackson, "Putting Race into Context: Race, Juvenile Justice Processing, and Urbanization," *Justice Quarterly* 15:487–504 (1998).

26. Robert Johnson, John Hoffman, and Dean Gerstein, *The Relationship Between Family Structure and Adolescent Substance Abuse* (Washington, DC: Office of Applied Studies, Substance Abuse and Mental Health Services Administration, 1996).

27. Sara McLanahan, "Father Absence and the Welfare of Children." Working paper (Chicago: John D. and Cathcrine T. MacArthur Research Foundation, 1998).

28. Cesar Rebellon, "Reconsidering the Broken Homes/Delinquency Relationship and Exploring Its Mediating Mechanism(s)," *Criminology* 40:103–135 (2002).

29. Ronald Simons, Kuei-Hsiu Lin, Leslie Gordon, Rand Conger, and Frederick Lorenz, "Explaining the Higher Incidence of Adjustment Problems Among Children of Divorce Compared with Those in Two-Parent Families," *Journal of Marriage and the Family* 61:131–148 (1999).

30. Sara Jaffee, Terrie Moffitt, Avshalom Caspi, and Alan Taylor, "Life with (or Without) Father: The Benefits of Living with Two Biological

Parents Depend on the Father's Antisocial Behavior," *Child Development* 74:109–117 (2003).

31. Judith Smetena, "Adolescents' and Parents' Reasoning About Actual Family Conflict," *Child Development* 60:1052–1067 (1989).

32. F. Ivan Nye, "Child Adjustment in Broken and Unhappy Unbroken Homes," *Marriage and Family* 19:356–361 (1957); idem, *Family Relationships and Delinquent Behavior* (New York: Wiley, 1958).

33. Michael Hershorn and Alan Rosenbaum, "Children of Marital Violence: A Closer Look at the Unintended Victims," *American Journal of Orthopsychiatry* 55:260–266 (1985).

34. Peter Jaffe, David Wolfe, Susan Wilson, and Lydia Zak, "Similarities in Behavior and Social Maladjustment Among Child Victims and Witnesses to Family Violence," *American Journal of Orthopsychiatry* 56:142–146 (1986).

35. Veronica Herrera, "Equals in Risk? The Differential Impact of Family Violence on Male and Female Delinquency." Paper presented at the American Society of Criminology meeting, San Diego, November 1997.

36. Henggeler, *Delinquency in Adolescence*, p. 39.

37. Jill Leslie Rosenbaum, "Family Dysfunction and Female Delinquency," *Crime and Delinquency* 35:41.

38. Paul Robinson, "Parents of 'Beyond Control' Adolescents," *Adolescence* 13:116–119 (1978).

39. Loeber and Stouthamer-Loeber, "Development of Juvenile Aggression and Violence," p. 251.

40. Carolyn Smith, Sung Joon Jang, and Susan Stern, "The Effect of Delinquency on Families," *Family and Corrections Network Report* 13:1–11 (1997).

41. Amato and Keith, "Parental Divorce and the Well-Being of Children."

42. Christopher Kierkus and Douglas Baer, "A Social Control Explanation of the Relationship Between Family Structure and Delinquent Behaviour," *Canadian Journal of Criminology,* 44:425–458 (2002).

43. John Paul Wright and Francis Cullen, "Parental Efficacy and Delinquent Behavior: Do Control and Support Matter?" *Criminology* 39:677–706 (2001).

44. Carter Hay, "Parenting, Self-Control, and Delinquency: A Test of Self-Control Theory," *Criminology* 39:707–736 (2001).

45. Roslyn Caldwell, Jenna Silverman, Noelle Lefforge, and Clayton Silver, "Adjudicated Mexican-American Adolescents: The Effects of Familial Emotional Support on Self-Esteem, Emotional Well-Being, and Delinquency," *American Journal of Family Therapy* 32:55–69 (2004).

46. Bill McCarthy and John Hagan, "Mean Streets: The Theoretical Significance of Situational Delinquency Among Homeless Youth," *American Journal of Sociology* 98:597–627 (1992).

47. Carolyn Smith, Alan Lizotte, Terence Thornberry, and Marvin Krohn, "Resilience to Delinquency," *Prevention Researcher* 4:4–7 (1997).

48. Sung Joon Jang and Carolyn Smith, "A Test of Reciprocal Causal Relationships Among Parental Supervision, Affective Ties, and Delinquency," *Journal of Research in Crime and Delinquency* 34:307–336 (1997).

49. Gerald Patterson and Magda Stouthamer-Loeber, "The Correlation of Family Management Practices and Delinquency," *Child Development* 55:1299–1307 (1984); Gerald R. Patterson, *A Social Learning Approach: Coercive Family Process,* vol. 3 (Eugene, OR: Castalia, 1982).

50. Christopher Ellison and Darren Sherkat, "Conservative Protestantism and Support for Corporal Punishment," *American Sociological Review* 58:131–144 (1993).

51. Murray Straus, "Discipline and Deviance: Physical Punishment of Children and Violence and Other Crime in Adulthood," *Social Problems* 38:101–123 (1991).

52. Murray A. Straus, "Spanking and the Making of a Violent Society: The Short- and Long-Term Consequences of Corporal Punishment," *Pediatrics* 98:837–843 (1996).

53. Ibid.

54. Loeber and Stouthamer-Loeber, "Development of Juvenile Aggression and Violence," p. 251.

55. Nathaniel Pallone and James Hennessy, "Brain Dysfunction and Criminal Violence," *Society* 35:21–27 (1998).

56. Nye, *Family Relationships and Delinquent Behavior.*

57. Rolf Loeber and Thomas Dishion, "Boys Who Fight at Home and School: Family Conditions Influencing Cross-Setting Consistency," *Journal of Consulting and Clinical Psychology* 52:759–768 (1984).

58. Lisa Broidy, "Direct Supervision and Delinquency: Assessing the Adequacy of Structural Proxies," *Journal of Criminal Justice* 23:541–554 (1995).

59. Jennifer Beyers, John Bates, Gregory Pettit, and Kenneth Dodge, "Neighborhood Structure, Parenting Processes, and the Development of Youths' Externalizing Behaviors: A Multilevel Analysis," *American Journal of Community Psychology* 31:35–53 (2003).

60. Douglas Downey, "Number of Siblings and Intellectual Development," *American Psychologist* 56:497–504 (2001); idem, "When Bigger Is Not Better: Family Size, Parental Resources, and Children's Educational Performance," *American Sociological Review* 60:746–761 (1995).

61. G. Rahav, "Birth Order and Delinquency," *British Journal of Criminology* 20:385–395 (1980); D. Viles and D. Challinger, "Family Size and Birth Order of Young Offenders," *International Journal of Offender Therapy and Comparative Criminology* 25:60–66 (1981).

62. Thomas Vander Ven, Francis Cullen, Mark Carrozza, and John Paul Wright, "Home Alone: The Impact of Maternal Employment on Delinquency," *Social Problems* 48:236–257 (2001).

63. For an early review, see Barbara Wooton, *Social Science and Social Pathology* (London: Allen and Unwin, 1959).

64. Daniel Shaw, "Advancing Our Understanding of Intergenerational Continuity in Antisocial Behavior," *Journal of Abnormal Child Psychology* 31:193–199 (2003).

65. Donald J. West and David P. Farrington, eds., "Who Becomes Delinquent?" in *The Delinquent Way of Life* (London: Heinemann, 1977); Donald J. West, *Delinquency: Its Roots, Careers, and Prospects* (Cambridge, MA: Harvard University Press, 1982).

66. West, *Delinquency*, p. 114.

67. David Farrington, "Understanding and Preventing Bullying," in Michael Tonry, ed., *Crime and Justice,* vol. 17 (Chicago: University of Chicago Press, 1993), pp. 381–457.

68. Leonore Simon, "Does Criminal Offender Treatment Work?" *Applied and Preventive Psychology,* Summer 1–22 (1998).

69. Philip Harden and Robert Pihl, "Cognitive Function, Cardiovascular Reactivity, and Behavior in Boys at High Risk for Alcoholism," *Journal of Abnormal Psychology* 104:94–103 (1995).

70. Laub and Sampson, "Unraveling Families and Delinquency," p. 370.

71. David P. Farrington, Gwen Gundry, and Donald J. West, "The Familial Transmission of Criminality," in Alan Lincoln and Murray Straus, eds., *Crime and the Family* (Springfield, IL: Charles C. Thomas, 1985), pp. 193–206.

72. Abigail Fagan and Jake Najman, "Sibling Influences on Adolescent Delinquent Behaviour: An Australian Longitudinal Study," *Journal of Adolescence* 26:546–558 (2003).

73. David Rowe and Bill Gulley, "Sibling Effects on Substance Use and Delinquency," *Criminology* 30:217–232 (1992); see also David Rowe, Joseph Rogers, and Sylvia Meseck-Bushey, "Sibling Delinquency and the Family Environment: Shared and Unshared Influences," *Child Development* 63:59–67 (1992).

74. Richard Gelles and Claire Pedrick Cornell, *Intimate Violence in Families,* 2nd ed. (Newbury Park, CA: Sage, 1990), p. 33.

75. Lois Hochhauser, "Child Abuse and the Law: A Mandate for Change," *Harvard Law Journal* 18:200 (1973); see also Douglas J. Besharov, "The Legal Aspects of Reporting Known and Suspected Child Abuse and Neglect," *Villanova Law Review* 23:458 (1978).

76. C. Henry Kempe, F. N. Silverman, B. F. Steele, W. Droegemueller, and H. K. Silver, "The Battered-Child Syndrome," *Journal of the American Medical Association* 181:17–24 (1962).

77. Brian G. Fraser, "A Glance at the Past, a Gaze at the Present, a Glimpse at the Future: A Critical Analysis of the Development of Child Abuse Reporting Statutes," *Chicago-Kent Law Review* 54:643 (1977–78).

78. See, especially, Inglis, *Sins of the Fathers,* ch. 8.

79. William Downs and Brenda Miller, "Relationships Between Experiences of Parental Violence During Childhood and Women's Self-Esteem," *Violence and Victims* 13:63–78 (1998).

80. Ruth S. Kempe and C. Henry Kempe, *Child Abuse* (Cambridge, MA: Harvard University Press, 1978), pp. 6–7.

81. Joseph Price and Kathy Glad, "Hostile Attributional Tendencies in Maltreated Children," *Journal of Abnormal Child Psychology* 31:329–344 (2003).

82. Herman Daldin, "The Fate of the Sexually Abused Child," *Clinical Social Work Journal* 16:20–26 (1988).

83. Judith Herman, Diana Russell, and Karen Trocki, "Long-Term Effects of Incestuous Abuse in Childhood," *American Journal of Psychiatry* 143:1293–1296 (1986).

84. Kathleen Kendall-Tackett, Linda Meyer Williams, and David Finkelhor, "Impact of Sexual Abuse on Children: A Review and Synthesis of Recent Empirical Studies," *Psychological Bulletin* 113:164–180 (1993).

85. Magnus Seng, "Child Sexual Abuse and Adolescent Prostitution: A Comparative Analysis," *Adolescence* 24:665–675 (1989); Dorothy Bracey, *Baby Pros: Preliminary Profiles of Juvenile Prostitutes* (New York: John Jay Press, 1979).

86. Xavier Coll, Fergus Law, Aurelio Tobias, Keith Hawton, and Josep Tomas, "Abuse and Deliberate Self-Poisoning in Women: A Matched Case-Control Study," *Child Abuse and Neglect* 25:1291–1293 (2001).

87. Murray Straus, Richard Gelles, and Suzanne Steinmentz, *Behind Closed Doors: Violence in the American Family* (Garden City, NY: Anchor Books, 1980); Richard Gelles and Murray Straus, "Violence in the American Family," *Journal of Social Issues* 35:15–39 (1979).

88. Gelles and Straus, "Violence in the American Family," p. 24.

89. Richard Gelles and Murray Straus, *The Causes and Consequences of Abuse in the American Family* (New York: Simon & Schuster, 1988); see also Murray A. Straus and Glenda Kaufman Kantor, "Trends in Physical Abuse by Parents from 1975 to 1992: A Comparison of Three National Surveys." Paper presented at the annual meeting of the American Society of Criminology, Boston, November 1995.

90. Murray A. Straus and Anita K. Mathur, "Social Change and Trends in Approval of Corporal Punishment by Parents from 1968 to 1994," in D. Frehsee, W. Horn, and K. Bussman, eds., *Violence Against Children* (New York: Aldine de Gruyter, 1996), pp. 91–105.

91. Richard Estes and Neil Alan Weiner, *The Commercial Sexual Exploitation of Children in the U.S., Canada and Mexico* (Philadelphia: University of Pennsylvania, 2001).

92. Lisa Jones and David Finkelhor, *The Decline in Child Sexual Abuse Cases* (Washington, DC: Office of Juvenile Justice and Delinquency Prevention, 2001).

93. Carolyn Webster-Stratton, "Comparison of Abusive and Non-abusive Families with Conduct-Disordered Children," *American Journal of Orthopsychiatry* 55:59–69 (1985); Brandt F. Steele and Carl B. Pollock, "A Psychiatric Study of Parents Who Abuse Infants and Small Children," in Ray Helfer and C. Henry Kempe, eds., *The Battered Child* (Chicago: University of Chicago Press, 1968), pp. 103–145.

94. Brandt F. Steele, "Violence Within the Family," in Ray E. Helfer and C. Henry Kempe, eds., *Child Abuse and Neglect: The Family and the Community* (Cambridge, MA: Ballinger, 1976), p. 13.

95. William Sack, Robert Mason, and James Higgins, "The Single-Parent Family and Abusive Punishment," *American Journal of Orthopsychiatry* 55:252–259 (1985).

96. Blair Justice and Rita Justice, *The Abusing Family* (New York: Human Sciences Press, 1976); Nanette Dembitz, "Preventing Youth Crime by Preventing Child Neglect," *American Bar Association Journal* 65:920–923 (1979).

97. Douglas Ruben, *Treating Adult Children of Alcoholics: A Behavioral Approach* (New York: Academic Press, 2000).

98. Martin Daly and Margo Wilson, "Violence Against Stepchildren," *Current Directions in Psychological Science* 5:77–81 (1996).

99. Ibid.

100. Margo Wilson, Martin Daly, and Atonietta Daniele, "Familicide: The Killing of Spouse and Children," *Aggressive Behavior* 21:275–291 (1995).

101. Richard Gelles, "Child Abuse and Violence in Single-Parent Families: Parent Absence and Economic Deprivation," *American Journal of Orthopsychiatry* 59:492–501 (1989).

102. Susan Napier and Mitchell Silverman, "Family Violence as a Function of Occupation Status, Socioeconomic Class, and Other Variables." Paper presented at the American Society of Criminology meeting, Boston, November 1995.

103. Robert Burgess and Patricia Draper, "The Explanation of Family Violence," in Lloyd Ohlin and Michael Tonry, eds., *Family Violence* (Chicago: University of Chicago Press, 1989), pp. 59–117.

104. Ibid., pp. 103–104.

105. *Troxel et vir. v. Granville* No. 99–138 (June 5, 2000).

106. 452 U.S. 18, 101 S.Ct. 2153 (1981); 455 U.S. 745, 102 S.Ct. 1388 (1982).

107. For a survey of each state's reporting requirements, abuse and neglect legislation, and available programs and agencies, see Costa and Nelson, *Child Abuse and Neglect*.

108. Linda Gordon, "Incest and Resistance: Patterns of Father-Daughter Incest, 1880–1930," *Social Problems* 33:253–267 (1986).

109. P.L. 93B247 (1974); P.L. 104B235 (1996).

110. Barbara Ryan, "Do You Suspect Child Abuse? The Story of 2-Year-Old Dominic James Made Headlines Not Only Because of His Tragic Death, But Because Criminal Charges Were Lodged Against a Nurse for Failing to Report His Suspicious Injuries. A Cautionary Tale," *RN* 66:73–76 (2003).

111. Robin Fretwell Wilson, "Children at Risk: The Sexual Exploitation of Female Children After Divorce," *Cornell Law Review* 86:251–327 (2001).

112. Sue Badeau and Sarah Gesiriech, *A Child's Journey Through the Child Welfare System* (Washington, DC: The Pew Commission on Children in Foster Care, December 13, 2003); Shirley Dobbin, Sophia Gatowski, and Margaret Springate, "Child Abuse and Neglect," *Juvenile and Family Court Journal* 48:43–54 (1997).

113. For an analysis of the accuracy of children's recollections of abuse, see Candace Kruttschnitt and Maude Dornfeld, "Will They Tell? Assessing Preadolescents' Reports of Family Violence," *Journal of Research in Crime and Delinquency* 29:136–147 (1992).

114. Ibid.

115. Debra Whitcomb, *When the Victim Is a Child* (Washington, DC: National Institute of Justice, 1992), p. 33.

116. *White v. Illinois*, 502 U.S. 346; 112 S.Ct. 736 (1992).

117. Myrna Raeder, "*White's* Effect on the Right to Confront One's Accuser," *Criminal Justice*, Winter 2–7 (1993).

118. *Coy v. Iowa*, 487 U.S. 1012 (1988).

119. *Maryland v. Craig*, 110 S.Ct. 3157 (1990).

120. *Walker v. Fagg*, 400 S.E. 2d 708 (Va. App. 1991).

121. Wendy Fisk, "Childhood Trauma and Dissociative Identity Disorder," *Child and Adolescent Psychiatric Clinics of North America* 5:431–447 (1996).

122. Mary Haskett and Janet Kistner, "Social Interactions and Peer Perceptions of Young Physically Abused Children," *Child Development* 62:679–690 (1991).

123. Gelles and Straus, "Violence in the American Family."

124. National Center on Child Abuse and Neglect, Department of Health, Education, and Welfare, *1977 Analysis of Child Abuse and Neglect Research* (Washington, DC: U.S. Government Printing Office, 1978), p. 29.

125. Steele, "Violence Within the Family," p. 22.

126. L. Bender and F. J. Curran, "Children and Adolescents Who Kill," *Journal of Criminal Psychopathology* 1:297 (1940), cited in Steele, "Violence Within the Family," p. 21.

127. W. M. Easson and R. M. Steinhilber, "Murderous Aggression by Children and Adolescents," *Archives of General Psychiatry* 4:1–11 (1961), cited in Steele, "Violence Within the Family," p. 22; see also J. Duncan and G. Duncan, "Murder in the Family: A Study of Some Homicidal Adolescents," *American Journal of Psychiatry* 127:1498–1502 (1971); C. King, "The Ego and Integration of Violence in Homicidal Youth," *American Journal of Orthopsychiatry* 45:134–145 (1975); James Sorrells, "Kids Who Kill," *Crime and Delinquency* 23:312–326 (1977).

128. Jose Alfaro, "Report of the Relationship Between Child Abuse and Neglect and Later Socially Deviant Behavior." Unpublished paper (Albany, NY: New York State Government, n.d.), pp. 175–219.

129. Cathy Spatz Widom, "Child Abuse, Neglect, and Violent Criminal Behavior," *Criminology* 27:251–271 (1989).

130. Cathy Spatz Widom, "The Cycle of Violence." *Science* 244(4901):160–166 (April 14, 1989).

131. Michael Maxfield and Cathy Spatz Widom, "Childhood Victimization and Patterns of Offending Through the Life Cycle: Early Onset and Continuation." Paper presented at the American Society of Criminology meeting, Boston, November 1995.

132. Jane Siegel and Linda Meyer Williams, "Violent Behavior Among Men Abused as Children." Paper presented at the American Society of Criminology meeting, Boston, November 1995; Jane Siegel and Linda Meyer Williams, "Aggressive Behavior Among Women Sexually Abused as Children." Paper presented at the American Society of Criminology meeting, Phoenix, 1993 (rev. version).

133. David Skuse, Arnon Bentovim, Jill Hodges, Jim Stevenson, Chriso Andreou, Monica Lanyado, Michelle New, Bryn Williams, and Dean McMillan, "Risk Factors for Development of Sexually Abusive Behaviour in Sexually Victimised Adolescent Boys: Cross Sectional Study," *British Medical Journal* 317:175–180 (1998).

134. Carolyn Smith and Terence Thornberry, "The Relationship Between Childhood Maltreatment and Adolescent Involvement in Delinquency," *Criminology* 33:451–477 (1995).

135. Widom, "Child Abuse, Neglect, and Violent Criminal Behavior," p. 267.

136. Matthew Zingraff, "Child Maltreatment and Youthful Problem Behavior," *Criminology* 31:173–202 (1993); Bruce Rind, Philip Tromovitch, and Robert Bauserman, "A Meta-Analytic Examination of Assumed Properties of Child Sexual Abuse Using College Samples," *Psychological Bulletin* 124:22–53 (1998); Kimberly Barletto, "Who's at Risk: Delinquent Trajectories of Children with Attention and Conduct Problems." Paper presented at the American Society of Criminology meeting, San Diego, 1997; Veronica Herrera, "Equals in Risk? The Differential Impact of Family Violence on Male and Female Delinquency." Paper presented at the American Society of Criminology meeting, San Diego, November, 1997.

137. Timothy Ireland, Carolyn Smith, and Terence Thornberry, "Developmental Issues in the Impact of Child Maltreatment on Later Delinquency and Drug Use," *Criminology* 40:359–401 (2002).

Chapter 8

1. For a general review, see Scott Cummings and Daniel Monti, *Gangs: The Origin and Impact of Contemporary Youth Gangs in the United States* (Albany: SUNY Press, 1993); this chapter also makes extensive use of George Knox et al., *Gang Prevention and Intervention: Preliminary Results from the 1995 Gang Research Task Force* (Chicago: National Gang Crime Research Center, 1995).

2. Paul Perrone and Meda Chesney-Lind, "Representations of Gangs and Delinquency: Wild in the Streets?" *Social Justice* 24:96–117 (1997).

3. Thomas Berndt and T. B. Perry, "Children's Perceptions of Friendships as Supportive Relationships," *Developmental Psychology* 22:640–648 (1986).

4. Spencer Rathus, *Understanding Child Development* (New York: Holt, Rinehart & Winston, 1988), p. 462.

5. Peggy Giordano, "The Wider Circle of Friends in Adolescence," *American Journal of Sociology* 101:661–697 (1995).

6. Shari Miller-Johnson, Philip Costanzo, John Coie, Mary Rose, Dorothy Browne, and Courtney Johnson, "Peer Social Structure and Risk-Taking Behaviors Among African-American Early Adolescents," *Journal of Youth and Adolescence* 32:375–384 (2003).

7. John Coie and Shari Miller-Johnson, "Peer Factors in Early Offending Behavior." In Rolf Loeber and David Farrington (eds.), *Child Delinquents* (Thousand Oaks, CA: Sage, 2001), pp. 191–210.

8. Ibid.

9. Judith Rich Harris, *The Nurture Assumption: Why Children Turn Out the Way They Do* (New York: Free Press, 1998).

10. Ibid., p. 463.

11. Albert Reiss, "Co-Offending and Criminal Careers," in Michael Tonry and Norval Morris, eds., *Crime and Justice*, vol. 10 (Chicago: University of Chicago Press, 1988).

12. Robert Agnew and Timothy Brezina, "Relational Problems with Peers, Gender, and Delinquency," *Youth and Society* 29:84–111 (1997).

13. Richard Felson and Dana Haynie, "Pubertal Development, Social Factors, and Delinquency Among Adolescent Boys," *Criminology* 40:967–989 (2002).

14. See Travis Hirschi, *Causes of Delinquency* (Berkeley: University of California Press, 1969).

15. James Short and Fred Strodtbeck, *Group Process and Gang Delinquency* (Chicago: Aldine de Gruyter, 1965).

16. Kate Keenan, Rolf Loeber, Quanwu Zhang, Magda Stouthamer-Loeber, and Welmoet Van Kammen, "The Influence of Deviant Peers on the Development of Boys' Disruptive and Delinquent Behavior: A Temporal Analysis," *Development and Psychopathology* 7:715–726 (1995).

17. John Cole, Robert Terry, Shari-Miller Johnson, and John Lochman, "Longitudinal Effects of Deviant Peer Groups on Criminal Offending in Late Adolescence." Paper presented at the American Society of Criminology meeting, Boston, November 1995.

18. Terence Thornberry and Marvin Krohn, "Peers, Drug Use, and Delinquency," in David Stoff, James Breiling, and Jack Maser, eds., *Handbook of Antisocial Behavior* (New York: Wiley, 1997), pp. 218–233; Thomas Dishion, Deborah Capaldi, Kathleen Spracklen, and Fuzhong Li, "Peer Ecology of Male Adolescent Drug Use," *Development and Psychopathology* 7:803–824 (1995).

19. Mark Warr, "Age, Peers, and Delinquency," *Criminology* 31:17–40 (1993).

20. Sara Battin, Karl Hill, Robert Abbott, Richard Catalano, and J. David Hawkins, "The Contribution of Gang Membership to Delinquency Beyond Delinquent Friends," *Criminology* 36:93–116 (1998).

21. Mark Warr, "Life-Course Transitions and Desistance from Crime," *Criminology* 36:502–536 (1998).

22. Stephen W. Baron, "Self-Control, Social Consequences, and Criminal Behavior: Street Youth and the General Theory of Crime," *Journal of Research in Crime and Delinquency* 40:403–425 (2003).

23. Daneen Deptula and Robert Cohen, "Aggressive, Rejected, and Delinquent Children and Adolescents: A Comparison of Their Friendships," *Aggression & Violent Behavior* 9:75–104 (2004).

24. David Farrington and Rolf Loeber, "Epidemiology of Juvenile Violence," *Child and Adolescent Psychiatric Clinics of North America* 9:733–748 (2000).

25. Peggy Giordano, Stephen Cernkovich, and M. D. Pugh, "Friendships and Delinquency," *American Journal of Sociology* 91:1170–1202 (1986).

26. Well-known movie representations of gangs include *The Wild Ones* and *Hell's Angels on Wheels*, which depict motorcycle gangs, and *Saturday Night Fever*, which focused on neighborhood street toughs; see also David Dawley, *A Nation of Lords* (Garden City, NY: Anchor, 1973).

27. For a recent review of gang research, see James Howell, "Recent Gang Research: Program and Policy Implications," *Crime and Delinquency* 40:495–515 (1994).

28. Walter Miller, *Violence by Youth Gangs and Youth Groups as a Crime Problem in Major American Cities* (Washington, DC: U.S. Government Printing Office, 1975).

29. Ibid., p. 20.

30. Malcolm Klein, *The American Street Gang: Its Nature, Prevalence, and Control* (New York: Oxford University Press, 1995), p. 30.

31. Irving Spergel, *The Youth Gang Problem: A Community Approach* (New York: Oxford University Press, 1995).

32. Ibid., p. 3.

33. Christopher Adamson, "Defensive Localism in White and Black: A Comparative History of European-American and African-American Youth Gangs," *Ethnic & Racial Studies*, 23: 272–298 (2000).

34. Frederick Thrasher, *The Gang* (Chicago: University of Chicago Press, 1927).

35. National Youth Gang Center, 2003. www.iir.com/nygc/faq.htm#q1.

36. Irving Spergel, *Street Gang Work: Theory and Practice* (Reading, MA: Addison-Wesley, 1966).

37. Miller, *Violence by Youth Gangs*, p. 2.

38. Miller, *Violence by Youth Gangs*, pp. 1–2.

39. Ibid.

40. C. Ronald Huff, "Youth Gangs and Public Policy," *Crime and Delinquency* 35:524–537 (1989).

41. Felix Padilla, *The Gang as an American Enterprise* (New Brunswick, NJ: Rutgers University Press, 1992), p. 3.

42. Pamela Irving Jackson, "Crime, Youth Gangs, and Urban Transition: The Social Dislocations of Postindustrial Economic Development," *Justice Quarterly* 8:379–897 (1991); Moore, *Going Down to the Barrio*, pp. 89–101.

43. Arlen Egley and Aline Major, *2001 Youth Gang Survey* (Washington, DC: Office of Juvenile Justice and Delinquency Prevention, 2003). Herein cited as 2001 National Youth Gang Survey; see also Arlen Egley, Aline Major, and James Howell, *National Youth Gang Survey: 1999–2001* (Tallahassee, FL: National Youth Gang Center, forthcoming 2004).

44. Arlen Egley, *National Youth Gang Survey Trends from 1996 to 2000.* Fact sheet (Washington, DC: Bureau of Justice Statistics, 2002).

45. Finn-Aage Esbensen and Elizabeth Deschenes, "A Multisite Examination of Gang Membership: Does Gender Matter?" *Criminology* 36:799–827 (1998).

46. William Julius Wilson, *The Truly Disadvantaged* (Chicago: University of Chicago Press, 1987).

47. Ibid.

48. 2001 National Youth Gang Survey.

49. Cheryl Maxson, *Gang Members on the Move.* Bulletin, Youth Gang Series (Washington, DC: Office of Juvenile Justice and Delinquency Prevention, 1998).

50. Ibid.

51. Fagan, "The Social Organization of Drug Use and Drug Dealing Among Urban Gangs."

52. Richard Cloward and Lloyd Ohlin, *Delinquency and Opportunity* (New York: Free Press, 1960), pp. 1–12

53. Fagan, "The Social Organization of Drug Use and Drug Dealing Among Urban Gangs."

54. Lewis Yablonsky, *The Violent Gang* (Baltimore: Penguin, 1966), p. 109.

55. James Diego Vigil, *Barrio Gangs* (Austin: Texas University Press, 1988), pp. 11–19.

56. Mark Warr, "Organization and Instigation in Delinquent Groups," *Criminology* 34:11–37 (1996).

57. Knox et al., *Gang Prevention and Intervention*, p. vii.

58. Ibid.

59. Wilson, *The Truly Disadvantaged.*

60. Ibid.

61. John Hagedorn, Jerome Wonders, Angelo Vega, and Joan Moore, "The Milwaukee Drug Posse Study," unpublished leaflet, n.d.

62. John M. Hagedorn, Jose Torres, Greg Giglio. "Cocaine, Kicks, and Strain: Patterns of Substance Use in Milwaukee Gangs," *Contemporary Drug Problems* 25:113–145 (1998).

63. Finn-Aage Esbensen, "Race and Gender Differences Between Gang and Nongang Youths: Results from a Multisite Survey," *Justice Quarterly* 15:504–525 (1998).

64. Ibid.

65. Cheryl Maxson and Monica Whitlock, "Joining the Gang: Gender Differences in Risk Factors for Gang Membership." In C. Ronald Huff, ed., *Gangs in America III* (Thousand Oaks, CA: Sage, 2002), pp. 19–35.

66. Karen Joe Laidler and Geoffrey Hunt, "Violence and Social Organization in Female Gangs," *Social Justice* 24:148–87 (1997); Moore, *Going Down to the Barrio;* Anne Campbell, *The Girls in the Gang* (Cambridge, MA: Basil Blackwell, 1984).

67. Karen Joe Laidler and Meda Chesney-Lind, "'Just Every Mother's Angel': An Analysis of Gender and Ethnic Variations in Youth Gang Membership," *Gender and Society* 9:408–430 (1995).

68. Jody Miller, *One of the Guys: Girls, Gangs, and Gender* (New York: Oxford University Press, 2001).

69. Ibid.

70. Joan Moore, James Diego Vigil, and Robert Garcia, "Residence and Territoriality in Chicano Gangs," *Social Problems* 31:182–194 (1983).

71. Mark Warr, "Organization and Instigation in Delinquent Groups," *Criminology* 34:11–37 (1996).

72. Malcolm Klein, "Impressions of Juvenile Gang Members," *Adolescence* 3:59 (1968).

73. Scott Decker, Tim Bynum, and Deborah Weisel, "A Tale of Two Cities: Gangs and Organized Crime Groups", *Justice Quarterly* 15:395–425 (1998).

74. 2001 National Youth Gang Survey.

75. Data provided by the National Youth Gang Center, 2003. www.iir.com/nygc/faq.htm#q6.

76. The following description of ethnic gangs leans heavily on the material developed in National School Safety Center, *Gangs in Schools*, pp. 11–23.

77. Spergel, *The Youth Gang Problem*, pp. 136–137.

78. Decker, Bynum, and Weisel, "A Tale of Two Cities."

79. Thomas Winfree Jr., Frances Bernat, Finn-Aage Esbensen, "Hispanic and Anglo Gang Membership in Two Southwestern Cities," *Social Science Journal* 38:105–118 (2001).

80. Los Angeles County Sheriff's Department, *Street Gangs of Los Angeles County.*

81. Ko-Lin Chin, *Chinese Subculture and Criminality: Nontraditional Crime Groups in America* (Westport, CT: Greenwood Press, 1990).

82. James Diego Vigil and Steve Chong Yun, "Vietnamese Youth Gangs in Southern California," in C. Ronald Huff, ed., *Gangs in America* (Newbury Park, CA: Sage, 1990), pp. 146–163.

83. See Glazier, "Small Town Delinquent Gangs."

84. For a review, see Lawrence Trostle, *The Stoners, Drugs, Demons and Delinquency* (New York: Garland, 1992).

85. Esbensen, "Race and Gender Differences Between Gang and Nongang Youths."

86. Terence Thornberry and James H. Burch, *Gang Members and Delinquent Behavior* (Washington, DC: Office of Juvenile Justice and Delinquency Prevention, 1997).

87. G. David Curry, Scott Decker, and Arlen Egley Jr., "Gang Involvement and Delinquency in a Middle School Population," *Justice Quarterly* 19:275–292 (2002).

88. Malcolm Klein, Cheryl Maxson, and Lea Cunningham, "Crack, Street Gangs, and Violence," *Criminology* 4:623–650 (1991); Mel Wallace, "The Gang-Drug Debate Revisited." Paper presented at the annual meeting of the American Society of Criminology, New Orleans, November 1992.

89. Kevin Thompson, David Brownfield, and Ann Marie Sorenson, "Specialization Patterns of Gang and Nongang Offending: A Latent Structure Analysis," *Journal of Gang Research* 3:25–35 (1996).

90. Sara Battin, Karl Hill, Robert Abbott, Richard Catalano, and J. David Hawkins, "The Contribution of Gang Membership to Delinquency Beyond Delinquent Friends," *Criminology* 36:93–116 (1998).

91. National Youth Gang Survey, 2001.

92. Geoffrey Hunt, Karen Joe Laidler, and Kristy Evans, "The Meaning and Gendered Culture of Getting High: Gang Girls and Drug Use Issues," *Contemporary Drug Problems* 29:375 (2002).

93. Terence P. Thornberry and James H. Burch, *Gang Members and Delinquent Behavior;* James C. Howell, "Youth Gang Drug Trafficking and Homicide: Policy and Program Implications," *Juvenile Justice Journal* 4:3–5 (1997).

94. Scott Decker, "Collective and Normative Features of Gang Violence," *Justice Quarterly* 13:243–264 (1996).

95. Terence Thornberry, Marvin Krohn, Alan Lizotte, Carolyn Smith, and Kimberly Tobin, *Gangs and Delinquency in Developmental Perspective* (New York: Cambridge University Press, 2003).

96. Ibid.

97. Ibid.

98. James C. Howell, "Youth Gang Drug Trafficking and Homicide: Policy and Program Implications," *Juvenile Justice Journal* 4:3–5 (1997).

99. Beth Bjerregaard and Alan Lizotte, "Gun Ownership and Gang Membership," *Journal of Criminal Law and Criminology* 86:37–53 (1995).

100. Ibid.

101. Pamela Lattimore, Richard Linster, and John MacDonald, "Risk of Death Among Serious Young Offenders," *Journal of Research in Crime and Delinquency* 34:187–209 (1997).

102. Decker, "Collective and Normative Features of Gang Violence."

103. Gini Sykes, *8 Ball Chicks: A Year in the Violent World of Girl Gangsters* (New York: Doubleday, 1998), pp. 2–11.

104. H. Range Hutson, Deirdre Anglin, and Michael Pratts Jr., "Adolescents and Children Injured or Killed in Drive-By Shootings in Los Angeles," *New England Journal of Medicine* 330:324–327 (1994).

Miller, *Violence by Youth Gangs*, pp. 2–26.

105. Herbert Block and Arthur Niederhoffer, *The Gang: A Study in Adolescent Behavior* (New York: Philosophical Library, 1958).

106. Ibid., p. 113.

107. Knox et al., *Gang Prevention and Intervention*, p. 44.

108. James Diego Vigil, "Group Processes and Street Identity: Adolescent Chicano Gang Members," *Ethos* 16:421–445 (1988).

109. James Diego Vigil and John Long, "Emic and Etic Perspectives on Gang Culture: The Chicano Case," in C. Ronald Huff, ed., *Gangs in America* (Newbury Park, CA: Sage, 1990), p. 66.

110. Albert Cohen, *Delinquent Boys* (New York: Free Press, 1955), pp. 1–19.

111. Irving Spergel, *Racketville, Slumtown, and Haulburg: An Exploratory Study of Delinquent Subcultures* (Chicago: University of Chicago Press, 1964).

112. Malcolm Klein, *Street Gangs and Street Workers* (Englewood Cliffs, NJ: Prentice-Hall, 1971), pp. 12–15.

113. Vigil, *Barrio Gangs*.

114. Vigil and Long, "Emic and Etic Perspectives on Gang Culture," p. 61.

115. David Brownfield, Kevin Thompson, and Ann Marie Sorenson, "Correlates of Gang Membership: A Test of Strain, Social Learning, and Social Control," *Journal of Gang Research* 4:11–22 (1997).

116. John Hagedorn, Jose Torres, and Greg Giglio, "Cocaine, Kicks, and Strain: Patterns of Substance Use in Milwaukee Gangs," *Contemporary Drug Problems* 25:113–145 (1998).

117. Spergel, *The Youth Gang Problem*, pp. 4–5.

118. Ibid.

119. Yablonsky, *The Violent Gang*, p. 237.

120. Ibid., pp. 239–241.

121. Klein, *The American Street Gang*.

122. Thornberry, Krohn, Lizotte, Smith, and Tobin, *Gangs and Delinquency in Developmental Perspective*.

123. Mercer Sullivan, *Getting Paid: Youth Crime and Work in the Inner City* (Ithaca, NY: Cornell University Press, 1989), pp. 244–245.

124. Finn-Aage Esbensen and David Huizinga, "Gangs, Drugs, and Delinquency in a Survey of Urban Youth," *Criminology* 31:565–587 (1993); G. David Curry and Irving Spergel, "Gang Involvement and Delinquency Among Hispanic and African-American Adolescent Males," *Journal of Research in Crime and Delinquency* 29:273–291 (1992).

125. Padilla, *The Gang as an American Enterprise*, p. 103.

126. Terence Thornberry, Marvin Krohn, Alan Lizotte, and Deborah Chard-Wierschem, "The Role of Juvenile Gangs in Facilitating Delinquent Behavior," *Journal of Research in Crime and Delinquency* 30:55–87 (1993).

127. Spergel, *The Youth Gang Problem*, pp. 93–94.

128. Miller, *One of the Guys.*

129. Ibid., p. 93.

130. L. Thomas Winfree Jr., Teresa Vigil Backstrom, and G. Larry Mays, "Social Learning Theory, Self-Reported Delinquency, and Youth Gangs: A New Twist on a General Theory of Crime and Delinquency," *Youth and Society* 26:147–177 (1994).

131. Karen Joe Laidler and Geoffrey Hunt, "Violence and Social Organization in Female Gangs," *Social Justice* 24:148–187 (1997).

132. Jerome Needle and W. Vaughan Stapleton, *Reports of the National Juvenile Justice Assessment Centers, Police Handling of Youth Gangs* (Washington, DC: Office of Juvenile Justice and Delinquency Prevention, 1983).

133. Scott Armstrong, "Los Angeles Seeks New Ways to Handle Gangs," *Christian Science Monitor*, 23 April 1988, p. 3.

134. Mark Moore and Mark A. R. Kleiman, *The Police and Drugs* (Washington, DC: National Institute of Justice, 1989), p. 8.

135. Barry Krisberg, "Preventing and Controlling Violent Youth Crime: The State of the Art," in Ira Schwartz, ed., *Violent Juvenile Crime* (Minneapolis: University of Minnesota, Hubert Humphrey Institute of Public Affairs, n.d.).

136. For a revisionist view of gang delinquency, see Hedy Bookin-Weiner and Ruth Horowitz, "The End of the Youth Gang," *Criminology* 21:585–602 (1983).

137. Quint Thurman, Andrew Giacomazzi, Michael Reisig, and David Mueller, "Community-Based Gang Prevention and Intervention: An Evaluation of the Neutral Zone," *Crime and Delinquency* 42:279–296 (1996).

138. Michael Agopian, "Evaluation of the Gang Alternative Prevention Program." Paper presented at the American Society of Criminology meeting, Boston, November 1995.

139. James Houston, "What Works: The Search for Excellence in Gang Intervention Programs." Paper presented at the American Society of Criminology meeting, Boston, November 1995.

140. Hagedorn, "Gangs, Neighborhoods, and Public Policy."

141. Curry and Spergel, "Gang Involvement and Delinquency Among Hispanic and African-American Adolescent Males."

Chapter 9

1. U.S. Senate Subcommittee on Delinquency, *Challenge for the Third Century: Education in a Safe Environment* (Washington, DC: U.S. Government Printing Office, 1977), p. 1.

2. Alexander Vazsonyi and Lloyd Pickering, "The Importance of Family and School Domains in Adolescent Deviance: African-American and Caucasian Youth," *Journal of Youth and Adolescence* 32:115–129 (2003); Delbert S. Eliott and Harwin L. Voss, *Delinquency and the Dropout* (Lexington, MA: Lexington Books, 1974), p. 204.

3. See, generally, Richard Lawrence, *School Crime and Juveniles* (New York: Oxford University Press, 1998).

4. U.S. Office of Education, *Digest of Educational Statistics* (Washington, DC: U.S. Government Printing Office, 1969), p. 25.

5. Kenneth Polk and Walter E. Schafer, eds., *Schools and Delinquency* (Englewood Cliffs, NJ: Prentice-Hall, 1972), p. 13.

6. Patrick Gonzales et al., National Center for Education Statistics, *Pursuing Excellence: Comparisons of Eighth-Grade Science and Mathematics Achievement from a U.S. Perspective, 1995–1999* (Washington, DC: U.S. Government Printing Office, 2000).

7. *National Education Goals Report, 1997* (Washington, DC: U.S. Government Printing Office, 1997).

8. For reviews see Bruce Wolford and LaDonna Koebel, "Kentucky Model for Youths at Risk," *Criminal Justice* 9:5–55 (1995); J. David Hawkins, Richard Catalano, Diane Morrison, Julie O'Donnell, Robert Abbott, and L. Edward Day, "The Seattle Social Development Project," in Joan McCord and Richard Tremblay, eds., *The Prevention of Antisocial Behavior in Children* (New York: Guilford Press, 1992), pp. 139–160.

9. Eugene Maguin and Rolf Loeber, "Academic Performance and Delinquency," in Michael Tonry, ed., *Crime and Justice: A Review of Research*, vol. 20 (Chicago: University of Chicago Press, 1995), pp. 145–264.

10. Terence Thornberry, Alan Lizotte, Marvin Krohn, Margaret Farnworth, and Sung Joon Jang, "Testing Interactional Theory: An Examination of Reciprocal Causal Relationships Among Family, School, and Delinquency," *Journal of Criminal Law and Criminology* 82:3–35 (1991).

11. Carolyn Smith, Alan Lizotte, Terence Thornberry, and Marvin Krohn, "Resilience to Delinquency," *Prevention Researcher* 4:4–7 (1997); Matthew Zingraff, Jeffrey Leiter, Matthew Johnsen, and Kristen Myers, "The Mediating Effect of Good School Performance on the Maltreatment-Delinquency Relationship," *Journal of Research in Crime and Delinquency* 31:62–91 (1994).

12. Lyle Shannon, *Assessing the Relationship of Adult Criminal Careers to Juvenile Careers: A Summary* (Washington, DC: U.S. Government Printing Office, 1982).

13. Marvin Wolfgang, Robert Figlio, and Thorsten Sellin, *Delinquency in a Birth Cohort* (Chicago: University of Chicago Press, 1972).

14. Ibid., p. 94.

15. Bureau of Justice Statistics, *Prisons and Prisoners* (Washington, DC: U.S. Government Printing Office, 1982), p. 2.

16. Martin Gold, "School Experiences, Self-Esteem, and Delinquent Behavior: A Theory for Alternative Schools," *Crime and Delinquency* 24:294–295 (1978).

17. Michael Gottfredson and Travis Hirschi, *A General Theory of Crime* (Stanford, CA: Stanford University Press, 1990); J. D. McKinney, "Longitudinal Research on the Behavioral Characteristics of Children with Learning Disabilities," *Journal of Learning Disabilities* 22:141–150 (1990).

18. Albert K. Cohen, *Delinquent Boys* (New York: Free Press, 1955); see also Kenneth Polk, Dean Frease, and F. Lynn Richmond, "Social Class, School Experience, and Delinquency," *Criminology* 12:84–95 (1974).
19. Jackson Toby, "Orientation to Education as a Factor in the School Maladjustment of Lower-Class Children," *Social Forces* 35:259–266 (1957).
20. John Paul Wright, Francis Cullen, and Nicolas Williams, "Working While in School and Delinquent Involvement: Implications for Social Policy," *Crime and Delinquency* 43:203–221 (1997).
21. Polk, Frease, and Richmond, "Social Class, School Experience, and Delinquency," p. 92.
22. Delos Kelly and Robert Balch, "Social Origins and School Failure," *Pacific Sociological Review* 14:413–430 (1971).
23. Lance Hannon, "Poverty, Delinquency, and Educational Attainment: Cumulative Disadvantage or Disadvantage Saturation?" *Sociological Inquiry* 73:575–595 (2003).
24. Jeannie Oakes, *Keeping Track: How Schools Structure Inequality* (New Haven, CT: Yale University Press, 1985), p. 48.
25. Delos Kelly, *Creating School Failure, Youth Crime, and Deviance* (Los Angeles: Trident Shop, 1982), p. 11.
26. Travis Hirschi, *Causes of Delinquency* (Berkeley: University of California Press, 1969), pp. 113–124, 132.
27. Richard Lawrence, "Parents, Peers, School and Delinquency." Paper presented at the American Society of Criminology meeting, Boston, November 1995.
28. Patricia Jenkins, "School Delinquency and the School Social Bond," *Journal of Research in Crime and Delinquency* 34:337–367 (1997).
29. Smith, Lizotte, Thornberry, and Krohn, "Resilience to Delinquency"; Zingraff, Leiter, Johnsen, and Myers, "The Mediating Effect of Good School Performance on the Maltreatment-Delinquency Relationship."
30. *Learning into the 21st Century, Report of Forum 5* (Washington, DC: White House Conference on Children, 1970).
31. Jay Teachman, Kathleen Paasch, and Karen Carver, "Social Capital and the Generation of Human Capital," *Social Forces* 75:1343–1360 (1997)
32. Spencer Rathus, *Voyages in Childhood* (Belmont, CA: Wadsworth, 2004).
33. Sherman Dorn, *Creating the Dropout* (New York: Praeger, 1996).
34. National Institute of Education, U.S. Department of Health, Education and Welfare, *Violent Schools–Safe Schools: The Safe Schools Study Report to the Congress,* vol. 1 (Washington, DC: U.S. Government Printing Office, 1977).
35. Jill DeVoe, Katharin Peter, Phillip Kaufman, Sally Ruddy, Amanda Miller, Mike Planty, Thomas Snyder, and Michael Rand, *Indicators of School Crime and Safety, 2002* (Washington, DC: U.S. Department of Education and Bureau of Justice Statistics, 2003).
36. Christine Kerres Malecki and Michelle Kilpatrick Demaray, "Carrying a Weapon to School and Perceptions of Social Support in an Urban Middle School," *Journal of Emotional and Behavioral Disorders,* 11:169–178 (2003).
37. Pamela Wilcox and Richard Clayton, "A Multilevel Analysis of School-Based Weapon Possession," *Justice Quarterly* 18:509–542 (2001).
38. Mark Anderson, Joanne Kaufman, Thomas Simon, Lisa Barrios, Len Paulozzi, George Ryan, Rodney Hammond, William Modzeleski, Thomas Feucht, Lloyd Potter, and the School-Associated Violent Deaths Study Group, "School-Associated Violent Deaths in the United States, 1994–1999," *Journal of the American Medical Association* 286:2695–2702 (2001).
39. Bryan Vossekuil, Marisa Reddy, Robert Fein, Randy Borum, and William Modzeleski, *Safe School Initiative: An Interim Report on the Prevention of Targeted Violence in Schools* (Washington, DC: United States Secret Service, 2000).
40. Gary Gottfredson and Denise Gottfredson, *Victimization in Schools* (New York: Plenum Press, 1985), p. 18.
41. Nancy Weishew and Samuel Peng, "Variables Predicting Students' Problem Behaviors," *Journal of Educational Research* 87:5–17 (1993).
42. James Q. Wilson, "Crime in Society and Schools," in J. M. McPartland and E. L. McDill, eds., *Violence in Schools: Perspective, Programs and Positions* (Lexington, MA: Heath, 1977), p. 48.
43. Joan McDermott, "Crime in the School and in the Community: Offenders, Victims, and Fearful Youth," *Crime and Delinquency* 29:270–283 (1983).
44. Ibid.
45. Ibid.
46. Daryl Hellman and Susan Beaton, "The Pattern of Violence in Urban Public Schools: The Influence of School and Community," *Journal of Research in Crime and Delinquency* 23:102–127 (1986).
47. Peter Lindstrom, "Patterns of School Crime: A Replication and Empirical Extension," *British Journal of Criminology* 37:121–131 (1997).
48. June L. Arnette and Marjorie C. Walsleben, *Combating Fear and Restoring Safety in Schools* (Washington, DC: Office of Juvenile Justice and Delinquency Prevention, 1998).
49. Sheila Heaviside, Cassandra Rowand, Catrina Williams, Elizabeth Burns, Shelley Burns, and Edith McArthur, *Violence and Discipline Problems in U.S. Public Schools: 1996–97* (Washington, D.C.: United States Government Printing Office, 1998).
50. Crystal A. Garcia, "School Safety Technology in America: Current Use and Perceived Effectiveness," *Criminal Justice Policy Review* 14:30–54 (2003).
51. Ibid.
52. Bruce Jacobs, "Anticipatory Undercover Targeting in High Schools," *Journal of Criminal Justice* 22:445–357 (1994).
53. Mike Kennedy, "Fighting Crime by Design," *American School & University,* 73:46–47 (2001).
54. Christopher Schreck, J. Mitchell Miller, and Chris Gibson, "Trouble in the Schoolyard: A Study of the Risk Factors of Victimization at School," *Crime & Delinquency,* 49:460–484 (2003).
55. National Commission on Excellence in Education, *A Nation at Risk* (Washington, DC: U.S. Government Printing Office, 1983).
56. Alexander Liazos, "Schools, Alienation, and Delinquency," *Crime and Delinquency* 24:355–361 (1978).
57. Stephen Cox, William Davidson, and Timothy Bynum, "A Meta-Analytic Assessment of Delinquency-Related Outcomes of Alternative Education Programs," *Crime and Delinquency* 41:219–234 (1995).
58. U.S. Senate Subcommittee on Delinquency, *Challenge for the Third Century,* p. 95.
59. "When School Is Out," *The Future of Children,* vol. 9 (Los Altos, CA: David and Lucile Packard Foundation, Fall 1999).
60. *New Jersey v. T.L.O.,* 469 U.S. 325, 105 S.Ct. 733 (1985).
61. *People v. Overton,* 24 N.Y.2d 522, 301 N.Y.S.2d 479, 249 N.E.2d 366 (1969); Brenda Walts, "*New Jersey v. T.L.O.:* Questions the Court Did Not Answer About School Searches," *Law and Education Journal* 14:421 (1985).
62. *Vernonia School District 47J v. Acton,* 115 S.Ct. 2394 (1995); Bernard James and Jonathan Pyatt, "Supreme Court Extends School's Authority to Search," *National School Safety Center News Journal* 26:29 (1995).
63. Michael Medaris, *A Guide to the Family Educational Rights and Privacy Act* (Washington, DC: Office of Juvenile Justice and Delinquency Prevention, 1998).
64. Ibid.
65. 393 U.S. 503, 89 S.Ct. 733 (1969).
66. Ibid.
67. *Bethel School District No. 403 v. Fraser,* 478 U.S. 675, 106 S.Ct. 3159, 92 L.Ed.2d 549 (1986).
68. *Hazelwood School District v. Kuhlmeier,* 484 U.S. 260, 108 S.Ct. 562, 98 L.Ed.2d 592 (1988).
69. Terry McManus, "Home Web Sites Thrust Students into Censorship Disputes," *New York Times,* 13 August 1998, p. E9.
70. *Santa Fe Independent School District, Petitioner v. Jane Doe,* individually and as next friend for her minor children, Jane and John Doe et al., No. 99–62 [June 19, 2000].
71. *Good News Club et al. v. Milford Central School* No. 99–2036 (2001).
72. *Ingraham v. Wright,* 430 U.S. 651, 97 S.Ct. 1401 (1977).
73. *Goss v. Lopez,* 419 U.S. 565, 95 S.Ct. 729 (1976).

Chapter 10

1. Thor Bjarnason, "European School Survey Project on Alcohol and Drugs." Press release (Albany: State University of New York, February

20, 2001); National Institute on Drug Abuse, Community Epidemiology Work Group, *Epidemiological Trends in Drug Abuse* (Washington, DC: National Institute on Drug Abuse, 1997).

2. "Ecstasy Use Among American Teens Drops for the First Time in Recent Years, and Overall Drug and Alcohol Use Also Decline in the Year After 9/11." News release (Ann Arbor: University of Michigan, Institute for Social Research, December 16, 2002), Table 1.

3. Peter Greenwood, "Substance Abuse Problems Among High-Risk Youth and Potential Interventions," *Crime and Delinquency* 38:444–458 (1992).

4. U.S. Department of Justice, *Drugs and Crime Facts, 1988* (Washington, DC: Bureau of Justice Statistics, 1989), pp. 3–4.

5. *Preliminary Data on Drug Use & Related Matters Among Adult Arrestees and Juvenile Detainees, 2002* (Washington, DC: Arrestee Drug Abuse Monitoring Program, National Institute of Justice, 2003).

6. Mary Ellen Mackesy-Amiti and Michael Fendrich, "Delinquent Behavior and Inhalant Use Among High School Students." Paper presented at the American Society of Criminology meeting, Boston, November 1995.

7. Dennis Coon, *Introduction to Psychology* (St. Paul, MN: West, 1992), p. 178.

8. Alan Neaigus, Aylin Atillasoy, Samuel Friedman, Xavier Andrade, Maureen Miller, Gilbert Ildefonso, and Don Des Jarlais, "Trends in the Noninjected Use of Heroin and Factors Associated with the Transition to Injecting," in James Inciardi and Lana Harrison, eds., *Heroin in the Age of Crack-Cocaine* (Thousand Oaks, CA: Sage, 1998), pp. 108–130.

9. "Ecstasy Use Among American Teens," Tables 1, 2.

10. "Drugs—The American Family in Crisis," *Juvenile and Family Court* 39:45–46 (Special issue, 1988).

11. Federal Bureau of Investigation, *Crime in the United States, 2001* (Washington, DC: U.S. Government Printing Office, 2002), Tables 29, 38.

12. Henrick J. Harwood, *Updating Estimates of the Economic Costs of Alcohol Abuse in the United States: Estimates, Update Methods, and Data.* Report prepared by the Lewin Group for the National Institute of Alcohol Abuse and Alcoholism (Rockville, MD: U.S. Department of Health and Human Services, 2000), Table 3.

13. D. J. Rohsenow, "Drinking Habits and Expectancies About Alcohol's Effects for Self Versus Others," *Journal of Consulting and Clinical Psychology* 51:75–76 (1983).

14. Spencer Rathus, *Psychology,* 4th ed. (New York: Holt, Rinehart & Winston, 1990), p. 161.

15. Mary Tabor, "'Ice' in an Island Paradise," *Boston Globe,* 8 December 1989, p. 3.

16. Paul Goldstein, "Anabolic Steroids: An Ethnographic Approach." Unpublished paper (Narcotics and Drug Research, Inc., March 1989).

17. *Center Facts About Access to Tobacco by Minors* (Atlanta, GA: Centers for Disease Control, May 23, 1997).

18. "Teen Smoking Declines Sharply in 2002, More Than Offsetting Large Increases in the Early 1990s." News release (University of Michigan, Institute for Social Research, December 16, 2002), Table 1.

19. Andrew Lang Golub and Bruce Johnson, "Crack's Decline: Some Surprises Across U.S. Cities," *National Institute of Justice Research in Brief* (Washington, DC: National Institute of Justice, 1997); Bruce Johnson, Andrew Lang Golub, and Jeffrey Fagan, "Careers in Crack, Drug Use, Drug Distribution, and Nondrug Criminality," *Crime and Delinquency* 41:275–295 (1995).

20. Ibid., p. 10.

21. Bruce Johnson, George Thomas, and Andrew Golub, "Trends in Heroin Use Among Manhattan Arrestees from the Heroin and Crack Era," in James Inciardi and Lana Harrison, eds., *Heroin in the Age of Crack-Cocaine* (Thousand Oaks, CA: Sage, 1998), pp. 108–130.

22. Robert Brooner, Donald Templer, Dace Svikis, Chester Schmidt, and Spyros Monopolis, "Dimensions of Alcoholism: A Multivariate Analysis," *Journal of Studies on Alcohol* 51:77–81 (1990).

23. *PRIDE Questionnaire Report for Grades 6 Through 12: 2002–2003 PRIDE Surveys National Summary/Total* (Bowling Green, KY: PRIDE Surveys, August 29, 2003), Tables 2.9, 2.10.

24. Diana C. Noone, "Drug Use Among Juvenile Detainees," in *Arrestee Drug Abuse Monitoring: 2000 Annual Report* (Washington, DC: National Institute of Justice, 2003), p. 135.

25. *Preliminary Data on Drug Use & Related Matters Among Adult Arrestees and Juvenile Detainees, 2002.*

26. G. E. Vallant, "Parent-Child Disparity and Drug Addiction," *Journal of Nervous and Mental Disease* 142:534–539 (1966).

27. Charles Winick, "Epidemiology of Narcotics Use," in D. Wilner and G. Kassenbaum, eds., *Narcotics* (New York: McGraw-Hill, 1965), pp. 3–18.

28. Delbert Elliott, David Huizinga, and Scott Menard, *Multiple Problem Youth: Delinquency, Substance Abuse, and Mental Health Problems* (New York: Springer-Verlag, 1989).

29. Peter Reuter, Robert MacCoun, and Patrick Murphy, *Money from Crime: A Study of the Economics of Drug Dealing in Washington, D.C.* (Santa Monica, CA: Rand, 1990).

30. Thomas Dishion, Deborah Capaldi, Kathleen Spracklen, and Fuzhong Li, "Peer Ecology of Male Adolescent Drug Use," *Development and Psychopathology* 7:803–824 (1995).

31. C. Bowden, "Determinants of Initial Use of Opioids," *Comprehensive Psychiatry* 12:136–140 (1971).

32. Terence Thornberry and Marvin Krohn, "Peers, Drug Use, and Delinquency," in David Stoff, James Breiling, and Jack Maser, eds., *Handbook of Antisocial Behavior* (New York: Wiley, 1997), pp. 218–233.

33. Richard Cloward and Lloyd Ohlin, *Delinquency and Opportunity: A Theory of Delinquent Gangs* (New York: Free Press, 1960).

34. Denise Kandel and Mark Davies, "Friendship Networks, Intimacy, and Illicit Drug Use in Young Adulthood: A Comparison of Two Competing Theories," *Criminology* 29:441–471 (1991).

35. James Inciardi, Ruth Horowitz, and Anne Pottieger, *Street Kids, Street Drugs, Street Crime: An Examination of Drug Use and Serious Delinquency in Miami* (Belmont, CA: Wadsworth, 1993), p. 43.

36. D. Baer and J. Corrado, "Heroin Addict Relationships with Parents During Childhood and Early Adolescent Years," *Journal of Genetic Psychology* 124:99–103 (1974).

37. Timothy Ireland and Cathy Spatz Widom, *Childhood Victimization and Risk for Alcohol and Drug Arrests* (Washington, DC: National Institute of Justice, 1995).

38. See S. F. Bucky, "The Relationship Between Background and Extent of Heroin Use," *American Journal of Psychiatry* 130:709–710 (1973); I. Chien, D. L. Gerard, R. Lee, and E. Rosenfield, *The Road to H: Narcotics Delinquency and Social Policy* (New York: Basic Books, 1964).

39. J. S. Mio, G. Nanjundappa, D. E. Verlur, and M. D. DeRios, "Drug Abuse and the Adolescent Sex Offender: A Preliminary Analysis," *Journal of Psychoactive Drugs* 18:65–72 (1986).

40. G. T. Wilson, "Cognitive Studies in Alcoholism," *Journal of Consulting and Clinical Psychology* 55:325–331 (1987).

41. John Hagedorn, Jose Torres, and Greg Giglio, "Cocaine, Kicks, and Strain: Patterns of Substance Use in Milwaukee Gangs," *Contemporary Drug Problems* 25:113–145 (1998).

42. For a thorough review, see Karol Kumpfer, "Impact of Maternal Characteristics and Parenting Processes on Children of Drug Abusers." Paper presented at the American Society of Criminology meeting, Boston, November 1995.

43. D. W. Goodwin, "Alcoholism and Genetics," *Archives of General Psychiatry* 42:171–174 (1985).

44. Ibid.

45. Patricia Dobkin, Richard Tremblay, Louise Masse, and Frank Vitaro, "Individual and Peer Characteristics in Predicting Boys' Early Onset of Substance Abuse: A Seven-Year Longitudinal Study," *Child Development* 66:1198–1214 (1995).

46. Ric Steele, Rex Forehand, Lisa Armistead, and Gene Brody, "Predicting Alcohol and Drug Use in Early Adulthood: The Role of Internalizing and Externalizing Behavior Problems in Early Adolescence," *American Journal of Orthopsychiatry* 65:380–387 (1995).

47. Ibid., pp. 380–381.

48. Jerome Platt and Christina Platt, *Heroin Addiction* (New York: Wiley, 1976), p. 127.

49. Rathus, *Psychology,* p. 158.

50. Eric Strain, "Antisocial Personality Disorder, Misbehavior, and Drug Abuse," *Journal of Nervous and Mental Disease* 163:162–165 (1995).

51. Dobkin, Tremblay, Masse, and Vitaro, "Individual and Peer Characteristics in Predicting Boys' Early Onset of Substance Abuse."

52. J. Shedler and J. Block, "Adolescent Drug Use and Psychological Health: A Longitudinal Inquiry," *American Psychologist* 45:612–630 (1990).

53. Greenwood, "Substance Abuse Problems Among High-Risk Youth and Potential Interventions," p. 448.

54. John Wallace and Jerald Bachman, "Explaining Racial/Ethnic Differences in Adolescent Drug Use: The Impact of Background and Lifestyle," *Social Problems* 38:333–357 (1991).

55. Marvin Krohn, Terence Thornberry, Lori Collins-Hall, and Alan Lizotte, "School Dropout, Delinquent Behavior, and Drug Use," in Howard Kaplan, ed., *Drugs, Crime, and Other Deviant Adaptations: Longitudinal Studies* (New York: Plenum Press, 1995), pp. 163–183.

56. B. A. Christiansen, G. T. Smith, P. V. Roehling, and M. S. Goldman, "Using Alcohol Expectancies to Predict Adolescent Drinking Behavior After One Year," *Journal of Counseling and Clinical Psychology* 57:93–99 (1989).

57. Inciardi, Horowitz, and Pottieger, *Street Kids, Street Drugs, Street Crime,* p. 135.

58. Ibid., p. 136.

59. Mary Ellen Mackesy-Amiti, Michael Fendrich, and Paul Goldstein, "Sequence of Drug Use Among Serious Drug Users: Typical vs. Atypical Progression," *Drug and Alcohol Dependence* 45:185–196 (1997).

60. The following sections lean heavily on Marcia Chaiken and Bruce Johnson, *Characteristics of Different Types of Drug-Involved Youth* (Washington, DC: National Institute of Justice, 1988).

61. Ibid., p. 100.

62. Inciardi, Horowitz, and Pottieger, *Street Kids, Street Drugs, Street Crime.*

63. Robert MacCoun and Peter Reuter, "Are the Wages of Sin $30 an Hour? Economic Aspects of Street-Level Drug Dealing," *Crime and Delinquency* 38:477–491 (1992).

64. Chaiken and Johnson, *Characteristics of Different Types of Drug-Involved Youth,* p. 12.

65. John Hagedorn, "Neighborhoods, Markets, and Gang Drug Organization," *Journal of Research in Crime and Delinquency* 31:264–294 (1994).

66. Chaiken and Johnson, *Characteristics of Different Types of Drug-Involved Youth,* p. 14.

67. Eric Baumer, Janet Lauritsen, Richard Rosenfeld, and Richard Wright, "The Influence of Crack Cocaine on Robbery, Burglary, and Homicide Rates: A Cross-City, Longitudinal Analysis," *Journal of Research in Crime and Delinquency* 35:316–340 (1998).

68. Ibid.

69. James Inciardi, "Heroin Use and Street Crime," *Crime and Delinquency* 25:335–346 (1979); idem, *The War on Drugs* (Palo Alto, CA: Mayfield, 1986); see also W. McGlothlin, M. Anglin, and B. Wilson, "Narcotic Addiction and Crime," *Criminology* 16:293–311 (1978); George Speckart and M. Douglas Anglin, "Narcotics Use and Crime: An Overview of Recent Research Advances," *Contemporary Drug Problems* 13:741–769 (1986); Charles Faupel and Carl Klockars, "Drugs-Crime Connections: Elaborations from the Life Histories of Hard-Core Heroin Addicts," *Social Problems* 34:54–68 (1987).

70. Eric Baumer, "Poverty, Crack, and Crime: A Cross-City Analysis," *Journal of Research in Crime and Delinquency* 31:311–327 (1994).

71. Marvin Dawkins, "Drug Use and Violent Crime Among Adolescents," *Adolescence* 32:395–406 (1997); Robert Peralta, "The Relationship Between Alcohol and Violence in an Adolescent Population: An Analysis of the Monitoring the Future Survey." Paper presented at the American Society of Criminology meeting, San Diego, November 1997; Helene Raskin White and Stephen Hansell, "The Moderating Effects of Gender and Hostility on the Alcohol-Aggression Relationship," *Journal of Research in Crime and Delinquency* 33:450–470 (1996); D. Wayne Osgood, "Drugs, Alcohol, and Adolescent Violence." Paper presented at the annual meeting of the American Society of Criminology, Miami, 1994.

72. *Preliminary Data on Drug Use & Related Matters Among Adult Arrestees and Juvenile Detainees, 2002,* Tables 2, 3; Fox Butterfield, "Justice Department Ends Testing of Criminals for Drug Use," *New York Times,* 28 January 2004.

73. David Cantor, "Drug Involvement and Offending of Incarcerated Youth." Paper presented at the American Society of Criminology meeting, Boston, November 1995.

74. B. D. Johnson, E. Wish, J. Schmeidler, and D. Huizinga, "Concentration of Delinquent Offending: Serious Drug Involvement and High Delinquency Rates," *Journal of Drug Issues* 21:205–229 (1991).

75. W. David Watts and Lloyd Wright, "The Relationship of Alcohol, Tobacco, Marijuana, and Other Illegal Drug Use to Delinquency Among Mexican-American, Black, and White Adolescent Males," *Adolescence* 25:38–54 (1990).

76. For a general review of this issue, see Helene Raskin White, "The Drug Use–Delinquency Connection in Adolescence," in Ralph Weisheit, ed., *Drugs, Crime and Criminal Justice* (Cincinnati: Anderson, 1990), pp. 215–256; Speckart and Anglin, "Narcotics Use and Crime"; Faupel and Klockars, "Drugs-Crime Connections."

77. Delbert Elliott, David Huizinga, and Susan Ageton, *Explaining Delinquency and Drug Abuse* (Beverly Hills, CA: Sage, 1985).

78. David Huizinga, Scott Menard, and Delbert Elliott, "Delinquency and Drug Use: Temporal and Developmental Patterns," *Justice Quarterly* 6:419–455 (1989).

79. Graham Farrell, "Drugs and Drug Control," in Graeme Newman, ed., *Global Report on Crime and Justice* (New York: Oxford University Press, 1999), p. 177.

80. *1998 International Narcotics Control Strategy Report* (Washington, DC: U.S. Department of State, February 1999).

81. Clifford Krauss, "Neighbors Worry About Colombian Aid," *New York Times,* 25 August 2000, pp. A3, A13.

82. Juan Forero with Tim Weiner, "Latin America Poppy Fields Undermine U.S. Drug Battle," *New York Times,* 8 August 2003, p. A1.

83. *National Drug Threat Assessment 2003* (Washington, DC: National Drug Intelligence Center, U.S. Department of Justice, 2003).

84. Farrell, "Drugs and Drug Control," pp. 179–180.

85. "Operation Webslinger Targets Illegal Internet Trafficking of Date-Rape Drug," *U.S. Customs Today* 38 (2002).

86. Gardiner Harris, "Two Agencies to Fight Online Narcotics Sales," *New York Times,* 18 October 2003.

87. Mark Moore, *Drug Trafficking* (Washington, DC: National Institute of Justice, 1988).

88. Melissa Sickmund, *Juveniles in Court* (Washington, DC: OJJDP National Report Series Bulletin, 2003), pp. 18, 20; Anne L. Stahl, *Drug Offense Cases in Juvenile Courts, 1990–1999.* Fact sheet (Washington, DC: Office of Juvenile Justice and Delinquency Prevention, 2003).

89. Ibid.

90. Phyllis L. Ellickson, Robert M. Bell, and K. McGuigan, "Preventing Adolescent Drug Use: Long-Term Results of a Junior High Program," *American Journal of Public Health* 83:856–861 (1993).

91. *Partnership Attitude Tracking Study 2003 Teens Study: Survey of Teens' Attitudes and Behaviors Toward Marijuana* (Washington, DC: RoperASW, 2003), pp. 11, 12.

92. Substance Abuse and Mental Health Services Administration, *Overview of Findings from the 2002 National Survey on Drug Use and Health* (Rockville, MD: Office of Applied Studies, 2003).

93. Brandon C. Welsh and Akemi Hoshi, "Communities and Crime Prevention," in Lawrence W. Sherman, David P. Farrington, Brandon C. Welsh, and Doris Layton MacKenzie, eds., *Evidence-Based Crime Prevention* (New York: Routledge, 2002), pp. 184–186.

94. Steven P. Schinke, Mario A. Orlandi, and Kristen C. Cole, "Boys & Girls Clubs in Public Housing Developments: Prevention Services for Youth at Risk," *Journal of Community Psychology, Office of Substance Abuse Prevention, Special Issue* (1992), p. 120.

95. Ibid, pp. 125–127.

96. Michele Spiess, *Juveniles and Drugs* (Washington, DC: Executive Office of the President, Office of National Drug Control Policy Fact Sheet, 2003), p. 5.

97. Scott W. Henggeler, Sonja K. Schoenwald, Charles M. Borduin, Melisa D. Rowland, and Phillippe B. Cunningham, *Multisystemic Treatment of Antisocial Behavior in Children and Adolescents* (New York: Guilford Press, 1998).

98. Scott W. Henggeler, W. Glenn Clingempeel, Michael J. Brondino, and Susan G. Pickrel, "Four-Year Follow-Up of Multisystemic Therapy with Substance-Abusing and Substance-Dependent

Juvenile Offenders," *Journal of the American Academy of Child and Adolescent Psychiatry* 41:868–874 (2002).

99. Eli Ginzberg, Howard Berliner, and Miriam Ostrow, *Young People at Risk: Is Prevention Possible?* (Boulder, CO: Westview Press, 1988), p. 99.

100. James C. Howell, *Preventing and Reducing Juvenile Delinquency: A Comprehensive Framework* (Thousand Oaks, CA: Sage, 2003), p. 139.

101. Ginzberg, Berliner, and Ostrow, *Young People at Risk: Is Prevention Possible?*

102. Donnie W. Watson, Lorrie Bisesi, Susie Tanamly, and Noemi Mai, "Comprehensive Residential Education, Arts, and Substance Abuse Treatment (CREASAT): A Model Treatment Program for Juvenile Offenders," *Youth Violence and Juvenile Justice* 1:388–401 (2003).

103. Kathryn Ann Farr, "Revitalizing the Drug Decriminalization Debate," *Crime and Delinquency* 36:223–237 (1990).

104. Reuter, MacCoun, and Murphy, *Money from Crime*, pp. 165–168.

New Directions in Preventing Delinquency: Secondary Prevention Efforts: Family and Community

1. James C. Howell, ed., *Guide for Implementing the Comprehensive Strategy for Serious, Violent, and Chronic Juvenile Offenders* (Washington, DC: Office of Juvenile Justice and Delinquency Prevention, U.S. Department of Justice, 1995), p. 90.

2. Joan McCord, Cathy Spatz-Widom, and Nancy A. Crowell, eds., *Juvenile Crime, Juvenile Justice* (Washington, DC: National Academy Press, Panel on Juvenile Crime: Prevention, Treatment, and Control, 2001), p. 147.

3. Andrew Hahn, "Extending the Time of Learning," in Douglas J. Besharov, ed., *America's Disconnected Youth: Toward a Preventive Strategy* (Washington, DC: Child Welfare League of America Press, 1999).

4. Andrew Hahn, *Evaluation of the Quantum Opportunities Program (QOP): Did the Program Work?* (Waltham, MA: Brandeis University, 1994).

5. Brandon C. Welsh and Akemi Hoshi, "Communities and Crime Prevention," in Lawrence W. Sherman, David P. Farrington, Brandon C. Welsh, and Doris Layton MacKenzie, eds., *Evidence-Based Crime Prevention* (London: Routledge, 2002); McCord, Widom, and Crowell, *Juvenile Crime, Juvenile Justice*.

6. McCord, Widom, and Crowell, *Juvenile Crime, Juvenile Justice*, p. 147.

7. "When School Is Out," *The Future of Children, vol. 9* (Los Altos, CA: David and Lucile Packard Foundation, Fall 1999), Executive Summary.

8. Steven P. Schinke, Mario A. Orlandi, and Kristin C. Cole, "Boys & Girls Clubs in Public Housing Developments: Prevention Services for Youth at Risk," *Journal of Community Psychology* (Special Issue, 1992), p. 120.

9. Ibid, pp. 125–127.

10. Lawrence W. Sherman, Denise C. Gottfredson, Doris Layton MacKenzie, John E. Eck, Peter Reuter, and Shawn D. Bushway, *Preventing Crime: What Works, What Doesn't, What's Promising* (Washington, DC: NIJ, 1997); Lawrence W. Sherman, Denise C. Gottfredson, Doris Layton MacKenzie, John E. Eck, Peter Reuter, and Shawn D. Bushway, *Preventing Crime: What Works, What Doesn't, What's Promising* (Washington, DC: NIJ Research in Brief, 1998).

11. Howard Snyder and Melissa Sickmund, *Juvenile Offenders and Victims: 1999 National Report* (Washington, DC: U.S. Department of Justice, Office of Juvenile Justice and Delinquency Prevention, 1999).

12. McCord, Widom, and Crowell, *Juvenile Crime, Juvenile Justice*, pp. 150–151.

13. Peter Z. Schochet, John Burghardt, and Steven Glazerman, *National Job Corps Study: The Short-Term Impacts of Job Corps on Participants' Employment and Related Outcomes: Executive Summary* (Princeton, NJ: Mathematica Policy Research, 2000), p. 3.

14. Lynn A. Curtis, *The State of Families: Family, Employment, and Reconstruction: Policy Based on What Works* (Milwaukee, WI: Families International, 1995).

15. Schochet, Burghardt, and Glazerman, *National Job Corps Study*.

16. David A. Long, Charles D. Mallar, and Craig V. D. Thornton, "Evaluating the Benefits and Costs of the Job Corps," *Journal of Policy Analysis and Management 1*:55–76 (1981).

17. Adele V. Harrell, Shannon E. Cavanagh, and Sanjeev Sridharan, *Evaluation of the Children At Risk Program: Results 1 Year After the End of the Program* (Washington, DC: NIJ Research in Brief, 1999).

18. Richard F. Catalano, Michael W. Arthur, J. David Hawkins, Lisa Berglund, and Jeffrey J. Olson, "Comprehensive Community- and School-Based Interventions to Prevent Antisocial Behavior," in Rolf Loeber and David P. Farrington, eds., *Serious and Violent Juvenile Offenders: Risk Factors and Successful Interventions* (Thousand Oaks, CA: Sage, 1998), p. 281.

19. James C. Howell and J. David Hawkins, "Prevention of Youth Violence," in Michael Tonry and Mark H. Moore, eds., *Youth Violence: Crime and Justice: A Review of Research*, vol. 24 (Chicago: University of Chicago Press, 1998), pp. 303–304.

20. J. David Hawkins, Richard F. Catalano, and Associates, *Communities That Care: Action for Drug Abuse Prevention* (San Francisco: Jossey-Bass, 1992).

21. Catalano, Arthur, Hawkins, Berglund, and Olson, "Comprehensive Community- and School-Based Interventions to Prevent Antisocial Behavior."

22. Bryan J. Vila, "Human Nature and Crime Control: Improving the Feasibility of Nurturant Strategies," *Politics and the Life Sciences 16*:3–21 (1997).

23. Richard A. Mendel, *Prevention or Pork? A Hard-Headed Look at Youth-Oriented Anti-Crime Programs* (Washington, DC: American Youth Policy Forum, 1995), p. 1.

24. David R. Offord, Helena Chmura Kraemer, Alan E. Kazdin, Peter S. Jensen, and Richard Harrington, "Lowering the Burden of Suffering from Child Psychiatric Disorder: Trade-Offs Among Clinical, Targeted, and Universal Interventions," *Journal of the American Academy of Child and Adolescent Psychiatry 37*:686–694 (1998).

Chapter 11

1. Robert M. Mennel, "Origins of the Juvenile Court: Changing Perspectives on the Legal Rights of Juvenile Delinquents," *Crime and Delinquency 18*:68–78 (1972).

2. Anthony Salerno, "The Child Saving Movement: Altruism or Conspiracy?" *Juvenile and Family Court Journal 42*:37 (1991).

3. Frank J. Coppa and Philip C. Dolce, *Cities in Transition: From the Ancient World to Urban America* (Chicago: Nelson Hall, 1974), p. 220.

4. Robert Mennel, "Attitudes and Policies Toward Juvenile Delinquency," in Michael Tonry and Norval Morris, eds., *Crime and Justice*, vol. 5 (Chicago: University of Chicago Press, 1983), p. 198.

5. Anthony M. Platt, *The Child Savers: The Invention of Delinquency* (Chicago: University of Chicago Press, 1969).

6. Ibid.

7. Sanford J. Fox, "Juvenile Justice Reform: A Historical Perspective," *Stanford Law Review 22*:1187 (1970).

8. Robert S. Pickett, *House of Refuge—Origins of Juvenile Reform in New York State, 1815–1857* (Syracuse, NY: Syracuse University Press, 1969).

9. Mennel, "Origins of the Juvenile Court," pp. 69–70.

10. Ibid., pp. 70–71.

11. Salerno, "The Child Saving Movement," p. 37.

12. Platt, *The Child Savers*.

13. Randall Shelden and Lynn Osborne, "'For Their Own Good': Class Interests and the Child Saving Movement in Memphis, Tennessee, 1900–1917," *Criminology 27*:747–767 (1989).

14. U.S. Department of Justice, Juvenile Justice and Delinquency Prevention, *Two Hundred Years of American Criminal Justice: An LEAA Bicentennial Study* (Washington, DC: Law Enforcement Assistance Administration, 1976).

15. Beverly Smith, "Female Admissions and Paroles of the Western House of Refuge in the 1880s: An Historical Example of Commu-

nity Corrections," *Journal of Research in Crime and Delinquency* 26:36–66 (1989).

16. Fox, "Juvenile Justice Reform," p. 1229.

17. Elizabeth Pleck, "Criminal Approaches to Family Violence, 1640–1980," in Lloyd Ohlin and Michael Tonry, eds., *Family Violence* (Chicago: University of Chicago Press, 1989), pp. 19–58.

18. Elizabeth Pleck, *Domestic Tyranny: The Making of Social Policy Against Family Violence from Colonial Times to the Present* (New York: Oxford University Press, 1987), pp. 28–30.

19. Linda Gordon, *Family Violence and Social Control* (New York: Viking, 1988).

20. Theodore Ferdinand, "Juvenile Delinquency or Juvenile Justice: Which Came First?" *Criminology* 27:79–106 (1989).

21. *In re Gault*, 387 U.S. 1, 87 S.Ct. 1428, 18 L.Ed.2d 527 (1967).

22. Mary Odem and Steven Schlossman, "Guardians of Virtue: The Juvenile Court and Female Delinquency in Early 20th-Century Los Angeles," *Crime and Delinquency* 37:186–203 (1991).

23. John Sutton, "Bureaucrats and Entrepreneurs: Institutional Responses to Deviant Children in the United States, 1890–1920," *American Journal of Sociology* 95:1367–1400 (1990).

24. Ibid., p. 1383.

25. Margueritte Rosenthal, "Reforming the Juvenile Correctional Institution: Efforts of the U.S. Children's Bureau in the 1930s," *Journal of Sociology and Social Welfare* 14:47–74 (1987); see also David Steinhart, "Status Offenses" in *The Future of Children: The Juvenile Court* (Los Altos, CA: David and Lucile Packard Foundation, Center for the Future of Children, 1996).

26. For an overview of these developments, see Theodore Ferdinand, "History Overtakes the Juvenile Justice System," *Crime and Delinquency* 37:204–224 (1991).

27. N.Y. Fam. Ct. Act, Art. 7, Sec. 712 (Consol. 1962).

28. *Kent v. United States*, 383 U.S. 541, 86 S.Ct. 1045, 16 L.Ed.2d 84 (1966); *in re Gault*, 387 U.S. 1, 87 S.Ct. 1428, 18 L.Ed.2d 527 (1967): Juveniles have the right to notice, counsel, confrontation, and cross-examination, and to the privileges against self-incrimination in juvenile court proceedings. *In re Winship*, 397 U.S. 358, 90 S.Ct. 1068, 25 L.Ed.2d 368 (1970): Proof beyond a reasonable doubt is necessary for conviction in juvenile proceedings. *Breed v. Jones*, 421 U.S. 519, 95 S.Ct. 1779, 44 L.Ed.2d 346 (1975): Jeopardy attaches in a juvenile court adjudicatory hearing, thus barring subsequent prosecution for the same offense as an adult.

29. Public Law 90–351, Title I—Omnibus Safe Streets and Crime Control Act of 1968, 90th Congress, June 1968.

30. National Advisory Commission on Criminal Justice Standards and Goals, *A National Strategy to Reduce Crime* (Washington, DC: U.S. Government Printing Office, 1973).

31. Juvenile Justice and Delinquency Prevention Act of 1974, Public Law 93–415 (1974). For a critique of this legislation, see Ira Schwartz, *Justice for Juveniles—Rethinking the Best Interests of the Child* (Lexington, MA: D.C. Heath, 1989), p. 175.

32. For an extensive summary of the Violent Crime Control and Law Enforcement Act of 1994, see *Criminal Law Reporter* 55:2305–2430 (1994).

33. Shay Bilchik, "A Juvenile Justice System for the 21st Century," *Crime and Delinquency* 44:89 (1998).

34. For a comprehensive view of juvenile law see, generally, Joseph J. Senna and Larry J. Siegel, *Juvenile Law: Cases and Comments,* 2nd ed. (St. Paul, MN: West, 1992).

35. For an excellent review of the juvenile process, see Adrienne Volenik, *Checklists for Use in Juvenile Delinquency Proceedings* (Washington, DC: American Bar Association, 1985); see also Jeffrey Butts and Gregory Halemba, *Waiting for Justice—Moving Young Offenders Through the Juvenile Court Process* (Pittsburgh, PA: National Center for Juvenile Justice, 1996).

36. Fox Butterfield, "Justice Besieged," *New York Times,* 21 July 1997, p. A16.

37. National Conference on State Legislatures, *A Legislator's Guide to Comprehensive Juvenile Justice, Juvenile Detention, and Corrections* (Denver: National Conference on State Legislators, 1996).

38. Joan McCord, Cathy Spatz Widom, and Nancy A. Crowell, eds., *Juvenile Crime, Juvenile Justice* (Washington, DC: National Acad-emy Press, Panel on Juvenile Crime: Prevention, Treatment, and Control, 2001).

39. Brandon C. Welsh and David P. Farrington, "Effective Programmes to Prevent Delinquency," in Joanna Adler, ed., *Forensic Psychology* (Cullompton, Devon, England: Willan, 2004).

40. *Youth Violence: A Report of the Surgeon General* (Rockville, MD: U.S. Department of Health and Human Services, 2001).

41. Laurence C. Novotney, Elizabeth Mertinko, James Lange, and Tara Kelly Baker, *Juvenile Mentoring Program: A Progress Review* (Washington, DC: OJJDP Juvenile Justice Bulletin, 2000).

42. James C. Howell, *Preventing and Reducing Juvenile Delinquency: A Comprehensive Framework* (Thousand Oaks, CA: Sage, 2003), p. 248.

43. Peter W. Greenwood, "Juvenile Crime and Juvenile Justice," in James Q. Wilson and Joan Petersilia, eds., *Crime: Public Policies for Crime Control* (Oakland, CA: Institute for Contemporary Studies Press, 2002), pp. 90–91.

44. "Implementation Status of Drug Court Programs" (Washington, DC: Office of Justice Programs Drug Court Clearinghouse at American University, September 8, 2003).

45. *Juvenile Drug Courts: Strategies in Practice* (Washington, DC: Bureau of Justice Assistance, 2003).

46. Barry C. Feld, "Criminology and the Juvenile Court: A Research Agenda for the 1990s," in Ira M. Schwartz, *Juvenile Justice and Public Policy—Toward a National Agenda* (New York: Lexington Books, 1992), p. 59.

47. Barry C. Feld, "Juvenile and Criminal Justice Systems' Responses to Youth Violence," in Michael Tonry and Mark H. Moore, eds., *Youth Violence: Crime and Justice: A Review of Research,* vol. 24 (Chicago: University of Chicago Press, 1998), p. 222.

48. Robert O. Dawson, "The Future of Juvenile Justice: Is It Time to Abolish the System?" *Journal of Criminal Law and Criminology* 81:136–155 (1990); see also Leonard P. Edwards, "The Future of the Juvenile Court: Promising New Directions in the Center for the Future of Children," in *The Future of Children: The Juvenile Court* (Los Altos, CA: David and Lucile Packard Foundation, Center for the Future of Children, 1996).

49. Hunter Hurst, "Juvenile Court: As We Enter the Millennium," *Juvenile and Family Court Journal* 50:21–27 (1999).

50. Carol J. DeFrances and Kevin Strom, *Juveniles Prosecuted in the State Criminal Courts* (Washington, DC: Bureau of Justice Statistics, 1997).

51. Franklin E. Zimring, *American Youth Violence* (New York: Oxford University Press, 1998).

52. Shay Bilchik, "A Juvenile Justice System for the 21st Century," *Crime and Delinquency* 44:89 (1998).

53. Patricia Torbet and Linda Szymanski, *State Legislative Responses to Violent Crime: 1996–97 Update* (Washington, DC: Office of Juvenile Justice and Delinquency Prevention, 1998).

54. Melissa Sickmund, *Juveniles in Court* (Washington, DC: Office of Juvenile Justice and Delinquency Prevention, U.S. Department of Justice, 2003), p. 7.

55. Stacy C. Moak and Lisa Hutchinson Wallace, "Legal Changes in Juvenile Justice: Then and Now," *Youth Violence and Juvenile Justice* 1:289–299 (2003), p. 292.

56. Torbet and Szymanski, *State Legislative Responses to Violent Crime.*

57. Hurst, "Juvenile Court: As We Enter the Millennium," p. 25.

58. McCord, Spatz Widom, and Crowell, *Juvenile Crime, Juvenile Justice,* p. 224.

59. Melissa M. Moon, Francis T. Cullen, and John Paul Wright, "It Takes a Village: Public Willingness to Help Wayward Youths," *Youth Violence and Juvenile Justice* 1:32–45 (2003).

60. Ibid, p. 152.

61. Greenwood, "Juvenile Crime and Juvenile Justice."

62. Alida Merlo, Peter Benekos, and William Cook, "The Juvenile Court at 100 Years: Celebration or Wake?" *Juvenile and Family Court Journal* 50:7 (1999).

63. Simon M. Fass and Chung-Ron Pi, "Getting Tough on Juvenile Crime: An Analysis of Costs and Benefits," *Journal of Research in Crime and Delinquency* 39:363–399 (2002).

1. This section relies on sources including Malcolm Sparrow, Mark Moore, and David Kennedy, *Beyond 911: A New Era for Policing* (New York: Basic Books, 1990); Daniel Devlin, *Police Procedure, Administration, and Organization* (London: Butterworth, 1966); Robert Fogelson, *Big City Police* (Cambridge, MA: Harvard University Press, 1977); Roger Lane, *Policing the City, Boston 1822–1885* (Cambridge, MA: Harvard University Press, 1967); Roger Lane, "Urban Police and Crime in Nineteenth-Century America," in Norval Morris and Michael Tonry, eds., *Crime and Justice*, vol. 2 (Chicago: University of Chicago Press, 1980), pp. 1–45; J. J. Tobias, *Crime and Industrial Society in the Nineteenth Century* (New York: Schocken Books, 1967); Samuel Walker, *A Critical History of Police Reform: The Emergence of Professionalism* (Lexington, MA: Lexington Books, 1977); idem, *Popular Justice* (New York: Oxford University Press, 1980); President's Commission on Law Enforcement and the Administration of Justice, *Task Force Report: The Police* (Washington, DC: U.S. Government Printing Office, 1967), pp. 1–9.

2. See, generally, Walker, *Popular Justice*, p. 61.

3. Law Enforcement Assistance Administration, *Two Hundred Years of American Criminal Justice* (Washington, DC: U.S. Government Printing Office, 1976).

4. August Vollmer, *The Police and Modern Society* (Berkeley: University of California Press, 1936).

5. O. W. Wilson, *Police Administration*, 2nd ed. (New York: McGraw-Hill, 1963).

6. Herman Goldstein, "Toward Community-Oriented Policing: Potential Basic Requirements and Threshold Questions," *Crime and Delinquency* 33:630 (1987); see also Janet Reno, "Taking America Back for Our Children," *Crime and Delinquency* 44:75 (1998).

7. Lawrence Sherman and Richard Berk, "The Specific Deterrent Effects of Arrest for Domestic Assault," *American Sociological Review* 49:261–272 (1984).

8. Yolander Hurst, James Frank, and Sandra Lee Browning, "The Attitudes of Juveniles Toward the Police: A Comparison of Black and White Youth," *Policing* 23:37–53 (2000).

9. Terrance J. Taylor, K. B. Turner, Finn-Aage Esbensen, and L. Thomas Winfree, Jr., "Coppin' an Attitude: Attitudinal Differences Among Juveniles Toward Police," *Journal of Criminal Justice* 29:295–305 (2001).

10. Denise C. Herz, "Improving Police Encounters with Juveniles: Does Training Make a Difference?" *Justice Research and Policy* 3:57–77 (2001).

11. Donald Black and Albert J. Reiss, Jr., "Police Control of Juveniles," *American Sociological Review* 35:63 (1970); Richard Lundman, Richard Sykes, and John Clark, "Police Control of Juveniles: A Replication," *Journal of Research on Crime and Delinquency* 15:74 (1978).

12. American Bar Association, *Standards Relating to Police Handling of Juvenile Problems* (Cambridge, MA: Ballinger, 1977), p. 1.

13. FBI, *Crime in the United States 2002* (Washington, DC: U.S. Government Printing Office, 2003), p. 291.

14. Samuel Walker, *The Police of America* (New York: McGraw-Hill, 1983), p. 133.

15. Karen A. Joe, "The Dynamics of Running Away: Deinstitutionalization Policies and the Police," *Juvenile Family Court Journal* 46:43–45 (1995).

16. Richard J. Lundman, *Prevention and Control of Juvenile Delinquency*, 3rd ed. (New York: Oxford University Press, 2001), p. 23.

17. *A Legislator's Guide to Comprehensive Juvenile Justice: Interventions for Youth at Risk* (Denver: National Conference on State Legislatures, 1996).

18. Lawrence W. Sherman and John E. Eck, "Policing for Crime Prevention," in Lawrence W. Sherman, David P. Farrington, Brandon C. Welsh, and Doris Layton MacKenzie, eds., *Evidence-Based Crime Prevention* (New York: Routledge, 2002), p. 321; for "hot spots" policing, see also Anthony A. Braga, "The Effects of Hot Spots Policing on Crime," in David P. Farrington and Brandon C. Welsh, eds., "What Works in Preventing Crime? Systematic Reviews of Experimental and Quasi-Experimental Research," *Annals of the American Academy of Political and Social Science* 578:104–125 (2001).

19. See, for example, Edmund F. McGarrell, Steven Chermak, Alexander Weiss, and Jeremy Wilson, "Reducing Firearms Violence Through Directed Police Patrol," *Criminology & Public Policy* 1:119–148 (2001).

20. Linda Szymanski, *Summary of Juvenile Code Purpose Clauses* (Pittsburgh: National Center for Juvenile Justice, 1988); see also, for example, GA Code Ann. 15; Iowa Code Ann. 232.2; Mass. Gen. Laws, ch. 119, 56.

21. Samuel M. Davis, *Rights of Juveniles—The Juvenile Justice System*, rev. (New York: Clark-Boardmen, June 1989), Sec. 3.3.

22. National Council of Juvenile and Family Court Judges, *Juvenile and Family Law Digest* 29:1–2 (1997).

23. See Fourth Amendment, U.S. Constitution.

24. *Chimel v. Cal.*, 395 U.S. 752, 89 S.Ct. 2034 (1969).

25. *United States v. Ross*, 456 U.S. 798, 102 S.Ct. 2157 (1982).

26. *Terry v. Ohio*, 392 U.S.1, 88 S.Ct. 1868 (1968).

27. *Bumper v. North Carolina*, 391 U.S. 543, 88 S.Ct. 1788 (1968).

28. *Miranda v. Arizona*, 384 U.S. 436, 86 S.Ct. 1602 (1966).

29. *Commonwealth v. Gaskins*, 471 Pa. 238, 369 A.2d 1285 (1977); *In re E.T.C.*, 141 Vt. 375, 449 A.2d 937 (1982).

30. *People v. Lara*, 67 Cal.2d 365, 62 Cal.Rptr. 586, 432 P.2d 202 (1967).

31. *West v. United States*, 399 F.2d 467 (5th Cir. 1968).

32. *Fare v. Michael C.*, 442 U.S. 707, 99 S.Ct. 2560 (1979).

33. *California v. Prysock*, 453 U.S. 355, 101 S.Ct. 2806 (1981).

34. See, for example, Larry Holtz, "*Miranda* in a Juvenile Setting—A Child's Right to Silence," *Journal of Criminal Law and Criminology* 79:534–556 (1987).

35. Kenneth C. Davis, *Discretionary Justice: A Preliminary Inquiry* (Baton Rouge: Louisiana State University Press, 1969); H. Ted Rubin, *Juvenile Justice: Police, Practice, and Law* (Santa Monica, CA: Goodyear, 1979).

36. Joseph Goldstein, "Police Discretion Not to Invoke the Criminal Process: Low-Visibility Decisions in the Administration of Justice," *Yale Law Journal* 69:544 (1960).

37. Victor Streib, *Juvenile Justice in America* (Port Washington, NY: Kennikat, 1978).

38. Herbert Packer, *The Limits of the Criminal Sanction* (Palo Alto, CA: Stanford University Press, 1968).

39. Black and Reiss, "Police Control of Juveniles"; Richard J. Lundman, "Routine Police Arrest Practices," *Social Problems* 22:127–141 (1974); Robert E. Worden and Stephanie M. Myers, *Police Encounters with Juvenile Suspects* (Albany: Hindelang Criminal Justice Research Center and School of Criminal Justice, State University of New York, 2001).

40. Nathan Goldman, *The Differential Selection of Juvenile Offenders for Court Appearance* (Washington, DC: National Council on Crime and Delinquency, 1963).

41. Irving Piliavin and Scott Briar, "Police Encounters with Juveniles," *American Journal of Sociology* 70:206–14 (1964); Theodore Ferdinand and Elmer Luchterhand, "Inner-City Youth, the Police, Juvenile Court, and Justice," *Social Problems* 8:510–526 (1970).

42. Paul Strasburg, *Violent Delinquents: Report to Ford Foundation from Vera Institute of Justice* (New York: Monarch, 1978), p. 11; Robert Terry, "The Screening of Juvenile Offenders," *Journal of Criminal Law, Criminology, and Police Science* 58:173–181 (1967).

43. Joan McCord, Cathy Spatz Widom, and Nancy A. Crowell, eds., *Juvenile Crime, Juvenile Justice* (Washington, DC: National Academy Press, Panel on Juvenile Crime: Prevention, Treatment, and Control, 2001), p. 163.

44. Worden and Myers, *Police Encounters with Juvenile Suspects*.

45. FBI, *Crime in the United States, 2002*.

46. Douglas Smith and Christy Visher, "Street-Level Justice: Situational Determinants of Police Arrest Decisions," *Social Problems* 29:167–178 (1981).

47. Douglas Smith and Jody Klein, "Police Control of Interpersonal Disputes," *Social Problems* 31:468–481 (1984).

48. Goldman, *The Differential Selection of Juvenile Offenders for Court Appearance*, p. 25; Norman Werner and Charles Willie, "Decisions of Juvenile Officers," *American Journal of Sociology* 77:199–214 (1971).

49. Aaron Cicourel, *The Social Organization of Juvenile Justice* (New York: Wiley, 1968).

50. Piliavin and Briar, "Police Encounters with Juveniles," p. 214.

51. David Klinger, "Demeanor or Crime? Why 'Hostile' Citizens Are More Likely to Be Arrested," *Criminology* 32:475–493 (1994).

52. Richard Lundman, "Demeanor or Crime? The Midwest City Police–Citizen Encounters Study," *Criminology* 32:631–653 (1994); Robert Worden and Robin Shepard, "On the Meaning, Measurement, and Estimated Effects of Suspects' Demeanor Toward the Police." Paper presented at the American Society of Criminology meeting, Miami, November 1994.

53. James Fyfe, David Klinger, and Jeanne Flaving, "Differential Police Treatment of Male-on-Female Spousal Violence," *Criminology* 35:455–73 (1997).

54. Dale Dannefer and Russel Schutt, "Race and Juvenile Justice Processing in Police and Court Agencies," *American Journal of Sociology* 87:1113–1132 (1982); Smith and Visher, "Street-Level Justice: Situational Determinants of Police Arrest Decisions"; see also, Ronald Weitzer, "Racial Discrimination in the Criminal Justice System: Findings and Problems in the Literature," *Journal of Criminal Justice* 24:309–322 (1996); Ronald Weitzer and Steven A. Tuch, "Perceptions of Racial Profiling: Race, Class, and Personal Experience," *Criminology* 40:435–456 (2002).

55. Richard J. Lundman and Robert L. Kaufman, "Driving While Black: Effects of Race, Ethnicity, and Gender on Citizen Self-Reports of Traffic Stops and Police Actions," *Criminology* 41:195–220 (2003).

56. Dan M. Kahan and Tracey L. Meares, "The Coming Crisis of Criminal Procedure," *Georgetown Law Journal* 86:1153–1184 (2000).

57. Randall Kennedy, *Race, Crime and the Law* (New York: Vintage, 1998).

58. Terence Thornberry, "Race, Socioeconomic Status, and Sentencing in the Juvenile Justice System," *Journal of Criminal Law and Criminology* 70:164–171 (1979); Dannefer and Schutt, "Race and Juvenile Justice Processing in Police and Court Agencies"; Jeffrey Fagan, Ellen Slaughter, and Eliot Hartstone, "Blind Justice? The Impact of Race on the Juvenile Justice Process," *Crime and Delinquency* 33:224–258 (1987).

59. Donna M. Bishop and Charles E. Frazier, "The Influence of Race in Juvenile Justice Processing," *Journal of Research in Crime and Delinquency* 25:242–261 (1988).

60. Ibid., p. 258; see also Melissa Sickmund, *Juvenile Court Statistics 1995* (Washington DC: OJJDP, 1998), p. 28.

61. *The Over-Representation of Minority Youth in the California Juvenile Justice System* (San Francisco: National Council on Crime and Delinquency, 1992).

62. Merry Morash, "Establishment of a Juvenile Record: The Influence of Individual and Peer Group Characteristics," *Criminology* 22:97–112 (1984).

63. Meda Chesney-Lind, "Judicial Enforcement of the Female Sex Role: The Family Court and Female Delinquency Issues," *Criminology* 8:51–71 (1973); idem, "Young Women in the Arms of Law," in L. Bowker, ed., *Women, Crime, and the Criminal Justice System,* 2nd ed. (Lexington, MA: Lexington Books, 1978).

64. Donna Bishop and Charles Frazier, "Gender Bias in Juvenile Justice Processing: Implications of the JJDP Act," *Journal of Criminal Law and Criminology* 82:1162–1186 (1992).

65. Douglas Smith, "The Organizational Context of Legal Control," *Criminology* 22:19–138 (1984); see also Stephen Mastrofski and Richard Ritti, "Police Training and the Effects of Organization on Drunk Driving Enforcement," *Justice Quarterly* 13:291–320 (1996).

66. John Irwin, *The Jail: Managing the Underclass in American Society* (Berkeley: University of California Press, 1985).

67. Darlene Conley, "Adding Color to a Black and White Picture: Using Qualitative Data to Explain Racial Disproportionality in the Juvenile Justice System," *Journal of Research in Crime and Delinquency* 31:135–148 (1994).

68. Robert Sampson, "Effects of Socioeconomic Context of Official Reaction to Juvenile Delinquency," *American Sociological Review* 51:876–885 (1986).

69. Ronald Weitzer "White, Black, or Blue Cops? Race and Citizen Assessments of Police Officers," *Journal of Criminal Justice* 28:313–324 (2000).

70. Thomas Priest and Deborah Brown Carter, "Evaluations of Police Performance in an African-American Sample," *Journal of Criminal Justice* 27:457–465 (1999); see also Matt De Lisi and Bob Regoli, "Race, Conventional Crime, and Criminal Justice: The Declining Importance of Skin Color," *Journal of Criminal Justice* 27:549–557 (1999).

71. Eric Fritsch, Tory Caeti, and Robert Taylor, "Gang Suppression Through Saturation Patrol, Aggressive Curfew, and Truancy Enforcement: A Quasi-Experimental Test of the Dallas Anti-Gang Initiative," *Crime and Delinquency* 45:122–139 (1999).

72. Matthew J. Hickman and Brian A. Reaves, *Local Police Departments, 2000* (Washington, DC: Bureau of Justice Statistics, 2003), p. 15.

73. Finn-Aage Esbensen, D. Wayne Osgood, Terrance J. Taylor, Dana Peterson, and Adrienne Freng, "How Great Is G.R.E.A.T.? Results from a Longitudinal Quasi-Experimental Design," *Criminology and Public Policy* 1:87–118 (2001).

74. Finn-Aage Esbensen and D. Wayne Osgood, "Gang Resistance Education and Training (G.R.E.A.T.): Results from the National Evaluation," *Journal of Research in Crime and Delinquency* 36:194–225 (1999).

75. Esbensen, Osgood, Taylor, Peterson, and Freng, "How Great Is G.R.E.A.T.?"

76. Yale University Child Study Center, *Community Outreach Through Police in Schools* (Washington, DC: Office for Victims of Crime Bulletin, 2003), p. 2.

77. Ibid, p. 3.

78. For an analysis of this position, see George Kelling and James Q. Wilson, "Broken Windows: The Police and Neighborhood Safety," *Atlantic Monthly* 249:29–38 (1982).

79. Robert Trojanowicz and Hazel Harden, *The Status of Contemporary Community Policing Programs* (East Lansing: Michigan State University Neighborhood Foot Patrol Center, 1985).

80. Hickman and Reaves, *Local Police Departments, 2000,* p. 15.

81. Terence Dunworth, *National Evaluation of the Youth Firearms Violence Initiative* (Washington, DC: NIJ Research in Brief, 2000), pp. 1, 4.

82. Ibid, p. 8.

83. Mark H. Moore, "Problem-Solving and Community Policing," in Michael Tonry and Norval Morris, eds., *Modern Policing. Crime and Justice: A Review of Research,* vol. 15 (Chicago: University of Chicago Press, 1992), p. 99.

84. Anthony A. Braga, *Problem Oriented Policing and Crime Prevention* (Monsey, NY: Criminal Justice Press, 2002), p. 10.

85. Moore, "Problem-Solving and Community Policing," p. 120.

86. Debra Cohen, *Problem-Solving Partnerships: Including the Community for a Change* (Washington, DC: Office of Community Oriented Policing Services, 2001), p. 2.

87. David Sheppard, Heath Grant, Wendy Rowe, and Nancy Jacobs, *Fighting Juvenile Gun Violence* (Washington, DC: OJJDP Juvenile Justice Bulletin, 2000), p. 2.

88. Ibid, p. 10.

89. Alan Lizotte and David Sheppard, *Gun Use by Male Juveniles: Research and Prevention* (Washington, DC: OJJDP Juvenile Justice Bulletin, 2001), p. 7.

90. Cohen, *Problem-Solving Partnerships,* p. 2.

91. Ibid, pp. 5–7.

Chapter 13

1. Kelly Dedel, "National Profile of the Organization of State Juvenile Corrections Systems," *Crime and Delinquency* 44:507–525 (1998). Herein cited as National Profile.

2. Anne L. Stahl, *Delinquency Cases in Juvenile Courts, 1999.* Fact sheet (Washington, DC: U.S. Department of Justice, Office of Juvenile Justice and Delinquency Prevention, 2003), p. 1.

3. Ibid, p. 2.

4. *Powell v. Alabama* 287 U.S. 45, 53 S.Ct. 55, 77, L.Ed.2d 158 (1932); *Gideon v. Wainwright* 372 U.S. 335, 83 S.Ct. 792, 9 L.Ed.2d 799 (1963); *Argersinger v. Hamlin* 407 U.S. 25, 92 S.Ct. 2006, 32 L.Ed.2d 530 (1972).

5. For a review of these studies, see T. Grisso, "The Competence of Adolescents as Trial Defendants," *Psychology, Public Policy, and Law* 3:3–32 (1997).

6. Christine Schnyder Pierce and Stanley L. Brodsky, "Trust and Understanding in the Attorney-Juvenile Relationship," *Behavioral Sciences and the Law* 20:89–107 (2002).

7. Ibid, p. 102.

8. Melinda G. Schmidt, N. Dickon Reppucci, and Jennifer L. Woolard, "Effectiveness of Participation as a Defendant: The Attorney-Juvenile Client Relationship," *Behavioral Sciences and the Law* 21:175–198 (2003).

9. Ibid, p. 193.

10. George W. Burruss, Jr. and Kimberly Kempf-Leonard, "The Questionable Advantage of Defense Counsel in Juvenile Court," *Justice Quarterly* 19:37–67 (2002).

11. Howard Davidson, "The Guardian *ad litem:* An Important Approach to the Protection of Children," *Children Today* 10:23 (1981); Daniel Golden, "Who Guards the Children?" *Boston Globe Magazine,* 27 December 1992, p. 12.

12. Chester Harhut, "An Expanded Role for the Guardian *ad litem,*" *Juvenile and Family Court Journal* 51:31–35 (2000).

13. Steve Riddell, "CASA: Child's Voice in Court," *Juvenile and Family Justice Today* 7:13–14 (1998).

14. American Bar Association, *A Call for Justice: An Assessment of Access to Counsel and Quality of Representation in Delinquency Proceedings* (Washington, DC: ABA Juvenile Justice Center, 1995).

15. Douglas C. Dodge, *Due Process Advocacy* (Washington, DC: Office of Juvenile Justice and Delinquency Prevention, 1997).

16. "ABA President Says New Report Shows 'Conveyor Belt Justice' Hurting Children and Undermining Public Safety." News release (Washington, DC: American Bar Association, October 21, 2003).

17. James Shine and Dwight Price, "Prosecutor and Juvenile Justice: New Roles and Perspectives," in Ira Schwartz, ed., *Juvenile Justice and Public Policy* (New York: Lexington Books, 1992), pp. 101–133.

18. James Backstrom and Gary Walker, "A Balanced Approach to Juvenile Justice: The Work of the Juvenile Justice Advisory Committee," *The Prosecutor* 32:37–39 (1988); see also *Prosecutors' Policy Recommendations on Serious, Violent, and Habitual Youthful Offenders* (Alexandria, VA: American Prosecutors' Institute, 1997).

19. Leonard P. Edwards, "The Juvenile Court and the Role of the Juvenile Court Judge," *Juvenile and Family Court Journal* 43:3–45 (1992); Lois Haight, "Why I Choose to Be a Juvenile Court Judge," *Juvenile and Family Justice Today* 7:7 (1998).

20. *Standards for Juvenile Detention Facilities* (Laurel, MD: American Correctional Association, 1991).

21. National Profile, p. 514.

22. Madeline Wordes and Sharon Jones, "Trends in Juvenile Detention and Steps Toward Reform," *Crime and Delinquency* 44:544–560 (1998).

23. Robert Shepard, *Juvenile Justice Standards Annotated: A Balanced Approach* (Chicago: American Bar Association, 1997).

24. Stahl, *Delinquency Cases in Juvenile Courts, 1999,* p. 2.

25. Paul Harms, *Detention in Delinquency Cases, 1990–1999.* Fact sheet (Washington, DC: U.S. Department of Justice, Office of Juvenile Justice and Delinquency Prevention, 2003), pp. 1–2.

26. Ibid.

27. Bohsiu Wu and Angel Ilarraza Fuentes, "The Entangled Effects of Race and Urban Poverty," *Juvenile and Family Court Journal* 49:41–51 (1998).

28. James Maupin and Lis Bond-Maupin, "Detention Decision Making in a Predominantly Hispanic Region: Rural and Non-Rural Differences," *Juvenile and Family Court Journal* 50:11–21 (1999).

29. Earl Dunlap and David Roush, "Juvenile Detention as Process and Place," *Juvenile and Family Court Journal* 46:1–16 (1995).

30. "OJJDP Helps States Remove Juveniles from Jails," *Juvenile Justice Bulletin* (Washington, DC: U.S. Department of Justice, 1990).

31. *The Jail Removal Initiative: A Summary Report* (Champaign, IL: Community Research Associates, 1987).

32. David Steinhart, "Status Offenses," *The Future of Children: The Juvenile Court,* vol. 6 (Los Altos, CA: David and Lucile Packard Foundation, 1996), p. 86–96.

33. Mark Soler, James Bell, Elizabeth Jameson, Carole Shauffer, Alice Shotton, and Loren Warboys, *Representing the Child Client* (New York: Matthew Bender, 1989), sec. 5.03b.

34. *Schall v. Martin,* 467 U.S. 253, (1984).

35. Jeffrey Fagan and Martin Guggenheim, "Preventive Detention for Juveniles: A Natural Experiment," *Journal of Criminal Law and Criminology, 86:*415–428 (1996).

36. Stahl, *Delinquency Cases in Juvenile Courts, 1999.*

37. Leona Lee, "Factors Influencing Intake Disposition in a Juvenile Court," *Juvenile and Family Court Journal* 46:43–62 (1995).

38. Edwin E. Lemert, "Diversion in Juvenile Justice: What Hath Been Wrought?" *Journal of Research in Crime and Delinquency* 18:34–46 (1981).

39. Don C. Gibbons and Gerald F. Blake, "Evaluating the Impact of Juvenile Diversion Programs," *Crime and Delinquency Journal* 22:411–419 (1976); Richard J. Lundman, "Will Diversion Reduce Recidivism?" *Crime and Delinquency Journal* 22:428–437 (1976); B. Bullington, J. Sprowls, D. Katkin, and M. Phillips, "A Critique of Diversionary Juvenile Justice," *Crime and Delinquency* 24:59–71 (1978); Thomas Blomberg, "Diversion and Accelerated Social Control," *Journal of Criminal Law and Criminology* 68:274–282 (1977); Sharla Rausch and Charles Logan, "Diversion from Juvenile Court: Panacea or Pandora's Box?" in J. Klugel, ed., *Evaluating Juvenile Justice* (Beverly Hills, CA: Sage, 1983), pp. 19–30.

40. Arnold Binder and Gilbert Geis, "Ad Populum Argumentation in Criminology: Juvenile Diversion as Rhetoric," *Criminology* 30:333–333 (1984).

41. Mark Ezell, "Juvenile Diversion: The Ongoing Search for Alternatives," in Ira M. Schwartz, ed., *Juvenile Justice and Public Policy* (New York: Lexington Books, 1992), pp. 45–59.

42. Albert W. Alschuler, "The Prosecutor's Role in Plea Bargaining," *University of Chicago Law Review* 36:50–112 (1968); Joyce Dougherty, "A Comparison of Adult Plea Bargaining and Juvenile Intake," *Federal Probation,* June 1988, pp. 72–79.

43. Sanford Fox, *Juvenile Courts in a Nutshell* (St. Paul, MN: West, 1985), pp. 154–156.

44. See Darlene Ewing, "Juvenile Plea Bargaining: A Case Study," *American Journal of Criminal Law* 6:167 (1978); Adrienne Volenik, *Checklists for Use in Juvenile Delinquency Proceedings* (Chicago: American Bar Association, 1985); Bruce Green, "Package Plea Bargaining and the Prosecutor's Duty of Good Faith," *Criminal Law Bulletin* 25:507–550 (1989).

45. Joseph Sanborn, *Plea Negotiations in Juvenile Court.* Ph.D. thesis (Albany: State University of New York, 1984); Joseph Sanborn, "Philosophical, Legal, and Systematic Aspects of Juvenile Court Plea Bargaining," *Crime and Delinquency* 39:509–527 (1993).

46. Charles M. Puzzanchera, *Delinquency Cases Waived to Criminal Court, 1990–1999.* Fact sheet (Washington, DC: U.S. Department of Justice, Office of Juvenile Justice and Delinquency Prevention, 2003), p. 1.

47. Gerard Rainville and Steven K. Smith, *Juvenile Felony Defendants in Criminal Courts: Survey of 40 Counties, 1998* (Washington, DC: Bureau of Justice Statistics, 2003).

48. Puzzanchera, *Delinquency Cases Waived to Criminal Court, 1990–1999,* p. 1.

49. Ind. Code Ann. 31-6-2(d) 1987; Ill.Ann.Stat. Ch. 37 Sec. 805 (1988); Penn. Stat. Ann. Title 42 6355(a) (1982); Patrick Griffin et al., *Trying Juveniles as Adults in Criminal Court: An Analysis of State Transfer Provisions* (Washington, DC: U.S. Department of Justice, Office of Juvenile Justice and Delinquency Prevention, 1998).

50. Joseph White, "The Waiver Decision: A Judicial, Prosecutorial, or Legislative Responsibility?" *Justice for Children* 2:28–30 (1987).

51. *Kent v. United States,* 383 U.S. 541, 86 S.Ct. 1045, 16 L.Ed.2d 84 (1966); *Breed v. Jones,* 421 U.S. 519, 95 S.Ct. 1179, 44 L.Ed.2d 346 (1975).

52. Barry Feld, "The Juvenile Court Meets the Principle of the Offense: Legislative Changes in Juvenile Waiver Statutes," *Journal of Criminal Law and Criminology* 78:471–534 (1987); Paul Marcotte, "Criminal Kids," *American Bar Association Journal* 76:60–66 (1990); Dale Parent et al., *Transferring Serious Juvenile Offenders to Adult Courts* (Washington DC: U.S. Department of Justice, National Institute of Justice, 1997).

53. Richard Redding, "Juvenile Offenders in Criminal Court and Adult Prison: Legal, Psychological, and Behavioral Outcomes," *Juvenile and Family Court Journal* 50:1–15 (1999); Craig A. Mason, Derek A. Chapman, Chang Shau, and Julie Simons, "Impacting Re-Arrest

Rates Among Youth Sentenced in Adult Court: An Epidemiology Examination of the Juvenile Sentencing Advocacy Project," *Journal of Clinical Child & Adolescent Psychology* 32:205–214 (2003); David L. Myers, "The Recidivism of Violent Youths in Juvenile and Adult Court: A Consideration of Selection Bias," *Youth Violence and Juvenile Justice* 1:79–101 (2003).

54. Redding, "Juvenile Offenders in Criminal Court and Adult Prison," p. 11; see also Richard E. Redding, "The Effects of Adjudicating and Sentencing Juveniles as Adults: Research and Policy Implications," *Youth Violence and Juvenile Justice* 1:128–155 (2003).

55. Emily Gaarder and Joanne Belknap, "Tenuous Borders: Girls Transferred to Adult Court," *Criminology* 40:481–517 (2002).

56. Redding, "Juvenile Offenders in Criminal Court and Adult Prison."

57. Howard N. Snyder and Melissa Sickmund, *Juvenile Offenders and Victims: 1999 National Report* (Washington, DC: U.S. Department of Justice, Office of Juvenile Justice and Delinquency Prevention, 1999), p. 177.

58. See Mason, Chapman, Shau, and Simons, "Impacting Re-Arrest Rates Among Youth Sentenced in Adult Court"; Myers, "The Recidivism of Violent Youths in Juvenile and Adult Court."

59. James Howell, "Juvenile Transfers to the Criminal Justice System: State of the Art," *Law & Policy* 18:17–60 (1996).

60. M. A. Bortner, "Traditional Rhetoric, Organizational Realities: Remand of Juveniles to Adult Court," *Crime and Delinquency* 32:53–73 (1986).

61. Puzzanchera, *Delinquency Cases Waived to Criminal Court, 1990–1999*; Jeffrey Fagan, Martin Forst, and T. Scott Vivona, "Racial Determinants of the Judicial Transfer Decision: Prosecuting Violent Youth in Criminal Court," *Crime and Delinquency* 33:359–386 (1987); J. Fagan, E. Slaughter, and E. Hartstone, "Blind Justice: The Impact of Race on the Juvenile Justice Process," *Crime and Delinquency* 53:224–258 (1987); J. Fagan and E. P. Deschenes, "Determinants of Judicial Waiver Decisions for Violent Juvenile Offenders," *Journal of Criminal Law and Criminology* 81:314–347 (1990); see also James Howell, "Juvenile Transfers to Criminal Court," *Juvenile and Family Justice Journal* 6:12–14 (1997).

62. Stahl, *Delinquency Cases in Juvenile Courts, 1999*, p. 2; Puzzanchera, *Delinquency Cases Waived to Criminal Court, 1990–1999*, p. 2.

63. Rainville and Smith, *Juvenile Felony Defendants in Criminal Courts.*

64. Puzzanchera, *Delinquency Cases Waived to Criminal Court, 1990–1999*, p. 2.

65. Barry Feld, "Delinquent Careers and Criminal Policy," *Criminology* 21:195–212 (1983).

66. Howard N. Snyder, Melissa Sickmund, and Eileen Poe-Yamagata, *Juvenile Transfers to Criminal Court in the 1990s: Lessons Learned from Four Studies* (Washington, DC: U.S. Department of Justice, Office of Juvenile Justice and Delinquency Prevention, 2000).

67. Rainville and Smith, *Juvenile Felony Defendants in Criminal Courts.*

68. Franklin E. Zimring, "Treatment of Hard Cases in American Juvenile Justice: In Defense of the Discretionary Waiver," *Notre Dame Journal of Law, Ethics, and Policy* 5:267–280 (1991); Lawrence Winner, Lonn Kaduce, Donna Bishop, and Charles Frazier, "The Transfer of Juveniles to Criminal Courts: Reexamining Recidivism Over the Long Term," *Crime and Delinquency* 43:548–564 (1997).

69. Robert Shepard, "The Rush to Waive Children to Adult Courts," *American Bar Association Journal of Criminal Justice* 10:39–42 (1995); see also Rainville and Smith, *Juvenile Felony Defendants in Criminal Courts.*

70. Institute of Judicial Administration, American Bar Association Joint Commission on Juvenile Justice Standards, *Standards Relating to Adjudication* (Cambridge, MA: Ballinger, 1980).

71. Joseph B. Sanborn Jr., "The Right to a Public Jury Trial—A Need for Today's Juvenile Court," *Judicature* 76:230–238 (1993). In the context of delinquency convictions to enhance criminal sentences, see Barry C. Feld, "The Constitutional Tension Between *Apprendi* and *McKeiver:* Sentence Enhancement Based on Delinquency Convictions and the Quality of Justice in Juvenile Courts," *Wake Forest Law Review* 38:1111–1224 (2003).

72. Linda Szymanski, *Juvenile Delinquents' Right to Counsel* (Pittsburgh, PA: National Center for Juvenile Justice, 1988).

73. *In re Winship*, 397 U.S. 358, 90 S.Ct. 1068 (1970).

74. *McKeiver v. Pennsylvania*, 403 U.S. 528, 91 S.Ct. 1976 (1971).

75. See, generally, R. T. Powell, "Disposition Concepts," *Juvenile and Family Court Journal* 34:7–18 (1983).

76. Fox, *Juvenile Courts in a Nutshell*, p. 221.

77. This section is adapted from Jack Haynes and Eugene Moore, "Particular Dispositions," *Juvenile and Family Court Journal* 34:41–48 (1983); see also Grant Grissom, "Dispositional Authority and the Future of the Juvenile Justice System," *Juvenile and Family Court Journal* 42:25–34 (1991).

78. Barry Krisberg, Elliot Currie, and David Onek, "What Works with Juvenile Offenders," *American Bar Association Journal on Criminal Justice* 10:20–24 (1995).

79. Stahl, *Delinquency Cases in Juvenile Courts, 1999*, p. 2.

80. Charles M. Puzzanchera, *Person Offenses in Juvenile Court, 1990–1999*. Fact sheet (Washington, DC: U.S. Department of Justice, Office of Juvenile Justice and Delinquency Prevention, 2003).

81. Stahl, *Delinquency Cases in Juvenile Courts, 1999*, p. 2.

82. Anthony Platt, *The Child Savers: The Invention of Delinquency* (Chicago: University of Chicago Press, 1969); David Rothman, *Conscience and Convenience: The Asylum and the Alternative in Progressive America* (Boston: Little, Brown, 1980).

83. Joseph Goldstein, Anna Freud, and Albert Solnit, *Beyond the Best Interests of the Child* (New York: Free Press, 1973).

84. See, for example, *in Interest on M.P.* 697 N.E. 2d 1153 (Il. App. 1998); *Matter of Welfare of CAW* 579 N.W. 2d 494 (MN. App. 1998).

85. See, for example, *Matter of Willis Alvin M.* 479 S.E. 2d. 871 (WV 1996).

86. Simon Singer and David McDowall, "Criminalizing Delinquency: The Deterrent Effects of NYJO Law," *Law and Society Review* 22:Sections 21–37 (1988).

87. Washington Juvenile Justice Reform Act of 1977, ch. 291; Wash. Rev. Code Ann. Title 9A, Sec. 1–91 (1977).

88. National Criminal Justice Association, *Juvenile Justice Reform Initiatives in the States, 1994–1996* (Washington, DC: U.S. Department of Justice, 1997).

89. Victor L. Streib, *The Juvenile Death Penalty Today: Death Sentences and Executions for Juvenile Crimes, January 1, 1973–September 30, 2003* (Ada, OH: Claude W. Pettit College of Law, Ohio Northern University, October 6, 2003), p. 3.

90. Lynn Cothern, *Juveniles and the Death Penalty* (Washington, DC: Office of Juvenile Justice and Delinquency Prevention, 2000).

91. Erica Goode, "Young Killer: Bad Seed or Work in Progress?" *New York Times*, 25 November 2003.

92. Victor L. Streib, *The Juvenile Death Penalty Today: Death Sentences and Executions for Juvenile Crimes, January 1, 1973–September 30, 2003.*

93. Steven Gerstein, "The Constitutionality of Executing Juvenile Offenders, *Thompson v. Oklahoma*," *Criminal Law Bulletin* 24:91–98 (1988); *Thompson v. Oklahoma*, 108 S.Ct. 2687 (1988).

94. 109 S.Ct. 2969 (1989); for a recent analysis of the *Wilkins* and *Stanford* cases, see the note in "*Stanford v. Kentucky* and *Wilkins v. Missouri:* Juveniles, Capital Crime, and Death Penalty," *Criminal Justice Journal* 11:240–266 (1989).

95. Victor Streib, "Excluding Juveniles from New York's Impendent Death Penalty," *Albany Law Review* 54:625–679 (1990).

96. Goode, "Young Killer."

97. Paul Piersma, Jeanette Ganousis, Adrienne E. Volenik, Harry F. Swanger, and Patricia Connell, *Law and Tactics in Juvenile Cases* (Philadelphia: American Law Institute, American Bar Association, Committee on Continuing Education, 1977), p. 397.

98. J. Addison Bowman, "Appeals from Juvenile Courts," *Crime and Delinquency Journal* 11:63–77 (1965).

99. *In re Gault*, 387 U.S. 1 87 S.Ct. 1428 (1967).

100. *Davis v. Alaska*, 415 U.S. 308 (1974); 94 S.Ct. 1105.

101. *Oklahoma Publishing Co. v. District Court*, 430 U.S. 97 (1977); 97 S.Ct. 1045.

102. *Smith v. Daily Mail Publishing Co.*, 443 U.S. 97, 99 S.Ct. 2667, 61 L.Ed.2d 399 (1979).

103. Linda Szymanski, *Confidentiality of Juvenile Court Records* (Pittsburgh, PA: National Center for Juvenile Justice, 1989).

104. Ira M. Schwartz, *Justice for Juveniles: Rethinking the Best Interests of the Child* (Lexington, MA: D. C. Heath, 1989), p. 172.

105. National Institute of Justice, *State Laws on Prosecutors' and Judges' Use of Juvenile Records.* Update (Washington, DC: Office of Justice Programs, 1995).

Chapter 14

1. Charles Murray and Louis B. Cox, *Beyond Probation* (Beverly Hills, CA: Sage, 1979).
2. Robert Shepard Jr., ed., *Juvenile Justice Standards, A Balanced Approach* (Chicago: American Bar Association, 1996).
3. George Killinger, Hazel Kerper, and Paul F. Cromwell Jr., *Probation and Parole in the Criminal Justice System* (St. Paul, MN: West, 1976), p. 45; National Advisory Commission on Criminal Justice Standards and Goals, *Corrections* (Washington, DC: U.S. Government Printing Office, 1983), p. 75.
4. Ibid.
5. Jerome Miller, *Last One Over the Wall: The Massachusetts Experiment in Closing Reform Schools* (Columbus: Ohio State University Press, 1998).
6. Bureau of Justice Statistics, *Report to the Nation on Crime and Justice* (Washington, DC: U.S. Government Printing Office, 1988), pp. 44–45; Peter Greenwood, "What Works with Juvenile Offenders: A Synthesis of the Literature and Experience," *Federal Probation* 58:63–67 (1994).
7. Charles Puzzanchera, Anne L. Stahl, Terrence A. Finnegan, Nancy Tierney, and Howard N. Snyder, *Juvenile Court Statistics 1999* (Pittsburgh, PA: National Center for Juvenile Justice, 2003).
8. Charles Puzzanchera, Anne L. Stahl, Terrence A. Finnegan, Howard N. Snyder, R. Poole, and Nancy Tierney, *Juvenile Court Statistics 1997* (Washington, DC: Office of Juvenile Justice and Delinquency Prevention, 2000).
9. *In re J.G.* 692 N.E. 2d 1226 (IL App. 1998).
10. *In Re Michael D.*, 264 CA Rptr 476 (CA App. 1989).
11. *Morrissey v. Brewer*, 408 U.S. 471, 92 S.Ct. 2593, 33 L.Ed.2d 484 (1972); *Gagnon v. Scarpelli*, 411 U.S. 778, 93 S.Ct. 1756, 36 L.Ed.2d 655 (1973).
12. Patricia McFall Torbet, *Juvenile Probation: The Workhorse of the Juvenile Justice System* (Washington, DC: Office of Juvenile Justice and Delinquency Prevention, 1996).
13. Richard Lawrence, "Reexamining Community Corrections Models," *Crime and Delinquency* 37:449–464 (1991).
14. See Matthew J. Giblin, "Using Police Officers to Enhance the Supervision of Juvenile Probationers: An Evaluation of the Anchorage CAN Program," *Crime & Delinquency* 48:116–137 (2002).
15. See Richard G. Wiebush, "Juvenile Intensive Supervision: The Impact on Felony Offenders Diverted from Institutional Placement," *Crime and Delinquency* 39:68–89 (1993); James Byrne, "The Control Controversy: A Preliminary Examination of Intensive Probation Supervision Programs in the United States," *Federal Probation* 50:4–16 (1986).
16. For a review of these programs, see James Byrne, ed., "Introduction," *Federal Probation* 50:2 (1986); see also Emily Walker, "The Community Intensive Treatment for Youth Program: A Specialized Community-Based Program for High-Risk Youth in Alabama," *Law and Psychology Review* 13:175–199 (1989).
17. James Ryan, "Who Gets Revoked? A Comparison of Intensive Supervision Successes and Failures in Vermont," *Crime and Delinquency* 43:104–118 (1997).
18. Angela A. Robertson, Paul W. Grimes, and Kevin E. Rogers, "A Short-Run Cost-Benefit Analysis of Community-Based Interventions for Juvenile Offenders," *Crime and Delinquency* 47:265–284 (2001).
19. Richard Ball and J. Robert Lilly, "A Theoretical Examination of Home Incarceration," *Federal Probation* 50:17–25 (1986); Joan Petersilia, "Exploring the Option of House Arrest," *Federal Probation* 50:50–56 (1986); Annesley Schmidt, "Electronic Monitors," *Federal Probation* 50:56–60 (1986); Michael Charles, "The Development of a Juvenile Electronic Monitoring Program," *Federal Probation* 53:3–12 (1989).
20. Sudipto Roy, "Five Years of Electronic Monitoring of Adults and Juveniles in Lake County, Indiana: A Comparative Study on Factors Related to Failure," *Journal of Crime and Justice* 20:141–160 (1997).

21. Joseph Papy and Richard Nimer, "Electronic Monitoring in Florida," *Federal Probation* 55:31–33 (1991); Annesley Schmidt, "Electronic Monitors: Realistically, What Can Be Expected?" *Federal Probation* 55:47–53 (1991).
22. Dennis Mahoney, Dennis Romig, and Troy Armstrong, "Juvenile Probation: The Balanced Approach," *Juvenile and Family Court Journal* 39:1–59 (1988).
23. Gordon Bazemore, "On Mission Statements and Reform in Juvenile Justice: The Case of the Balanced Approach," *Federal Probation* 61:64–70 (1992); Gordon Bazemore and Mark Umbreit, *Balanced and Restorative Justice* (Washington, DC: Office of Juvenile Justice and Delinquency Prevention, 1994).
24. Office of Juvenile Justice and Delinquency Prevention, *The 8% Solution.* Fact sheet (Washington, DC: U.S. Department of Justice, Office of Juvenile Justice and Delinquency Prevention, 2001).
25. Ibid., pp. 1–2.
26. Anne L. Schneider, ed., *Guide to Juvenile Restitution* (Washington, DC: U.S. Department of Justice, 1985); Anne Schneider and Jean Warner, *National Trends in Juvenile Restitution Programming* (Washington, DC: U.S. Government Printing Office, 1989).
27. Gordon Bazemore, "New Concepts and Alternative Practice in Community Supervision of Juvenile Offenders: Rediscovering Work Experience and Competency Development," *Journal of Crime and Justice* 14:27–45 (1991); Jeffrey Butts and Howard Snyder, *Restitution and Juvenile Recidivism* (Washington, DC: U.S. Department of Justice, 1992).
28. Anne Schneider, "Restitution and Recidivism Rates of Juvenile Offenders: Results from Four Experimental Studies," *Criminology* 24:533–552 (1986).
29. Shay Bilchik, *A Juvenile Justice System for the 21st Century* (Washington, DC: Office of Juvenile Justice and Delinquency Prevention, 1998).
30. Peter Schneider, William Griffith, and Anne Schneider, *Juvenile Restitution as a Sole Sanction or Condition of Probation: An Empirical Analysis* (Eugene, OR: Institute for Policy Analysis, 1980); S. Roy, "Juvenile Restitution and Recidivism in a Midwestern County," *Federal Probation* 57:55–62 (1995).
31. Anne Schneider, "Restitution and Recidivism Rates of Juvenile Offenders," *Directory of Restitution Programs* (Washington, DC: OJJDP Juvenile Justice Clearinghouse, 1996). This directory contains information on more than five hundred restitution programs across the country.
32. Greenwood, "What Works with Juvenile Offenders."
33. Sharon Mihalic, Katherine Irwin, Delbert Elliott, Abigail Fagan, and Dianne Hansen, *Blueprints for Violence Prevention* (Washington, DC: OJJDP Juvenile Justice Bulletin, 2001), p. 10.
34. Patricia Chamberlain and John B. Reid, "Comparison of Two Community Alternatives to Incarceration," *Journal of Consulting and Clinical Psychology* 66:624–633 (1998).
35. *Children in Custody 1975–1985: Census of Public and Private Juvenile Detention, Correctional, and Shelter Facilities* (Washington, DC: U.S. Department of Justice, 1989), p. 4.
36. For a detailed description of juvenile delinquency in the 1800s, see J. Hawes, *Children in Urban Society: Juvenile Delinquency in Nineteenth-Century America* (New York: Oxford University Press, 1971).
37. D. Jarvis, *Institutional Treatment of the Offender* (New York: McGraw-Hill, 1978), p. 101.
38. Margaret Werner Cahalan, *Historical Corrections Statistics in the United States, 1850–1984* (Washington, DC: U.S. Department of Justice, 1986), pp. 104–105.
39. Clemons Bartollas, Stuart J. Miller, and Simon Dinitiz, *Juvenile Victimization: The Institutional Paradox* (New York: Wiley, 1976), p. 6.
40. LaMar T. Empey, *American Delinquency—Its Meaning and Construction* (Homewood, IL: Dorsey, 1978), p. 515.
41. Edward Eldefonso and Walter Hartinger, *Control, Treatment, and Rehabilitation of Juvenile Offenders* (Beverly Hills, CA: Glencoe, 1976), p. 151.
42. Ibid., p. 152.

43. M. Rosenthal, "Reforming the Justice Correctional Institution: Efforts of U.S. Children's Bureau in the 1930s," *Journal of Sociology and Social Welfare* 14:47–73 (1987).

44. Bureau of Justice Statistics, *Fact Sheet on Children in Custody* (Washington, DC: U.S. Department of Justice, 1989); Barbara Allen-Hagen, *Public Juvenile Facilities—Children in Custody, 1989* (Washington, DC: Office of Juvenile Justice and Delinquency Prevention, 1991); James Austin et al., *Juveniles Taken into Custody, 1993* (Washington, DC: Office of Juvenile Justice and Delinquency Prevention, 1995).

45. National Conference on State Legislatures, *A Legislator's Guide to Comprehensive Juvenile Justice, Juvenile Detention, and Corrections* (Denver: National Conference on State Legislatures, 1996).

46. Ibid.

47. Hunter Hurst and Patricia Torbet, *Organization and Administration of Juvenile Services: Probation, Aftercare, and State Delinquent Institutions* (Pittsburgh: National Center for Juvenile Justice, 1993), p. 4.

48. Melissa Sickmund, *Juveniles in Corrections* (Washington, DC: Office of Juvenile Justice and Delinquency Prevention, 2004); Melissa Sickmund, *Juvenile Residential Facility Census, 2000: Selected Findings* (Washington, DC: Office of Juvenile Justice and Delinquency Prevention, 2002), p. 2.

49. Sickmund, *Juveniles in Corrections*.

50. Ibid.

51. Ira Schwartz, Marilyn Jackson-Beck, and Roger Anderson, "The 'Hidden' System of Juvenile Control," *Crime and Delinquency* 30:371–385 (1984).

52. Rebecca Craig and Andrea Paterson, "State Involuntary Commitment Laws: Beyond Deinstitutionalization," *National Conference of State Legislative Reports* 13:1–10 (1988).

53. Sickmund, *Juvenile Residential Facility Census, 2000*, p. 3.

54. Ibid., p. 3.

55. Alan Breed and Barry Krisberg, "Is There a Future?" *Corrections Today* 48:14–26 (1986); John M. Broder, "Dismal California Prisons Hold Juvenile Offenders: Report Documents Long List of Mistreatment," *New York Times*, 15 February 2004, p. A12.

56. Sickmund, *Juveniles in Corrections*.

57. Howard N. Snyder and Melissa Sickmund, *Juvenile Offenders and Victims: 1999 National Report* (Pittsburgh, PA: National Center for Juvenile Justice, 1999), p. 192.

58. Ibid., p. 195.

59. Rodney L. Engen, Sara Steen, and George S. Bridges, "Racial Disparities in the Punishment of Youth: A Theoretical and Empirical Assessment of the Literature," *Social Problems* 49:194–220 (2002).

60. Barry Krisberg, Ira Schwartz, G. Fishman, Z. Eisikovits, and E. Gitman, "The Incarceration of Minority Youth," *Crime and Delinquency* 33:173–205 (1987).

61. Craig Fischer, ed., "Washington State Moves to End Juvenile Justice Race Disparity," *Criminal Justice Newsletter* 27:1–8 (1996).

62. Sickmund, *Juveniles in Corrections*.

63. See David M. Halbfinger, "Care of Juvenile Offenders in Mississippi Is Faulted," *New York Times*, 1 September 2003.

64. Snyder and Sickmund, *Juvenile Offenders and Victims: 1999 National Report*, p. 200.

65. Bartollas, Miller, and Dinitz, *Juvenile Victimization*, sec. C.

66. Christopher Sieverdes and Clemens Bartollas, "Security Level and Adjustment Patterns in Juvenile Institutions," *Journal of Criminal Justice* 14:135–145 (1986).

67. Several authors have written about this sexual double standard. See E. A. Anderson, "The Chivalrous Treatment of the Female Offender in the Arms of the Criminal Justice System: A Review of the Literature," *Social Problems* 23:350–357 (1976); G. Armstrong, "Females Under the Law: Protected but Unequal," *Crime and Delinquency* 23:109–120 (1977); Meda Chesney-Lind, "Judicial Enforcement of the Female Sex Role: The Family Court and the Female Delinquent," *Issues in Criminology* 8:51–59 (1973); idem, "Juvenile Delinquency: The Sexualization of Female Crime," *Psychology Today* 19:43–46 (1974); Allan Conway and Carol Bogdan, "Sexual Delinquency: The Persistence of a Double Standard," *Crime and Delinquency* 23:13–135 (1977); Meda Chesney-Lind, *Girls, Delin-*

quency, and the Juvenile Justice System* (Pacific Grove, CA: Brooks/Cole, 1991).

68. Snyder and Sickmund, *Juvenile Offenders and Victims: 1999 National Report*, p. 200.

69. See Emily Gaarder and Joanne Belknap, "Tenuous Borders: Girls Transferred to Adult Court," *Criminology* 40:481–518 (2002).

70. Leslie Acoca, "Outside/Inside: The Violation of American Girls at Home, on the Streets, and in the Juvenile Justice System," *Crime and Delinquency* 44:561–589 (1998).

71. Barbara Bloom, Barbara Owen, Elizabeth Piper Deschenes, and Jill Rosenbaum, "Improving Juvenile Justice for Females: A Statewide Assessment in California," *Crime & Delinquency* 48:526–552 (2002), p. 548.

72. For a historical analysis of a girls' reformatory, see Barbara Brenzel, *Daughters of the State* (Cambridge, MA: MIT Press, 1983).

73. Ilene R. Bergsmann, "The Forgotten Few Juvenile Female Offenders," *Federal Probation* 53:73–79 (1989).

74. *Justice by Gender: The Lack of Appropriate Prevention, Diversion, and Treatment Alternatives for Girls in the Justice System: A Report* (Chicago: American Bar Association and National Bar Association, 2001), pp. 27–29.

75. Doris Layton MacKenzie, "Reducing the Criminal Activities of Known Offenders and Delinquents: Crime Prevention in the Courts and Corrections," in Lawrence W. Sherman, David P. Farrington, Brandon C. Welsh, and Doris Layton MacKenzie, eds., *Evidence-Based Crime Prevention* (New York: Routledge, 2002), p. 352.

76. For an interesting article highlighting the debate over the effectiveness of correctional treatment, see John Whitehead and Steven Lab, "Meta-Analysis of Juvenile Correctional Treatment," *Journal of Research in Crime and Delinquency* 26:276–295 (1989).

77. National Conference on State Legislatures, *A Legislator's Guide to Comprehensive Juvenile Justice, Juvenile Detention, and Corrections*.

78. Robert Shepard Jr., "State Pen or Playpen? Is Prevention 'Pork' or Simply Good Sense?" *American Bar Association Journal of Criminal Justice* 10:34–37 (1995); James Howell, ed., *Guide for Implementing the Comprehensive Strategy for Serious, Violent, and Chronic Juvenile Offenders* (Washington, DC: U.S. Department of Justice, Office of Juvenile Justice and Delinquency Prevention, 1995).

79. Louise Sas and Peter Jaffe, "Understanding Depression in Juvenile Delinquency: Implications for Institutional Admission Policies and Treatment Programs," *Juvenile and Family Court Journal* 37:49–58 (1985–86).

80. See, generally, William Glasser, "Reality Therapy: A Realistic Approach to the Young Offender," in Robert Schaste and Jo Wallach, eds., *Readings in Delinquency and Treatment* (Los Angeles: Delinquency Prevention Training Project, Youth Studies Center, University of Southern California, 1965); see also Richard Rachin, "Reality Therapy: Helping People Help Themselves," *Crime and Delinquency* 16:143 (1974).

81. Helen A. Klein, "Toward More Effective Behavior Programs for Juvenile Offenders," *Federal Probation* 41:45–50 (1977); Albert Bandura, *Principles of Behavior Modification* (New York: Holt, Rinehart & Winston, 1969); H. A. Klein, "Behavior Modification as Therapeutic Paradox," *American Journal of Orthopsychiatry* 44:353 (1974).

82. Thomas J. Dishion, Joan McCord, and François Poulin, "When Interventions Harm: Peer Groups and Problem Behavior," *American Psychologist* 54:755–764 (1999); Joan McCord, "Cures That Harm: Unanticipated Outcomes of Crime Prevention Programs," *Annals of the American Academy of Political and Social Science* 587:16–30 (2003).

83. Larry Brendtero and Arlin Ness, "Perspectives on Peer Group Treatment: The Use and Abuses of Guided Group Interaction/Positive Peer Culture," *Child and Youth Services Review* 4:307–324 (1982).

84. Elaine Traynelis-Yurek and George A. Giacobbe, "Communication Rehabilitation Regime for Incarcerated Youth: Positive Peer Culture," *Journal of Offender Rehabilitation* 26:157–167 (1998).

85. Bruno Bettelheim, *The Empty Fortress* (New York: Free Press, 1967).

86. *CYA Newsletter*, "Ventura School for Juvenile Female Offenders" (Ventura, CA: California Youth Authority, 1988).

87. Kate O'Sullivan, Nancy Rose, and Thomas Murphy, *PEPNet: Connecting Juvenile Offenders to Education and Employment.* Fact sheet (Washington, DC: U.S. Department of Justice, Office of Juvenile Justice and Delinquency Prevention, 2001), p. 1.

88. Doris Layton MacKenzie, "Reducing the Criminal Activities of Known Offenders and Delinquents: Crime Prevention in the Courts and Corrections," p. 355; Doris Layton MacKenzie, "Evidence-Based Corrections: Identifying What Works," *Crime and Delinquency* 46:457–471 (2000).

89. Thomas Castellano and Irina Soderstrom, "Therapeutic Wilderness Programs and Juvenile Recidivism: A Program Evaluation," *Journal of Offender Rehabilitation* 17:19–46 (1992).

90. MacKenzie, "Reducing the Criminal Activities of Known Offenders and Delinquents," p. 355.

91. Jerald Burns and Gennaro Vito, "An Impact Analysis of the Alabama Boot Camp Program," *Federal Probation* 59:63–67 (1995).

92. Ronald Corbett and Joan Petersilia, eds., "The Results of a Multi-Site Study of Boot Camps," *Federal Probation* 58:60–66 (1995).

93. Doris Layton MacKenzie, Angela R. Gover, Gaylene Styve Armstrong, and Ojmarrh Mitchell, *A National Study Comparing the Environments of Boot Camps with Traditional Facilities for Juvenile Offenders* (Washington, DC: NIJ Research in Brief, 2001), pp. 1–2.

94. Doris Layton MacKenzie, David B. Wilson, and Suzanne B. Kider, "Effects of Correctional Boot Camps on Offending," in *What Works in Preventing Crime? Systematic Reviews of Experimental and Quasi-Experimental Research*, edited by David P. Farrington and Brandon C. Welsh, *Annals of the American Academy of Political and Social Science* 578:126–143 (2001).

95. Ibid., p. 134.

96. MacKenzie, "Reducing the Criminal Activities of Known Offenders and Delinquents," p. 348.

97. Dale G. Parent, *Correctional Boot Camps: Lessons Learned from a Decade of Research* (Washington, DC: National Institute of Justice, 2003).

98. Anthony Salerno, "Boot Camps—A Critique and Proposed Alternative," *Journal of Offender Rehabilitation* 20:147–158 (1994).

99. Joanne Ardovini-Brooker and Lewis Walker, "Juvenile Boot Camps and the Reclamation of Our Youth: Some Food for Thought," *Juvenile and Family Court Journal* 51:12–28 (2000).

100. Morton Birnbaum, "The Right to Treatment," *American Bar Association Journal* 46:499 (1960).

101. See for example, *Matter of Welfare of CAW* 579 N.W. 2d 494 (MN App. 1998).

102. *Inmates of the Boys' Training School v. Affleck,* 346 F. Supp. 1354 (D.R.I. 1972).

103. Ibid., p. 1343.

104. *Nelson v. Heyne,* 491. F. 2d 353 (1974).

105. *Morales v. Turman,* 383 F. Supp. 53 (E.D. Texas 1974).

106. *Pena v. New York State Division for Youth,* 419 F. Supp. 203 (S.D.N.Y. 1976).

107. *Ralston v. Robinson,* 102 S.Ct. 233 (1981).

108. Patricia Puritz and Mary Ann Scali, *Beyond the Walls: Improving Conditions of Confinement for Youth in Custody* (Washington, DC: Office of Juvenile Justice and Delinquency Prevention, 1998).

109. Joan McCord, Cathy Spatz Widom, and Nancy A. Crowell, eds., *Juvenile Crime, Juvenile Justice.* (Washington, DC: National Academy Press, Panel on Juvenile Crime: Prevention, Treatment, and Control, 2001), p. 194.

110. Michael Norman, "Discretionary Justice: Decision Making in a State Juvenile Parole Board," *Juvenile and Family Court Journal* 37:19–26 (1985–86).

111. James Maupin, "Risk Classification Systems and the Provisions of Juvenile Aftercare," *Crime and Delinquency* 39:90–105 (1993).

112. David M. Altschuler and Troy L. Armstrong, "Juvenile Corrections and Continuity of Care in a Community Context: The Evidence and Promising Directions," *Federal Probation* 66:72–77 (2002).

113. David M. Altschuler and Troy L. Armstrong, "Intensive Aftercare for High-Risk Juveniles: A Community Care Model" (Washington, DC: Office of Juvenile Justice and Delinquency Prevention, 1994).

114. David M. Altschuler and Troy Armstrong, "Reintegrating Juvenile Offenders: Translating the Intensive Aftercare Program Model into Performance Standards." Paper presented at the American Society of Criminology meeting, San Francisco, November 2000.

115. See *Morrissey v. Brewer,* 408 U.S. 471, 92 S.Ct. 2593, 33 L.Ed.2d 484 (1972).

New Directions in Preventing Delinquency: Tertiary Prevention Efforts: The Role of the Juvenile Justice System

1. Barry C. Feld, "Juvenile and Criminal Justice Systems' Responses to Youth Violence," in Michael Tonry and Mark H. Moore, eds., *Youth Violence: Crime and Justice: A Review of Research*, vol. 24 (Chicago: University of Chicago Press, 1998), p. 222.

2. Anthony A. Braga, David M. Kennedy, Elin J. Waring, and Anne Morrison Piehl, "Problem-Oriented Policing Deterrence and Youth Violence: An Evaluation of Boston's Operation Ceasefire," *Journal of Research in Crime and Delinquency* 38:195–225 (2001).

3. David Sheppard, Heath Grant, Wendy Rowe, and Nancy Jacobs, *Fighting Juvenile Gun Violence* (Washington, DC: Office of Juvenile Justice and Delinquency Prevention, Juvenile Justice Bulletin, 2000), p. 2.

4. Jeffrey A. Butts, "Encouraging Findings from the OJJDP Evaluation," *In Session: The Newsletter of the National Youth Court Center* 2(3):1, 7 (Summer 2002).

5. Peter W. Greenwood, "Juvenile Crime and Juvenile Justice," in James Q. Wilson and Joan Petersilia, eds., *Crime: Public Policies for Crime Control* (Oakland, CA: Institute for Contemporary Studies, 2002), pp. 90–91.

6. Rolf Loeber and David P. Farrington, "Never Too Early, Never Too Late: Risk Factors and Successful Interventions for Serious and Violent Juvenile Offenders," *Studies on Crime and Crime Prevention* 7:7–30 (1998).

Glossary

abandonment: Parents physically leave their children with the intention of completely severing the parent-child relationship.

academic achievement: Being successful in a school environment.

active speech: Expressing an opinion by speaking or writing; freedom of speech is a protected right under the First Amendment to the U.S. Constitution.

addict: A person with an overpowering physical or psychological need to continue taking a particular substance or drug.

addiction-prone personality: The view that the cause of substance abuse can be traced to a personality that has a compulsion for mood-altering drugs.

adjudicatory hearing: The fact-finding process wherein the juvenile court determines whether there is sufficient evidence to sustain the allegations in a petition.

adolescent-limited: Offender who follows the most common delinquent trajectory, in which antisocial behavior peaks in adolescence and then diminishes.

advisement hearing: A preliminary protective or temporary custody hearing in which the court will review the facts, determine whether removal of the child is justified, and notify parents of the charges against them.

aftercare: Transitional assistance to juveniles equivalent to adult parole to help youths adjust to community life.

age of onset: Age at which youths begin their delinquent careers; early onset is believed to be linked with chronic offending patterns.

aging-out process (also known as desistance or spontaneous remission): The tendency for youths to reduce the frequency of their offending behavior as they age; aging out is thought to occur among all groups of offenders.

alcohol: Fermented or distilled liquids containing ethanol, an intoxicating substance.

anabolic steroids: Drugs used by athletes and bodybuilders to gain muscle bulk and strength.

anesthetic drugs: Nervous system depressants.

anomie: Normlessness produced by rapidly shifting moral values; according to Merton, anomie occurs when personal goals cannot be achieved using available means.

appellate process: Allows the juvenile an opportunity to have the case brought before a reviewing court after it has been heard in juvenile or family court.

arrest: Taking a person into the custody of the law to restrain the accused until he or she can be held accountable for the offense in court proceedings.

at-risk youths: Young people who are extremely vulnerable to the negative consequences of school failure, substance abuse, and early sexuality.

authority conflict pathway: Pathway to delinquent deviance that begins at an early age with stubborn behavior and leads to defiance and then to authority avoidance.

bail: Amount of money that must be paid as a condition of pretrial release to ensure that the accused will return for subsequent proceedings; bail is normally set by the judge at the initial appearance, and if unable to make bail the accused is detained in jail.

balanced probation: Programs that integrate community protection, accountability of the juvenile offender, competency, and individualized attention to the juvenile offender; based on the principle that juvenile offenders must accept responsibility for their behavior.

balancing-of-the-interests approach: Efforts of the courts to balance the parents' natural right to raise a child with the child's right to grow into adulthood free from physical abuse or emotional harm.

barrio: A Latino word meaning "neighborhood."

battered child syndrome: Nonaccidental physical injury of children by their parents or guardians.

behavior modification: A technique for shaping desired behaviors through a system of rewards and punishments.

behaviorism: Branch of psychology concerned with the study of observable behavior rather than unconscious processes; focuses on particular stimuli and responses to them.

best interests of the child: A philosophical viewpoint that encourages the state to take control of wayward children and provide care, custody, and treatment to remedy delinquent behavior.

bifurcated process: The procedure of separating adjudicatory and dispositionary hearings so different levels of evidence can be heard at each.

biosocial theory: The view that both thought and behavior have biological and social bases.

bipolar disorder: A psychological condition producing mood swings between wild elation and deep depression.

blended families: Nuclear families that are the product of divorce and remarriage, blending one parent from each of two families and their combined children into one family unit.

boot camps: Programs that combine get-tough elements with education, substance abuse treatment, and social skills training.

broken home: Home in which one or both parents is absent due to divorce or separation; children in such an environment may be prone to antisocial behavior.

chancery courts: Court proceedings created in fifteenth-century England to oversee the lives of highborn minors who were orphaned or otherwise could not care for themselves.

child abuse: Any physical, emotional, or sexual trauma to a child, including neglecting to give proper care and attention, for which no reasonable explanation can be found.

child savers: Nineteenth-century reformers who developed programs for troubled youth and influenced legislation creating the juvenile justice system; today some critics view them as being more concerned with control of the poor than with their welfare.

Children's Aid Society: Child-saving organization that took children from the streets of large cities and placed them with farm families on the prairie.

chivalry hypothesis (also known as paternalism hypothesis): The view that low female crime and delinquency rates are a reflection of the leniency with which police treat female offenders.

choice theory: Holds that youths will engage in delinquent and criminal behavior after weighing the consequences and benefits of their actions; delinquent behavior is a rational choice made by a motivated offender who perceives that the chances of gain outweigh any possible punishment or loss.

chronic juvenile offenders (also known as chronic delinquent offenders, chronic delinquents, or chronic recidivists): Youths who have been arrested four or more times during their minority and perpetuate a striking majority of serious criminal acts; this small group, known as the "chronic 6 percent," is believed to engage in a significant portion of all delinquent behavior; these youths do not age out of crime but continue their criminal behavior into adulthood.

classical criminology: Holds that decisions to violate the law are weighed against possible punishments and to deter crime the pain of punishment must outweigh the benefit of illegal gain; led to graduated punishments based on seriousness of the crime (let the punishment fit the crime).

cliques: Small groups of friends who share intimate knowledge and confidences.

cocaine: A powerful natural stimulant derived from the coca plant.

cognitive theory: The branch of psychology that studies the perception of reality and the mental processes required to understand the world we live in.

collective efficacy: A process in which mutual trust and a willingness to intervene in the supervision of children and help maintain public order creates a sense of well being in a neighborhood and helps control antisocial activities.

community policing: Police strategy that emphasizes fear reduction, community organization, and order maintenance rather than crime fighting.

community service restitution: Offenders assist some worthwhile community organization for a period of time.

community treatment: Using nonsecure and noninstitutional residences, counseling services, victim restitution programs, and other community services to treat juveniles in their own communities.

complaint: Report made by the police or some other agency to the court that initiates the intake process.

conditions of probation: Rules and regulations mandating that a juvenile on probation behave in a particular way.

confidentiality: Restricting information in juvenile court proceedings in the interest of protecting the privacy of the juvenile.

continuity of crime: The idea that chronic juvenile offenders are likely to continue violating the law as adults.

controversial status youth: Aggressive kids who are either highly liked or intensely disliked by their peers and who are the ones most likely to become engaged in antisocial behavior.

co-offending: Committing criminal acts in groups.

cottage system: Housing in a compound of small cottages, each of which accommodates twenty to forty children.

covert pathway: Pathway to a delinquent career that begins with minor underhanded behavior, leads to property damage, and eventually escalates to more serious forms of theft and fraud.

crack: A highly addictive crystalline form of cocaine containing remnants of hydrochloride and sodium bicarbonate; it makes a crackling sound when smoked.

crackdown: A law enforcement operation that is designed to reduce or eliminate a particular criminal activity through the application of aggressive police tactics, usually involving a larger than usual contingent of police officers.

criminal atavism: The idea that delinquents manifest physical anomalies that make them biologically and physiologically similar to our primitive ancestors, savage throwbacks to an earlier stage of human evolution.

critical feminists: Hold that gender inequality stems from the unequal power of men and women and the subsequent exploitation of women by men; the cause of female delinquency originates with the onset of male supremacy and the efforts of males to control females' sexuality.

crowds: Loosely organized groups who share interests and activities.

cultural deviance theory: Links delinquent acts to the formation of independent subcultures with a unique set of values that clash with the mainstream culture.

cultural transmission: The process of passing on deviant traditions and delinquent values from one generation to the next.

culture conflict: When the values of a subculture clash with those of the dominant culture.

culture of poverty: View that lower-class people form a separate culture with their own values and norms, which are sometimes in conflict with conventional society.

custodial interrogation: Questions posed by the police to a suspect held in custody in the prejudicial stage of the juvenile justice process; juveniles have the same rights against self-incrimination as adults when being questioned.

dark figures of crime: Incidents of crime and delinquency that go undetected by police.

deinstitutionalization: Removing juveniles from adult jails and placing them in community-based programs to avoid the stigma attached to these facilities.

delinquent: Juvenile who has been adjudicated by a judicial officer of a juvenile court as having committed a delinquent act.

designer drugs: Lab-made drugs designed to avoid existing drug laws.

detached street workers: Social workers who go out into the community and establish close relationships with juvenile gangs with the goal of modifying gang behavior to conform to conventional behaviors and help gang members get jobs and educational opportunities.

detention hearing: A hearing by a judicial officer of a juvenile court to determine whether a juvenile is to be detained or released while proceedings are pending in the case.

determinate sentence: Specifies a fixed term of detention that must be served.

developmental theory: The view that criminality is a dynamic process, influenced by social experiences as well as individual characteristics.

differential association theory: Asserts that criminal behavior is learned primarily in interpersonal groups and that youths will become delinquent if definitions they learn in those groups that are favorable to violating the law exceed definitions favorable to obeying the law.

disaggregated: Analyzing the relationship between two or more independent variables (such as murder convictions and death sentence) while controlling for the influence of a dependent variable (such as race).

discretion: Use of personal decision making and choice in carrying out operations in the criminal justice system, such as deciding whether to make an arrest or accept a plea bargain.

disorganized neighborhood: Inner-city areas of extreme poverty where the critical social control mechanisms have broken down.

disposition: For juvenile offenders, the equivalent of sentencing for adult offenders; juvenile dispositions should be more rehabilitative than retributive.

disposition hearing: The social service agency presents its case plan and recommendations for care of the child and treatment of the parents, including incarceration and counseling or other treatment.

diversion: Officially halting or suspending a formal criminal or juvenile justice proceeding at any legally prescribed processing point after a recorded justice system entry, and referral of that person to a treatment or care program or a recommendation that the person be released.

drop out: To leave school before completing the required program of education.

drug courts: Courts whose focus is providing treatment for youths accused of drug-related acts.

due process: Basic constitutional principle based on the concept of the primacy of the individual and the complementary concept of limitation on governmental power; safeguards the individual from unfair state procedures in judicial or administrative proceedings; due process rights have been extended to juvenile trials.

early onset: The view that kids who begin engaging in antisocial behaviors at a very early age are the ones most at risk for a delinquency career.

egalitarian families: Husband and wife share power at home; daughters gain a kind of freedom similar to that of sons and their law-violating behaviors mirror those of their brothers.

ego identity: According to Erik Erikson, ego identity is formed when persons develop a firm sense of who they are and what they stand for.

electronic monitoring: Active monitoring systems consist of a radio transmitter worn by the offender that sends a continuous signal to the probation department computer; passive systems employ computer-generated random phone calls that must be answered in a certain period of time from a particular phone.

extraversion: Impulsive behavior without the ability to examine motives and behavior.

familicide: Mass murders in which a spouse and one or more children are slain.

family group homes: A combination of foster care and group home; they are run by a single family rather than by professional staff.

Federal Bureau of Investigation (FBI): Arm of the U.S. Department of Justice that investigates violations of federal law, gathers crime statistics, runs a comprehensive crime laboratory, and helps train local law enforcement officers.

final order: Order that ends litigation between two parties by determining all their rights and disposing of all the issues.

foster care programs: Placement with families who provide attention, guidance, and care.

free will: The view that youths are in charge of their own destinies and are free to make personal behavior choices unencumbered by environmental factors.

gang: Group of youths who collectively engage in delinquent behaviors.

gateway drug: A substance that leads to use of more serious drugs; alcohol use has long been thought to lead to more serious drug abuse.

gender-schema theory: A theory of development that holds that children internalize gender scripts that reflect the gender-related social practices of the culture. Once internalized, these gender scripts predispose the kids to construct a self-identity that is consistent with them.

general deterrence: Crime control policies that depend on the fear of criminal penalties, such as long prison sentences for violent crimes; the aim is to convince law violators that the pain outweighs the benefit of criminal activity.

general strain theory: Links delinquency to the strain of being locked out of the economic mainstream, which creates the anger and frustration that lead to delinquent acts.

general theory of crime (GTC): A developmental theory that modifies social control theory by integrating concepts from biosocial, psychological, routine activities, and rational choice theories.

gentrified: A lower-class area transformed into a middle-class enclave through property rehabilitation.

graffiti: Inscriptions or drawings made on a wall or structure and used by delinquents for gang messages and turf definition.

group homes: Nonsecured, structured residences that provide counseling, education, job training, and family living.

group therapy: Counseling several individuals together in a group session.

guardian *ad litem:* A court-appointed attorney who protects the interests of the child in cases involving the child's welfare.

guided group interaction (GGI): Through group interactions a delinquent can acknowledge and solve personal problems with support from other group members.

hallucinogens: Natural or synthetic substances that produce vivid distortions of the senses without greatly disturbing consciousness.

hashish: A concentrated form of cannabis made from unadulterated resin from the female cannabis plant.

hearsay: Out-of-court statements made by one person and recounted in court by another; such statements are generally not allowed as evidence except in child abuse cases wherein a child's statements to social workers, teachers, or police may be admissible.

heroin: A narcotic made from opium and then cut with sugar or some other neutral substance until it is only 1 to 4 percent pure.

hot spot: A particular location or address that is the site of repeated and frequent criminal activity.

house arrest: Offender is required to stay home during specific periods of time; monitoring is done by random phone calls and visits or by electronic devices.

House of Refuge: A care facility developed by the child savers to protect potential criminal youths by taking them off the street and providing a family-like environment.

identity crisis: Psychological state, identified by Erikson, in which youth face inner turmoil and uncertainty about life roles.

impulsive: Lacking in thought or deliberation in decision making. An impulsive person lacks close attention to details, has organizational problems, is distracted and forgetful.

in loco parentis: In the place of the parent; rights given to schools that allow them to assume parental duties in disciplining students.

indeterminate sentence: Does not specify the length of time the juvenile must be held; rather, correctional authorities decide when the juvenile is ready to return to society.

individual counseling: Counselors help juveniles understand and solve their current adjustment problems.

inhalants: Volatile liquids that give off a vapor, which is inhaled, producing short-term excitement and euphoria followed by a period of disorientation.

intake: Process during which a juvenile referral is received and a decision made to file a petition in juvenile court to release the juvenile, to place the juvenile under supervision, or to refer the juvenile elsewhere.

Intensive Aftercare Program (IAP): A balanced, highly structured, comprehensive continuum of intervention for serious and violent juvenile offenders returning to the community.

interactional theory: A developmental theory that attributes delinquent trajectories to mutual reinforcement between delinquents and significant others over the life course—family in early adolescence, school and friends in mid-adolescence, and social peers and one's own nuclear family in adulthood.

interstitial group: Delinquent group that fills a crack in the social fabric and maintains standard group practices.

intrafamily violence: An environment of discord and conflict within the family; children who grow up in dysfunctional homes often exhibit delinquent behaviors, having learned at a young age that aggression pays off.

juvenile court judge: A judge elected or appointed to preside over juvenile cases whose decisions can only be reviewed by a judge of a higher court.

juvenile defense attorneys: Represent children in juvenile court and play an active role at all stages of the proceedings.

juvenile delinquency: Participation in illegal behavior by a minor who falls under a statutory age limit.

juvenile intensive probation supervision (JIPS): A true alternative to incarceration that involves almost daily supervision of the juvenile by the probation officer assigned to the case.

juvenile justice process: Under the *parens patriae* philosophy, juvenile justice procedures are informal and nonadversarial, invoked for juvenile offenders rather than against them; a petition instead of a complaint is filed; courts make findings of involvement or adjudication of delinquency instead of convictions; and juvenile offenders receive dispositions instead of sentences.

juvenile justice system: The segment of the justice system including law enforcement officers, the courts, and correctional agencies that is designed to treat youthful offenders.

juvenile officers: Police officers who specialize in dealing with juvenile offenders; they may operate alone or as part of a juvenile police unit in the department.

juvenile probation officer: Officer of the court involved in all four stages of the court process—intake, predisposition, postadjudication, and postdisposition—who assists the court and supervises juveniles placed on probation.

juvenile prosecutor: Government attorney responsible for representing the interests of the state and bringing the case against the accused juvenile.

klikas: Subgroups of same-aged youths in Hispanic gangs that remain together and have separate names and a unique identity in the gang.

labeling theory: Posits that society creates deviance through a system of social control agencies that designate (or label) certain individuals as delinquent, thereby stigmatizing them and encouraging them to accept this negative personal identity.

latent trait: A stable feature, characteristic, property, or condition, such as defective intelligence or impulsive personality, that makes some people delinquency-prone over the life course.

latent trait theory: The view that delinquent behavior is controlled by a "master trait," present at birth or soon after, that remains stable and unchanging throughout a person's lifetime.

Law Enforcement Assistance Administration (LEAA): Unit in the U.S. Department of Justice established by the Omnibus Crime Control and Safe Streets Act of 1968 to administer grants and provide guidance for crime prevention policy and programs.

learning disabilities (LD): Neurological dysfunctions that prevent an individual from learning to his or her potential.

least detrimental alternative: A program that will best foster a child's growth and development.

least restrictive alternative: A program with the least restrictive or secure setting that will benefit the child.

legalization of drugs: Decriminalizing drug use to reduce the association between drug use and crime.

liberal feminism: Asserts that females are less delinquent than males because their social roles provide them with fewer opportunities to commit crimes; as the roles of girls and women become more similar to those of boys and men, so too will their crime patterns.

life course persister: One of the small group of offenders whose delinquent career continues well into adulthood.

life course theory: A developmental theory that focuses on changes in behavior as people travel along the path of life and how these changes affect crime and delinquency.

mandatory sentences: Sentences are defined by a statutory requirement that states the penalty to be set for all cases of a specific offense.

marijuana: The dried leaves of the cannabis plant.

masculinity hypothesis: View that women who commit crimes have biological and psychological traits similar to those of men.

metanalysis: An analysis technique that synthesizes results across many programs over time.

milieu therapy: All aspects of the environment are part of the treatment, and meaningful change, increased growth, and satisfactory adjustment are encouraged.

minimal brain dysfunction (MBD): Damage to the brain itself that causes antisocial behavior injurious to the individual's lifestyle and social adjustment.

***Miranda* warning:** Supreme Court decisions require police officers to inform individuals under arrest of their constitutional rights; warnings must also be given when suspicion begins to focus on an individual in the accusatory stage.

monetary restitution: Offenders compensate crime victims for out-of-pocket losses caused by the crime, including property damage, lost wages, and medical expenses.

multisystemic treatment (MST): Addresses a variety of family, peer, and psychological problems.

nature theory: The view that intelligence is inherited and is a function of genetic makeup.

near-groups: Clusters of youth who, outwardly, seem unified but actually have limited cohesion, impermanence, minimal consensus of norms, shifting membership, disturbed leadership, and limited definitions of membership expectations.

need for treatment: The criteria on which juvenile sentencing is based. Ideally, juveniles are treated according to their need for treatment and not for the seriousness of the delinquent act they committed.

negative affective states: Anger, depression, disappointment, fear, and other adverse emotions that derive from strain.

neglect: Passive neglect by a parent or guardian, depriving children of food, shelter, health care, and love.

neuroticism: A personality trait marked by unfounded anxiety, tension, and emotional instability.

nuclear family: A family unit composed of parents and their children; this smaller family structure is subject to great stress due to the intense, close contact between parents and children.

nurture theory: The view that intelligence is determined by environmental stimulation and socialization.

Office of Juvenile Justice and Delinquency Prevention (OJJDP): Branch of the U.S. Justice Department charged with shaping national juvenile justice policy through disbursement of federal aid and research funds.

orphan train: A practice of the Children's Aid Society in which urban youths were sent West for adoption with local farm couples.

overt pathway: Pathway to a delinquent career that begins with minor aggression, leads to physical fighting, and eventually escalates to violent delinquency.

parens patriae: The power of the state to act on behalf of the child and provide care and protection equivalent to that of a parent.

parental efficacy: Parents are said to have parental efficacy when they are supportive and effectively control their children in a noncoercive fashion.

parole guidelines: Recommended length of confinement and kinds of aftercare assistance most effective for a juvenile who committed a specific offense.

Part I offenses (also known as index crimes): Offenses including homicide and nonnegligent manslaughter, forcible rape, robbery, aggravated assault, burglary, larceny, arson, and motor vehicle theft; recorded by local law enforcement officers, these crimes are tallied quarterly and sent to the FBI for inclusion in the UCR.

Part II offenses: All crimes other than Part I offenses; recorded by local law enforcement officers, arrests for these crimes are tallied quarterly and sent to the FBI for inclusion in the UCR.

passive speech: A form of expression protected by the First Amendment but not associated with actually speaking words; examples include wearing symbols or protest messages on buttons or signs.

paternalistic family: A family style wherein the father is the final authority on all family matters and exercises complete control over his wife and children.

petition: Document filed in juvenile court alleging that a juvenile is a delinquent, a status offender, or a dependent and asking that the court assume jurisdiction over the juvenile.

plea bargaining: The exchange of prosecutorial and judicial concessions for a guilty plea by the accused; plea bargaining usually results in a reduced charge or a more lenient sentence.

pledge system: Early English system in which neighbors protected each other from thieves and warring groups.

Poor Laws: English statutes that allowed the courts to appoint overseers for destitute and neglected children, allowing placement of these children as servants in the homes of the affluent.

positive peer culture (PPC): Counseling program in which peer leaders encourage other group members to modify their behavior and peers help reinforce acceptable behaviors.

power-control theory: Holds that gender differences in the delinquency rate are a function of class differences and economic conditions that influence the structure of family life.

precocious sexuality: Sexual experimentation in early adolescence.

predatory crimes: Violent crimes against persons and crimes in which an offender attempts to steal an object directly from its holder.

prestige crimes: Stealing or assaulting someone to gain prestige in the neighborhood; often part of gang initiation rites.

pretrial conference: The attorney for the social services agency presents an overview of the case, and a plea bargain or negotiated settlement can be agreed to in a consent decree.

preventive detention: Keeping the accused in custody prior to trial because the accused is suspected of being a danger to the community.

probable cause: Reasonable ground to believe the existence of facts that an offense was committed and that the accused committed that offense.

probation: Nonpunitive, legal disposition of juveniles emphasizing community treatment in which the juvenile is closely supervised by an officer of the court and must adhere to a strict set of rules to avoid incarceration.

problem behavior syndrome (PBS): A cluster of antisocial behaviors that may include family dysfunction, substance abuse, smoking, precocious sexuality and early pregnancy, educational underachievement, suicide attempts, sensation seeking, and unemployment, as well as delinquency.

problem-oriented policing: Law enforcement that focuses on addressing the problems underlying incidents of juvenile delinquency rather than the incidents alone.

prosocial bonds: Socialized attachment to conventional institutions, activities, and beliefs.

pseudomaturity: Characteristic of life course persisters, who tend to engage in early sexuality and drug use.

psychodynamic theory: Branch of psychology that holds that the human personality is controlled by unconscious mental processes developed early in childhood.

psychopathic personality (also known as sociopathic or antisocial personality): A person lacking in warmth, exhibiting inappropriate behavior responses, and unable to learn from experience; the condition is defined by persistent violations of social norms, including lying, stealing, truancy, inconsistent work behavior, and traffic arrests.

psychotherapy: Highly structured counseling in which a therapist helps a juvenile solve conflicts and make a more positive adjustment to society.

public defender: An attorney who works in a public agency or under private contractual agreement as defense counsel to indigent defendants.

reality therapy: A form of counseling that emphasizes current behavior and requires the individual to accept responsibility for all of his or her actions.

reform schools: Institutions in which educational and psychological services are used in an effort to improve the conduct of juveniles who are forcibly detained.

relative deprivation: Condition that exists when people of wealth and poverty live in close proximity to one another; the relatively deprived are apt to have feelings of anger and hostility, which may produce criminal behavior.

representing: Tossing or flashing gang signs in the presence of rivals, often escalating into a verbal or physical confrontation.

residential programs: Residential, nonsecure facilities such as a group home, foster home, family group home, or rural home where the juvenile can be closely monitored and develop close relationships with staff members.

resource dilution: A condition that occurs when parents have such large families that their resources, such as time and money, are spread too thin, causing lack of familial support and control.

restorative justice: Nonpunitive strategies for dealing with juvenile offenders that make the justice system a healing process rather than a punishment process.

retreatists: Gangs whose members actively engage in substance abuse.

review hearings: Periodic meetings to determine whether the conditions of the case plan for an abused child are being met by the parents or guardians of the child.

right to treatment: Philosophy espoused by many courts that juvenile offenders have a statutory right to treatment while under the jurisdiction of the courts.

role conflicts: Conflicts police officers face that revolve around the requirement to perform their primary duty of law enforcement and a desire to aid in rehabilitating youthful offenders.

role diffusion: According to Erik Erikson, role diffusion occurs when youths spread themselves too thin, experience personal uncertainty, and place themselves at the mercy of leaders who promise to give them a sense of identity they cannot develop for themselves.

routine activities theory: The view that crime is a "normal" function of the routine activities of modern living; offenses can be expected if there is a motivated offender and a suitable target that is not protected by capable guardians.

rural programs: Specific recreational and work opportunities provided for juveniles in a rural setting such as a forestry camp, a farm, or a ranch.

school failure: Failing to achieve success in school can result in frustration, anger, and reduced self-esteem, which may contribute to delinquent behavior.

search and seizure: The U.S. Constitution protects citizens from any search and seizure by police without a lawfully obtained search warrant; such warrants are issued when there is probable cause to believe that an offense has been committed.

sedatives: Drugs of the barbiturate family that depress the central nervous system into a sleeplike condition.

self-control: Refers to a person's ability to exercise restraint and control over his or her feelings, emotions, reactions, and behaviors.

self-fulfilling prophecy: Deviant behavior patterns that are a response to an earlier labeling experience; youths act out these social roles even if they were falsely bestowed.

self-labeling: The process by which a person who has been negatively labeled accepts the label as a personal role or identity.

self-reports: Questionnaire or survey technique that asks subjects to reveal their own participation in delinquent or criminal acts.

shelter care: A place for temporary care of children in physically unrestricting facilities.

situational crime prevention: A crime prevention method that relies on reducing the opportunity to commit criminal acts by making them more difficult to perform, reducing their reward, and increasing their risks.

skinhead: Member of White supremacist gang, identified by a shaved skull and Nazi or Ku Klux Klan markings.

social bond: Ties a person to the institutions and processes of society; elements of the bond include attachment, commitment, involvement, and belief.

social capital: Positive relations with individuals and institutions, as in a successful marriage or a successful career, that support conventional behavior and inhibit deviant behavior.

social conflict theories: The view that intergroup conflict, born out of the unequal distribution of wealth and power, is the root cause of delinquency.

social control: Ability of social institutions to influence human behavior; the justice system is the primary agency of formal social control.

social control theories: Posit that delinquency results from a weakened commitment to the major social institutions (family, peers, and school); lack of such commitment allows youths to exercise antisocial behavioral choices.

social development model (SDM): A developmental theory that attributes delinquent behavior patterns to childhood socialization and pro- or antisocial attachments over the life course.

social disorganization: Neighborhood or area marked by culture conflict, lack of cohesiveness, a transient population, and insufficient social organizations; these problems are reflected in the problems at schools in these areas.

social investigation report (also known as predisposition report): Developed by the juvenile probation officer, this report includes clinical diagnosis of the juvenile and the need for court assistance, relevant environmental and personality factors, and other information to assist the court in developing a treatment plan.

social learning theories: Posit that delinquency is learned through close relationships with others, assert that children are born "good" and learn to be "bad" from others.

social structure theories: Those theories which suggest that social and economic forces operating in deteriorated lower-class areas, including disorganization, stress, and cultural deviance, push residents into criminal behavior patterns.

socialization: The process of learning the values and norms of the society or the subculture to which the individual belongs.

Society for the Prevention of Cruelty to Children (SPCC): First established in 1874, these organizations protected children subjected to cruelty and neglect at home or at school.

specific deterrence: Sending convicted offenders to secure incarceration facilities so that punishment is severe enough to convince them not to repeat their criminal activity.

status offense: Conduct that is illegal only because the child is under age.

stigmatized: People who have been negatively labeled because of their participation, or alleged participation, in deviant or outlawed behaviors.

stimulants: Synthetic substances that produce an intense physical reaction by stimulating the central nervous system.

strain: A condition caused by the failure to achieve one's social goals.

substance abuse: Using drugs or alcohol in such a way as to cause physical harm to oneself.

suppression effect: A reduction of the number of arrests per year for youths who have been incarcerated or otherwise punished.

teen courts: Courts that make use of peer juries to decide nonserious delinquency cases.

tracking: Dividing students into groups according to their ability and achievement levels.

trait theory: Holds that youths engage in delinquent or criminal behavior due to aberrant physical or psychological traits that govern behavioral choices; delinquent actions are impulsive or instinctual rather than rational choices.

tranquilizers: Drugs that reduce anxiety and promote relaxation.

transfer process: Transferring a juvenile offender from the jurisdiction of juvenile court to adult criminal court.

transitional neighborhood: Area undergoing a shift in population and structure, usually from middle-class residential to lower-class mixed use.

truant: Being out of school without permission.

truly disadvantaged: According to William Julius Wilson, those people who are left out of the economic mainstream and reduced to living in the most deteriorated inner-city areas.

turning points: Critical life events, such as career and marriage, that may enable adult offenders to desist from delinquency.

underachievers: Those who do not achieve success in school at the level of their expectations.

underclass: Group of urban poor whose members have little chance of upward mobility or improvement.

Uniform Crime Report (UCR): Compiled by the FBI, the UCR is the most widely used source of national crime and delinquency statistics.

utilitarians: Those who believe that people weigh the benefits and consequences of their future actions before deciding on a course of behavior.

victim service restitution: Offenders provide some service directly to the crime victim.

victimization: The number of people who are victims of criminal acts; young teens are fifteen times more likely than older adults (age sixty-five and over) to be victims of crimes.

waiver (also known as bindover or removal): Transferring legal jurisdiction over the most serious and experienced juvenile offenders to the adult court for criminal prosecution.

watch system: Replaced the pledge system in England; watchmen patrolled urban areas at night to provide protection from harm.

wayward minors: Early legal designation of youths who violate the law because of their minority status; now referred to as status offenders.

widening the net: Phenomenon that occurs when programs created to divert youths from the justice system actually involve them more deeply in the official process.

wilderness probation: Programs involving outdoor expeditions that provide opportunities for juveniles to confront the difficulties of their lives while achieving positive personal satisfaction.

writ of habeus corpus: Judicial order requesting that a person detaining another produce the body of the prisoner and give reasons for his or her capture and detention.

zero tolerance policy: Mandating specific consequences or punishments for delinquent acts and not allowing anyone to avoid these consequences.

Name Index

Webb, Barry, 375n53
Webster, Pamela, 381n44, n51
Webster-Stratton, Carolyn, 387n93
Wei, Evelyn, 380n19
Weikart, David P., 382n17
Weiner, Neil Alan, 169, 387n91
Weiner, Tim, 394n82
Weis, Joseph, 114, 372n12, 381n33
Weisburd, David, 375n58
Weisel, Deborah, 389n73, n78
Weisheit, Ralph, 393n76
Weishew, Nancy, 391n41
Weiss, Alexander, 396n19
Weisstub, David N., 362
Weisz, John, 171
Weitekamp, Elmar, 374n3, 379n57, 380n15
Weitzer, Ronald, 299, 397n54, n69
Wells, James, 281
Wells, L. Edward, 374n73
Wells, Nancy, 371n16
Wells, William, 29
Welsh, Brandon C., 291, 375n54, n55,
    382n10, 394n5, n93, 395n39, 396n18,
    401n75, 402n94, n95
Werner, Norman, 397n48
West, Donald J., 64, 164, 373n44, n59,
    376n98, n99, 386n65, n66, 387n71
Wheaton, Blair, 381n48
Wheeler, Etta Angell, 165, 166
Whitbeck, Les, 372n68
Whitcomb, Debra, 388n115
White, Helene Raskin, 377n152
White, Jennifer, 373n64, 377n168
White, Joseph, 399n50
White, Michael, 374n35
White, Susan, 381n39
White, Thomas, 377n171
Whitehead, Barbara Dafoe, 385n16
Whitehead, John, 371n24, 401n76
Whitlock, Monica, 382n3 (ch. 6), 389n65
Widom, Cathy Spatz, 178–179, 388n129,
    n130, n131, 135, 393n37, 394n2, n5, n6,
    n12, 395n38, 396n58, 397n73, 402n109
Wiebe, Richard, 382n74
Wiebush, Richard G., 365, 400n15
Wiener, Jörg A., 375n77
Wiersema, Brian, 374n71
Wiesner, Margit, 380n25

Wilbanks, William, 372n24
Wilcox, Pamela, 391n37
Will, Jeffery, 378n30
Williams, Bryn, 388n133
Williams, Catrina, 391n49
Williams, Charles, 210
Williams, Linda Meyer, 385n113, 387n84,
    388n132
Williams, Mark, 377n134
Williams, Nicolas, 391n20
Williamson, Deborah, 281
Willie, Charles, 397n48
Wilner, D., 392n27
Wilson, B., 393n69
Wilson, David B., 402n94, n95
Wilson, Edmond O., 375n69
Wilson, G. T., 393n40
Wilson, James Q., 121, 374n7, 381n56,
    391n42, 395n43, 397n78, 402n5
Wilson, Janet, 374n11, 384n93
Wilson, Jeremy, 396n19
Wilson, John, 374n69, 379n94
Wilson, Margo, 373n46, 378n31, 387n98,
    n99, n100
Wilson, Mary Ellen, 165, 166
Wilson, O. W., 396n5
Wilson, Robin Fretwell, 387n111
Wilson, Susan, 386n34
Wilson, William Julius, 84, 191, 378n10,
    n19, 389n46, n47, n59, n60
Windham, Amy M., 382n9
Windle, Michael, 384n71
Wines, Enoch, 262
Winfree, L. Thomas, Jr., 389n79, 390n130,
    396n9
Winick, Charles, 392n27
Winneke, Gerhard, 375n77
Winner, Lawrence, 399n67
Winston (drug user), 246
Wise, Nancy, 384n100
Wish, E., 393n74
Wislar, Joseph S., 372n11
Witmer, Helen, 372n8
Wofford, Sharon, 382n77
Wolfe, David, 386n34
Wolfgang, Marvin, 39, 40, 45, 212, 372n16,
    373n44, n50, n57, n58, n60, 374n2,
    375n61, 386n24, 391n13, n14

Wolfinger, Nicholas, 162
Wolford, Bruce, 391n8
Wonders, Jerome, 389n61
Wong, Frank, 73
Wong, Janelle, 29
Wood, Peter, 127n6
Wood, Wendy, 73
Woolard, Jennifer L., 398n8, n9
Wooton, Barbara, 376n97, 386n63
Worden, Robert E., 295, 397n39, n44, n52
Worder, Madeline, 398n22
Wright, Bradley Entner, 128, 129, 381n53,
    382n83, n84
Wright, John Paul, 379n60, n70, 386n43,
    n62, 391n20, 396n59, 60
Wright, Lloyd, 393n75
Wright, Richard, 393n67, n68
Wu, Bohsiu, 398n27
Wu, Chyi-In, 379n59, 380n12
Wundram, Sabine, 375n77
Wundt, Wilhelm, 71
Wung, Phen, 380n26

Yablonsky, Lewis, 201, 377n151, 389n54,
    390n119, n120
Yeung, W. Jean, 371n8, 378n12, n13
Young, Kimball, 377n163
Young, Lise A., 328
Yun, Steve Chong, 389n82
Yun Soo Kim, Julia, 372n11

Zak, Lydia, 386n34
Zantop, Half, xiii
Zantop, Susanne, xiii
Zaslaw, Jay, 380n104
Zeeb, Linda, 385n17
Zernike, Kate, 252
Zhang, Lening, 127n1, n11, 379n80
Zhang, Quanwu, 388n16
Zhao, Jihong, 378n36
Zimmerman, Joel, 376n88
Zimmerman, Rick, 252
Zimring, Franklin E., 325, 396n51, 399n68
Zingraff, Matthew, 388n136, 391n11, n29
Zlotnick, S. Jack, 376n110, n121

Subject Index

social learning theory
  child abuse and neglect and, 178
  view of, 70–71, 94–95, 99, 102, 105
social process theories
  social control, 94, 95–99, 102, 105, 177
  social learning, 70–71, 94–95, 99, 102, 105
  social reaction theory, 94, 98–99, 102–105
  and socialization, 91–94, 101–103, 105
  summary of, 99
social reaction theory, 94, 98–99, 102–105
social stigma
  and adult court transfer, 323
  and social reaction theory, 94, 98–99, 105
  of status offenders, 16–17, 20, 274
  treatment/prevention programs and, 78, 259
social structure theories
  anomie/strain, 88–90
  cultural deviance, 91
  factors in, 83–85
  overview of, 82–83, 85–86, 91, 105
  and prevention, 101
  social disorganization, 86–88
socialization
  and cognitive theory, 71–74, 94
  elements and influence of, 50, 91–94, 99, 105
  and family, 158
  gender differences and, 137, 144–148, 151, 153
  peers and, 184, 201
  and prevention, 101–103
  and schools, 211–212, 229
  social development model, 114–115
Society for the Prevention of Cruelty to Children (SPCC), 264–265, 266
Society for the Prevention of Pauperism, 262
sociobiology, 60
source control, 249–250
Southwestern Pennsylvania Costs of Services in Medicaid Study, 134
SPCC (Society for the Prevention of Cruelty to Children), 264–265, 266
Spectrum Wilderness Program, 359
Stanford v. Kentucky, 269, 332, 335
State Attorney's Office, Jacksonville (FL), 218
states
  ADAM survey results and, 247–248
  and child abuse intervention, 173–175, 180
  control of juveniles/parents, 18–19
  incarceration statistics, 351, 352
  institution conditions, 351
  minimum age for waiver, 279, 280
  parental liability laws, 18–19
  participation in IAP, 365
  reform of status offense laws, 17–19

treatment of status offenders by, 15–18
statistics. *See* crime rate
status offenders, historical treatment of, 15–19, 270, 314–315
stealing. *See* theft
steroids, 235, 237
Stockholm (Sweden), 222
strain
  general strain theory, 89–91, 102, 105, 178
  nature and results of, 88–89, 97
stimulants, 234
substance abuse. *See* drug abuse
Substance Abuse and Mental Health Services Administration's Center for Substance Abuse Prevention, 117
Suffer the Children (Young), 328
Suffolk County Probation Department's South Country Truancy Reduction Program, 219
Supreme Court. *See* U.S. Supreme Court
Synar Amendment of 1992, 236
synthetic drugs, 236
Syracuse University Family Development Research Program's Quality Infant and Toddler Caregiving Workshop, 132–133

T

tattoos, 196, 200
teen courts, 261, 280–281
teen pregnancy, 5, 29, 146–147
tertiary prevention, 131, 368–369
Texas, 244, 355
theft
  and gender, 33
  and the NCVS, 42, 43
  and race, 34
  and self-report, 30, 31
theories
  behavioral, 70–71, 76, 77, 79
  biosocial, 60–67, 79
  choice, 48, 49–51, 53–58, 79
  cognitive, 71–74, 76, 77, 79
  developmental, 108, 128–129
  feminist, 148–151, 153
  on gang involvement, 199–202
  general crime, 121–128
  interactional, 116, 118, 121, 128
  latent trait, 108, 121–128
  life course, 108, 109–115
  nature/nurture, 75
  psychodynamic, 68–70, 76, 77
  routine activities, 51–53, 58, 79
  social conflict theories, 99–100, 104–105
  social control, 94, 95–98, 99
  social learning, 70–71, 94, 95, 99
  social process, 101–103
  social reaction, 94, 98–99, 103–104
  social structure, 82–83, 85–91, 101, 105
  trait, 58–60, 76–78, 79
Thompson v. Oklahoma, 269, 332

Tinker v. Des Moines Independent Community School District, 227–228
Title III of the JJDPA, 16–17
T.L.O., New Jersey v., 227, 269
totality of the circumstances doctrine, 293–294
trait theory
  behavioral, 70–71
  biochemical factors and, 60–62
  cognitive, 72–74
  critiques of, 76
  and gender differences, 142–144, 153
  genetic influences and, 64–67
  and intelligence, 75–76
  neurological dysfunction and, 62–63
  past and present, 59–60
  personality, 74–75
  premise of, 48–49, 58–59, 79
  and prevention, 76–78
  psychodynamic, 68–70
  psychological, 67–68
  See also latent trait theory
transfer. *See* waiver
tranquilizers, 235
treatment
  boot camp, 338, 359–361
  challenges of, 356–357, 369
  and chronic offenders, 41
  diversion, 316–318
  educational, vocational, and recreational, 358–359
  group correctional, 357–358
  individual correctional, 357
  individualized model, 330
  juvenile justice process and, 273–274, 282
  legal right to, 14, 361–362, 366
  as opposed to punishment, 14, 20, 103
  for substance abuse, 253–254
  trait theory, 77–78
  types of, 338–339
Troxel v. Granville, 172
truancy
  as a status offense, 16, 17, 19
  and school failure, 216, 218–219
  and self-reports, 30
  Suffolk County Probation Department's South Country Truancy Reduction Program, 219
Turman, Morales v., 361
turning points, 118
Twenty-First Century Community Learning Centers, 226
twin studies, 65–67

U

UCLA's Comprehensive Residential Education, Arts, and Substance Abuse Treatment (CREASAT) program, 254
UCR (Uniform Crime Report)
  data and methods of, 23–24, 31, 45, 149